W9-DEF-538

Houghton Mifflin
Math

symmetry

HOUGHTON MIFFLIN

BOSTON

Education Place® is a registered trademark of Houghton Mifflin Company.

Weekly Reader® is a federally registered trademark of Weekly Reader Corp.

Copyright ©2007 by Houghton Mifflin Company. All rights reserved.

No part of this work may be reproduced or transmitted in any form or by any means, electronic or mechanical, including photocopying or recording, or by any information storage or retrieval system without the prior written permission of Houghton Mifflin Company unless such copying is expressly permitted by federal copyright law. Address inquiries to School Permissions, Houghton Mifflin Company, 222 Berkeley Street, Boston, MA 02116.

Printed in the U.S.A.
ISBN-13: 978-0-618-59093-3
ISBN-10: 0-618-59093-5

3456789-KDL-14 13 12 11 10 09 08 07 06

Houghton Mifflin Math

Program Authors & Consultants

Authors

Dr. Carole Greenes

Professor of Mathematics
Education

Boston University
Boston, MA

Dr. Matt Larson

Curriculum Specialist for
Mathematics

Lincoln Public Schools
Lincoln, NE

Dr. Miriam A. Leiva

Distinguished Professor of
Mathematics Emerita

University of
North Carolina
Charlotte, NC

Dr. Jean M. Shaw

Professor Emerita of
Curriculum and Instruction

University of Mississippi
Oxford, MS

Dr. Lee Stiff

Professor of Mathematics
Education

North Carolina State University
Raleigh, NC

Dr. Bruce R. Vogeli

Clifford Brewster Upton
Professor of Mathematics

Teachers College, Columbia
University
New York, NY

Karol Yeatts

Associate Professor

Barry University
Miami, FL

Consultants

Strategic Consultant

Dr. Liping Ma

Senior Scholar

Carnegie Foundation
for the Advancement
of Teaching
Palo Alto, CA

**Language and
Vocabulary Consultant**

Dr. David Chard

Professor of Reading

University of Oregon
Eugene, OR

Reviewers

Grade K

Hilda Kendrick
W E Wilson
Elementary School
Jefferson, IN

Debby Nagel
Assumption
Elementary School
Cincinnati, OH

Jen Payet
Lake Ave. Elementary School
Saratoga Springs, NY

Karen Sue Hinton
Washington Elementary
School
Ponca City, OK

Grade 1

Karen Wood
Clay Elementary School
Clay, AL

Paula Rowland
Bixby North Elementary
School
Bixby, OK

Stephanie McDaniel
B. Everett Jordan
Elementary School
Graham, NC

Juan Melgar
Lowrie Elementary School
Elgin, IL

Sharon O'Brien
Echo Mountain School
Phoenix, AZ

Grade 2

Sally Bales
Akron Elementary School
Akron, IN

Rose Marie Bruno
Mawbey Street Elementary
School
Woodbridge, NJ

Kiesha Doster
Berry Elementary School
Detroit, MI

Marci Galazkiewicz
North Elementary School
Waukegan, IL

Ana Gaspar
Lowrie Elementary School
Elgin, IL

Elana Heinoren
Beechfield Elementary
School
Baltimore, MD

Kim Terry
Woodland Elementary School
West
Gages Lake, IL

Megan Burton
Valley Elementary School
Pelham, AL

Kristy Ford
Eisenhower Elementary
School
Norman, OK

Grade 3

Jenny Chang
North Elementary School
Waukegan, IL

Patricia Heintz
Harry T. Stewart
Elementary School
Corona, NY

Shannon Hopper
White Lick Elementary School
Brownsburg, IN

Allison White
Kingsley Elementary School
Naperville, IL

Amy Simpson
Broadmoore Elementary
School
Moore, OK

Reviewers

Grade 4

Barbara O'Hanlon
Maurice & Everett Haines
Elementary School
Medford, NJ

Connie Rapp
Oakland Elementary School
Bloomington, IL

Pam Rettig
Solheim Elementary School
Bismarck, ND

Tracy Smith
Blanche Kelso Bruce
Academy
Detroit, MI

Brenda Hancock
Clay Elementary School
Clay, AL

Karen Scroggins
Rock Quarry Elementary
School
Tuscaloosa, AL

Lynn Fox
Kendall-Whittier Elementary
School
Tulsa, OK

Grade 5

Jim Archer
Maplewood Elementary
School
Indianapolis, IN

Maggie Dunning
Horizon Elementary School
Hanover Park, IL

Mike Intoccia
McNichols Plaza
Scranton, PA

Jennifer LaBelle
Washington Elementary
School
Waukegan, IL

Anne McDonald
St. Luke The Evangelist
School
Glenside, PA

Ellen O'Rourke
Bower Elementary School
Warrenville, IL

Gary Smith
Thomas H. Ford Elementary
School
Reading, PA

Linda Carlson
Van Buren Elementary
School
Oklahoma City, OK

Grade 6

Robin Akers
Sonoran Sky Elementary
School
Scottsdale, AZ

Ellen Greenman
Daniel Webster Middle
School
Waukegan, IL

Angela McCray
Abbott Middle School
West Bloomfield, MI

Mary Popovich
Horizon Elementary School
Hanover Park, IL

Debbie Taylor
Sonoran Sky Elementary
School
Scottsdale, AZ

Across Grades

Jacqueline Lampley
Hewitt Elementary School
Trussville, AL

Rose Smith
Five Points Elementary
School
Orrville, AL

Winnie Tepper
Morgan County Schools
Decatur, AL

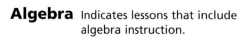

Algebra Indicates lessons that include algebra instruction.

UNIT 1 **Place Value and Money**

vi

Addition and Subtraction

Algebra Indicates lessons that include algebra instruction.

5 Subtract Whole Numbers

Unit 2
Literature
Connection
Bird Feeder
page 646

Data and Probability

UNIT 3   Data and Probability

x

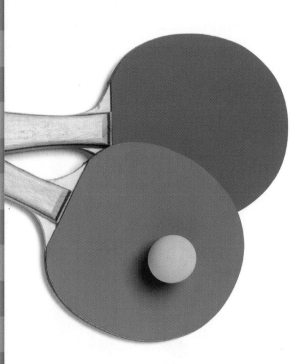

Algebra Indicates lessons that include algebra instruction.

7 Probability

Unit 3
Literature
Connection
Frog or Toad
page 648

Multiplication and Division Basic Facts

Algebra Indicates lessons that include algebra instruction.

(WR) Indicates **WEEKLY (WR) READER** eduplace.com/map

Measurement

Algebra Indicates lessons that include algebra instruction.

14 Metric Measurement

Unit 5
Literature
Connection
The Big Chill
page 651

Geometry and Measurement

UNIT 6 **Geometry and Measurement**

xvi

Algebra Indicates lessons that include algebra instruction.

17 Perimeter, Area, and Volume

Unit 6
Literature
Connection
Snowflakes
page 653

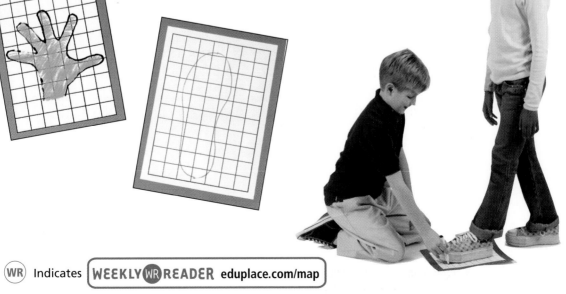

Fractions and Decimals

Algebra Indicates lessons that
include algebra instruction.

20 Decimals

FINISHING THE UNIT

Unit 7
Literature
Connection
Ice-Skating Contest
page 654

Multiplication and Division by 1-Digit Numbers

Algebra Indicates lessons that include algebra instruction.

xx

22 Divide by 1-Digit Divisors

FINISHING THE UNIT

Unit 8
Literature
Connection
Elephants on the Move
page 656

STUDENT RESOURCES

 Indicates WEEKLY (WR) READER eduplace.com/map

Welcome!

This year in math you'll learn about numbers, patterns, shapes, and different ways to measure. Scientists, cooks, builders, and artists all use math every day—and you will too. You'll use the mathematics you know to solve problems and describe objects and patterns you see. You can get started by finding out about yourself as a mathematician and about the other students in your class.

Real Life Connection
Collecting Data

About Me

Write your math autobiography by writing two or three things about each question. You can also draw a picture of yourself doing math, if you want.

- What do you like best about math class?
- What are you good at in math class?
- What would you like to know more about?
- How do you (or how does someone in your family) use math outside of math class?

About My Class

Your classmates may be just like you in some ways but different in other ways. You can collect data to find out something about the whole class.

- Think of one topic you'd like to know about all your classmates.
- Write a survey question for your topic.
- Take a survey among your classmates. Use tally marks to collect the data.
- Make a bar or picture graph to show your results.
- Use your graph and data to write what you learned about your class.

What is your favorite playground area or equipment?

Swings	
climbing structure	II
basketball court	┼┼┼
slide	

Lesson | Problem Solving and Numbers

Objective Review basic number and problem solving skills.

Review and Remember

You know about adding and subtracting with whole numbers. You also know a lot about money. On this page, you will review both concepts.

Look at the coins at the right. Is their value less than (<) or greater than (>) one dollar?

One way to find out is to put the coins in order of their value. Then count on to find the total value.

| 25¢ | 50¢ | 75¢ | 85¢ | 95¢ | 96¢ |

96¢ is less than $1.00.   96¢ < $1.00

Guided Practice

Find the value of each group of coins.

1.    2.

3. Use < or > to compare the values of the groups of coins in Exercises 1 and 2.

4. If you combine the coins in Exercises 1 and 2, how much money would you have?

Ask Yourself

- What is the value of each coin?
- Did I count the money in order from greatest to least value?

Explain Your Thinking ▶ Suppose you pay for a pencil that costs 32¢ with 2 quarters. Explain two different ways to find how much change you should get.

Practice and Problem Solving

Find the value of each group of coins.

5.

6.

7. Use < or > to compare the values of the groups of coins in Exercises 5 and 6.

8. Suppose you combine the coins in Exercises 5 and 6. How much money would you have?

Use the pictures at the right. Solve each problem.

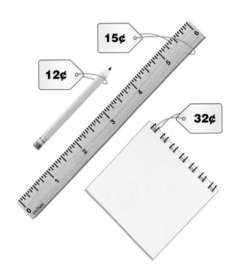

9. How much would it cost to buy a pencil and a ruler?

10. You pay for a pencil with a quarter. How much change should you get?

11. How much more does a notebook cost than a pencil?

12. **Create Your Own** Write a problem about money. Trade problems with a classmate and solve.

Mixed Review and Test Prep

Open Response

Write the next 3 numbers to continue each pattern. (Grade 2)

13. 5 10 15 20 25 30 __, __, __

14. 50 48 46 44 42 __, __, __

Multiple Choice

15. How much money do you need to buy one of each of the three items shown above? (Grade 2)

A 47¢   C 79¢

B 59¢   D 95¢

Measurement

Objective Review basic measurement skills needed to start third grade.

Work Together

Materials
inch ruler

In some lessons, you will learn as you do an activity. In this activity you will work with a partner to measure objects in the classroom.

STEP 1 Estimate then measure the length of the pencil above to the nearest inch.

STEP 2 Line up the left end of the pencil with the zero mark of the inch ruler.

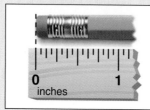

On some rulers there is no zero mark. The left end of the ruler is zero.

STEP 3 Find the inch mark closest to the right end of the pencil.

- What is the length of the pencil to the nearest inch?
- How close is your measurement to your estimate?

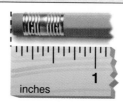

On Your Own

Estimate the length of each pencil. Then measure to the nearest inch.

1.

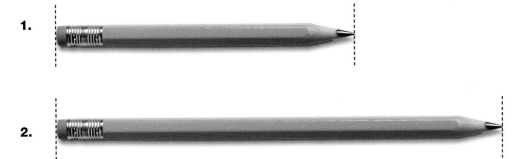

2.

Use an inch ruler to solve.

3. Collect 5 pencils from people in your class. Measure each to the nearest inch.

4. Write the lengths from Exercise 3 in order from shortest to longest.

5. Find an object that you estimate is about 6 inches long. Measure the object. Write the name and length of the object.

6. Draw a line segment that is 4 inches long.

Talk About It • Write About It

7. **What's Wrong?** Jacob says that the pencil below is about 5 inches long. What did he do wrong? Explain your answer.

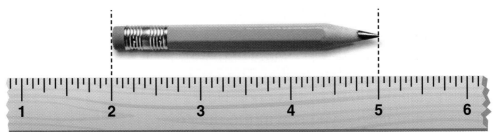

8. A yardstick is 36 inches long. List 3 things in your classroom that would be easier to measure with a yardstick than with a 12-inch ruler.

Visual Thinking
Going Geometric

What looks like a bus, but is not a bus? The answer is a trolley coach! It runs on electricity instead of gasoline. Some cities use trolleys to take people from place to place.

Many different shapes are used in drawing the picture above.

1. Look at the shapes with 4 sides. Write the names of as many of those shapes as you can. If you cannot name one, then just draw the shape.

2. Name or draw any shapes with more or fewer than 4 sides.

3. Look at the door of the trolley. The artist used rectangles to draw the door. How many rectangles do you see in the door?

4. In Exercises 1–3 you worked with plane shapes. Now look at the drawing and name any solid shapes you see.

UNIT 1

Place Value and Money

Reading Mathematics

Reviewing Vocabulary

Here are some math vocabulary words that you should know.

cent sign (¢)	the symbol used to show cents
decimal point (.)	the symbol used to separate dollars and cents
dollar sign ($)	the symbol used to show dollars
is greater than (>)	the symbol used to compare two numbers when the greater number is written first
is less than (<)	the symbol used to compare two numbers when the lesser number is written first

Reading Words and Symbols

Numbers can be shown in many different ways.

Models: 3 hundreds blocks
2 tens rods
4 ones cubes.

Words: three hundred twenty-four

Symbols: 324

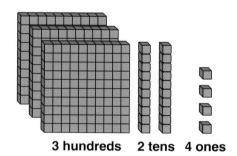

3 hundreds   2 tens   4 ones

Use words and symbols to show each number.

1. 63

2. 742

Reading Test Questions

Choose the correct answer for each.

3. Which number does the model show?

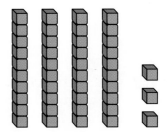

   a. 33   **c.** 43

   b. 34   **d.** 44

Model means "picture" or "example."

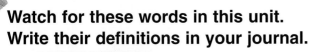

4. Which coin has a value of 5¢?

  a.   **c.**

  b.   **d.**

Value means "worth" or "amount."

5. Which symbol correctly compares 8 tens ● 6 tens?

  a. $=$ **c.** $<$

  b. $>$ **d.** $+$

A **symbol** is a "sign" or a "mark" used instead of words.

Learning Vocabulary

Watch for these words in this unit. Write their definitions in your journal.

ordinal numbers

expanded form

standard form

word form

half-dollar

equivalent amounts

Education Place

At **eduplace.com/map** see eGlossary and eGames—Math Lingo.

Literature Connection

Read "A is for Abacus" on Page 645. Then work with a partner to answer the questions about the story.

Place Value

INVESTIGATION

Using Data

This student is inside an "anti-gravity" chamber at the U.S. Space Camp in Huntsville, Alabama. Look at the sign. Which numbers are used to count? Which numbers are used to label? Give examples of numbers that are used to count or label in other kinds of camps.

Space Camp

- Founded in **1982**.
- Over **300,000** people have graduated.
- **9-year-olds** and older may attend.
- It costs about **$700.00** for **5** days.

Use What You Know

Use this page to review and remember what you need to know for this chapter.

VOCABULARY

Choose the best word to complete each sentence.

Vocabulary
tens
ones
digits
hundreds

1. The number 8,562 has four ____.

2. The number 309 has 3 hundreds and 9 ____.

3. The number 390 has 3 hundreds and 9 ____.

CONCEPTS AND SKILLS

Write the number for each.

4.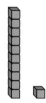

5.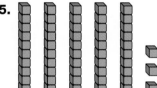

6.

7. 60 + 4

8. 100 + 50

9. 300 + 70 + 2

Write the missing numbers.

10. 86, 87, ____, 89, ____, ____, 92

11. 90, 80, ____, 60, 50, 40, ____

12. 100, ____, 300, 400, 500, ____, 700

13. 222, 223, ____, 225, 226, ____

Write About It

14. Think about the number 904. Describe the number in at least 3 different ways.

15. **What's Wrong?** Sara says that the digit 0 stands for nothing. So she decides not to write the 0 in 740. Why is that wrong?

Facts Practice, See page 665.

Uses of Numbers

Objective Use numbers in different ways.

Vocabulary
ordinal numbers

Learn About It

There are 9 planets in our solar system. You can use **ordinal numbers** to describe the position of each planet. Saturn is the sixth planet from the sun.

The picture at the right shows the planets in our solar system.

Here are some other ways to use numbers.

▶ **You can use numbers to count.**

- You can count the number of people in a group.

- You can count the number of objects in a group.

There were 7 astronauts in the first NASA program called Project Mercury.

▶ **You can use numbers to measure.**

- You can measure distance.

- You can measure temperature.

The planet Saturn is about 750 million miles from Earth.

▶ **You can use numbers to label.**

- You can label the time or date.

- You can label a building or flight.

NASA launched the Cassini Orbiter on October 15, 1997 to explore Saturn.

Tell how each number is used. Write *position,* *count, measure,* or *label* for each.

1.

2.

3. 18 marbles   4. 25 Elm Street   5. 37 inches

Explain Your Thinking ▶ How are numbers used in your classroom? Give 3 examples.

Practice and Problem Solving

Tell how each number is used. Write *position,* *count, measure,* or *label* for each.

6.

7.

8.

9. fifth in line   10. 19 buttons   11. 54 pounds

Complete.

12. first, _____, third, fourth

13. fourth, _____, sixth, _____

14. There are 3 students giving reports about Saturn. Zack is before Ben. Mona is not first. Ben is not third. In what order do they give their reports?

 15. **Write About It** Andy says the most important use of numbers is for counting. Ethan says numbers are most useful as labels. What do you think?

Mixed Review and Test Prep ✓

Open Response

Add or subtract. (Grade 2)

16. 3 + 4   17. 10 + 2

18. 7 − 7   19. 16 − 9

20. Rita lives 2 floors above Jonah. Jonah lives on the fifth floor. What floor does Rita live on? Explain how you know.

(Ch.1, Lesson 1)

Audio Tutor 1/2 Listen and Understand

Place Value: Ones, Tens, and Hundreds

Objective Identify values of digits in numbers to 999.

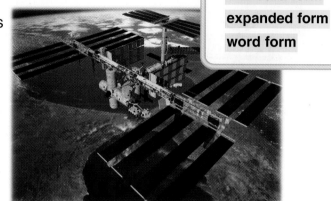

Vocabulary
digits
place value
standard form
expanded form
word form

Learn About It

Numbers are made up of **digits**. The value of each digit depends on its place in a number.

The International Space Station is about 361 feet wide.

▶ A **place-value** chart can help explain what this number means.

hundreds	tens	ones
3	6	1

The value of the 3 is 300.   The value of the 6 is 60.   The value of the 1 is 1.

▶ There are different ways to write 361.

Different Ways to Write a Number	
You can use **standard form** .	361
You can use **expanded form** .	300 + 60 + 1
You can use **word form** .	three hundred sixty-one

Guided Practice

Write each number in two other ways.
Use standard form, expanded form, and word form.

1. 700 + 10 + 7

2. two hundred fifty-four

3. 929

4. 1 hundred 9 tens 2 ones

Ask Yourself
• What is the value of each digit?
• Do any places have zeros?

Explain Your Thinking ▶ In the number 507, what is the meaning of the zero in the tens place?

Extra Help at **eduplace.com/map**

Practice and Problem Solving

Write each number in standard form.

5.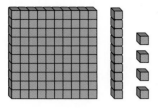

6.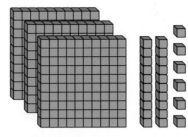

7.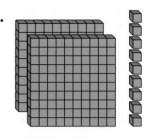

8. $900 + 80 + 6$

9. $400 + 60$

10. $700 + 20 + 3$

11. one hundred eleven

12. four hundred twenty

13. six hundred eight

Write the place of the underlined digit. Then write its value.

14. 1<u>7</u>6

15. 89<u>3</u>

16. 3<u>1</u>0

17. 42<u>7</u>

18. <u>5</u>51

19. <u>2</u>67

20. 35<u>6</u>

21. <u>9</u>28

22. 64<u>0</u>

23. 4<u>0</u>7

 Algebra • Equations Find the value of ■.

24. $100 + 30 + ■ = 136$

25. $200 + ■ + 5 = 245$

26. $■ + 70 + 9 = 579$

27. $300 + ■ = 380$

Data Use the table for Problems 28–30.

28. **Analyze** Which number has a 6 in the tens place?

29. How would you write the number of days for Mission 3 in expanded form?

30. **What's Wrong?** Juan says the Mission 1 crew spent the most time in outer space because that number has the most ones. Explain why he is wrong.

Time in Outer Space	
Mission	**Days**
Mission 1	139 days
Mission 2	167 days
Mission 3	131 days
Mission 4	196 days

Mixed Review and Test Prep

Open Response

Add. (Grade 2)

31. $\begin{array}{r} 26 \\ + 33 \\ \hline \end{array}$

32. $\begin{array}{r} 56 \\ + 12 \\ \hline \end{array}$

33. $\begin{array}{r} 36 \\ + 51 \\ \hline \end{array}$

Multiple Choice

34. Which shows three hundred five? (Ch. 1, Lesson 2)

A 35

B 305

C 350

D 503

How Big Is One Thousand?

Objective Relate one thousand to hundreds and tens.

Vocabulary
thousand

Materials
10 x 10 Grid Paper
 (LT 5)
crayons
scissors
tape

Work Together

Look at the paper square on the right. Suppose you made a line of 1,000 squares this size. How long would your line be? How would your line compare to one with 10 squares? 100 squares?

Paper Square

You can use grid paper to explore one thousand .

STEP 1

Make a table like the one shown. Choose a color for your team.

- Color a strip of 10 squares on grid paper.

- Cut out the strip. Repeat for 9 more strips.

- Estimate: Name something in your class that may be about 10 squares long, 100 squares long, and 1000 squares long.

Number of Teams	Number of Strips	Number of Squares
1		
2		
3		
4		
5		
6		
7		
8		
9		
10		

STEP 2

- How many strips do you have?
- How many squares do you have?

Fill in the first row of your table.

STEP 3

- Tape your team's 10 strips end to end.
- Now join another team and tape both teams' strips together. Then fill in the second row of your table.

STEP 4

Work as a class to tape all of the strips together. Then complete your table.

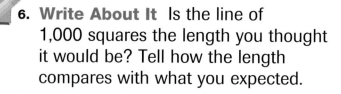

On Your Own

Use your completed table to help you answer each question.

1. How many squares are in each strip?

2. How many strips does each team have?

3. How many squares does each team have?

4. Together how many strips do all 10 teams make?

5. How many squares are there in all?

 6. **Write About It** Is the line of 1,000 squares the length you thought it would be? Tell how the length compares with what you expected.

Tell if each is _greater than, less than,_ or _equal to_ 1,000.

7. 8 boxes of 100 pencils

8. 9 boxes of 1,000 craft sticks

9. 10 trays of 10 muffins

10. 10 bags of 100 letters

Talk About It • Write About It

You have learned how 1,000 is related to 10 and 100.

11. Look at the table you completed. What pattern do you notice in each row? in each column?

12. If you know how many tens there are in 100, how can you find the number of tens in 700?

13. For which would you need a larger container: 1,000 grains of sand or 1,000 marbles? Explain your thinking.

Audio Tutor 1/3 Listen and Understand

Place Value Through Thousands

Vocabulary
thousands

Objective Identify values of digits in numbers to 9,999.

Learn About It

When the Space Shuttle returns to Earth, it gets very hot. That is why the shuttle is made of materials that can stand temperatures of more than 2,390°F!

▶ **A place-value chart can help explain what this number means.**

thousands	hundreds	tens	ones
2	3	9	0

The value of the 2 is 2,000. The value of the 3 is 300. The value of the 9 is 90. The value of the 0 is 0.

▶ **There are different ways to write 2,390.**

Different Ways to Write a Number	
You can use **standard form**.	2,390
You can use **expanded form**.	2,000 + 300 + 90
You can use **word form**.	two thousand, three hundred ninety

Guided Practice

Write each number in two other ways.
Use standard form, expanded form, and word form.

1. 1,000 + 700 + 8
2. seven thousand, thirty-six
3. 2,039
4. four thousand, one hundred five

Ask Yourself
- What is the value of each digit in the number?
- Do any places have zeros?

Explain Your Thinking ▶ In what ways are 2,390 and 3,290 similar? In what ways are they different?

Write each number in two other ways. Use standard form, expanded form, and word form

5. $8,000 + 7$

6. $9,000 + 30$

7. $4,000 + 900 + 10 + 6$

8. $2,000 + 100 + 30 + 2$

9. five thousand, one hundred thirty

10. six thousand, ninety-four

11. five thousand, three hundred

12. one thousand, seven hundred thirteen

13. seven thousand, sixteen

14. two thousand, nine hundred one

Write the place of the underlined digit. Then write its value. Use your place value workmat if you need help.

15. 3,650

16. 1,098

17. 5,751

18. 6,709

19. 4,184

20. 9,276

21. 7,537

22. 2,670

Solve.

23. **Analyze** Use these clues to find the year of the first Space Shuttle launch:

   • It has an 8 in the tens place.

   • The ones digit is the same as the thousands digit.

   • The hundreds digit is greater than the tens digit.

24. Some astronauts have spent over 1,347 hours in space. Is that number closer to 1,000 or 2,000? Explain how you know.

Go On

Choose the number or numbers that match each statement.

25. There is a 2 in the hundreds place.

2,487   1,240   234

26. There is a 5 in the tens place.

4,525   4,050   532

27. There is a 6 in the thousands place.

6,490   6,371   1,639

28. There is a 0 in the ones place.

4,390   3,094   430

29. There is a number greater than 1 in the thousands place.

4,086   2,400   459

30. There is a number less than 7 in the hundreds place.

6,890   1,350   680

Make the greatest possible number using each set of digits. Then make the least possible number.

31. 4, 7, 9, 0   **32.** 1, 8, 6, 5   **33.** 3, 5, 2, 6   **34.** 3, 5, 9, 6

35. 8, 1, 9, 8   **36.** 5, 4, 2, 7   **37.** 6, 0, 9, 3   **38.** 4, 0, 2, 0

 Data Use the table for Problems 39–42.

39. Write the number of visitors to the Space Shot exhibit in expanded form.

40. Analyze Which exhibit has a 7 in the ones place and a 4 in the tens place?

41. Which exhibit had the greatest number of visitors? Write the number of visitors to that exhibit in word form.

42. Create and Solve Use the table to create a math problem. Then give it to a classmate to solve.

43. Reasoning Three movies are showing at the Spacedome Theater. *Blue Planet* is showing before *Space Station*. *Destiny in Space* is not first or last. Write the movies in the order that they will be shown.

Exhibit	Number of Visitors
Space Shot	1,467
Lunar Lander	2,047
Outpost in Space	1,974
Mars Mission	3,091

Extra Practice See page 25, Set C.

Calculator Connection
Broken Calculator

This calculator is broken.
Only these four keys are working:

To show 123 using the keys above, press:

Write the keys you need to press to show each number. Remember, you can only use the 1, 0, + and = keys.

1. 42   **2.** 50   **3.** 215   **4.** 333   **5.** 2,136

Check your understanding of Lessons 1–4.

Tell how each number is used. Write *position*, *count*, *measure*, or *label* for each. (Lesson 1)

1.

2.

3.

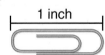
1 inch

Write each number in standard form. (Lessons 2, 4)

4. 300 + 60 + 8   **5.** 4,000 + 200 + 10 + 7   **6.** two thousand eighteen

Tell if each is *greater than*, *less than*, or *equal to* 1,000. (Lesson 3)

7. 2 boxes of 1,000 beads   **8.** 9 books of 100 pages

Problem-Solving Strategy
Find a Number Pattern

Objective Solve problems by finding a number pattern.

Problem The year is 2099. You and your family are on vacation at a hotel—in space! Each floor of the Cosmic Hotel has more rooms than the floor below it. The first floor has 500 rooms. The floors above it have 501, 503, and 506 rooms.

If the pattern continues, how many rooms are on the sixth floor?

 **UNDERSTAND**

What do you know?

- The first floor has 500 rooms, the second floor has 501 rooms, the third has 503 rooms, and the fourth has 506 rooms.

PLAN

You can look for a pattern to help you solve the problem.

SOLVE

Find a pattern.

500 $\xrightarrow{+1}$ 501 $\xrightarrow{+2}$ 503 $\xrightarrow{+3}$ 506

- Add 1, then add 2, then add 3, then add 4, then add 5, and so on.

- Use the pattern to find the next two numbers. The next two numbers are 510 and 515.

Solution: The sixth floor will have 515 rooms.

LOOK BACK

Look back at the problem.

Does the solution answer the question that was asked?

Guided Practice

Use the Ask Yourself questions to help you solve each problem.

1. The first tower in front of the Mars Motel is 3,475 feet tall. The second tower is 3,465 feet tall and the third tower is 3,455 feet tall. If the pattern continues, how tall is the fifth tower?

   (Hint) Which digit in the number is changing?

2. Your space ship's computer counts the number of stars you pass each minute. The last four counts were 812, 813, 815, and 818. If the pattern continues, what will the next count be?

Ask Yourself

UNDERSTAND
• **What facts do I know?**

PLAN
• **What is the pattern?**

SOLVE
• **How can I use the pattern to answer the question?**

LOOK BACK
• **Does the solution make sense?**

Independent Practice

Use a number pattern to solve each problem.

3. A small drink at the Lunar Diner is 54¢. A medium drink is 60¢ and a large drink is 66¢. If the pattern continues, how much is an extra large drink likely to be?

4. Moon rocks are sold in different size bags. The smallest bag contains 5 rocks. The number of rocks in the bag increases in this order: 5, 6, 8, 11. If the pattern continues, how many moon rocks are in the next two bags?

5. The first 3 moon racers you see are wearing the numbers 6103, 6110, and 6117. If the pattern continues, what number is the next moon racer likely to be wearing?

6. What are the next two numbers in the pattern below likely to be?

   534, 530, 526, ____, ____

7. Look at the numbers below. What is the next number likely to be?

   5, 10, 15, 20, ____

Go On

Mixed Problem Solving

Solve. Show your work. Tell what strategy you used.

8. **Multistep** There are 2,563 trees in Paula's town. There are 500 oak trees, 2,000 maple trees, and 60 spruce trees. The rest are birch trees. How many birch trees are there?

9. What is the greatest four-digit number that can be made with the digits 3, 1, 6, and 4?

10. Juice boxes come in packs of 6 each. Mr. Meyers took 4 of these packs on a field trip. How many juice boxes did he take?

You Choose

Strategy
- Make a Table
- Find a Pattern
- Make an Organized List
- Write a Number Sentence.
- Use Logical Reasoning

Computation Method
- Mental Math
- Estimation
- Paper and Pencil
- Calculator

Data Use the graph for Problems 11–14. Then tell which method you chose.

Mrs. Vega's class is visiting the bakery near their school. The graph shows how many loaves of each kind of bread the bakery made today.

11. How many loaves of raisin bread did the bakery make today?

12. The bakery made equal numbers of two kinds of bread. Which ones?

13. How many more loaves of rye than wheat are there?

14. Yesterday the bakery made 35 loaves of Italian bread. How many more loaves did they make yesterday than they made today?

Loaves of Bread Baked Today

Rye	
Raisin	
Italian	
Wheat	

Each stands for 5 loaves.

Problem Solving on Tests

Choose the letter of the correct answer.

1. Maria wrote the number 356 in four ways. Which way is **not** correct?

   A 300 + 50 + 6

   B 100 + 100 + 100 + 50 + 6

   C three hundred fifty-six

   D 3 hundreds 50 tens 6 ones

   (Chapter 1, Lesson 2)

2. Mrs. Nygen asks four students to get in line. Who is third?

   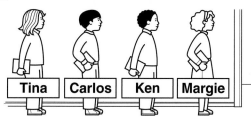

   F Ken   G Margie   H Carlos   J Tina

   (Chapter 1, Lesson 1)

Open Response

Solve each problem.

3. Kate has 9 sheets of 100 stickers. Is the number of stickers she has greater than 1,000? Explain.

   (Chapter 1, Lesson 3)

4. Paul draws 2 dots, 5 dots, 8 dots, and 11 dots. If he continues the pattern, how many dots will he draw next?

   (Chapter 1, Lesson 5)

Extended Response

5. The table shows the heights of some famous buildings in the United States.

Building	Height (in feet)
Library Tower Los Angeles, CA	1,018
Citicorp Center New York City	915
Bank of America Plaza Atlanta, GA	1,023
Empire State Building New York City	1,250
John Hancock Center Chicago, IL	1,127

a. Write the heights of the buildings in order from least to greatest. Explain how understanding place value helped you do this.

b. Mr. Black told his family that the Sears Tower in Chicago was built in 1974. It is one thousand, four hundred fifty feet tall. Write the height of the Sears Tower in standard and expanded form.

c. The Plaza Tower in New Orleans is 531 feet tall. The LL&E Tower is 481 feet tall. Which tower is taller? How do you know?

(Chapter 1, Lesson 4)

Education Place

See **eduplace.com/map** for more Test-Taking Tips.

Place Value Through Ten Thousands

Objective Identify values of digits in numbers through 99,999.

Vocabulary
ten thousands

Learn About It

About 25,040 students from all over the world polished mirrors to help create the satellite, Starshine 1.

▶ **A place-value chart can help explain what this number means.**

ten thousands	thousands	hundreds	tens	ones
2	5	0	4	0

▶ **There are different ways to write 25,040.**

Different Ways to Write a Number	
You can use **standard form**.	25,040
You can use **expanded form**.	20,000 + 5,000 + 40
You can use **word form**.	twenty-five thousand, forty

Guided Practice

Write each number in standard form.

1. 30,000 + 700 + 8
2. ten thousand, three hundred seven
3. 60,000 + 50 + 2
4. forty-two thousand, two hundred

Ask Yourself

• What is the value of each digit in the number?

• Do any places have zeros?

Explain Your Thinking ▶ If a five-digit number has no hundreds, is there a digit in the hundreds place? Use a place-value chart to explain.

Write each number in standard form.

5. 60,000 + 30 + 1

6. 80,000 + 3,000 + 900 + 20 + 5

7. 70,000 + 2,000 + 4

8. 8,000 + 300 + 5

9. eighty thousand, eighty

10. ten thousand, two hundred seventy-five

11. ninety-two thousand, three

12. sixty-five thousand, seventy-one

Write the place of the underlined digit.
Then write its value.
Use your place value workmat if you need help.

13. <u>1</u>3,500

14. <u>8</u>21

15. 7,03<u>2</u>

16. <u>6</u>1,496

17. 85<u>,</u>177

18. <u>7</u>9,343

19. <u>7</u>9

20. 33,<u>3</u>33

 Data **Use the table for Problems 21–23.**

21. When a planet orbits the sun, it travels around it. Look at the number of days it takes Saturn to orbit the sun. Write that number in word form.

22. Write the number of days it takes Pluto to orbit the sun in expanded form.

23. **Estimate** Which planet takes almost twice as long to orbit the sun as Uranus?

Days To Orbit The Sun

Planet	Number Of Days
Saturn	10,759 days
Uranus	30,685 days
Neptune	60,148 days
Pluto	90,735 days

Mixed Review and Test Prep

Open Response

Write the time. (Grade 2)

24.

25.

26.

Multiple Choice

27. Which is another way to write 40,283? (Ch.1, Lesson 6)

A 40,000 + 2,000 + 800 + 3

B 40,000 + 2,000 + 80 + 3

C 40,000 + 200 + 80 + 3

D 4,000 + 200 + 80 + 3

Extra Practice See page 25, Set D.

Place Value Through Hundred Thousands

Vocabulary
hundred thousands

Objective Identify values of digits in greater numbers.

Learn About It

Have you ever wondered how far away the moon really is? The moon is about 238,900 miles from Earth.

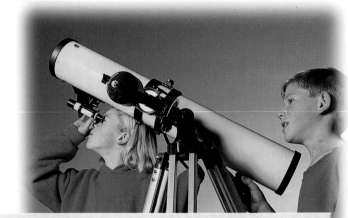

▶ **A place-value chart can help explain what this number means.**

hundred thousands	ten thousands	thousands	hundreds	tens	ones
2	3	8	9	0	0

▶ **There are different ways to write 238,900.**

Different Ways to Write a Number	
You can use **standard form**.	238,900
You can use **expanded form**.	200,000 + 30,000 + 8,000 + 900
You can use **word form**.	two hundred thirty-eight thousand, nine hundred

Guided Practice

Write each number in standard form.

1. 500,000 + 20,000 + 7,000 + 800

2. two hundred twenty-eight thousand, six

Write the place of the underlined digit. Then write its value.

3. 4̲51,097   **4.** 953̲,860   **5.** 320,2̲05   **6.** 22̲7,193

Ask Yourself
- What is the value of each digit?
- Do any places have zeros?

Explain Your Thinking ▶ Why is it important to write zeros in the ones and tens places of 238,900?

Practice and Problem Solving

Write each number in standard form.

7. 600,000 + 9,000 + 200 + 10 + 5

8. 400,000 + 300 + 90 + 8

9. 800,000 + 60,000 + 2,000 + 10 + 9

10. 100,000 + 30,000 + 2,000 + 800 + 50 + 4

11. two hundred twenty-nine thousand, five hundred thirty-three

12. nine hundred six thousand, eight hundred twenty-nine

13. five hundred thousand, seven hundred sixteen

14. four hundred ninety-four thousand, seven hundred fifty

Write the place of the underlined digit. Then write its value.

15. 3̲67,901   16. 731,4̲52   17. 80̲3,544   18. 9̲3̲2,761

19. 99̲3,609   20. 2̲52,880   21. 760,2̲33   22. 127,6̲48

Solve.

23. **What's Wrong?** Look at the poster at the right. Hal says that there were forty-two hundred thousand entries last year. Explain his mistake.

24. The Sun's diameter is about eight hundred sixty-five thousand miles. How would you write that number in standard form?

25. **Analyze** Use the clues to guess the 5-digit number Maria wrote.
    • All of the digits are odd numbers.
    • None of the digits are the same.
    • It is the greatest number that can be made.

Match each number in standard form to its expanded or word form.

26. 11,430   **a.** 100,000 + 10,000 + 4,000 + 300

27. 35,600   **b.** eleven thousand, four hundred thirty

28. 114,300   **c.** 30,000 + 5,000 + 600

29. 36,500   **d.** three hundred fifty-six thousand

30. 356,000   **e.** 30,000 + 6,000 + 500

 Data **Use the table for Problems 31–33.**

Jupiter has more than sixty moons.
The distances to four of its moons
are shown in the table at the right.

31. Write the distance from Jupiter to
Metis in word form.

32. Find the moon farthest away
from Jupiter. How would you
write that distance in expanded
form?

33. The distance of which moon
has the same digit in the
hundreds place, the thousands
place, and the hundred
thousands place?

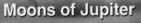

Moons of Jupiter

Moon	Miles From Jupiter
Europa	416,940 miles
Io	262,219 miles
Metis	79,636 miles
Thebe	137,944 miles

Mixed Review and Test Prep

Open Response

**Write the next three numbers in each
pattern.** (Ch. 1, Lesson 5)

34. 2, 6, 10, 14, _____, _____, _____

35. 19, 17, 15, 13, _____, _____, _____

36. 22, 24, 26, 28, _____, _____, _____

Multiple Choice

37. Which shows the following
number in standard form?
300,000 + 6,000 + 90 + 2

A 3,692   **C** 306,092

B 300,692   **D** 369,200

Extra Practice See page 25, Set E.

Algebraic Thinking
Odds and Evens

You can make patterns with even and odd numbers.

Even numbers end in 2, 4, 6, 8, or 0.	Odd numbers end in 1, 3, 5, 7, or 9.
12, 14, 16, 18, 20 ... is a pattern.	5, 7, 9, 11, 13 … is another pattern.

1. This chart is missing all the odd numbers. What are the missing numbers?

100		102		104		106		108	
110		112		114		116		118	

2. Look at the mailbox numbers. Are the numbers even or odd? What is the next number likely to be?

3. Look at this pattern.

   14, 16, 18, 20, 22, 24, _____

   Are the numbers even or odd? What is the next number likely to be?

4. Look at this pattern.

   47, 45, 43, 41, 39, 37, _____

   Are the numbers even or odd? What is the next number likely to be?

Solve.

5. Write a 5-digit even number in which 4 of the digits are odd.

6. Write a 6-digit odd number that has more even digits than odd digits.

7. What is the greatest odd number you can make using these number cards?

Chapter Review/Test

VOCABULARY

Choose the correct term to complete each sentence.

> **Vocabulary**
> thousands
> standard form
> ten thousands
> expanded form

1. $200,000 + 30 + 5$ is the ____ of 200,035.

2. In the number 638,351 the 8 is in the ____ place.

3. In the number 594,082 the 9 is in the ____ place.

CONCEPTS AND SKILLS

Tell how each number is used. Write *position, count, measure,* or *label* for each. (Lesson 1, pp. 4–5)

4. 8 feet   5. first place   6. 14 people   7. 46 Oak Street

Write each number in standard form. (Lessons 2–4, 6–7, pp. 6–13, 18–23)

8. $500 + 40 + 8$ 9. $7,000 + 800 + 40 + 2$

10. nine hundred twenty-four   11. $300,000 + 40,000 + 5,000 + 20 + 9$

12. four hundred sixty-eight   13. eighty-two thousand, six hundred fifty

Write the place of the underlined digit. Then write its value.

(Lesson 2–4, 6–7, pp. 6–13, 18–23)

14. <u>7</u>14   15. 1,<u>5</u>97   16. 6<u>1</u>2,800

17. 1<u>3</u>,329   18. 40,6<u>3</u>7   19. <u>4</u>25,912

PROBLEM SOLVING

Use a number pattern to solve.

(Lesson 5, pp. 14–16)

20. Sam read 3 books one summer. He read 5 books the next summer, then 7 books the summer after that. If the pattern continues, how many books will Sam read the next summer?

Write About It

Show You Understand

Lois said "nine thousand, fifteen" is the word form for 90,150.

Explain why she is wrong, and write the correct word form for 90,150.

Extra Practice

Set A (Lesson 1, pp. 4–5)

Write *position, count, measure,* or *label* for each.

1. 6 pints   **2.** 16 coins   **3.** second floor   **4.** room 310

Set B (Lesson 2, pp. 6–7)

Write each number in standard form.

1. six hundred seven   **2.** four hundred ten   **3.** two hundred forty-one

4. 300 + 20 + 7   **5.** 100 + 6   **6.** 100 + 80 + 2

Set C (Lessons 3, 4, pp. 8–13)

Write the place of the underlined digit. Then write its value.

1. 1,71$\underline{2}$ **2.** $\underline{6}$,341   **3.** 3,$\underline{4}$98   **4.** 8,2$\underline{5}$6   **5.** $\underline{5}$,134   **6.** 4,47$\underline{8}$

Set D (Lesson 6, pp. 18–19)

Write each number in standard form.

1. 50,000 + 7,000 + 40 + 3   **2.** 20,000 + 500 + 80 + 1

3. seventy thousand, forty-seven   **4.** ninety thousand, five hundred six

Write the place of the underlined digit. Then write its value.

5. 41,$\underline{2}$21   **6.** 1$\underline{0}$,507   **7.** 12,63$\underline{4}$ **8.** $\underline{7}$8,104   **9.** 45,$\underline{2}$21   **10.** 1$\underline{4}$,092

Set E (Lesson 7, pp. 20–23)

Write each number in standard form.

1. 700,000 + 5,000 + 30 + 5   **2.** six hundred ninety-three thousand

Write the place of the underlined digit. Then write its value.

3. 8$\underline{2}$0,209   **4.** $\underline{7}$64,392   **5.** 115,21$\underline{9}$ **6.** 541,$\underline{3}$82   **7.** $\underline{1}$67,134

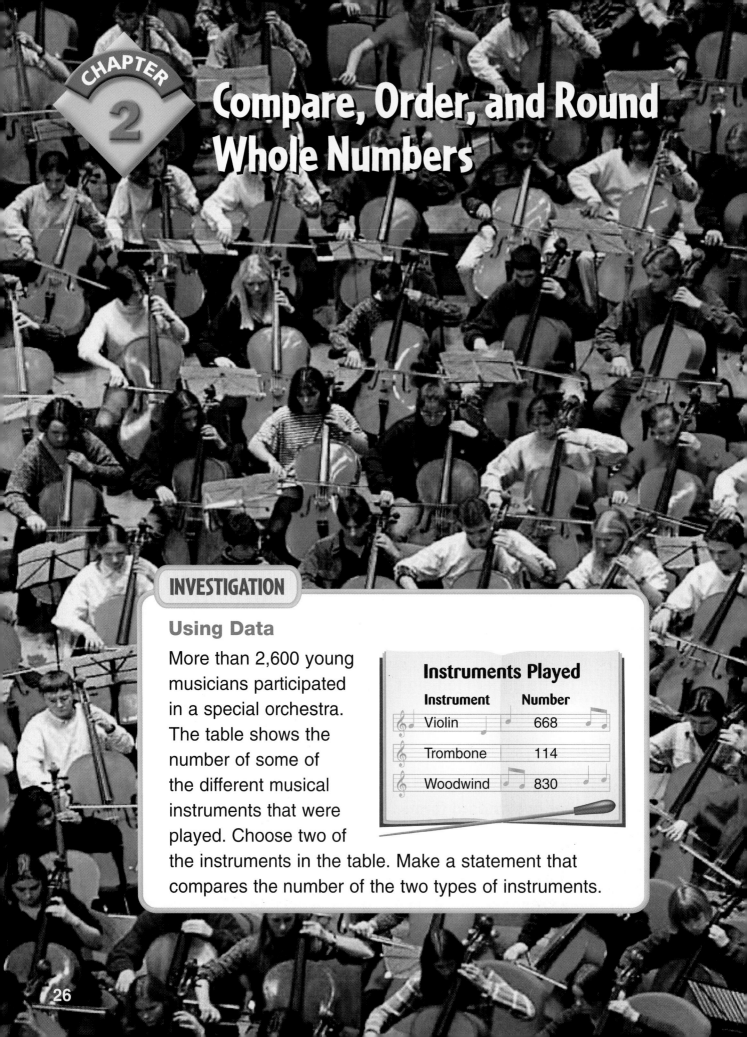

Compare, Order, and Round Whole Numbers

INVESTIGATION

Using Data

More than 2,600 young musicians participated in a special orchestra. The table shows the number of some of the different musical instruments that were played. Choose two of the instruments in the table. Make a statement that compares the number of the two types of instruments.

Instruments Played

Instrument	Number
Violin	668
Trombone	114
Woodwind	830

Use this page to review and remember
what you need to know for this chapter.

VOCABULARY

Choose the best term to complete each sentence.

1. Seven _____ eight plus three.

2. Eight is between seven and nine on a _____.

3. Eleven _____ six plus four.

Vocabulary

compare

number line

is less than

is greater than

CONCEPTS AND SKILLS

Write the place of the underlined digit. Then write its value.

4. 4<u>3</u> 5. 7<u>8</u> 6. 18<u>5</u> 7. <u>8</u>90 8. 6<u>7</u>2 9. <u>1</u>,348 10. 3,<u>7</u>42

Use the number line for Questions 11–14.

220 222 224 226 228 230 232 234 236

11. What number is between 232 and 234?

12. What number is between 225 and 227?

13. Which number, 223 or 228, is closer to 220?

14. Which number, 223 or 228, is closer to 230?

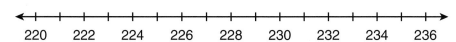
Write About It

15. Look at the number line below. Is any
   number as close to 50 as it is to 60? If so,
   which number? Explain how you know.

   50 51 52 53 54 55 56 57 58 59 60

Facts Practice, See page 666.

Audio Tutor 1/4 Listen and Understand

Compare Numbers

Objective Use number lines and place value to compare numbers.

Vocabulary

is less than (<)

is greater than (>)

is not equal to (≠)

Learn About It

It's finally time for the yearly dance recital! There are 124 ballet dancers and 128 tap dancers in the recital. Do the two groups have equal numbers of dancers? If not, which group is greater?

Different Ways to Compare 124 and 128

Way ➊ Use a place-value chart.

hundreds	tens	ones
1	2	4
1	2	8

↑ same   ↑ same   ↑ 8 ones > 4 ones

Since the digit in the ones place is greater in one of the numbers, the numbers are not equal.

124 ≠ 128

↑ is not equal to

No, the two groups do not have equal numbers.

Way ➋ Use a number line.

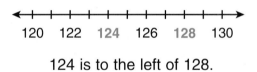

124 is to the left of 128.

124 < 128 and 128 > 124.

↑ is less than   ↑ is greater than

The number of tap dancers is greater.

Solution: The groups are not equal. Since 128 is greater than 124, there are more tap dancers than ballet dancers.

Another Example

Four-Digit Numbers

Which is less, 2,758 or 2,798?

2,758 < 2,798
2,758 is less.

thousands	hundreds	tens	ones
2	7	5	8
2	7	9	8

↑ same   ↑ same   ↑ 5 tens < 9 tens

Compare. Write >, <, or = for each ●.

1. 35 ● 37   2. 77 ● 97   3. 190 ● 109

4. 239 ● 156   5. 1,157 ● 1,157   6. 2,347 ● 2,357

Ask Yourself

• Should I use a number line or a place-value chart?

• Which digits should I compare first?

Explain Your Thinking ▶ Suppose you are comparing 468 and 493. Do you need to compare the digits in the ones place? Why or why not?

Practice and Problem Solving

Compare. Write >, <, or = for each ●.

7. 50 ● 98   8. 70 ● 70   9. 100 ● 98   10. 105 ● 150

11. 78 ● 89   12. 199 ● 201   13. 5,683 ● 5,683   14. 3,497 ● 4,271

X **Algebra** • **Symbols Write = or ≠ for each ●.**

15. 15 + 4 ● 19   16. 70 + 5 ● 72   17. 60 + 4 ● 66

18. 100 + 40 ● 140   19. 300 + 9 ● 390   20. 700 + 80 ● 870

Solve.

21. A dance school has 165 jazz dancers and 156 folk dancers. Are there more jazz dancers or folk dancers?

22. **Multistep** A prima ballerina uses 2 new pairs of ballet shoes for each performance. How many pairs does she use if she performs 4 times?

Mixed Review and Test Prep

Open Response

Skip count by 2s, 5s, or 10s to complete. (Grade 2)

23. 2, 4, 6, 8, _____, _____, _____

24. 10, 20, 30, 40, _____, _____, _____

25. 5, 10, 15, 20, _____, _____, _____

26. 24, 26, 28, 30, _____, _____, _____

Multiple Choice

27. Which of the following is true? (Ch. 2, Lesson 1)

A 87 > 97

B 894 < 898

C 1,143 = 1,144

D 3,098 > 3,098

Extra Practice See page 43, Set A.

Audio Tutor 1/5 Listen and Understand

Order Numbers

Objective Use place value and number lines to order numbers.

Learn About It

The third graders at First Street School are putting on a class play! On which day were the greatest number of tickets sold?

You can compare and order the numbers to find which is the greatest number.

Day of Performance	Tickets Sold
Friday	207
Saturday	223
Sunday	196

▶ **Use a place-value chart to help you order 207, 223, and 196 from least to greatest.**

- Start at the left to compare digits in the greatest place first.

- Continue comparing digits in the tens and ones places.

The order of the numbers from least to greatest is:

196   207   223

hundreds	tens	ones
2	0	7
2	2	3
1	9	6

1 hundred < 2 hundreds, so 196 is the least number.

0 tens < 2 tens, so 223 is the greatest number.

Solution: The greatest number of tickets were sold on Saturday.

Another Example

Use a Number Line.

Order these numbers from greatest to least: 564   749   620.

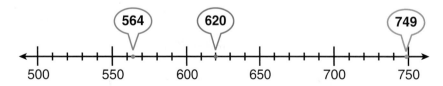

The order from greatest to least is: 749   620   564.

Write the numbers in order from greatest to least.

1. 99 89 92

2. 165 1,257 309

Ask Yourself

- Which place should I look at first?
- Which number is greatest?

Explain Your Thinking ▶ Why is 1,752 greater than 564 even though 5 is greater than 1?

Practice and Problem Solving

Write the numbers in order from least to greatest.

3. 71 89 30

4. 561 34 87

5. 5,790 1,484 1,348

Write the numbers in order from greatest to least.

6. 19 16 61

7. 129 347 12

8. 1,976 1,944 1,960

 Data Use the table for Problems 9–11.

9. Write the number of people at the Spring Concert in expanded form.

10. Order the number of people at the events from greatest to least. Which event had the greatest number of people in the audience?

 11. **Write About It** Suppose ten more people had attended the Talent Show. Would that affect the order of the numbers you wrote for Problem 10? Explain your thinking.

Attendance at School Performances	
Event	**Number of People**
Musical	436
Winter Concert	518
Spring Concert	420
Talent Show	419

Mixed Review and Test Prep

Open Response

Find each sum. (Grade 2)

12.
```
  3
  2
+ 4
```

13.
```
  5
  7
+ 1
```

14.
```
  9
  3
+ 6
```

15. Order these numbers from least to greatest. (Ch. 2, Lesson 2)

812 793 821

Explain your answer.

Round Two-Digit and Three-Digit Numbers

Objective Round numbers to the nearest ten or the nearest hundred.

Learn About It

The Little Theatre of the Deaf performs shows for school children across the country. During one season they performed 451 shows.

Rounded to the nearest hundred, how many shows did the theatre company perform in the season?

The Little Theatre of the Deaf combines Sign Language and spoken words in their performances.

Round **451 to the nearest hundred.**

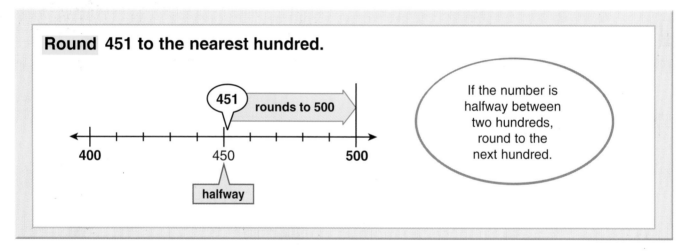

If the number is halfway between two hundreds, round to the next hundred.

Solution: Rounded to the nearest hundred, they performed 500 shows.

Another Example

To the Nearest Ten

Round 354 to the nearest ten.

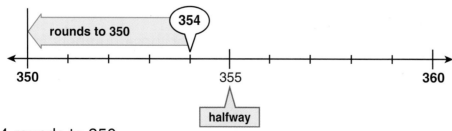

354 rounds to 350.

32

Guided Practice

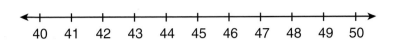

Round each number to the nearest ten.

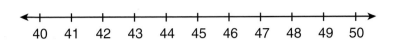

1. 48   **2.** 46   **3.** 44   **4.** 45

Round each number to the nearest hundred.

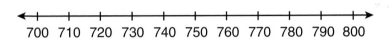

5. 791   **6.** 736   **7.** 743   **8.** 750

Explain Your Thinking ▶ Will a three-digit number rounded to the nearest ten and to the nearest hundred ever be the same?

Practice and Problem Solving

Round each number to the nearest ten.

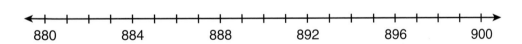

9. 889   **10.** 881   **11.** 883   **12.** 892

13. 897   **14.** 885   **15.** 894   **16.** 895

For each number, write the 2 tens the number is between. Then round to the nearest ten.

17. 81   **18.** 79   **19.** 47   **20.** 42

21. 68   **22.** 283   **23.** 456   **24.** 534

25. 334   **26.** 182   **27.** 714   **28.** 853

Go On

Ask Yourself
• To what place am I rounding?
• What should I do if the number is halfway between two tens or two hundreds?

For each number, write the 2 hundreds the number is between. Then round to the nearest hundred.

29. 466

30. 735

31. 243

32. 195

33. 856

34. 654

35. 588

36. 349

37. 306

38. 384

39. 415

40. 333

Round to the place of the underlined digit.

41. <u>3</u>4

42. 1<u>8</u>9

43. <u>9</u>27

44. <u>5</u>5

45. <u>7</u>93

46. <u>2</u>43

47. 3<u>5</u>6

48. <u>1</u>50

Solve.

49. The National Theatre of the Deaf has given 64 national tours and 31 international tours since it began giving performances. What is each number rounded to the nearest ten?

50. Mr. Adams has 185 movie posters and 212 music posters. He says that he has about 200 of each type of poster. Why does he use the same estimate for each type of poster?

51. **Analyze** Rounded to the nearest ten, the number of shows given by a puppet theater was 120. What is the least number of shows that could have been given? Explain.

52. **Multistep** In the school chorus there are 22 third-graders and 17 second-graders. Fourteen of these students also play the piano. How many do *not* play the piano?

The Little Theatre of the Deaf performing Dragon Stories.

Extra Practice See page 43, Set C.

Social Studies Connection
Abacus

The abacus has been used in Asian countries for centuries to solve problems.

To show numbers on an abacus:

- Push the beads to the crossbar.

- In the upper section beads touching the crossbar stand for 5.

- In the lower section beads touching the crossbar stand for 1.

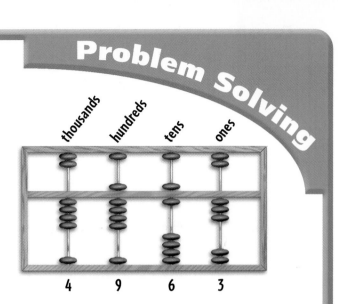

thousands hundreds tens ones

4   9   6   3

This abacus shows 4,963.

Write the numbers each abacus shows.

1.

2.

3.

WEEKLY WR READER   eduplace.com/map

Check your understanding of Lessons 1–3.

Compare. Write >, <, or = for each ⬤. (Lesson 1)

1. 76 ⬤ 67   2. 372 ⬤ 365   3. 4,306 ⬤ 4,308

Write the numbers in order from greatest to least. (Lesson 2)

4. 694   784   690   5. 6,543   7,595   6,595

Round each number to the place of the underlined digit. (Lesson 3)

6. 5̲4   7. 6̲8   8. 4̲2   9. 7̲50

10. 3̲49   11. 48̲2   12. 67̲6   13. 5̲18

Round Four-Digit Numbers

Objective Round four-digit numbers to the nearest thousand, hundred, or ten.

Learn About It

The musical *Cats* was one of the longest-running shows on Broadway. It ran almost 20 years with 7,485 performances. To the nearest thousand, about how many performances did *Cats* have on Broadway?

Cats on Broadway in New York City

Different Ways to Round 7,485

Way 1 **Use a number line.**

Find 7,485 on the number line.

7,485 is closer to 7,000 than to 8,000.

So round 7,485 to 7,000.

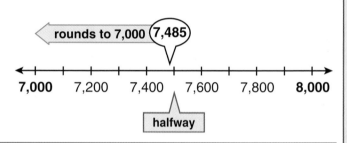

rounds to 7,000 (7,485)

7,000   7,200   7,400   7,600   7,800   8,000

halfway

Way 2 **Use rounding rules.**

STEP 1 Underline the digit in the place you are rounding to.

7, 4 8 5
↑
thousands place

STEP 2 Circle the digit to the right of the underlined digit.

7,④8 5
↑
circled digit

STEP 3 If the circled digit is 5 or greater, round up.

If the circled digit is less than 5, round down.

7,④8 5   4 < 5, so round down.
↓
7,0 0 0

Solution: To the nearest thousand, there were about 7,000 performances.

Other Examples

A. To the Nearest Hundred

1, 5③7 < 3 < 5

↑ hundreds place

1,537 rounds to⟩ 1,500

B. To the Nearest Ten

1, 5 3⑦ < 7 > 5

↑ tens place

1,537 rounds to⟩ 1,540

Guided Practice

Round to the place of the underlined digit.

1. 4,1<u>0</u>9
2. 6,<u>5</u>88
3. <u>2</u>,857
4. 4,6<u>2</u>4

5. 8,9<u>4</u>3
6. <u>1</u>,445
7. 1,9<u>1</u>5
8. 5,<u>6</u>82

Ask Yourself

• To what place am I rounding?

• What digit is to the right of the place being rounded to?

Explain Your Thinking ▶ Can a three-digit number round to 1,000? Explain why or why not.

Practice and Problem Solving

Round to the place of the underlined digit.

9. 4,<u>3</u>99
10. 9,8<u>0</u>9
11. <u>8</u>,250
12. <u>2</u>,885

13. <u>1</u>36
14. 1,0<u>3</u>4
15. <u>3</u>,491
16. <u>5</u>,658

17. <u>9</u>,483
18. 3,<u>4</u>85
19. 3,<u>5</u>11
20. <u>1</u>,539

Solve.

21. There were 1,385 people who attended a performance of *Annie*. What was the attendance to the nearest thousand? to the nearest hundred? to the nearest ten?

22. The newspaper said 2,862 people went to a show on Broadway. Felix said about 3,000 people went. Explain why both the newspaper and Felix could be correct.

Mixed Review and Test Prep

Open Response

Add. (Grade 2)

23. 4 + 3 + 7
24. 5 + 2 + 1
25. 8 + 8 + 9
26. 6 + 7 + 4
27. 6 + 4 + 2
28. 3 + 8 + 2

29. Jasmine figured out that she is 3,952 days old. To the nearest hundred, how many days old is she? Explain. (Ch. 2, Lesson 4)

Problem-Solving Application
Use a Bar Graph

Objective Use information in bar graphs to solve problems.

You can use information from a bar graph to help you solve problems.

Problem A student art show was held on four nights. Look at the bar graph. On which night did the most people attend the art show? How many people attended on that night?

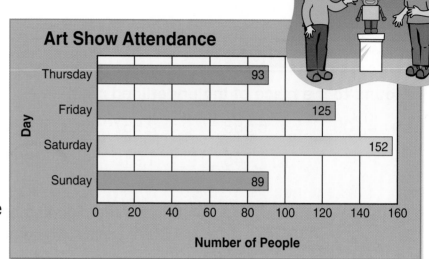

Art Show Attendance

Day	Number of People
Thursday	93
Friday	125
Saturday	152
Sunday	89

Number of People

UNDERSTAND

This is what you know.

- The art show was held on four nights.
- The graph shows how many people attended each night.

PLAN

Use the bar graph to compare the number of people who attended each night.

SOLVE

- Look at the bars for the four days. The bar that is the longest shows the night most people attended.
- Read the number at the end of that bar to find out how many people attended that night.

Solution: The most people attended on Saturday night. On Saturday, 152 people attended the art show.

LOOK BACK

Look back at the bar graph.

Does the solution seem reasonable?

Use the bar graph on Page 38 to solve each problem.

1. On which night did the least number of people attend the art show? How many people attended on that night?

2. To the nearest hundred, how many people attended the Friday night art show?

3. Which two nights had about the same number of people attend?

   (Hint) Which two bars are about the same length?

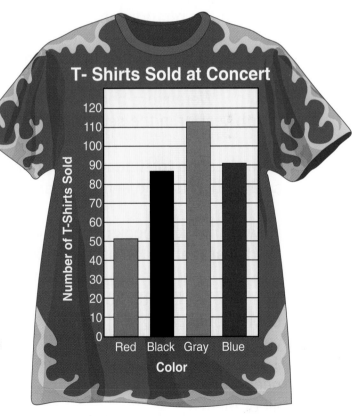

Ask Yourself

UNDERSTAND **What facts do I know?**

PLAN **Can I find the information I need on the graph?**

SOLVE • **Do I compare the length of the bars to solve?**

• **Do I need to use numbers to solve?**

LOOK BACK **Does my answer make sense?**

Independent Practice

The graph on the right shows the number of T-shirts sold to raise money for the art club. Use the bar graph for Problems 4–7.

4. To the nearest ten, about how many blue T-shirts were sold?

5. To the nearest ten, how many black T-shirts were sold?

6. **Explain** Which two T-shirt colors had about the same number of sales? How can you tell from the graph?

7. About how many more grey T-shirts were sold than black T-shirts?

8. **Create and Solve** Use real or made-up data to create a bar graph of your own. Then write and solve a problem about the graph you drew.

Mixed Problem Solving

Solve. Show your work. Tell what strategy you used.

9. Mr. Bridge gives guitar lessons. If each lesson is a half-hour long, how many students could he teach in 3 hours?

10. **Money** Together, a small and a large music poster cost $12. A large poster costs $4 more than a small one. How much does each poster cost?

11. One week Min rode her bike 2 miles. The next week she rode it 6 miles. The third week she rode it 10 miles. If Min continues the pattern, how many miles will she ride in the fifth week?

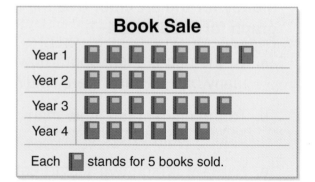

You Choose

Strategy
- Find a Pattern
- Draw a Picture
- Make a Table
- Solve a Simpler Problem
- Write a Number Sentence

Computation Method
- Mental Math
- Estimation
- Paper and Pencil
- Calculator

Data Use the pictograph for Problems 12–15.

12. In which year were the most books sold?

13. **Explain** Were more books sold in the fourth year or in the second year?

14. What was the total number of books sold in the first and second years?

15. How many more books were sold in the third year than in the second year?

Book Sale

Year 1	▯ ▯ ▯ ▯ ▯ ▯ ▯ ▯
Year 2	▯ ▯ ▯ ▯ ▯
Year 3	▯ ▯ ▯ ▯ ▯ ▯ ▯
Year 4	▯ ▯ ▯ ▯ ▯ ▯

Each ▯ stands for 5 books sold.

16. **You Decide** Decide how many books you want to sell at next year's sale. If each person buys 1 or 2 books, how many people need to buy books to sell all of them?

Math Challenge
Place Value Puzzler

Use the clues to match each girl with her home town.

- The population of Selene's town has a 3 in the hundreds place.

- The population of Meg's town has a 3 in the thousands place.

- The population of Terry's town has a 7 in the ones place.

Who lives in each town?

Social Studies Connection
Order the Heights

Here are the heights of some of the world's famous mountains. Write them in order from the tallest mountain to the shortest mountain.

Annapurna (Nepal)	26,504 ft
Cotopaxi (Ecuador)	19,347 ft
McKinley (U.S.)	20,320 ft
Fuji (Japan)	12,388 ft
Kilimanjaro (Tanzania)	19,340 ft

Brain Teaser

Try the number riddles!

Follow the clues below to answer the riddles.

- The number has 4 digits.

- All of its digits are odd.

- The sum of its ones and tens digits is 8.

- The sum of its hundreds and thousands digits is 12.

What's the greatest number it could be?

What's the least number it could be?

Education Place

Check out
eduplace.com/map
for more brain teasers.

Chapter Review/Test

VOCABULARY

Choose the best term to complete each sentence.

1. When we list numbers from greatest to least, we are putting them in ____.

2. When we do not need a number to be exact, we can ____ the number.

Vocabulary

compare

order

round

CONCEPTS AND SKILLS

Compare. Write >, <, or = for each ⬤. (Lesson 1, pp. 28–29)

3. 89 ⬤ 98   4. 301 ⬤ 299   5. 5,678 ⬤ 5,678

Write the numbers in order from least to greatest. (Lesson 2, pp. 30–31)

6. 63 67 61   7. 732 772 734   8. 1,856 1,854 1,850

Round to the place of the underlined digit. (Lessons 3–4, pp. 32–37)

9. 4̲4   10. 1̲99   11. 9̲3̲2   12. 2̲56   13. 6̲24

14. 3,3̲99   15. 6,8̲0̲9   16. 2̲,244   17. 5̲,056   18. 3̲,511

PROBLEM SOLVING

Solve. Use the bar graph. (Lesson 5, pp. 38–41)

19. About how many of each smoothie were sold?

20. Which smoothie was sold the least?

Show You Understand

A mile is 5,280 ft. Alex says this is about 5,300 ft. Dave says this is about 5,000 ft. Are they both correct? Explain your answer.

Extra Practice

Set A (Lesson 1, pp. 28–29)

Compare. Write <, >, or = for each ⬤.

1. 69 ⬤ 64   **2.** 39 ⬤ 39   **3.** 438 ⬤ 483   **4.** 79 ⬤ 67

5. 53 ⬤ 153   **6.** 794 ⬤ 794   **7.** 285 ⬤ 852   **8.** 5,442 ⬤ 4,452

Write = or ≠ for each ⬤.

9. 16 + 5 ⬤ 17   **10.** 31 + 4 ⬤ 32   **11.** 50 + 4 ⬤ 56

12. 100 + 60 ⬤ 160   **13.** 200 + 8 ⬤ 280   **14.** 600 + 40 ⬤ 460

Set B (Lesson 2, pp. 30–31)

Write the numbers in order from least to greatest.

1. 93 76 91   **2.** 327 312 302   **3.** 3,822 3,288 3,832

Write the numbers in order from greatest to least.

4. 45 54 42   **5.** 381 318 338   **6.** 9,669 9,996 9,696

Set C (Lesson 3, pp. 32–34)

Round to the nearest ten.

1. 71   **2.** 69   **3.** 51   **4.** 77   **5.** 33

Round to the nearest hundred.

6. 304   **7.** 960   **8.** 452   **9.** 805   **10.** 600

Set D (Lesson 4, pp. 36–37)

Round to the place of the underlined digit.

1. <u>7</u>,400   **2.** <u>2</u>,501   **3.** 4,<u>9</u>21   **4.** 9,<u>5</u>31   **5.** <u>7</u>,147

6. 9,8<u>1</u>5   **7.** 7,4<u>4</u>9   **8.** 9,<u>3</u>30   **9.** <u>1</u>,349   **10.** 9,1<u>9</u>5

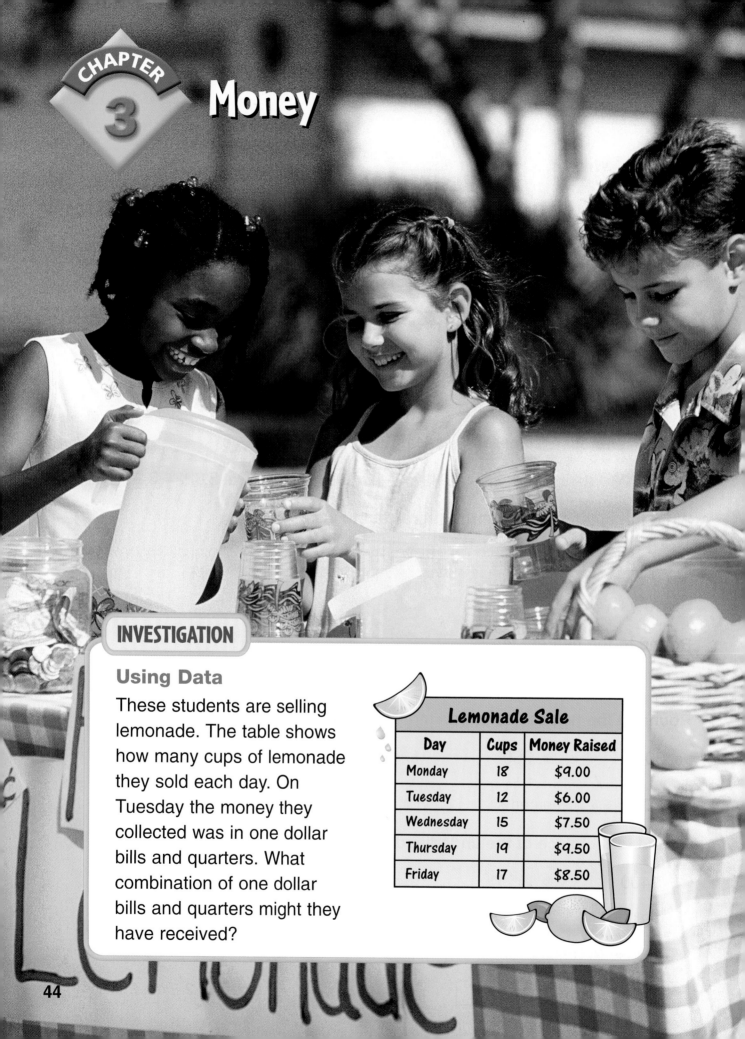

Money

INVESTIGATION

Using Data

These students are selling lemonade. The table shows how many cups of lemonade they sold each day. On Tuesday the money they collected was in one dollar bills and quarters. What combination of one dollar bills and quarters might they have received?

Lemonade Sale		
Day	Cups	Money Raised
Monday	18	$9.00
Tuesday	12	$6.00
Wednesday	15	$7.50
Thursday	19	$9.50
Friday	17	$8.50

Use What You Know

**Use this page to review and remember
what you need to know for this chapter.**

VOCABULARY

Choose the best term to complete each sentence.

1. One _____ is worth 10¢.

2. The $ symbol is called a _____.

3. Five pennies is equal to 1 _____.

4. A _____ has a value of 1¢.

5. One hundred cents is equal to 1 _____.

Vocabulary
dime

penny

nickel

dollar

cent sign

dollar sign

CONCEPTS AND SKILLS

Write the value of each coin.

6.   7.   8.   9.

Write each amount using a cent sign.

10.

11.

12. twenty-three cents   13. eight cents   14. sixty-two cents

Write About It

15. Name three different sets
of coins that you could
use to buy this book.

 75¢

Facts Practice, See page 667.

Value of Money

Objective Understand the value of dollars, dimes, and pennies.

Vocabulary
dollar
dime
penny
dollar sign ($)
decimal point (.)

Learn About It

Blake has some money to spend at the school fair. He has 1 dollar, 1 dime, and 1 penny. What is the total value of the money?

Dollars	Dimes	Pennies
1	1	1

1 dollar
100 cents
100¢

1 dime
10 cents
10¢

1 penny
1 cent
1¢

one dollar and eleven cents
$1.11

dollar sign ↑ ↑ decimal point

Solution: The total value is $1.11.

Other Examples

A. Zero Dollars

Dollars	Dimes	Pennies
0	3	4

thirty-four cents
$0.34 or 34¢

B. Zero Dimes

Dollars	Dimes	Pennies
2	0	4

two dollars and four cents
$2.04

C. Zero Pennies

Dollars	Dimes	Pennies
6	2	0

six dollars and twenty cents
$6.20

Guided Practice

Write each amount using a dollar sign and a decimal point.

1.

2.

Ask Yourself

• Did I place the decimal point between the dollars and cents?

• Did I write the dollar sign?

Explain Your Thinking ▶ Is there a way to write the amount for Exercise 2 without using a dollar sign? If so, how?

Practice and Problem Solving

Write each amount, using a dollar sign and a decimal point.

3.

4.

5. eight dollars and forty-four cents

6. eleven dollars and six cents

Solve.

7. **Analyze** Taylor had 8 dimes and 30 pennies in her purse. She spent half of the dimes. What is the value of the money left in her purse?

8. Ryan has $6.15 in his bank. How much will he have if he adds 1 dollar, 2 dimes, and 1 penny?

Mixed Review and Test Prep

Open Response

Order the numbers from least to greatest. (Ch. 2, Lesson 2)

9. 127 201 152

10. 65 39 90

11. 100 83 76

12. 1,204 24 402

13. 56 359 185

14. 129 140 121

15. 246 624 264

16. 385 358 835

Multiple Choice

17. Wanda has 1 dollar, 5 dimes, and 2 pennies. What is the total value of her money?
(Ch.3, Lesson 1)

A $1.25

c $2.15

B $1.52

D $2.51

Audio Tutor 1/7 Listen and Understand

Count Coins and Bills

Objective Name and count coins and bills.

Vocabulary
half-dollar
quarter
nickel

Learn About It

Kendal handed Mr. Jefferson the coins shown below to pay for a used book at the school book sale. What is the total value of the coins?

half-dollar	quarter	dime	nickel	penny
fifty cents	twenty-five cents	ten cents	five cents	one cent
50¢ $0.50	25¢ $0.25	10¢ $0.10	5¢ $0.05	1¢ $0.01

$0.50 ⟹ $0.75 ⟹ $0.85 ⟹ $0.90 ⟹ $0.91

Start with the coin of greatest value.
Continue counting coins from greatest to least value.

Solution: The total value of the coins is $0.91.

Another Example

Count Bills and Coins

$10.00 ⟹ $15.00 ⟹ $15.50 ⟹ $15.75 ⟹ $15.85 ⟹ $15.90

The total value of the bills and coins is $15.90.

Guided Practice

Write each amount using a dollar sign and a decimal point.

1.

2.

Ask Yourself

• What is the value of each bill and coin?

• Did I count the money in order from greatest to least value?

Explain Your Thinking ▶ Why do people often start with the bill or coin of greatest value when they count money?

Write each amount, using a dollar sign and a decimal point.

3.

4.

5. 1 dollar, 1 half-dollar, 7 nickels

6. 3 half-dollars, 1 quarter, 3 pennies

7. 1 five-dollar bill, 1 half-dollar, 2 quarters, 4 nickels

8. 6 quarters, 2 dimes, 1 nickel, 3 pennies

9. 4 one-dollar bills, 2 quarters, 1 nickel, 4 pennies

10. 2 one-dollar bills, 2 half-dollars, 1 nickel, 1 penny

 Data Use the book sale sign for Problems 11–12.

11. Michel paid for a book with a one-dollar bill, 2 dimes, 2 nickels, and 5 pennies. What type of book did Michel buy?

12. Multistep Mina bought a book. She paid with a one-dollar bill and 5 dimes and one nickel. Which type of book did she buy?

13. Reasoning Celso has 5 coins that total 96¢. What are the five coins?

Used Books

Type of Book	Cost
Biography	$1.55
Mystery	$1.80
Poetry	$1.35
Craft	$0.99

Mixed Review and Test Prep

Open Response

Round each number to the nearest ten. (Ch. 2, Lessons 3–4)

14. 48   **15.** 752   **16.** 1,336

17. 523   **18.** 399   **19.** 2,065

20. 333   **21.** 859   **22.** 1,407

23. Dana has 2 quarters, 3 dimes, and 4 nickels. Veronica has 1 half-dollar, 1 quarter, 1 dime, and 10 pennies. Who has more money? Explain how you got your answer. (Ch.3, Lesson 2)

Audio Tutor 1/8 Listen and Understand

Problem-Solving Application
Make Change

Objective Make change from a given amount.

You can count up from the cost of something to find out how much change you should receive.

Problem Ilyse and her mother go to the grocery store. They buy a box of raisins for $2.35 and pay with a five-dollar bill. How much change should they receive?

UNDERSTAND

What do you know?

- The raisins cost $2.35.
- They pay with a five-dollar bill.

PLAN

Count up from the cost of the raisins to the amount paid.

SOLVE

- Start with the total cost of the raisins.
- Count up from that amount. Count coins and bills until you reach five dollars.

Cost of snack						Amount paid
$2.35 ⇨	$2.40 ⇨	$2.50 ⇨	$2.75 ⇨	$3.00 ⇨	$4.00 ⇨	$5.00

- Then count the bills and coins used to make the change.

Solution: They should receive $2.65 in change.

LOOK BACK

Look back at the problem.

Does your answer seem reasonable?

Extra Help at **eduplace.com/map**

Use the Ask Yourself questions to help you solve each problem.

1. Inez spends $1.40 for carrot sticks. She pays $2.00. How much change should she receive?

2. Paolo buys juice for $0.89. He pays with a five-dollar bill. How much change should he receive?

   Hint Will Paolo receive more than one dollar in change?

Ask Yourself

UNDERSTAND What does the question ask me to find?

PLAN Do I know which amount to begin with, and which amount to count to?

SOLVE What coins and bills do I need?

LOOK BACK Did I solve the problem?

Independent Practice

Use the items at the right for Problems 3–6.

3. Alan buys a tube of toothpaste. He pays $3.00. How much change should he receive?

4. Meg buys a bag of bird seed. She pays with a ten-dollar bill. How much change should she receive? List the coins and bills she might receive as change.

5. **Multistep** Jamil buys a notepad. He pays $1.00. Then he uses his change to buy an eraser. How much money does Jamil have left?

6. Anita buys a cooking magazine. She pays $5.00. Does she have enough money left to buy a puzzle magazine that costs $2.00? Explain why or why not.

Bird Seed $ 7.65

CROSSWORDS GAMES & PUZZLES $ 2.00

Cooking $ 3.20

$ 0.45

TOOTHPASTE $ 2.78

$ 0.35

Compare Money Amounts

Objective Compare amounts of money.

Vocabulary
equivalent amounts

Learn About It

Bob and Dora are buying slices of fruit breads at the school bake sale. Which kind of bread costs more?

STEP 1 Find the value of each group of coins.

Bob uses these coins to buy banana bread.

25¢ ⟹ 50¢ ⟹ 55¢

The banana bread costs 55¢.

Dora uses these coins to buy apple bread.

25¢ ⟹ 35¢ ⟹ 45¢ ⟹ 50¢

The apple bread costs 50¢.

STEP 2 Compare the money values.

55¢ > 50¢

Solution: The banana bread costs more.

Another Example

The money amounts below are **equivalent amounts**. This means they are equal in value. Both groups show $11.25.

Ask Yourself
- What is the value of each bill or coin?
- What is the total amount?
- How do the amounts compare?

Compare. Write >, <, or = for each .

1.

2.

Explain Your Thinking ▶ Look back at Exercises 1–2. Which exercise shows equivalent amounts? Explain how you know.

Practice and Problem Solving

Compare. Write >, <, or = for each ●.

3.

4.

Solve.

5. Sara, Ben, and Tory buy baked goods at the sale. Sara spends $3.65, Ben spends $3.05, and Tory spends $3.55. Put the amounts in order from greatest to least. Who spends the most?

6. **Challenge** Luc has 2 half-dollars, 3 dimes, and 4 nickels. Martha has 3 quarters, 2 dimes, 2 nickels, and 5 pennies. Does the person with more coins have more money? Explain your thinking.

Go On

Find the total value of the bills and coins.
Then write the letter of the equivalent amount.

7. 1 half-dollar, 2 dimes, 2 nickels

A.

8. 15 one-dollar bills, 2 quarters

9. 8 dimes

B.

10. 1 dollar, 5 quarters

11. 9 quarters

C.

12. 3 five-dollar bills, 5 dimes

Use the fewest number of coins and bills to show
each amount.

13. 13¢   14. 60¢   15. 95¢   16. $14.00   17. $5.35

18. 75¢   19. $10.60   20. 30¢   21. $13.05   22. 47¢

📊 **Data** Use the sign for Problems 23–26.

23. Samantha wants to buy 1 brownie and 1 corn muffin. She has $3.00. Does she have enough to buy both items? How do you know?

24. Suppose you have quarters, dimes, and nickels. What is the fewest number of coins you could use to buy an oatmeal cookie?

25. **What's Wrong?** Suppose Oscar uses 2 one-dollar bills to pay for a brownie. He receives 4 dimes in change. What's wrong?

26. **Analyze** Diana used 5 coins to buy a lemon bar. She did not receive change. What coins could Diana have used?

Bake Sale

Oatmeal Cookie	$0.65
Corn Muffin	$0.95
Lemon Bar	$0.85
Brownie	$1.05

Extra Practice See page 61, Set C.

Math Challenge
Even Steven

Steven has three banks in his room. He wants each bank to hold the same amount of money. Help Steven move coins from one bank to another so each bank has the same amount.

1. How should the coins be moved?

2. Draw a picture to show what coins should be in each bank.

3. Write the amount that each bank now holds.

Check your understanding of Lessons 1–4.

Write each amount. (Lessons 1–2)

1.

2.

Compare. Write >, <, or = for each **.** (Lesson 4)

3. 3 dimes ⬤ 1 quarter

4. 3 quarters ⬤ 1 dollar

5. 2 quarters ⬤ 6 nickels

6. 8 nickels ⬤ 4 dimes

Solve. (Lesson 3)

7. Emilio buys a poster that costs $2.65. He gives the clerk $5.00. What is his change? List the bills and coins that Emilio might receive.

Round Money

Objective Round money to the nearest dollar and nearest ten dollars.

Learn About It

Members of the Computer Club are selling plants to raise money for new software. The club sells each plant for $7.65. About how much does each plant cost?

You can round the amount to the nearest dollar or ten dollars to tell about how much money each plant costs.

Different Ways to Round $7.65

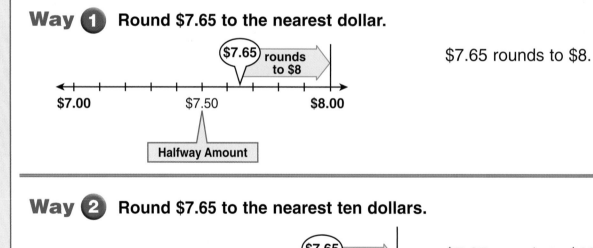

Way 1 Round $7.65 to the nearest dollar.

$7.65 rounds to $8

$7.00 $7.50 $8.00

Halfway Amount

$7.65 rounds to $8.

Way 2 Round $7.65 to the nearest ten dollars.

$7.65 rounds to $10

$0 $1 $2 $3 $4 $5 $6 $7 $8 $9 $10

Halfway Amount

$7.65 rounds to $10.

Solution: If you round to the nearest dollar, the club sells each plant for about $8.

If you round to the nearest ten dollars, the club sells each plant for about $10.

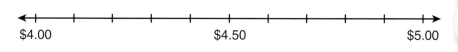

Guided Practice

Round to the nearest dollar.

$4.00 $4.50 $5.00

1. $4.29   **2.** $4.81   **3.** $4.50

Round to the nearest ten dollars.

$50 $51 $52 $53 $54 $55 $56 $57 $58 $59 $60

4. $53.82   **5.** $59.76   **6.** $50.73

Explain Your Thinking ▶ Which usually gives you a closer estimate, rounding to the nearest dollar or rounding to the nearest ten dollars?

Practice and Problem Solving

Round to the nearest dollar.

$6.00 $6.50 $7.00

7. $6.51   **8.** $6.83   **9.** $6.07

10. $6.90   **11.** $6.50   **12.** $6.38

Round to the nearest ten dollars.

$40 $41 $42 $43 $44 $45 $46 $47 $48 $49 $50

13. $42.09   **14.** $48.35   **15.** $49.79

16. $41.50   **17.** $44.98   **18.** $47.18

Ask Yourself
- Which dollar amount is the amount closer to?
- What should I do if the amount is halfway between the dollar amounts?

Go On

Round each amount to the place of the underlined digit.

19. $\underline{3}.59

20. $\underline{1}5.23

21. $1\underline{2}.38

22. $\underline{2}4.61

Round each amount to the nearest dollar. Then compare.
Write >, <, or = for each ⬤.

23. $5.47 ⬤ $5.90

24. $4.05 ⬤ $4.60

25. $2.91 ⬤ $2.91

26. $1.42 ⬤ $1.48

27. $3.27 ⬤ $3.22

28. $7.30 ⬤ $7.50

Solve.

29. The soccer team is raising money for new uniforms. Benito raises $18.45, Will raises $17.25, and Tanya raises $17.95. Which students raise about $18 each?

30. Fran raised $8.55 one week and $9.20 the next. She says that she has raised about $9 each week. Why is she correct?

31. Multistep Jessica donates 4 quarters, 4 dimes, and 1 nickel. George donates 5 quarters, 3 dimes, and 3 nickels. Who donates more? How much more?

 32. Write About It When you round an amount to the nearest dollar and to the nearest 10 dollars, can the rounded amounts be the same?

Mixed Review and Test Prep ✓

Open Response

Add or subtract. (Grade 2)

33. 300 + 200

34. 400 + 300

35. 600 + 100

36. 700 − 500

37. 400 − 200

38. 800 − 100

Multiple Choice

39. Which shows $4.38 rounded to the nearest dollar?
(Ch.3, Lesson 5)

A $3.00

C $4.50

B $4.00

D $5.00

Extra Practice See page 61, Set D.

Activity

Count it up!

Practice counting money amounts by playing this game with a partner. Try to be the first person to reach the "target amount"!

2 Players

What You'll Need • a number cube labeled 1 to 6, play money (1¢, 5¢, 10¢, 25¢, and 50¢ coins; 6 of each)

How to Play

1. Players decide on a target amount from the list.

2. Each player rolls the number cube. The number rolled is the number of coins the player has to pick. The player can pick any of the coins.

3. Each player counts his or her money and records the total value of the coins.

4. After each turn, players add the new amount to the amount already recorded by counting the coins. The first player to reach or pass the target amount wins!

Target Amounts
$2.37
$2.95
$3.09
$3.42
$3.61
$4.20
$4.78
$4.83
$4.99

Chapter Review/Test

VOCABULARY

Choose the best term to complete each sentence.

1. Ten pennies is equal to one ____.

2. Between the digits for the dollars and cents you need to write a ____.

3. Four quarters is equal to one ____.

4. Five dimes is equal to one ____.

Vocabulary
- dime
- dollar
- dollar sign
- half-dollar
- decimal point

CONCEPTS AND SKILLS

Write each amount. (Lessons 1–2, pp. 46–49)

5. four dollars and three cents

6. 1 five-dollar bill, 2 dimes, 3 nickels

7. three dollars and sixty cents

8. 1 ten-dollar bill, 2 quarters

Compare. Write >, <, or = for each ●. (Lesson 4, pp. 52–54)

9. 2 quarters ● 6 dimes

10. 3 dimes ● 6 nickels

Round each amount to the place of the underlined digit. (Lesson 5, pp. 56–58)

11. $2.11

12. $7.85

13. $5.27

14. $4.50

15. $36.25

16. $28.53

17. $44.79

18. $51.00

PROBLEM SOLVING

Solve. (Lesson 3, pp. 50–51)

19. Anika buys a bag of popcorn for $1.25. She pays with a five-dollar bill. How much change should she receive?

20. Jared buys a pretzel for $2.75. He pays with a ten-dollar bill. How much change should he receive?

Write About It

Show You Understand

Mick and Paco are comparing money. Mick says to Paco, "I have six coins, and you only have three, so I have more money than you do." Is Mick right or wrong?

Explain your answer.

Extra Practice

Set A (Lesson 1, pp. 46–47)

Write each amount, using a dollar sign and a decimal point.

1.

2.

3. four dollars and two cents

4. five dollars and seventy-one cents

Set B (Lesson 2, pp. 48–49)

Write each amount, using a dollar sign and a decimal point.

1. 1 five-dollar bill, 3 one-dollar bills, 1 half-dollar, 6 nickels

2. 1 ten-dollar bill, 1 five-dollar bill, 3 quarters, 1 dime, 4 pennies

3. 3 five-dollar bills, 2 one-dollar bills, 4 dimes, 6 pennies

4. 6 one-dollar bills, 2 half-dollars, 2 quarters, 6 dimes

Set C (Lesson 4, pp. 52–54)

Compare. Write >, <, or = for each ⬤.

1.

2.

Set D (Lesson 5, pp. 56–58)

Round to the nearest dollar.

1. $4.86   **2.** $2.91   **3.** $8.17   **4.** $6.43   **5.** $2.27

Round to the nearest ten dollars.

6. $54.33   **7.** $59.13   **8.** $71.78   **9.** $55.60   **10.** $79.12

When in Rome...

The Romans developed a number system using letters to stand for numbers. The table shows some Roman numerals from 1 to 1,000.

To read most Roman numerals you must add the values of the letters to find the value of the number. Look at these examples.

III = 1 + 1 + 1, or 3
VI = 5 + 1, or 6
LII = 50 + 2, or 52

For some Roman numerals, **I** appears before a greater number. To read these numbers you must *subtract* the value of **I**, or 1, from the greater number. Here are some examples.

IV = 5 – 1, or 4
IX = 10 – 1, or 9

Roman numerals are still used today. You might see them on a building or on the face of a clock.

1	I
2	II
3	III
4	IV
5	V
6	VI
7	VII
8	VIII
9	IX
10	X
50	L
100	C
500	D
1,000	M

Problem Solving

Suppose you lived in ancient Rome and had to send packages to four friends. Their addresses are shown using our number system. Write each address using Roman numerals.

1. 6 Caesar Street

2. 18 Doric Boulevard

3. 65 Aqueduct Way

4. 59 Empire Road

Imagine you found packages addressed to people who lived in ancient Rome. Their addresses are shown in Roman numerals. Write each address using our number system.

5. LVII Coliseum Way

6. XXI Rome Road

7. DXI Julius Street

Education Place
Visit Weekly Reader Connections at **eduplace.com/map** for more on this topic.

8. C Virgil Lane

How Many?

Have you ever tried to guess how many marbles are in a full jar?

Sometimes you can use an amount you already know to help you estimate. This amount is called a **reference set**.

Jar A

There are 50 marbles in Jar A. Use this as a reference set.

Jar B

How many marbles are in Jar B? Estimate to decide.

Think: The reference set is 50 marbles. There are about two times as many marbles in Jar B. So, there are about 100 marbles in Jar B.

Try These!

Choose the best estimate for each jar below. Use the jars at the right as reference sets.

75 Marbles

200 Marbles

1

a. 25   **b.** 75

2

a. 100   **b.** 200

3

a. 200   **b.** 300

Money Matters

Jacob puts 2 one-dollar bills and 3 quarters into his piggy bank. His brother Sam puts 1 one-dollar bill, 6 quarters, and 2 dimes into his bank. Who puts more money into his bank?

You can use the coin and bill models found on Education Place at **eduplace.com/map** to help you compare.

- At the pictures of the workmats choose **Two Numbers.**

- To show Jacob's money:
  Put your pointer over the **Stamp** tool.
  Then click the dollar bill 2 times.
  Next, click the quarter 3 times.

- Click anywhere in the right workspace.

- Follow the steps above to show Sam's money.

- Click **[1 2 3]**.

Solution: Jacob has $2.75 and Sam has $2.70.
So, Jacob has more money.

Use the coin and bills models. Write >, <, or = for each ⬤.

1. 3 one-dollar bills, 3 quarters, and 3 pennies ⬤ 3 one-dollar bills, 2 quarters, 2 dimes, and 1 nickel

2. 1 five-dollar bill, 2 quarters, 2 dimes and 1 nickel ⬤ 1 five-dollar bill, 3 quarters, 1 nickel, and 2 pennies

3. 2 one-dollar bills and 3 dimes ⬤ 2 one-dollar bills and 3 nickels

4. **Challenge** Show $3.43 four different ways.
   Show two ways on the mat. Then clear it and show two more ways.

✓ Unit 1 Test

⬤ Open Response

Choose the correct term to complete each sentence.

Vocabulary
is less than
is greater than
standard form
equivalent amounts

1. The symbol > means ____.

2. The number 67 is written in ____.

3. Three dimes and thirty pennies are ____.

CONCEPTS AND SKILLS ⬤ Open Response

Tell how each number is used. Write *position*, *count*, *measure*, or *label* for each. (Chapter 1)

4. 101 Dalmatians

5. 26 feet

6. 5th in line

7. 14 Grove Street

Write each number in standard form. (Chapters 1–2)

8. 300 + 40 + 2

9. 2,000 + 500 + 7

10. fifty-six thousand, two hundred sixty

11. eight hundred thousand, sixty

Write the numbers in order from greatest to least. (Chapter 2)

12. 234 340 276

13. 9,567 9,999 7,445

**Write the place of the underlined digit.
Then write its value.** (Chapters 1–2)

14. 3<u>6</u>7

15. <u>1</u>34

16. <u>4</u>,849

17. 7,9<u>8</u>3

18. 6,4<u>3</u>2

19. 5<u>6</u>3,981

Round to the place of the underlined digit. (Chapters 2–3)

20. <u>7</u>2

21. 4<u>5</u>2

22. <u>6</u>,859

23. $3.<u>6</u>5

24. $<u>8</u>.43

25. $4<u>7</u>.50

Compare. Write >, <, or = for each ⬤. (Chapters 2–3)

26. 45 ⬤ 35

27. 209 ⬤ 290

28. $35.98 ⬤ $24.99

Write each amount using a dollar sign and decimal point. (Chapter 3)

29.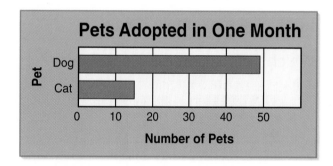

30. 3 one-dollar bills, 1 quarter, 2 dimes

PROBLEM SOLVING (Open Response)

31. Julia saved 3 pennies on Monday, 6 on Tuesday, and 9 on Wednesday. If she continues the pattern, how many pennies should she save on Friday?

32. Sara buys a T-shirt that costs $9.59. She gives the clerk a ten-dollar bill. The clerk gives her four coins for her change. List the coins Sara receives.

33. Use the bar graph to solve the problem.

   To the nearest ten, about how many dogs were adopted? About how many cats?

Pets Adopted in One Month

Pet: Dog, Cat

Number of Pets: 0 10 20 30 40 50

Performance Assessment

(Extended Response)

Task The Eastside Pep Club was raising money for charity. They held a contest in which people had to guess the number of marbles in a jar.

As a club member, you need to decide how many marbles to put in the jar. Use the information at the right to help you. Then, write the clues for the contest.

Explain your thinking.

Information You Need

- One clue gives the number rounded to the nearest hundred.

- One clue gives the number rounded to the nearest ten.

- One clue uses a greater than or less than statement.

Cumulative Test Prep

Solve Problems 1–10.

Test-Taking Tip

Use number sense to eliminate answers that are obviously wrong.

Look at the example below.

Which number do the blocks show?

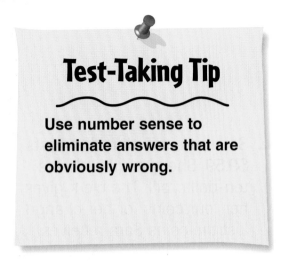

A 134	**C** 1,340
B 143	**D** 1,430

THINK

Choices C and D cannot be correct. They are much greater than the number of blocks shown. Eliminate those answers.

1. Ray is first in line. Celia is behind Denzel. You-Hee is between Ray and Denzel. Who is third in line?

   A Denzel **C** Celia

   B You-Hee **D** Ray

   (Chapter 1, Lesson 1)

2. Which number has a 6 in the ten thousands place?

   F 160 **H** 16,509

   G 615 **J** 62,530

   (Chapter 1, Lesson 6)

3. Which number makes this number sentence true?

   $$500 + \underline{} + 7 = 597$$

   A 9 **C** 9,000

   B 90 **D** 90,000

   (Chapter 1, Lesson 2)

4. Tonya had $7.57 in her pocket. She took 3 quarters, 7 dimes, 1 nickel, and 11 pennies out of her pocket. How much money is left in her pocket?

   F $1.61 **H** $5.96

   G $5.86 **J** $6.01

   (Chapter 3, Lesson 3)

For Test-Taking Tips, see page 659.

Open Response

5. Write 102,101 in word form.

(Chapter 1, Lesson 7)

6. Don says that the number of coins in a jar is about 400. If he rounded to the nearest ten, what is the least number of coins that can be in the jar?

(Chapter 2, Lesson 3)

7. List four odd numbers that are less than 65 and greater than 50.

(Chapter 2, Lesson 1)

8. Look at Timo's and Lori's money below.

Timo	Lori

Who has more money?

(Chapter 3, Lesson 4)

9. What number is next in the pattern?

1, 2, 4, 7, 11, 16, ___

(Chapter 1, Lesson 5)

Extended Response

10. The bar graph shows the number of shirts sold in one week at Jay's Clothing Store.

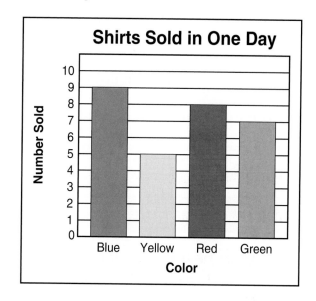

A How many yellow shirts were sold?

B Which shirt color was the most popular? How can you tell?

C Sales for which color shirt were closest to 10?

D Were more green shirts or yellow shirts sold? Explain how you got your answer.

(Chapter 2, Lesson 5)

Education Place

Look for Cumulative Test Prep at **eduplace.com/map** for test prep practice.

Vocabulary Wrap-Up for **Unit 1**

Look back at the big ideas and vocabulary in this unit.

Big Ideas

You can use place value to compare numbers.

You can round numbers to the nearest ten, nearest hundred, or nearest thousand.

You can count coins and bills.

Key Vocabulary
place value
compare
round

Math Conversations

Use your new vocabulary to discuss these big ideas.

1. Explain how the place value of 8 in 286 compares to the place value of 8 in 13,784.

2. Explain how to order these numbers from least to greatest.

   4,927   4,709   4,972

3. Explain how to find the change if you spend $0.83 and you pay with a one-dollar bill.

4. **Write About It** If you bought a bag of carrots for $1.29, how could you find the change you should receive if you pay with a $5 bill? Write the coins and bills you might receive.

The 2 in 1,254 is in the hundreds place.

Right, so that digit's value is 2 hundreds, or 200.

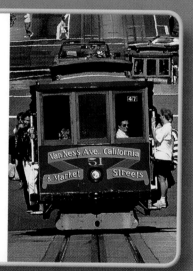
UNIT 2

Addition and Subtraction

Reading Mathematics

Reviewing Vocabulary

Here are some math vocabulary words that you should know.

addition	an operation on two or more numbers that gives the sum
subtraction	an operation on two numbers that gives the difference
addend	a number that is added
sum	the answer to an addition problem
difference	the answer to a subtraction problem

Reading Words and Symbols

You can use words and symbols to describe addition and subtraction.

2 plus 3 equals 5.

$$2 + 3 = 5$$

↑
sum

5 minus 3 equals 2.

$$5 - 3 = 2$$

↑
difference

Use words and symbols to describe each picture.

1.

2.

Reading Test Questions

Choose the correct answer for each.

3. Which number sentence best describes the picture?

   a. $8 + 1 = 9$ **c.** $9 - 4 = 5$

   b. $4 + 5 = 9$ **d.** $9 - 5 = 4$

Describes means "tells about" or "explains."

---

4. Which of the following is not equivalent to 6?

   a. $12 - 6$

   b. $8 - 4$

   c. $5 + 1$

   d. $4 + 2$

Not equivalent means "not equal."

5. Which of the following is false?

   a. In $6 + 1 = 7$, the 6 is an addend.

   b. In $4 = 2 + 2$, the 4 is the sum.

   c. In $6 - 5 = 1$, the 1 is the difference.

   d. In $5 = 8 - 3$, the 8 is the difference.

False means "not true" or "wrong."

Learning Vocabulary

Watch for these words in this unit. Write their definitions in your journal.

- regroup
- estimate
- Commutative Property
- Zero Property
- Associative Property
- fact family

Education Place

At **eduplace.com/map** see eGlossary and eGames—Math Lingo.

Literature Connection

Read "The School is One Big Bird Feeder" on Pages 646–647. Then work with a partner to answer the questions about the story.

CHAPTER 4 Add Whole Numbers

INVESTIGATION

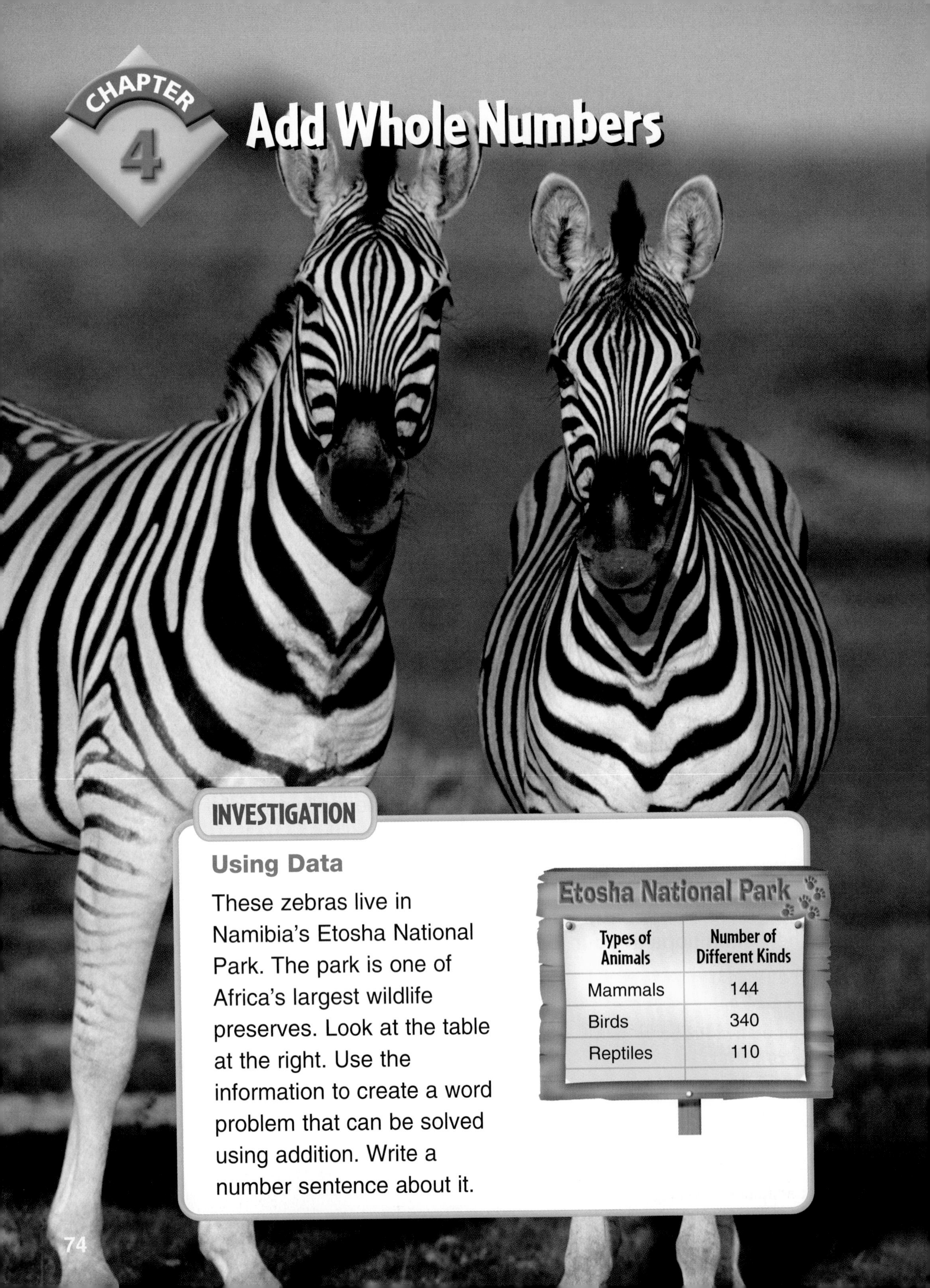

Using Data

These zebras live in Namibia's Etosha National Park. The park is one of Africa's largest wildlife preserves. Look at the table at the right. Use the information to create a word problem that can be solved using addition. Write a number sentence about it.

Etosha National Park

Types of Animals	Number of Different Kinds
Mammals	144
Birds	340
Reptiles	110

Use What You Know

Use this page to review and remember
what you need to know for this chapter.

VOCABULARY

Choose the best term to complete each sentence.

Vocabulary
sum
digit
addend
addition
difference
regroup

1. An operation that gives a sum is called ____.

2. In the number 289, the symbol 2 is called a ____.

3. The answer when you add is the ____.

4. The answer when you subtract is called the ____.

5. The number that is added is called the ____.

CONCEPTS AND SKILLS

Add.

6.
$$\begin{array}{r} 8 \\ + 9 \\ \hline \end{array}$$

7.
$$\begin{array}{r} 5 \\ + 8 \\ \hline \end{array}$$

8.
$$\begin{array}{r} 9 \\ + 2 \\ \hline \end{array}$$

9.
$$\begin{array}{r} 4 \\ + 3 \\ \hline \end{array}$$

10.
$$\begin{array}{r} 5 \\ + 6 \\ \hline \end{array}$$

11.
$$\begin{array}{r} 2 \\ + 8 \\ \hline \end{array}$$

12. $7 + 8$

13. $9 + 5$

14. $2 + 8$

15. $8 + 4$

16. $4 + 7$

Find the sum.

17.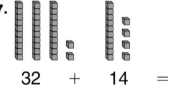

$$32 \quad + \quad 14 \quad = \quad \blacksquare$$

18.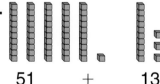

$$51 \quad + \quad 13 \quad = \quad \blacksquare$$

Write About It

19. Explain how to use $3 + 6$ to find $30 + 60$.

20. Explain how to use $2 + 8$ to find $20 + 80$.

Facts Practice, See page 665.

Addition Properties

Objective   Use addition properties to add.

Vocabulary

sum

Commutative Property

Zero Property

Associative Property

Learn About It

Using addition properties can help you find a sum .

Commutative Property

▶ **Changing the order that numbers are added does not change the sum.**

$$5 + 3 = 8$$

↑ addend   ↑ addend   ↑ sum

You can add down.
$$\begin{array}{r} 5 \\ + 3 \\ \hline \end{array} \downarrow$$

$$3 + 5 = 8$$

↑ addend   ↑ addend   ↑ sum

You can add up.
$$\begin{array}{r} 3 \\ + 5 \\ \hline \end{array} \uparrow$$

Zero Property

▶ **The sum of any number and zero is that number.**

$$4 + 0 = 4$$

Associative Property

▶ **Changing the way that addends are grouped does not change the sum.**

$$(6 + 4) + 3 \qquad 6 + (4 + 3)$$
$$10 + 3 = 13 \qquad 6 + 7 = 13$$

Parentheses show which numbers to add first.

Use addition properties to help find a sum using mental math.

You can change the order, the grouping, or both to make it easier to add. Also look to make a 10, add doubles, or any other way to add you find useful.

$$2 + 6 + 8 \qquad\qquad 7 + 5 + 7 \qquad\qquad 8 + 9 + 8 + 1$$
$$10 + 6 = 16 \qquad 14 + 5 = 19 \qquad 16 + 10 = 26$$

Extra Help at **eduplace.com/map**

Find each sum.

1. 6 + 3
   3 + 6

2. 0 + 7
   7 + 0

3. (7 + 3) + 5
   7 + (3 + 5)

Ask Yourself

• Which addition property can I use?

• How can I group the addends so that they are easier to add?

Explain Your Thinking ▶ Describe three ways to find 8 + 2 + 6 using mental math. Is one way easier than the others? Explain.

Practice and Problem Solving

Find each sum.

4. 2
    0
  + 9

5. 1
    5
  + 4

6. 3
    2
  + 1

7. 2
    7
  + 8

8. 5
    8
  + 3

9. 2
    7
  + 4

10. 5 + (2 + 8)

11. (3 + 2) + 6

12. 4 + 2 + (5 + 5)

13. (4 + 6) + 2 + 2 + 4

14. 5 + 4 + 7 + 2 + 1

15. 3 + 7 + 6 + 2 + 3

16. **Multistep** Ken's family caught 6 trout, 5 bass, 4 pike, and 1 catfish. After they gave away 2 trout, 2 bass, and 1 catfish, how many fish did they have left?

17. Think about solving 6 + 4 + 9. Which two numbers would you add first? Explain your thinking.

Mixed Review and Test Prep

Open Response

Skip count to find each missing number. (Ch. 1, Lesson 1)

18. 8, 10, _____, 14, 16

19. 60, 70, 80, 90, _____

20. 8,000, 9,000, _____, 11,000

Multiple Choice

21. Which of the following shows the Zero Property of Addition? (Ch. 4, Lesson 1)

   A 6 + 2 = 8

   B 10 + 0 = 10

   C (1 + 8) + 4 = 13

   D 4 + 3 + 4 = 11

Extra Practice See page 105, Set A.

Lesson 2

 Audio Tutor 1/10 Listen and Understand

Estimate Sums

Objective Estimate sums by rounding numbers or using compatible numbers.

Vocabulary

estimate

compatible numbers

 **Learn About It**

In a park in Wyoming, 227 visitors reported seeing a moose last year. This year 77 visitors reported seeing a moose. About how many visitors reported seeing moose in the two years?

If you do not need an exact answer, you can estimate. When you **estimate**, you find an answer that is close to the exact answer.

Different Ways to Estimate 227 + 77

Way ❶ Use rounding.

Round each number to the greatest place. Then add.

$$
\begin{array}{r}
227 \text{ rounds to } 200 \\
+\ 77 \text{ rounds to } +\ 80 \\
\hline
280
\end{array}
$$

227 + 77 is about 280.

Way ❷ Use compatible numbers.

Compatible numbers are numbers that are easy to compute mentally.

$$
\begin{array}{r}
227 \text{ is about } 225 \\
+\ 77 \text{ is about } +\ 75 \\
\hline
300
\end{array}
$$

227 + 77 is about 300.

Solution: Using rounding, about 280 visitors saw a moose.
Using compatible numbers, about 300 people saw a moose.

Other Examples

A. Estimate Money Using Rounding

$$
\begin{array}{r}
\$1.53 \text{ rounds to } \$2.00 \\
+\ 3.21 \text{ rounds to } +\ 3.00 \\
\hline
\$5.00
\end{array}
$$

$1.53 + $3.21 is *about* $5.00.

B. Estimate Money Using Compatible Numbers

$$
\begin{array}{r}
\$1.53 \text{ is about } \$1.50 \\
+\ 3.21 \text{ is about } +\ 3.00 \\
\hline
\$4.50
\end{array}
$$

$1.53 + $3.21 is *about* $4.50.

78

Ask Yourself

- To what place should I round each number?
- What numbers would be easy to add mentally?

Guided Practice

Round each number to the greatest place. Then add.

1. 54 + 65   **2.** 268 + 343   **3.** $3.32 + $1.42

Tell what compatible numbers you would use. Then add.

4. 46 + 53   **5.** 24 + 27   **6.** 327 + 58   **7.** $2.17 + $0.45

Explain Your Thinking ▶ How can you tell if an estimated sum is greater or less than the exact answer?

Practice and Problem Solving

Round each number to the greatest place. Then add.

8. 47	**9.** 29	**10.** 53	**11.** 71	**12.** 36
+ 53	+ 37	+ 49	+ 17	+ 42

13. 346	**14.** $2.84	**15.** 384	**16.** $6.55	**17.** 164
+ 389	+ 1.72	+ 525	+ 1.07	+ 837

18. $8.52 + $2.84   **19.** 311 + 818   **20.** 963 + 572   **21.** $6.84 + $2.75

Tell what compatible numbers you would use. Then add.

22. 26	**23.** 14	**24.** 26	**25.** 64	**26.** 48
+ 53	+ 37	+ 35	+ 38	+ 53

27. 22	**28.** $1.62	**29.** 162	**30.** 221	**31.** 163
+ 145	+ 0.23	+ 23	+ 307	+ 122

Go On

Round each number in the box to the greatest place. Then use the rounded numbers to answer Exercises 32–34.

32. Which numbers have a sum of about 900?

33. Which numbers have a sum of about 700?

34. Which numbers have a sum of about 600?

127	715
210	502

Data Use the sign for Problems 35–36.

35. Estimate About how many campsites near the park can Andrew's family choose from?

36. How much would it cost Andrew and his family to enter the park and spend 3 nights at Indian Creek?

37. Andrew's family spent $185 for food and $120 for gas on the trip. About how much did the family spend for food and gas?

Welcome to
Yellowstone National Park
Entrance Fee
$20 per car

Campsites Nearby
Indian Creek–75 sites
$10 per night

Pebble Creek–32 sites
$10 per night

Mixed Review and Test Prep

Open Response
Write the place of the underlined digit. Then write its value. (Ch. 1, Lesson 7)

38. <u>4</u>33,716

39. 852,3<u>8</u>5

40. 345,<u>2</u>08

41. 9<u>2</u>3,623

42. Suppose you want to buy two items that cost $8.12 and $1.43. How would you estimate to be sure that you had enough money? Explain.
(Ch. 4, Lesson 2)

Extra Practice See page 105, Set B.

Math Reasoning

Front-End Estimation

Another way to estimate sums is to add the front digits of the numbers. This is called **front-end estimation** .

Vocabulary

front-end estimation

Here are some examples of front-end estimation.

Two-Digit Numbers

The front digits are tens.
Add the tens.

$$43 \rightarrow 40$$
$$+ 26 \rightarrow + 20$$
$$\overline{ 60}$$

So 43 + 26 is about 60.

Dimes

The front digits are dimes.
Add the dimes.

$$\$0.59 \rightarrow \$0.50$$
$$+ 0.36 \rightarrow + 0.30$$
$$\overline{ \$0.80}$$

So $0.59 + $0.36 is about $0.80.

Three-Digit Numbers

The front digits are hundreds.
Add the hundreds.

$$536 \rightarrow 500$$
$$+ 245 \rightarrow + 200$$
$$\overline{ 700}$$

So 536 + 245 is about 700.

Dollars

The front digits are dollars.
Add the dollars.

$$\$7.39 \rightarrow \$7.00$$
$$+ 3.76 \rightarrow + 3.00$$
$$\overline{ \$10.00}$$

So $7.39 + $3.76 is about $10.00.

For each problem, estimate the sum using front-end estimation.

1. $\begin{array}{r} 73 \\ + 66 \\ \hline \end{array}$

2. $\begin{array}{r} 48 \\ + 44 \\ \hline \end{array}$

3. $\begin{array}{r} 273 \\ + 432 \\ \hline \end{array}$

4. $\begin{array}{r} \$0.52 \\ + 0.38 \\ \hline \end{array}$

5. $\begin{array}{r} \$8.42 \\ + 3.58 \\ \hline \end{array}$

6. Compare your estimates and the actual sum for Problems 1–5.
   Are the estimates greater than or less than the sums?
   Explain why.

7. **Analyze** Look at the examples to the right. In which one would you get the same estimate using rounding and front-end estimation?

   84 + 47 = ◼

   22 + 44 = ◼

Regroup Ones

Objective Regroup ones to add.

Vocabulary
regroup

Learn About It

Felipe belongs to a bird-watching club. Last April, Felipe's club spotted 159 birds. Then in May, they saw 118 birds. How many birds did the club see in those two months?

Add. 159 + 118 = ▥

STEP 1 Show 159 and 118.

$$159$$
$$+\ 118$$

STEP 2 Add the ones.

9 ones + 8 ones = 17 ones

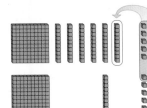

$$\overset{1}{1}59$$
$$+\ 118$$
$$\overline{7}$$

> **Regroup** 17 ones as 1 ten 7 ones.

STEP 3 Add the tens.

1 ten + 5 tens + 1 ten = 7 tens

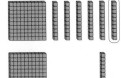

$$\overset{1}{1}59$$
$$+\ 118$$
$$\overline{77}$$

STEP 4 Add the hundreds.

1 hundred + 1 hundred = 2 hundreds

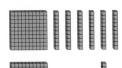

$$\overset{1}{1}59$$
$$+\ 118$$
$$\overline{277}$$

Estimate to Check

159	rounds to	200
+ 118	rounds to	+ 100
277		300

The answer is reasonable.

Solution: The club saw 277 birds.

Other Examples

A. Two-Digit Numbers

$$\begin{array}{r} \overset{1}{2}5 \\ + 37 \\ \hline 62 \end{array}$$

Regroup 12 ones as 1 ten 2 ones.

B. Money

$$\begin{array}{r} \overset{1}{\$2}.48 \\ + 3.36 \\ \hline \$5.84 \end{array}$$

Regroup 14 ones as 1 ten 4 ones.

Guided Practice

Find each sum. Estimate to check.

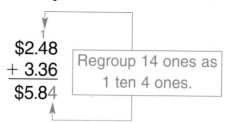

Ask Yourself

- What is the sum of the ones?
- Do I need to regroup ones?

1. $\begin{array}{r} 658 \\ + 234 \\ \hline \end{array}$

2. $\begin{array}{r} 268 \\ + 124 \\ \hline \end{array}$

3. $\begin{array}{r} \$31 \\ + 27 \\ \hline \end{array}$

4. $52 + 27$

5. $643 + 221$

6. $\$3.37 + \$3.18$

Add. Then write *yes* for each exercise where you regrouped ones to make a ten.

7. $\begin{array}{r} 34 \\ + 62 \\ \hline \end{array}$

8. $\begin{array}{r} 23 \\ + 68 \\ \hline \end{array}$

9. $\begin{array}{r} 354 \\ + 127 \\ \hline \end{array}$

10. $\begin{array}{r} 438 \\ + 224 \\ \hline \end{array}$

Explain Your Thinking ▶ How can you tell when to regroup?

Practice and Problem Solving

Find each sum. Estimate to check.

11. $\begin{array}{r} \$19 \\ + 75 \\ \hline \end{array}$

12. $\begin{array}{r} 17 \\ + 39 \\ \hline \end{array}$

13. $\begin{array}{r} \$37 \\ + 19 \\ \hline \end{array}$

14. $\begin{array}{r} \$837 \\ + 142 \\ \hline \end{array}$

15. $\begin{array}{r} 243 \\ + 548 \\ \hline \end{array}$

16. $\begin{array}{r} 205 \\ + 107 \\ \hline \end{array}$

17. $354 + 213$

18. $362 + 29$

19. $\$541 + \$317$

Go On

Algebra • **Functions** **Complete each table by following the rule.**

Rule: Add 28	
Input	Output
20.	54	
21.	47	
22.	65	
23.	31	

Rule: Add 126	
Input	Output
24.	337	
25.	112	
26.	568	
27.	324	

Rule: Add $135	
Input	Output
28.	$437	
29.	$229	
30.	$564	
31.	$820	

Solve.

32. One day, 165 birds came to the Nature Center feeder. The next day, 127 birds came to the feeder. How many birds came to the feeder during both days?

33. At a Nature Center store, Sharma spent $4 on a gift for her sister and $3 on cards. If Sharma had $10 at the start, how much money does she have left?

34. **Estimate** The store has 33 books on the birds of North America, 21 books on Eastern birds, and 44 books on Western birds. About how many bird books is that?

35. **Multistep** Jason has 245 bird cards. Talika has 128 cards more than Jason. Miguel has 309 cards. Who has the least number of cards?

Mixed Review and Test Prep

Open Response

Write each amount, using a dollar sign and a decimal point. (Ch. 3, Lesson 2)

36. 5 quarters, 2 nickels, 1 penny

37. 1 dollar, 4 dimes, 3 nickels

Multiple Choice

38. What is the sum of 527 + 169?
(Ch. 4, Lesson 3)

A 606   **C** 706

B 696   **D** 796

Extra Practice See page 105, Set C.

Math Reasoning
Adding in Different Ways

Here are two different ways to add.

▶ **This is how Ken did these two addition problems.**

Ken

$$57 = 50 + 7$$
$$+\ 22 = 20 + 2$$
$$70 + 9 = 79$$

Ken

$$46 = 40 + 6$$
$$+\ 35 = 30 + 5$$
$$70 + 11 = 81$$

- How does writing 57 as 50 + 7 and 22 as 20 + 2 help Ken add?

- How does writing 46 as 40 + 6 and 35 as 30 + 5 help Ken add?

▶ **This is how Donna does the same two problems using mental math.**

Donna

$$\begin{array}{r} 57 \\ +\ 22 \\ \hline \end{array} \qquad \begin{array}{r} 57 \\ +\ 20 \\ \hline 77 \\ +\ 2 \\ \hline 79 \end{array}$$

Donna thinks of 22 as 20 + 2

Donna

$$\begin{array}{r} 46 \\ +\ 35 \\ \hline \end{array} \qquad \begin{array}{r} 46 \\ +\ 30 \\ \hline 76 \\ +\ 5 \\ \hline 81 \end{array}$$

Donna thinks of 35 as 30 + 5

- How does thinking of 22 as 20 + 2 help Donna add?

- How does thinking of 35 as 30 + 5 help Donna add?

Find each sum. Use Ken's, Donna's, and the standard method.

1. $\begin{array}{r} 27 \\ +\ 57 \\ \hline \end{array}$
2. $\begin{array}{r} 81 \\ +\ 14 \\ \hline \end{array}$
3. $\begin{array}{r} 66 \\ +\ 28 \\ \hline \end{array}$
4. $\begin{array}{r} 32 \\ +\ 44 \\ \hline \end{array}$
5. $\begin{array}{r} 63 \\ +\ 29 \\ \hline \end{array}$

6. **Explain** How are the three methods alike? How are they different?

Regroup Ones and Tens

Objective Regroup both ones and tens to add.

Vocabulary
regroup

Learn About It

In one week a giant panda ate 272 pounds of bamboo. The next week, the panda ate 378 pounds. How many pounds of bamboo did the panda eat in two weeks?

Sometimes you have to **regroup** the ones <u>and</u> the tens.

Add.   272 + 378 = ▪

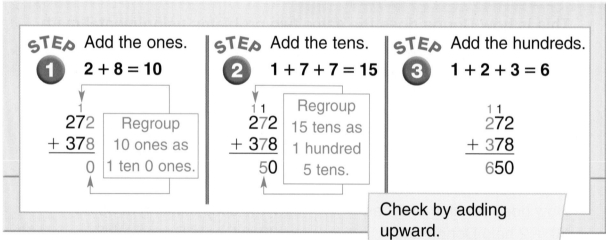

STEP 1 Add the ones.

2 + 8 = 10

$$\begin{array}{r} {\overset{1}{2}72} \\ +\ 378 \\ \hline 0 \end{array}$$

Regroup 10 ones as 1 ten 0 ones.

STEP 2 Add the tens.

1 + 7 + 7 = 15

$$\begin{array}{r} {\overset{1\ 1}{2}72} \\ +\ 378 \\ \hline 50 \end{array}$$

Regroup 15 tens as 1 hundred 5 tens.

STEP 3 Add the hundreds.

1 + 2 + 3 = 6

$$\begin{array}{r} {\overset{1\ 1}{2}72} \\ +\ 378 \\ \hline 650 \end{array}$$

Check by adding upward.

$$\begin{array}{r} 272 \\ +\ 378 \\ \hline 650 \end{array}$$

Solution: The panda ate 650 pounds of bamboo in two weeks.

Other Examples

A. Two-Digit Numbers

$$\begin{array}{r} {\overset{1}{7}9} \\ +\ 58 \\ \hline 137 \end{array}$$

B. Money

$$\begin{array}{r} {\overset{1\ 1}{\$3}.45} \\ +\ 2.98 \\ \hline \$6.43 \end{array}$$

Bring down the decimal point and the dollar sign.

Find each sum.

1. 67
    + 75

2. 374
    + 148

3. $2.94
    + 6.76

4. $4.28
    + 1.79

Ask Yourself

• What is the sum of the ones? Do I need to regroup?

• What is the sum of the tens? Do I need to regroup?

5. $1.28 + $3.85

6. 265 + 176

Explain Your Thinking ▶ Why do you sometimes need to regroup when you add?

Practice and Problem Solving

Add. Check by adding upward.

7. 313
    + 485

8. $1.51
    + 3.28

9. $4.23
    + 1.72

10. 135
    + 649

11. 134
    + 183

12. 636
    + 192

13. $3.82
    + 5.65

14. 243
    + 498

15. 234 + 498

16. 477 + 239

17. 149 + 778

18. 657 + 264

19. 585 + 326

20. 372 + 479

𝒳 Algebra • **Functions** Follow the rule to complete each table.

Rule: Add 58	
Input	Output
21. 73	▢
22. 87	▢
23. 56	▢
24. 62	▢

Rule: Add 248	
Input	Output
25. 176	▢
26. 463	▢
27. 298	▢
28. 564	▢

Go On

Mental Math **Find each sum.**

29. $3 + 5 = \blacksquare$
$30 + 50 = \blacksquare$
$300 + 500 = \blacksquare$
$3,000 + 5,000 = \blacksquare$

30. $7 + 5 = \blacksquare$
$70 + 50 = \blacksquare$
$700 + 500 = \blacksquare$
$7,000 + 5,000 = \blacksquare$

✖ Algebra • Properties **Find the missing numbers.**

31. $328 + 69 = \blacksquare + 328$

32. $237 + 0 = \blacksquare$

33. $(555 + 6) + 39 = (6 + 39) + \blacksquare$

34. $(440 + 8) + 35 = (35 + \blacksquare) + 8$

📊 Data **Use the map for Problem 35.**

35. To study giant pandas in China, scientists flew from Beijing to Xi'an and then to Chengdu. About how many miles did they fly from Beijing to Chengdu?

36. The scientists traveled 76 miles by bus to one panda reserve and then 96 miles by bus to another reserve. How far did they travel by bus?

37. A baby panda opens its eyes when it is about 45 days old. It begins to crawl about 30 days later. About how many days old is the baby panda when it begins to crawl?

38. **What's Wrong?** This is how Chang found the sum of $58 + 83$. What did Chang do wrong?

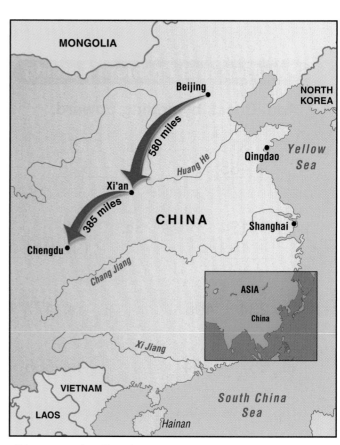

Giant pandas live in remote mountain areas in China.

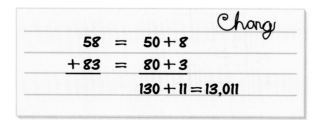

Chang
$58 = 50 + 8$
$+ 83 = 80 + 3$
$130 + 11 = 13,011$

Extra Practice See page 105, Set D.

Calculator Connection

Nifty Nines

Use a calculator to find patterns when adding 99.

1. Press  [+] [9] [9]. Then press [=] 6 times. Record each sum.

2. What is the pattern for the:
   • hundreds place?
   • tens place?
   • ones place?

3. What is the sum of the ones digit and the hundreds digit for each number?

4. **Predict** What will the next 4 numbers in the pattern be? Press [=] 4 times to check.

Check your understanding of Lessons 1–4.

Find the value of ■. (Lesson 1)

1. $3 + 6 = 6 + ■$

2. $5 + ■ = 5$

3. $(2 + 5) + 5 = 2 + (■ + 5)$

4. $6 + (3 + 2) = 3 + (6 + ■)$

Estimate each sum. (Lesson 2)

5. $16 + 34$

6. $23 + 58$

7. $33 + 36$

Add. (Lessons 3, 4)

8. $\begin{array}{r} 37 \\ + 28 \\ \hline \end{array}$

9. $\begin{array}{r} 567 \\ + 226 \\ \hline \end{array}$

10. $\begin{array}{r} \$3.64 \\ + 2.58 \\ \hline \end{array}$

Extra Practice at **eduplace.com/map**

Problem-Solving Strategy
Guess and Check

Objective Use the guess and check strategy to solve problems.

Problem You want to draw the moth and the butterfly in their actual size and side by side. You know the total length of their wingspan is 62 centimeters. You also know that the wingspan of the butterfly is 2 centimeters longer than the moth's. What is the wingspan of each?

Queen Alexandra's Birdwing

Atlas Moth

The actual wingspans of the moth and butterfly are each longer than the width of this page!

UNDERSTAND

This is what you know.

• The two lengths total 62 centimeters.

• The wingspan of the butterfly is 2 centimeters longer than that of the moth.

PLAN

Guess two numbers that have a difference of 2. Then add to check if their sum is 62. Continue guessing and checking until you find numbers that work.

SOLVE

First Guess: 31 and 29	**Second Guess: 32 and 30**
Check: $31 + 29 = 60$	Check: $32 + 30 = 62$
$60 < 62$	$32 - 30 = 2$
60 is too small. Guess again.	30 and 32 are correct.

Solution: The wingspan of the butterfly is 32 cm.
The wingspan of the moth is 30 cm.

LOOK BACK

Look back at the problem.

How can you use the result of one guess to decide what your next guess should be?

Use the Ask Yourself questions to help you solve each problem.

1. Lin has 6 more moth pictures than Bea. Together they have 22 moth pictures. How many moth pictures does each girl have?

2. Emily and Jacob found books about insects. Emily found 4 more books than Jacob. Together they found 18 books. How many books did each find?

(Hint) How much greater is one number than the other?

Ask Yourself

UNDERSTAND **What facts do I know?**

PLAN **Did I think of two numbers whose sum is less than the total?**

SOLVE **Did I use the guess and check strategy?**

LOOK BACK **Did I solve the problem?**

Independent Practice

Use guess and check to solve each problem.

3. The United States had 5 more endangered species of butterflies than beetles. Together the total is 29. How many endangered species of beetles were there?

4. Dylan has collected 21 insects. There are beetles and moths in his collection. If there are 3 more beetles than moths, how many of each kind of insect are there?

5. Harrison has 39 pictures of butterflies in his collection. There are 7 more pictures of monarchs than swallowtails. How many pictures of each kind of butterfly does he have?

Northeastern Beach Tiger Beetle

Karner Blue Butterfly

Schaus Swallowtail Butterfly

Go On

Mixed Problem Solving

Solve. Show your work. Tell what strategy you used.

6. Hannah has 56 red beads and 87 blue beads. She needs 150 beads to make a necklace. Does she have enough? Explain.

7. **Multistep** The market is 23 miles from Ben's house. The flower shop is 9 miles beyond the market. How many miles does Ben travel from home to the flower shop and back?

 **Data** Use the graph for Problems 8–12.

The graph shows the number of vegetable plants in Mr. Fisher's garden this year.

8. Mr. Fisher planted about the same number of which two vegetable plants?

9. Next year Mr. Fisher plans to plant 10 more bean plants than he planted this year. How many bean plants will Mr. Fisher plant next year?

10. **Mental Math** How many more tomatoes than squash did Mr. Fisher plant?

11. How many vegetable plants did Mr. Fisher plant altogether?

12. **Create and Solve** Use the data to write a problem of your own. Give it to a classmate to solve.

You Choose

Strategy
- Draw a Picture
- Solve a Simpler Problem
- Use Logical Reasoning
- Work Backward
- Write a Number Sentence

Computation Method
- Mental Math
- Estimation
- Paper and Pencil
- Calculator

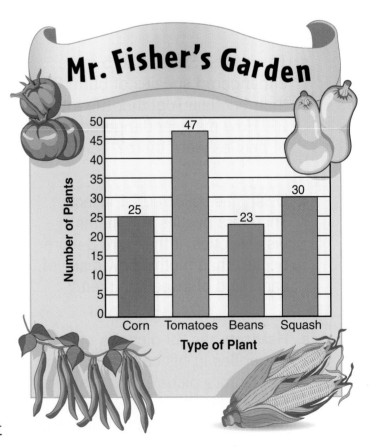

Mr. Fisher's Garden

Problem Solving on Tests

Choose the letter of the correct answer. If the correct answer is not here, choose NH.

1. Mia sold 113 raffle tickets. Kyle sold 168 raffle tickets. About how many tickets were sold in all?

   A 100   **B** 150   **C** 250   **D** NH

   (Chapter 4, Lesson 2)

2. Geraldo bought an orange for 59¢. He paid for it with a $5-bill. How much change should he receive?

   F $4.41   **H** $4.61

   G $4.51   **J** NH

   (Chapter 3, Lesson 3)

Open Response

Solve each problem.

3. Sunny Farms ships crates of peaches each week.

   Week 1   Week 2   Week 3

   Explain In which week were the most crates shipped?

   (Chapter 2, Lesson 2)

4. Mr. Owen has 4 red, 3 blue, and 5 green caps. He gives out 2 red, 1 blue, and 3 green caps. How many caps does he still have?

   (Grade 2)

Extended Response

5. You and your friend have a total of $12 to spend at the Sandwich Shop.

• Sandwich Shop Menu •		
Sandwiches		
Roast beef sandwich	———	$3.29
Tuna sandwich	———	$2.99
Grilled chicken sandwich	——	$2.95
Snacks		
Granola Bar	———	$0.99
Apple	———	$0.75

Drinks	Large	Small
Juice ———	$1.00	$0.75
Milk ———	$1.00	$0.75

a. Each of you buy a different sandwich, snack, and drink. What can you buy from the menu? Explain your choices.

b. Whose meal costs more? Show your work.

c. Suppose your sister buys a small milk, a granola bar, and one other item. She pays with 4 one-dollar bills, 2 quarters, 2 dimes, and 3 pennies. She receives no change. What is the other item she buys?

(Chapter 4, Lesson 4)

 Education Place

See **eduplace.com/map** for more Test-Taking Tips.

Column Addition

Objective Add three or more addends.

Learn About It

At a reptile exhibit, there are 124 snakes, 78 lizards, and 52 turtles. How many reptiles are there in all?

Add. $124 + 78 + 52 = \blacksquare$

STEP 1 Add the ones.

$4 + 8 + 2 = 14$ **ones**

$$
\begin{array}{r}
1 \\
12\overset{}{4} \\
78 \\
+\ 52 \\
\hline
4
\end{array}
$$

Regroup 14 ones as 1 ten 4 ones.

Be sure to line up the numbers correctly.

STEP 2 Add the tens.

$1 + 2 + 7 + 5 = 15$

$$
\begin{array}{r}
1\ 1 \\
124 \\
78 \\
+\ 52 \\
\hline
54
\end{array}
$$

Regroup 15 tens as 1 hundred 5 tens.

STEP 3 Add the hundreds.

$1 + 1 = 2$

$$
\begin{array}{r}
1\ 1 \\
124 \\
78 \\
+\ 52 \\
\hline
254
\end{array}
$$

Check your work.

You can check by adding upward.

$$
\begin{array}{r}
1\ 1 \\
124 \\
78 \\
+\ 52 \\
\hline
254
\end{array}
$$

Solution: There are 254 reptiles in the exhibit.

Other Examples

A. Money

$$
\begin{array}{r}
2\ 1 \\
\$1.62 \\
2.99 \\
+\ 4.76 \\
\hline
\$9.37
\end{array}
$$

B. Regroup Hundreds

$$
\begin{array}{r}
1 \\
231 \\
612 \\
854 \\
+\ 101 \\
\hline
1{,}798
\end{array}
$$

Regroup 17 hundreds as 1 thousand 7 hundreds.

Guided Practice

Ask Yourself

• What is the sum of the ones? Do I need to regroup?

• What is the sum of the tens? Do I need to regroup?

Find each sum.

1. $\begin{array}{r} 62 \\ 15 \\ +\ 17 \\ \hline \end{array}$

2. $\begin{array}{r} \$1.54 \\ 2.18 \\ +\ 4.63 \\ \hline \end{array}$

3. $\begin{array}{r} 18 \\ 243 \\ +\ 71 \\ \hline \end{array}$

4. $\begin{array}{r} 245 \\ 601 \\ 319 \\ +\ 172 \\ \hline \end{array}$

5. $32 + 28 + 41 + 36$

6. $370 + 320 + 345$

Explain Your Thinking ▶ What is the greatest number of ones you would regroup when you add three numbers?

Practice and Problem Solving

Add. Check by adding in a different order.

7. $\begin{array}{r} 12 \\ 14 \\ +\ 42 \\ \hline \end{array}$

8. $\begin{array}{r} \$42 \\ 33 \\ +\ 13 \\ \hline \end{array}$

9. $\begin{array}{r} 25 \\ 25 \\ +\ 45 \\ \hline \end{array}$

10. $\begin{array}{r} \$3.06 \\ 1.09 \\ +\ 2.50 \\ \hline \end{array}$

11. $\begin{array}{r} 704 \\ 372 \\ +\ 118 \\ \hline \end{array}$

12. $\begin{array}{r} 549 \\ 735 \\ +\ 76 \\ \hline \end{array}$

13. $\begin{array}{r} 23 \\ 238 \\ 340 \\ +\ 152 \\ \hline \end{array}$

14. $\begin{array}{r} 121 \\ 225 \\ 321 \\ +\ 425 \\ \hline \end{array}$

15. $23 + 24 + 41$

16. $134 + 16 + 32 + 40$

17. $142 + 68 + 13$

18. $184 + 15 + 79 + 12$

Write *true* or *false*. Give an example to support your answer.

19. Changing the order of the addends changes the sum.

20. The sum of two numbers is never equal to one of the addends.

Go On

Algebra • Symbols Use what you know about properties to solve.
Write >, <, or = for each ⬤.

21. $36 + 0$ ⬤ $36 - 0$ **22.** $18 + 6$ ⬤ $18 - 6$

23. $24 + 5$ ⬤ $24 + 6$ **24.** $54 - 3$ ⬤ $54 - 4$

25. $29 + 34$ ⬤ $34 + 29$ **26.** $23 + 38$ ⬤ $19 + 42$

27. $19 + 45$ ⬤ $31 + 27$ **28.** $47 + 22$ ⬤ $35 + 31$

Solve.

29. A boa constrictor is 96 inches long. A python is 204 inches longer than the boa. An anaconda is 36 inches longer than the python. How long is the anaconda?

30. On Monday, 3 buses arrived at the zoo. The buses held 45 students, 39 students, and 27 students. How many students visited on Monday?

31. **Estimate** The zoo shop has 267 toys, 423 books, and 215 games in stock. About how many items does the shop have in stock?

32. **Create and Solve** Write a word problem in which the answer is the sum of 100. Use 3 addends in your word problem.

Anacondas can be 30 feet long, as long as 2 car lengths!

Mixed Review and Test Prep

Open Response

Compare. Write >, <, or = for each ⬤.
(Ch. 3, Lesson 4)

33. $9.50 ⬤ 9 dollars, 2 quarters

34. 6 half-dollars ⬤ $3.25

35. $15.85 ⬤ $15.50

36. Mrs. Kane drove 57 miles to a friend's house. She drove home, then drove another 28 miles to the next town. How far did she drive? (Ch. 4, Lesson 6)

Extra Practice See page 105, Set E.

Add It Up!

2 Players

What You'll Need • Number cube labeled 1 to 6
• Number cube labeled 4 to 9

How to Play

1. The first player rolls both number cubes and writes a two-digit number using the rolled numbers. Then he or she rolls both cubes again and writes another two-digit number.

2. The first player then finds the sum of the two numbers. The other player checks that the addition is correct. The ones digit of the sum is the number of points that the first player earns for this turn.

3. Players take turns repeating Steps 1 and 2. Each player keeps a record of his or her total number of points. The first player to reach a total of 50 points wins.

Lesson 7

Add Greater Numbers

Objective Find the sum of two 4-digit numbers.

Learn About It

There are 1,248 bison in one herd. Another herd is made up of 1,664 bison. How many bison are in the two herds?

The American bison were hunted almost to extinction. Now, many thousands roam the Great Plains.

Add. 1,248 + 1,664 = ■

STEP 1 Add the ones.

8 + 4 = 12

```
   1
 1,248
+ 1,664
     2
```

Regroup 12 ones as 1 ten 2 ones.

STEP 2 Add the tens

1 + 4 + 6 = 11

```
  11
 1,248
+ 1,664
    12
```

Regroup 11 tens as 1 hundred 1 ten.

STEP 3 Add the hundreds.

1 + 2 + 6 = 9

```
  11
 1,248
+ 1,664
   912
```

STEP 4 Add the thousands.

1 + 1 = 2

```
  11
 1,248
+ 1,664
 2,912
```

Check your work. Estimate to the nearest hundred.

```
  1,248   rounds to      1,200
+ 1,664   rounds to    + 1,700
                         2,900
```

2,912 is a reasonable answer.

Solution: There are 2,912 bison in the two herds.

Other Examples

A. Money

```
 11 1
$23.45
+ 19.79
$43.24
```

B. Zeros

```
 1  1
1,603
+ 3,509
5,112
```

C. To Ten Thousand

```
 1 11
5,678
+ 4,322
10,000
```

98

Guided Practice

Find each sum. Estimate to check.

1. 3,838
+ 2,165

2. $79.25
+ 11.54

3. 4,025
+ 3,082

Ask Yourself
- What is the sum of the digits in each column?
- Do I need to regroup?

Explain Your Thinking ▶ Why can you add numbers in a different order to check that your sum is correct?

Practice and Problem Solving

Find each sum. Estimate to check.

4. 1,345
3,223
+ 1,211

5. 128
354
+ 215

6. 5,380
+ 1,046

7. 3,192
+ 5,466

8. 3,103
+ 1,903

9. $15.99
+ 23.25

10. $24.68
+ 12.99

11. 1,709
+ 3,402

12. 3,834
+ 2,788

13. One year at Yellowstone National Park 637 grizzly bears, 489 black bears, and 49 unidentified bears were seen. How many bears were seen altogether?

14. California rangers tracked 3,492 wild horses. Wyoming rangers tracked 4,123 more wild horses. How many wild horses were tracked in Wyoming?

Mixed Review and Test Prep

Open Response

Compare. Write >, <, or =. (Ch. 2, Lesson 1)

15. 57 ● 75

16. 69 ● 71

17. 437 ● 419

18. 780 ● 870

19. 563 ● 653

20. 824 ● 880

21. 958 ● 684

22. 256 ● 256

23. A large pile of lumber has 2,689 boards. Added to the pile are 1,467 more boards. How many boards are there now?
(Ch. 4, Lesson 7)

Extra Practice See page 105, Set F.

Choose a Method

Objective Decide what method to use to solve problems.

Learn About It

Elena's father is a wildlife photographer. He took 200 photos in Hawaii Volcanoes National Park and 336 photos in Haleakala National Park.

Before you solve a problem you need to decide what method to use.

> Dear Elena,
> Hello from Hawaii.
> I'm almost finished with my photo shoot. To get here I flew 596 miles from Washington, D.C. to Chicago, and another 4,256 miles to Honolulu.
>
> Love, Dad

Elena Brown
155 Cliffton Street
Washington, DC
01349

▶ **You can use mental math to find how many photos Elena's father took.**

200 + 336 = ■

Think
336 = 300 + 36
So 200 + 300 = 500
500 + 36 = 536

Solution: Elena's father took 536 photos.

Nene, Hawaii's State Bird

▶ **You can use paper and pencil to find how many miles Elena's father flew.**

```
   1 1
   596
+ 4,256
  4,852
```

▶ **You can use a calculator to find how many miles Elena's father flew.**

Enter: [5] [9] [6]

Press: [+]

Enter: [4] [2] [5] [6]

Press: [=]

Solution: 4852

Solution: Elena's father flew 4,852 miles.

Add. Choose mental math, paper and pencil, or calculator. Explain your choice.

1. $52 + 81$ **2.** $90 + 210$ **3.** $3,050 + 295$

Ask Yourself

• Can I add the numbers in my head?

• Should I use pencil and paper or a calculator?

Explain Your Thinking ▶ Look back at Exercises 1–3. Which ones were you able to solve using mental math?

Practice and Problem Solving

Add. Choose mental math, paper and pencil, or calculator. Explain your choice.

4.	**5.**	**6.**	**7.**	**8.**
11	45	333	520	480
+ 22	+ 55	+ 444	+ 375	+ 320

9. $252 + 198$ **10.** $987 + 529$ **11.** $1,230 + 1,635$ **12.** $6,050 + 2,010$

Solve.

13. On Friday 335 people visited the bird sanctuary, on Saturday 475 people visited, and on Sunday 525 people visited. How many people visited in the three days?

14. **Multistep** Tickets for the bird sanctuary cost $4.75 for adults and $2.35 for children. Mrs. Gallo buys tickets for herself and her 2 children. How much does she spend?

Mixed Review and Test Prep ✓

Open Response
Skip count to find the missing numbers. (Ch. 1, Lesson 5)

15. 15, 20, _____, 30, 35

16. 40, 45, 50, _____, 60, _____, 70

17. 30, 40, 50, 60, _____, _____

18. What method would you use to find $482 + 346$? (Ch. 4, Lesson 8)

Explain your choice.

Problem-Solving Decision
Estimate or Exact Answer

Objective Decide if an estimate or an exact answer is needed to solve a problem.

Before solving a problem, you must decide whether you need an estimate or an exact answer.

This female lion weighs 338 pounds. This male lion weighs 157 pounds more than the female lion.

▶ **Sometimes you need an exact answer to solve a problem.**

Suppose someone asks you, "How much does the male lion weigh?"

Since the question asks for the exact weight, you need to add 338 pounds and 157 pounds.

$$\begin{array}{r} 338 \\ + 157 \\ \hline 495 \end{array}$$

The male lion weighs 495 pounds.

▶ **Sometimes you need an estimate to solve a problem.**

Suppose someone asks you, "About how much does the male lion weigh?"

Since the question asks "about how much," you can estimate to solve the problem.

$$\begin{array}{r} 338 \;\text{rounds to}\; 300 \\ + 157 \;\text{rounds to}\; + 200 \\ \hline 495 \qquad\qquad 500 \end{array}$$

The male lion weighs about 500 pounds.

Solve. Tell whether you need an exact answer or an estimate.

1. **Multistep** Two young zebras weigh 357 pounds each. An adult zebra weighs 765 pounds. Do the young zebras together weigh more or less than the adult? Explain.

2. An Asian male elephant weighs about 8,000 pounds more than a female giraffe, which weighs 2,790 pounds. About how much does the male elephant weigh?

Algebraic Thinking
What Are the Numbers?

Different shapes can stand for different numbers.
Same shapes can stand for the same number.

★ + ★ = 10

Each star represents the same
number so ★ must equal 5.

♥ + ★ = 8

Since the ★ equals 5
we know the ♥ must equal 3.

Find the value of each shape to make the number sentence true.

1. ▲ + ▲ + 30 = 130

2. ▲ + ▲ + 6 = 106

3. ■ + ■ + 6 = 46

4. ■ + ■ + 8 = 48

5. ● + ● + 8 = 88

6. ▲ + ● = 90

7. ▲ + ■ + 5 = 75

8. ● + ■ + 10 = 70

9. ▲ + ● + ■ = 110

▲ = ?	■ = ?	● = ?

Different letters can also be used to stand for different numbers.
Same letters stand for the same number.

10. $a + a = 40$

11. $a + b = 55$

12. $a + c = 60$

13. $b + b = 70$

14. $b + c + 10 = 85$

15. $a + b + 10 = 65$

16. $c + c + 2 = 82$

17. $a + a + a = 60$

18. $a + b + c = 95$

$a = ?$	$b = ?$	$c = ?$

Chapter Review/Test

VOCABULARY

Choose the best term to complete each sentence.

1. If you group the addends so they are easier to add, you are using the ____.

2. When you add 0 and 3 you use the ____.

3. When you do not need the exact answer, you can ____.

Vocabulary

regroup

estimate

Associative Property

Zero Property

CONCEPTS AND SKILLS

Estimate each sum. (Lesson 2, pp. 78–80)

4.	5.	6.	7.
37 + 42	45 + 38	843 + 486	$7.84 + 1.18

Add. (Lessons 1, 3–4, and 6–8, pp. 76–77, 82–88, 94–101)

8.	9.	10.	11.	12.
47 + 38	17 + 55	158 + 347	$43.86 + 23.59	2,158 + 4,591

13. $4 + (3 + 6)$

14. $4 + 3 + 7 + 6$

15. $18 + 65 + 39$

16. $(1 + 5) + 7$

17. $3 + 9 + 1 + 3$

18. $77 + 13 + 49$

PROBLEM SOLVING

Solve. (Lessons 5, 9, pp. 90–93, 102)

19. Together Ken and Amy have 36 coins. Ken has 4 more coins than Amy. How many coins does Amy have?

20. There are 318 mystery books at the Grove Library. The Fox Library has 297 mystery books. How many mystery books do both libraries have?

Write About It

Show You Understand

Van saw this addition problem.

$$5,048 \\ + 1,011$$

He said he needed a calculator because he couldn't add these numbers in his head. Do you agree? Why or why not?

Extra Practice

Set A (Lesson 1, pp. 76–77)

Find each sum.

  1. $3 + 2 + (8 + 2)$ **2.** $9 + (3 + 6 + 1)$ **3.** $(2 + 5 + 3) + 2$

....

Set B (Lesson 2, pp. 78–80)

Estimate each sum.

  1. $48 + 55$ **2.** $67 + 99$ **3.** $726 + 109$ **4.** $\$4.85 + \$3.25$

....

Set C (Lesson 3, pp. 82–84)

Add.

  1. $27 + 68$ **2.** $64 + 28$ **3.** $139 + 351$ **4.** $\$5.46 + \$2.07$

....

Set D (Lesson 4, pp. 86–88)

Find each sum.

1.	**2.**	**3.**	**4.**	**5.**
46	428	$4.86	122	319
+ 87	+ 491	+ 3.29	+ 799	+ 293

....

Set E (Lesson 6, pp. 94–96)

Add. Check by adding in a different order.

1.	**2.**	**3.**	**4.**	**5.**
22	47	36	251	271
28	31	149	27	316
+ 33	+ 12	+ 12	+ 403	511
				+ 104

....

Set F (Lesson 7, pp. 98–99)

Find each sum. Estimate to check.

1.	**2.**	**3.**	**4.**	**5.**
$21.79	8,873	$30.57	1,287	6,803
+ 33.26	+ 1,029	+ 54.61	+ 6,765	+ 2,197

....

Set G (Lesson 8, pp. 100–101)

Add. Choose mental math, paper and pencil, or calculator.

  1. $15 + 13$ **2.** $185 + 200$ **3.** $501 + 710$ **4.** $6,395 + 5,463$

Subtract Whole Numbers

INVESTIGATION

Using Data

Cable cars in San Francisco "grip" cables under the street and are pulled along at about 10 miles an hour. Look at the table. Use the information to write a number sentence to show the number of years that passed between any two events.

San Francisco's Cable Cars

1873	First cable car system tested.
1878	Cable cars go into service.
1951	Cable cars are shut down.
1984	Cable car system is rebuilt.

Use What You Know

Use this page to review and remember what you need to know for this chapter.

VOCABULARY

Choose the best term to complete each sentence.

Vocabulary
- regroup
- estimate
- hundreds
- thousands
- difference

1. To find an answer that is close to the exact answer, you can ____.

2. You can ____ 10 ones blocks as 1 tens block to show a number in another way.

3. In the number sentence $9 - 4 = 5$, the number 5 is the ____.

4. The number 832 is equal to 7 ____, 13 tens, and 2 ones.

CONCEPTS AND SKILLS

Subtract. Regroup if you need to.

5. $\begin{array}{r} 13 \\ -\ 4 \\ \hline \end{array}$
6. $\begin{array}{r} 15 \\ -\ 7 \\ \hline \end{array}$
7. $\begin{array}{r} 17 \\ -\ 8 \\ \hline \end{array}$
8. $\begin{array}{r} 12 \\ -\ 5 \\ \hline \end{array}$
9. $\begin{array}{r} 14 \\ -\ 9 \\ \hline \end{array}$

10. $\begin{array}{r} 60 \\ -\ 50 \\ \hline \end{array}$
11. $\begin{array}{r} 70 \\ -\ 30 \\ \hline \end{array}$
12. $\begin{array}{r} 90 \\ -\ 20 \\ \hline \end{array}$
13. $\begin{array}{r} 30 \\ -\ 20 \\ \hline \end{array}$
14. $\begin{array}{r} 50 \\ -\ 30 \\ \hline \end{array}$

15. $\begin{array}{r} 43 \\ -\ 12 \\ \hline \end{array}$
16. $\begin{array}{r} 67 \\ -\ 53 \\ \hline \end{array}$
17. $\begin{array}{r} 72 \\ -\ 26 \\ \hline \end{array}$
18. $\begin{array}{r} 84 \\ -\ 65 \\ \hline \end{array}$
19. $\begin{array}{r} 53 \\ -\ 47 \\ \hline \end{array}$

 Write About It

20. Look at Roger's work on the right. What did he do wrong? Subtract the numbers correctly.

Roger

$\begin{array}{r} 27 \\ -18 \\ \hline 11 \end{array}$

Facts Practice, See page 666.

Subtraction Rules

Objective Use subtraction rules
to find differences.

Vocabulary

difference

Learn About It

Subtraction rules and a good mental
picture can often help you find a
solution.

Subtraction Rules

Subtract Zero	Subtract a Number from Itself
Three people step onto an empty elevator. No one gets on or off at the next floor. How many people are on the elevator?	Six people step onto an empty elevator. All 6 get off at the next floor and no one gets on. How many people are on the elevator?
There are still 3 people on the elevator.	There are 0 people on the elevator.
When you subtract 0 from a number, the **difference** is that number.	When you subtract a number from itself, the difference is zero.
$3 - 0 = 3$	$6 - 6 = 0$

Guided Practice

Find each difference.

1. $\begin{array}{r} 12 \\ -12 \\ \hline \end{array}$
2. $\begin{array}{r} 1 \\ -0 \\ \hline \end{array}$
3. $\begin{array}{r} 20 \\ -20 \\ \hline \end{array}$
4. $\begin{array}{r} 10 \\ -0 \\ \hline \end{array}$

5. $7 - 4 - 3$ 6. $35 - 0$ 7. $15 - 15$ 8. $40 + 4 - 4$

Ask Yourself

• Are the numbers
the same?

• Am I subtracting
zero?

Explain Your Thinking ▶ If there were 10 counters on a table and
you took 10 away, how many would be
left on the table? Explain how you know.

108

Subtract. Use subtraction rules when you can.

9. $11 - 1$

10. $15 - 0$

11. $13 - 10$

12. $18 - 18$

13. $19 - 7$

14. $26 - 0$

15. $37 - 17$

16. $14 - 0$

17. $29 - 14$

18. $77 - 77$

19. $13 - 13$

20. $16 - 0$

21. $12 - 3$

22. $53 - 21$

 Algebra • **Properties Find each missing number.**

23. $13 - \blacksquare = 13$

24. $\blacksquare - 15 = 0$

25. $0 = 16 - \blacksquare$

26. $\blacksquare - 0 = 18$

27. $\blacksquare - 14 = 0$

28. $\blacksquare - 20 = 0$

29. $25 - \blacksquare = 25$

30. $0 = \blacksquare - 31$

31. $\blacksquare = 52 - 52$

Solve.

32. I am the difference when 0 is subtracted from 24. What number am I?

33. The difference is 21 when 0 is subtracted from me. What number am I?

34. I am the difference when 35 is subtracted from 35. What number am I?

35. **Multistep** Seven people get on an empty elevator at floor 1. Three people get off at floor 2. Three people get on at floor 2. How many people are on the elevator now?

Mixed Review and Test Prep

Open Response

Find each sum. (Ch. 4, Lesson 1)

36. $6 + 3 = \blacksquare$
    $3 + 6 = \blacksquare$

37. $4 + 0 = \blacksquare$
    $0 + 4 = \blacksquare$

38. $2 + (7 + 3)$

39. $8 + (2 + 5)$

40. Sue had 32 stamps. Then she collected 29 more stamps. Sue gave 61 stamps away. How many stamps did she have left? (Ch. 5, Lesson 1)

Relate Addition and Subtraction

Objective Learn how addition and subtraction are related.

Learn About It

A school bus makes 10 stops on the way to school. The bus has already made 4 stops. How many more stops will the bus make?

Addition and subtraction are related. You can use either operation to find the answer.

Different Ways to Find the Difference Between 10 and 4

Way 1 Write an addition sentence. Find the missing addend.	**Way 2** Write a subtraction sentence. Find the difference.
$4 + \blacksquare = 10$	$10 - 4 = \blacksquare$
stops made · remaining stops · total stops (sum)	total stops · stops made · remaining stops (difference)

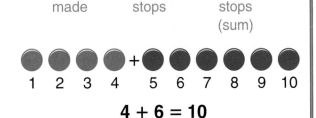

Solution: The bus will make 6 more stops.

A **fact family** is a group of number sentences that use the same numbers.

Fact families show how addition and subtraction are related.

Fact Family for 4, 6, and 10

$$4 + 6 = 10 \qquad 10 - 4 = 6$$
$$6 + 4 = 10 \qquad 10 - 6 = 4$$

Extra Help at eduplace.com/map

Guided Practice

Ask Yourself
- How can the given fact help me find the missing number?
- Do I need to find a missing addend or the difference?

Use counters to find each missing number.

1. 3 + ■ = 7
   7 − 3 = 4

2. ■ + 10 = 22
   22 − 10 = 12

3. 40 + ■ = 60
   60 − 40 = 20

Explain Your Thinking ▶ There are only two facts in the fact family for 3, 3, and 6. Explain why.

Practice and Problem Solving

Use counters to find each missing number.

4. ■ + 3 = 8
   8 − 3 = 5

5. ■ + 7 = 15
   15 − 7 = 8

6. 14 + ■ = 24
   24 − 14 = 10

7. 6 + ■ = 15
   15 − 6 = 9

Complete each fact family.

8. 6 + 8 = 14
   8 + ■ = 14
   14 − 8 = ■
   14 − ■ = 8

9. 7 + 9 = 16
   9 + 7 = ■
   16 − 9 = ■
   16 − ■ = 9

10. 2 + 8 = 10
    ■ + 2 = 10
    10 − 2 = ■
    ■ − 8 = 2

11. 4 + 5 = 9
    5 + ■ = 9
    ■ − 5 = 4
    9 − ■ = 5

Solve.

12. **Represent** Twenty-eight students take the bus to school. Nineteen students take the bus home. Write an addition sentence to find how many more students take the bus in the morning.

13. Write a simple word problem that can be modeled by using the counters shown below.

Mixed Review and Test Prep ✓

Open Response
Round each to the nearest dollar.
(Ch. 3, Lesson 5)

14. $7.08
15. $1.81
16. $3.45

17. $5.27
18. $8.69
19. $2.50

20. $0.79
21. $3.09
22. $6.22

23. Antonio wrote 39 − 18 = 21. What addition sentence could he use to check his answer?
(Ch. 5, Lesson 2)

Lesson 3

Estimate Differences

Objective Round numbers to estimate differences.

Learn About It

Bobby lives in Orlando, Florida. His friend lives in Sarasota, Florida and his uncle lives in Jasper, Florida. About how much farther does Bobby live from his uncle than from his friend?

The word *about* tells you that you do not need an exact answer.

Estimate how many more miles it is from Orlando to Jasper than from Orlando to Sarasota.

Estimate 168 − 108.

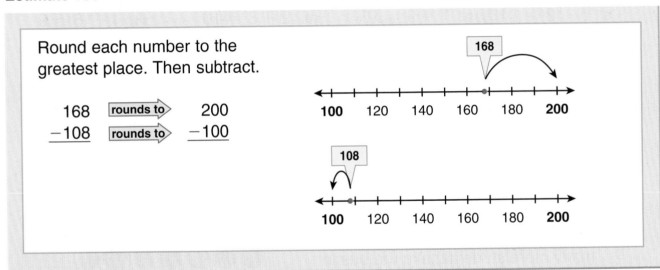

Round each number to the greatest place. Then subtract.

168 rounds to 200
−108 rounds to −100

Solution: Bobby lives about 100 miles farther from his uncle than from his friend.

Other Examples

A. Two-Digit Numbers

85 rounds to 90
− 57 rounds to − 60
           30

Remember Since the ones digit in 85 is 5, 85 rounds to 90.

85 − 57 is about 30.

B. Money

$4.35 rounds to $4.00
− 2.27 rounds to −2.00
              $2.00

$4.35 − $2.27 is about $2.00.

Guided Practice

Round each number to the greatest place. Then subtract.

Ask Yourself

• What place should I round each number to?

• How many zeros should my estimate have?

1. 528
   − 364

2. 78
   − 61

3. 234
   − 132

4. $6.25 − $2.87

5. 736 − 187

Explain Your Thinking ▶ Is it reasonable to say that 439 − 199 is about 500? Explain.

Practice and Problem Solving

Round each number to the greatest place. Then subtract.

6. 84
   − 61

7. 91
   − 44

8. 42
   − 24

9. 39
   − 12

10. 48
    − 22

11. $8.83
    − 5.59

12. 777
    − 192

13. $709
    − 612

14. 941
    − 811

15. $7.85
    − 4.70

16. 57 − 41

17. 82 − 54

18. 842 − 714

19. $932 − $321

20. $6.75 − $3.19

21. 742 − 211

22. Bobby's grandparents are driving 420 miles to Orlando. They drove 185 miles and then stopped for lunch. About how many more miles do they have to travel?

23. **Multistep** On their way to Orlando, Bobby's grandmother bought 2 T-shirts and 3 bottles of sunblock. About how much change should she receive from a fifty-dollar bill?

24. **Money** Bobby has 7 one-dollar bills, 9 quarters, 5 dimes, and 3 nickels. Does Bobby have enough to buy a T-shirt? Explain your reasoning.

Go On

Decide if each estimate is reasonable. If the estimate is not reasonable, name an estimate that is.

25. 832 − 214 is about 600

26. 49 − 12 is about 20

27. 908 − 582 is about 500

28. 92 − 11 is about 80

 Data The table shows the distances the Martinez family traveled on their vacation. Use the table for Problems 29–32.

29. About how many more miles did the Martinez family travel to the beach than to the campground?

30. The Martinezes could have visited a cousin who lives 384 miles away. About how many more miles is that than the distance to their aunt's house?

31. **Create and Solve** Use the information in the table to write your own problem. Then give it to a classmate to solve.

 32. **Write About It** When might it be important to know the exact number of miles it is to each place?

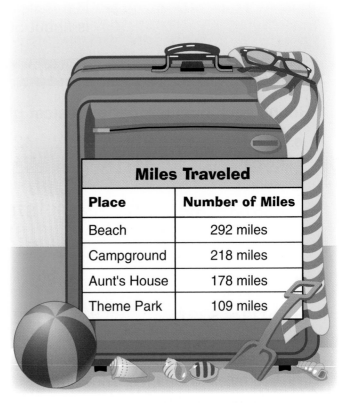

Miles Traveled	
Place	**Number of Miles**
Beach	292 miles
Campground	218 miles
Aunt's House	178 miles
Theme Park	109 miles

Mixed Review and Test Prep

Open Response

Decide if each object weighs more than or less than 1 pound. (Grade 2)

33.    **34.**   **35.**

36. There are 51 trees in the community park. Ten years ago, the first 18 trees were planted there. About how many more trees are in the park now? Explain how you got your answer. (Ch. 5, Lesson 3)

Extra Practice See page 133, Set C.

Math Reasoning

Front-End Estimation

Rounding is not the only way to estimate differences. Another way is to subtract the front digits of the numbers. This is called **front-end estimation.**

Vocabulary

front-end estimation

Here are some examples of front-end estimation.

Two-Digit Numbers

The front digits are tens.
Subtract the tens.

$$
\begin{array}{r}
65 \rightarrow 60 \\
-44 \rightarrow -40 \\
\hline
20
\end{array}
$$

So 65 − 44 is about 20.

Dimes

The front digits are dimes.
Subtract the dimes.

$$
\begin{array}{r}
\$0.52 \rightarrow \$0.50 \\
-0.16 \rightarrow -0.10 \\
\hline
\$0.40
\end{array}
$$

So $0.52 − $0.16 is about $0.40.

Three-Digit Numbers

The front digits are hundreds.
Subtract the hundreds.

$$
\begin{array}{r}
547 \rightarrow 500 \\
-266 \rightarrow -200 \\
\hline
300
\end{array}
$$

So 547 − 266 is about 300.

Dollars

The front digits are dollars.
Subtract the dollars.

$$
\begin{array}{r}
\$8.49 \rightarrow \$8.00 \\
-2.78 \rightarrow -2.00 \\
\hline
\$6.00
\end{array}
$$

So $8.49 − $2.78 is about $6.00.

For each exercise, estimate the difference using front-end estimation.

1.
$$
\begin{array}{r} 76 \\ -64 \\ \hline \end{array}
$$

2.
$$
\begin{array}{r} 36 \\ -33 \\ \hline \end{array}
$$

3.
$$
\begin{array}{r} 241 \\ -183 \\ \hline \end{array}
$$

4.
$$
\begin{array}{r} 868 \\ -459 \\ \hline \end{array}
$$

5.
$$
\begin{array}{r} \$5.45 \\ -3.67 \\ \hline \end{array}
$$

6. Compare your estimates and the actual differences for Exercises 1–5. Are the estimates greater than or less than the differences?

7. **Analyze** Look at the examples to the right. In which one would you get the same estimate using rounding and front-end estimation?

$$884 - 245 = \blacksquare$$

$$538 - 125 = \blacksquare$$

Audio Tutor 1/15 Listen and Understand
Regroup Tens
Objective Regroup tens as ones when you subtract.

Learn About It

This ferry is transporting passengers from the North Carolina coast to an island of the Outer Banks. It is carrying 245 people. If 119 people get off the ferry, how many people are still on the ferry?

Subtract. 245 − 119 = ▮

STEP 1
Show 245 with base-ten blocks.

$$\begin{array}{r} 245 \\ -\,119 \end{array}$$

STEP 2
9 > 5, so there are not enough ones to subtract.

Regroup 1 ten as 10 ones. There are 3 tens left.

10 ones + 5 ones = 15 ones

$$\begin{array}{r} 2\,\overset{3\,15}{\cancel{45}} \\ -\,1\,1\,9 \end{array}$$

STEP 3
Now you can subtract the ones.

15 ones − 9 ones = 6 ones

$$\begin{array}{r} 2\,\overset{3\,15}{\cancel{45}} \\ -\,1\,1\,9 \\ \hline 6 \end{array}$$

STEP 4
Subtract the tens.

3 tens − 1 ten = 2 tens

$$\begin{array}{r} 2\,\overset{3\,15}{\cancel{45}} \\ -\,1\,1\,9 \\ \hline 2\,6 \end{array}$$

STEP 5
Subtract the hundreds.

2 hundreds − 1 hundred = 1 hundred

$$\begin{array}{r} 2\,\overset{3\,15}{\cancel{45}} \\ -\,1\,1\,9 \\ \hline 1\,2\,6 \end{array}$$

Solution: 126 people are still on the ferry.

Open Response

Round each amount to the nearest ten dollars. (Ch. 3, Lesson 5)

41. $11.87   **42.** $54.52

43. $7.25   **44.** $67.14

45. $25.96   **46.** $73.44

47. This year, 785 people participated in a walk-a-thon. Last year, 469 people participated. How many more people took part this year than last year? (Ch. 5, Lesson 4)

Social Studies Connection
United States Landmarks

Problem Solving

Use the table to solve the riddles.

1. I am the only landmark whose height does not round to 600 feet, when rounded to the nearest hundred.

2. If you subtracted 25 feet from my height, I would be the size of a Seattle landmark.

3. I am about 400 feet taller than one landmark and 50 feet shorter than another.

4. If you added my height and the height of a New York statue, the sum would be 757 feet.

5. I am not the tallest or the shortest landmark on the list. One of my digits is a zero.

U.S. Landmark	Height
Gateway Arch St. Louis, Missouri	630 feet
Statue of Liberty Liberty Island, New York	152 feet
Space Needle Seattle, Washington	605 feet
Washington Monument Washington, D.C.	555 feet

Regroup Tens and Hundreds

Objective Regroup tens and hundreds to subtract.

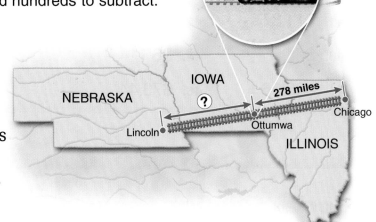

Learn About It

Hector's mom is a train conductor on the route from Chicago, Illinois to Lincoln, Nebraska. It is 557 miles from Chicago to Lincoln. The train has just stopped at Ottumwa, Iowa. How much farther is it to Lincoln?

Subtract. $557 - 278 = $ ■

STEP 1 8 > 7, so you need to regroup 1 ten as 10 ones.

$$
\begin{array}{r}
{}^{4}5\overset{17}{\cancel{5}}7 \\
-278 \\
\hline
\end{array}
$$

STEP 2 Subtract the ones.

$$17 - 8 = 9$$

$$
\begin{array}{r}
{}^{4}5\overset{17}{\cancel{5}}7 \\
-278 \\
\hline
9
\end{array}
$$

STEP 3 7 > 4, so you need to regroup 1 hundred as 10 tens.

$$
\begin{array}{r}
{}^{4}\,{}^{14}\cancel{5}\overset{17}{\cancel{5}}7 \\
-278 \\
\hline
9
\end{array}
$$

STEP 4 Subtract the tens.

$$14 - 7 = 7$$

$$
\begin{array}{r}
{}^{4}\,{}^{14}\cancel{5}\overset{17}{\cancel{5}}7 \\
-278 \\
\hline
79
\end{array}
$$

STEP 5 Subtract the hundreds.

$$4 - 2 = 2$$

$$
\begin{array}{r}
{}^{4}\,{}^{14}\cancel{5}\overset{17}{\cancel{5}}7 \\
-278 \\
\hline
279
\end{array}
$$

Use addition to check.

$$
\begin{array}{r}
557 \\
-278 \\
\hline
279
\end{array}
\qquad
\begin{array}{r}
279 \\
+278 \\
\hline
557
\end{array}
$$

Solution: It is 279 miles farther to Lincoln.

Another Example

Money

$$
\begin{array}{r}
{}^{8}\,{}^{\overset{12}{2}}\,{}^{14}\$\cancel{9}.\cancel{3}\cancel{4} \\
-\;3.45 \\
\hline
\$5.89
\end{array}
$$

Bring down the decimal point and the dollar sign.

Find each difference.

Ask Yourself
- Are there enough ones to subtract?
- Are there enough tens to subtract?

1. 624
    − 378

2. $8.52
    − 1.74

3. 962
    − 141

4. $7.28
    − 3.49

5. 315 − 248

6. $9.56 − $6.37

7. 752 − 268

Explain Your Thinking ▶ Why do you sometimes need to regroup in more than one place?

Practice and Problem Solving

Subtract. Check by adding.

8.   436
    − 158

9. $7.23
    − 2.35

10. 542
    − 167

11. 824
    − 537

12. $9.53
    − 4.78

13. 318
    − 139

14. 764
    − 291

15. 687
    − 353

16. 458 − 121

17. $8.42 − $1.79

18. 574 − 268

19. 536 − 289

20. 764 − 132

21. 692 − 263

Estimate by rounding. Then choose the correct answer.

22. 315 − 186

a. 129   b. 229

23. 786 − 459

a. 427   b. 327

24. 634 − 265

a. 369   b. 469

Solve.

25. Shara will travel 650 miles on a train trip. She has traveled 365 miles so far. How many more miles will she travel?

26. **Write About It** Cameron took 162 pictures on his train trip to California and 128 pictures on the way back. Can he make 2 collages that each use 150 pictures? Explain.

Go On

27. 35 + 20 ● 55 − 10

28. 15 + 15 ● 50 − 10

29. 45 + 20 ● 90 − 25

30. 100 − 70 ● 23 + 17

31. 13 + 13 ● 45 − 20

32. 85 − 45 ● 16 + 24

Solve.

33. A total of 243 people signed up for a trip to Bruneau Canyon. If 154 of them are adults, how many children signed up for the trip?

34. Money Janice has $10. If hiking maps of the canyon cost $3 each, will Janice have enough money to buy 3 maps?

35. Janice is hiking a trail in Bruneau Canyon. She has 240 feet more to hike. If she hikes 165 feet and then stops for water, how many more feet does she have to hike?

Bruneau Canyon, Idaho

Mixed Review and Test Prep ✓

Open Response

Find each sum. (Ch. 4, Lesson 6)

36.
```
   15
   69
 + 25
```

37.
```
   26
   32
 + 40
```

38.
```
  293
  415
+ 137
```

39.
```
 $1.83
  5.06
+ 2.70
```

Multiple Choice

40. Leticia has a jigsaw puzzle with 422 pieces. So far, she has put together 293 pieces. How many pieces still need to be put together? (Ch. 5, Lesson 5)

A 229

C 129

B 139

D 121

Extra Practice See page 133, Set E.

Math Reasoning
Subtracting in Different Ways

Here are two different ways to use mental math to subtract.

▶ **Colby breaks numbers apart to subtract easier numbers.**

$$
\begin{array}{r} 67 \\ -\ 9 \\ \hline \end{array}
\qquad
\begin{array}{r} 67 \\ -\ 7 \\ \hline 60 \\ -\ 2 \\ \hline 58 \end{array}
$$

Colby thinks of 9 as 7 + 2.

$$
\begin{array}{r} 52 \\ -\ 37 \\ \hline \end{array}
\qquad
\begin{array}{r} 52 \\ -\ 2 \\ \hline 50 \\ -\ 30 \\ \hline 20 \\ -\ 5 \\ \hline 15 \end{array}
$$

Colby thinks of 37 as 2 + 30 + 5.

- How does thinking of 9 as 7 + 2 help Colby subtract?

- How does thinking of 37 as 2 + 30 + 5 help Colby subtract?

▶ **Tim finds easier numbers by adding on.**

$$
\begin{array}{r} 67 \\ -\ 9 \\ \hline \end{array}
\qquad
\begin{array}{r} 68 \\ -\ 10 \\ \hline 58 \end{array}
$$

Tim adds 1 to each number.

$$
\begin{array}{r} 52 \\ -\ 37 \\ \hline \end{array}
\qquad
\begin{array}{r} 55 \\ -\ 40 \\ \hline 15 \end{array}
$$

Tim adds 3 to each number.

- How does adding 1 to each number help Tim subtract?

- How does adding 3 to each number help Tim subtract?

Find each difference. Use Colby's, Tim's, and the standard method.

1. $\begin{array}{r} 43 \\ -7 \\ \hline \end{array}$
2. $\begin{array}{r} 22 \\ -9 \\ \hline \end{array}$
3. $\begin{array}{r} 54 \\ -6 \\ \hline \end{array}$
4. $\begin{array}{r} 87 \\ -28 \\ \hline \end{array}$
5. $\begin{array}{r} 52 \\ -36 \\ \hline \end{array}$

6. **Explain** Why does Tim's method work for subtraction?

Subtract Greater Numbers

Objective Learn how to subtract four-digit numbers.

Learn About It

Three jumbo jets land at an airport. The jets carry a total of 1,445 passengers and 2,932 pieces of luggage. How many more pieces of luggage are there than passengers?

Subtract. 2,932 − 1,445 = ▇

Different Ways to Subtract 1,445 From 2,932

Way ❶ Use pencil and paper.

STEP 1 5 > 2, so you need to regroup 1 ten as 10 ones.

$$\begin{array}{r} {\scriptstyle 2\,12} \\ 2,9\cancel{3}\cancel{2} \\ -\,1,4\,4\,5 \\ \hline \end{array}$$

STEP 2 Subtract the ones.

12 − 5 = 7

$$\begin{array}{r} {\scriptstyle 2\,12} \\ 2,9\cancel{3}\cancel{2} \\ -\,1,4\,4\,5 \\ \hline 7 \end{array}$$

STEP 3 4 > 2, so you need to regroup 1 hundred as 10 tens.

$$\begin{array}{r} {\scriptstyle 8\ \overset{12}{\cancel{2}}\,12} \\ 2,\cancel{9}\cancel{3}\cancel{2} \\ -\,1,4\,4\,5 \\ \hline 7 \end{array}$$

STEP 4 Subtract the tens.

12 − 4 = 8

$$\begin{array}{r} {\scriptstyle 8\ \overset{12}{\cancel{2}}\,12} \\ 2,\cancel{9}\cancel{3}\cancel{2} \\ -\,1,4\,4\,5 \\ \hline 8\,7 \end{array}$$

STEP 5 Subtract the hundreds.

8 − 4 = 4

$$\begin{array}{r} {\scriptstyle 8\ \overset{12}{\cancel{2}}\,12} \\ 2,\cancel{9}\cancel{3}\cancel{2} \\ -\,1,4\,4\,5 \\ \hline 4\,8\,7 \end{array}$$

STEP 6 Subtract the thousands.

2 − 1 = 1

$$\begin{array}{r} {\scriptstyle 8\ \overset{12}{\cancel{2}}\,12} \\ 2,\cancel{9}\cancel{3}\cancel{2} \\ -\,1,4\,4\,5 \\ \hline 1,4\,8\,7 \end{array}$$

Way ❷ Use a calculator.

Press: [2] [9] [3] [2] [−] [1] [4] [4] [5] [=]

Solution: | 1487 |

Solution: There are 1,487 more pieces of luggage than passengers.

Other Examples

A. Three-Digit Difference

$$\begin{array}{r} 5\ \overset{14}{\cancel{4}}\ 13 \\ 8,\cancel{6}\cancel{5}\cancel{3} \\ -8,489 \\ \hline 164 \end{array}$$

B. Money

$$\begin{array}{r} 3\ \overset{12}{\cancel{2}}\ 14 \\ \$4\cancel{3}.\cancel{4}6 \\ -28.54 \\ \hline \$14.92 \end{array}$$

Guided Practice

Subtract.

1. 8,482
    − 2,845

2. 6,287
    − 1,402

3. $79.18
    − 24.26

Ask Yourself

- Do I need to regroup?
- Did I subtract ones, tens, hundreds, and thousands in that order?

Explain Your Thinking ▶ How would you check to see if your answer is reasonable?

Practice and Problem Solving

Find each difference. Check by adding or estimating.

4. 4,828
    − 1,476

5. 8,726
    − 3,579

6. 3,594
    − 1,678

7. $69.25
    − 28.39

8. 5,388
    − 2,679

9. 9,824
    − 6,912

10. $89.72
    − 65.95

11. 4,828
    − 4,539

12. 7,985
    − 4,502

13. $29.25
    − 15.12

14. 5,827
    − 1,911

15. 7,254
    − 3,108

16. 7,629
    − 3,108

17. $46.58
    − 43.62

18. 8,928
    − 1,476

19. There were 1,149 people at the airshow on Friday. On Saturday, there were 3,428 people. How many more people were at the airshow on Saturday?

20. **Algebra** The airshow has 5 more biplanes than gliders. Together there are 23 flying machines. How many biplanes are there?

Go On ▶

Mental Math **Look for a pattern to subtract these numbers.**

21. 4 − 2 = ■
    40 − 20 = ■
    400 − 200 = ■
    4,000 − 2,000 = ■

22. 6 − 5 = ■
    60 − 50 = ■
    600 − 500 = ■
    6,000 − 5,000 = ■

23. 7 − 1 = ■
    70 − 10 = ■
    700 − 100 = ■
    7,000 − 1,000 = ■

24. 8 − 3 = ■
    80 − 30 = ■
    800 − 300 = ■
    8,000 − 3,000 = ■

25. 9 − 2 = ■
    90 − 20 = ■
    900 − 200 = ■
    9,000 − 2,000 = ■
    90,000 − 20,000 = ■

26. 6 − 3 = ■
    60 − 30 = ■
    600 − 300 = ■
    6,000 − 3,000 = ■
    60,000 − 30,000 = ■

Choose a Computation Method

Mental Math • Estimation • Paper and Pencil • Calculator

Data Use the chart for Problems 27–29.
Then explain which method you chose.

27. **Multistep** Mark ordered pasta and juice at the café. He then ordered one more item. If he spent a total of $13.85, what other item did he buy?

28. Which items can be bought for exactly $5.00?

29. **You Decide** Decide what you and a friend would order at the café. Then find the total cost.

Sam's Café
Sandwich $5.35
Fruit Salad $3.60
Pasta $8.85
Juice $1.40

30. Last week, the café served 910 lunches and 793 dinners. About how many more lunches did the café serve?

31. Sari needs 1,487 menus. So far, 1,220 copies have been printed. How many menus still need to be printed?

Extra Practice See page 133, Set F.

Calculator Connection

Mystery Numbers

Use your calculator to find each mystery number.

1.

What's My Number?

The number is less
than 721 − 291.
↓
The number is greater
than 321 + 97.
↓
The tens digit
is even.
↓
The sum of the
digits is 11.

2.

What's My Number?

The number
is odd.
↓
The number is greater
than 369 − 215.
↓
The number is less
than 411 − 246.
↓
The sum of the
digits is 15.

3.

What's My Number?

The number is greater
than 68 + 119 + 43.
↓
The number is less
than 810 − 571.
↓
The number
is odd.
↓
The ones digit is 4 more
than the tens digit.

Quick Check

Check your understanding of Lessons 1–6.

Complete each fact family. (Lesson 2)

1. $3 + 6 = $ ■ $9 − $ ■ $ = 6$ **2.** $5 + 2 = $ ■   ■ $ − 2 = 5$
■ $ + 3 = 9$ ■ $ − 6 = 3$ ■ $ + 5 = 7$ $7 − $ ■ $ = 2$

Estimate each difference. Tell how you estimated. (Lesson 3)

3. $82 − 38$ **4.** $\$5.87 − \$2.76$ **5.** $768 − 219$

Subtract. (Lessons 1, 4–6)

6. $\begin{array}{r} 47 \\ -47 \\ \hline \end{array}$ **7.** $\begin{array}{r} 36 \\ -12 \\ \hline \end{array}$ **8.** $\begin{array}{r} 652 \\ -313 \\ \hline \end{array}$ **9.** $\begin{array}{r} \$496 \\ -496 \\ \hline \end{array}$

10. $\begin{array}{r} 413 \\ -254 \\ \hline \end{array}$ **11.** $\begin{array}{r} 862 \\ -695 \\ \hline \end{array}$ **12.** $\begin{array}{r} 2{,}423 \\ -1{,}285 \\ \hline \end{array}$ **13.** $\begin{array}{r} \$31.54 \\ -13.27 \\ \hline \end{array}$

 **Audio Tutor** 1/16 Listen and Understand

Subtract Across Zeros

Objective Learn how to subtract across zeros.

Vocabulary
regroup

Learn About It

A taxi company owns 300 taxis. There are 128 taxis on duty today. How many taxis are not on duty?

Subtract. 300 − 128 = ■

STEP 1 There are no ones or tens to subtract from. **Regroup** 3 hundreds as 2 hundreds 10 tens.	**STEP 2** Regroup 10 tens as 9 tens 10 ones.	**STEP 3** Subtract ones, tens, and hundreds.
$\begin{array}{r} \overset{2\ 10}{\cancel{3}\cancel{0}}0 \\ -\ 128 \\ \hline \end{array}$	$\begin{array}{r} \overset{2\ \overset{9}{10}\ 10}{\cancel{3}\cancel{0}\cancel{0}} \\ -\ 128 \\ \hline \end{array}$	$\begin{array}{r} \overset{2\ \overset{9}{10}\ 10}{\cancel{3}\cancel{0}\cancel{0}} \\ -128 \\ \hline 172 \end{array}$

Solution: 172 taxis are not on duty.

▶ Use the same steps when you subtract four-digit numbers.

Find 4,302 − 1,155.

STEP 1 2 < 5, so you need to regroup. There are no tens to regroup. So regroup 3 hundreds as 2 hundreds 10 tens.	**STEP 2** Regroup 10 tens as 9 tens 10 ones. **10 ones + 2 ones = 12 ones**	**STEP 3** Subtract ones, tens, hundreds, and thousands.
$\begin{array}{r} \overset{2\ 10}{4,\cancel{3}\cancel{0}2} \\ -1,155 \\ \hline \end{array}$	$\begin{array}{r} \overset{2\ \overset{9}{10}\ 12}{4,\cancel{3}\cancel{0}\cancel{2}} \\ -1,155 \\ \hline \end{array}$	$\begin{array}{r} \overset{2\ \overset{9}{10}\ 12}{4,\cancel{3}\cancel{0}\cancel{2}} \\ -1,155 \\ \hline 3,147 \end{array}$

Solution: 3,147

Guided Practice

Find each difference.

Ask Yourself
- Are there zeros in the number I am subtracting from?
- If so, what do I do?

1. 504
    − 239

2. 900
    − 647

3. 800
    − 726

4. 3,405
    − 1,267

Explain Your Thinking ▶ How is regrouping to find 504 − 239 different from regrouping to find 514 − 239?

Practice and Problem Solving

Subtract. Check by adding or estimating.

5. 707
    − 353

6. 802
    − 577

7. 900
    − 652

8. 700
    − 436

9. 800
    − 725

10. 808 − 566

11. 500 − 288

12. 4,702 − 1,391

13. 5,609 − 2,365

14. 9,304 − 5,637

15. 8,700 − 4,279

Solve.

16. During Arnaldo's trip to the city he spent $9 on 2 taxicab rides. He spent $4.25 on his second ride. How much did he spend on his first ride?

17. The City Taxi Service made 2,000 trips yesterday. They made 1,542 trips today. How many more trips did they make yesterday?

18. **Multistep** A taxi company had 1,065 cabs. Then they bought 1,035 cabs. If 255 cabs are sold, how many cabs would the company have?

Mixed Review and Test Prep

Open Response

Tell if the object is more than or less than a pound. (Grade 2)

19.

20.

21. The students' goal is to collect 1,000 recyclable cans. They have collected 568 cans. How many more cans do they need?
(Ch. 5, Lesson 7)

Problem-Solving Decision
Explain Your Answer

Objective Describe how to solve a problem.

Sometimes you need to tell what you did to solve a problem.

Problem A helicopter is flying at an altitude of 450 feet. If its altitude decreases by 134 feet, what will its new altitude be? Explain.

Here are two ways students described how they solved the problem above.

The height above sea level at which a helicopter flies is called its altitude.

Briana drew a picture.

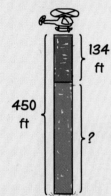

- The long rectangle shows the whole altitude of 450 ft.
- The blue shows the part you know, 134 ft.
- You subtract to find the missing part.

  450 − 134 = 316

So 316 feet is the new altitude.

Scott labeled his work.

I subtracted 134 from 450.

$$
\begin{array}{r}
4\ \ 10 \\
4\cancel{5}\cancel{0} \\
-134 \\
\hline
316
\end{array}
$$

← altitude of helicopter (ft)
← number of feet altitude decreased
← new altitude (ft)

So 316 feet is the new altitude.

- Did Briana and Scott both fully describe how they solved the problem?

Try These

Solve. Explain how you solved each problem with a picture or labels.

1. A helicopter flew to a hospital 44 miles away. The helicopter then flew another 27 miles. How many miles did the helicopter fly?

2. A helicopter pilot flies no higher than 1,000 feet. If she is currently flying at 224 feet, how many feet higher can she fly?

3. A company built 382 helicopters. It painted 234 helicopters. How many helicopters still need to be painted?

4. There are 205 packages in the helicopter. If 138 are delivered, how many are still in the helicopter?

Challenge
Target Practice

Use the digits around the outside of each target to write subtraction sentences with two-digit numbers. Arrange the numbers so the difference is the number in the bull's eye.

___ ___ − ___ ___ = 7

___ ___ − ___ ___ = 6

Math Reasoning
Which Way?

Write the words *greater than* or *less than* to complete each sentence.

1. Think about 44 − 19. The difference is ____ 44.

2. Think about 248 + 32. The sum is ____ 248.

3. Think about 12 + 580. The sum is ____ 12.

4. Think about 892 − 31. The difference is ____ 892.

Brain Teaser

Find each missing number.

1. $535 - 76 = \blacksquare - 248$

2. $139 - 137 = \blacksquare - 153$

3. $332 - 322 = \blacksquare - 663$

4. $401 - 359 = \blacksquare - 79$

Arrange the answers on the lines below to make the number sentence true.

___ − ___ + ___ − ___ = 0

Education Place
Check out **eduplace.com/map** for more brain teasers.

Chapter Review/Test

VOCABULARY

Choose the best term to complete each sentence.

1. A group of number sentences that use the same numbers is called a ____.

2. The answer to a subtraction problem is called the ____.

3. The answer to an addition problem is called the ____.

Vocabulary

sum

regroup

difference

fact family

CONCEPTS AND SKILLS

Find each missing number. (Lesson 2, pp. 110–111)

4. $25 + 10 = 35$
   $35 - \blacksquare = 25$

5. $17 + 5 = 22$
   $22 - 17 = \blacksquare$

6. $13 + 19 = 32$
   $\blacksquare - 19 = 13$

Round each number to the greatest place.
Then subtract. (Lesson 3, pp. 112–114)

7. $69 - 57$

8. $311 - 230$

9. $918 - 488$

Find each difference. Check each answer by estimating.

(Lessons 1, 4–7, pp. 108–109, 116–129)

10. $\begin{array}{r} 34 \\ -\ 34 \\ \hline \end{array}$

11. $\begin{array}{r} 92 \\ -\ 61 \\ \hline \end{array}$

12. $\begin{array}{r} 45 \\ -\ 38 \\ \hline \end{array}$

13. $\begin{array}{r} 596 \\ -\ 189 \\ \hline \end{array}$

14. $\begin{array}{r} \$7.53 \\ -\ 5.27 \\ \hline \end{array}$

15. $\begin{array}{r} 402 \\ -\ 298 \\ \hline \end{array}$

16. $\begin{array}{r} \$43.36 \\ -\ 23.59 \\ \hline \end{array}$

17. $\begin{array}{r} 382 \\ -\ 195 \\ \hline \end{array}$

18. $\begin{array}{r} 9,901 \\ -\ 7,865 \\ \hline \end{array}$

19. $\begin{array}{r} 4,500 \\ -\ 2,468 \\ \hline \end{array}$

PROBLEM SOLVING

Solve. Explain your answer. (Lesson 8, p. 130)

20. The bicycle was invented in 1791. The car was invented in 1885. How many years after the bicycle was the car invented?

Write About It

Show You Understand

Look at the problem below.

$\begin{array}{r} 79 \\ -\ 32 \\ \hline \end{array}$

Will rounding or front-end estimation give a closer estimate of the difference?

Extra Practice

Set A (Lesson 1, pp. 108–109)

Subtract.

1. $\begin{array}{r} 16 \\ -\ 0 \\ \hline \end{array}$
2. $\begin{array}{r} 32 \\ -\ 32 \\ \hline \end{array}$
3. $\begin{array}{r} 75 \\ -\ 0 \\ \hline \end{array}$
4. $\begin{array}{r} 24 \\ -\ 24 \\ \hline \end{array}$

Set B (Lesson 2, pp. 110–111)

Find each missing number.

1. 42 + 13 = 55
   55 − ■ = 13
2. 7 + 12 = 19
   ■ − 12 = 7
3. 39 + 21 = 60
   60 − 21 = ■

Set C (Lesson 3, pp. 112–114)

Round each number to the greatest place. Then subtract.

1. 67 − 31
2. $4.91 − $1.86
3. 276 − 158
4. $8.53 − $4.29

Set D (Lesson 4, pp. 116–118)

Find each difference.

1. 62 − 28
2. 76 − 29
3. $443 − $225
4. 594 − 288

Set E (Lesson 5, pp. 120–122)

Subtract.

1. $4.23 − $2.46
2. 741 − 526
3. 391 − 172
4. 634 − 479

Set F (Lesson 6, pp. 124–126)

Find each difference.

1. 4,642 − 2,158
2. 6,393 − 2,295
3. 9,717 − 3,925
4. 3,471 − 1,968

Set G (Lesson 7, pp. 128–129)

Subtract.

1. 5,302 − 3,291
2. 8,600 − 4,125
3. 7,008 − 5,137
4. 4,005 − 1,372

Extra Practice at **eduplace.com/map**

Go Fly a Kite!

Kites have been part of Japanese culture for about two thousand years. In Japan people try to set kite-flying records. In 1998 Japanese junior high school students set a kite record. They flew 15,585 kites on one string.

Each year there are many kite festivals, each with its own theme. One kite festival features giant kites. Some giant kites weigh more than 1,900 pounds and need teams of about 100 people to fly them!

134

Problem Solving

The table shows data about one kite from each of four giant kite festivals. Use the table for Problems 1–3.

 1 What is the difference in length between the longest and the shortest kite?

 2 How many of the Shirone kites are needed to equal the length of 2 Sagami kites?

Amazing Japanese Kites		
Giant Kite Festival	Kite Length (in meters)	Kite Weight (in kilograms)
Sagami	14	880
Sanjo	5	9
Shirone	7	30
Showamchi	16	800

 3 Which of the Japanese kites is the heaviest? How much heavier is this kite than the combined weight of the other 3 kites?

 4 The Shirone kite cost about $12,675 to make. The Sagami kite cost about $15,379. What was the total cost of the two kites?

Education Place
Visit Weekly Reader Connections at **eduplace.com/map** for more on this topic.

Enrichment: Palindromes

Vocabulary

palindrome

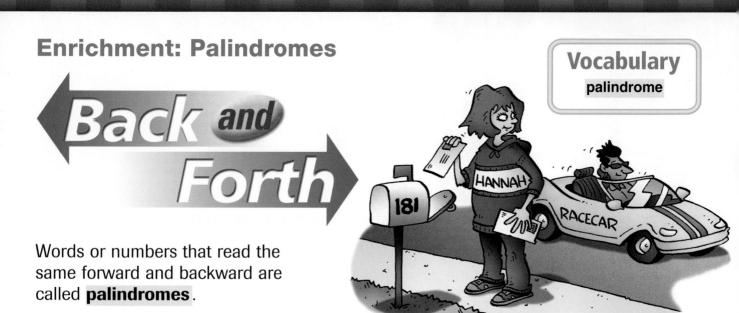

Words or numbers that read the same forward and backward are called **palindromes**.

▶ **You can turn any number into a palindrome.**

Here's how to turn 81 into a palindrome.

• Start with the number.	81
• Reverse the digits.	+ 18
• Find the sum.	99 ← This is a palindrome.

▶ **Sometimes you need to follow the steps more than once.**

Here's how to turn 67 into a palindrome.

• Start with the number.	67
• Reverse the digits.	+ 76
• Find the sum.	143
• Reverse the digits.	+ 341
• Find the sum.	484 ← This is a palindrome.

Try These!

Use addition to turn each number into a palindrome.

1. 18   **2.** 34   **3.** 48   **4.** 87   **5.** 124

6. 156   **7.** 423   **8.** 2,009   **9.** 4,217   **10.** 5,612

Block It Out!

You can use the base-ten blocks found on Education Place at **eduplace.com/kids/mw/** to practice addition.

Follow these steps to find 175 + 246.

- Use **Change Mat** to choose **Two Numbers**.

- To show 175:
  Put your pointer over the **Stamp** tool.
  Click the hundreds block.
  Then click the tens block 7 times.
  Next, click the ones block 5 times.

- Click anywhere in the bottom workspace.

- Follow the steps above to show 246.

- Drag blocks from bottom to top.

- To regroup 10 ones as 1 ten, click the left arrow above the ones column.

- To regroup 10 tens as 1 hundred, click the left arrow above the tens column.

- Click **[1 2 3]**.

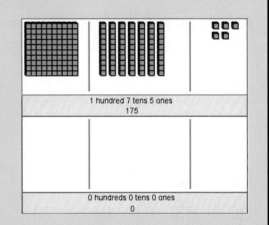

1 hundred 7 tens 5 ones
175

0 hundreds 0 tens 0 ones
0

Solution: There are 4 hundreds blocks, 2 tens blocks, and 1 ones block. So, 175 + 246 = 421.

Use the base-ten blocks to find each sum.

1. 62 + 48
2. 85 + 33
3. $75 + $49
4. 49 + 98
5. 422 + 18
6. 139 + 196
7. 234 + 182
8. $277 + $181

9. **Analyze** Which blocks do you regroup when adding 647 and 159?

Unit 2 Test

VOCABULARY (Open Response)

Choose the best term to complete each sentence.

Vocabulary
- difference
- fact family
- Associative Property
- Commutative Property

1. The number sentence 6 + 3 can be rewritten as 3 + 6 using the ____.

2. When you subtract 6 from 10, the ____ is 4.

3. The number sentences 6 + 7 = 13 and 13 − 6 = 7 belong to one ____.

CONCEPTS AND SKILLS (Open Response)

Round each number to the greatest place.
Then add or subtract to find each estimate. (Chapters 4, 5)

4.
```
   18
 + 27
```

5.
```
   87
 − 26
```

6.
```
   531
 − 215
```

7.
```
   112
 + 381
```

8.
```
 $6.55
 − 4.11
```

Add or subtract. (Chapters 4, 5)

9.
```
   83
 − 83
```

10.
```
   73
 − 32
```

11.
```
   13
 + 28
```

12.
```
   97
 − 36
```

13.
```
   46
 + 39
```

14.
```
   43
 − 27
```

15.
```
   70
 − 38
```

16.
```
   222
 + 379
```

17.
```
 $5.64
 + 1.88
```

18.
```
   549
 − 203
```

19.
```
   652
 + 258
```

20.
```
 $6.14
 − 3.15
```

21.
```
   2,198
 + 3,822
```

22.
```
   9,023
 − 4,172
```

23.
```
   4,629
 + 1,383
```

24. (6 + 4) + 8

25. (5 + 2 + 3) + 5

26. 23 + 33 + 41

27. 91 − 12

28. 753 − 219

29. $5.97 − $2.73

PROBLEM SOLVING (Open Response)

30. During the summer, Tamika and Sara read a total of 87 books. Tamika read 39 books. How many books did Sara read?

31. Rafi has 105 stamps. Peng has 67 stamps. Peng's brother gave him 53 more stamps. Do the two boys have more than 200 stamps?

32. David has 12 coins. He only has dimes and quarters. He has 6 more dimes than quarters. How many of each kind of coin does David have?

33. In many schools in the U.S., the school year is 180 days. In China, the school year is 251 days. How many days longer is the school year in China than in the U.S.?

Performance Assessment

(Constructed Response)

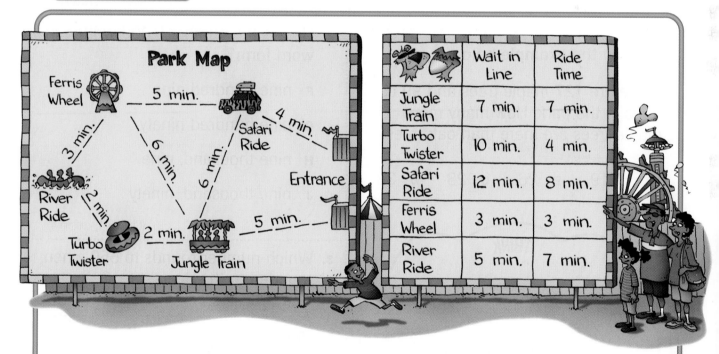

Task You and your family are at the amusement park. You are at the entrance looking at the sign that tells you about each ride. Next to the sign is a map of the park.

Use the signs and the information at the right. Decide which rides you will go on in the time you have left. Explain your thinking.

Information You Need

- You have 90 minutes left until the park closes.
- You want to go on at least 3 different rides.
- When the park closes you need to be back at the entrance.
- The map shows how long it takes to walk on the paths from ride to ride.

Cumulative Test Prep

Solve Problems 1–10.

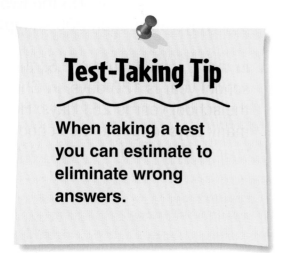

Test-Taking Tip

When taking a test you can estimate to eliminate wrong answers.

Look at the example below.

There are 127 maple trees and 99 oak trees in the park. How many more maple trees are there than oak trees?

A 19   **B** 26   **C** 28   **D** 38

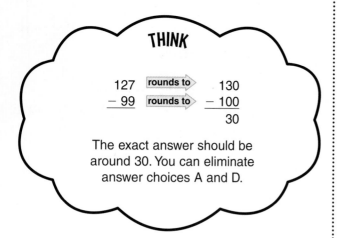

THINK

$$\begin{array}{r} 127 \\ -\ 99 \\ \end{array} \quad \begin{array}{c} \text{rounds to} \\ \text{rounds to} \end{array} \quad \begin{array}{r} 130 \\ -\ 100 \\ \hline 30 \end{array}$$

The exact answer should be around 30. You can eliminate answer choices A and D.

Multiple Choice

1. What is the missing number that completes the pattern?

98, 100, 102, 104, ___, 108

A 107   **C** 105

B 106   **D** 104

(Chapter 1, Lesson 5)

2. How is the number 9,009 written in word form?

F nine hundred nine

G nine hundred ninety

H nine thousand, nine

J nine thousand, ninety

(Chapter 1, Lesson 4)

3. Which number rounds to 550 when rounded to the nearest ten?

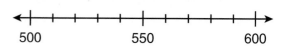

A 527   **C** 561

B 548   **D** 582

(Chapter 2, Lesson 3)

4. What is the sum of $2.73 + $1.96?

F $3.60   **H** $4.60

G $3.69   **J** $4.69

(Chapter 4, Lesson 4)

For Test-Taking Tips, see page 659.

5. Write the number for the base-ten blocks shown.

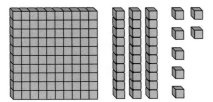

(Chapter 1, Lesson 2)

6. Rounded to the nearest ten, the Elm School cafeteria sold 150 cartons of milk. What is the greatest number of cartons that could have been sold?

(Chapter 2, Lesson 3)

7. Darnel pays $20 for a shirt that costs $18.68. What is the least number of pennies Darnel could receive in change?

(Chapter 3, Lesson 3)

8. Kate has 102 red, 54 white, and 145 blue stickers in her collection. How many stickers does Kate have?

(Chapter 4, Lesson 6)

9. The science club has 389 photos of insects. They want 1,000 photos by the end of the year. How many more do they need?

(Chapter 5, Lesson 7)

10. Julie's school collected canned food for a pet shelter. The table shows the number of cans collected.

Can Collection		
	Grade 3	Grade 4
Week 1	198	87
Week 2	199	98
Week 3	187	99

A. What is the total number of cans collected each week?

B. How many more cans were collected during Week 2 than during Week 1?

C. Round to the nearest hundred to estimate the total number of cans the fourth grade collected in the three weeks.

D. Did the students in the fourth grade collect more or fewer cans than the estimated amount? Explain how you know.

(Chapter 4, Lesson 2;
Chapter 4, Lesson 4)

Education Place
Look for Cumulative Test Prep at **eduplace.com/map** for more practice.

Vocabulary Wrap-Up for Unit 2

Look back at the big ideas and vocabulary in this unit.

Big Ideas

Addition and subtraction are related.

You can round numbers to estimate sums and differences.

Regrouping is sometimes necessary when you add or subtract.

Key Vocabulary

estimate

sum

difference

regrouping

Math Conversations

Use your new vocabulary to discuss these big ideas.

1. Explain how to regroup tens and ones to find $200 - 173$.

2. Explain how finding $15 - 8$ is the same as finding a missing addend.

3. Explain how fact families help show that addition and subtraction are related.

4. Explain why changing the order in which numbers are added does not change the sum.

5. **Write About It** The three elementary schools in Smallville have 115 students, 220 students, and 389 students. How could you estimate the total number of students in Smallville?

About how much is $692 + 413$?

Round the numbers to the nearest hundred. Then add the rounded numbers.

CHAPTER 6

Graph and Analyze Data

page 146

CHAPTER 7

Probability

page 174

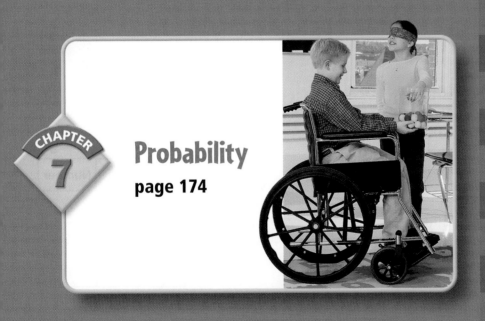

Data and Probability

Reading Mathematics

Reviewing Vocabulary

Here are some math vocabulary words that you should know.

bar graph	a graph that uses bars to show data
pictograph	a graph that uses pictures to show data
tally chart	a chart used to record data
tally mark	a mark on a tally chart that stands for 1 of something

Reading Words And Symbols

You can use words and symbols to describe the marbles.

- There are 5 red, 2 blue, and 3 green marbles in the bag.
- Each tally mark in the chart stands for one marble.
- Five tally marks can be written as 𝍸.

Marbles in Bag		
Color	**Tally**	**Number**
Red	𝍸	5
Green	|||	3
Blue	||	2

Use words or symbols to answer the questions.

1. Write two sentences to describe the marbles in the bag at the right.
2. Create a tally chart to describe the marbles in the bag.

Reading Test Questions

Choose the correct answer for each.

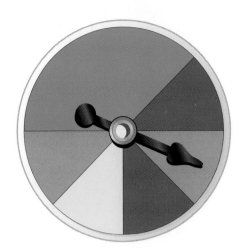

3. On which color is the spinner most likely to land?

    a. orange   **c.** yellow

    b. green   **d.** purple

Most likely means "having the greatest chance."

4. On which color is the spinner least likely to land?

    a. orange   **c.** green

    b. yellow   **d.** purple

Least likely means "having the smallest chance."

5. What is the chance that the spinner will land on red?

    a. likely   **c.** unlikely

    b. certain   **d.** impossible

Chance means "how likely it is that something will happen."

Learning Vocabulary

Watch for these words in this unit. Write their definitions in your journal.

- median
- mode
- range
- ordered pair
- probability

Literature Connection

Read "Frog or Toad" on Page 648. Then work with a partner to answer the questions about the story.

Education Place

At **eduplace.com/map** see eGlossary and eGames—Math Lingo.

Graph and Analyze Data

INVESTIGATION

Using Data

This softball player is waiting for the perfect pitch! Meanwhile, her coach is keeping track of how the team is doing. Look at the chart. Make a statement that compares some of the data shown in the chart.

Coach's Tally	
Walks	IIII
Runs	IIII III
Home Runs	II
Stolen Bases	III

Use What You Know

**Use this page to review and remember
what you need to know for this chapter.**

VOCABULARY

Choose the best term to complete each sentence.

1. A graph that uses bars to show data is a ____.

2. To keep track of what you are counting you can
   make ____.

3. A graph that shows information with pictures is
   a ____.

Vocabulary

bar graph

pictograph

tally marks

number line

CONCEPTS AND SKILLS

**The pictograph below shows the number of different sports
jerseys in a box. Use the pictograph for Questions 4–6.**

4. How many soccer and hockey jerseys
   are there?

5. How many more hockey jerseys than
   football jerseys are there?

6. What is the total number of jerseys?

Sports Jerseys

Soccer	👕 👕 👕
Hockey	👕 👕 👕 👕
Football	👕 👕

Each 👕 stands for 2 jerseys.

**Write the numbers in order from least
to greatest.**

7. 7   3   19   8. 57   93   84   9. 107   217   16

Write About It

10. How are bar graphs similar to pictographs?
    How are they different?

Facts Practice, See page 667.

Collect and Organize Data

Objective Conduct a survey and record the results.

Work Together

One way to collect **data**, or information, is to conduct a **survey**. When you conduct a survey, you ask people a question and you record their answers.

You can use a tally chart to record answers. This tally chart shows the survey results. The question was "Which color do you like best?"

- Which color was chosen most often?
- Which color was chosen least often?

A tally mark stands for one vote.
| stands for 1.
卌 stands for 5.

Favorite Colors

Color	Tally	Number
Red	卌	5
Blue	|||	3
Green	卌 ||	7
Purple	||||	4

Work with a group to conduct a survey in your class.

STEP 1 Write a survey question that has three or four possible answers. Use the tally chart above as a model to make your own tally chart.

- What is the title of your tally chart?
- What headings did you use?

STEP 2 Conduct a survey in your class. Record the results in the tally chart you made.

STEP 3 Count the tally marks for each choice.

- Which choice has the greatest number of tallies?
- Which choice has the least number of tallies?

On Your Own

Use the tally chart at the right for Questions 1–3.

1. How many students chose football?

2. How many more students chose football than baseball?

3. How many students chose either tennis or hockey?

Favorite Sport to Watch		
Sport	Tally	Number
Baseball	ⲏⲏ	5
Hockey	ⅠⅠ	2
Tennis	ⅠⅠⅠ	3
Football	ⲏⲏ ⅠⅠ	7

Use your Workmat or make a tally chart like the one below.
Record the information from the list using tallies.
Then use your tally chart for Questions 4–6.

Our Favorite Sports		
Sport	Tally	Number
Bicycling		
Skateboarding		
Soccer		
Volleyball		

Our Favorite Sports

Sue	Skateboarding
Mary	Bicycling
Carlos	Skateboarding
Bob	Soccer
Kim	Soccer
Roger	Volleyball
Alyssa	Soccer
Cynthia	Bicycling
Rex	Soccer
Maggie	Soccer

4. How many students were surveyed?

5. Which is the least favorite sport?

6. How many students chose either skateboarding or bicycling?

Talk About It • Write About It

You learned how to make tally charts to record data.

7. Look at your completed tally chart and the list above. Is it easier to see which sport is the favorite by looking at the tally chart or the list? Explain.

8. Look at the data in the list. Did more students choose team sports or individual sports? Make another tally chart to show this information.

Explore Range, Median, Mode, and Mean

Objective Use models to find the range, median, mode, and mean of a set of numbers.

Materials
snap cubes
sheet of paper

Work Together

Work with a partner to learn how to describe data in different ways. Use snap cubes to represent the numbers in the table.

Swimming Races	
Type of Race	**Number of Swimmers**
Backstroke	2
Sidestroke	5
Crawl	2
Butterfly	4
Freestyle	7

 STEP 1 Look at the table. Make 5 stacks of snap cubes to show the number of swimmers in each race. Place the stacks of cubes on the sheet of paper.

- How many stacks did you make?

- How many cubes are in each stack?

 STEP 2 Now put the stacks in order starting with the stack that has the least number of cubes and ending with the stack that has the greatest number of cubes.

The difference between the greatest number and the least number is called the **range**.

- What is the least number of cubes in a stack?

- What is the greatest number?

- Subtract the least number from the greatest. What is the difference? This is the range of the data.

STEP 3

Look at the stacks of cubes again.

When a set of data is ordered from least to greatest, the middle number is called the **median**.

- How many cubes are in the middle stack?

- What is the median of the data?

STEP 4

Now look at the cubes to see if a number appears more than once. The number that occurs most often in a set of data is called the **mode**.

- What number of cubes occurs most often?

- What is the mode of the data?

STEP 5

Move cubes from one stack to another, so all the stacks have the same number of cubes. Record the new number of cubes in each stack.

When the stacks have the same number of cubes, the number in each stack is called the **mean**.

- How many cubes are in each stack?

- What is the mean of the data?

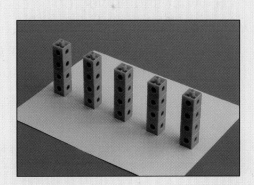

Go On

The table shows the number of swim classes taught on weekdays. Use snap cubes to show this information. Then use the cubes to answer Questions 1–4.

Swim Classes Taught	
Day of the Week	Number of Classes
Monday	5
Tuesday	4
Wednesday	9
Thursday	4
Friday	8

1. How many stacks of cubes did you make? Explain why you made that number of stacks.

2. How many cubes are in each stack?

3. Rearrange the stacks of cubes in order from least to greatest.

   a. What is the range of the data?
   b. What is the median?
   c. What is the mode?

4. Move the cubes to find the mean.

   a. What should you do to each stack to find the mean?
   b. What is the mean number of classes taught each weekday?

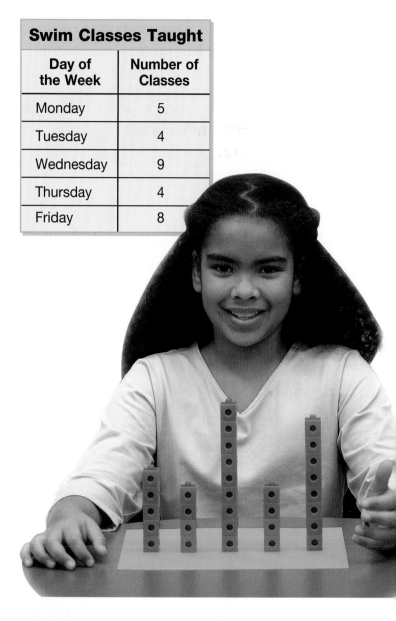

 Talk About It • Write About It

You have learned how to find the range, median, mode, and mean of a set of data.

5. Look at the cubes at the right. Explain how you know what the mean is.

6. Explain what you would do to find the mean, median, mode, and range of the data.

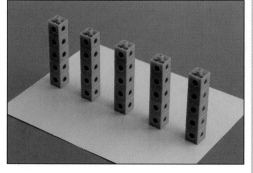

Algebraic Thinking
Mean, Median, Mode — Match!

Look at the pictures of snap cubes. Write *red*, *blue*, or *orange* to tell the set of cubes that shows each of the following.

1. A mean of 3.

2. A median of 4.

3. A mode of 5.

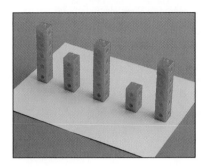  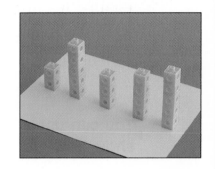

Visual Thinking
Tally Trouble!

A waitress used these tally marks to take an order.

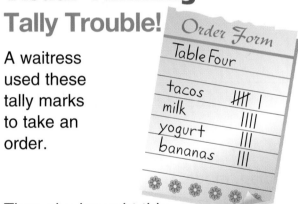

Order Form
Table Four

tacos	IIII I
milk	IIII
yogurt	III
bananas	III

Then she brought this tray of food. What is wrong?

Draw a tray that shows the right amount of each kind of food.

Brain Teaser

Ann took a survey of her friends. She asked how many books each friend read last month. The list below shows the number of books her friends read.

$$2, 4, 4, 4, 6$$

• What is the mode of Ann's data?

• What is the mean of Ann's data?

• What is the median of Ann's data?

 Education Place

Check out **eduplace.com/map** for more brain teasers.

Line Plots

Objective Read and make line plots.

Vocabulary

line plot
median
mode
range

Learn About It

Ali conducted a survey of 9 baseball players to find out how many home runs each player hit last season.

The table at the right shows the results of her survey.

Home Runs Last Season

Rick	1	John	0	Jess	1
Sally	4	Luis	2	Lynn	4
Max	3	Yoko	4	Mike	6

▶ **You can use a line plot to show how often something happens.**

Read the line plot to find how many players hit 1 home run.

- Find 1 on the line plot. It stands for 1 home run.

- Then count the number of X's above 1. Each X stands for 1 player. There are 2 X's above 1. So 2 players hit 1 home run.

```
                              X
              X               X
    X    X    X    X    X               X
    |    |    |    |    |    |    |
    0    1    2    3    4    5    6
```

Number of Home Runs Hit

▶ **You can use the line plot to find the median, mode, and range.**

To find the **median**, list the data in order from least to greatest.

    0 1 1 2 3 4 4 4 6

The middle number is 3.

The median is 3.

To find the **mode**, look for the number that has the most X's.

The number 4 has three X's. The number of home runs that occurred most often was 4.

The mode is 4.

To find the **range**, subtract the least number on the line plot from the greatest number.

The range is 6.

$$6 - 0 = 6$$

    ↑   ↑   ↑
  greatest least range
  number number

Try this activity to make a line plot.

The table at the right shows the number of games won by different teams. Follow the steps below to make a line plot to show the data in the table.

Number of Games Won					
Lasers	2	Sparks	1	Wings	3
Bears	1	Falcons	1	Suns	4
Comets	5	Hawks	4	Foxes	1

 STEP 1 Use the title *Number of Games Won* for the line plot. Draw and label a number line.

- What is the least number of games won? What is the greatest number?

- How do the answers to those questions help you label the number line?

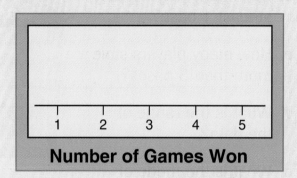

Number of Games Won

 STEP 2 Draw an X above each number for each team that has won that many games.

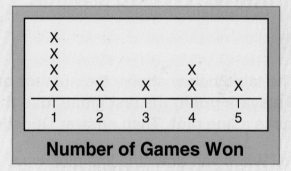

Number of Games Won

Guided Practice

Use your line plot to answer Questions 1–3.

1. How many teams won exactly 4 games?

2. What is the median of the data?

3. What is the range of the data?

Ask Yourself
- What do the X's above the numbers stand for?

Explain Your Thinking ▶ Is it easier to use the table or the line plot to find the mode?

Sara asked her teammates how many bases they each stole last season. This line plot shows the results. Use the line plot to answer Questions 4–9.

4. How many players stole exactly 3 bases?

5. How many players stole at least 1 base?

6. How many players stole more than 3 bases?

7. What is the range of the data?

8. What is the mode of the data?

9. **Reasoning** Suppose one more player says she stole 6 bases. Will the range of the data change? Explain.

The table below shows the number of hits that 5 players got in the last game. Use the data to make a line plot. Then answer Questions 10–16.

10. When you draw the line plot, what numbers will you use for the number line?

11. What do the X's on your line plot stand for?

12. How many players got more than 1 hit?

13. How many players got exactly three hits?

14. What is the range of the data?

15. What is the mode of the data?

16. **Reasoning** Suppose Carl had 3 hits in the last game. Would the mode of the data change? Explain.

Hits Last Game	
Name of Player	Number of Hits
Sally	5
Max	4
Yoko	1
Amy	3
Edie	3

Extra Practice See page 173, Set A.

Science Connection
Animal Number Puzzle

Human adults can have up to 32 teeth. Kids usually have 20 teeth. (Unless the loose ones have fallen out, that is!) What about animals?

Use these clues to complete the table.

- A raccoon has twice as many teeth as a beaver.

- A cat has fewer teeth than a raccoon but more than a beaver. The number of teeth a cat has ends in 0.

- A horse has 4 more teeth than a raccoon.

- A squirrel has half the number of teeth a horse has.

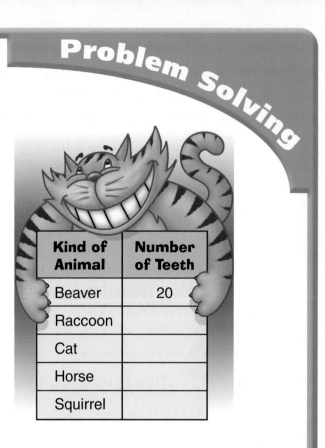

Kind of Animal	Number of Teeth
Beaver	20
Raccoon	
Cat	
Horse	
Squirrel	

WEEKLY WR READER eduplace.com/map

Check your understanding of Lessons 1–3.

Use the tally chart for Questions 1–3. (Lesson 1)

1. How many students were surveyed?

2. What is the most popular color?

3. How many more students chose red than blue?

This line plot shows the number of goals scored by 13 soccer players. Use the line plot for Questions 4–5. (Lessons 2–3)

4. What is the median of the data?

5. What was the greatest number of goals scored?

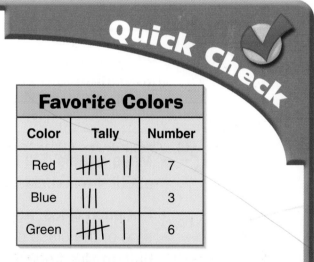

Favorite Colors		
Color	Tally	Number
Red	卌 ‖	7
Blue	‖‖	3
Green	卌 ‖	6

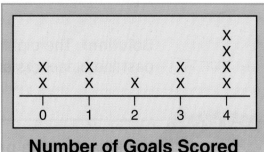

Number of Goals Scored

Lesson 4

Problem-Solving Strategy
Make a Table

Objective Make a table to solve a problem.

Problem The first class in the Field Day Parade marches past the bleachers at 2:05 P.M. Each class passes the parents in the bleachers 2 minutes after the class in front of it. When does the eighth class march past the bleachers?

UNDERSTAND

This is what you know:

- The first class marches past the bleachers at 2:05 P.M.

- Each class passes the bleachers 2 minutes after the class in front of it.

PLAN

You can make a table to organize the information and solve the problem.

SOLVE

- Make a table. Fill in what you know about the first class.

- For each class, add 2 minutes to the time of the class before it. Use this pattern to complete the table.

Solution: The eighth class will march past the bleachers at 2:19 P.M.

Class	Time
First	2:05 P.M.
Second	2:07 P.M.
Third	2:09 P.M.
Fourth	2:11 P.M.
Fifth	2:13 P.M.
Sixth	2:15 P.M.
Seventh	2:17 P.M.
Eighth	2:19 P.M.

LOOK BACK

Look back at the problem.
Does the answer make sense?

Guided Practice

Use the Ask Yourself questions to help solve each problem.

1. Katy runs 100 yards in the relay race. Each of her 3 teammates runs 50 more yards than the runner before. How many yards will Katy's team run in all?

2. Joe stacks the cans in the Pitch Ball game. The bottom row has 12 cans. Each row has 2 fewer cans than the row below it. How many cans will be in the fifth row?

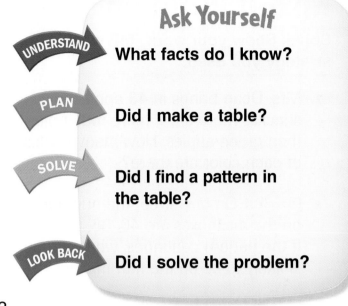

Ask Yourself

UNDERSTAND → **What facts do I know?**

PLAN → **Did I make a table?**

SOLVE → **Did I find a pattern in the table?**

LOOK BACK → **Did I solve the problem?**

Independent Practice

Make a table to solve each problem.

3. In a game, Sonya runs to Flag A and collects 3 tennis balls. Then she runs to Flags B, C, D, and E and collects 2 more tennis balls than she did at the flag before. How many tennis balls should she collect at Flag D?

4. **Multistep** Terrell counts 12 legs in the 3-legged race. Each team of 2 students runs on 3 legs. How many students are in the race?

5. The first number in a number pattern is 18. Each number in the pattern is 4 less than the number before it. What is the fourth number in the pattern?

6. **Multistep** Jaime saved $1.25 one week. Each week after that he saves $0.75 more than the week before. What will his total savings be at the end of 4 weeks?

Go On

Mixed Problem Solving

Solve. Show your work. Tell what strategy you used.

7. Mrs. Dean brings in 43 apples for snacks. There are 7 more red apples than green apples. How many apples of each color are there?

8. **Predict** On one street the numbers on the mailboxes are 40, 38, and 36. If the pattern continues, what number is likely to be on the fifth mailbox?

9. Marco is building stairs with blocks. The picture below shows the blocks he used for 2, 3, and 4 steps. If the pattern continues, how many blocks will he need for 6 steps?

| 2 steps | 3 steps | 4 steps |

You Choose

Strategy
- Act It Out
- Draw a Picture
- Find a Pattern
- Guess and Check
- Make a Table

Computation Method
- Mental Math
- Estimation
- Paper and Pencil
- Calculator

Data **Use the pictograph to solve Problems 10–12.**

Mr. Lundberg's science class is studying butterflies. The pictograph shows the number of each kind of butterfly they found.

10. The class found the most of which kind of butterfly?

11. How many more monarchs than admirals did the class find?

12. **Explain** Suppose the class finds 4 more swallowtail butterflies. How many more symbols will they need to place in the pictograph?

Butterflies Collected

Monarch	X X X X X X
Swallowtail	X X X
Admiral	X X
White	X X X X
Each **X** stands for 1 butterfly	

Problem Solving on Tests

Multiple Choice

Choose the letter of the correct answer. If the correct answer is not here, choose NH.

1. Mr. Stein writes a check for ten dollars and six cents. Which shows this amount using a dollar sign and a decimal point?

   A \$100.16 **C** \$10.06

   B \$10.60 **D** \$1.06

   (Chapter 3, Lesson 2)

2. Emily's birthday is in 37 days. Tan's birthday is 16 days after Emily's. In how many days is Tan's birthday?

   F 53 **G** 43 **H** 21 **J** NH

   (Chapter 4, Lesson 3)

Open Response

Solve each problem.

3. A moving truck travels 389 miles from Vermont to Maine. Then it returns to Vermont by the same route. How many miles less than 1,000 miles does the truck travel?

   (Chapter 5, Lesson 7)

4. Delia buys a toy for \$1.39. She pays with the bills shown.

   Explain What is the least number of coins she can receive for change? What are the coins?

   (Chapter 3, Lesson 3)

Constructed Response

5. Jenny and Pete help their mom at a garden center. A shipment of plants has just arrived by truck.

Truck Delivery of New Plants

Type	Tally	Number
Azaleas	卌 卌 |	11
Tulips		18
Daffodils	卌 卌 卌 卌 卌	
Jonquils	卌 卌 卌 ||	
Hyacinths		20

   a. Copy and complete the tally chart.

   b. The garden center had 7 azalea plants and 13 jonquils before the new shipment. Pete needs to know how many azalea and jonquil plants they have now. **Explain** How can you decide how many they have now?

   c. Jenny and Pete's mom wants to know the total of all the plants in the garden center after the shipment. How many plants do they have? Show a way that Jenny can find the answer.

   (Chapter 6, Lesson 1)

Education Place

See **eduplace.com/map** for more Test-Taking Tips.

Make a Pictograph

Objective Read and make pictographs.

Vocabulary
pictograph
key

Materials
Workmat 4 (Tables)

Work Together

The students in Lee's gymnastics class chose their favorite floor exercises. The table at the right shows the results of the survey.

Work with a partner. Make a pictograph to show the data in the table in a different way. A **pictograph** uses pictures or symbols to represent data.

Favorite Floor Exercises

Exercise	Number of Students
Splits	10
Flips	6
Cartwheels	4
Handstands	5

STEP 1 Draw an outline for the pictograph. Write in the title and the name of each exercise.

- How many rows will your pictograph have?

Favorite Floor Exercises

Splits	
Flips	
Cartwheels	
Handstands	

STEP 2 Decide on a symbol and the number it represents.

Let ♀ stand for 2 students. Write the **key** on your graph.

- How do you know how many ♀ to draw for splits?

Key → Each ♀ stands for 2 students.

STEP 3 Draw the correct number of ♀ for each exercise.

Since each ♀ stands for 2 students, half a symbol, ♀, stands for 1 student.

- How many symbols will you use to show the number of students who chose handstands?

Favorite Floor Exercises

Splits	♀ ♀ ♀ ♀ ♀
Flips	
Cartwheels	
Handstands	

Each ♀ stands for 2 students.

Make a pictograph of the data in this table. Use a key where each ▭ stands for 5 tickets sold. Then use your pictograph to answer Questions 1–3.

1. What is the title of your pictograph?

2. How many pictures will you draw for each of the 4 days?

3. **Write About It** Write a question that could be answered using the information in your pictograph.

Tickets Sold for Gymnastics Show	
Day 1	35
Day 2	20
Day 3	15
Day 4	30

The information below describes the results of a survey about gymnastics.

4. Use the information to copy and complete the pictograph.

- Six people like to use the balance beam.

- Eight more people like to use the trampoline than those who like to use the balance beam.

- The same number of people like to use the trampoline as those who like to use the vault.

- The number of people who like to use the trampoline is the same as the total number of people who like to use the balance beam and the uneven bars.

Favorite Gymnastics Activities	
Balance Beam	
Trampoline	
Vault	
Uneven Bars	

Each ♀ stands for 2 people.

Talk About It • Write About It

You learned how to read and make a pictograph.

5. Suppose there are 20 wristbands, 25 warm-up suits, and 40 kneepads. Would a key where each picture stands for 10 items be a good choice for a pictograph? Explain why or why not.

Extra Practice See page 173, Set B.

Make a Bar Graph

Objective Make a bar graph to represent data.

Vocabulary

bar graph

scale

Materials
colored pencils
10×10 grid
(Workmat 7;
Learning Tool 5)

 Work Together

The Winter Olympics in 2002 took place in
Salt Lake City, Utah. The table shows the
number of medals won by four countries.

Medals Won	
Country	**Number of Medals**
Canada	17
Italy	12
France	11
China	8

Work with a partner.
Make a **bar graph** to show the data in
the table. Use a 10×10 grid.

STEP 1
- Write the title.
- Label the side and the bottom of the graph.

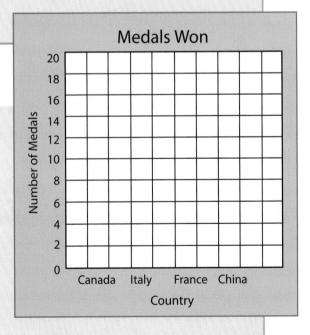

STEP 2
Choose a **scale** for your graph
to show the number of medals.

Use a scale of 2. Start with 0.
Complete the scale.

- How did you complete
  the scale on your graph?

- What is the greatest
  number on your scale?
  Explain why.

STEP 3 Draw the bars. Some of the bars may end halfway between two numbers because you used a scale of 2.

- Where does the bar for Canada end?
- Where does the bar for France end?

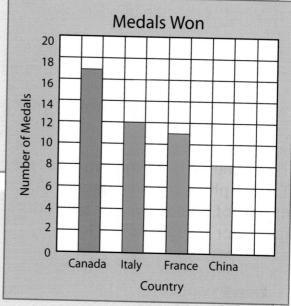

STEP 4 Look back at the table. Compare the bars of your graph to the data in the table.

- Is each bar of your graph the correct height? Explain.

On Your Own

The graph below is a horizontal bar graph. Use it for Questions 1–4.

1. What is the scale on this graph?

2. Which country won the most swimming medals?

3. Which country won the least number of medals? How many medals did that country win?

4. Which country won twice as many medals as Bulgaria? Explain your answer.

Make a vertical or horizontal bar graph of the data in this table. Use a scale of 5.

5. What is the title of your graph?

6. What is the greatest number on your scale? What is the least number?

7. What labels did you use for your graph?

Favorite Winter Olympic Events

Event	Number of Spectators
Figure Skating	40
Speed Skating	20
Ski Jump	35
Bobsled	15

The scale is missing from this vertical bar graph. The graph shows the favorite Summer Olympic events of some Olympic spectators. Use the graph for Questions 8–11.

8. Which summer event is the most popular?

9. **Estimate** Which event is about half as popular as track?

10. **Analyze** Which two events combined were as popular as gymnastics?

11. Suppose the number of spectators that chose gymnastics is 60. About how many spectators chose track?

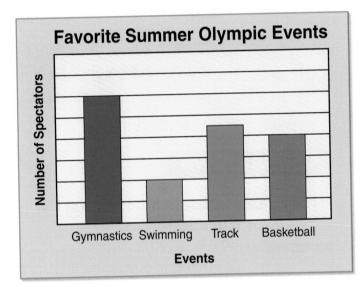

Talk About It • Write About It

You learned how to make a bar graph to organize data.

12. Does displaying data on a horizontal bar graph instead of a vertical bar graph change the meaning of the data? Explain why or why not.

13. Conduct a survey of the students in your class. What are their favorite Summer Olympic events? Make a bar graph to show the results of your survey.

Extra Practice See page 173, Set C.

Math Reasoning
Choose a Graph to Display Data

Miguel collected data about a Ping Pong Tournament in his school. Then he displayed the data in the following ways.

▶ Miguel made a pictograph to show the number of students who attended. It is easy to show large numbers in a pictograph.

- Would Miguel's data be easy to read if he used a tally chart? Why or why not?

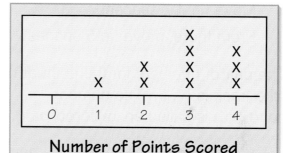

Tournament Attendance	
Third Graders	🧍 🧍 🧍 🧍 🧍
Fourth Graders	🧍 🧍 🧍 🧍 🧍
Fifth Graders	🧍 🧍 🧍 🧍 🧍 🧍

Each 🧍 stands for 10 students.

▶ Miguel made a line plot to show the scores of some of the ping pong rounds. A line plot is good for comparing small amounts of data.

- Could you show the data on a pictograph? Why or why not?

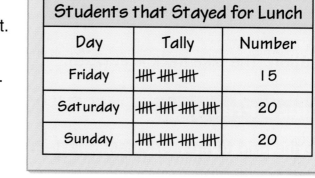

Number of Points Scored

▶ Miguel made a tally chart to show the number of students who stayed for lunch on each day of the tournament.

- Use the data to make a line plot, bar graph, or a pictograph.

Students that Stayed for Lunch		
Day	Tally	Number
Friday	卌 卌 卌	15
Saturday	卌 卌 卌 卌	20
Sunday	卌 卌 卌 卌	20

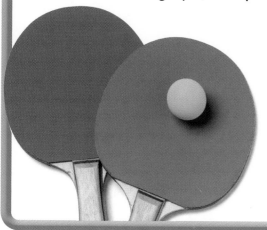

Explain Which way did you choose to display the data from the tally chart? Why did you choose that way?

Read Graphs With Ordered Pairs

Objective Use ordered pairs to locate points on a grid.

Vocabulary
ordered pair

Learn About It

A bike path system makes it easy to ride your bicycle just about anywhere! The grid below shows some places you can bike to in Lisa's town. Where is the bike track?

Count spaces on the grid to find out.

- Start at 0.
- Move right 7 spaces.
- From there, move up 5 spaces.

The pair of numbers for the point at the bike track is (7, 5). The number pair (7, 5) is called an **ordered pair**.

- The first number of an ordered pair tells how far to the right to move.
- The second number tells how far up to move.

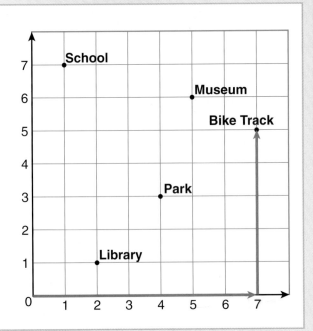

Solution: The bike track is at (7, 5).

Guided Practice

Use the grid to answer Questions 1–3.

1. What ordered pair tells where the park is?
2. What ordered pair tells where the library is?
3. What is located at (1, 7)?

Ask Yourself
- Did I move to the right first?
- Did I move up next?

Explain Your Thinking ▶ Do (7, 5) and (5, 7) show the same place? Explain your thinking.

Extra Help at **eduplace.com/map**

Use the grid at the right. Write the ordered pair for each point.

4. *G*   **5.** *H*   **6.** *D*   **7.** *A*

8. *B*   **9.** *E*   **10.** *F*   **11.** *C*

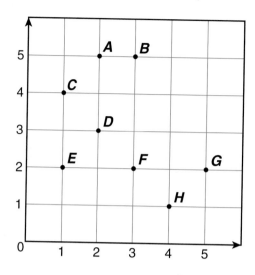

Write the letter for the point named by each ordered pair.

12. (3, 5)   **13.** (5, 2)   **14.** (1, 4)   **15.** (3, 2)

16. (1, 2)   **17.** (2, 5)   **18.** (4, 1)   **19.** (2, 3)

20. Start at Point B. Move down to Point F. Move from Point F to Point G. How long is the path?

Solve.

21. Make a grid like the one at the right. Draw dots on your grid to show the points for each ordered pair.

    (5, 1) (5, 3) (1, 3) (1, 1)

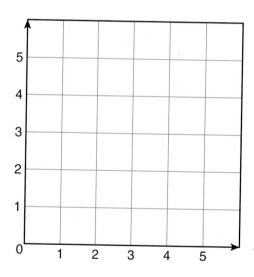

22. Connect the points in order. Connect the last point to the first. What figure did you draw?

23. What ordered pairs could you choose to make a square? Explain your reasoning.

24. Create and Solve Choose points that can be connected in order to make a shape.

- Write ordered pairs for the points.

- Describe to a classmate how to draw the shape. Use words like, Start at (5, 2). Then move left to (2, 3).

Go On

The grid shows the places Mickel and his dad visited on their bikes. Use the grid for Problems 25–29.

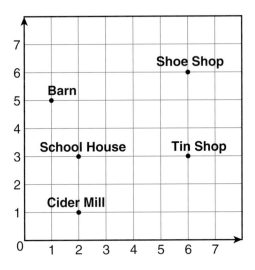

25. Mickel rode his bike first to the place located at (6, 3) on the grid. Where did Mickel bike to first?

26. Mickel and his dad had a picnic lunch under a tree at the cider mill. What ordered pair shows where they had lunch?

27. **What's Wrong?** Mickel said the ordered pair for the Tin Shop is (3, 6). What mistake did he make?

28. **Reasoning** Mickel used these clues to describe his favorite place.

   • The sum of the numbers in the ordered pair is 5.

   • The first number is less than the second.

   What is Mickel's favorite place?

29. **You Decide** Make a list of ordered pairs to show a bike path you might take through the historic village using the grid. Record your path on a grid.

Mixed Review and Test Prep

Open Response

Find each missing number.

(Ch. 5, Lesson 1)

30. $5 - \blacksquare = 0$

31. $7 - 0 = \blacksquare$

32. $\blacksquare - 2 = 0$

33. $6 - \blacksquare = 6$

34. Which ordered pair describes moving right 3 spaces and up 6 spaces? (Ch. 6, Lesson 7)

Extra Practice See page 173, Set D.

Real World Connection
Line Graphs

A **line graph** shows how data changes over time.

This line graph shows the daily low temperature in Town A for one week in January. What was the temperature on Thursday?

- Find Thursday on the bottom of the graph. Put your finger on it.

- Go up to the point.

- Go across to the left side of the graph to find the temperature.

Solution: It was 25°F on Thursday in Town A.

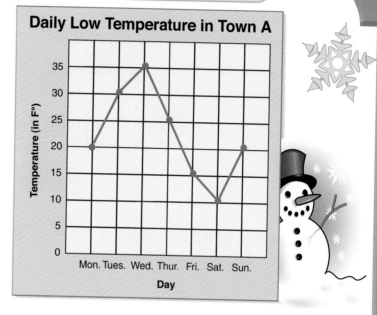

Did the daily low temperature increase or decrease from Thursday to Friday? How do you know?

Use Workmat 7 to make a line graph for the data in this table.

	Mon.	Tues.	Wed.	Thur.	Fri.	Sat.	Sun.
Town B	10°F	15°F	30°F	15°F	5°F	10°F	20°F

- Write a title.

- Label the side and bottom of the graph.

- Choose a scale. Use a scale of 5. Start with 0.

- Place the points for each day of the week.

- Now draw a line to connect the days.

Use your graph to answer these questions.

1. Which day was the coldest? What was the temperature?

2. Did the daily low temperature increase or decrease from Monday to Wednesday? How do you know?

Chapter Review/Test

VOCABULARY

Choose the best term to complete each sentence.

Vocabulary
- mean
- mode
- range
- median

1. The difference between the greatest number and the least number in a set of data is called the _____.

2. The number that occurs the most often in a set of data is called the _____.

3. When a set of data is ordered from least to greatest, the middle number is called the _____.

CONCEPTS AND SKILLS

Use the line plot for Questions 4–5.

(Lessons 2–3, pp. 150–156)

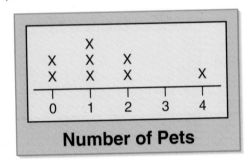

Number of Pets

Use the table for Exercises 6–7.

(Lessons 5–6, pp. 162–166)

Lunch Count	
Kind of Food	Number of Students
Pizza	7
Hamburger	5
Chicken	2

4. How many students have 4 pets?

5. What is the mode of data?

6. Draw a pictograph to show the data.

7. Draw a bar graph to show the data.

Use grid paper to make a grid for Problems 8–9. (Lesson 7, pp. 168–170)

8. Label point *A* at (0, 5).

9. Label point *B* at (4, 1).

PROBLEM SOLVING

Solve. (Lesson 4, pp. 158–160)

10. A marching band has 2 students in the first row. Each row has 3 more students than the row before it. How many students are in the fifth row?

Write About It

Show You Understand

Look at the pictograph and bar graph you made. How did you decide on a key and a scale? Explain your reasoning.

Extra Practice

Set A (Lessons 2–3, pp. 150–156)

Use the line plot to answer the questions.

1. In how many games were 0 runs scored?

2. What was the greatest number of runs scored?

3. How many games were played?

4. What is the mode of the data?

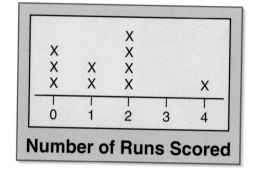

Number of Runs Scored

Set B (Lesson 5, pp. 162–163)

Use the table to make a pictograph.
Use ♀ to stand for 4 people.

1. What is the title of your pictograph?

2. How many ♀ did you use for *Play Sports*?

3. For which activities did you use ⚦ ?

Favorite Activity	
Activity	**Number of Students**
Play Sports	32
Visit Friends	30
Make Crafts	26
Read a Book	12

Set C (Lesson 6, pp. 164–166)

Use the table to make a bar graph.

1. How many bars does your graph have?

2. What scale did you use?

3. How did you choose your scale?

Favorite Subject	
Subject	**Number of Students**
Math	17
Reading	15
Science	12
Social Studies	9

Set D (Lesson 7, pp. 168-170)

Use the grid for Exercises 1–6.
Write the ordered pair for each point.

1. X 2. Y 3. Z

What letter names each point?

4. (7, 3)   5. (6, 4)   6. (7, 7)

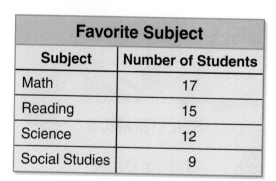

Extra Practice at **eduplace.com/map**

CHAPTER 7

Probability

INVESTIGATION

Using Data

These students are playing a game using a jar of different colored balls. The chart shows how many times each color was picked. The jar contains 32 balls. About how many of each color could be in the jar? Why do you think so?

Color	Number of Times Picked
Red	IIII
Yellow	HHT II
Green	III
Blue	II

Use What You Know

Use this page to review and remember what you need to know for this chapter.

VOCABULARY

Choose the best phrase to complete each sentence.

1. A bag has 3 black tiles and 7 white tiles. The chance of picking a white tile is ____.

2. A bag has 5 green marbles and 1 white marble. The chance of picking a white marble is ____.

Vocabulary
impossible
less likely
more likely

CONCEPTS AND SKILLS

Name the color that you are more likely to spin.

3.   4.   5.   6.

The line plot at the right shows the number of books one class read in 1 week. Use the line plot for Questions 7–9.

7. How many students read 5 books during the week?

8. How many students read more than 1 book?

9. How many students didn't read any books?

 **Write About It**

10. Suppose you picked a marble from a bag and then returned it. If you picked a red marble 9 times and a blue marble once, do you think the bag holds more red or blue marbles? Explain.

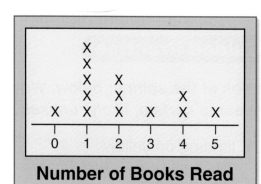

Number of Books Read

Facts Practice, See page 665

Audio Tutor 1/20 Listen and Understand

Understand Probability

Objective Decide if an event is certain, likely, unlikely, or impossible.

Learn About It

Probability describes how likely it is that an event will happen. Using words, you can describe the probability of an event as *certain, likely, unlikely,* or *impossible.*

Carla and Connor are playing a Grab Bag Game using blue and red cubes. What is the probability of picking a blue cube from each bag?

Bag A	Bag B	Bag C	Bag D

The probability of picking a blue cube is **certain**.	The probability of picking a blue cube is **likely**.	The probability of picking a blue cube is **unlikely**.	The probability of picking a blue cube is **impossible**.

Guided Practice

Look at the spinner below. Write whether the event is *certain, likely, unlikely,* or *impossible.*

1. landing on yellow

2. landing on red

3. landing on yellow or green

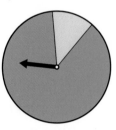

Ask Yourself

- Which color covers more of the spinner?
- Which color covers less of the spinner?

Explain Your Thinking ▶ Why is it possible, but unlikely, that the spinner will land on yellow?

Practice and Problem Solving

Write the word *certain*, *likely*, *unlikely*, or *impossible* to describe the probability of picking a green cube.

4.    **5.**    **6.**    **7.**

Draw a set of cubes to represent each statement.

8. Picking a red cube is certain.

9. Picking a blue cube is impossible.

10. Picking a blue cube is likely.

11. Picking a red cube is possible, but unlikely.

12. Picking a red cube is likely.

13. Picking a blue cube is possible, but unlikely.

Write whether each event is *certain*, *likely*, *unlikely*, or *impossible*. Explain your answer.

14. May will follow April.

15. It will be sunny in Florida.

16. A horse will fly.

17. You will win a million dollars today.

Solve.

18. Look at the spinner on the right. How could you change it to make it certain to land on orange?

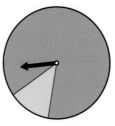

19. **Represent** Draw a spinner on which it is unlikely you will land on green and likely you will land on red.

20. Is it possible that the sum of any two 1-digit numbers will be 24? Explain your reasoning.

Open Response

Subtract. (Ch. 5, Lessons 4, 5, 7)

21. $55 - 19$

22. $636 - 45$

23. $323 - 139$

24. $502 - 234$

25. A bag is filled with 9 black tiles and 1 white tile. Describe the probability of picking a white tile. (Ch. 7, Lesson 1)

Extra Practice See page 191, Set A.

Identify Outcomes

Objective Record and display the results of probability experiments.

Vocabulary
outcome
equally likely

Materials

For each pair:
penny or other coin
chart (Learning Tool 9)
spinners (Learning Tools 10 and 11)

Work Together

Activities such as spinning a spinner, rolling a number cube, and tossing a coin are used in probability experiments.

If you toss a coin, there are two possible **outcomes**, or results.

- The coin can land heads up.
- The coin can land tails up.

You are **equally likely** to get heads or tails. This means that heads and tails have the same probability of occurring.

heads   **tails**

Work with a partner.

STEP 1
Take turns tossing a coin 50 times. Record a tally mark for each outcome.

- How many possible outcomes are there?

Coin-Toss Experiment		
Outcome	Tally	Number
Heads		
Tails		

STEP 2
Record the total number of times each outcome occurred.

- How many times did the coin land heads up?
- How many times did the coin land tails up?
- Did heads land up about as often as tails?

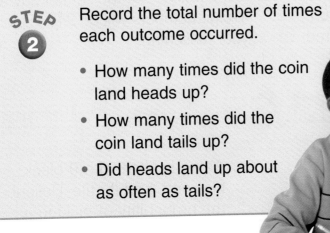

Now look at the results of a number-cube experiment.

Suppose Brian rolls two number cubes 100 times. Each time, he records the sum of the two numbers that are on the top faces of the cubes.

Each cube is numbered from 1–6.

The possible outcomes are:
2, 3, 4, 5, 6, 7, 8, 9, 10, 11, 12.

Brian's results are shown in the table below.

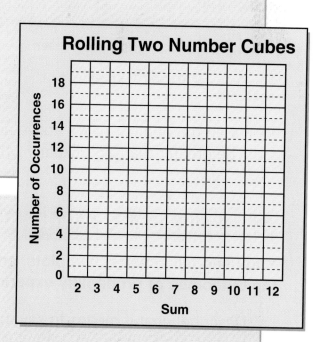

Rolling Two Number Cubes											
Outcome (Sum)	2	3	4	5	6	7	8	9	10	11	12
Number of Times It Happened	3	5	8	12	13	18	13	12	8	5	3

Work with your partner to show the results of Brian's experiment in a bar graph.

STEP 1
Make a bar graph to show the outcomes.

- How many bars do you need in your graph?

- Where will the bar end for the sum 2?

STEP 2
Use the graph to tell about the results.

- Which sum occurred most often?

- What do you notice about the other sums?

Rolling Two Number Cubes

Number of Occurrences (vertical axis): 0, 2, 4, 6, 8, 10, 12, 14, 16, 18

Sum (horizontal axis): 2, 3, 4, 5, 6, 7, 8, 9, 10, 11, 12

Go On

Complete these spinner experiments.

1. **Experiment 1** Use a spinner like the one below.
   Make 25 spins. Record your results in a tally chart.

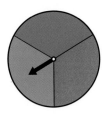

Spinner Experiment		
Outcome	Tally	Number
Blue		
Red		
Green		

- How many possible outcomes are there?

- Did the spinner land on each color about an equal number of times?

2. **Experiment 2** Use a spinner like the one below.
   Make 25 spins. Record your results on a line plot.

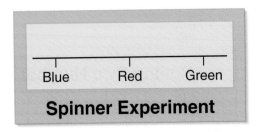

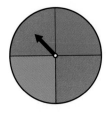

- Can the number of X's above any of the colors be greater than 25? Explain why or why not.

Talk About It • Write About It

You used tally charts, line plots, and bar graphs to record the outcomes of probability experiments.

3. Describe what it means to say that landing on red, blue, or green in Experiment 1 is *equally likely*.

4. Think about your results for Experiments 1 and 2 above. Were the results the same for both experiments? Explain why or why not.

Pick and Predict

2 Players

What You'll Need • a paper bag, paper squares (Learning Tool 12) or 7 red and 7 blue paper squares

How to Play

1 The first player secretly places any number of the 14 squares in the bag and puts the rest of the squares out of sight.

2 The second player picks a square from the bag without looking. The first player records its color in a tally chart. Then the second player puts the square back into the bag.

3 Players repeat Step 2 nineteen times. The second player then uses the tally chart to predict the color he or she will pick next. After predicting, the second player picks a paper square from the bag. If the prediction is correct, the player gets 1 point.

4 Players take turns repeating Steps 1 to 3. The first player to get 5 points wins.

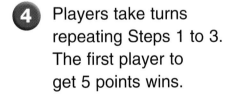

Audio Tutor 1/21 Listen and Understand

Outcomes and Probability

Objective Calculate the probability of an event.

Learn About It

Carol and her friend are playing a probability game with the cards shown below.

The cards will be turned face down and mixed up. Carol wants to find the probability of picking an L.

▶ First Carol counts the **number of L's** in the word:

ILLINOIS

There are **2** L's.

▶ Then Carol counts the **number of letters** in the word:

ILLINOIS

There are **8** letters or possible outcomes.

There are **2 out of 8** chances of picking an L.

Solution: The probability of picking an L is 2 out of 8.

Guided Practice

Suppose the letter cards below are face down and mixed up. Write the probability of picking each letter.

1. A   **2.** N   **3.** T   **4.** S

Ask Yourself

- Did I count the number of each letter?
- Did I count all possible outcomes?

Explain Your Thinking ▶ Look back at the cards for KANSAS. Suppose you lost the N card just before you picked. Would the probability of picking an S change? Why or why not?

Extra Help at **eduplace.com/map**

Write the probability of picking each letter.

| M | O | N | T | A | N | A |

| A | L | A | S | K | A |

5. A   **6.** N   **7.** T   **8.** A   **9.** S   **10.** N

Write the probability of spinning each symbol.

11. ▲   **12.** ★   **13.** ■

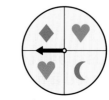

14. ◆   **15.** ☾   **16.** ♥

17. ■   **18.** ♥   **19.** ★

20. ◆   **21.** ☾   **22.** ▲

Solve.

23. Analyze Stephen puts the cards shown face down and mixes them up. Then he picks a card. What is the probability that he picks a letter from A through L? Explain how you found the answer.

Open Response

Write each time. (Grade 2)

24.

25.

26. A bag of tiles holds 1 black, 3 red, and 6 white tiles. If you pick without looking, what is the probability of choosing a red tile? (Ch. 7, Lesson 3)

Make Predictions

Objective Use the results of experiments to predict outcomes.

Learn About It

You can use data from a probability experiment to make a prediction about what is likely to happen if the experiment is repeated.

▶ Drew has a bag of 10 marbles. Without looking, Drew picked a marble from the bag 25 times. The marble was put back each time. This tally chart shows the results of Drew's experiment.

Picking a Marble From a Bag		
Outcome	Tally	Number
Red	|||| |||| |||| |||| |||	23
Blue	||	2

> A red marble was picked much more often than a blue marble.

These results suggest that if Drew picks another marble, it is more likely to be red than blue.

• Would you predict that there are 5 red marbles and 5 blue marbles in the bag? Why or why not?

▶ This line plot shows the results of another experiment in which Marcia tossed a number cube 30 times.

• Why do you think Marcia never tossed a 1?

• Why do you think the line plot shows almost double the number of 2s as the other numbers?

• Do you think it is reasonable to predict that the number cube had these numbers: 2, 2, 3, 4, 5, and 6? Why?

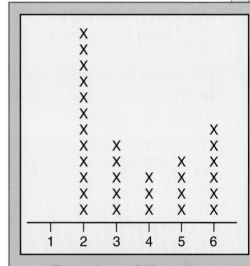

Results of Number Cube Toss

The tally chart shows the results of picking cubes from a bag 25 times and replacing the cube each time. Use the chart to answer Questions 1 and 2.

Picking Cubes From a Bag		
Outcome	Tally	Number
Yellow	卌 卌 卌	15
Green	卌 |||	8
Blue	||	2

Ask Yourself

• What color cube has the greatest number of tally marks?

• Are 15 yellow cubes about twice as much as 8 green cubes?

1. Suppose you pick another cube. What color is it most likely to be? Why?

2. Would you predict that there are about double the number of yellow cubes as green cubes in the bag? How do you know?

Explain Your Thinking ▶ If there are 10 cubes in the bag above, how many of each color do you think there would be? How did you decide?

Practice and Problem Solving

Catherine spun a spinner 30 times and recorded the results in a bar graph. Use the graph for Questions 3–5.

3. How many times did she spin each color?

4. Do you think the chance of spinning each color is equally likely? Explain.

5. What color do you predict she will spin next?

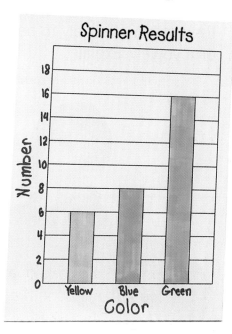

Go On ➡

Solve each problem.

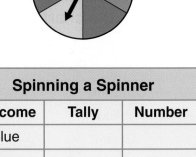

6. Look at the spinner on the right. Suppose you make 50 spins. Which color do you predict the spinner is likely to land on most often?

7. Make a spinner like the one above. Make 50 spins. Record the results. Then make a bar graph. Was your prediction correct?

Spinning a Spinner		
Outcome	Tally	Number
Blue		
Green		
Red		
Yellow		

8. Two hundred students write their names on identical slips of paper and put them into a box. If 35 of the names are girls' names, who is more likely to be chosen on the first pick, a girl or a boy?

9. **Analyze** A bag has 10 marbles. Joe picks a marble from the bag 50 times without looking. Each time he puts it back. The results are 30 red, 10 blue, and 10 green. How many of each color do you think are in the bag?

10. **Write About It** Suppose each letter of the alphabet is written on an identical slip of paper and put into a bag. If a person picks a slip without looking, is the letter more likely to be a consonant or a vowel? Explain.

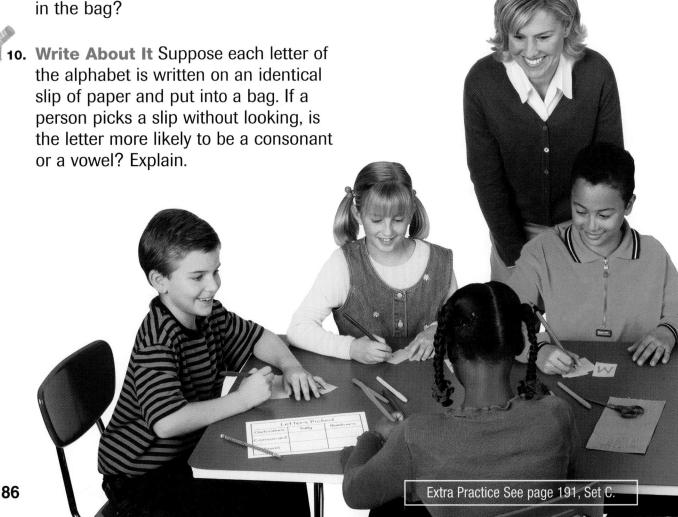

186

Extra Practice See page 191, Set C.

Math Reasoning
Mapping Paths

Tao and his family are at an amusement park. They want to go on all the rides once. They do not want to walk past a ride they have already visited.

Find 3 different paths that Tao's family could take that would include all the rides. They can begin at any one of the rides.

Record the paths by writing the letters in order.

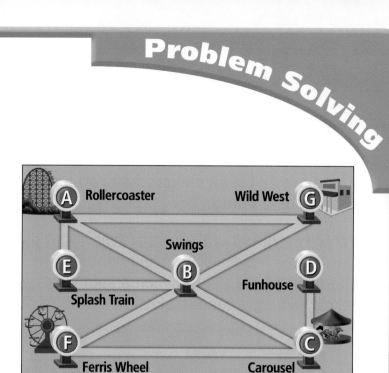

Check your understanding of Lessons 1–4.

Write whether it is *certain*, *likely*, *unlikely*, or *impossible* to land on green. (Lesson 1)

1. 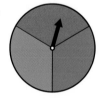 **2.**   **3.**   **4.**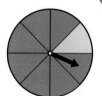

Write the probability of each event.

(Lessons 2–3)

5. spinning a 1   **6.** spinning a 2

7. spinning a 3   **8.** spinning a 4

9. spinning a number less than 4

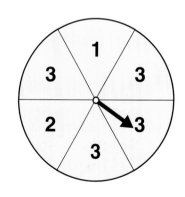

Solve. (Lesson 4)

10. Suppose you spin the number spinner above 10 times. Predict which number it is likely to land on most often.

Problem-Solving Application
Use Probability

Objective Use probability to decide if a game is fair or unfair.

A game is fair if all players have an equal chance of winning.

Problem Alfred and Maria are playing a game. One player moves when a spin lands on green. The other player moves when a spin lands on yellow. Which spinner makes the game fair?

Spinner 1

Spinner 2

Spinner 3

UNDERSTAND

What is the question?

Which spinner makes the game fair?

What do you know?

- Each spinner is separated into equal sections that are colored green or yellow.

PLAN

Count the number of equal sections on each spinner. Then compare the number of yellow sections to the number of green sections.

SOLVE

There are an equal number of green and yellow sections on Spinner 2.

Solution: Spinner 2 makes the game fair.

LOOK BACK

Look back at the problem.

Why do spinners 1 and 3 make the game unfair?

Guided Practice

Solve each problem. Use the spinners on Page 188.

1. Suppose you and a friend are playing a game with Spinner 1. Which color would you choose to have a better chance of winning?

2. Suppose Alfred and Maria want to use Spinner 3 for their game. How can the spinner be changed to make it fair?

(**Hint**) Which color sections need to be changed?

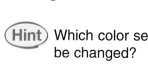

Ask Yourself

UNDERSTAND — **What does the question ask me to find?**

PLAN — **Did I compare the green and yellow sections?**

SOLVE — **Are more of the sections green or yellow?**

LOOK BACK — **Did I answer the question?**

Independent Practice

Solve.

3. Look at the spinner. Is the probability of spinning yellow the same as the probability of spinning green? Explain.

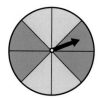

4. Jody, Ashur, and Dena are playing a game, using this spinner. Write a rule that makes the game fair.

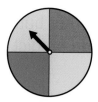

5. **Represent** Draw a spinner with 3 different colors. Make two of the colors equally likely to occur. Compare your drawing to a classmate's drawing. Is there more than one way to draw this spinner? Explain.

6. **Write About It** Is each outcome equally likely to occur?

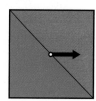

Chapter Review/Test

VOCABULARY

Choose the best term to complete each sentence.

Vocabulary

outcomes

probability

equally likely

1. ____ describes how likely it is that an event will occur.

2. When you toss a coin, heads or tails are ____ to occur.

CONCEPTS AND SKILLS

Write *certain, likely, unlikely,* or *impossible* to describe the probability of the spinner landing on green. (Lesson 1, pp. 176–177)

3.

4.

5.

Suppose a number cube is numbered from 1–6. Write each probability. (Lessons 2–3, pp. 178–183)

6. tossing a 5

7. tossing a 2 or a 3

Use the bar graph for Questions 8–9. The buttons are replaced after every pick.

(Lesson 4, pp. 184–186)

8. Does the bar graph tell you how many buttons are in the bag? Explain.

9. If another button is picked, what color do you predict it will be? Explain.

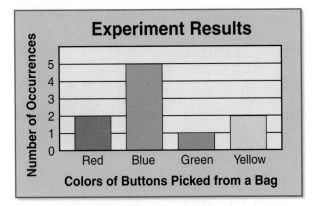

PROBLEM SOLVING

Solve. (Lesson 5, pp. 188–189)

10. A game spinner has 4 equal sections— 2 blue, 1 green, and 1 yellow. Each player chooses a color and gets 1 space every time his color is spun. Is the game fair?

Write About It

Show You Understand

A spinner is divided into 2 unequal sections. How can you tell which section the spinner is more likely to land on?

Extra Practice

Set A (Lesson 1, pp. 176–177)

Write *certain, likely, unlikely,* or *impossible* to describe the probability of landing on blue.

1. 　　2. 　　3. 　　4.

Write *certain, likely, unlikely,* or *impossible.*

5. You will travel in space.　　6. Monday will follow Sunday.

Set B (Lesson 3, pp. 182–183)

Write the probability of spinning each color.

1. yellow　　2. green　　3. blue　　4. red

5. yellow　　6. red　　7. orange　　8. white

Set C (Lesson 5, pp. 184–186)

Use the bar graph to answer the questions.

The bar graph shows the results of Kelley picking a marble from a bag without looking and then replacing it.

1. How many times did Kelley pick each color?

2. If another marble is picked from the bag, what color do you predict it will be? How did you decide?

3. Would you predict there are about the same number of red and green marbles in the bag? How did you decide?

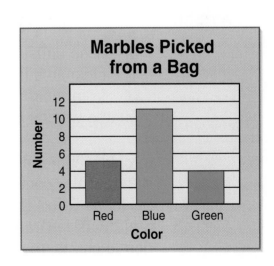

Extra Practice at **eduplace.com/map**

Migrating Manatees

These unusual underwater animals are manatees. Their nickname is "Florida's gentle giants." The name comes from their large size and calm nature. The average manatee weighs between 800 and 1,500 pounds.

In cold weather manatees migrate, or move to warmer waters. When winter comes, manatees leave the chilled waters of the St. Johns River. They move to the warm waters of Blue Spring State Park in Orange City, Florida. Park visitors can view these gentle giants from a boardwalk next to the spring.

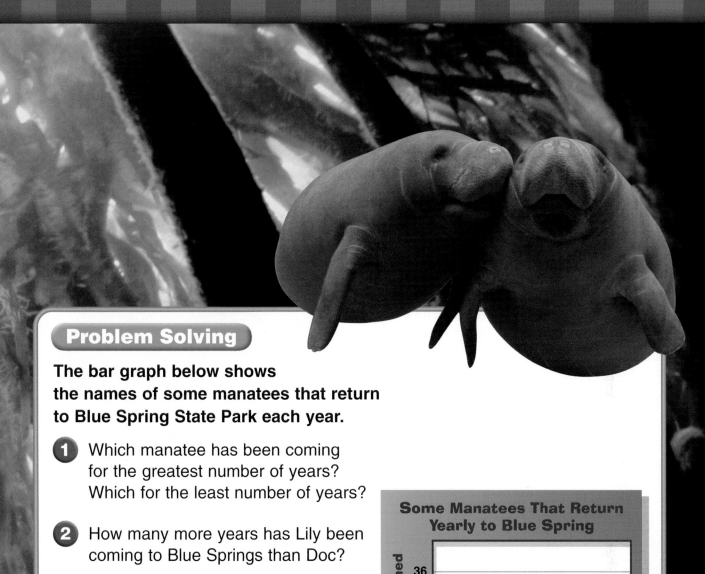

Problem Solving

The bar graph below shows the names of some manatees that return to Blue Spring State Park each year.

1 Which manatee has been coming for the greatest number of years? Which for the least number of years?

2 How many more years has Lily been coming to Blue Springs than Doc?

3 If both Floyd and Brutus return for another 8 years, how many years will each manatee have come to Blue Spring?

4 What is the range of the data in the bar graph?

5 What is the median number of years that a manatee has returned to Blue Spring?

Education Place

Visit Weekly Reader Connections at **eduplace.com/map** for more on this topic.

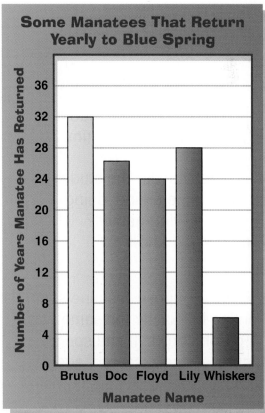

Some Manatees That Return Yearly to Blue Spring

Number of Years Manatee Has Returned

36
32
28
24
20
16
12
8
4
0

Brutus Doc Floyd Lily Whiskers

Manatee Name

Enrichment: Circle Graphs

Web Browsers

A circle graph is made up of a circle divided into parts. Use a circle graph when you want to compare parts of a whole.

One hundred students were asked how they used the Internet. The circle graph shows their responses.

Look at the section of the circle graph that is labeled "Using E-mail." It is the largest part of the circle. This means that students spent most of their online time using e-mail.

Time Spent Online

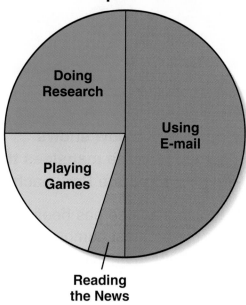

Try These!

Use the circle graph for Problems 1–5.

1. On which activity did the students spend the least amount of time?

2. What does the yellow section in the circle graph represent?

3. On which activity did the students spend more time online: doing research or playing games? Explain how you know.

4. Look at the size of the section for doing research. How does it compare to the size of the section for e-mail? What does this mean?

5. **Challenge** Suppose Jasmine spent time online in exactly the same way as the graph shows. If she spent 20 minutes doing research, about how much time did she spend using e-mail? How can you tell?

Technology Time

Favorite Food Survey

You are going to take part in a survey. Then you will be able to see a bar graph of many students' answers including yours.

Go to Data Place at eduplace.com/map.

- Click on "Favorite Meal"
- Click on the button under your favorite.
- Click "Submit".
- View the result shown in the bar graph

Each time someone takes part in the survey the bar graph changes. Make sure you write down the numbers for the meal choices on the day you take the survey.

○ hamburger and fries

○ turkey dinner

○ soup and sandwich

○ pizza

○ toast and cereal

○ spaghetti and salad

Use the bar graph that shows the results of the Favorite Food Survey to answer Problems 1-6.

1. In the survey which food is the students' favorite?

2. Which food do the fewest number of students prefer?

3. How many students did not choose pizza as their favorite?

4. What is the range of the data?

5. How many students participated in the survey? How can you tell?

6. **Create and Solve** Write your own question using the data in the graph.

Unit 3 Test

VOCABULARY (Open Response)

Choose the best term to complete each sentence.

1. A pair of numbers that names a point on a grid is called an ____.

2. A graph that uses pictures to represent data is called a ____.

3. When you ask people a question and record their answers you are conducting a ____.

> **Vocabulary**
> survey
> line plot
> pictograph
> ordered pair

CONCEPTS AND SKILLS (Open Response)

Use the line plot for Problems 4–5. (Chapter 6)

The line plot shows the number of shells Lynn found on each of 8 days during her vacation.

4. On how many days did Lynn find two or more shells?

5. What is the range of the data? What is the mode of the data?

```
          X
          X           X
      X   X   X       X   X
     ┬───┬───┬───┬───┬───┬───┬
     0   1   2   3   4   5   6
```
Number of Shells

Use the information in the table to make a pictograph. Then answer Questions 6–8. (Chapter 6)

Favorite Vacation Activites	
Activity	**Number of Votes**
Swimming	35
Hiking	20
Sightseeing	40

6. How many votes in all?

7. Why did you choose the number you did for the key?

8. How many more people voted for swimming than for hiking?

Use the information in the table to make a bar graph. Then answer Questions 9–11. (Chapter 6)

Birds Cindy Saw	
Type of Bird	**Number Seen**
Crow	4
Gull	9
Robin	11

9. How many birds did Cindy see?

10. Why did you choose the scale you did?

11. How many more robins than crows did Cindy see?

Use the grid for Problems 12–15. Write the ordered pair for each point. (Chapter 6)

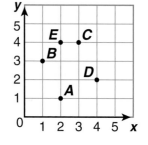

12. *A* **13.** *E* **14.** *D* **15.** *C*

Write whether each event is *certain, likely, unlikely,* **or** *impossible.* (Chapter 7)

16. Raindrops are wet. **17.** A cow has wings. **18.** You will fly to the moon.

PROBLEM SOLVING Open Response

19. Matt earns $5 a week for each dog he walks. He walks 3 dogs the first week. If he adds 1 dog each week, how much will he have earned in total by the end of the sixth week?

20. Sam and Dan are playing a game. Sam receives a point if the spinner lands on yellow. Dan receives a point if it lands on blue. Draw a spinner so that the game is fair.

Performance Assessment

Constructed Response

Cups of Lemonade Andrea Sold Last Week

Task Andrea has a lemonade stand. Use the bar graph and the information at the right to decide how many bags of cups and canisters of lemonade powder Andrea should buy for next week. Explain your thinking.

Information You Need

- Each bag contains 25 cups.
- When mixed with water, a canister of powder will make about 40 cups of lemonade.
- This is the last week Andrea will sell lemonade.

Cumulative Test Prep

Solve Problems 1–10.

Test-Taking Tip

Sometimes one of the first answers given might seem correct. Read all the answers before making your final choice.

Look at the example below.

Which shows all the odd numbers from 1 through 11?

   A 1, 2, 5, 6, 10, 11

   B 1, 3, 5, 7, 9

   C 2, 4, 6, 8, 10

   D 1, 3, 5, 7, 9, 11

THINK

You might stop at choice B and think that it is correct. However, it is missing the number 11. If you read all of the answer choices, you see that choice D has a complete list of all the odd numbers from 1 through 11.

Multiple Choice

1. Carlos had $7.02 and gave $1.25 to Tamara and $1.50 to Emily. How much money does Carlos have now?

  A $4.27   **C** $5.27

  B $4.73   **D** $5.73

(Chapter 5, Lesson 7)

2. A concert hall can hold 17,892 fans. Write 17,892 in expanded form.

  F 10,000 + 7,000 + 800 + 2

  G 10,000 + 7,000 + 90 + 2

  H 10,000 + 7,000 + 800 + 90 + 2

  J 10,000 + 7,000 + 900 + 80 + 2

(Chapter 1, Lesson 6)

3. Frank's test scores are 98, 87, 84, 90, and 91. What is his median score?

  A 89   **C** 93

  B 90   **D** 98

(Chapter 6, Lesson 2)

4. Tia bought a box of 25 pens. She already had 16 pens at home. How many pens does she have now?

  F 9   **H** 31

  G 11   **J** 41

(Chapter 4, Lesson 3)

For Test-Taking Tips, see page 659.

5. What is the least whole number you can make using these digits?

5	3	9	1

(Chapter 2, Lesson 2)

6. Suppose you picked one card without looking from the bag shown. What is the probability that it will be an E?

(Chapter 7, Lesson 3)

7. Write two number sentences in the same fact family using the numbers 8, 12, and 4.

(Chapter 5, Lesson 2)

8.

Number of Apples Picked

Hao	🍎 🍎 🍎 🍎 🍎 🍎
Marisol	🍎 🍎 🍎 🍎

Each 🍎 stands for 2 apples.

How many more apples did Hao pick than Marisol?

(Chapter 6, Lesson 5)

9. There are 27 students in Mr. Daled's class and 26 in Mrs. Vega's class. How many students are in the two classes?

(Chapter 4, Lesson 3)

10. Amy bought a gallon of milk. The clerk gave her $1.87 back in coins. While putting the money away, Amy dropped some of the coins on the floor. The picture below shows the coins she dropped.

A Amy paid for the milk with a five-dollar bill. How much did the milk cost? Explain your thinking.

B What is the value of the change Amy did not drop?

C What coins could make up the amount of money that Amy did not drop? Describe as many ways as you can to show that amount.

(Chapter 3, Lesson 3)

Education Place

Look for Cumulative Test Prep at **eduplace.com/map** for more practice.

Vocabulary Wrap-Up for Unit 3

Look back at the big ideas and vocabulary in this unit.

Big Ideas

A line plot can be used to show how often something happens.

Probability describes how likely it is that an event will happen.

Key Vocabulary
line plot

probability

Math Conversations

Use your new vocabulary to discuss these big ideas.

1. Describe 2 differences between pictographs and bar graphs.

2. Explain how to draw a dot on a grid to show the ordered pair (2, 5).

3. **Write About It** What type of data display would you use to show the number of goals scored by members of a soccer team? Why is this the best display method?

I have a cube numbered 1 to 6.

It is equally likely that you will roll an even number or an odd number.

CHAPTER **8**

Multiplication Concepts
page 204

CHAPTER **9**

Multiplication Facts and Patterns
page 230

CHAPTER **10**

Division Concepts
page 258

CHAPTER **11**

Division Facts and Patterns
page 284

UNIT 4

Multiplication and Division Basic Facts

Reading Mathematics

Reviewing Vocabulary

Here are some math vocabulary words that you should know.

multiplication	an operation that finds the total number of items that are in equal groups
division	an operation that separates objects into equal groups
product	the answer in a multiplication problem
quotient	the answer in a division problem

Reading Words and Symbols

You can use words and symbols to describe multiplication and division.

2 times 3 equals 6.

$$2 \times 3 = 6$$

↑
product

6 divided by 2 equals 3.

$$6 \div 2 = 3$$

↑
quotient

Use words and symbols to describe each picture.

1.

2.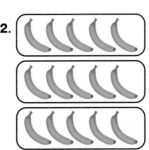

Reading Test Questions

Choose the correct answer for each.

3. Which number sentence represents the picture?

    a. $3 \times 1 = 3$ **c.** $3 \times 3 = 9$

    b. $3 \times 2 = 6$ **d.** $3 \times 4 = 12$

Represents means "stands for" or "shows."

---

4. Which number sentence is incorrect?

    a. $9 + 1 = 10$

    b. $12 - 5 = 8$

    c. $4 \times 2 = 8$

    d. $4 \div 2 = 2$

Incorrect means "false" or "wrong."

5. Which two pictures show equivalent amounts?

a.   **c.**

b.   **d.**

Equivalent means "equal."

Learning Vocabulary

Watch for these words in this unit. Write their definitions in your journal.

Commutative Property

factors

divisor

dividend

square number

 Education Place

At **eduplace.com/map** see eGlossary and eGames— Math Lingo.

Literature Connection

Read "Leaders of the Pack" on Pages 649–650. Then work with a partner to answer the questions about the story.

Multiplication Concepts

Golden
Replicas
of
United
States
Stamps

INVESTIGATION

Using Data

Yoshi and his dad collect stamps. They organize their stamps into equal rows as shown in the table. Yoshi's uncle gives him 24 president stamps. How might Yoshi place them in equal rows?

Stamp Collection		
Type of Stamp	Number of Rows	Stamps in Each Row
Flag	2	10
Flower	4	3
Animal	7	8

Use What You Know

**Use this page to review and remember
what you need to know for this chapter.**

VOCABULARY

Choose the best term to complete each sentence.

Vocabulary

sum

addend

difference

equal groups

1. A number being added is an ____.

2. The ____ is the answer in an addition problem.

3. Groups that have the same number of objects are called ____.

CONCEPTS AND SKILLS

Skip count to complete.

4. 3, 6, 9, 12, ____, ____, 21

5. 5, 10, 15, 20, ____, ____, 35

Find each sum.

6. 2 + 2 + 2 + 2 + 2

7. 10 + 10 + 10

Does the picture show equal groups? Write *yes* or *no*.

8.

9.

Write About It

10. Look back at the picture for Exercise 9. How is finding this sum different from finding the sum for Exercise 8?

Facts Practice, See page 667.

 Audio Tutor 1/22 Listen and Understand

Model Multiplication as Repeated Addition

Objective Use repeated addition to model multiplication.

Vocabulary
multiplication

Materials
For each pair:
36 counters
6 pieces of paper

Work Together

Work with a partner to model **multiplication**.

Look at the 3 strips of stickers shown on the right. There are 5 stickers on each strip. How can you find the number of stickers there are in all?

STEP 1
Use pieces of paper to stand for the strips.
Use counters to stand for the stickers.
Put 5 counters on each piece of paper.

STEP 2
Find the total number of counters.
You can find the total number in different ways.

Write an addition sentence.

Think
I can use repeated addition.
3 groups of 5 = 15.

$$5 + 5 + 5 = 15$$

Write a **multiplication** sentence.

Think
3 groups of 5 = 15.

$$3 \times 5 = 15$$

Read: Three times five equals fifteen.

• How many counters are there in all?

• How many stickers are there in all?

Extra Help at **eduplace.com/map**

STEP 3

Now use counters to make other equal groups. Find the total number of counters. Make a table like the one below. Draw a picture of your groups of counters. Then describe your picture in words, with an addition sentence, and with a multiplication sentence.

Draw the Equal Groups	Think	Addition Sentence	Multiplication Sentence
⦿ ⦿ ⦿	3 groups of 5	$5 + 5 + 5 = 15$	$3 \times 5 = 15$

STEP 4

Repeat Step 3 several times. Record your work in your table.

On Your Own

Model each set with counters. Then write an addition sentence and a multiplication sentence for each.

1. 4 groups of 3

2. 5 groups of 2

3. 2 groups of 7

4. 5 groups of 4

5. 3 groups of 6

6. 2 groups of 10

Write a multiplication sentence for each.

7. $4 + 4 + 4 = 12$

8. $3 + 3 + 3 + 3 + 3 + 3 = 18$

9. $7 + 7 + 7 + 7 = 28$

10. $5 + 5 + 5 + 5 + 5 + 5 + 5 = 35$

Talk About It • Write About It

You have learned how to use repeated addition to find answers to multiplication problems.

11. Can you write a multiplication sentence to describe this picture? Explain why or why not.

12. Suppose you buy 3 identical packages of stickers. What must you know before you can multiply to find the total number of stickers?

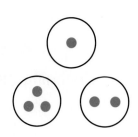

Algebra

Arrays and Multiplication

Objective Use arrays to multiply.

Vocabulary

array

Commutative Property

factors

product

Learn About It

Kevin puts stamps he collects in an album. How many stamps are on this page of his album?

The stamps are arranged in an array. An **array** shows objects arranged in rows and columns. Each row has an equal number of stamps. Each column has an equal number of stamps.

3 columns

6 rows

▶ **Multiply to find the total number of stamps.**

$$6 \quad \times \quad 3 \quad = \quad 18$$

rows   stamps in each row   total number of stamps

6 columns

▶ **Suppose the page is turned. Does the total number of stamps change?**

$$3 \quad \times \quad 6 \quad = \quad 18$$

rows   stamps in each row   total number of stamps

3 rows

Solution: There are 18 stamps on the page. The total does not change.

Commutative Property of Multiplication

Changing the order of the **factors** does not change the **product**.

$$6 \quad \times \quad 3 \quad = \quad 18$$

factor   factor   product

$$3 \quad \times \quad 6 \quad = \quad 18$$

factor   factor   product

Write a multiplication sentence for each array.

Ask Yourself
- How many rows are there?
- How many are in each row?

1.

2.

Explain Your Thinking ▶ How can knowing $4 \times 6 = 24$ help you find 6×4?

Practice and Problem Solving

Write a multiplication sentence for each array.

3. ♥ ♥ ♥   ♥ ♥
   ♥ ♥ ♥   ♥ ♥
   ♥ ♥

4. ▲ ▲ ▲ ▲   ▲ ▲
   ▲ ▲ ▲ ▲   ▲ ▲
               ▲ ▲
               ▲ ▲

5.

𝒙 Algebra • Properties Find each missing number.

6. $2 \times 6 = 12$
   $6 \times \blacksquare = 12$

7. $8 = 4 \times 2$
   $\blacksquare = 2 \times 4$

8. $21 = 7 \times 3$
   $21 = 3 \times \blacksquare$

9. $3 \times 4 = 12$
   $4 \times \blacksquare = 12$

10. Alyssa bought a sheet of stamps that has 4 rows of 5 stamps. How many stamps did she buy?

11. Teva had 2 rows of stamps with 7 stamps in each row. She gave away 3 stamps. How many stamps are left?

12. **Analyze** Melissa would like to display her collection of 12 stamps in an array. What are all the different ways she can do that?

Mixed Review and Test Prep ✓

Open Response

Add. (Ch. 4, Lesson 7)

13.
```
  496
+ 782
```

14.
```
  923
+ 608
```

15.
```
 $26.64
+ 33.78
```

16. Which number should be in the box to make this number sentence true? Explain how you know. (Ch. 8, Lesson 2)

$$4 \times \blacksquare = 2 \times 4$$

Extra Practice See page 229, Set A.

Audio Tutor 1/23 Listen and Understand

Multiply With 2

Objective Use different ways to multiply when 2 is a factor.

Learn About It

Rachel collects state quarters. She has 2 quarters from each of 6 different states. How many state quarters does she have?

Multiply. $6 \times 2 = \blacksquare$ or

$$\begin{array}{r} 2 \leftarrow \text{factor} \\ \times 6 \leftarrow \text{factor} \\ \hline \blacksquare \leftarrow \text{product} \end{array}$$

factor   factor   product

Different Ways to Find 6 x 2

Way ❶ Skip count.

Skip count by 2s until you say 6 numbers.

Say: 2, 4, 6, 8, 10, 12.

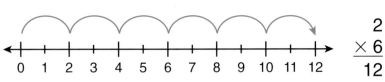

0 1 2 3 4 5 6 7 8 9 10 11 12

$$\begin{array}{r} 2 \\ \times 6 \\ \hline 12 \end{array}$$

Way ❷ Draw a picture.

Then use repeated addition.

$2 + 2 + 2 + 2 + 2 + 2 = 12$

Way ❸ Write a multiplication sentence.

$6 \times 2 = \blacksquare$

$6 \times 2 = 12$

Think 6 groups of 2 = 12.

Solution: Rachel has 12 state quarters.

Guided Practice

Multiply.

1. $\begin{array}{r} 2 \\ \times 4 \\ \hline \end{array}$

2. $\begin{array}{r} 7 \\ \times 2 \\ \hline \end{array}$

3. $\begin{array}{r} 8 \\ \times 2 \\ \hline \end{array}$

4. $\begin{array}{r} 2 \\ \times 9 \\ \hline \end{array}$

Ask Yourself

- Can skip counting help me?
- Can changing the order of the factors help me?

Explain Your Thinking ▶ Why does 6×3 equal 3×6?

Write a multiplication sentence for each picture.

5.

6.

7.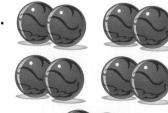

Multiply.

8. 3
   × 2

9. 2
   × 6

10. 5
    × 2

11. 10
    × 2

12. 8
    × 2

13. 6
    × 2

14. 2
    × 4

15. 2
    × 3

16. 7
    × 2

17. 9
    × 2

18. 1
    × 2

19. 2
    × 2

20. 2×9

21. 4×2

22. 7×2

23. 8×2

24. 2×10

Solve.

25. Matt puts 8 coins in each box. He uses 2 boxes. How many coins does Matt have?

26. **Money** Natalie has 2 dimes and 2 nickels. How much money does she have?

27. In Exercises 8–24, the number 2 is one of the factors. Is the product of each exercise odd or even? Explain why.

28. Ruth has 7 foreign coins. Her 3 cousins each give her 2 more. How many foreign coins does Ruth have now?

Mixed Review and Test Prep

Open Response

Subtract. (Ch. 5, Lesson 6)

29.   7,243
    − 3,768

30.   5,117
    − 3,208

31. $46.51
    − 29.37

32.   7,381
    − 5,199

Multiple Choice

33. A toothbrush costs $2. If Mark and his sister each used 4 toothbrushes last year, how much did that cost?

(Ch. 8, Lesson 3)

A $4   B $6   C $8   D $16

Multiply With 4

Objective Use different ways to multiply when 4 is a factor.

Learn About It

A group of 3 friends wants to trade their favorite sports cards. Each friend brings 4 sports cards. How many sports cards do the friends have to trade?

Multiply.

$$3 \times 4 = \blacksquare$$

factor   factor   product

or

$$\begin{array}{r} 4 \leftarrow \text{factor} \\ \times\, 3 \leftarrow \text{factor} \\ \hline \blacksquare \leftarrow \text{product} \end{array}$$

Different Ways to Find 3 x 4

Way 1 Skip count.

Skip count by 4s until you say 3 numbers.

Say: 4, 8, 12.

0   4   8   12

$$\begin{array}{r} 4 \\ \times\, 3 \\ \hline 12 \end{array}$$

Way 2 Draw a picture.

Then use repeated addition.

4 + 4 + 4 = 12

Way 3 Multiply with 2 and double the product.

Multiply with 2. $3 \times 2 = 6$

Then double the product. Think: $6 + 6 = 12$ or $6 \times 2 = 12$

Way 4 Write a multiplication sentence.

$3 \times 4 = \blacksquare$

$3 \times 4 = 12$

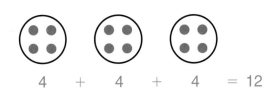

Think
3 groups of 4 = 12.

Solution: The friends have 12 sports cards to trade.

Write a multiplication sentence for each picture.

1.   2.

Ask Yourself
- How many groups are there?
- How many are in each group?

Multiply.

3. 2
   × 4

4. 4
   × 5

5. 7
   × 4

6. 4
   × 9

Explain Your Thinking ▶ How can knowing 7 × 2 = 14 help you find 7 × 4?

Practice and Problem Solving

Write a multiplication sentence for each picture.

7.   8.   9.

Find each product.

10.   1
    × 4

11.   4
    × 4

12.   4
    × 3

13.   6
    × 4

14.   9
    × 4

15.   4
    × 8

16. 10
    × 4

17.   4
    × 2

18. 4 × 10

19. 1 × 4

20. 9 × 2

21. 5 × 4

22. 3 × 4

23. 4 × 8

24. 5 × 2

25. 7 × 4

26. 8 × 2

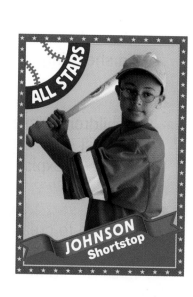

Go On

✗ Algebra • Properties **Find each missing number.**

27. $2 \times 5 = 10$
    $5 \times 2 = $ ■

28. $4 \times 8 = 32$
    $8 \times 4 = $ ■

29. $16 = 8 \times 2$
    ■ $= 2 \times 8$

30. $12 = 6 \times 2$
    $12 = 2 \times $ ■

31. $4 \times 9 = 36$
    $9 \times $ ■ $= 36$

32. $28 = 4 \times 7$
    $28 = 7 \times $ ■

33. $3 \times 2 = 6$
    $2 \times 3 = $ ■

34. $24 = 4 \times 6$
    $24 = 6 \times $ ■

35. $2 \times 4 = 8$
    $4 \times $ ■ $= 8$

📊 Data **Use the sign for Problems 36–41.**

36. What is the total cost for 5 adults?

37. What is the total cost for 7 children's tickets?

38. How much do tickets for 3 children, 2 adults, and 1 senior citizen cost altogether?

39. **Analyze** Mrs. Lu buys 7 baseball cards for $4 each. She has $6 left after paying for the cards and her adult admission. How much money did she bring to the Expo?

40. **Represent** Show why the cost of 4 children's tickets is the same as the cost of 2 adult tickets. Draw a picture to explain your reasoning.

41. **Create and Solve** Use data from the sign to create your own word problem. Then give your problem to a classmate to solve.

TRADING CARD EXPO

Saturday Only!
9 A.M. – 9 P.M.

Ticket Prices
Child............................ $ 2
Adult............................ $ 4
Senior Citizen............. $ 3

Extra Practice See page 229, Set C.

Algebraic Thinking
What's My Rule?

Look at this magical adding machine. It adds 5 to the input number.

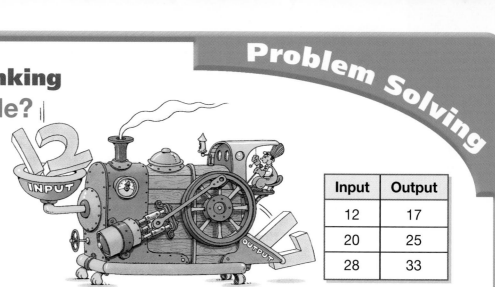

Input	Output
12	17
20	25
28	33

Look at each machine and table. Then write the rule and complete the table.

1.

Input	Output
16	13
28	25
37	▨
▨	50

2.

Input	Output
3	12
6	24
8	▨
▨	36

Check your understanding of Lessons 1–4.

Write an addition sentence and a multiplication sentence for each array. (Lessons 1–2)

1.

2.

3.

Multiply. (Lessons 3–4)

4. 3
   × 2

5. 4
   × 4

6. 2
   × 4

7. 10
   × 2

8. 9
   × 4

9. 4
   × 5

10. 2
    × 8

Multiply With 5

Objective Use different ways to multiply when 5 is a factor.

Learn About It

Yuji collects unusual rocks. He brings 4 boxes to science class. Each box holds 5 rocks. How many rocks does Yuji bring?

Multiply. $4 \times 5 = \blacksquare$ or $\begin{array}{r} 5 \\ \times 4 \\ \hline \blacksquare \end{array}$

Different Ways to Find 4 x 5

Way 1 Skip count.

Skip count by 5s.

Say: 5, 10, 15, 20.

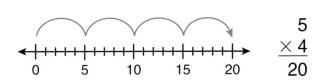

$\begin{array}{r} 5 \\ \times 4 \\ \hline 20 \end{array}$

Way 2 Draw a picture.

Then use repeated addition.

5 + 5 + 5 + 5 = 20

Way 3 Draw an array.

4 rows of 5 = 20

Way 4 You can write a multiplication sentence.

$4 \times 5 = \blacksquare$
$4 \times 5 = 20$

Think
4 groups of 5 = 20.

Solution: Yuji brings 20 rocks to science class.

Guided Practice

Find each product.

1. $\begin{array}{r} 5 \\ \times 3 \\ \hline \end{array}$ 2. $\begin{array}{r} 4 \\ \times 5 \\ \hline \end{array}$ 3. $\begin{array}{r} 5 \\ \times 2 \\ \hline \end{array}$ 4. $\begin{array}{r} 7 \\ \times 5 \\ \hline \end{array}$

Ask Yourself

• Can changing the order help me?

• Can I count by 5s?

Explain Your Thinking ▶ When you multiply a number by 5, can the product have a 2 in the ones place? Why or why not?

Practice and Problem Solving

Find each product.

5.	6.	7.	8.	9.	10.
$\begin{array}{r} 5 \\ \times\, 2 \\ \hline \end{array}$	$\begin{array}{r} 1 \\ \times\, 5 \\ \hline \end{array}$	$\begin{array}{r} 3 \\ \times\, 5 \\ \hline \end{array}$	$\begin{array}{r} 5 \\ \times\, 9 \\ \hline \end{array}$	$\begin{array}{r} 5 \\ \times\, 6 \\ \hline \end{array}$	$\begin{array}{r} 4 \\ \times\, 5 \\ \hline \end{array}$

11.	12.	13.	14.	15.	16.
$\begin{array}{r} 5 \\ \times\, 5 \\ \hline \end{array}$	$\begin{array}{r} 5 \\ \times\, 7 \\ \hline \end{array}$	$\begin{array}{r} 6 \\ \times\, 5 \\ \hline \end{array}$	$\begin{array}{r} 5 \\ \times\, 1 \\ \hline \end{array}$	$\begin{array}{r} 2 \\ \times\, 5 \\ \hline \end{array}$	$\begin{array}{r} 8 \\ \times\, 5 \\ \hline \end{array}$

17. 2×8 **18.** 5×10 **19.** 4×4 **20.** 3×5 **21.** 4×7

Algebra • Equations Find each missing factor.

22. $5 \times \blacksquare = 10$ **23.** $\blacksquare \times 5 = 25$ **24.** $5 \times \blacksquare = 40$ **25.** $45 = \blacksquare \times 5$

26. $30 = 5 \times \blacksquare$ **27.** $5 \times \blacksquare = 50$ **28.** $5 = 1 \times \blacksquare$ **29.** $35 = 5 \times \blacksquare$

Solve.

30. Amelia puts 5 rocks in each of 4 bags. She has 3 rocks left over. How many rocks did Amelia start with?

31. **What's Wrong** Ben wants to know how many are in 6 groups of 5. Look at Ben's work below. What did he do wrong?

32. Evan's rock display has 7 rows of 5 striped rocks. It also has 8 rows of 4 black rocks. Does Evan have more striped rocks or more black rocks?

> Ben
>
> 6 + 5 = 11

Mixed Review and Test Prep

Open Response

Find the perimeter of each figure.

(Grade 2)

33.

10 ft

6 ft ⬜ 6 ft

10 ft

34.

3 cm 5 cm

4 cm

35. Jacob wants to buy some comic books that cost $5 each. He has $18. What is the greatest number of comic books he can buy? Explain how you got your answer. (Ch. 8, Lesson 5)

Multiply With 10

Objective Use different ways to multiply when 10 is a factor.

Vocabulary
product

Learn About It

At the Model Train Show, Ken displayed his collection of model trains. He put 10 train cars on each of 4 tables. How many train cars did he display?

Multiply. $4 \times 10 = $ ▪ or $\begin{array}{r} 10 \\ \times\ 4 \\ \hline \text{▪} \end{array}$

Different Ways to Find 4 × 10

Way ① Skip count.

Skip count by 10s.

Say: 10, 20, 30, 40.

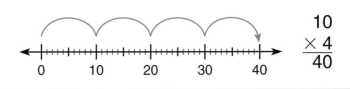

$\begin{array}{r} 10 \\ \times\ 4 \\ \hline 40 \end{array}$

Way ② Use a pattern.

When a number is multiplied by 10, write a zero after the number to show the **product**.

$1 \times 10 = 10$

$2 \times 10 = 20$

$3 \times 10 = 30$

$4 \times 10 = 40$

> **Think**
> $4 \times 1 = 4$
> So, $4 \times 10 = 40$

Way ③ Write a multiplication sentence.

$4 \times 10 = $ ▪

$4 \times 10 = 40$

> **Think**
> 4 groups of 10 = 40

Solution: Ken displayed 40 model train cars.

Guided Practice

Multiply.

1. 3×10 **2.** 10×6 **3.** 7×10 **4.** 10×9

Ask Yourself

- Can I use a pattern to help me?
- Can I skip count by 10s?

Explain Your Thinking ▶ The product of 10 and another number is 80. What is the other number? Explain how you know.

Find each product.

5. 10
×4

6. 10
×6

7. 10
×8

8. 10
×7

9. 10
×3

10. 10
×10

11. 2×10

12. 5×10

13. 10×1

14. 3×10

15. 10×4

16. 7×10

17. 10×10

18. 9×10

19. 6×10

20. 8×10

X Algebra • Functions Complete each table by following the rule.

Rule: Multiply by 2	
Input	Output
6	12
21. 3	
22. 5	
23.	14

Rule: Multiply by 5	
Input	Output
24. 4	
25. 8	
26.	30
27. 10	

Rule: Multiply by 10	
Input	Output
28.	20
29. 7	
30.	90
31.	100

Data Use the pictograph for Problems 32–34.

32. How many biplane models were at the model airplane show?

33. Half of the glider models at the show were made of wood. How many models is that?

34. **Represent** How many more symbols would be needed to show 90 model jets on the pictograph?

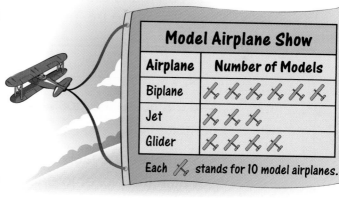

Model Airplane Show	
Airplane	Number of Models
Biplane	✈ ✈ ✈ ✈ ✈
Jet	✈ ✈ ✈
Glider	✈ ✈ ✈ ✈

Each ✈ stands for 10 model airplanes.

Mixed Review and Test Prep

Open Response

Tell if each item weighs more or less than a kilogram. (Grade 2)

35.

36.

Multiple Choice

37. There are 4 boxes of markers. Each box has 10 markers. How many markers are there?
(Ch. 8, Lesson 6)

A 14   B 40   C 44   D 48

Lesson 7

Problem-Solving Strategy
Make an Organized List

Objective Make an organized list to solve a problem.

Problem Elena has 4 hats in her hat collection. She also has 2 jackets. How many different combinations of a jacket and a hat can she wear?

UNDERSTAND

This is what you know.

- Elena has 4 different hats.

- She has 2 different color jackets.

PLAN

You can make an organized list to help you solve the problem.

SOLVE

Make a list of the possible combinations.

- Start with one jacket. Match the jacket to each hat.

- Then match the other jacket to each hat.

Count the number of different combinations.

Solution: Elena can wear 8 different combinations of a jacket and a hat.

Possible Combinations
yellow jacket → blue hat
yellow jacket → straw hat
yellow jacket → pink hat
yellow jacket → floral cap
denim jacket → blue hat
denim jacket → straw hat
denim jacket → pink hat
denim jacket → floral cap

LOOK BACK

Look back at the problem. Does the solution make sense?

Use the Ask Yourself questions to help you solve each problem.

1. Walt has a red, a blue, and a green cap in his hat collection. He has a tan, a white, and a yellow shirt. How many different combinations of one shirt and one cap can he wear?

2. Sabrina has a purple, a yellow, a pink, and a black hat. She has a red, a green, and a blue scarf. How many different combinations of one scarf and one hat can she wear?

Ask Yourself

UNDERSTAND What facts do I know?

PLAN How can I list all of the different combinations?

SOLVE
• Did I list all of the colors of the first item and of the second item?

• Did I count all of the combinations?

LOOK BACK Did I find all of the combinations?

Independent Practice

Make an organized list to solve each problem.

3. Sidra has a leather belt and a cloth belt. She has skirts made of cotton, denim, or corduroy. How many combinations of belts and skirts can Sidra wear?

4. Al is making sandwiches. He can use either rye or white bread. He can use either tuna or ham. How many different types of sandwiches can he make?

5. Neil won a prize at the fair. He can get a stuffed bear, a dog, or a cat. Each animal comes in black, white, brown, or gray. How many different types of stuffed animals can he choose?

6. Chay has 2 vests. One is blue and one is brown. He has 6 baseball caps from different teams. How many different combinations of one vest and one hat can he wear?

Mixed Problem Solving

Solve. Show your work. Tell what strategy you used.

7. Ben picked 6 more apples than Judy. Together they picked 62 apples. How many apples did each person pick?

8. Steven, Daniel, and Anna are lining up to use the sink. In how many different ways can they form a line?

9. Kim took 5 marbles out of a bag. Then she put 2 marbles back in. If there are 15 marbles in the bag now, how many marbles were in the bag when Kim started?

You Choose

Strategy
- Act It Out
- Draw a Picture
- Guess and Check
- Make an Organized List
- Work Backward

Computation Method
- Mental Math
- Estimation
- Paper and Pencil
- Calculator

Data Use the graph to solve Problems 10–14. Then tell which computation method you used.

A survey asked a group of dog owners about their pet dogs. The bar graph shows the results of the survey.

10. Which kind of dog do most people own?

11. Which kind of dog do 15 people own?

12. How many more people own a terrier than a collie?

13. How many people own hounds or poodles?

14. Which two kinds of dogs were chosen by 50 people?

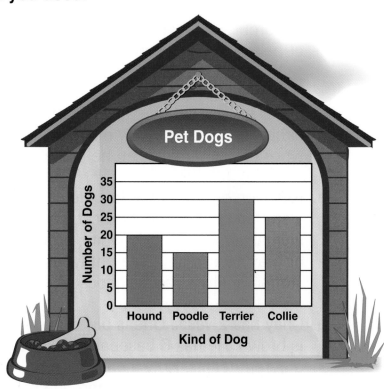

222

Problem Solving on Tests

Multiple Choice

Choose the letter of the correct answer.

1. Which number sentence is not correct?

   A $4 \times 9 = 36$ C $4 \times 3 = 7$

   B $6 \times 4 = 24$ D $1 \times 4 = 4$

   (Chapter 8, Lesson 4)

2. Ron made a line plot to show the number of hits each player made. How many players got 5 hits?

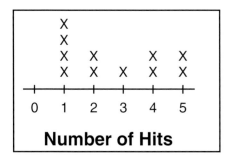

   F 1   G 2   H 3   J 5

   (Chapter 6, Lesson 3)

Open Response

Solve each problem.

3. Would you describe the probability of landing on red or blue with this spinner as equally likely? Explain.

   (Chapter 7, Lesson 2)

4. Find the value for the box.

   $8 + \blacksquare = 13$

   (Chapter 5, Lesson 2)

Extended Response

5. The tally chart shows the number of goals scored by 5 players on the Bears team during one season. Use the tally chart to answer the questions.

Soccer Goals	
Player	Tally
Laurie	III
Janet	I
Debbie	II
Michelle	HHT III
Karla	HHT I

   a. Who scored the greatest number of goals? Who scored the least number? What is the range of this data?

   b. How many more goals were scored by Debbie and Michelle than by Laurie and Karla? Explain how you know.

   c. Use the tally chart to make a bar graph. Label your graph, choose a scale, and give your graph a title.

   (Chapter 6, Lesson 6)

 Education Place

See **eduplace.com/map** for more Test-Taking Tips.

Audio Tutor 1/25 Listen and Understand

Algebra

Multiply With 1 and 0

Objective Use special properties to multiply when 1 or 0 is a factor.

Vocabulary
Property of One
Zero Property

Learn About It

Jake's grandparents brought him some new marbles for his collection.

You can use special properties to help you multiply. Look at the multiplication properties below.

Property of One

When 1 is a factor, the product is always equal to the other factor.

Jake has 6 bags of marbles. Each bag has 1 red marble in it. How many red marbles are in the bags?

Multiply.

$6 \times 1 = \blacksquare$ or $\begin{array}{r} 1 \\ \times 6 \\ \hline \blacksquare \end{array}$

$6 \times 1 = 6$

There are 6 red marbles in all.

Zero Property

When 0 is a factor, the product is always 0.

Jake has 4 empty marble bags. If there are 0 marbles in each bag, how many marbles are in the bags?

Multiply.

$4 \times 0 = \blacksquare$ or $\begin{array}{r} 0 \\ \times 4 \\ \hline \blacksquare \end{array}$

$4 \times 0 = 0$

There are 0 marbles in the four bags.

Guided Practice

Multiply.

1. $\begin{array}{r} 1 \\ \times\,6 \\ \hline \end{array}$
2. $\begin{array}{r} 0 \\ \times\,7 \\ \hline \end{array}$
3. $\begin{array}{r} 1 \\ \times\,5 \\ \hline \end{array}$
4. $\begin{array}{r} 0 \\ \times\,9 \\ \hline \end{array}$

5. 4×1
6. 8×0
7. 0×2
8. 1×3

Ask Yourself
- If 1 is a factor, what must the product be?
- If 0 is a factor, what must the product be?

Explain Your Thinking ▶ The number sentence 3×0 means 3 groups of 0. Why does it make sense that the product is zero?

Practice and Problem Solving

Multiply.

9. $\begin{array}{r} 0 \\ \times\,8 \\ \hline \end{array}$
10. $\begin{array}{r} 1 \\ \times\,7 \\ \hline \end{array}$
11. $\begin{array}{r} 0 \\ \times\,2 \\ \hline \end{array}$
12. $\begin{array}{r} 1 \\ \times\,9 \\ \hline \end{array}$
13. $\begin{array}{r} 5 \\ \times\,1 \\ \hline \end{array}$
14. $\begin{array}{r} 0 \\ \times\,4 \\ \hline \end{array}$

15. $\begin{array}{r} 7 \\ \times\,0 \\ \hline \end{array}$
16. $\begin{array}{r} 1 \\ \times\,6 \\ \hline \end{array}$
17. $\begin{array}{r} 8 \\ \times\,1 \\ \hline \end{array}$
18. $\begin{array}{r} 0 \\ \times\,1 \\ \hline \end{array}$
19. $\begin{array}{r} 5 \\ \times\,0 \\ \hline \end{array}$
20. $\begin{array}{r} 10 \\ \times\,1 \\ \hline \end{array}$

21. 6×0
22. 1×7
23. 1×1
24. 0×3
25. 10×0

26. 1×9
27. 4×0
28. 5×1
29. 1×0
30. 0×7

Use the number sentences at the right for Problems 31–33.

31. What number does each shape stand for?

32. Suppose Marisa has 8 empty boxes. Which multiplication sentence shows how many marbles she has?

33. Steve collects crystals. He gave 1 crystal to each of his 4 friends. Which multiplication sentence shows how many crystals he gave to his friends?

$4 \times \blacktriangle = 4$

$2 \times \bullet = 0$

$8 \times \blacksquare = 0$

$\blacklozenge \times 8 = 8$

Go On

Solve.

34. What's Wrong? Look at the picture Marly drew to the right.

Marly wrote the number sentence $4 \times 0 = 0$ to describe her picture. What did she do wrong?

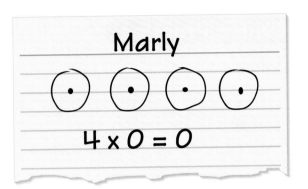

Marly

$4 \times 0 = 0$

 Algebra • Properties Find each missing number.

35. $4 \times 0 = \blacksquare \times 4$

36. $3 \times \blacksquare = 0$

37. $1 \times 6 = 6 \times \blacksquare$

38. $8 \times \blacksquare = 8$

39. $\blacksquare \times 7 = 0$

40. $8 \times \blacksquare = 7 \times 0$

41. $1 \times 9 = \blacksquare \times 1$

42. $\blacksquare \times 1 = 6$

43. $5 \times \blacksquare = 1 \times 5$

44. $\blacksquare \times 9 = 4 \times 0$

45. $10 \times 0 = 5 \times \blacksquare$

46. $2 \times 3 = \blacksquare \times 6$

Data Use the table to Solve Problems 47–49.

Manny's Marble Shop sells bags filled with marbles. The table shows the number of different marbles in one bag.

47. Sharon bought 2 bags of marbles. How many blue marbles did she get?

48. Jared bought 5 bags of marbles from Manny's Marble Shop. Did he get a greater number of clear marbles or green marbles?

49. Analyze Brandon bought 4 bags of marbles and gave some of them to his sister. He has 6 clear marbles left. How many clear marbles did he give to his sister?

 50. Write About It Is it easier to find 5×0 than 598×0? Explain why.

Manny's Marble Bag	
Types of Marbles	**Number of Marbles**
Cat's Eye	3
Green	4
Red	5
Blue	7
Clear	2

226

Extra Practice See page 229, Set F.

Open Response

What comes next in the pattern?

(Ch. 1, Lesson 5)

51. 10, 12, 14, 16, _____

52. 1, 2, 4, 7, 11, _____

Multiple Choice

53. Which of the following is true?

(Ch. 8, Lesson 8)

A $1 \times 8 = 9$ B $0 \times 5 = 5$

C $10 \times 1 = 10$ D $1 \times 1 = 2$

Problem Solving

Social Studies Connection
Greek Numbers

Since people began to count long ago, they have used different symbols for numbers. These are some of the symbols that people in Greece used as numbers.

Use the Greek symbols to find each product.

1. $\beta \times \varepsilon$

2. $\beta \times 0$

3. $\delta \times 6$

4. $\alpha \times 9$

5. $\beta \times \alpha$

6. $\varepsilon \times 5$

7. $\delta \times 7$

8. $\varepsilon \times 9$

9. $\beta \times \beta$

10. $\varepsilon \times \varepsilon$

Greek Symbols

$\alpha = 1$ $\beta = 2$

$\delta = 4$ $\varepsilon = 5$

Chapter Review/Test

VOCABULARY

Choose the correct term to complete each sentence.

Vocabulary

factors

product

Commutative Property

Zero Property

1. When you multiply two numbers, you get a ____.

2. Since 3 × 4 = 12, 3 and 4 are ____ of 12.

3. The number sentences 2 × 5 = 10 and 5 × 2 = 10 are an example of the ____.

CONCEPTS AND SKILLS

Write a multiplication sentence for each array. (Lesson 1–2, pp. 206–209)

4. ▲ ▲ ▲ ▲ ▲
   ▲ ▲ ▲ ▲ ▲
   ▲ ▲ ▲ ▲ ▲

5. ● ● ● ● ● ● ●
   ● ● ● ● ● ● ●

6. ★ ★ ★ ★ ★ ★ ★ ★ ★

7. ■ ■ ■ ■
   ■ ■ ■ ■
   ■ ■ ■ ■

Find each product. (Lessons 3–6, 8, pp. 210–219, 224–226)

8. $\begin{array}{r} 7 \\ \times 2 \\ \hline \end{array}$
9. $\begin{array}{r} 6 \\ \times 2 \\ \hline \end{array}$
10. $\begin{array}{r} 3 \\ \times 2 \\ \hline \end{array}$
11. $\begin{array}{r} 4 \\ \times 4 \\ \hline \end{array}$
12. $\begin{array}{r} 3 \\ \times 4 \\ \hline \end{array}$
13. $\begin{array}{r} 9 \\ \times 4 \\ \hline \end{array}$

14. $\begin{array}{r} 4 \\ \times 5 \\ \hline \end{array}$
15. $\begin{array}{r} 7 \\ \times 5 \\ \hline \end{array}$
16. $\begin{array}{r} 6 \\ \times 5 \\ \hline \end{array}$
17. $\begin{array}{r} 10 \\ \times 5 \\ \hline \end{array}$
18. $\begin{array}{r} 10 \\ \times 3 \\ \hline \end{array}$
19. $\begin{array}{r} 10 \\ \times 9 \\ \hline \end{array}$

20. 0 × 5
21. 3 × 0
22. 4 × 1
23. 1 × 9
24. 1 × 0

PROBLEM SOLVING

Solve. (Lesson 7, pp. 220–222)

25. Hank has white sneakers, black sneakers, and red sneakers. He has blue pants and black pants. How many combinations of sneakers and pants can Hank wear?

Write About It

Show You Understand

Jan and Eri are looking at a multiplication problem.

• Eri says one of the factors is 7.
• Jan says the product is 7.

If they are both right, what is the multiplication problem? Explain how you know.

Extra Practice

Set A (Lesson 2, pp. 208–209)

Write a multiplication sentence for each array.

1. 😊😊😊😊😊
   😊😊😊😊😊

2. ▲ ▲
   ▲ ▲
   ▲ ▲

3. ■ ■ ■ ■
   ■ ■ ■ ■
   ■ ■ ■ ■

4. ★ ★
   ★ ★

Set B (Lesson 3, pp. 210–211)

Find each product.

1. $\begin{array}{r} 5 \\ \times\ 2 \\ \hline \end{array}$
2. $\begin{array}{r} 8 \\ \times\ 2 \\ \hline \end{array}$
3. $\begin{array}{r} 10 \\ \times\ 2 \\ \hline \end{array}$
4. $\begin{array}{r} 2 \\ \times\ 2 \\ \hline \end{array}$
5. $\begin{array}{r} 9 \\ \times\ 2 \\ \hline \end{array}$
6. $\begin{array}{r} 6 \\ \times\ 2 \\ \hline \end{array}$

Set C (Lesson 4, pp. 212–214)

Multiply.

1. $\begin{array}{r} 4 \\ \times\ 6 \\ \hline \end{array}$
2. $\begin{array}{r} 4 \\ \times\ 7 \\ \hline \end{array}$
3. $\begin{array}{r} 10 \\ \times\ 4 \\ \hline \end{array}$
4. $\begin{array}{r} 4 \\ \times\ 5 \\ \hline \end{array}$
5. $\begin{array}{r} 4 \\ \times\ 4 \\ \hline \end{array}$
6. $\begin{array}{r} 9 \\ \times\ 4 \\ \hline \end{array}$

Set D (Lesson 5, pp. 216–217)

Find each product.

1. $\begin{array}{r} 5 \\ \times\ 5 \\ \hline \end{array}$
2. $\begin{array}{r} 3 \\ \times\ 5 \\ \hline \end{array}$
3. $\begin{array}{r} 7 \\ \times\ 5 \\ \hline \end{array}$
4. $\begin{array}{r} 9 \\ \times\ 5 \\ \hline \end{array}$
5. $\begin{array}{r} 4 \\ \times\ 5 \\ \hline \end{array}$
6. $\begin{array}{r} 8 \\ \times\ 5 \\ \hline \end{array}$

Set E (Lesson 6, pp. 218–219)

Multiply.

1. 10×6
2. 10×1
3. 10×4
4. 10×8
5. 7×10

Set F (Lesson 8, pp. 224–226)

Find each product.

1. 2×0
2. 0×1
3. 1×4
4. 3×0
5. 7×1

Extra Practice at **eduplace.com/map**

CHAPTER

9

Multiplication Facts and Patterns

Using Data

These five macaws enjoy the moist tropical rainforest in Peru's Manu National Park. Look at the sign. Suppose each macaw laid eggs at the same time. Write and solve a word problem about the number of eggs more than one bird might have laid.

Macaw Facts

Life span: about 50 years

Size: about 35 inches

Weight: about 2 pounds

Eggs: 2-4 laid at the same time

Use What You Know

Use this page to review and remember what you need to know for this chapter.

VOCABULARY

Choose the best word to complete each sentence.

Vocabulary
array
factors
product
multiply
Commutative
Property

1. To find the total number of objects that are in equal groups, you can ____.

2. A group of objects arranged in rows and columns is called an ____.

3. You multiply two numbers to find the ____.

4. Numbers that are multiplied are called ____.

CONCEPTS AND SKILLS

Write a multiplication sentence for each picture.

5. 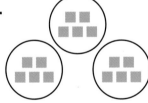   6.    7.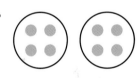

Find each product.

8. $\begin{array}{r} 4 \\ \times\ 2 \\ \hline \end{array}$ 9. $\begin{array}{r} 7 \\ \times\ 1 \\ \hline \end{array}$ 10. $\begin{array}{r} 2 \\ \times\ 9 \\ \hline \end{array}$ 11. $\begin{array}{r} 8 \\ \times\ 0 \\ \hline \end{array}$

12. 1×0 13. 4×6 14. 3×10 15. 4×1

16. 7×10 17. 5×5 18. 9×4 19. 6×2

 **Write About It**

20. There are 9 groups of 10 tiles each. Is it quicker to multiply or add to find the total number of tiles? Explain.

Facts Practice, See page 668.

Audio Tutor 1/26 Listen and Understand

Use a Multiplication Table

Objective Find patterns in a multiplication table.

Materials
grid paper or
Learning Tool 14

Work Together

You can find patterns in a multiplication table.

STEP 1 Use grid paper to make a **multiplication** table like the one on the right. Include the numbers shown.

STEP 2 The numbers along the top and side are **factors**. Find the row for 2 and the column for 4. Then find the square where the row and column meet. Write the **product** of 2 × 4 in that square.

column ↓

×	0	1	2	3	4	5	6	7	8	9	10
0	0	0	0	0	0						
1	0	1	2	3	4						
2	0	2	4	6	8						
3											
4											
5											
6											
7											
8											
9											
10											

row →

2 x 4 = 8

STEP 3 Fill in all the other squares that have products you know.

STEP 4 Look for patterns in the table.

- Which row and column have the same number in every square?

- Which row has the same numbers as the column for 4?

- Which row and column show products that increase by two each time?

- Which rows and columns have even numbers only?

Use your multiplication table to answer each question.

1. When you multiply a number by 0, what is the product?

2. When you multiply a number by 1, what is the product?

3. What do all the products in the column for 10 have in common?

4. Look for other patterns in the table. Describe two patterns that you find.

**Below are parts of a multiplication table.
In which row or column is each part found?**

5.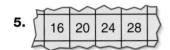

6.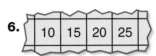

7.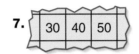

8.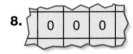

9.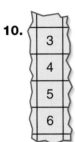

10.

| 3 |
| 4 |
| 5 |
| 6 |

11.

| 30 |
| 35 |
| 40 |

12.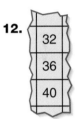

**Write *true* or *false* for each statement.
Give examples to support your answers.**

13. The product will always be 0 when you multiply by 0.

14. The product will always be 1 when you multiply by 1.

15. Each product appears at least two times in the multiplication table.

Talk About It • Write About It

You have learned to find patterns in a multiplication table.

16. How could you use the products in the row for 2 to help you find the products in the row for 4?

17. For each row, is there a column that has the same products? Why or why not?

Audio Tutor 1/3 Listen and Understand
Multiply With 3

Objective Use different ways to multiply when 3 is a factor.

Vocabulary
array

Learn About It

The nature club is going to take a hike in a rainforest. Each member of the club will bring 3 bottles of water. If there are 5 members, how many bottles of water will they bring?

Multiply. $5 \times 3 = \blacksquare$ or
$$\begin{array}{r} 3 \\ \times\ 5 \\ \hline \blacksquare \end{array}$$

Different Ways to Find 5×3

Way ① Skip count.

Skip count by 3s.
Say: 3, 6, 9, 12, 15.

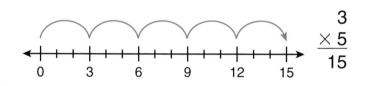

$$\begin{array}{r} 3 \\ \times\ 5 \\ \hline 15 \end{array}$$

Way ② Draw a picture.

Then use repeated addition.

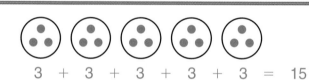

$3 + 3 + 3 + 3 + 3 = 15$

Way ③ Draw an array.

5 rows of 3 is 15.

Way ④ You can write a multiplication sentence.

$5 \times 3 = \blacksquare$
$5 \times 3 = 15$

Think 5 groups of 3 is 15.

Solution: The nature club will bring 15 bottles of water.

Guided Practice

Multiply.

1. $\begin{array}{r} 3 \\ \times\ 2 \\ \hline \end{array}$
2. $\begin{array}{r} 1 \\ \times\ 3 \\ \hline \end{array}$
3. $\begin{array}{r} 3 \\ \times\ 3 \\ \hline \end{array}$
4. $\begin{array}{r} 5 \\ \times\ 3 \\ \hline \end{array}$

Ask Yourself
• How can I use the Commutative Property?

Explain Your Thinking ▶ How can knowing $2 \times 4 = 8$ help you find 3×4?

Extra Help at **eduplace.com/map**

Find each product.

5. 3
    × 6

6. 3
    × 4

7. 3
    × 8

8. 9
    × 3

9. 7
    × 3

10. 3
    × 1

11. 5
    × 3

12. 3
    × 3

13. 2
    × 3

14. 10
    × 3

15. 6
    × 3

16. 3
    × 0

Draw an array for each. Then copy and complete each multiplication sentence.

17. $5 \times 3 = \blacksquare$

18. $4 \times 3 = \blacksquare$

19. $3 \times 6 = \blacksquare$

20. $3 \times 2 = \blacksquare$

Solve.

21. A park ranger led 3 groups of hikers. There were 4 people in each group. How many hikers did she lead?

22. Tyrone planted 3 seeds every day for 5 days. Mina planted a total of 12 seeds. How many more seeds did Tyrone plant than Mina?

23. Lucia buys 3 sheets of nature stickers. Each sheet has 8 stickers. Does she have 24 stickers? Use words, pictures, or numbers to explain.

Mixed Review and Test Prep

Open Response
Write the value of the underlined digit. (Ch. 1, Lesson 7)

24. 12<u>4</u>,893

25. 518,<u>6</u>27

26. 9<u>3</u>6,204

27. <u>2</u>05,978

28. What number will make this number sentence true?

(Ch. 9, Lesson 2)

$$3 \times \blacksquare = 2 \times 3$$

Explain how you know.

Multiply With 6

Objective Use different ways to multiply when 6 is a factor.

Vocabulary
product

Learn About It

An adventure group is rafting on a rainforest river. Each raft holds 6 people. There are 7 rafts in the group. How many people are rafting?

Multiply. $7 \times 6 = $ ■ or $\begin{array}{r} 6 \\ \times 7 \\ \hline ■ \end{array}$

Different Ways to Find 7×6

Way ❶ Use doubling.

6 is double 3, so 7×6 is double 7×3.

$7 \times 3 = 21$

$7 \times 6 = 21 + 21$

$\boxed{21 + 21 = 42}$

So $7 \times 6 = 42$.

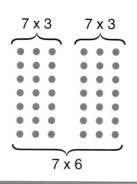

7 x 3   7 x 3

7 x 6

Way ❷ Use repeated addition.

$6 + 6 + 6 + 6 + 6 + 6 + 6 = 42$

Way ❸ Write a multiplication sentence.

$7 \times 6 = $ ■

$7 \times 6 = 42$

Think
7 groups of 6 is 42.

Solution: There are 42 people rafting.

Guided Practice

Multiply.

1. $\begin{array}{r} 6 \\ \times 2 \\ \hline \end{array}$

2. $\begin{array}{r} 5 \\ \times 6 \\ \hline \end{array}$

3. $\begin{array}{r} 6 \\ \times 4 \\ \hline \end{array}$

4. $\begin{array}{r} 9 \\ \times 6 \\ \hline \end{array}$

Ask Yourself

• What 3s fact can I use to find the **product**?

• Is there another fact I can use?

Explain Your Thinking ▶ Why is 6×8 greater than 5×8?

Find each product.

5. $\begin{array}{r} 6 \\ \times\ 1 \\ \hline \end{array}$
6. $\begin{array}{r} 6 \\ \times\ 3 \\ \hline \end{array}$
7. $\begin{array}{r} 5 \\ \times\ 6 \\ \hline \end{array}$
8. $\begin{array}{r} 10 \\ \times\ 6 \\ \hline \end{array}$
9. $\begin{array}{r} 6 \\ \times\ 7 \\ \hline \end{array}$

10. $\begin{array}{r} 4 \\ \times\ 6 \\ \hline \end{array}$
11. $\begin{array}{r} 6 \\ \times\ 0 \\ \hline \end{array}$
12. $\begin{array}{r} 6 \\ \times\ 6 \\ \hline \end{array}$
13. $\begin{array}{r} 6 \\ \times\ 8 \\ \hline \end{array}$
14. $\begin{array}{r} 6 \\ \times\ 2 \\ \hline \end{array}$

15. 8×6
16. 6×3
17. 9×6
18. 1×6

19. 4×6
20. 2×6
21. 6×7
22. 6×9

 Algebra • **Functions** Copy and complete each table.

Rule: Multiply by 6	
Input	Output
2	12
23. 4	■
24. 6	■
25. ■	60

26.
Rule: Multiply by ■	
Input	Output
2	6
4	12
7	21
27. 8	■

**Write *true* or *false* for each statement.
If the statement is false, explain why.**

28. Since $6 + 6 + 6 + 6 = 24$, 6×6 must equal 24.

29. To find 5×6, you can add $6 + 6 + 6 + 6 + 6$.

30. You can use 8 groups of 6 objects to show 8×6.

31. Since $3 \times 3 = 9$, the product of 6×3 must be twice as much.

Go On

Algebra • Symbols Write >, <, or = for each .

32. 2 × 6 ● 15

33. 60 ● 6 × 10

34. 5 × 6 ● 25

35. 50 ● 9 × 6

36. 6 × 6 ● 34

37. 6 × 1 ● 7

 Data Use the recipe to solve problems 38–41.

Antoine created a recipe for Nature Mix. The recipe on the right will make one batch.

38. Antoine decides to make 6 batches of this mix. How many cups of oat cereal will he need?

39. Almonds and cashews are nuts. How many cups of nuts are needed to make 2 batches?

40. Darlene wants to make 6 batches of Nature Mix. She says that she needs 15 cups of dried pineapple. Is she correct? Explain how you know.

41. Write About It Suppose you want to make 5 batches of Nature Mix. Why is it easier to multiply than to add to find how many cups of each ingredient are needed?

Nature Mix

2 cups almonds

1 cup cashews

3 cups dried pineapple

4 cups oat cereal

1. Mix ingredients in a bowl.
2. Scoop a serving into a plastic bag.
3. Eat and enjoy on your next outdoor trip.

Mixed Review and Test Prep

Open Response

Add or subtract. (Ch. 4, Lessons 3, 4)
(Ch. 5, Lesson 4)

42. $628
− 209

43. $5.56
+ 3.44

Multiple Choice

44. Mrs. Lee ordered 4 salads. Each salad costs $6, including tax. What is the total cost of the salads? (Ch. 9, Lesson 3)

A $18

c $24

B $20

D $26

Extra Practice See page 257, Set B.

Number Sense
Multiplying in Different Ways

There are many different ways to find a product.

Vocabulary

Distributive Property

Sean uses doubles.

5×6 is double 5×3.

$5 \times 6 = (5 \times 3) + (5 \times 3)$

$5 \times 6 = 15 + 15$

$5 \times 6 = 30$

Parentheses show which operation should be done first.

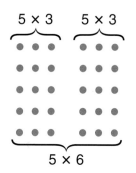

5×3 5×3

5×6

Theresa uses the Distributive Property. She thinks of 6 as 4 + 2.

$5 \times 6 = 5 \times (4 + 2)$

$5 \times 6 = (5 \times 4) + (5 \times 2)$

$5 \times 6 = 20 + 10$

$5 \times 6 = 30$

Think $6 = 4 + 2$.

Bob also uses the Distributive Property. But he thinks of 6 as 5 + 1.

$5 \times 6 = 5 \times (5 + 1)$

$5 \times 6 = (5 \times 5) + (5 \times 1)$

$5 \times 6 = 25 + 5$

$5 \times 6 = 30$

Think $6 = 5 + 1$.

Use doubles to find each product.

1. 2×4　　　　**2.** 3×6　　　　**3.** 4×8　　　　**4.** 5×10

Use the Distributive Property to find each product.
Copy and complete each set of exercises.

5. $8 \times 6 = 8 \times (3 + 3)$
$8 \times 6 = (8 \times 3) + (\blacksquare \times \blacksquare)$
$8 \times 6 = \blacksquare + \blacksquare$
$8 \times 6 = \blacksquare$

6. $2 \times 13 = 2 \times (10 + 3)$
$2 \times 13 = (2 \times 10) + (2 \times 3)$
$2 \times 13 = \blacksquare + \blacksquare$
$2 \times 13 = \blacksquare$

7. Analyze You can use the Distributive Property to write $4 \times 7 = 4 \times (3 + 4)$. Can you also write $4 \times 7 = (3 + 1) \times 7$? Explain why or why not.

Audio Tutor 1/28 Listen and Understand

Multiply With 7

Objective Learn different ways to multiply when 7 is a factor.

Learn About It

The nature center exhibit has tanks of different types of rainforest frogs. Each tank has 7 frogs. There are 5 tanks. How many frogs are in the exhibit?

Multiply. $5 \times 7 = \blacksquare$ or $\begin{array}{r} 7 \\ \times\ 5 \\ \hline \blacksquare \end{array}$

Different Ways to Find 5 × 7

Way ❶ Use repeated addition.

$7 + 7 + 7 + 7 + 7 = 35$

Way ❷ Draw an array.

5 rows of 7 is 35.

Way ❸ Use a fact you know.

You know that $7 \times 5 = 35$,
so $5 \times 7 = 35$.

Remember
The order you use to multiply factors does not change the product. The product remains the same.

Solution: There are 35 frogs in the exhibit.

Guided Practice

Multiply.

1. $\begin{array}{r} 7 \\ \times\ 6 \\ \hline \end{array}$
2. $\begin{array}{r} 5 \\ \times\ 7 \\ \hline \end{array}$
3. $\begin{array}{r} 7 \\ \times\ 2 \\ \hline \end{array}$
4. $\begin{array}{r} 10 \\ \times\ 7 \\ \hline \end{array}$

5. 8×7
6. 7×3
7. 4×7
8. 7×7

Ask Yourself
• What other fact can I use to find the product?

Explain Your Thinking ▶ Why is it useful to know that you can multiply factors in any order?

Find each product.

9. 7
×2

10. 7
×5

11. 7
×8

12. 4
×7

13. 7
×7

14. 3
×7

15. 0
×7

16. 7
×9

17. 10
×7

18. 7
×1

19. 7
×6

20. 5
×7

21. 7×3

22. 9×7

23. 8×7

24. 1×7

25. 7×7

Algebra • Symbols Compare. Write >, <, or = for each .

26. 4×7 ⬭ 5×7

27. 7×7 ⬭ 6×6

28. 0×7 ⬭ 1×7

29. 6×2 ⬭ 2×7

30. 8×5 ⬭ 9×6

31. 4×3 ⬭ 3×4

Solve.

32. The students who visited the nature center drew pictures of the animals they saw. A group of 7 students drew 4 pictures each. How many pictures is this?

33. Yuriko saw 15 insects during a walk outside. Together, Yuriko and Bob saw a total of 29 insects during the walk. How many insects did Bob see?

34. On the gift shop counter, there are 3 packs of 7 reptile cards. There are 18 mammal cards. How many cards are on the counter?

Mixed Review and Test Prep

Open Response
Find each product. (Ch. 8, Lessons 3, 4, 6)

35. 2
×8

36. 9
×10

37. 5
×4

38. Explain how you know that 7 is a factor of 56. Use words, pictures or numbers to explain.
(Ch. 9, Lesson 4)

Multiply With 8

Objective Learn different ways to multiply when 8 is a factor.

Learn About It

Did you know that a tarantula has eight legs? How many legs do 6 tarantulas have?

Multiply. $6 \times 8 = \blacksquare$ or $\begin{array}{r} 8 \\ \times\ 6 \\ \hline \blacksquare \end{array}$

Different types of tarantulas live in the world's rainforests.

Different Ways to Find 6×8

Way 1 **Use doubling.**

6×8 is double 6×4.

$6 \times 4 = 24$

$6 \times 8 = 24 + 24$

$\boxed{24 + 24 = 48}$

So $6 \times 8 = 48$.

6 x 4   6 x 4

6 x 8

Way 2 **Use repeated addition.**

$8 + 8 + 8 + 8 + 8 + 8 = 48$

Way 3 **Use a fact you know.**

You know that $8 \times 6 = 48$,
so $6 \times 8 = 48$.

Remember
Changing the order of the factors does not change the product.

Solution: Six tarantulas have a total of 48 legs.

► **You can use facts you know to find a fact you don't know.**

Jeff and Elena found 9 × 8 in different ways.

Jeff did it this way since he knew 8 × 8 = 64.

Jeff

$9 \times 8 = ?$

$8 \times 8 = 64$

$64 + 8 = 72$

So $9 \times 8 = 72$.

> Jeff added a group of 8.

Elena did it this way since she knew 10 × 8 = 80.

Elena

$9 \times 8 = ?$

$10 \times 8 = 80$

$80 - 8 = 72$

So $9 \times 8 = 72$.

> Elena subtracted a group of 8.

- Why did Jeff add a group of 8?

- Why did Elena subtract a group of 8?

- Is Jeff's or Elena's way of finding 9 × 8 easier? Explain why you think so.

Guided Practice

Find each product.

1. $\begin{array}{r} 8 \\ \times 3 \\ \hline \end{array}$

2. $\begin{array}{r} 7 \\ \times 8 \\ \hline \end{array}$

3. $\begin{array}{r} 8 \\ \times 1 \\ \hline \end{array}$

4. $\begin{array}{r} 5 \\ \times 8 \\ \hline \end{array}$

5. $\begin{array}{r} 6 \\ \times 8 \\ \hline \end{array}$

6. $\begin{array}{r} 8 \\ \times 0 \\ \hline \end{array}$

7. $\begin{array}{r} 8 \\ \times 8 \\ \hline \end{array}$

8. $\begin{array}{r} 4 \\ \times 8 \\ \hline \end{array}$

9. 8×2

10. 1×8

11. 8×9

12. 7×8

13. 8×10

14. 8×8

15. 0×8

16. 5×8

Ask Yourself

- What 4s fact can I use to find the product?
- Is there another fact I can use?

Explain Your Thinking ► How can you use 10 × 8 to find 11 × 8?

Go On

Multiply.

17. 8×7

18. 8×2

19. 1×8

20. 3×8

21. 8×9

22. 8×0

23. 6×8

24. 5×8

25. 8×8

26. 2×8

27. 8×3

28. 7×8

29. 8×5

30. 9×8

31. 10×8

32. 8×6

33. 8×1

34. 8×4

𝑿 Algebra • Functions Copy and complete each table.

Rule: Multiply by 8	
Input	Output
8	64
35. ▨	40
36. 3	▨
37. ▨	16

38.

Rule: Multiply by ▨	
Input	Output
3	18
5	30
6	36
39. 9	▨

📊 Data The pictograph shows some students' favorite rainforest animals. Use the pictograph for Problems 40–43.

40. How many students chose the sloth?

41. How many more students chose the anteater than the bat?

42. **Predict** Suppose each student put the name of his or her favorite animal in a hat. Which animal is least likely to be picked?

43. **Create and Solve** Write a word problem using the information from the graph. Give it to a classmate to solve.

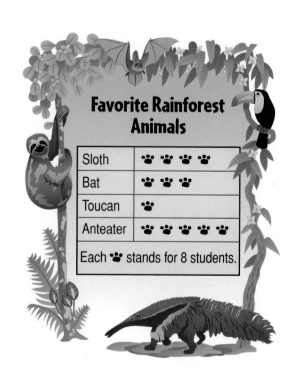

Favorite Rainforest Animals

Sloth	🐾 🐾 🐾 🐾
Bat	🐾 🐾 🐾
Toucan	🐾
Anteater	🐾 🐾 🐾 🐾 🐾

Each 🐾 stands for 8 students.

Extra Practice See page 257, Set D.

Algebraic Thinking
Shapes in Equations

Find the value of each shape. Different shapes stand for different numbers. Same shapes stand for same numbers.

1. ■ − ▲ = 2

   ■ × ▲ = 48

2. ★ − ● = 4

   ★ × ● = 45

3. ◆ + ◆ = 16

   ◆ × ◆ = 64

■ = ?   ★ = ?   ◆ = ?

▲ = ?   ● = ?

4. **Create and Solve** Make up your own number sentence puzzle. Use the same shapes as above or invent your own. Then give your puzzle to a classmate to solve.

Check your understanding of Lessons 1–5.

Find each product. (Lessons 1–5)

1. $\begin{array}{r} 5 \\ \times\ 3 \\ \hline \end{array}$

2. $\begin{array}{r} 3 \\ \times\ 7 \\ \hline \end{array}$

3. $\begin{array}{r} 4 \\ \times\ 6 \\ \hline \end{array}$

4. $\begin{array}{r} 9 \\ \times\ 6 \\ \hline \end{array}$

5. 7×7

6. 7×4

7. 8×3

8. 8×7

Solve. (Lessons 1–5)

9. Andy's scrapbook contains photographs of the rainforest. Each page has 3 photographs. How many photographs are on 6 pages?

10. A female orangutan may have 2 or 3 babies. If 2 orangutans each have 3 babies, how many babies will there be?

Multiply With 9

Objective Learn different ways to multiply when 9 is a factor.

Factors	Product
<u>1</u> × 9 =	9
<u>2</u> × 9 =	18
<u>3</u> × 9 =	27
<u>4</u> × 9 =	36
<u>5</u> × 9 =	45
<u>6</u> × 9 =	54
<u>7</u> × 9 =	63
<u>8</u> × 9 =	■
<u>9</u> × 9 =	■
<u>10</u> × 9 =	■

Learn About It

This table shows most of the products of the 9s facts. The next fact in the table is $8 \times 9 = ■$. What is 8×9?

Multiply. $8 \times 9 = ■$ or $\begin{array}{r} 9 \\ \times 8 \\ \hline ■ \end{array}$

▶ **You can use patterns to find 9s facts.**

- Look at each row in the table. Notice that the tens digit of the product is always 1 less than the underlined factor.

  $\underline{7} \times 9 = 63$

- Look at each product in the table. Notice that the sum of the digits is always 9.

  $7 \times 9 = \boxed{63} \rightarrow 6 + 3 = 9$

▶ **Now use these patterns to find 8×9.**

$8 \times 9 = \underline{7}\_$

$8 - 1 = 7$

Think
The tens digit will be 1 less than the factor you are multiplying by 9.

$8 \times 9 = \underline{7}\,\underline{2}$

$7 + 2 = 9$

Think
The sum of the digits in the product will be 9.

Solution: $8 \times 9 = 72$

Guided Practice

Multiply.

1. $\begin{array}{r} 9 \\ \times 3 \\ \hline \end{array}$

2. $\begin{array}{r} 7 \\ \times 9 \\ \hline \end{array}$

3. $\begin{array}{r} 9 \\ \times 2 \\ \hline \end{array}$

4. $\begin{array}{r} 5 \\ \times 9 \\ \hline \end{array}$

5. 4×9

6. 1×9

7. 6×9

8. 10×9

Ask Yourself
- How can I use patterns to find the product?

Explain Your Thinking ▶ How can you use patterns to help you find 9×9?

Practice and Problem Solving

Multiply.

9. $\begin{array}{r} 9 \\ \times 2 \\ \hline \end{array}$
10. $\begin{array}{r} 9 \\ \times 6 \\ \hline \end{array}$
11. $\begin{array}{r} 4 \\ \times 9 \\ \hline \end{array}$
12. $\begin{array}{r} 9 \\ \times 0 \\ \hline \end{array}$
13. $\begin{array}{r} 1 \\ \times 9 \\ \hline \end{array}$
14. $\begin{array}{r} 9 \\ \times 5 \\ \hline \end{array}$

15. $\begin{array}{r} 3 \\ \times 9 \\ \hline \end{array}$
16. $\begin{array}{r} 9 \\ \times 8 \\ \hline \end{array}$
17. $\begin{array}{r} 9 \\ \times 7 \\ \hline \end{array}$
18. $\begin{array}{r} 10 \\ \times 9 \\ \hline \end{array}$
19. $\begin{array}{r} 9 \\ \times 9 \\ \hline \end{array}$
20. $\begin{array}{r} 6 \\ \times 9 \\ \hline \end{array}$

21. 4×9
22. 10×9
23. 2×9
24. 9×3
25. 5×9

✗ Algebra • Equations Find each missing number.

26. $3 \times 5 = \blacksquare \times 3$
27. $6 \times \blacksquare = 8 \times 3$
28. $8 \times 5 = 10 \times \blacksquare$

29. $9 \times 1 = \blacksquare \times 3$
30. $2 \times \blacksquare = 5 \times 4$
31. $7 \times 4 = 4 \times \blacksquare$

Solve.

32. Mr. Miller bought 9 books about the rainforest for each of 3 classrooms. How many rainforest books did he buy?

33. **Estimate** Mario bought a jaguar poster for $6.97. Mia bought a macaw poster for $3.85. About how much more did Mario spend?

34. Elia used 9 sheets of paper for a book report on the rainforest. She used twice as many for an art project. What is the total number of sheets Elia used?

Mixed Review and Test Prep

Open Response

Multiply. (Ch. 8, Lessons 5, 8)

35. 6×0
36. 0×10

37. 5×7
38. 5×4

39. 8×1
40. 1×3

Multiple Choice

41. At Mr. Ramirez's party there are 7 full tables. Each table seats 9 people. How many people are at the party? (Ch. 9, Lesson 6)

   A 16   **B** 54   **c** 63   **D** 72

Fast Facts Practice

Find each product as quickly as you can!

1.   6
    × 5

2.   9
    × 2

3.   4
    × 7

4. 10
    × 8

5.   4
    × 6

6.   5
    × 7

7.   1
    × 7

8.   2
    × 6

9.   4
    × 5

10.   6
    × 8

11.   9
    × 7

12.   0
    × 6

13.   3
    × 1

14.   8
    × 8

15.   9
    × 4

16.   4
    × 0

17.   2
    × 7

18.   1
    × 9

19.   6
    × 6

20.   5
    × 3

21.   9
    × 6

22.   8
    × 3

23.   7
    × 8

24.   3
    × 3

25.   6
    × 0

26.   1
    × 8

27.   5
    × 9

28.   5
    × 8

29.   0
    × 1

30.   8
    × 6

31. 4×2
32. 0×3
33. 8×1
34. 3×6
35. 10×9

36. 10×3
37. 5×5
38. 9×8
39. 6×8
40. 5×0

41. 4×7
42. 6×4
43. 3×9
44. 10×5
45. 1×6

46. 8×3
47. 7×6
48. 7×7
49. 6×9
50. 9×9

Algebra • Functions Copy and complete each table. Find the rule for each.

51.

number of marker boxes	1	2	3	4	5	6	7	8	9	10
number of markers	6	12	■	24	■	■	■	■	■	■

52.

number of crayon boxes	1	2	3	4	5	6	7	8	9	10
number of crayons	8	16	■	32	■	■	■	■	■	■

Coloring Counts

2 Players

What You'll Need • 2 sets of index cards labeled 2 to 9
• 2 hundred charts (Learning Tool 16 or Workmat 2)

How to Play

1 Shuffle the cards and place them facedown in a pile. Each player takes a hundred chart and crayon.

2 The first player picks the top card from the pile. The player can use the number picked in one of these ways.

- Color all numbers on the chart that have the number as a factor.

- Color all numbers on the chart that have the number in the ones place.

- Color all numbers on the chart that have the number in the tens place.

3 Players take turns repeating Step 2 until all of the cards have been used. The player with more squares colored at the end of the game wins!

Audio Tutor 1/29 Listen and Understand

Patterns on a Multiplication Table

Objective Find patterns using a multiplication table.

Vocabulary
multiple
square number

Materials
grid paper or
Learning Tool 15

Work Together

You can use a multiplication table to see different patterns.

STEP 1
Copy and complete the multiplication table on the right. Use patterns to fill in the products for 11 and 12.

×	0	1	2	3	4	5	6	7	8	9	10	11	12
0	0	0	0	0	0	0	0	0	0	0			
1	0	1	2	3	4	5	6	7	8	9	10		
2	0	2	4	6	8	10	12	14	16	18	20		
3	0	3	6	9	12	15	18	21	24	27	30		
4	0	4	8	12	16	20	24	28	32	36	40		
5	0	5	10	15	20	25	30	35	40	45	50		
6	0	6	12	18	24	30	36	42	48	54	60		
7	0	7	14	21	28	35	42	49	56	63	70		
8	0	8	16	24	32	40	48	56	64	72	80		
9	0	9	18	27	36	45	54	63	72	81	90		
10	0	10	20	30	40	50	60	70	80	90	100		
11													
12													

STEP 2
Look at the row for 2. All numbers in this row are multiples of 2.

A **multiple** of 2 is any product that has 2 as a factor.

0, 2, 4, 6, 8, and so on are multiples of 2.

The factors of 12 are 1, 2, 3, 4, 6, and 12, because 1 × 12 = 12, 2 × 6 = 12, and 3 × 4 = 12.

STEP 3
List the multiples of 2. Then list the multiples of 4 shown in the row for 4. Compare the numbers in both lists.

• What pattern can you find?

Now repeat this for the multiples of 3 and 6.

• What other pairs of numbers form a similar pattern?

Look at the shaded products in the table shown at the right. Then look at their factors.

- What can you say about the factors that form each of these products?

When the two factors of a product are the same, the product is a **square number.** 1, 4, 9, 16, and so on are square numbers. Zero is not a square number.

×	0	1	2	3	4	5
0	0	0	0	0	0	0
1	0	1	2	3	4	5
2	0	2	4	6	8	10
3	0	3	6	9	12	15
4	0	4	8	12	16	20
5	0	5	10	15	20	25

- Shade the square numbers on your table.

- How could you find some other square numbers that are not in the table?

On Your Own

Write *true* or *false* for each statement.
Give an example to support each answer.

1. Any multiple of 4 is also a multiple of 2.

2. If a number is odd, all of its multiples will be odd.

3. If a number is even, all of its multiples will be even.

Write whether each array shows a square number.
If not, find the fewest squares that could be added
to make it show a square number.

4.

5.

6.

Talk About It • Write About It

You learned that you can use a multiplication table to find patterns.

7. How can you use a multiplication table to show that you can multiply factors in any order?

8. In the table, why is the number above a square number the same as the number to the left of that square number?

Multiply Three Numbers

Objective Learn to group factors in any order to find the product of 3 or more numbers.

Learn About It

Mr. Levin's students are tasting foods grown in rainforests. He put 5 pieces of mango on each plate and put 2 plates on each table. There are 3 tables. How many pieces of mango are there?

$$5 \times 2 \times 3 = \blacksquare$$

pieces of mango   number of plates   number of tables

Associative Property of Multiplication

The way factors are grouped does not change the product.

▶ **You can multiply 5 × 2 first.**

$(5 \times 2) \times 3 = \blacksquare$
$10 \times 3 = 30$

▶ **You can multiply 2 × 3 first.**

$5 \times (2 \times 3) = \blacksquare$
$5 \times 6 = 30$

No matter which two factors are multiplied first, the product will be the same.

> **Remember**
> The parentheses ( ) tell you which factors to multiply first.

Solution: There are 30 pieces of mango.

Guided Practice

Find each product. Multiply factors in parentheses first.

1. $6 \times (1 \times 7) = \blacksquare$
$(6 \times 1) \times 7 = \blacksquare$

2. $3 \times (2 \times 4) = \blacksquare$
$(3 \times 2) \times 4 = \blacksquare$

Ask Yourself
- Which two numbers will I multiply first?

Explain Your Thinking ▶ In which order would you multiply $3 \times 2 \times 6$? Explain why.

Find each product. Multiply factors in parentheses first.

3. $(3 \times 1) \times 2 = $ ■

4. $4 \times (9 \times 0) = $ ■

5. $3 \times (3 \times 2) = $ ■

6. $(5 \times 2) \times 3 = $ ■

7. $(9 \times 1) \times 8 = $ ■

8. $(0 \times 7) \times 4 = $ ■

✗ Algebra • Properties Use the Associative Property
to find each missing factor.

9. $1 \times (2 \times $ ■ $) = 10$

10. $(1 \times $ ■ $) \times 3 = 9$

11. $(3 \times $ ■ $) \times 2 = 12$

12. $9 \times ($ ■ $ \times 2) = 36$

13. $7 \times ($ ■ $ \times 5) = 35$

14. $($ ■ $ \times 2) \times 6 = 48$

Solve.

15. If $3 \times 9 \times 4 = 108$,
then what is $9 \times 4 \times 3$?

16. If $4 \times 7 \times 8 = 224$
then what is $8 \times 4 \times 7$?

📊 Data Use the list at the right to answer Problems 17–18.

17. The third grade is having rainforest parties
in 3 different classrooms. How many mango
halves are needed for all of the parties?

18. How many bags of nuts are needed for all
3 parties?

19. You Decide You need 60 paper plates
for the parties. Plates come in bags of
15 and bags of 20. How many of each
size bag will you buy? Explain.

Food Needed for
Each Party

4 mango halves

2 pineapples

2 bags of cashew nuts

1 bag of brazil nuts

Mixed Review and Test Prep ✓

**Write each amount using a dollar sign
and a decimal point.** (Ch. 3, Lesson 2)

20.

21. 7 quarters, 1 dime, 3 nickels,
and 4 pennies

22. There are 3 tables with
3 students at each table. Each
student has 2 books. Write a
number sentence to show how
to find the total number of
books. (Ch. 9, Lesson 8)

Problem-Solving Decision
Multistep Problems

Objective Learn to solve problems that have more than one step.

Jaguar

Bornean Horned Frog

White-Bellied Parrot

Black Lemur

Rosa's uncle studies the rainforest. Every week he sends Rosa post cards of animals that live in the rainforest.

Problem Rosa has 4 post cards of fish. She has 8 times as many post cards of birds. How many post cards of fish and birds does she have?

Decide what to do. Then do each step in order.

STEP 1 Find the number of bird post cards.

$$\begin{array}{r} 4 \leftarrow \text{fish post cards} \\ \times\ 8 \\ \hline 32 \leftarrow \text{bird post cards} \end{array}$$

Rosa has 32 bird post cards.

STEP 2 Add the number of bird post cards and the number of fish post cards.

$$\begin{array}{r} 32 \leftarrow \text{bird post cards} \\ +\ 4 \leftarrow \text{fish post cards} \\ \hline 36 \leftarrow \text{total number of post cards} \end{array}$$

Rosa has 36 post cards.

Solution: Rosa has a total of 36 post cards.

Try These

1. Rosa received 2 post cards of snakes and 2 post cards of monkeys each month for 3 months. How many post cards is that?

2. Maria saw 7 butterflies. Andrew saw 3 times as many butterflies as Maria. What is the total number of butterflies the two friends saw?

3. The library has 2 videos about the rainforest. It has 8 times as many books about the rainforest. How many more books than videos about the rainforest does the library have?

4. At a Save the Rainforest fundraiser, Mrs. Brown's class sold 9 pencils. The class sold 3 times as many erasers. How many more erasers than pencils did the class sell?

Use the price list at the right to answer Problems 5–7.

5. Mike's dad bought 4 key chains and 3 packs of postcards. How much did Mike's dad spend?

6. Yuri had $20 to spend at the fundraiser. He bought 2 packs of pencils and 5 erasers. How much change did Yuri get after his purchase?

7. Each pack of pencils contains 8 pencils. Sari bought 3 packs. She gave away 10 pencils to her friends. How many pencils does Sari have left?

Rainforest Fundraiser	
Item	**Costs**
Pack of pencils	$4
Pack postcards	$2
Key chains	$5
Erasers	$1

Reading Connection
Haiku Poetry

Haiku is a Japanese form of poetry. Haiku poems are 3 lines long.

The first line has 5 syllables, the second line has 7 syllables, and the third line has 5 syllables. The number of syllables in these lines is always the same.

Suppose you and 5 of your classmates each wrote a haiku.

1. How many syllables would be in one haiku?

2. Explain how you could find the number of syllables in all of the haiku.

old and quiet pond ← 5 syllables
suddenly a frog plops in— ← 7 syllables
a deep water sound ← 5 syllables

Matsuo Basho was a famous Japanese poet who lived from 1644–1694. He wrote the haiku above.

Chapter Review/Test

VOCABULARY

Choose the best term to complete each sentence.

Vocabulary

array

factors

product

multiples

1. The answer to a multiplication problem is called the ____.

2. An ____ shows objects arranged in rows and columns.

3. The numbers 6, 9, 12, and 15 are all ____ of 3.

CONCEPTS AND SKILLS

Multiply. (Lessons 1–7, pp. 232–251)

4. $\begin{array}{r} 4 \\ \times\ 9 \\ \hline \end{array}$
5. $\begin{array}{r} 0 \\ \times\ 6 \\ \hline \end{array}$
6. $\begin{array}{r} 4 \\ \times\ 4 \\ \hline \end{array}$
7. $\begin{array}{r} 8 \\ \times\ 2 \\ \hline \end{array}$
8. $\begin{array}{r} 8 \\ \times\ 0 \\ \hline \end{array}$
9. $\begin{array}{r} 2 \\ \times\ 9 \\ \hline \end{array}$

10. $\begin{array}{r} 1 \\ \times\ 6 \\ \hline \end{array}$
11. $\begin{array}{r} 8 \\ \times\ 5 \\ \hline \end{array}$
12. $\begin{array}{r} 7 \\ \times\ 4 \\ \hline \end{array}$
13. $\begin{array}{r} 3 \\ \times\ 6 \\ \hline \end{array}$
14. $\begin{array}{r} 9 \\ \times\ 9 \\ \hline \end{array}$
15. $\begin{array}{r} 5 \\ \times\ 7 \\ \hline \end{array}$

16. 6×9
17. 5×3
18. 8×4

Find each product. (Lesson 8, pp. 252–253)

19. $(1 \times 8) \times 5 = \blacksquare$
20. $7 \times (2 \times 3) = \blacksquare$
21. $4 \times (4 \times 0) = \blacksquare$

22. $3 \times (4 \times 2) = \blacksquare$
23. $(6 \times 1) \times 7 = \blacksquare$
24. $(2 \times 1) \times 7 = \blacksquare$

PROBLEM SOLVING

Solve. (Lesson 9, pp. 254–255)

25. Carla put 10 oatmeal cookies on a plate. Then she put twice as many peanut butter cookies on the plate. How many cookies are on the plate?

 Write About It

Show You Understand

Craig says he can draw 4 different arrays to show a product of 25. Is he correct? Explain.

Extra Practice

Set A (Lesson 2, pp. 234–235)

Multiply.

1. 3×1
2. 2×3
3. 9×3
4. 3×10
5. 5×3
6. 3×8

Set B (Lesson 3, pp. 236–238)

Find each product.

1. 6×7
2. 5×6
3. 6×8
4. 10×6
5. 9×6

Set C (Lesson 4, pp. 240–241)

Multiply.

1. 6×7
2. 7×8
3. 3×7
4. 7×7
5. 7×9
6. 5×7

Set D (Lesson 5, pp. 242–244)

Find each product.

1. 8×9
2. 0×8
3. 7×8
4. 1×8
5. 8×3

Set E (Lesson 6, pp. 246–247)

Multiply.

1. 9×1
2. 5×9
3. 8×9
4. 10×9
5. 9×3
6. 7×9

Set F (Lesson 8, pp. 252–253)

Multiply.

1. $(2 \times 3) \times 5$
2. $(6 \times 1) \times 3$
3. $7 \times (2 \times 3)$
4. $8 \times (3 \times 2)$
5. $0 \times (9 \times 1)$
6. $(2 \times 5) \times 6$

CHAPTER 10

Division Concepts

INVESTIGATION

Using Data

Deana and her mom go to the store to buy some pet care products for her dog. They have $10 to spend. What can they buy?

Polly's Pet Products

Item	Price
Grooming Brush	$4
Doggy Shears	$3
Shampoo	$2
Comb	$1

Use What You Know

Use this page to review and remember
what you need to know for this chapter.

VOCABULARY

Choose the best term to complete each sentence.

1. In the number sentence $2 \times 4 = 8$, 2 is a ____.

2. You can draw an ____ to find a product.

3. You can use repeated addition to help you ____.

Vocabulary

array

factor

multiply

product

CONCEPTS AND SKILLS

Write two multiplication sentences for each array.

4.

5.

6.

Multiply.

7.   7
   $\times\ 2$

8.   8
   $\times\ 5$

9.   3
   $\times\ 5$

10. 10
   $\times\ 2$

11.   6
   $\times\ 2$

12.   6
   $\times\ 7$

13.   8
   $\times\ 3$

14. 10
   $\times\ 5$

15.   9
   $\times\ 2$

16.   7
   $\times\ 10$

17. 5×7

18. 3×9

19. 8×7

 Write About It

20. Why can't you write a multiplication
    sentence for this picture?

Facts Practice, See page 669.

Audio Tutor 1/30 Listen and Understand

The Meaning of Division

Objective Use models to explore two ways to think about division.

Vocabulary

equal groups

division

divide

Work Together

When you divide you separate items into **equal groups**.

Work with a partner to model two different ways to think about **division**.

Materials
For each pair:
30 counters

STEP 1

You can **divide** to find the number to put into each group.

Suppose you have 18 counters and want to make 6 equal groups.

Draw 6 circles on a sheet of paper.

Share 18 counters equally among them.

- How many groups did you make?

- How many counters are in each group?

$$18 \div 6 = 3$$

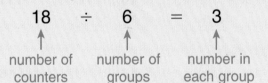

| number of counters | number of groups | number in each group |

STEP 2

You also divide to find the number of equal groups.

Suppose you have 18 counters and want to put them into groups of 6.

Put 18 counters into groups of 6.

- How many counters are in each group?

- How many groups did you make?

$$18 \div 6 = 3$$

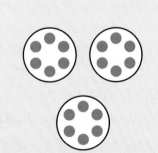

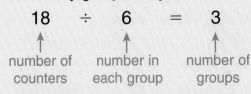

| number of counters | number in each group | number of groups |

Use counters to find the number in each equal group.
Then complete each division sentence.

	Number of Counters	Number of Equal Groups	Number in Each Group	Division Sentence
1.	6	2	■	$6 \div 2 = $ ■
2.	18	3	■	$18 \div 3 = $ ■
3.	16	4	■	$16 \div 4 = $ ■

Use counters to find the number of equal groups.
Then complete each division sentence.

	Number of Counters	Number of Equal Groups	Number in Each Group	Division Sentence
4.	9	■	3	$9 \div 3 = $ ■
5.	14	■	2	$14 \div 2 = $ ■
6.	30	■	6	$30 \div 6 = $ ■

Write a division sentence to describe each picture.

7.   8.

9.   10.

Talk About It • Write About It

You have explored two ways to think about division.

11. Describe two ways to divide 8 objects into equal groups.

12. Ella wants to share 15 counters by dividing them into equal groups. She puts more than one counter in each group. What is the greatest number of equal groups Ella can make if she uses all the counters?

Audio Tutor 1/31 Listen and Understand

Model Division as Repeated Subtraction

Objective Use repeated subtraction to find quotients.

Learn About It

Students have 15 carrots to feed 5 rabbits. They want to feed the same number of carrots to each rabbit. How many carrots will each rabbit get?

Find 15 ÷ 5.

You can use repeated subtraction to find a quotient.

Skip count backward on a number line to show repeated subtraction.

- Start at 15.
- Count back by 5s until you reach 0.
- Count the number of times you subtracted.

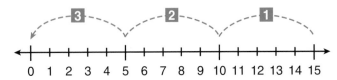

You subtracted 5 three times. There are 3 carrots in each group.

So 15 ÷ 5 = 3. ← quotient

Solution: Each rabbit will get 3 carrots.

Guided Practice

Use repeated subtraction to find each quotient.

1.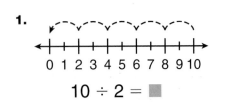

   10 ÷ 2 = ■

2.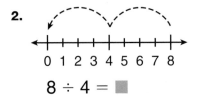

   8 ÷ 4 = ■

Ask Yourself
- What number am I subtracting?
- Where do I start?
- How many times did I subtract?

Explain Your Thinking ▶ How is using a number line to help you divide like using a number line to help you multiply? How is it different?

Extra Help at **eduplace.com/map**

Use repeated subtraction to find each quotient.

3.
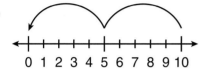

$$8 \div 2 = \blacksquare$$

4.
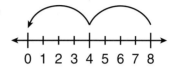

$$12 \div 3 = \blacksquare$$

Match each number line with the correct division sentence. Solve.

5.
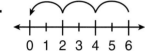

6.

7.

8.
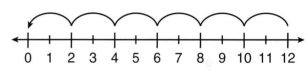

a. $6 \div 2 = \blacksquare$ **b.** $10 \div 5 = \blacksquare$ **c.** $12 \div 2 = \blacksquare$ **d.** $8 \div 4 = \blacksquare$

9. Denise has 4 pet rabbits. If she has an equal number of lop rabbits and angora rabbits, how many angora rabbits does she have?

10. Four rabbits share some carrots equally. If each rabbit has 6 carrots, how many carrots are there?

11. **Represent** Draw a picture to show $9 \div 3$. Then draw a number line to show $9 \div 3$. Describe how each drawing shows $9 \div 3$.

Mixed Review and Test Prep

Open Response

Write the name of each figure. (Grade 2)

12.

13.

14.

15.

Multiple Choice

16. Which division sentence does the number line show?

(Ch. 10, Lesson 2)

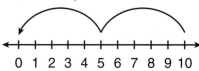

A $10 \div 2 = 5$ C $10 \div 5 = 2$

B $10 \div 10 = 1$ D $15 \div 5 = 3$

Algebra

Relate Multiplication and Division

Objective Use arrays to relate multiplication and division.

Vocabulary
dividend
divisor
quotient

Learn About It

The 12 pictures of kittens shown on the right form an array.

You can use arrays to help you understand how multiplication and division are related.

Multiply to find the number of pictures in all.

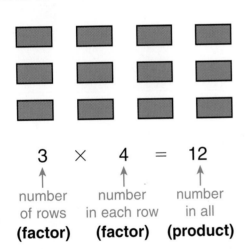

$$3 \times 4 = 12$$

number of rows **(factor)**   number in each row **(factor)**   number in all **(product)**

Divide to find the number of pictures in each row.

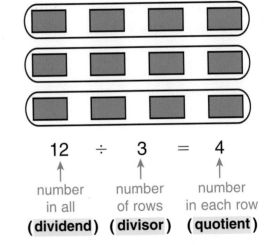

$$12 \div 3 = 4$$

number in all **(dividend)**   number of rows **(divisor)**   number in each row **(quotient)**

▶ Multiplication and division are opposite operations.

Look at these arrays of 16 counters.

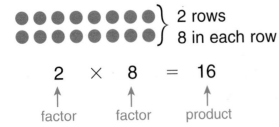

2 rows
8 in each row

$$2 \times 8 = 16$$

factor   factor   product

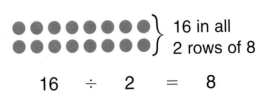

16 in all
2 rows of 8

$$16 \div 2 = 8$$

dividend   divisor   quotient

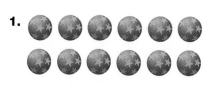

Guided Practice

Use the array to complete each number sentence.

1.

■ × 6 = 12

■ ÷ 2 = 6

2.

3 × ■ = 15

15 ÷ ■ = 5

Ask Yourself

- How many rows are there?
- How many are in each row?
- How many are there in all?

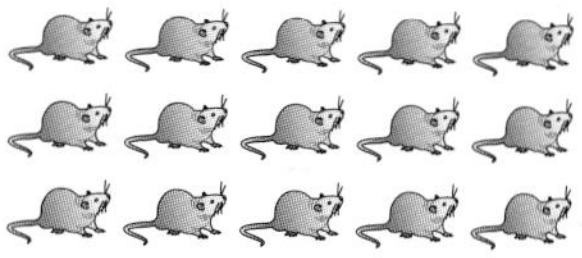

Explain Your Thinking ▶ Look at each pair of number sentences above. Why are the product and the dividend the same in each pair?

Practice and Problem Solving

Use the array to complete each number sentence.

3.

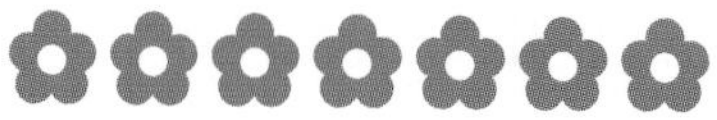

1 × ■ = 7

7 ÷ ■ = 7

4.

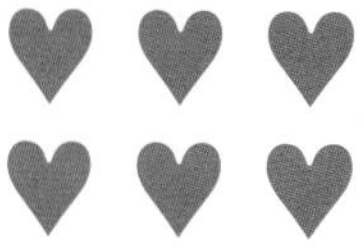

■ × 3 = 6

■ ÷ 2 = 3

5.

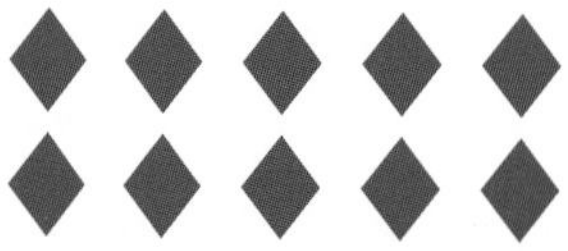

■ × 5 = 10

■ ÷ 2 = 5

Draw an array for each multiplication sentence. Then write a related division sentence.

6. 3 × 2 = 6 **7.** 4 × 3 = 12 **8.** 1 × 7 = 7 **9.** 2 × 7 = 14

10. 2 × 10 = 20 **11.** 3 × 9 = 27 **12.** 3 × 8 = 24 **13.** 4 × 9 = 36

Mixed Review and Test Prep

Open Response

Tell how each number is used. Write *position, count,* or *measure*.
(Ch. 1, Lesson 1)

14. sixth letter **15.** 12 feet

16. 24 pencils **17.** third row

18. How many different rectangular arrays can you make with 12 counters? (Ch. 10, Lesson 3)

Explain how you got your answer.

Extra Practice See page 283, Set B.

Audio Tutor 1/32 Listen and Understand

Divide by 2

Objective Use different ways to divide by 2.

Learn About It

The pet store has 12 gerbils. If Kim puts 2 gerbils in each cage, how many cages will she need?

$$12 \div 2 = 6 \quad \text{or} \quad 2\overline{)12}$$

6 ← quotient

2)12 ← dividend

↑ dividend   ↑ divisor   ↑ quotient   ↑ divisor

Different Ways to Find 12 ÷ 2

Way 1 Use repeated subtraction.

• Start at 12.

• Count back by 2s to 0.

• Count the number of 2s you subtracted.   You subtracted 2 six times.   So 12 ÷ 2 = 6.

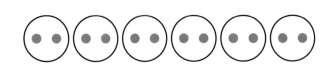

0 1 2 3 4 5 6 7 8 9 10 11 12

Way 2 Make equal groups.

• Use 12 counters.

• Put 2 counters in each group.

• Count the number of equal groups.   There are 6 groups of 2.   So 12 ÷ 2 = 6.

Way 3 Use a related multiplication fact.

12 ÷ 2 = ■   Think 2 × ■ = 12   So 12 ÷ 2 = 6.
2 × 6 = 12

Solution: Kim will need 6 cages.

Guided Practice

Use the multiplication fact to find each quotient.

1. 2 × 4 = 8
   8 ÷ 2 = ■

2. 2 × 5 = 10
   10 ÷ 2 = ■

Ask Yourself

• How does a multiplication fact help me find a quotient?

Explain Your Thinking ▶ How can a number line help you find 4 ÷ 2?

Use the picture to find each quotient.

3.

0 1 2 3 4 5 6

$6 \div 2$

4.

$14 \div 2$

5.

$4 \div 2$

Use the multiplication fact to find each quotient.

6. $1 \times 2 = 2$
   $2 \div 2 = \blacksquare$

7. $5 \times 2 = 10$
   $10 \div 2 = \blacksquare$

8. $2 \times 2 = 4$
   $4 \div 2 = \blacksquare$

9. $7 \times 2 = 14$
   $14 \div 2 = \blacksquare$

10. $6 \times 2 = 12$
    $12 \div 2 = \blacksquare$

11. $8 \times 2 = 16$
    $16 \div 2 = \blacksquare$

12. $3 \times 2 = 6$
    $6 \div 2 = \blacksquare$

13. $9 \times 2 = 18$
    $18 \div 2 = \blacksquare$

Divide.

14. $2\overline{)18}$

15. $2\overline{)2}$

16. $2\overline{)12}$

17. $2\overline{)4}$

18. $2\overline{)10}$

19. $2\overline{)14}$

20. $2\overline{)8}$

21. $2\overline{)16}$

22. $2\overline{)20}$

23. $2\overline{)6}$

Solve.

24. There are 8 hamsters. If Kyle feeds 2 pieces of lettuce to each hamster, how many pieces of lettuce will he need?

25. A hamster cage weighs 6 pounds. A lizard cage weighs 2 times as much as the hamster cage. Does the lizard cage weigh more or less than 10 pounds? Explain your reasoning.

Open Response

Find the missing numbers.

(Ch. 4, Lesson 1)

26. $5 + (6 + 2) = (5 + \blacksquare) + 2$

27. $(1 + 7) + 6 = 1 + (7 + \blacksquare)$

28. $(8 + \blacksquare) + 4 = 8 + (3 + 4)$

Multiple Choice

29. Tickets to the fair cost $2 each. How many tickets can Ron buy with $10? (Ch. 10, Lesson 4)

A 5

C 8

B 12

D 20

Extra Practice See page 283, Set C.

Problem-Solving Decision
Choose the Operation

Objective Decide what operations to use to solve problems.

Sometimes you need to decide what operation to use to solve a problem.

The class field trip to a petting zoo included a picnic lunch.

Sometimes you add to find the total.

In a pen are 17 goats and 26 sheep. How many animals are in the pen?

$$\begin{array}{r} 17 \leftarrow \text{goats} \\ + 26 \leftarrow \text{sheep} \\ \hline 43 \leftarrow \text{total number of animals} \end{array}$$

Solution: 43 animals are in the pen.

You subtract to find the difference.

There are 13 tuna and 17 ham sandwiches. How many more ham sandwiches are there?

$$\begin{array}{r} 17 \leftarrow \text{ham sandwiches} \\ - 13 \leftarrow \text{tuna sandwiches} \\ \hline 4 \leftarrow \text{more ham sandwiches} \end{array}$$

Solution: There are 4 more ham sandwiches.

Sometimes you multiply to find the total.

Five apple pies are each cut into 6 slices. How many slices are there?

$$\begin{array}{r} 6 \leftarrow \text{slices in 1 pie} \\ \times 5 \leftarrow \text{pies} \\ \hline 30 \leftarrow \text{total number of slices} \end{array}$$

Solution: There are 30 slices of pie.

You divide to find equal groups.

Five students can sit at each picnic table. How many tables do 30 students need?

$$30 \div 5 = 6$$

number of students   number at each table   number of tables

Solution: They need 6 tables.

Try These

Solve. Tell which operation you used.

1. The teacher brought 4 bags of oranges. Each bag contained 10 oranges. How many oranges were there?

2. Two students at a time can pet the lambs. If there are 12 students waiting, how many groups of 2 are waiting?

3. In a pen are 18 cows and 22 donkeys. How many more donkeys than cows are there?

4. Each cow drinks 28 gallons of water a day. How many gallons do 2 cows drink?

Social Studies Connection
Ancient Brahmi Numerals

Brahmi (BRAH mee) is an ancient Indian writing system that is thousands of years old.

- In Brahmi, the number sentence 8 ÷ 2 = 4 would look like this:

- The problem 3 ÷ 3 = 1 might look like this in Brahmi:

1. Write three division sentences using 1–10 in our number system. Then write the same sentences using Brahmi numbers.

2. **Create and Solve** Make up other division problems of your own using only the Brahmi numbers. Give them to a classmate to solve.

WEEKLY ⓌⓇ READER   eduplace.com/map

Check your understanding of Lessons 1–5.

Write a related division sentence. (Lessons 1–3)

1. 5 × 2 = 10   **2.** 3 × 7 = 21   **3.** 4 × 8 = 32   **4.** 3 × 5 = 15

Divide. (Lesson 4)

5. 2)‾14   **6.** 2)‾8   **7.** 2)‾18   **8.** 2)‾12

Solve. Tell which operation you used. (Lesson 5)

9. The library has 8 computers. If 4 students are at each computer, how many students are at the computers?

10. Nell, Kate, and Jerry share 15 seashells equally. How many seashells does each friend have?

Divide by 5

Objective Use different ways to divide by 5.

Learn About It

There are 20 puppy treats for the puppies in a training class. If each puppy gets 5 treats, how many puppies are there in the class?

Divide. $20 \div 5 = n$ or $5\overline{)20}$

Different Ways to Find 20 ÷ 5

Way ❶ Use repeated subtraction.

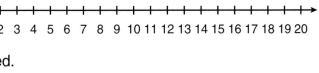

- Start at 20.
- Count back by 5s to 0.
- Count the number of 5s you subtracted.
- You subtracted 5 four times. So $20 \div 5 = 4$.

Way ❷ Make equal groups.

- Use 20 counters.
- Put 5 counters in each group.
- Count the number of equal groups
- There are 4 groups of 5. So $20 \div 5 = 4$.

Solution: There are 4 puppies in the training class.

Guided Practice

Find each quotient.

1.

    $10 \div 5 = \blacksquare$

2.

    $15 \div 5 = \blacksquare$

Ask Yourself

- How many equal groups can I make?
- What multiplication fact can help me?

Explain Your Thinking ▶ How does knowing that $5 \times 6 = 30$ help you find $30 \div 5$?

Use the array to help you find the quotient.

3.

$25 \div 5 = \blacksquare$

4.

$15 \div 5 = \blacksquare$

5.

$30 \div 5 = \blacksquare$

Divide.

6. $5\overline{)10}$

7. $2\overline{)4}$

8. $5\overline{)5}$

9. $5\overline{)15}$

10. $5\overline{)30}$

11. $5\overline{)25}$

12. $2\overline{)10}$

13. $5\overline{)40}$

14. $5\overline{)20}$

15. $2\overline{)8}$

16. $2\overline{)14}$

17. $5\overline{)35}$

18. $2\overline{)18}$

19. $2\overline{)16}$

20. $5\overline{)45}$

21. $35 \div 5$

22. $45 \div 5$

23. $15 \div 5$

24. $14 \div 2$

25. $30 \div 5$

Solve.

26. There are 30 dogs competing in a dog show. Each trainer takes care of 5 dogs. How many trainers take care of the 30 dogs?

27. Three dogs are lined up for the show. The Bulldog is behind the Chow and in front of the Poodle. How are the dogs lined up?

28. Jo trains her dog for 10 minutes twice a day. How much time does she spend training in 5 days?

 29. **Write About It** Can you divide 27 into equal groups of 5? Explain why or why not.

Mixed Review and Test Prep

Open Response

Name each figure. (Grade 2)

30.

31.

32.

33.

34. There are 40 students who want to play basketball. If 5 players are on a team, how many teams are there? Explain how you got your answer. (Ch. 10, Lesson 6)

Audio Tutor 1/33 Listen and Understand

Divide by 10

Objective Use different ways to divide by 10.

Vocabulary
fact

Learn About It

There are 40 horses at Sunset Horse Farm. There are 10 horse stalls in each stable. How many stables are there at Sunset Horse Farm?

Divide. $40 \div 10 = $ ▪ or $10\overline{)40}$

Different Ways to Find $40 \div 10$

Way ❶ Use repeated subtraction.

- Start at 40. Count back by 10s to 0.
- Count the number of 10s you subtracted.

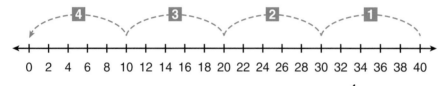

You subtracted four 10s. So $40 \div 10 = 4$ or $10\overline{)40}$.

Way ❷ Use a related multiplication fact.

$40 \div 10 = $ ▪   Think: $10 \times $ ▪ $= 40$ So $40 \div 10 = 4.$
 $10 \times 4 = 40$

Solution: There are 4 stables at Sunset Horse Farm.

Guided Practice

Find each quotient.

1. $10 \div 10$ 　　2. $30 \div 10$ 　　3. $20 \div 10$

4. $10\overline{)60}$ 　　5. $10\overline{)100}$ 　　6. $10\overline{)90}$

Ask Yourself
- How many equal groups can I make?
- What multiplication fact can help me?

Explain Your Thinking ▶ How can thinking of 60 as 6 tens help you find $60 \div 10$?

Fnd each quotient.

7. $10\overline{)100}$ 　　8. $10\overline{)30}$ 　　9. $10\overline{)10}$ 　　10. $10\overline{)50}$ 　　11. $10\overline{)80}$

12. $10\overline{)20}$ 　　13. $10\overline{)40}$ 　　14. $10\overline{)60}$ 　　15. $10\overline{)90}$ 　　16. $10\overline{)70}$

17. $100 \div 10$ 　18. $50 \div 10$ 　19. $90 \div 10$ 　20. $80 \div 10$ 　21. $30 \div 10$

22. $10 \div 10$ 　23. $70 \div 10$ 　24. $40 \div 10$ 　25. $20 \div 10$ 　26. $60 \div 10$

𝒳 Algebra • Equations Find each missing number.

27. $50 \div \blacksquare = 5$ 　28. $\blacksquare \div 5 = 7$ 　　29. $5 \times \blacksquare = 15$ 　30. $\blacksquare \times 4 = 40$

31. $12 = \blacksquare \times 6$ 　32. $2 = 10 \div \blacksquare$ 　33. $\blacksquare \times 8 = 56$ 　34. $9 = 45 \div \blacksquare$

📊 Data Use the sign for Problems 35–37.

35. Jesse is selling horse treats at the farm today. Larisa has 30¢ to spend. How many apples can she buy?

36. Irina wants to buy 6 biscuits, 3 carrots, and 3 apples. How much money does she need?

37. **Analyze** Fong spent exactly 21¢ on treats for his favorite horse. He bought the greatest number of treats he could. What did he buy?

Treats for Your Favorite Horse
Apple 10¢
Carrot 5¢
Biscuit 2¢

Mixed Review and Test Prep ✓

Open Response

Multiply. (Ch. 9, Lessons 3–7)

38. 7×4 　　39. 8×6 　　40. 9×9

41. 3×9 　　42. 5×5 　　43. 9×2

44. 8×7 　　45. 9×4 　　46. 9×1

Multiple Choice

47. Ken uses 10 beads for each key chain. How many key chains can he make with 70 beads?

(Ch. 10, Lesson 7)

A 7 　**B** 60 　**C** 8 　**D** 80

Problem-Solving Strategy

Write a Number Sentence

Objective Write a number sentence to solve a problem.

Problem Pete's Pet Palace has 5 cages of canaries. Each cage has the same number of canaries. If there are 35 canaries, how many canaries are in each cage?

'Pete's Pet Palace'

 **UNDERSTAND**

This is what you know.

- There are 35 canaries.
- There are 5 cages.
- Each cage has the same number of canaries.

 PLAN

Write a number sentence to help solve the problem.

SOLVE

- Decide which operation to use.

- Choose a letter to represent what you are trying to find. Let *n* represent that number.

- Write a number sentence. Use it to solve the problem.

$$35 \div 5 = n$$

↑	↑	↑
number of canaries	number of cages	number in each cage

$35 \div 5 = 7$

Solution: There are 7 canaries in each cage.

LOOK BACK

Look back at the problem. Is there a multiplication sentence you could write to solve the problem?

Guided Practice

Use the Ask Yourself questions to help you solve each problem.

1. There are 6 terrariums at Pete's Pet Palace. Each terrarium has 2 lizards. How many lizards are there in all?

2. Last week Pete's Pet Palace sold 17 dog bones and 3 times as many dog collars as cat collars. If they sold 7 cat collars, how many dog collars did they sell?

 Hint What information do you need?

Ask Yourself

UNDERSTAND **What facts do I know?**

PLAN **Do I choose a letter to represent what I am trying to find?**

SOLVE **Do I write a number sentence?**

LOOK BACK **Did I solve the problem?**

Independent Practice

Write a number sentence to solve each problem.

3. Pete wants to display 35 bird feeders. He plans to put 5 bird feeders on each shelf. How many shelves will he use?

4. Last week 95 people visited a bird shelter. This week 113 people visited. How many more people visited this week than last week?

5. Martin and his father went bird watching last weekend. They spotted 28 birds on Saturday and 43 on Sunday. How many birds did they see?

Go On

Mixed Problem Solving

Solve. Show your work. Tell what strategy you used.

6. **Money** Renzo had $15. He spent $4.75 for a ticket to the movies and $2.50 on snacks at the movie. How much money does Renzo have left?

7. Tracie lives 5 blocks from the library. Noel lives 3 times as far from the library as Tracie. How far does Noel live from the library?

8. **Multistep** Marcus has 45 marbles that are 5 different colors. He has the same number of each color. He buys 2 more yellow marbles. How many yellow marbles does he have?

You Choose

Strategy
- Act It Out
- Draw a Picture
- Make a Table
- Solve a Simpler Problem
- Write a Number Sentence

Computation Method
- Mental Math
- Estimation
- Paper and Pencil
- Calculator

Data Use the line plot to solve Problems 9–13.

The line plot shows the ages in years of the actors who appeared in the school play.

9. What is the age of the greatest number of actors in the play?

10. For which ages are there the same number of actors?

11. How many more 13-year-old actors are there than 11-year-old actors?

12. How many student actors are in the play?

13. How many actors are younger than 11 years old?

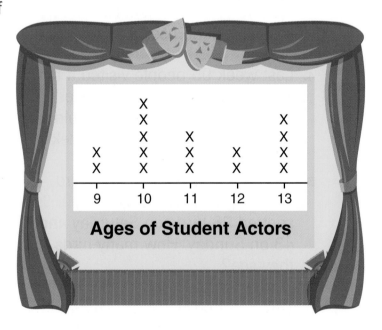

Ages of Student Actors

276

Problem Solving on Tests

Choose the letter of the correct answer. If correct answer is not here, choose NH.

1. Ali is drawing a design using stars. He draws 4 rows of 3 stars. How many stars will he draw altogether?

   A 7 stars   **C** 14 stars

   B 12 stars   **D** 16 stars

   (Chapter 9, Lesson 2)

2. Mrs. Gamio buys 2 boxes of pineapples. Each box has 9 pineapples. How many pineapples does she buy?

   F 18 pineapples

   G 16 pineapples

   H 11 pineapples

   J NH

   (Chapter 8, Lesson 3)

Open Response

Solve each problem.

3. Julie drew this array of dots. Write the number sentences it represents.

   (Chapter 8, Lesson 4)

4. **Represent** Suppose you need to make a fair spinner for a game.

   Draw and color a four-part spinner. Explain the rules for a fair game using your spinner.

   (Chapter 7, Lesson 4)

Constructed Response

5. Look at the target and balls below. The object of the game is to score as close to 100 points as possible without going over 100 points.

   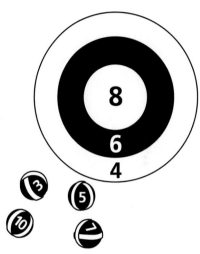

   • You may throw 3 or 4 of the balls shown, one at a time each.

   • Multiply the number on each ball by the number in the ring it hits. Then add the points from all your throws.

   a. What is the best score you can get?

   b. How can you throw the balls to get the best score?

   (Chapter 9, Lessons 2–10)

Education Place

See **eduplace.com/map** for more Test-Taking Tips.

Algebra

Division Rules

Objective Use special rules when you divide with 0 and 1.

Learn About It

George bought 3 heat rocks for his 3 iguanas, Iris, Ira, and Isaac. How many heat rocks did he buy for each iguana?

Divide. $3 \div 3 = 1$

He bought 1 heat rock for each iguana.

Here are some rules for dividing with 0 and 1.

Division Rules

When any number except 0 is divided by itself, the quotient is 1.	Put 3 counters into 3 groups. There is 1 counter in each group.	Think $3 \div 3 = 1$
When any number is divided by 1, the quotient is that number.	Put 3 counters into 1 group. There are 3 counters in the group.	Think $3 \div 1 = 3$
When 0 is divided by any number except 0, the quotient is 0.	Put 0 counters into 3 groups. There are 0 counters in each group.	Think $0 \div 3 = 0$
You cannot divide a number by 0.	Try to put 3 counters into 0 groups. It is not possible to put 3 counters into 0 groups.	$3 \div 0 = \square$

Guided Practice

Divide.

1. $2 \div 1$ **2.** $1 \div 1$ **3.** $0 \div 9$

4. $6\overline{)6}$ **5.** $8\overline{)0}$ **6.** $7\overline{)7}$

Ask Yourself

What is the rule for

• dividing by 1?
• dividing 0 by a number?
• dividing a number by itself?

Explain Your Thinking ▶ Which division rule could help you find $486 \div 1$?

Practice and Problem Solving

Divide.

7. $10\overline{)10}$ **8.** $1\overline{)9}$ **9.** $7\overline{)7}$ **10.** $2\overline{)8}$

11. $1\overline{)1}$ **12.** $2\overline{)6}$ **13.** $5\overline{)20}$ **14.** $10\overline{)50}$

15. $2\overline{)10}$ **16.** $5\overline{)30}$ **17.** $3\overline{)3}$ **18.** $10\overline{)100}$

19. $4 \div 4$ **20.** $4 \div 2$ **21.** $12 \div 2$ **22.** $18 \div 2$

23. $15 \div 5$ **24.** $0 \div 3$ **25.** $30 \div 10$ **26.** $5 \div 5$

Match each division sentence with the division rule that helps you solve it.

27. When any number except 0 is divided by itself the quotient is 1.

28. When any number is divided by 1, the quotient is that number.

29. When 0 is divided by any number except 0, the quotient is 0.

a. $689 \div 1 = n$

b. $2,385 \div 2,385 = n$

c. $0 \div 5,288 = n$

Go On ▶

Algebra • **Functions** Follow the rule to complete each table.

Rule: Divide by 1.		
	Input	**Output**
30.	0	■
31.	1	■
32.	■	4
33.	■	8
34.	10	■

Rule: Divide by 5.		
	Input	**Output**
35.	0	■
36.	■	1
37.	40	■
38.	■	4
39.	■	7

Algebra • **Symbols** Write >, <, or = for each ●.

40. 2×8 ● $8 \div 8$

41. $2 \div 2$ ● $5 \div 5$

42. $10 \div 2$ ● $15 \div 5$

43. $12 \div 2$ ● $14 \div 2$

44. $40 \div 5$ ● 10×2

45. 6×6 ● $36 \div 1$

46. 5×9 ● $287 \div 287$

47. 2×4 ● $45 \div 5$

Write *true* or *false* for each sentence. Draw or write an example to support your answer.

48. When the divisor and the dividend are the same, the quotient is always 1.

49. You cannot divide 0 by 1.

50. When you divide by 1, the answer is always the same as the dividend.

51. You can never divide by 0.

52. The quotient is always less than the divisor.

True or false?

Extra Practice See page 283, Set F.

Open Response

Find each missing number.

(Ch. 9, Lesson 6)

53. $3 \times 5 = \blacksquare \times 3$

54. $6 \times \blacksquare = 8 \times 3$

Multiple Choice

55. Which statement is not true?

(Ch. 10, Lesson 9)

A $10 \div 10 = 1$ B $9 \div 1 = 9$

c $10 \div 5 = 2$ D $1 \div 1 = 0$

Algebraic Thinking
Shapes in Equations

Problem Solving

Write the value of each shape. Use what you
know about multiplication and division facts to solve.

1. $4 \div \triangle = \triangle$

2. $16 \div \bullet = \bullet$

3. $25 \div \blacklozenge = \blacklozenge$

4. $36 \div \blacksquare = \blacksquare$

5. $\blacksquare \times \blacklozenge = \blacksquare$

6. $\blacksquare \div \bigstar = 3$

7. $\bigstar \times 3 = \blacksquare$

8. $\blacksquare \div \triangle = 15$

9. $\bullet \times \blacklozenge = 20$

10. $\blacksquare \div \blacksquare = \blacklozenge$

11. $\triangle \times \blacklozenge = \bigstar$

12. $\bigstar \div \triangle = \blacklozenge$

$\triangle$ =	$\blacklozenge$ =	$\blacksquare$ =
$\bullet$ =	$\blacksquare$ =	$\bigstar$ =

Chapter Review/Test

VOCABULARY

Choose the best term to complete each sentence.

Vocabulary
divide
factor
divisor
quotient
dividend

1. The answer to a division problem is the ____.

2. If you break a set into equal groups you ____.

3. In the problem $3)\overline{15}$ the ____ is 15.

4. In the problem $15 \div 3$ the ____ is 3.

CONCEPTS AND SKILLS

Find each quotient. (Lessons 1–2, pp. 260–263)

5.

0 1 2 3 4 5 6

$6 \div 3 = \blacksquare$

6.

0 1 2 3 4 5 6 7 8 9 10 11 12

$12 \div 4 = \blacksquare$

Use the array to complete each number sentence. (Lesson 3, pp. 264–265)

7. $3 \times \blacksquare = 15$
   $15 \div \blacksquare = 3$

8. $\blacksquare \times 6 = 24$
   $24 \div \blacksquare = 6$

Divide. (Lessons 4, 6–7, 9, pp. 266–267, 270–273, 278–280)

9. $2)\overline{16}$ 10. $10)\overline{30}$ 11. $5)\overline{25}$ 12. $5)\overline{30}$ 13. $2)\overline{18}$

14. $2 \div 2$ 15. $14 \div 2$ 16. $10 \div 1$ 17. $5 \div 1$ 18. $0 \div 2$

PROBLEM SOLVING

Solve. (Lessons 5, 8, pp. 268, 274–276)

19. Mrs. Lee placed her 28 students into 4 groups. How many students were in each group?

20. Jared made 20 pancakes for breakfast. He and his family ate 16. How many were left over?

Show You Understand

Marcus and Al write multiplication sentences that relate to $18 \div 6 = 3$. Marcus writes $6 \times 3 = 18$. Al writes $3 \times 6 = 18$. Who is correct? Explain.

Extra Practice

Set A (Lesson 2, pp. 262–263)

Match each number line with the correct division sentence. Solve.

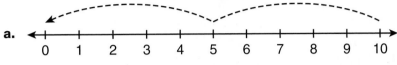

a.

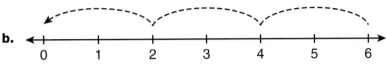

b.

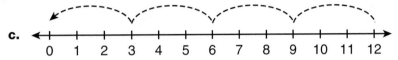

c.

1. $6 \div 2 = \blacksquare$

2. $10 \div 5 = \blacksquare$

3. $12 \div 3 = \blacksquare$

Set B (Lesson 3, pp. 264–265)

Use the array to complete each number sentence.

1.
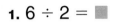

$2 \times \blacksquare = 18$

$18 \div \blacksquare = 9$

2.

$\blacksquare \times 6 = 12$

$12 \div \blacksquare = 2$

3.

$4 \times \blacksquare = 28$

$\blacksquare \div 7 = 4$

Set C (Lesson 4, pp. 266–267)

Divide.

1. $2\overline{)12}$ **2.** $2\overline{)20}$ **3.** $2\overline{)16}$ **4.** $2\overline{)14}$ **5.** $2\overline{)8}$

Set D (Lesson 6, pp. 270–271)

Find each quotient.

1. $50 \div 5$ **2.** $25 \div 5$ **3.** $35 \div 5$ **4.** $40 \div 5$ **5.** $5 \div 5$

Set E (Lesson 7, pp. 272–273)

Divide.

1. $10\overline{)20}$ **2.** $10\overline{)50}$ **3.** $10\overline{)100}$ **4.** $10\overline{)40}$ **5.** $10\overline{)10}$

Set F (Lesson 9, pp. 278–280)

Find each quotient.

1. $0 \div 4$ **2.** $9 \div 1$ **3.** $10 \div 10$ **4.** $3 \div 1$ **5.** $0 \div 1$

Extra Practice at **eduplace.com/map**

CHAPTER 11

Division Facts and Patterns

FDN
GONE. NOT FOR
09-11-*

INVESTIGATION

Using Data

Depending on the career you choose, you may work short or long days. Look at the table. Write and solve a word problem about the number of hours a group of firefighters worked in one day.

Work Hours

Worker	Hours per Day
Firefighter	8
Teacher	9
Journalist	10
Store Owner	12

Use What You Know

**Use this page to review and remember
what you need to know for this chapter.**

VOCABULARY

Choose the best term to complete each sentence.

Vocabulary
divide
factor
divisor
division
quotient
dividend

1. Multiplication and _____ are opposite operations.

2. In the number sentence 14 ÷ 2 = 7, the 2 is the _____.

3. The answer in a division problem is called the _____.

4. When you _____, you separate items into equal groups.

5. In the number sentence 40 ÷ 5 = 8, the _____ is 40.

CONCEPTS AND SKILLS

Write a multiplication sentence and a division sentence for each array.

6.   7.   8.    9.

Divide.

10. $5\overline{)10}$ 11. $2\overline{)4}$ 12. $1\overline{)8}$ 13. $6\overline{)0}$ 14. $10\overline{)30}$

15. $4 \div 1$ 16. $16 \div 2$ 17. $90 \div 10$ 18. $35 \div 5$ 19. $0 \div 3$

 Write About It

20. Omar wants to divide 20 berries equally among 5 bags. Sally wants to divide 20 berries equally among 2 bags. Are both possible? Explain why or why not.

Facts Practice, See page 670.

Audio Tutor 1/34 Listen and Understand

Divide Using a Multiplication Table

Objective Use a multiplication table to see how divisors, dividends, and quotients are related.

Vocabulary
divisor
dividend
quotient

Materials
Multiplication Table
(Learning Tool 17)

Work Together

You have used a multiplication table to figure out products. You can also use it to help you divide.

STEP 1

Use the table to find 30 ÷ 5. First, find the row marked 5. This number is the **divisor**.

Move across this row to the column that shows 30. This number is the **dividend**.

Look at the number 6 at the top of the column. This number is the **quotient**.

• Why can you use the table to divide?

column

×	0	1	2	3	4	5	6	7	8	9	10
0	0	0	0	0	0	0	0	0	0	0	0
1	0	1	2	3	4	5	6	7	8	9	10
2	0	2	4	6	8	10	12	14	16	18	20
3	0	3	6	9	12	15	18	21	24	27	30
4	0	4	8	12	16	20	24	28	32	36	40
5	0	5	10	15	20	25	30	35	40	45	50
6	0	6	12	18	24	30	36	42	48	54	60
7	0	7	14	21	28	35	42	49	56	63	70
8	0	8	16	24	32	40	48	56	64	72	80
9	0	9	18	27	36	45	54	63	72	81	90
10	0	10	20	30	40	50	60	70	80	90	100

row →

STEP 2

Make and complete a chart like the one below. Use the multiplication table to help you.

Example	Divisor	Dividend	Quotient
24 ÷ 6			
35 ÷ 7			
56 ÷ 8			
81 ÷ 9			

Extra Help at **eduplace.com/map**

STEP 3

Find the number 20 in 4 different places in the table. Use 20 as the dividend. Record the divisors and quotients in your chart. Then use your chart to help you write division sentences for each.

- How are your division sentences the same?

- How are they different?

STEP 4

Now find the number 25 in the table.

Write a division sentence with 25 as the dividend. Write a related multiplication sentence.

What do you notice about the factors, the divisor, and the quotient of the related sentences?

On Your Own

Use the multiplication table to find each quotient.

1. $12 \div 2$ 2. $9 \div 1$ 3. $36 \div 4$ 4. $0 \div 5$ 5. $15 \div 5$ 6. $28 \div 4$

7. $30 \div 6$ 8. $28 \div 7$ 9. $16 \div 8$ 10. $27 \div 9$ 11. $45 \div 9$ 12. $49 \div 7$

Talk About It • Write About It

You learned how to use a multiplication table to help you divide.

13. Explain how you can use a multiplication table to find $32 \div 4$.

14. If the dividend and the divisor are both even numbers, must the quotient also be an even number? Give examples to support your answer.

Fact Families

Objective Use fact families to show how multiplication and division are related.

Learn About It

A cartoonist drew these squirrels. How many rows of squirrels has the cartoonist drawn? How many squirrels are in each row? How many squirrels are there in all?

You can use the fact family for 3, 4, and 12 to tell about the squirrels.

A **fact family** is a group of number sentences that use the same numbers. Fact families show how multiplication and division are related.

Fact Family for 3, 4, and 12

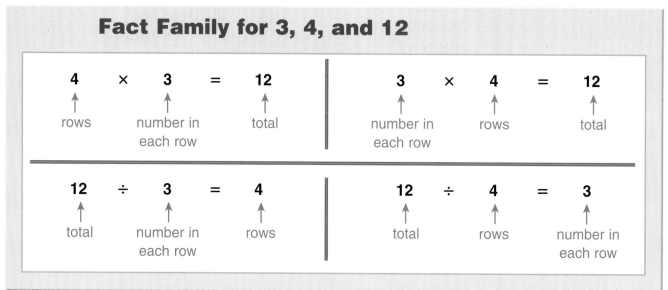

4	×	3	=	12
↑ rows		↑ number in each row		↑ total

3	×	4	=	12
↑ number in each row		↑ rows		↑ total

12	÷	3	=	4
↑ total		↑ number in each row		↑ rows

12	÷	4	=	3
↑ total		↑ rows		↑ number in each row

Solution: There are 12 squirrels in all. There are 3 squirrels in each row. There are 4 rows of squirrels.

Another Example

Fact Family for 4, 4, and 16

$4 \times 4 = 16$
$16 \div 4 = 4$

Copy and complete each fact family.

1. $3 \times 3 = 9$
$9 \div 3 = \blacksquare$

2. $2 \times 4 = 8$
$4 \times 2 = \blacksquare$
$8 \div 4 = \blacksquare$
$8 \div 2 = \blacksquare$

Ask Yourself

• Do I need to find the number of rows or the number of columns?

• Do I need to find the total?

Explain Your Thinking ▶ How are the products and dividends related in each fact family?

Practice and Problem Solving

Copy and complete each fact family.

3. $1 \times 8 = 8$
$8 \times \blacksquare = 8$
$8 \div 1 = \blacksquare$
$8 \div \blacksquare = 1$

4. $5 \times 9 = 45$
$\blacksquare \times 5 = 45$
$45 \div \blacksquare = 9$
$45 \div 9 = \blacksquare$

5. $3 \times 10 = 30$
$\blacksquare \times 3 = 30$
$30 \div \blacksquare = 10$
$30 \div \blacksquare = 3$

6. $6 \times 5 = 30$
$\blacksquare \times 6 = 30$
$30 \div \blacksquare = 5$
$30 \div \blacksquare = 6$

Write a fact family for each set of numbers.

7. 2, 3, 6
8. 10, 2, 20
9. 8, 3, 24
10. 4, 9, 36
11. 1, 5, 5
12. 5, 7, 35
13. 7, 7, 49
14. 6, 8, 48
15. 3, 7, 21
16. 3, 6, 18
17. 4, 5, 20
18. 2, 8, 16

Solve.

19. **What's Wrong?** Shelley says that $4 \times 8 = 32$ and $8 \div 4 = 2$ are in the same fact family. Explain why she is wrong. Then write the correct fact family with 4, 8, and 32.

20. Suppose you make two arrays. One array is 4 rows and 2 columns. The other is 3 rows and 4 columns. Which array shows the greatest dividend? Explain.

Mixed Review and Test Prep

Open Response

Find each missing number.

(Ch. 9, Lessons 2, 3)

21. $3 \times \blacksquare = 27$
22. $3 \times \blacksquare = 21$
23. $6 \times \blacksquare = 24$
24. $6 \times \blacksquare = 42$
25. $3 \times \blacksquare = 18$
26. $6 \times \blacksquare = 30$

27. Greg knows $2 \times 10 = 20$. Write a fact that belongs to the same fact family.

(Ch. 11, Lesson 2)

Extra Practice See page 315, Set A.

Audio Tutor 1/36 Listen and Understand

Divide by 3

Objective Learn different ways to divide by 3.

Learn About It

A landscaper plants 15 trees in 3 rows.
Each row has the same number of trees.
How many trees are in each row?

$$15 \div 3 = \blacksquare \quad \text{or} \quad 3\overline{)15}$$

Different Ways to Find $15 \div 3$

Way ① Use repeated subtraction.

- Start at 15 on a number line.
- Count back by 3s to 0.
- Count the number of 3s you subtracted.

You subtracted five 3s.

So $15 \div 3 = 5$.

Way ② Use a related multiplication fact.

$15 \div 3 = \blacksquare$ Think $3 \times \blacksquare = 15$ So $15 \div 3 = 5$.
$3 \times 5 = 15$

Solution: There are 5 trees in each row.

Guided Practice

Ask Yourself

- What multiplication fact can help me?

Find each quotient.

1. $3\overline{)9}$ 2. $3\overline{)3}$ 3. $3\overline{)27}$ 4. $3\overline{)0}$

5. $6 \div 3$ 6. $12 \div 3$ 7. $24 \div 3$ 8. $18 \div 3$

Explain Your Thinking ▶ Can you plant 19 trees in 3 equal rows?
Explain why or why not.

Divide.

9. $3\overline{)6}$ 10. $3\overline{)9}$ 11. $3\overline{)0}$ 12. $3\overline{)12}$ 13. $3\overline{)18}$

14. $3\overline{)15}$ 15. $3\overline{)24}$ 16. $3\overline{)3}$ 17. $3\overline{)21}$ 18. $3\overline{)27}$

19. $0 \div 3$ 20. $9 \div 3$ 21. $15 \div 3$ 22. $3 \div 3$ 23. $18 \div 3$

24. $30 \div 3$ 25. $12 \div 3$ 26. $24 \div 3$ 27. $21 \div 3$ 28. $6 \div 3$

✖ **Algebra • Symbols** Write >, <, or = for each ⬤.

29. $15 \div 3$ ⬤ $15 + 3$ 30. $5 \div 5$ ⬤ $3 - 3$ 31. 4×2 ⬤ $16 \div 2$

32. $45 \div 5$ ⬤ 7×3 33. $21 - 3$ ⬤ $21 \div 3$ 34. $18 \div 2$ ⬤ 2×10

35. Hal planted 27 rose bushes. The colors of the roses are red, yellow, or white. There is the same number of each color bush. How many bushes are red?

36. One seed pack cost $6 and a bottle of weed killer cost $3. If you bought 2 seed packs and 3 bottles of weed killer, how much did you spend?

37. **Analyze** Ann picked 27 orange flowers, 21 blue flowers, and 24 pink flowers. How can she put the flowers in 3 vases so that each vase has the same number of flowers of each color?

Open Response

Divide. (Ch. 10, Lessons 4, 6)

38. $10 \div 2$ 39. $20 \div 5$

40. $18 \div 2$ 41. $35 \div 5$

42. $25 \div 5$ 43. $16 \div 2$

44. $40 \div 5$ 45. $2 \div 2$

46. A class can be in 2 equal groups and in 3 equal groups. There are more than 12 and fewer than 20 students. How many students are in the class?
(Ch. 11, Lesson 3)

Extra Practice See page 315, Set B.

Divide by 4

Objective Learn different ways to divide by 4.

Vocabulary
equal groups

Learn About It

A baker makes 24 loaves of fresh bread. If she puts the same number of loaves into each of 4 bins, how many loaves will be in each bin?

$24 \div 4 = \blacksquare$ or $4\overline{)24}$

Different Ways to Find 24 ÷ 4

Way ❶ Make equal groups.

- Use 24 counters.
- Divide them into 4 equal groups.
- Count the number in each group.

There are 6 counters in each group. So 24 ÷ 4 = 6.

Way ❷ Use a related multiplication fact.

$24 \div 4 = \blacksquare$ Think $4 \times \blacksquare = 24$ So 24 ÷ 4 = 6.
                                   $4 \times 6 = 24$

Solution: The baker will put 6 loaves in each bin.

Guided Practice

Divide.

1. $4\overline{)36}$
2. $4\overline{)28}$
3. $4\overline{)16}$
4. $4\overline{)20}$

5. $8 \div 4$
6. $0 \div 4$
7. $12 \div 4$
8. $32 \div 4$

Ask Yourself
- What multiplication fact can help me?
- Can I make equal groups?

Explain Your Thinking ▶ How are the dividends, divisors, and quotients related in the problems $16 \div 2 = 8$ and $32 \div 4 = 8$?

Find each factor and quotient.

9. $4 \times \blacksquare = 12$
$12 \div 4 = \blacksquare$

10. $4 \times \blacksquare = 20$
$20 \div 4 = \blacksquare$

11. $4 \times \blacksquare = 8$
$8 \div 4 = \blacksquare$

12. $4 \times \blacksquare = 32$
$32 \div 4 = \blacksquare$

13. $4 \times \blacksquare = 36$
$36 \div 4 = \blacksquare$

14. $4 \times \blacksquare = 0$
$0 \div 4 = \blacksquare$

15. $4 \times \blacksquare = 4$
$4 \div 4 = \blacksquare$

16. $4 \times \blacksquare = 24$
$24 \div 4 = \blacksquare$

17. $4 \times \blacksquare = 28$
$28 \div 4 = \blacksquare$

Find the quotient.

18. $4\overline{)12}$

19. $4\overline{)0}$

20. $4\overline{)20}$

21. $4\overline{)36}$

22. $4\overline{)28}$

23. $4\overline{)24}$

24. $4\overline{)32}$

25. $4\overline{)16}$

26. $4 \div 4$

27. $36 \div 4$

28. $24 \div 4$

29. $8 \div 4$

✖ Algebra • Functions Complete each table. If the rule is not given, write the rule and complete the table.

Rule: Divide by 4.	
Input	**Output**
30. 0	$\blacksquare$
31. $\blacksquare$	1
32. 16	$\blacksquare$
33. $\blacksquare$	6
34. 32	$\blacksquare$

35.

Rule: _____.	
Input	**Output**
45	9
35	7
25	5
36. 20	$\blacksquare$
37. 30	$\blacksquare$

Use ÷ or × to complete each number sentence.

38. 4 ● 3 = 6 ● 2

39. 36 ● 6 = 3 ● 2

40. 16 ● 4 = 4 ● 1

41. 35 ● 1 = 5 ● 7

42. 3 ● 3 = 45 ● 5

43. 4 ● 6 = 24 ● 1

44. 8 ● 2 = 16 ● 4

45. 9 ● 1 = 18 ● 2

46. Calculator Suppose the number 4 key on your calculator is broken. How could you use the calculator to find 588 ÷ 4? Explain.

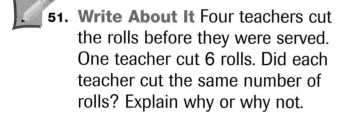 **Data** The third grade is having a special breakfast. Use the graph for Problems 47–51.

47. The students who brought muffins brought 4 muffins each. How many students brought muffins?

48. Three students brought in all the rolls. They each brought in the same number of rolls. How many rolls did each student bring?

49. If 42 people come for breakfast, can each person have either a roll or a bagel? Explain your answer.

50. Analyze The bagels are plain, whole wheat, blueberry, or cranberry. If there are the same number of each kind, how many whole wheat bagels are there?

51. Write About It Four teachers cut the rolls before they were served. One teacher cut 6 rolls. Did each teacher cut the same number of rolls? Explain why or why not.

Foods Bought for Breakfast

Number: 0, 4, 8, 12, 16, 20, 24, 28, 32

Muffins   Rolls   Bagels

Extra Practice See page 315, Set C.

Social Studies Connection
One Star for Each State

In 1818 it was decided that the United States flag would have one star for each state. The stars could be arranged in any way.

Over the years the United States flag changed as more states joined and more stars were added.

20-star Flag (1818)

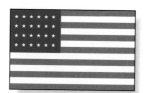
24-star Flag (1822)

48-star Flag (1912–1959)

Use the flags above for Questions 1–2.

> Remember that an array shows objects in rows and columns. Each row has an equal number of objects.

1. Arrange the stars in the 1818 flag in a different way using an array. What arrays can you make?

2. Make as many other arrays as you can for the 24-star and the 48-star flags.

WEEKLY **WR** READER eduplace.com/map

Quick Check

Check your understanding of Lessons 1–4.

Copy and complete each fact family. (Lesson 2)

1. $3 \times 5 = 15$ $15 \div 3 = \blacksquare$
   $5 \times \blacksquare = 15$ $15 \div \blacksquare = 3$

2. $4 \times 10 = 40$ $40 \div \blacksquare = 10$
   $\blacksquare \times 4 = 40$ $40 \div \blacksquare = 4$

Divide. (Lessons 1, 3, and 4)

3. $3\overline{)18}$ 4. $4\overline{)36}$ 5. $9\overline{)36}$ 6. $4\overline{)28}$

7. $21 \div 3$ 8. $15 \div 3$ 9. $16 \div 4$ 10. $24 \div 4$

Extra Practice at eduplace.com/map

Divide by 6

Objective Learn different ways to divide by 6.

Learn About It

A photographer took 24 pictures of 6 different children. She took the same number of pictures of each child. How many pictures of each child did she take?

$24 \div 6 = \blacksquare$ or $6\overline{)24}$

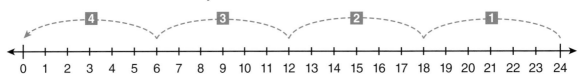

Different Ways to Find $24 \div 6$

Way ❶ Use repeated subtraction.

- Start at 24 on a number line.
- Count back by 6s to 0.
- Count the number of times you subtracted 6.

4   **3**   **2**   **1**

0 1 2 3 4 5 6 7 8 9 10 11 12 13 14 15 16 17 18 19 20 21 22 23 24

You subtracted four 6s.

So $24 \div 6 = 4$.

Way ❷ Make equal groups.

- Use 24 counters.
- Divide them into 6 equal groups.
- Count the number in each group.

There are 4 counters in each group.

So $24 \div 6 = 4$.

Way ❸ Use a related multiplication fact.

Think $6 \times \blacksquare = 24$
$6 \times 4 = 24$
So $24 \div 6 = 4$.

Way ❹ Use a related division fact.

Think $24 \div \blacksquare = 6$
$24 \div 4 = 6$
So $24 \div 6 = 4$.

Solution: She took 4 pictures of each child.

Guided Practice

Divide.

Ask Yourself

- What multiplication fact can help me?
- What related division fact can help me?

1. $6\overline{)36}$ 2. $6\overline{)60}$ 3. $6\overline{)42}$ 4. $6\overline{)54}$

5. $6 \div 6$ 6. $0 \div 6$ 7. $12 \div 6$ 8. $48 \div 6$

Explain Your Thinking ▶ What related multiplication and division facts can you use to help you find $30 \div 6$?

Practice and Problem Solving

Find the quotient.

9. $6\overline{)0}$ 10. $6\overline{)18}$ 11. $6\overline{)6}$ 12. $6\overline{)24}$ 13. $6\overline{)12}$

14. $6\overline{)42}$ 15. $6\overline{)54}$ 16. $6\overline{)48}$ 17. $6\overline{)30}$ 18. $6\overline{)36}$

19. $18 \div 6$ 20. $36 \div 6$ 21. $0 \div 6$ 22. $30 \div 6$ 23. $6 \div 6$

24. $48 \div 6$ 25. $24 \div 6$ 26. $54 \div 6$ 27. $42 \div 6$ 28. $18 \div 6$

𝒳 Algebra • Symbols Use $<$, $>$, or $=$ for each ⬤.

29. $25 \div 5$ ⬤ 25 30. $24 \div 3$ ⬤ 18 31. $0 \div 6$ ⬤ 6×0

32. 24 ⬤ $20 \div 4$ 33. 5×3 ⬤ $54 \div 6$ 34. $36 \div 6$ ⬤ 2×3

35. $30 \div 6$ ⬤ 2×4 36. $28 \div 4$ ⬤ 2×2 37. 48 ⬤ $24 \div 6$

38. Candace has 48 photos to put in her album. If she puts 6 photos on each album page, how many album pages will she use?

39. Lori has 2 old cameras. One weighs 4 pounds more than the other. Together they weigh 26 pounds. What are the weights of the 2 cameras?

40. **Analyze** In a photography class, two people can sit on each side of a square table. If 2 square tables are pushed together, how many people can sit at the tables?

Go On ▶

Choose the better estimate. (Grade 2)

41. About how long is a real pencil?

6 inches   6 feet

42. About how heavy is a real bike?

30 pounds   3 pounds

Multiple Choice

43. Which number sentence describes the array?

(Ch. 11, Lesson 5)

A $2 \times 6 = \blacksquare$ c $2 + 6 = \blacksquare$

B $2 \times 8 = \blacksquare$ D $6 + 2 = \blacksquare$

Problem Solving

Algebraic Thinking
Missing Numbers

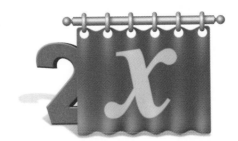

You can use a symbol like a ▉ or any letter to stand for an unknown number.

Look at these examples.

The box stands for the unknown number.	The letter *x* stands for the unknown number.	The letter *a* stands for the unknown number.
$2 \times \blacksquare = 6$	$4 \times 3 = x$	$8 \div a = 4$
Think $2 \times 3 = 6$	Think $4 \times 3 = 12$	Think $8 \div 2 = 4$
So $\blacksquare = 3$.	So $x = 12$.	So $a = 2$.

Find each missing number.

1. $2 \times \blacksquare = 4$

2. $5 \times \blacksquare = 10$

3. $2 = 10 \div \blacksquare$

4. $4 = 2 + n$

5. $9 - n = 8$

6. $1 \times b = 4$

7. $8 + 1 = 10 - n$

8. $18 \div 3 = 1 + a$

9. $3 \times 2 = 12 \div a$

Extra Practice See page 315, Set D.

Logical Reasoning
Using a Venn Diagram

The circles of a Venn diagram show how different sets are related. Look at the Venn diagram at the right. One circle shows all the red objects. The other circle shows all the stars.

Use the Venn diagram.

1. How many red objects are not stars?

2. How many red objects are stars?

3. How many stars are not red?

4. Where are the red stars?

5. **Challenge** Make a Venn diagram of your own. Write 3 or 4 questions about it and give them to a friend to answer.

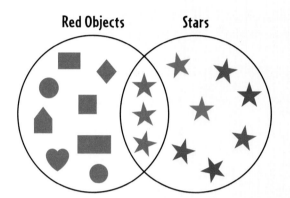

Red Objects   Stars

Algebraic Thinking
Facts and Patterns

Use division facts and patterns to find the missing numbers.

÷	32	40	■	56
8	4	■	6	■

÷	27	36	■	54
9	3	■	5	■

÷	30	■	■	45
5	6	■	■	■

Brain Teaser

You want to show the number 36 on your calculator. But the keys for 3 and 6 are broken. How can you show the number without using those keys?

Hint: You can use any of the operation signs: +, −, ×, ÷.

Education Place

Check out **eduplace.com/map** for more brain teasers.

Lesson 6

Problem-Solving Strategy
Draw a Picture
Objective Draw a picture to solve a problem.

Problem Linda's mom is a carpenter. She cuts a 24-inch board into 3 equal pieces. Then she cuts each of those pieces in half. How many pieces of wood are there? How long is each piece?

UNDERSTAND

This is what you know.

- The board is 24 inches long.
- Linda's mom cuts the board into 3 equal pieces.
- Then she cuts each of those pieces in half.

PLAN

You can draw a picture to help you solve the problem.

SOLVE

- Draw a rectangle to show the 24-inch board. Divide it into 3 equal parts.

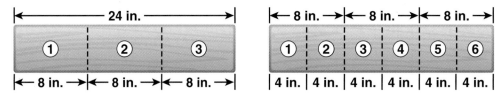

$$24 \div 3 = 8$$

- Now divide each 8-inch piece in half.

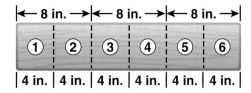

$$8 \div 2 = 4$$

Solution: There are 6 small pieces of wood. Each piece is 4 inches long.

LOOK BACK

Look back at the problem. How does drawing a picture help you answer the question?

Use the Ask Yourself questions to help you solve each problem.

1. Linda's mom makes birdhouses. First she cut a 36-inch piece of wood in half. Then she cut each piece into 3 equal pieces. How many pieces did Linda's mom have then?

2. Linda's mom cut a wooden rod for bird perches. She cut it into 9 pieces. How many cuts did she make?

 Hint The answer is **not** 9.

Ask Yourself

UNDERSTAND **What facts do I know?**

PLAN **Did I draw a rectangle to show the wood?**

SOLVE
- **Did I divide the rectangle into equal parts?**
- **Did I label the parts?**
- **Did I find how many pieces in all?**

LOOK BACK **Does my answer make sense?**

Independent Practice

Draw a picture to solve each problem.

3. Linda paints birdhouses red, yellow, or green. One day she painted 12 houses. She painted every third house green. How many houses did Linda paint green that day?

4. Natalie arranged 27 pictures of birds by color. The birds were white, brown, or blue. Every third bird was white. How many pictures of white birds were there?

5. Chip marks a board to divide it into 15 sections. He also puts 1 mark at each end of the board. How many marks does Chip make in all?

6. **Reasoning** Abdul has 4 red bricks and 6 blue bricks. He wants to stack one brick on top of another so that no bricks of the same color are touching. Will any bricks be left over? Explain.

Mixed Problem Solving

Solve. Show your work. Tell what strategy you used.

7. **Money** Ryan spent $12 on 3 jars of glitter. Each jar cost the same. If Ryan had only bought 2 jars, how much would he have paid?

8. Lee paints 3 glass vases the first week. If she paints 1 more vase each week than the week before, how many vases will she paint in the sixth week?

9. Ana spent 20 minutes cutting stars for a collage. Then she spent 15 minutes gluing them in place. If Ana finished at 2:15 P.M., what time did she start?

You Choose

Strategy
- Draw a Picture
- Find a Pattern
- Make a Table
- Work Backward
- Write a Number Sequence

Computation Method
- Mental Math
- Estimation
- Paper and Pencil
- Calculator

Independent Practice

 Data Use the pictograph to solve Problems 10–13.

Eduardo builds and sells furniture. The pictograph shows how many pieces of furniture he built and sold last year.

10. If each person who bought armchairs bought two of them, how many people bought armchairs?

11. How many more bookcases than tables were sold?

12. It costs $6.00 for supplies to put a finish on each table. How much did it cost Eduardo to put a finish on all the tables sold?

13. **Write About It** Can you tell from the graph how much money Eduardo earned selling this furniture? Explain.

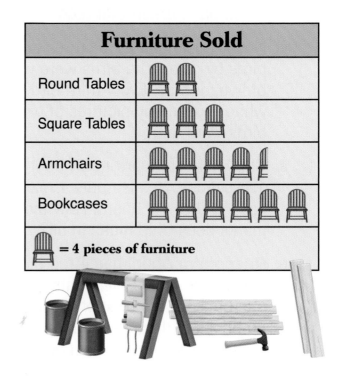

Furniture Sold

Round Tables	🪑🪑
Square Tables	🪑🪑🪑
Armchairs	🪑🪑🪑🪑🪑
Bookcases	🪑🪑🪑🪑🪑🪑🪑

🪑 = 4 pieces of furniture

302

Problem Solving on Tests

Choose the letter of the correct answer. If correct answer is not here, choose NH.

1. Look at the rows of marbles. Which numbers would you use to write a fact family for this array?

   ⊘⊘⊘⊘⊘⊘⊘⊘⊘
   ⊘⊘⊘⊘⊘⊘⊘⊘⊘
   ⊘⊘⊘⊘⊘⊘⊘⊘⊘

   A 1, 9, 9   **B** 3, 6, 18

   C 3, 3, 9   **D** NH

   (Chapter 11, Lesson 2)

2. Four students each brought 6 muffins to the meeting. How many muffins did they have in all?

   F 16   **G** 24   **H** 30   **J** 36

   (Chapter 8, Lesson 4)

Open Response

Solve each problem.

3. Use the table below. Mrs. Lee and 3 of her students are going to the aquarium. How much will it cost?

Price of Aquarium Tickets	
Teachers	**Students**
$4.25	$3.50

   (Chapter 4, Lesson 8)

4. Tom has 7 stamps. Megan has 3 times as many stamps as Tom. Jane has twice as many as Megan. How many stamps does Jane have?

   (Chapter 9, Lesson 4)

Constructed Response

5. A music program will take place in Mr. Hale's room. He is setting up 24 chairs for the audience.

   a. Each row should have the same number of chairs. What are some different ways he can arrange the chairs?

   b. Suppose there is extra space left to walk down the middle of the rows of chairs. Each side of the space should have the same number of chairs. How many chairs should there be on each side?

   c. The principal suggested using a larger room. He said you could put 60 chairs in the room and leave a space to walk down the middle of the rows. How many chairs would you have on each side?
   Represent What are some of the different ways each side could be arranged?

   (Chapter 9, Lesson 6)

Education Place

See **eduplace.com/map** for more Test-Taking Tips.

Divide by 7

Objective Learn different ways to divide by 7.

Learn About It

The head of a dancing school is planning a dance for 21 students. For part of the dance, he places 7 students in each row. How many rows are there?

$$21 \div 7 = n \quad \text{or} \quad 7\overline{)21}^{\,n}$$

Different Ways to find $21 \div 7$

Way 1 Make equal groups.

- Use 21 counters.
- Put 7 counters in each group.
- Count the number of groups.

There are 3 groups of 7 counters each.

So $21 \div 7 = 3$.

Way 2 Use a related multiplication fact.

Think $7 \times n = 21$
$7 \times 3 = 21$

So $21 \div 7 = 3$.

Way 3 Use a related division fact.

Think $21 \div n = 7$
$21 \div 3 = 7$

So $21 \div 7 = 3$.

Solution: There are 3 rows.

Guided Practice

Find each quotient.

1. $7\overline{)14}$
2. $7\overline{)49}$
3. $7\overline{)56}$
4. $7\overline{)28}$

5. $21 \div 7$
6. $70 \div 7$
7. $42 \div 7$
8. $35 \div 7$

Ask Yourself

- What multiplication fact can help me?
- What division fact can help me?

Explain Your Thinking ▶ What multiplication fact can you use to find $63 \div 7$?

Practice and Problem Solving

Divide.

9. $7\overline{)28}$　　　**10.** $7\overline{)63}$　　　**11.** $7\overline{)35}$　　　**12.** $7\overline{)14}$　　　**13.** $7\overline{)42}$

14. $7\overline{)0}$　　　**15.** $7\overline{)21}$　　　**16.** $7\overline{)56}$　　　**17.** $7\overline{)28}$　　　**18.** $7\overline{)7}$

19. $63 \div 9$　　**20.** $28 \div 7$　　**21.** $14 \div 7$　　**22.** $0 \div 7$　　**23.** $21 \div 7$

24. $56 \div 7$　　**25.** $7 \div 7$　　**26.** $49 \div 7$　　**27.** $35 \div 7$　　**28.** $63 \div 7$

✗ Algebra • Symbols Write +, −, ×, or ÷ for each ●.

29. $20 \, ● \, 4 = 5$　　　　**30.** $20 \, ● \, 4 = 16$　　　　**31.** $20 \, ● \, 4 = 24$

32. $21 \, ● \, 7 = 3$　　　　**33.** $21 \, ● \, 7 = 28$　　　　**34.** $21 \, ● \, 7 = 14$

Solve.

35. The dance school orders 56 dance costumes in 7 different colors. If the same number of each color is ordered, how many of each color are ordered?

36. The students practiced the new dance for 2 hours each week. If they practiced for 6 weeks, how many hours did they practice altogether?

37. The dance teacher runs with his dog 4 times a week. They run 2 miles each time. How many miles do the teacher and his dog run in 3 weeks?

Mixed Review and Test Prep

Open Response

Divide. (Ch. 10, Lessons 7, 9)

38. $4 \div 1$　　　　**39.** $20 \div 10$

40. $60 \div 10$　　　**41.** $9 \div 1$

42. $0 \div 5$　　　　**43.** $0 \div 8$

44. Andy practices piano 4 times a week for 2 hours each time. Mark practices for 1 hour every day. Who practices more hours in 5 weeks? Explain your answer. (Ch. 11, Lesson 7)

Divide by 8

Objective Learn different ways to divide by 8.

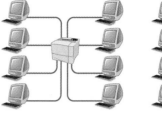

Learn About It

Ms. Schultz is the computer expert at her company. She is connecting 8 computers to each printer that the company owns. If there are 32 computers, how many printers are there?

$$32 \div 8 = \frac{n}{\blacksquare} \quad \text{or} \quad 8\overline{)32}^{\,n}$$

Different Ways to Find $32 \div 8$

Way ① Make equal groups.

- Use 32 counters.
- Put 8 in each group.
- Count the number of equal groups.

There are 4 groups of 8.

So $32 \div 8 = 4$.

Way ② Use a related multiplication fact.

Think $8 \times n = 32$
        $8 \times 4 = 32$

So $32 \div 8 = 4$.

Way ③ Use a related division fact.

Think $32 \div n = 8$
        $32 \div 4 = 8$

So $32 \div 8 = 4$.

Solution: The company has 4 printers.

Guided Practice

Find each quotient.

1. $8\overline{)8}$
2. $8\overline{)24}$
3. $8\overline{)48}$
4. $16 \div 8$

5. $0 \div 8$
6. $64 \div 8$
7. $56 \div 8$
8. $32 \div 8$

Ask Yourself

- How many equal groups of 8 can I make?
- What multiplication fact can help me?

Explain Your Thinking ▶ How can knowing $40 \div 8 = 5$ help you find $48 \div 8$?

Divide.

9. $8\overline{)16}$ 10. $8\overline{)32}$ 11. $8\overline{)64}$ 12. $8\overline{)0}$

13. $8\overline{)40}$ 14. $8\overline{)80}$ 15. $8\overline{)56}$ 16. $8\overline{)48}$

17. $8 \div 8$ 18. $24 \div 8$ 19. $32 \div 8$ 20. $72 \div 8$

Find each missing number.

21. $42 \div 7 = n$ 22. $8 \times b = 24$ 23. $5 \times 7 = \blacksquare$ 24. $36 \div a = 6$

25. $49 \div \blacksquare = 7$ 26. $40 \div n = 5$ 27. $20 \div 2 = a$ 28. $56 \div 8 = n$

Solve.

29. The first day, Rosa has 2 e-mails. Every day after that, she has twice as many e-mails as the day before. How many e-mails does she have on the fifth day?

31. Jimmy prints 8 copies of a story he wrote on his computer. He prints a total of 40 pages. How many pages is the story?

32. There are 3 groups of 8 students sitting in the computer lab. There are 78 seats in the lab. How many seats are empty?

30. **You Decide** Colored pencils come in packs of 4, 6, or 8 pencils. Each pack has pencils of only 1 color—red, green, or blue. Suppose you need exactly 20 pencils. What packs of each color will you buy? Explain your thinking.

Mixed Review and Test Prep

Open Response
Solve each problem.
(Ch. 4, Lessons 4, 7, Ch. 5, Lessons 5, 7)

33. 178
    +312

34. 4,749
    +3,318

35. 867
    −492

36. 5,904
    −1,628

Multiple Choice

37. Which number sentence is NOT true? (Ch. 11, Lesson 8)

    A $16 \div 8 = 2$ C $56 \div 8 = 7$

    B $24 \div 8 = 3$ D $72 \div 8 = 8$

Go On

Fast Fact Practice

**Find the quotients as quickly as you can!
Write only the answer.**

1. 6)42 2. 3)27 3. 8)8 4. 10)70 5. 7)56 6. 5)15

7. 8)32 8. 7)35 9. 10)20 10. 6)30 11. 8)56 12. 7)63

13. 5)45 14. 6)18 15. 7)49 16. 8)64 17. 3)9 18. 4)16

19. 8)48 20. 7)28 21. 6)54 22. 4)36 23. 7)42 24. 3)12

25. 7)21 26. 6)60 27. 8)72 28. 4)24 29. 3)6 30. 6)36

31. $70 \div 7$ 32. $24 \div 8$ 33. $60 \div 10$ 34. $10 \div 2$ 35. $80 \div 10$

36. $42 \div 7$ 37. $27 \div 3$ 38. $16 \div 8$ 39. $36 \div 6$ 40. $25 \div 5$

41. $24 \div 6$ 42. $14 \div 7$ 43. $9 \div 3$ 44. $40 \div 8$ 45. $12 \div 6$

46. $8 \div 2$ 47. $7 \div 7$ 48. $0 \div 4$ 49. $56 \div 7$ 50. $54 \div 9$

51. $30 \div 10$ 52. $18 \div 3$ 53. $48 \div 6$ 54. $10 \div 10$ 55. $16 \div 4$

Complete each table. If the rule is not given, write the rule.

Rule: Divide by 6.	
Input	**Output**
56. ■	5
57. 54	■
58. 36	■
59. ■	7

Rule: Divide by 7.	
Input	**Output**
60. 70	■
61. ■	3
62. 56	■
63. 14	■

Rule: Divide by 8.	
Input	**Output**
64. 48	■
65. ■	9
66. 16	■
67. ■	4

68. Rule: ____.	
Input	**Output**
42	7
30	5
69. 18	■
70. ■	4

71. Rule: ____.	
Input	**Output**
70	7
72. 30	■
50	5
73. ■	8

74. Rule: ____.	
Input	**Output**
24	3
75. 64	■
8	1
76. 40	■

Math Scramble

2 Players

What You'll Need • 3 sets of number cards labeled 0 to 9 (Learning Tool 18) • 15 cards for each of these symbols: $\times$, $\div$, and $=$ (Learning Tools 19 and 20)

How to Play

1 Player 1 deals all the number cards. Players take symbol cards as needed.

2 Player 1 builds a multiplication or division sentence using the number cards and any symbol cards needed.

3 Player 2 builds a number sentence onto Player 1's number sentence.

4 Players take turns building connecting number sentences until one of the following happens.

• One player has used all of his or her number cards.

• Neither player is able to build another number sentence.

The player who runs out of cards first wins. If both players have cards left, the player with fewer cards wins.

Divide by 9

Objective Learn different ways to divide by 9.

Learn About It

Mr. Nakane has 63 paintings to hang in 9 rooms of the museum. He hangs the same number of paintings in each room. How many paintings are hung in each room?

$$63 \div 9 = \blacksquare \quad \text{or} \quad 9\overline{)63}^{\,n}$$

Different Ways to Find 63 ÷ 9

Way ❶ Make equal groups.

- Use 63 counters.
- Divide them into 9 equal groups.
- Count the number in each group.

There are 7 counters in each group.

So $63 \div 9 = 7$.

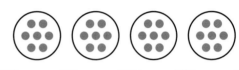

Way ❷ Use a related multiplication fact.

Think $9 \times n = 63$
$9 \times 7 = 63$

So $63 \div 9 = 7$.

Way ❸ Use a related division fact.

Think $63 \div n = 9$
$63 \div 7 = 9$

So $63 \div 9 = 7$.

Solution: Seven paintings are hung in each room.

Guided Practice

Find each quotient.

1. $9\overline{)72}$
2. $9\overline{)63}$
3. $81 \div 9$
4. $9 \div 9$

Ask Yourself

- How many items are in each of 9 equal groups?
- What division fact can help me?

Explain Your Thinking ▶ Without dividing, how can you tell that $36 \div 9$ is greater than $27 \div 9$?

Find each factor and quotient.

5. $9 \times \blacksquare = 36$
$36 \div 9 = \blacksquare$

6. $9 \times \blacksquare = 45$
$45 \div 9 = \blacksquare$

7. $9 \times \blacksquare = 18$
$18 \div 9 = \blacksquare$

8. $9 \times \blacksquare = 72$
$72 \div 9 = \blacksquare$

9. $9 \times \blacksquare = 27$
$27 \div 9 = \blacksquare$

10. $9 \times \blacksquare = 63$
$63 \div 9 = \blacksquare$

Divide.

11. $9\overline{)0}$ **12.** $9\overline{)27}$ **13.** $9\overline{)90}$ **14.** $9\overline{)54}$

15. $4\overline{)36}$ **16.** $7\overline{)56}$ **17.** $6\overline{)36}$ **18.** $8\overline{)64}$

19. $18 \div 9$ **20.** $63 \div 9$ **21.** $81 \div 9$ **22.** $36 \div 9$

23. $72 \div 9$ **24.** $9 \div 9$ **25.** $42 \div 7$ **26.** $45 \div 9$

✗ Algebra • Functions **Find the rule. Then complete each table.**

27.

Rule: ____.	
Input	**Output**
45	5
18	2
36	4
28. ■	9
29. 9	■

30.

Rule: ____.	
Input	**Output**
18	6
27	9
9	3
31. 15	■
32. 6	■

33. Mr. Nakane has 36 small carvings to display in a case. If he puts 9 carvings in each row, how many rows will he have?

34. **Analyze** Mr. Nakane gets 4 more small carvings. He wants to arrange all the carvings he has in one case, with an equal number of carvings in each row. How can he do it?

Go On

✳ Algebra • Symbols Write +, −, ×, or ÷ for each ⬤.

35. 24 ⬤ 6 = 8 ⬤ 4

36. 8 ⬤ 3 = 24 ⬤ 0

37. 5 ⬤ 5 = 5 ⬤ 20

38. 56 ⬤ 7 = 10 ⬤ 2

39. 6 ⬤ 6 = 5 ⬤ 4

40. 2 ⬤ 1 = 16 ⬤ 8

Write *always*, *never*, or *sometimes* to complete each sentence about division with basic facts.

41. The quotient and the divisor are _____ the same number.

42. The divisor can _____ be zero.

43. The divisor is _____ greater than the dividend.

44. A number is _____ even if it can be divided evenly by 2.

45. A number is _____ odd if it can be divided evenly by 5.

📊 Data Use the table for Problems 46–49.

46. Suzi read all of her books in 9 months. If she read the same number of books each month, how many books did she read each month?

47. **Analyze** Sebastian read chapter books and picture books. He read twice as many chapter books as picture books. How many of each type did he read?

48. Students fill out forms to record the total number of books read. The form has room for 9 books. How many forms will Jean-Marie need to list all of his books? Explain.

49. **Create and Solve** Write a number sentence that includes division by 9. Create a word problem that can be solved using your number sentence.

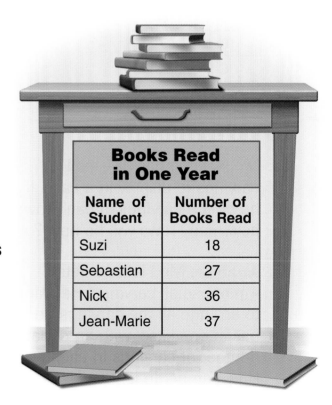

Books Read in One Year	
Name of Student	**Number of Books Read**
Suzi	18
Sebastian	27
Nick	36
Jean-Marie	37

Extra Practice See page 315, Set G.

Open Response

Round each amount to the nearest ten dollars. (Ch. 11, Lesson 9)

50. $11.87

51. $54.52

52. $7.25

53. $67.14

54. Find each factor and quotient.
(Ch. 11, Lesson 9)

$$9 \times \blacksquare = 54$$

$$54 \div 9 = \blacksquare$$

Calculator Connection
What's Your Sign?

Problem Solving

The math professor has dropped her bag of signs.

Use your calculator to help her figure out which signs will make the number sentences true. You can use $+$, $-$, $\times$, and $\div$.

1. 8 ● 2 ● 6 = 22

8 ● 2 ● 6 = 24

8 ● 2 ● 6 = 12

8 ● 2 ● 6 = 10

2. 9 ● 3 ● 7 = 20

9 ● 3 ● 7 = 21

9 ● 3 ● 7 = 13

9 ● 3 ● 7 = 10

3. 10 ● 2 ● 3 = 11

10 ● 2 ● 3 = 9

10 ● 2 ● 3 = 17

10 ● 2 ● 3 = 15

4. 2 ● 3 ● 4 ● 5 = 4

2 ● 3 ● 4 ● 5 = 19

5. 6 ● 3 ● 2 ● 10 = 40

6 ● 3 ● 2 ● 10 = 70

6. Create and Solve Use your calculator to help you make a set of number sentences like those above. Then give them to a classmate to solve.

Chapter Review/Test

VOCABULARY

Choose the best term to complete each sentence.

Vocabulary

product

divisor

quotient

dividend

fact family

1. In the sentence 36 ÷ 9 = 4, the _____ is 4.

2. A group of number sentences that use the same numbers is a _____.

3. In the sentence 20 ÷ 4 = 5, the _____ is 4.

4. In the sentence 12 ÷ 3 = 4, the _____ is 12.

CONCEPTS AND SKILLS

Write a fact family for each set of numbers. (Lesson 2, pp. 288–289)

5. 3, 5, 15   **6.** 2, 6, 12   **7.** 4, 6, 24   **8.** 2, 3, 6   **9.** 3, 9, 27

Divide. (Lessons 3–5, 7–9, pp. 290–298, 304–312)

10. 4)$\overline{36}$ **11.** 3)$\overline{24}$ **12.** 6)$\overline{36}$ **13.** 7)$\overline{49}$ **14.** 8)$\overline{24}$

15. 9)$\overline{0}$ **16.** 9)$\overline{54}$ **17.** 4)$\overline{16}$ **18.** 48 ÷ 6   **19.** 7 ÷ 7

20. 80 ÷ 8   **21.** 12 ÷ 4   **22.** 81 ÷ 9   **23.** 30 ÷ 3   **24.** 72 ÷ 8

PROBLEM SOLVING

Draw a picture to solve the problem.

(Lesson 6, pp. 300–302)

25. Jonathan is making coin patterns. He sets out the coins in a row in this order: penny, nickel, dime, quarter. Then he sets out more coins. If he continues the pattern, what will the tenth coin be?

Write About It

Do You Understand?

Lisa is planning a dinner party.

- There will be 24 people and 3 tables.
- Each table will have the same number of people.
- A vase at each table will have 2 flowers for each person.

Explain how Lisa knows how many flowers she needs for each vase.

Extra Practice

Set A (Lesson 2, pp. 288–289)

Write a fact family for each set of numbers.

1. 2, 4, 8   **2.** 4, 8, 32   **3.** 3, 4, 12   **4.** 10, 3, 30

Set B (Lesson 3, pp. 290–291)

Divide.

1. $3\overline{)24}$ **2.** $3\overline{)15}$ **3.** $3\overline{)30}$ **4.** $3\overline{)3}$ **5.** $3\overline{)0}$

Set C (Lesson 4, pp. 292–295)

Find the quotient.

1. $36 \div 4$ **2.** $32 \div 4$ **3.** $8 \div 4$ **4.** $12 \div 4$ **5.** $0 \div 4$

Set D (Lesson 5, pp. 296–298)

Divide.

1. $6\overline{)30}$ **2.** $6\overline{)18}$ **3.** $6\overline{)48}$ **4.** $6\overline{)36}$ **5.** $6\overline{)0}$

Set E (Lesson 7, pp. 304–305)

Find the quotient.

1. $56 \div 7$ **2.** $49 \div 7$ **3.** $14 \div 7$ **4.** $42 \div 7$ **5.** $28 \div 7$

Set F (Lesson 8, pp. 306–309)

Divide.

1. $8\overline{)24}$ **2.** $8\overline{)80}$ **3.** $8\overline{)16}$ **4.** $8\overline{)40}$ **5.** $8\overline{)64}$

Set G (Lesson 9, pp. 310–313)

Find the quotient.

1. $72 \div 9$ **2.** $63 \div 9$ **3.** $18 \div 9$ **4.** $54 \div 9$ **5.** $36 \div 9$

Monarchs on the Move

Have you ever watched one of these colorful insects? A monarch butterfly may be small, but many travel over 2,000 miles to reach their winter home.

Every year in the fall, monarchs from all over eastern North America fly south. They gather in a forest high in the mountains of Mexico.

Scientists study monarchs. They worry that humans may damage the monarchs' Mexican habitat. Some people are trying to find ways to protect these hardy travelers.

Problem Solving

Mr. Denson's students are raising monarch butterflies in observation tents. They will release them after they hatch.

1 Mr. Denson's class has a total of 48 butterflies. He divides them equally into 6 tents. How many butterflies are in each tent?

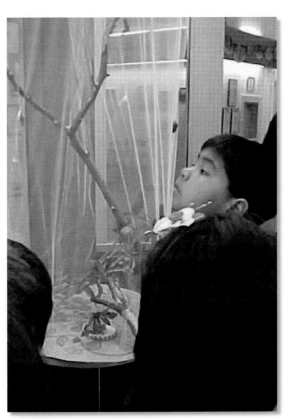

2 Male monarchs have 1 black spot on each of their wings. Female monarchs have no spots. When 8 of the monarchs hatch, Tonio counts 12 black spots. How many of the monarchs are males?

3 When the monarchs are released, they land on 4 milkweed plants. Cathy counts 4 monarchs on each plant. How many monarchs is that?

4 **Represent** Myra says she saw 5 butterflies, each with 2 spots. Draw a picture of what Myra saw and write the multiplication sentence for the number of spots.

Education Place

Visit Weekly Reader Connections at **eduplace.com/map** for more on this topic.

Enrichment: Unit Costs

BARGAIN HUNTING

Some stores offer lower prices if a customer buys more than one of an item. You can decide if the offer saves money by finding the cost of one item, or the **unit cost**.

Problem Omar wants to buy some balloons. Balloon Express sells 4 balloons for 36¢. Party Palace sells the same balloons at 6 for 48¢. Which store has the better price?

First find the **unit cost** of the balloons at each store. Then compare the costs.

STEP **1**	STEP **2**	STEP **3**
Find how much 1 balloon costs at Balloon Express.	Find how much 1 balloon costs at Party Palace.	Compare.
36¢ ÷ 4 = 9¢	**48¢ ÷ 6 = 8¢**	**8¢ < 9¢**
The balloons at Balloon Express cost 9¢ each.	The balloons at Party Palace cost 8¢ each.	Since 8¢ is less than 9¢, Party Palace has the better price because it is the lower price.
The unit cost is 9¢.	The unit cost is 8¢.	

Try These!

Decide which store has the lower price.

1. Store A: 3 party hats for 18¢
   Store B: 7 party hats for 35¢

2. Store A: 4 toy whistles for 32¢
   Store B: 5 toy whistles for 45¢

3. Store A: 4 streamers for 16¢
   Store B: 6 streamers for 42¢

318 Unit 4 Enrichment

Calculator Capers

Use 5, 6 and 7

□ × □ + □ = 41

5×6+7=?

6×7+5=?

5×7+6=?

Use a calculator to help you arrange each set of numbers to make the number sentences true. Use each number only once.

Use 2, 4, and 7

1. ▪ × ▪ + ▪ = 30

Use 3, 6, and 7

2. ▪ × ▪ − ▪ = 15

Use 4, 5, and 6

3. ▪ × ▪ + ▪ = 29

Use 4, 3, and 24

4. ▪ ÷ ▪ − ▪ = 4

Use 2, 3, and 18

5. ▪ ÷ ▪ + ▪ = 12

Use 4, 7, and 56

6. ▪ ÷ ▪ − ▪ = 4

Use 3, 4, and 12

7. ▪ ÷ ▪ + ▪ = 6

Use 4, 6, and 36

8. ▪ ÷ ▪ − ▪ = 2

Use 5, 6, and 9

9. ▪ × ▪ − ▪ = 39

Use 6, 7, and 10

10. ▪ × ▪ − ▪ = 53

Unit 4 Test

VOCABULARY ⬭Open Response⬭

Choose the best term to complete each sentence.

1. When you multiply the answer is called the ____.

2. When you divide 48 by 6, 48 is called the ____.

3. The answer to $56 \div 7 = 8$ is called the ____.

4. The number sentences $16 \div 2 = 8$ and $2 \times 8 = 16$ belong to the same ____.

> **Vocabulary**
> factor
> product
> quotient
> dividend
> fact family

CONCEPTS AND SKILLS ⬭Open Response⬭

Multiply. (Chapters 8–9)

5. 0×5 6. 10×1 7. 2×9 8. 4×5

9. 6×4 10. 7×7 11. 3×8 12. 9×7

Find each missing factor. (Chapter 9)

13. $(2 \times \blacksquare) \times 3 = 30$ 14. $\blacksquare \times (2 \times 4) = 32$ 15. $(\blacksquare \times 3) \times 5 = 45$

16. $2 \times (\blacksquare \times 7) = 14$ 17. $(4 \times 2) \times \blacksquare = 24$ 18. $(\blacksquare \times 1) \times 6 = 18$

Divide. (Chapters 10–11)

19. $0 \div 6$ 20. $5\overline{)5}$ 21. $2\overline{)18}$ 22. $30 \div 10$

23. $9\overline{)54}$ 24. $28 \div 4$ 25. $63 \div 7$ 26. $8\overline{)64}$

Write a fact family for each array. (Chapter 11)

27. ★ ★
    ★ ★
    ★ ★

28. ★ ★ ★ ★ ★
    ★ ★ ★ ★ ★

29. ★ ★ ★
    ★ ★ ★
    ★ ★ ★
    ★ ★ ★

30. Bo has 3 kinds of wrapping paper and 4 kinds of ribbon. How many different ways can he wrap a present if he uses one kind of paper and one kind of ribbon?

31. Joe gave away all of the 24 paper roses he made. He gave an equal number to his mother, aunt and cousin. How many roses did he give to each person?

32. Beth is making a necklace. She has 8 red beads and 6 white beads. She has 4 times as many blue beads as red beads. How many beads does Beth have in all?

33. Kim made a row of tiles. The first tile is green, the second is red, and the third is yellow. She repeated the pattern 3 times. What color is the eighth tile?

Performance Assessment

Extended Response

PARTY BAGS	High-Bounce Balls	Bubbles	MINI YO-YO'S	FUNNY GLASSES	Crazy Straws
6 for $1	4 for $3	4 for $1	6 for $4	3 for $2	6 for $2

Task Marisa and her mom are planning to make 12 party bags.

Use the prices above and the information at the right. List the 3 toys you think they should buy. Find the total cost of the 12 filled party bags including the cost of the bags. Explain your thinking.

Information You Need

- They want to put 3 toys in each bag.
- They would like each of the 12 party bags to be exactly alike.
- They want the total cost of the 12 party bags (including the bags) to be under $25.

Cumulative Test Prep

Solve Problems 1–10.

Test-Taking Tip

When you take a test it is important to read the question carefully. Be sure you know what you are asked to find.

Look at the example below.

Phoebe has $2.31 in a jar. Jason has $1.02 in a jar. Rounded to the nearest dollar, what is the total amount of money in both jars?

   A $1.00   **c** $3.00

   B $1.29   **D** $3.33

THINK

If you do not read the question carefully, you may think the answer is $3.33, or **D**.

But the question asks for the total amount *rounded to the nearest dollar*. You need to find an estimate. So the correct answer is $3.00 or **C**.

Multiple Choice

1. Eight math teams play in a town league. Each team has 6 players. Rounded to the nearest ten, how many players are in the league?

   A 14   **B** 40   **c** 48   **D** 50

(Chapter 2, Lesson 3; Chapter 9, Lesson 3)

2. Which two numbers are missing in the pattern below?

$$3, 6, 9, 12, \underline{}, 18, \underline{}$$

   F 14 and 20   **H** 15 and 21

   G 15 and 20   **J** 21 and 24

(Chapter 9, Lesson 2)

3. Owen uses 3 quarters to pay for a pencil that costs $0.55. How much change should he get?

   A 25¢   **c** 15¢

   B 20¢   **D** 10¢

(Chapter 3, Lesson 3)

4. Soon-Jin read 17 pages in a book on Saturday. She read 28 pages on Sunday. Rounded to the nearest ten, how many pages did she read?

   F 60   **H** 45

   G 50   **J** 10

(Chapter 2, Lesson 3; Chapter 4, Lesson 2)

For Test-Taking Tips, see page 659.

5. There are 5 rows of marbles. Each row has 4 marbles. If the marbles are moved into 4 rows, how many will be in each row? Explain.

(Chapter 8, Lesson 2)

6. Ivan paid for 5 stickers with $1.00. Suppose the stickers cost 9¢ each. How much change should Ivan get?

(Chapter 3, Lesson 3; Chapter 8, Lesson 5)

7. Rose puts 15 books on shelves. How many shelves does Rose use if she puts 5 books on each shelf? Write a number sentence to show how you got your answer.

(Chapter 10, Lesson 8)

8. Which instruments have fewer than 8 strings, but more strings than a violin?

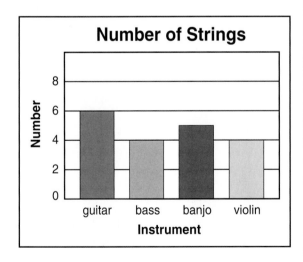

(Chapter 6, Lesson 6)

9. Jamal has a bag of tiles: 2 red, 3 blue, and 1 yellow. What is the probability Jamal will pick a red tile if he takes one without looking?

(Chapter 7, Lesson 3)

10. Look at this Venn diagram.

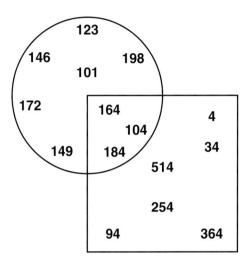

A What do all of the numbers inside the circle have in common?

B List three more numbers that can be placed inside the circle.

C What do all of the numbers inside the square have in common?

D List three more numbers that can be placed inside the square.

E What rule can be used to describe the numbers inside both the circle and the square?

(Chapter 1, Lesson 2)

Education Place

Look for Cumulative Test Prep at **eduplace.com/map** for more practice.

Vocabulary Wrap-Up for **Unit 4**

Look back at the big ideas and vocabulary in this unit.

Big Ideas

Multiplication and division are opposite operations.

You can think of multiplication as repeated addition, or adding equal groups.

You can think of division as repeated subtraction, or subtracting equal groups.

Key Vocabulary
- **multiplication**
- **division**
- **equal groups**

Math Conversations

Use your new vocabulary to discuss these big ideas.

1. Explain why writing $3 + 3 + 3 + 3 + 3$ is the same as writing 5×3.

2. Explain how $3 \times 5 = 15$ and $15 \div 3 = 5$ are related.

3. Explain why 3×5 is equal to 5×3.

4. **Write About It** Amit is making an Indian dish called Saag Aloo that serves 4 people. What if Amit wants to make enough for 12 people? Explain how he could use multiplication to adjust the recipe.

How can we write 3×4 as an addition sentence?

We could add 4 to itself 3 times. $4 + 4 + 4$

UNIT 5

Measurement

Reading Mathematics

Reviewing Vocabulary

Here are some math vocabulary words that you should know.

hour	a unit of time equal to 60 minutes
calendar	a table showing the months, days, and weeks for one year
thermometer	a tool used to measure temperature
inch (in.)	a unit of length in the customary system
foot (ft)	a unit of length in the customary system, made up of 12 inches

Reading Words and Symbols

You can use words and symbols to describe measurements. Look at these measuring tools.

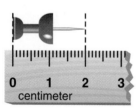

Read: The push pin is two centimeters long.

Write symbols: 2 cm

Read: The apples weigh four pounds.

Write symbols: 4 lb

Use words and symbols to describe each measurement.

1.

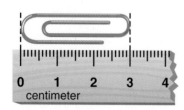

2.

Reading Test Questions

Choose the correct answer for each.

3. Which unit of measure is best used to weigh a polar bear?

   a. ounces

   b. pounds

   c. inches

   d. quarts

   Unit of measure means "the kind of standard measure."

4. Which would probably be measured in feet?

   a. the length of a stamp

   b. the length of a highway

   c. the length of a pencil

   d. the length of a room

   Probably means "most likely."

5. Approximately how long is the crayon?

   a. 7 cm   **c.** 10 cm

   b. 9 cm   **d.** 11 cm

Approximately means "close to," or "about."

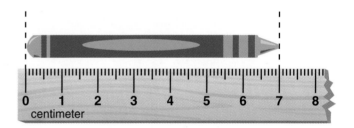

Learning Vocabulary

Watch for these words in this unit. Write their definitions in your journal.

ordinal number

half inch

ounce (oz)

kilogram (kg)

mass

gram (g)

Education Place

At **eduplace.com/map** see eGlossary and eGames—Math Lingo.

Literature Connection

Read "The Big Chill" on Pages 651–652. Then work with a partner to answer the questions about the story.

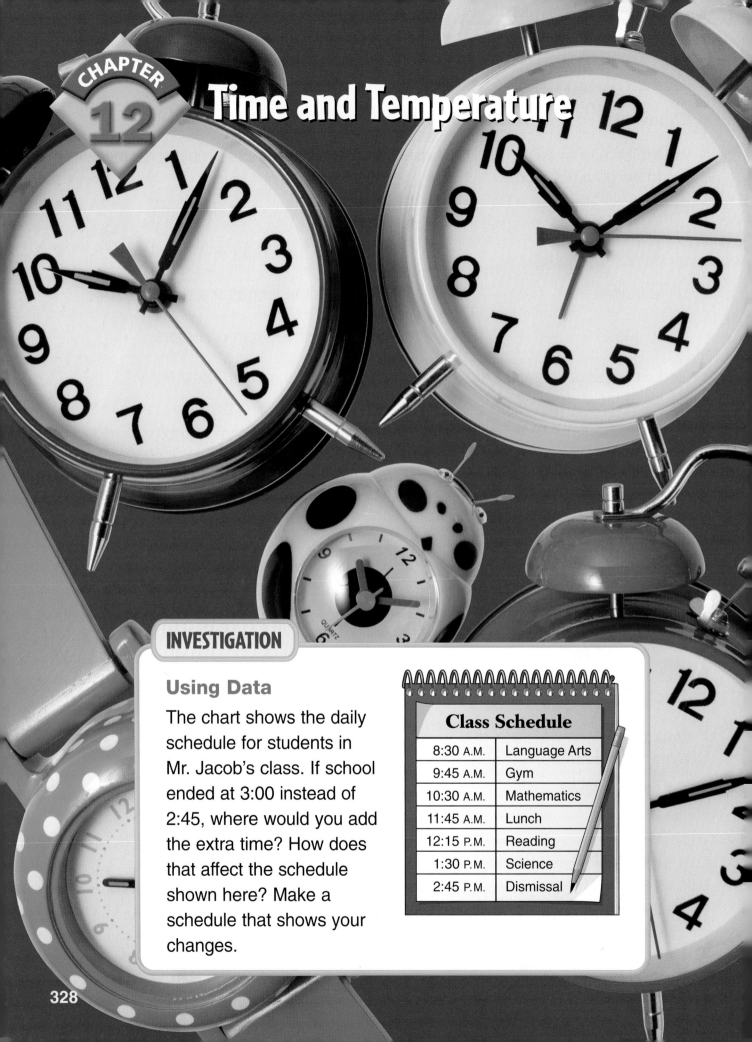

INVESTIGATION

Using Data

The chart shows the daily schedule for students in Mr. Jacob's class. If school ended at 3:00 instead of 2:45, where would you add the extra time? How does that affect the schedule shown here? Make a schedule that shows your changes.

Class Schedule	
8:30 A.M.	Language Arts
9:45 A.M.	Gym
10:30 A.M.	Mathematics
11:45 A.M.	Lunch
12:15 P.M.	Reading
1:30 P.M.	Science
2:45 P.M.	Dismissal

Use What You Know

**Use this page to review and remember
what you need to know for this chapter.**

VOCABULARY

Choose the best term to complete each sentence.

Vocabulary

day

hour

half-hour

calendar

1. There are 24 hours in a ____.

2. A ____ shows the days, weeks, and months of the year.

3. There are 60 minutes in a(n) ____.

CONCEPTS AND SKILLS

Write the time.

4.

5.

6.

Use the calendar to answer the questions.

7. How many days in August are Mondays?

8. Which day of the week is August 12?

9. What is the date of the last Tuesday in August?

	August					
Sun.	Mon.	Tue.	Wed.	Thu.	Fri.	Sat.
	1	2	3	4	5	6
7	8	9	10	11	12	13
14	15	16	17	18	19	20
21	22	23	24	25	26	27
28	29	30	31			

 **Write About It**

10. Which is longer, 2 weeks or 15 days? Explain how you know.

Facts Practice, See page 667.

Hour, Half-Hour, Quarter-Hour

Objective Tell time to the hour, half-hour, and quarter-hour.

Learn About It

Connor has a busy schedule. You can see his morning activities below. Look at the clocks. The short hand shows **hours**. The long hand shows **minutes**.

Units of Time
1 day = 24 hours
1 hour = 60 minutes
1 half-hour = 30 minutes
1 quarter-hour = 15 minutes

Getting Up

Write:
• 6:15

Read: 6:15
• six-fifteen
• fifteen minutes after six
• quarter after six

Getting Dressed

Write:
• 6:30

Read: 6:30
• six-thirty
• thirty minutes after six
• half past six

Eating Breakfast

Write:
• 6:45

Read: 6:45
• six forty-five
• forty-five minutes after six
• quarter to seven

On Bus to School

Write:
• 7:00

Read: 7:00
• seven o'clock

A.M. is used for the hours 12 midnight (12 A.M.) until 12 noon.

11:00 A.M.

P.M. is used for the hours 12 noon (12 P.M.) to 12 midnight.

11:00 P.M.

Ask Yourself
- How many hours does the clock show?
- How many minutes does the clock show?

Guided Practice

Describe each time in at least two ways.

1.

2.

3.

Explain Your Thinking ▶ How many times will Connor's watch show 7:00 in one day?

Practice and Problem Solving

Describe each time in at least two ways.

4.

5.

6.

7.

Write each time using numbers.

8. two o'clock

9. half past seven

10. quarter after five

11. quarter to four

12. quarter after one

13. half past twelve

Choose the most reasonable time to start each activity.

14. getting up
   a. 7:00 A.M.
   b. 7:00 P.M.

15. doing homework
   a. 3:30 A.M.
   b. 3:30 P.M.

16. eating dinner
   a. 6:15 A.M.
   b. 6:15 P.M.

Solve.

17. **Patterns** School buses leave at 2:45 P.M., 3:00 P.M., and 3:15 P.M. If the pattern continues, what time does the next bus leave?

18. Which time is closer to five o'clock, half past five or 4:45? Explain how you got your answer.

Mixed Review and Test Prep

Open Response

Add or subtract. (Grade 2)

19. 35¢ + 42¢

20. 64¢ − 23¢

21. 98¢ − 50¢

22. 25¢ + 72¢

23. Describe the time 2:45 in at least three different ways.
(Ch. 12, Lesson 1)

Extra Practice See page 351, Set A.

Time to Five Minutes

Objective Tell time to five minutes.

Learn About It

Connor's teacher gave him a schedule that lists when each class starts. Connor sees that it is time for math class.

How can you read the time shown on the clock?

Different Ways to Tell Time

Way ❶ You can tell time by the number of minutes **after an hour**.

- The **hour hand** is between 9 and 10, so the time is after 9 o'clock.
- The **minute hand** is on 7. Start at 12 and count ahead by 5-minute steps.

Write: 9:35
Read: nine thirty-five, or 35 minutes after 9.

> **Remember** It takes 5 minutes for the minute hand to move from one number to the next.

Way ❷ You can tell time by the number of minutes **before an hour**.

- The **hour hand** is between 9 and 10, so the time is before 10 o'clock.
- The **minute hand** is on 7. Start at 12 and count back to 7 by 5-minute steps.

Write: 9:35
Read: 25 minutes before 10.

Solution: The time 9:35 can be read as:
- nine thirty-five
- 35 minutes after 9
- 25 minutes before 10

Guided Practice

Describe each time as minutes after an hour and minutes before an hour.

1.   2.   3.

Ask Yourself
- Where is the hour hand pointing?
- Where do I start counting by 5-minute steps? Where do I stop?

Explain Your Thinking ▶ How long does it take for the minute hand to move from one number to the next?

Practice and Problem Solving

Describe each time as minutes after an hour and minutes before an hour.

4.   5.   6.   7.

Solve.

8. The hour hand on a clock points between 10 and 11. The minute hand points at 8. What time is it?

9. Carlos spent 1,542 minutes at school this week. How long is that to the nearest hundred?

10. **What's Wrong?** Rita's train arrives at the station at 2:40 P.M. She told a friend to meet her there at 20 minutes before 2:00. What should Rita have told her?

Mixed Review and Test Prep

Open Response

Complete each pattern. (Ch. 1, Lesson 5)

11. 15, 30, 45, _____

12. 30, 35, 40, _____, 50

13. 346, 348, _____, 352, _____

14. 505, _____, 525 ,535, _____

Multiple Choice

15. The sun is rising when Trudy gets out of bed at ten minutes after six. What time does Trudy get up? (Ch. 12, Lesson 2)

   A 5:50 P.M.   C 6:10 A.M.

   B 6:50 A.M.   D 6:10 P.M.

Time to the Minute

Objective Tell the number of minutes after the hour and before the hour.

Learn About It

Connor just finished writing a story and is recording it on tape. The time that Connor started recording his story is shown on the clock in the picture. How can you read the time shown on the clock?

Different Ways to Tell Time

Way 1 Here's how to tell the number of minutes **after an hour**.

- Start at the 12.
- Count ahead by 5-minute steps.
- Then count the remaining minutes.

Write: 1:42
Read: 42 minutes after 1

> **Remember** Each small mark between the numbers on the clock stands for 1 minute.

Way 2 Here's how to tell the number of minutes **before an hour**.

- Start at the 12.
- Count back by 5-minute steps.
- Then count the remaining minutes.

Write: 1:42
Read: 18 minutes before 2

Solution: You can read the time 1:42 as
- one forty-two
- 42 minutes after 1
- 18 minutes before 2

Write each time as minutes after an hour and minutes before an hour.

1.

2.

3.

Ask Yourself
- Where do I start counting by 5-minute steps? Where do I stop?
- What do I count by next?

Explain Your Thinking ▶ Why does 24 minutes after 6 tell the same time as 36 minutes before 7?

Practice and Problem Solving

Describe each time two ways.

4.

5.

6.

7.

Describe each time in words.

8. 7:31   9. 9:59   10. 11:17   11. 5:43   12. 8:46

 Data Use the table for Problems 13–14.

13. Which students started to record their stories between 1:30 and 2:00? between 2:00 and 2:30?

14. **Compare** List the students in order from the first student to start recording to the last student.

Recording Times	
Name	**Starting Time**
Anita	2:05 P.M.
Tyler	1:42 P.M.
Malik	2:54 P.M.
Kali	1:18 P.M.
Miguel	2:28 P.M.
Pedro	2:59 P.M.

Mixed Review and Test Prep

Open Response
Tell whether the number is even or odd. (Ch. 1, Lesson 7)

15. 9   16. 25   17. 34

18. 87   19. 126   20. 520

21. A baseball game began at 20 minutes before 3. Avery arrived at two fifty-five. Was he on time? Explain your answer.

(Ch. 12, Lesson 3)

Extra Practice See page 351, Set C.

Audio Tutor 2/1 Listen and Understand

Elapsed Time

Objective Use a clock to help you tell how long an activity will last.

Learn About It

Connor volunteers with his mom at an animal shelter every Wednesday. He arrives at 4:00 P.M. and leaves at 5:30 P.M. How long is he at the animal shelter?

▶ **If you know the starting time and the ending time, you can figure out how long Connor volunteers.**

Start at 4:00.

Count the hours.
4:00 to 5:00 is 1 hour.

Then count the minutes.
5:00 to 5:30 is 30 minutes.

Solution: Connor is at the animal shelter for 1 hour and 30 minutes.

Suppose Connor gets to the animal shelter at 4:15 P.M. and stays for 40 minutes. What time does he leave?

▶ **If you know when he gets to the animal shelter and how long he stays, you can figure out the time he leaves.**

Start at 4:15.

Count ahead 40 minutes to 4:55.

Solution: He leaves at 4:55 P.M.

Guided Practice

Tell what time it will be.

1. in 3 hours   **2.** in 20 minutes   **3.** in 45 minutes

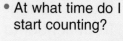
Ask Yourself
- At what time do I start counting?
- Do I need to count hours?
- Do I need to count minutes?

Explain Your Thinking ▶ Visiting hours at the animal shelter are from 9:00 A.M. to 11:30 A.M. on Saturday. How long is that?

Practice and Problem Solving

Tell what time it will be.

4. in 5 minutes   **5.** in 35 minutes   **6.** in 1 hour   **7.** in 3 hours

Write the time using numbers. Label each time A.M. or P.M.

8. 2 minutes before noon

9. 4 hours before 1 P.M.

10. One hour after 11:30 A.M.

11. 45 minutes after midnight

12. 18 minutes after noon

Remember
A.M. is used for the hours from 12 midnight to 12 noon. P.M. is used for the hours from 12 noon to 12 midnight.

Look at each pair of times. Write how much time has passed.

13. Start: 7:30 A.M.
    End: 7:40 A.M.

14. Start: 10:10 P.M.
    End: 10:55 P.M.

15. Start: 9:30 A.M.
    End: 11:30 A.M.

16. Start: 2:45 P.M.
    End: 3:30 P.M.

17. Start: 6:20 A.M.
    End: 6:42 A.M.

18. Start: 3:10 P.M.
    End: 4:13 P.M.

Solve.

19. It took Connor 6 minutes to walk from school to the animal shelter. If he left at 3:37 P.M., what time did he get to the shelter?

20. Twana bought a book about dogs for $16.75. She gave the store clerk a $20 bill. How much change did she receive?

21. Andy groomed 3 dogs starting at 4:00 P.M. and ending at 4:45 P.M. Each dog took 15 minutes to groom. What times did Andy begin grooming each dog?

22. There are 4 dogs, 4 cats, and 2 birds at the shelter. If Kan spent 3 minutes feeding each animal, how long did it take him to feed all the animals?

Estimate. Use the times on the sign at the right to complete the story.

23. Jody's family is going camping. She can hardly wait to go! Jody gets up early and takes _____ to eat breakfast.

24. Everyone helps pack the car. The campsite is in a National Park in another state. The family drives for _____ to get there.

25. Finally Jody can relax and enjoy the campsite. She and her family will be on vacation for _____.

10 days

6 hours

15 minutes

Use the clues to find each time.

26. The time is between 5 A.M. and 7 A.M.

- The hour digit is an even number.
- The sum of the minute digits is 6.
- You say the number of minutes when you count by 5s.

27. The time is between 6 P.M. and 8 P.M.

- The hour digit is an odd number.
- The minute hand is between 2 and 3.
- The sum of the minute digits is 3.

Extra Practice See page 351, Set D.

Real World Connection
Estimate Time

Sometimes you don't need to know an exact time. You can just estimate how much time has passed.

The clocks show what time the movie starts and ends. About how long is the movie?

Estimate how many hours pass.

The movie is about 2 hours long.

The sign shows the times for several events at a 4-H Fair. About how long does each event last?

1. Rabbit Show

2. Dairy Show

3. Arts and Crafts display

Start Time	End Time

Daily Events

Pancake Breakfast	7:00 A.M. – 8:45 A.M.
Dairy Show	9:30 A.M. – 1:45 P.M.
Arts and Crafts Display	9:00 A.M. – 4:15 P.M.
Rabbit Show	10:00 A.M. – 11:15 P.M.

Check your understanding for Lessons 1–4.

Write the time in at least two ways. (Lessons 1–3)

1.
2.
3.
4.

Write how much time has passed. (Lesson 4)

5. A game starts at 4:30 P.M. It ends at 6:00 P.M.

6. A phone call starts at 11:05 A.M. It ends at 11:17 A.M.

7. A movie starts at 7:30 P.M. It ends at 8:45 P.M.

8. A meeting starts at 11:30 A.M. It ends at 1:15 P.M.

Use a Calendar

Objective Read and use a calendar.

Vocabulary

ordinal numbers

leap year

Learn About It

A calendar shows the days of the week and months of the year. Connor and Hannah are in a school play. They start rehearsing Thursday, January 9. The play is on January 23. How many days do they have to rehearse?

Calendar Units	
1 week = 7 days	
1 year = 12 months	
1 year = 52 weeks	
1 year = 365 days	

Find Thursday, January 9 on the calendar.

Now find January 23. Count the number of days from January 9 to January 23.

There are 14 days or 2 weeks.

January

Sun.	Mon.	Tue.	Wed.	Thu.	Fri.	Sat.
			1	2	3	4
5	6	7	8	9	10	11
12	13	14	15	16	17	18
19	20	21	22	23	24	25
26	27	28	29	30	31	

Write: January 9
Read: January ninth

Solution: They have 14 days, or 2 weeks, to rehearse.

Ordinal numbers are used to show order or position.

1st first	2nd second	3rd third	4th fourth	5th fifth	6th sixth	7th seventh
8th eighth	9th ninth	10th tenth	11th eleventh	12th twelfth	13th thirteenth	14th fourteenth
15th fifteenth	16th sixteenth	17th seventeenth	18th eighteenth	19th nineteenth	20th twentieth	21st twenty-first
22nd twenty-second	23rd twenty-third	24th twenty-fourth	25th twenty-fifth	26th twenty-sixth	27th twenty-seventh	28th twenty-eighth
29th twenty-ninth	30th thirtieth	31st thirty-first				

Ordinal numbers are often used when talking about the days on a calendar.

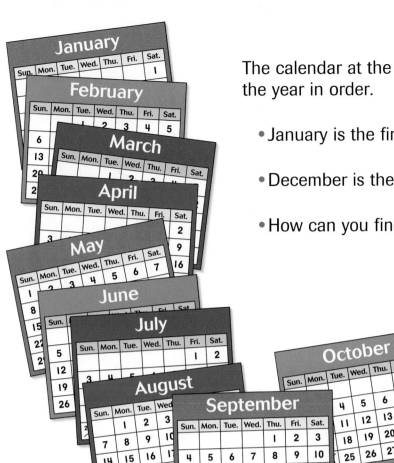

The calendar at the left shows the months of the year in order.

- January is the first month of the year.

- December is the twelfth month.

- How can you find the fifth month?

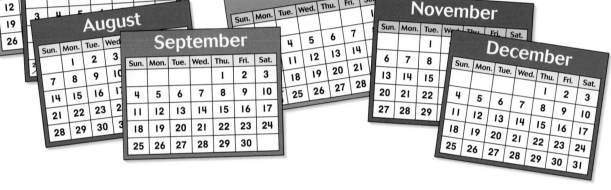

Guided Practice

Use the calendar on page 340 to write the day of the week.

1. January 3
2. January 11
3. January 20

Write the name of each month.

4. fourth month
5. ninth month
6. sixth month

7. What is the date of the thirteenth day of the seventh month?

Explain Your Thinking ▶ Look back at the January calendar on page 340. Why is the number of Tuesdays different from the number of Wednesdays? Why doesn't each month of a calendar start on a Sunday?

Ask Yourself

- How do I find the day of the week when I know the date?

- How can I use ordinal numbers to find the month?

Go On

Practice and Problem Solving

Use the calendar for Exercises 8–12.

8. What date is Memorial Day?

9. What day of the week is May 17?

10. What date is Mother's Day?

11. What is the date a week after May 20?

12. What date comes after May 31?

			May			
Sun.	Mon.	Tue.	Wed.	Thu.	Fri.	Sat.
1	2	3	4	5	6	7
8 Mother's Day	9	10	11	12	13	14
15	16	17	18	19	20	21
22	23	24	25	26	27	28
29	30 Memorial Day	31				

Write the name of the month that is 2 months after each month.

13. May   14. August   15. March   16. December

Write the name of the month that is 3 months before each month.

17. June   18. November   19. April   20. February

Write the name of the date.

21. fifth day of the tenth month

22. thirty-first day of the seventh month

23. twentieth day of the third month

24. sixteenth day of the first month

Use the calendar above for Problems 25–27.

25. Ms. Landry is the theater director at a school. If she gets paid every Friday, how many paychecks will she get in May?

26. **Estimate** Look at the calendar for May. About how many weeks are there between Mother's Day and Memorial Day?

27. Jamal went to the museum on Friday, May 6. Paul went 1 week later. If Miko went to the museum 3 days before Paul, what date did she go?

28. **Write Your Own** Use ordinal numbers to write three questions using the January calendar on page 340. Give your questions to a classmate to answer.

Extra Practice, See page 351, Set E.

Open Response

Complete each pattern. (Ch. 1, Lesson 5)

29. 9, 12, 15, 18, _____, 24

30. 98, 103, 108, 113, 118, _____

31. 45, 40, 35, 30, _____, _____

32. 107, 109, _____, 113, 115, 117

Multiple Choice

33. There are 31 days in March. If March 29 is a Tuesday, what day of the week is April 1?

(Ch. 12, Lesson 5)

A Tuesday   **C** Thursday

B Wednesday   **D** Friday

Problem Solving

Science Connection

Leap Year

Connor was born on February 29. His birthday is special because it takes place only in a leap year.

A **leap year** is a year that has one more day than an ordinary year. It has 366 days.

Our calendar usually has 365 days in a year. This is how long it takes the earth to circle the sun—almost. To keep time with the sun, every four years we add an extra day to February.

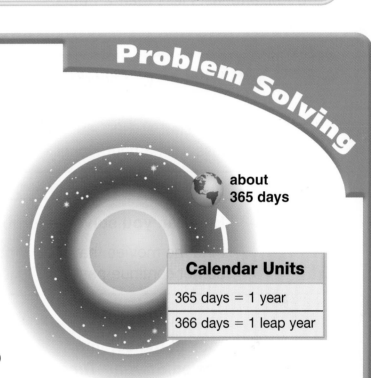

about 365 days

Calendar Units
365 days = 1 year
366 days = 1 leap year

1. The years 2000 and 2004 were leap years. When will the next three leap years occur?

2. Suppose it is a leap year. If February 27 is a Tuesday, what day is March 2?

3. Connor was born on February 29, 1996. How many actual birthdays will he have celebrated by 2005?

People born on February 29 don't have a birthday every year. Stolen base leader John "Pepper" Martin died when he was 61 years old, but he had only 15 birthdays!

Problem-Solving Application

Use a Schedule

Objective Read and use a schedule.

Movie Schedule

Movie	Starting Time	Ending Time
Mister Fritter	1:50 P.M.	2:55 P.M.
Looking for Larry	1:00 P.M.	3:15 P.M.
Wonder Dog	1:00 P.M.	2:45 P.M.
Zombies	12:00 P.M.	2:30 P.M.
Godzilla in Love	1:00 P.M.	3:30 P.M.
To Catch a Fish	12:00 P.M.	1:40 P.M.

A schedule is a table that lists the times for events or activities.

Problem Connor and his friends are going to the movies for his birthday. They need to find a movie that starts at 1:00 P.M. and lasts less than 2 hours. Which movie should they choose?

UNDERSTAND

What do you need to find?

You need to find the movies that start at 1:00 P.M. and are less than 2 hours long.

PLAN

How can you solve the problem?

Find the movies that start at 1:00 P.M. and do not continue past 3:00 P.M.

SOLVE

Look at the column labeled *Starting Time*.

Three movies start at 1:00 P.M.

- *Looking for Larry*
- *Wonder Dog*
- *Godzilla in Love*

Now look at the column labeled *Ending Time*.

The movies end at different times.

- *Looking for Larry* ends at 3:15 P.M.
- *Wonder Dog* ends at 2:45 P.M.
- *Godzilla in Love* ends at 3:30 P.M.

Wonder Dog starts at 1:00 P.M. and lasts for less than 2 hours, so Connor and his friends should see that movie.

LOOK BACK

Mister Fritter also lasts less than 2 hours. Why couldn't Connor and his friends see that movie?

Ask Yourself
- Did I check the starting time for each movie?
- Did I check the ending time for each movie?

Use the schedule on page 344 for Problems 1 and 2.

1. The movie theater cancels the movie that starts at 1:00 P.M. and ends at 3:30 P.M. Which movie is canceled?

2. If you arrived at the movie theater at noon and wanted to see 2 movies before 3:00 P.M., which movies could you see?

   (Hint) Look for the shortest movie that starts at 12:00 P.M.

Independent Practice

Use the schedule below for Problems 3–6.

3. Hannah's schedule is hard to read. Her activities should be listed from the earliest starting time to the latest. How should they appear?

4. Hannah wants to have lunch with her grandmother from noon to 1:00 P.M. Between which two activities should she have lunch?

5. Suppose Hannah decides to practice the piano for twice as much time as her schedule shows. How long would she practice the piano?

6. If Hannah's soccer game runs half an hour late, how much time will she have to clean her room before she has to go to the library?

7. **Create Your Own** Make a schedule that shows what you will do after school today. Then compare your schedule with that of a classmate.

Hannah
Saturday Schedule

Activity	Starting Time	Ending Time
Practice piano	9:30 A.M.	10:00 A.M.
Eat breakfast	8:00 A.M.	8:20 A.M.
Play soccer	1:15 P.M.	2:30 P.M.
Clean room	2:45 P.M.	3:15 P.M.
Help run errands	11:00 A.M.	11:45 A.M.
Go to library	3:15 P.M.	4:00 P.M.

Audio Tutor 2/2 Listen and Understand

Temperature: Degrees Fahrenheit and Celsius

Objective Tell temperature in degrees Fahrenheit and degrees Celsius.

Vocabulary

degrees
  Fahrenheit (°F)

degrees
  Celsius (°C)

negative

Materials
Thermometer

Learn About It

A thermometer is used to measure temperature. It shows how warm or cold something is.

You can measure temperature:
  • in customary units as
    degrees Fahrenheit (°F)
  • in metric units as
    degrees Celsius (°C)

Look at the thermometer to the right. What temperature does it show?

Solution: The temperature is 35°Celsius or 95°Fahrenheit.

▶ When temperatures are very cold, the thermometer may show numbers below zero. Then the temperature is written as a **negative** number. The thermometer below shows −5°F.

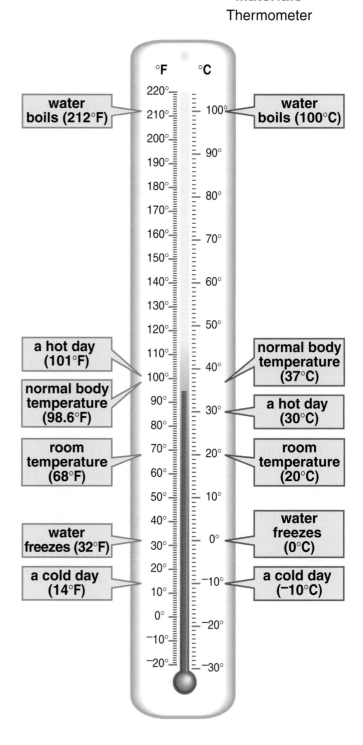

Extra Help at **eduplace.com/map**

Try this activity to compare temperatures.

The red line in a thermometer is really a liquid. It moves up when it is warm, and down when it is cool.

Use a thermometer to measure:

- The temperature of cold water from the sink
- The temperature of hot water from the sink
- Your classroom air temperature

Then measure the temperature outside each day for a week.

How did the temperature change?

Does it matter what time of day you look at the thermometer?

Guided Practice

Ask Yourself

- Where is the top of the red bar?
- What temperature describes hot? warm? cool? cold?

Write each temperature using °C. Then write *hot, warm, cool,* or *cold* to describe the temperature.

1.
2.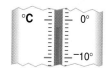
3.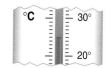

Write each temperature using °F. Then write *hot, warm, cool,* or *cold* to describe the temperature.

4.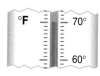
5.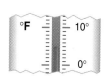
6.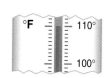

Explain Your Thinking ▶ Which feels colder, 10°F or ⁻10°F? Explain.

Which feels warmer, 10°F or 10°C? Explain.

Go On

Write each temperature using °F or °C. Then write *hot, warm, cool,* or *cold* to describe the temperature.

7.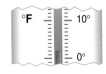

8.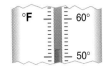

9.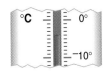

10.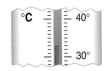

Write these temperatures in order from coldest to warmest.

11. 32°F, 0°F, ⁻1°F

12. 43°C, ⁻12°C, 10°C

13. 10°F, 100°C, 100°F

14. 17°C, ⁻17°C, 7°C

15. 0°C, 0°F, 100°C

16. 3°F, 53°F, ⁻3°F

Choose the better estimate of the temperature.

17.

a. 0°C   b. 30°C

18.

a. 70°F   b. 20°F

19.

a. 50°F   b. 100°F

Solve.

20. The temperature in one swimming pool is 20°F. The temperature in another is 20°C. Choose the swimming pool where you would rather swim.

21. When Cole went to school in the morning the temperature was 56°F. When he got home it was 73°F. How many degrees did the temperature rise?

22. **Write About It** Suppose you are outside, and the temperature is 28°C. Describe an activity you might do and the clothes you would wear.

23. The temperature rose 10° from 10 A.M. to 3 P.M. If it rose the same amount each hour, how much higher was the temperature at noon than at 10 A.M.?

Extra Practice See page 351, Set F.

Open Response

Find each product. Multiply factors in parentheses first. (Ch. 9, Lesson 8)

24. $3 \times (5 \times 2) = $ ____.

25. $(3 \times 3) \times 4 = $ ____.

26. $(0 \times 7) \times 3 = $ ____.

27. Sonia visited her aunt last winter for three days. On Friday the temperature was 5°F. On Saturday it was 2°F and on Sunday it was ⁻5°F. Put the days in order from coldest to warmest. (Ch. 12, Lesson 7)

Problem Solving

Visual Thinking
Using a Time Line

You can use a time line to show when things happen. The time line below shows the 24 hours in a day.

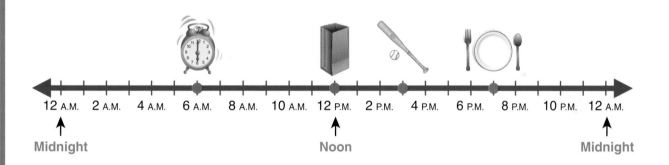

Write the time for each of the activities shown on the time line. Use A.M. and P.M.

1. play ball

2. eat dinner

3. wake up

4. eat lunch

5. How much time passed between waking up and having lunch?

6. Bedtime is 2 hours after dinner. What time is bedtime?

 7. Write Your Own Make your own time line for a day.

Chapter Review/Test

VOCABULARY

Vocabulary

minute

degrees Celsius

leap year

ordinal number

1. The temperature 25°C means twenty-five ____.
2. There are 366 days in a ____.
3. A unit of time that is shorter than an hour is a ____.

CONCEPTS AND SKILLS

Describe each time as minutes before and after an hour. (Lessons 1–3, pp. 330–335)

4.

5.

6.

7.

Name each month or date. (Lesson 5, pp. 340–343)

8. sixth month
9. eleventh month
10. 3 months after October
11. 4 months before June
12. fourth day of the seventh month
13. twenty-fifth day of the ninth month

Write the temperatures in order from coldest to warmest. (Lesson 7, pp. 346–348)

14. 5°C, 10°C, 0°C
15. 1°F, 11°F, ⁻1°F
16. 33°C, 3°C, 13°C
17. 12°F, 2°F, 20°F

PROBLEM SOLVING

Use the schedule to solve. (Lessons 4, 6, pp. 336–338, 344–345)

Cole's Saturday Schedule

Activity	Start Time	End Time
swimming	10:00 A.M.	11:00 A.M.
lunch	11:45 A.M.	12:30 P.M.
movies	1:00 P.M.	3:15 P.M.

18. How long is lunch?
19. Which activity lasts 1 hour?
20. For how long can Cole read between lunch and the movies?

Write About It

Show You Understand

Sue and her father went on a fishing trip. Explain how you can use the clues below to figure out the day and date they returned.

- July 1 is a Friday.
- They left for the lake on July 8.
- They were gone for two weeks and one day.

Extra Practice

Set A (Lesson 1, pp. 330–331)

Write each time using numbers.

1. three o'clock   **2.** half past nine   **3.** quarter after two   **4.** one-fifteen

---

Set B (Lesson 2, pp. 332–333)

Describe each time as minutes before and after an hour.

1.    **2.**    **3.**    **4.**

Set C (Lesson 3, pp. 334–335)

Describe each time as minutes before and after an hour.

1.    **2.** 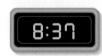   **3.**    **4.**

Set D (Lesson 4, pp. 336–338)

Look at each pair of times. Write how much time has passed.

1. Start: 11:45 A.M.
　　 End: 12:40 P.M.

2. Start: 2:45 P.M.
　　 End: 3:02 P.M.

3. Start:　8:06 A.M.
　　 End:　11:52 A.M.

Set E (Lesson 5, pp. 340–343)

Name each month or date.

1. 4 months after June   **2.** fifth day of the fifth month   **3.** 8 months before May

---

Set F (Lesson 7, pp. 346–348)

Write each temperature using °F or °C. Then write *hot, warm, cool,* or *cold.*

1. 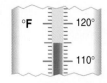   **2.** 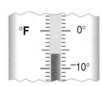   **3.**    **4.**

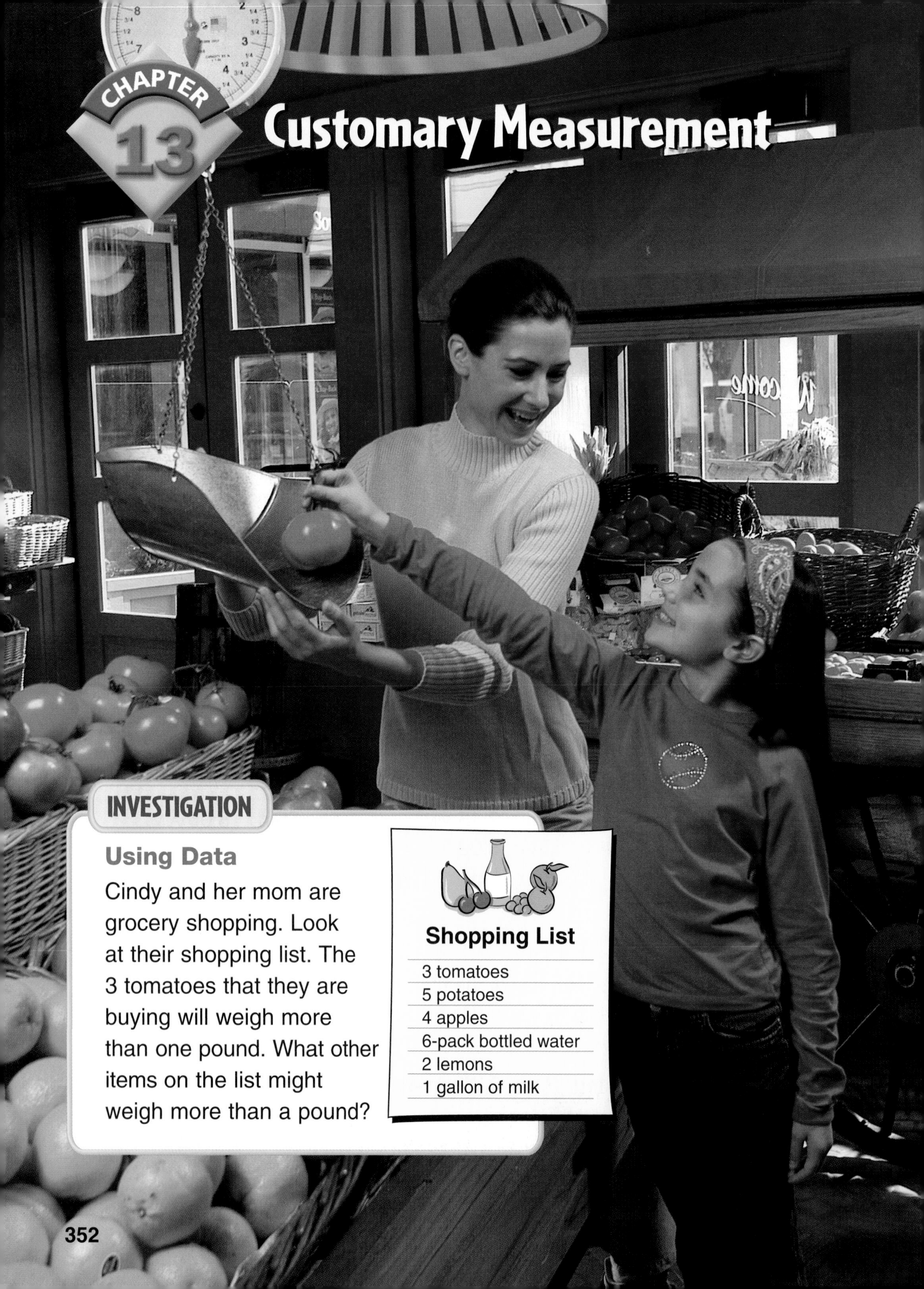

CHAPTER 13

Customary Measurement

INVESTIGATION

Using Data

Cindy and her mom are grocery shopping. Look at their shopping list. The 3 tomatoes that they are buying will weigh more than one pound. What other items on the list might weigh more than a pound?

Shopping List

- 3 tomatoes
- 5 potatoes
- 4 apples
- 6-pack bottled water
- 2 lemons
- 1 gallon of milk

Use What You Know

**Use this page to review and remember
what you need to know for this chapter.**

VOCABULARY

Choose the best term to complete each sentence.

Vocabulary
ruler
pound
scale
measuring cup

1. You use a _____ to find how much something weighs.

2. You use a _____ to find how long something is.

3. You use a _____ to find how much liquid
a container holds.

CONCEPTS AND SKILLS

Measure to the nearest inch.

4.

5. Green

6.

7.

Choose the better estimate

8. **a.** 8 inches long
b. 8 feet long

9. **a.** 7 inches tall
b. 7 feet tall

Write About It

10. Bo drew a line 1 foot long. Dell drew
a line 11 inches long. Whose line is
longer? Explain how you know.

Facts Practice, See page 668.

Measure to the Nearest Inch

Objective Estimate and measure length to the nearest inch.

Vocabulary
inch (in.)

Materials
inch ruler
classroom objects
small paper clips
1 piece of string

Work Together

There are many ways to estimate and measure the length of objects. One way is to use a nonstandard unit such as your hand or paper clips.

Work with a partner. Estimate and then measure the length of the pencil below. Use your hand and paper clips.

 STEP 1 Use the width of your hand to measure the pencil.

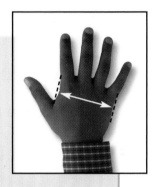

- Estimate: _____ hand widths
- How many hand widths long is the pencil?
- How close is that to your estimate?

 STEP 2 Estimate the length of the pencil in paper clips. Then lay paper clips end to end along the picture of the pencil.

- How many paper clips long is the pencil?
- How close is that to your estimate?
- Which measurement do you think is better for measuring a pencil? Explain.

▶ Another way to measure length is to use an inch ruler. An **inch (in.)** is a standard unit used to measure length in the customary measurement system.

Estimate and then measure the length of the pencil below to the nearest inch.

> Some rulers have a zero on them. That kind of a ruler uses the zero as the starting point to measure.

STEP 1 Line up the left end of the pencil with the left end of the ruler.

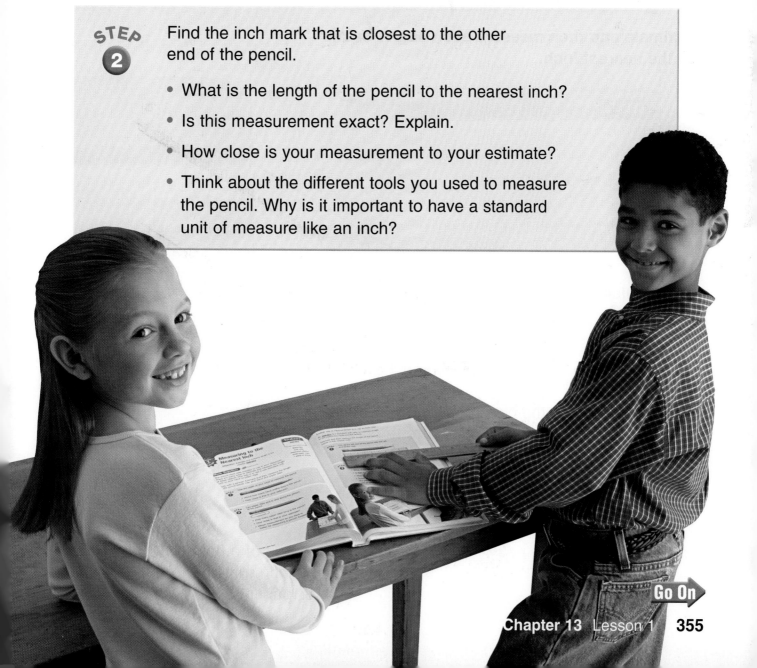

STEP 2 Find the inch mark that is closest to the other end of the pencil.

- What is the length of the pencil to the nearest inch?

- Is this measurement exact? Explain.

- How close is your measurement to your estimate?

- Think about the different tools you used to measure the pencil. Why is it important to have a standard unit of measure like an inch?

Go On

Follow these directions.

- Find 5 classroom objects to measure.

- Estimate and then measure the length of each object to the nearest inch.

- Record your work in a table like the one below.

	Object	My Estimate	Length to the Nearest Inch
1.			
2.			
3.			
4.			
5.			

Estimate and then measure each object below to the nearest inch.

6.

7.

8.

9.

Use a ruler. Draw a line of each length.

10. 3 inches   **11.** 10 inches   **12.** 7 inches   **13.** 5 inches

14. Name three objects that are about 1 inch long or wide.

15. Find objects in the classroom that you think are about 6 inches long. Measure the objects to check your estimates.

Choose the better unit to measure each item. Explain your reasoning.

16. length of a desk
   a. paper clips
   b. hand widths

17. height of a box
   a. inch ruler
   b. paper clips

18. What's Wrong? Mary said the pencil below is about 4 inches long. What did she do wrong? Explain your answer.

19. Carly wants to build a birdhouse. She needs to cut a 9-inch strip of wood. Does she need an exact measure or an estimate? Explain.

20. Kevin wants to make a sign. He needs to cut a length of paper. Does he need an exact measure or an estimate? Explain.

21. Pick an object. Estimate its length and then measure. Explain why you chose the tool you used and how you measured.

22. Measure your shoe, your math book, and your thumb using an inch ruler. Order the measurements you made from least to greatest.

Talk About It • Write About It

You learned how to measure using nonstandard units and using the standard unit of inches.

You can use string and a ruler to measure curved paths.

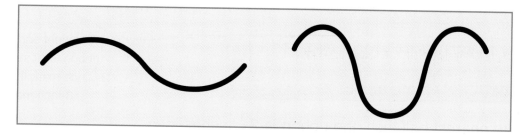

• Put the string along one of the paths. Then straighten the string and measure it with a ruler.

• Repeat for the other path.

23. Explain How can you use the strings to compare the lengths of the designs?

24. Why couldn't you use just a ruler to measure these paths?

Measure to the Nearest Half Inch

Objective Measure objects to the nearest half inch.

Learn About It

Ms. Sanchez owns a craft shop. She is measuring a piece of ribbon for a customer. The ribbon needs to be $8\frac{1}{2}$ inches long.

You can use an inch ruler to measure to the nearest **half inch**.

▶ **How long is this ribbon to the nearest half inch?**

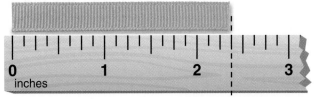

To the nearest half inch, the ribbon is $2\frac{1}{2}$ inches long.

The right end of the ribbon is closer to the $2\frac{1}{2}$-inch mark than to either the 2-inch mark or the 3-inch mark.

▶ **How long is this ribbon to the nearest half inch?**

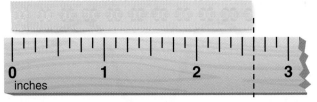

To the nearest half inch, the ribbon is $2\frac{1}{2}$ inches long.

The right end of this ribbon is closer to the $2\frac{1}{2}$-inch mark than to the 3-inch mark.

Another Example

Sometimes a measurement to the nearest half inch is a whole number.

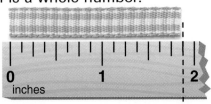

To the nearest half inch, this ribbon is 2 inches long.

Extra Help at **eduplace.com/map**

Guided Practice

Measure each to the nearest half inch.

Ask Yourself
- Which mark on the ruler is closest to the end of the object?

1.

2.

Use an inch ruler. Draw a line of each length.

3. $5\frac{1}{2}$ in.   4. 7 in.   5. $2\frac{1}{2}$ in.   6. 4 in.

Explain Your Thinking ▶ Why might it be better to measure to the nearest half inch than to the nearest inch?

Practice and Problem Solving

Measure each to the nearest half inch.

7.

8.

Use an inch ruler. Draw a line of each length.

9. $\frac{1}{2}$ in.   10. $3\frac{1}{2}$ in.   11. 5 in.   12. $7\frac{1}{2}$ in.

Solve.

13. One line is 2 inches long. Another is $3\frac{1}{2}$ inches long. A third is 4 inches long. How long are the 3 lines if you connect them end to end?

14. Mateo cut a $2\frac{1}{2}$-inch piece of thread. Karen cut a piece of thread that is 2 inches longer than Mateo's. How long is Karen's thread?

15. **Analyze** A ribbon measures $3\frac{1}{2}$ inches long. One end of the ribbon lies on the 2-inch mark of a ruler. Where does the other end lie?

Mixed Review and Test Prep

Open Response

Write how much time has passed.

(Ch. 12, Lesson 4)

16. Start: 8:30 A.M.   17. Start: 9:00 P.M.
    End: 8:50 A.M.   End: 10:30 P.M.

18. A white ribbon is $1\frac{1}{2}$ inches long. A pink ribbon is 3 inches longer. How long is the pink ribbon? (Ch. 13, Lesson 2)

Audio Tutor 2/4 Listen and Understand

Customary Units of Length

Objective Measure the lengths of objects using customary units.

Learn About It

Alex wants to buy a robot that is a foot tall. Robot Rita is 6 inches tall. Robot Rick is 12 inches tall. Which robot should Alex buy?

Since 1 foot equals 12 inches, Alex should buy Robot Rick.

Customary Units of Length
1 foot = 12 inches
1 yard = 3 feet
1 yard = 36 inches
1 mile = 1,760 yards
1 mile = 5,280 feet

▶ You can measure objects of many different sizes using customary units of length.

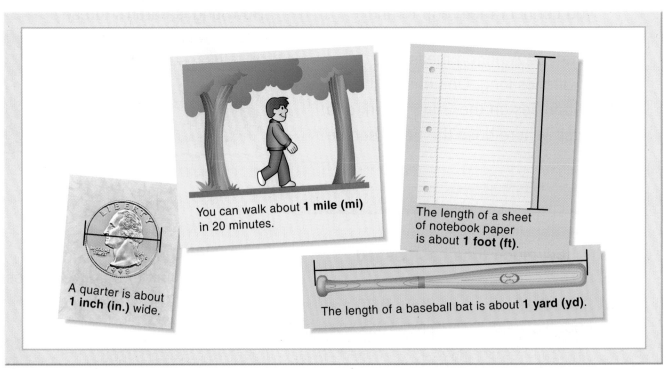

A quarter is about **1 inch (in.)** wide.

You can walk about **1 mile (mi)** in 20 minutes.

The length of a sheet of notebook paper is about **1 foot (ft)**.

The length of a baseball bat is about **1 yard (yd)**.

Guided Practice

Choose the unit you would use to measure each.
Write *inch*, *foot*, *yard,* or *mile*.

1. the width of a piece of note paper

2. the distance from your home to an airport

3. the length of a football field

Choose the better estimate.

4. the width of a shopping bag
   a. 2 feet   **b.** 2 inches

5. the length of a classroom
   a. 12 yards   **b.** 12 inches

6. the width of a postcard
   a. 3 feet   **b.** 3 inches

7. the distance across a lake
   a. 4 yards   **b.** 4 miles

Explain Your Thinking ▶ Why do people use miles instead of feet to measure the distance between cities?

Ask Yourself
- Do I need to use a small, medium, or large unit of measure?

Practice and Problem Solving

Choose the better estimate.

8. the height of a building
   a. 50 miles   **b.** 50 yards

9. the length of a car
   a. 12 yards   **b.** 12 feet

10. the length of a boat
   a. 24 feet   **b.** 24 miles

11. the distance between two cities
   a. 35 miles   **b.** 35 inches

12. the width of your hand
   a. 4 inches   **b.** 40 feet

13. the depth of a swimming pool
   a. 80 feet   **b.** 8 feet

Algebra • Functions Copy and complete each table. Write the rule you used.

14.

Feet	1	2	3	4	5
Inches	12	24	■	■	■

15.

Yards	1	2	3	4	5	6
Feet	3	6	9	■	■	■

Go On

Copy and complete.

16. 15 ft = _____ yd   **17.** 6 yd = _____ ft   **18.** 2 ft = _____ in.

19. 36 in. = _____ ft   **20.** 4 ft = _____ in.   **21.** 6 in. = _____ ft

22. 3 ft = _____ yd   **23.** 10 yd = _____ ft   **24.** 18 in. = _____ ft

Compare. Write >, <, or = for each ●.

25. 2 yd ● 2 ft   **26.** 5,280 ft ● 1 mi   **27.** 1 ft ● 10 in.

28. 1 mile ● 1,750 yd   **29.** 12 in. ● 12 ft   **30.** 1 yd ● 3 ft

31. 24 in. ● 1 ft   **32.** 3 ft ● 2 yd   **33.** 5 yd ● 18 ft

Order from shortest to longest.

34. 6 in.   2 yd   3 ft   **35.** 1 mi   6,000 ft   10 yd

36. 50 yd   50 mi   50 ft   **37.** 15 yd   30 ft   100 in.

Calculator • Complete the table. Use a calculator if needed.

38.

12 inches = 1 foot × 12
24 inches = 2 feet × 12
36 inches = _____ feet × 12
48 inches = _____ feet × 12

39.

3 feet = 1 yard × 3
6 feet = 2 yards × 3
9 feet = _____ yards × 3
12 feet = _____ yards × 3

40.

36 inches = 1 yard × 36
72 inches = 2 yards × 36
108 inches = _____ yards × 36
144 inches = _____ yards × 36

Extra Practice See page 379, Set B.

Science Connection
Measuring Geckos

Geckos grow up to 9 inches long! How long is this gecko to the nearest quarter inch?

The gecko is about $5\frac{1}{4}$ inches long.

Try This!

• Find 3 objects in your classroom. Estimate their length to the nearest inch. Then measure them to the nearest quarter inch.

> The end of the gecko's nose is closer to the $5\frac{1}{4}$-inch mark than to the 5-inch mark.

Check your understanding of Lessons 1–3.

Use an inch ruler. Draw a line of each length. (Lessons 1, 2)

1. 2 in.   **2.** 7 in.   **3.** $4\frac{1}{2}$ in.   **4.** $8\frac{1}{2}$ in.

Measure each feather to the nearest half inch. (Lesson 2)

5.    **6.**

Choose the unit you would use to measure each.
Write _inch_, _foot_, _yard_, or _mile_. (Lesson 3)

7. the height of a flagpole   **8.** the width of a stamp

9. the length of a sneaker   **10.** the distance across the ocean

---

Extra Practice at **eduplace.com/map**

Chapter 13 Lesson 3   **363**

Problem-Solving Strategy
Use Logical Reasoning

Objective Use logical reasoning to solve problems.

Problem Sam, Joella, and Ming each bought a model airplane. Ming's airplane is 9 inches long. It is 4 inches longer than Sam's airplane. Sam's airplane is 2 inches shorter than Joella's. How long is Joella's airplane?

UNDERSTAND

This is what you know.

- Ming's airplane is 9 inches long.

- Ming's airplane is 4 inches longer than Sam's.

- Sam's airplane is 2 inches shorter than Joella's.

PLAN

Use logical reasoning to help you solve the problem.

SOLVE

Start with what you know.

- **Ming's airplane** is 9 inches long.

- **Sam's airplane** is 4 inches shorter than Ming's airplane.

    Subtract.   9 in. − 4 in. = 5 in.

Sam's airplane is 5 inches long.

- **Joella's airplane** is 2 inches longer than Sam's airplane.

    Add.   5 in. + 2 in. = 7 in.

Solution: Joella's airplane is 7 inches long.

LOOK BACK

Reread the problem. Does the solution match the facts in the problem?

Use the **Ask Yourself** questions to help you solve each problem.

1. Bill, Liz, and Rosa each bought a model train. The trains are 12 inches, 15 inches, and 18 inches long. Rosa's train is not as long as Bill's. Liz's train is the longest. How long is each train?

   (Hint) How long is Liz's train?

2. Joe's model ship is 25 inches longer than Amy's. Amy's model ship is 50 inches long. Ty's is twice as long as Joe's. How long is each model ship?

Ask Yourself

UNDERSTAND → **What facts do I know?**

PLAN → **How can I organize the facts?**

SOLVE → **Did I start with a given fact and use it to find a missing fact?**

LOOK BACK → **Does my answer match the facts in the problem?**

Independent Practice

Use logical reasoning to solve each problem.

3. Sue, Andy, Lu, and Carlos each bought a hobby book. The books cost $3, $5, $6, and $8. Andy spent $6. Sue spent less than Lu did. Carlos spent the most. How much did each of them spend?

4. Alexi, Lila, Sarah, and Josh measured their heights. They are 49 inches, 51 inches, 54 inches, and 38 inches tall. Alexi is the tallest. Josh is 49 inches tall. Sarah is taller than Josh. What are their heights?

5. Beth, Maya, Jill, and Di are in line to buy movie tickets. Jill is ahead of Beth. Maya is behind Beth. Di is second. What is their order in line from first to last?

Mixed Problem Solving

Solve. Show your work. Tell what strategy you used.

6. **Multistep** Gina added new stickers to her album. On one page she put 5 rows of 7 stickers each. On the next page, she put 6 rows of 7 stickers each. How many new stickers did Gina add?

7. Jodi has 8 more markers than Dede. Together they have 20 markers. How many markers does each girl have?

8. **Represent** You want to display 16 stuffed animals in equal groups of 2 or more. What are the different ways the 16 stuffed animals can be grouped?

You Choose

Strategy
- Act It Out
- Draw a Picture
- Guess and Check
- Write a Number Sentence
- Use Logical Reasoning

Computation Method
- Mental Math
- Estimation
- Paper and Pencil
- Calculator

Data Use the sign to solve Problems 9–12.

9. Lee and Elena go to the zoo at 1:00 P.M. They want to take a zoo tour. What movies can they see?

10. Kenny goes on the zoo tour at 12:00 P.M. Linda goes to see the first show of *All About Elephants*. What is the earliest time they can meet for lunch?

11. If Zach and Hal take the 10:00 A.M. zoo tour, which showing of *Reptiles Are Cool* can they see?

12. **You Decide** Plan a trip to the zoo. Use the data to make a schedule of what you will do.

At the ZOO

Zoo Hours	9:30 AM–6:00 PM
Zoo Tours	10:00 AM
(All tours	12:00 PM
last 1 hour.)	2:00 PM

Movies

Reptiles Are Cool	10:30 AM, 2:30 PM
Animals of the Deep	11:30 AM, 3:30 PM
All About Elephants	12:30 PM, 4:30 PM

(All movies last 30 minutes.)

Cafeteria Hours	11:00 AM–2:30 PM

Problem Solving on Tests

Multiple Choice

Choose the letter of the correct answer.

1. What is the length of Cindy's barrette to the nearest half inch?

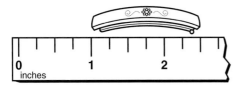

   A $1\frac{1}{2}$ in.   **C** $2\frac{1}{2}$ in.

   B 2 in.   **D** 3 in.

   (Chapter 13, Lesson 2)

2. Two sisters are making fruit salad cups. They have 54 grapes. If they make 9 equal servings, how many grapes will they put in each cup?

   F 9   **G** 7   **H** 8   **J** 6

   (Chapter 11, Lesson 9)

Open Response

Solve each problem.

3. Kate made this spinner. Why is it more likely that the spinner will land on the letter A?

   (Chapter 7, Lesson 1)

4. Deena wants to give 56 balloons equally to 8 people. What multiplication fact can help her solve this problem?

   (Chapter 11, Lesson 8)

Extended Response

5. Using a schedule can help you plan your time. Write your schedule for a typical school day. Use the sample schedule to help you.

MY SCHEDULE			
Activity	Start Time	End Time	Amount of Time
Get Ready for School			
School			
Soccer Practice			
Dinner			
Homework			
Free Time			
Get Ready for Bed			
Sleep			

   a. Write each activity, its start time, and its end time.

   b. Find the amount of time it takes to do each activity. Fill in the last column.

   c. Which activity takes the most time?

   d. Does the last column of your schedule add up to 24 hours? Why or why not?

   (Chapter 12, Lesson 6)

Education Place

See **eduplace.com/map** for more Test-Taking Tips.

Estimate and Measure Capacity

Objective Estimate and measure the amount a
container can hold.

Vocabulary
- **cup (c)**
- **pint (pt)**
- **quart (qt)**
- **gallon (gal)**

Materials
cup, pint, quart,
  gallon containers

different-size
  containers

Work Together

Capacity is the amount a container can hold. In the
customary system, **cup (c)**, **pint (pt)**, **quart (qt)**, and
gallon (gal) are measures of capacity.

STEP 1

Use the cup container to fill the pint
container. In a chart like the one
shown, record how many cups are
needed to fill the pint.

- How many cups are there in a pint?

Capacity			
	Pint	Quart	Gallon
Cups	2		
Pints			
Quarts			

STEP 2

Estimate the number of cups needed to fill the quart
and gallon containers. Use the cup container to check
your estimates. Record your results in the table.

- How many cups are there in a quart? a gallon?

STEP 3

Now estimate the number of pints needed to
fill the quart and gallon containers. Use the
pint container to check your estimates.
Record your results in the chart.

- How many pints are there in a
quart? a gallon?

STEP 4

Estimate the number of quarts needed to fill
the gallon container. Check your estimate
and record your results in the chart.

- How many quarts are there
in a gallon?

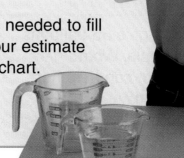

368

STEP 5 Now choose a different-size container. Estimate how many cups, pints, quarts, or gallons it holds. Then measure to check your estimate.

- Did the container hold more or less than you estimated?

STEP 6 Estimate and then measure the capacity of all the other containers.

On Your Own

Use your chart to find the missing measure.

1. 1 gal = ____ qt

2. 1 pt = ____ c

3. 1 qt = ____ pt

4. 2 qt = ____ pt

5. 3 pt = ____ c

6. 2 gal = ____ qt

7. 3 qt = ____ pt

8. 3 gal = ____ qt

9. 1 gal = ____ pt

10. **Explain** How can you find the number of quarts when you know the number of gallons?

Talk About It • Write About It

You have learned to estimate and measure the capacity of different-size containers.

11. Could these containers have the same capacity? Explain your thinking. Then describe a way to find out.

12. Suppose you pour 1 gallon of water into pint containers. Then you pour 1 gallon of water into quart containers. Would you use more pint containers or more quart containers? Explain.

Lesson 6

Customary Units of Capacity

Objective Measure and compare the amount a container can hold in customary units.

Learn About It

The Juice Bar at the mall sells juice in one-pint, one-quart, and one-gallon containers.

You can use customary units to measure capacity.

Customary Units of Capacity
1 pint = 2 cups
1 quart = 2 pints
1 gallon = 4 quarts

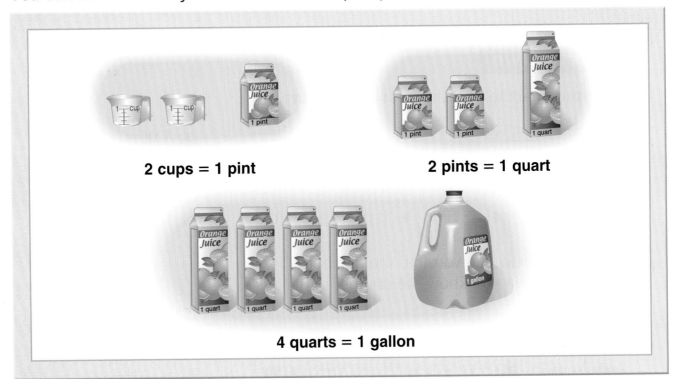

2 cups = 1 pint

2 pints = 1 quart

4 quarts = 1 gallon

Guided Practice

Choose the unit you would use to measure the capacity of each. Write *cup, pint, quart,* or *gallon*.

1.

2.

3.

4. Compare the capacities of the containers in Exercises 1–3. Write them in order from greatest to least capacity.

Ask Yourself

- Are you measuring a small, medium, or large container?
- Which is the smallest unit of measure? the largest?

Explain Your Thinking ▶ Is a quart greater than or less than 5 cups?

Choose the unit you would use. Write *cup, pint, quart,* or *gallon*.

5.

6.

7.

8.

Choose the better estimate.

9. baby pool
   a. 20 gal   b. 20 c

10. watering can
    a. 2 qt   b. 200 pt

11. glass of juice
    a. 1 qt   b. 1 c

Write in order from least capacity to greatest capacity.

12. 1 qt   3 c   1 pt

13. 1 gal   5 qt   6 pt

Copy and complete.

14. 2 pt = ____ c

15. 4 qt = ____ gal

16. 3 qt = ____ pt

17. 2 pt = ____ qt

18. 8 c = ____ pt

19. 3 gal = ____ pt

Complete the table.

20.
4 pints = 1 quart × 2
8 pints = 2 quarts × 2
12 pints = ____ quarts × 2
16 pints = ____ quarts × 2

21.
16 quarts = 1 gallon × 4
32 quarts = 2 gallons × 4
48 quarts = ____ gallons × 4
64 quarts = ____ gallons × 4

22. For field day, 10 gallons of juice were donated to the school. How many quarts of juice is that?

Mixed Review and Test Prep

Open Response
Round each number to the greatest place. Then solve. (Ch. 5, Lesson 3)

23. 519 − 321

24. 681 − 129

25. $8.67 − $2.48

26. 5,100 − 1,922

Multiple Choice
27. What is the best estimate for the capacity of a kitchen sink? (Ch. 13, Lesson 6)

   A 10 cups   c 10 quarts

   B 10 pints   D 10 gallons

Hands On Lesson 7

Customary Units of Weight

Objective Measure the weights of objects in customary units.

Vocabulary
pound (lb)
ounce (oz)

Materials
balance scale
1-pound weight

Learn About It

At the Country Bakery, Mr. Macintosh sells his famous apple cookies by the pound.

Pound (lb) and **ounce (oz)** are customary units used when measuring weight.

Measure things that are very light—a paper clip, a key, or a slice of bread—in ounces.

Measure things that are heavy—a bicycle, a chair, or a loaf of bread—in pounds.

Customary Units of Weight
1 pound = 16 ounces

1 ounce

1 pound

16 one-ounce slices of bread have the same weight as a 1-pound loaf of bread.

Try this activity to estimate and measure weight.

STEP 1 Find five small objects in your classroom. Predict which objects weigh less than, more than, or about one pound. Record your work.

STEP 2 Use the balance scale and the 1-pound weight to check your predictions.

372

Choose the unit you would use to measure the weight of each. Write *ounce* or *pound*.

Ask Yourself

- Do I need a small or large unit of measure?
- Which is the smaller unit of measure? the larger unit?

1.

2.

3.

4.

5.

6.

Explain Your Thinking ▶ Which is heavier: a pound of flour or a pound of bricks? Explain.

Practice and Problem Solving

Choose the unit you would use to measure the weight. Write *ounce* or *pound*.

7.

8.

9.

10. refrigerator   11. cracker   12. paper towel

13. pencil   14. piano   15. sponge

Choose the better estimate.

16. a pizza
    a. 2 lb   b. 2 oz

17. a banana
    a. 6 lb   b. 6 oz

18. a slice of cheese
    a. 1 lb   b. 1 oz

19. a wooden spoon
    a. 10 oz   b. 100 oz

20. a turkey
    a. 2 lb   b. 20 lb

21. a television set
    a. 20 oz   b. 20 lb

Write in order from the least weight to the greatest weight.

22. 20 oz   1 lb   12 oz

23. 2 lb   25 oz   40 oz

24. 25 oz   50 oz   3 lb

25. $\frac{1}{2}$ lb   9 oz   7 oz

Go On

Find the missing measure.

26. 1 lb = ____ oz

27. 3 lb = ____ oz

28. 32 oz = ____ lb

29. 2 lb = ____ oz

30. 48 oz = ____ lb

31. $\frac{1}{2}$ lb = ____ oz

32. 8 oz = ____ lb

33. 4 lb = ____ oz

34. 16 oz = ____ lb

35. 5 lb = ____ oz

36. 64 oz = ____ lb

37. $1\frac{1}{2}$ lb = ____ oz

 Data Use the table for Problems 38–41.

38. Which box of cookies is heavier, pumpkin or blueberry? Explain how you know.

39. Which box of cookies is the heaviest? How many ounces does it weigh?

40. Write the boxes of cookies in order from heaviest to lightest.

41. Analyze Suppose a box of lemon cookies weighs 20 ounces. Is it heavier or lighter than the box of apple cookies? How much heavier or lighter?

 42. Write Your Own Write a rule that tells how to find the number of ounces when you know the number of pounds.

Country Bakery Cookies

Cookies	Weight
Apple	2 pounds
Chocolate	24 ounces
Pumpkin	8 ounces
Blueberry	1 pound

Mixed Review and Test Prep

Open Response

Add. (Ch. 4, Lesson 6)

43.
```
  125
   79
+  30
```

44.
```
 $3.09
  5.96
+ 7.25
```

45.
```
 $2.89
  0.15
+ 5.36
```

46. A bag of potatoes weighs 2 pounds 7 ounces. What is the weight of the bag in ounces? Explain how you know. (Ch. 13, Lesson 7)

Extra Practice See page 379, Set D.

Activity

Match the Measure

2 players

What You'll Need • Learning Tool 25 or 20 index cards

How to Play

1 Use Learning Tool 25 or make a set of cards like those shown in Set A and 2 sets of cards like those shown in Set B.

2 Shuffle all of the cards. Lay them face down in a 4 × 5 array.

3 Take turns turning over 2 cards at a time. A player makes a match when a unit of measure matches something that would normally be measured in that unit. For example, "feet" and "length of your classroom."

If a player makes a match, the player keeps the cards. If a player does not make a match, the player turns the cards back over.

4 Continue taking turns until all cards have been matched. The player with the most matches wins.

Set A

length of your classroom	distance to the store
weight of a cat	water in a sink
height of a third grader	distance to the moon
water in a pool	milk in a small carton
juice in a glass	weight of a desk

Set B

feet	cups
pounds	gallons
miles	

Problem-Solving Decision

Too Much or Too Little Information

Objective Use logical thinking to solve problems.

Before you can solve a problem you need to decide what information you need and if you have that information.

At Super Rocks a small bag of rocks weighs 8 ounces and a medium bag weighs 12 ounces. Large rocks cost $3 each.

Problem A	Problem B
How much will two small bags of rocks weigh?	How much will a medium bag of rocks and two large rocks weigh?
You have too much information. What facts do you need?	**You have too little information. What facts do you need?**
• weight of small bag of rocks (8 oz)	• weight of medium bag of rocks (12 oz) • weight of a large rock (not given)
There is more information in the problem, but it is not needed.	There is not enough information given in the problem.
Solve. $2 \times 8 = 16$ So, the two small bags of rocks weigh 16 ounces.	**Solve.** It isn't possible since the weight of a large rock isn't given.

Try These

Solve. If you can't solve the problem, tell what information you need.

1. Mimi bought 6 small bags of rocks. How much did all the bags of rocks weigh?

2. Cal bought 2 small bags of rocks and 5 large rocks. How much money did he spend?

3. Lee bought a medium bag and 3 large rocks. How much did all the rocks weigh?

4. Amanda bought a medium and a small bag of rocks. Did she buy more or less than a pound of rocks?

Solve. If you can't solve the problem, tell what information you need.

Colored Stones

5. Jared bought 4 bags of colored stones for a project. He paid with a ten-dollar bill. How much change did he get back?

6. Sarah paid using 3 one-dollar bills and 3 quarters for 2 bags of colored stones. She received no change. Which bags did she buy?

7. Fran needs 100 stones for a project. She already has a bag of stones. Which size bags should she buy so that she gets at least 100 stones but as few extras as possible?

Logical Thinking
Non-Standard Units

Problem Solving

You can measure with a dollar bill when you don't have a ruler handy. A dollar bill is about 6 inches long.

1. Farmer Mac grew a 30-inch-long squash. How many dollar bills long is it?

2. Farmer Mac's chickens weigh 7 pounds each. His dog weighs 42 pounds. How many chickens does his dog weigh?

3. Farmer Mac has a 294-pound pig. How many dogs does his pig weigh? Use a calculator if you wish.

Chapter Review/Test

VOCABULARY

Choose the best term to complete each sentence.

Vocabulary

cup

foot

pint

miles

pounds

1. The length of a sheet of paper is about a ____.

2. A small glass of juice is about the same as a ____.

3. The distance between cities is measured in ____.

4. A cat could weigh about nine _____.

CONCEPTS AND SKILLS

Measure to the nearest half inch. (Lesson 2, pp. 358–359)

5. ▬▬▬▬▬

6. ▬▬▬▬▬

7. ▬▬▬

Choose the unit you would use to measure each.
Write *inch, foot, cup, gallon, ounce*, or *pound*. (Lessons 3, 6–7, pp. 360–362, 370–374)

8. length of a finger

9. capacity of a pool

10. the weight of a dog

Choose the better estimate. (Lessons 3, 6–7, pp. 360–362, 370–374)

11. height of a house
    a. 25 ft   b. 25 yd

12. capacity of a bathtub
    a. 15 c   b. 15 gal

13. box of toothpicks
    a. 2 oz   b. 2 lb

Copy and complete. (Lessons 3, 5–7, pp. 360–362, 368–374)

14. ____ qt = 4 gal

15. 2 pt = ____ c

16. ____ oz = 3 lb

17. 2 gal = ____ pt

18. ____ ft = 9 yd

19. 32 oz = ____ lb

PROBLEM SOLVING

Solve. (Lessons 4, 8, pp. 364–366, 376–377)

20. Sandra is 2 inches taller than Tabitha and 4 inches shorter than Ted and Amy. Ted is an inch taller than Samson. Samson is 61 inches tall. How tall is Tabitha?

Write About It

Show You Understand

Suppose you have 2 gallons of cider for 15 people. If you serve the cider in 1-cup glasses, could everyone have 2 glasses each?

Extra Practice

Measure each to the nearest half inch.

1. ▬▬▬▬▬▬▬▬▬   2. ▬▬▬▬▬▬   3. ▬▬▬▬▬

Set B (Lesson 3, pp. 360–362)

Choose the better estimate.

1. length of your foot
   a. 10 inches   **b.** 10 feet

2. length of a piece of spaghetti
   a. 1 foot   **b.** 1 yard

Find the missing measure.

3. 3 ft = ____ in.   **4.** ____ yd = 9 ft   **5.** 36 in. = ____ yd   **6.** 4 yd = ____ ft

7. ____ ft = 24 in.   **8.** 6 in. = ____ ft   **9.** ____ yd = 30 ft   **10.** 5 ft = ____ in.

Set C (Lesson 6, pp. 370–371)

Choose the better estimate.

1. glass of milk
   a. 1 c   **b.** 1 qt

2. bottle of water
   a. 3 c   **b.** 3 gal

3. baby pool
   a. 75 c   **b.** 75 gal

Copy and complete.

4. 3 pt = ____ c   **5.** ____ pt = 6 gal   **6.** 4 gal = ____ qt   **7.** 4 pt = ____ qt

Set D (Lesson 7, pp. 372–374)

Choose the better estimate.

1. calculator
   a. 12 lb   **b.** 12 oz

2. baby
   a. 8 lb   **b.** 8 oz

3. key
   a. 1 oz   **b.** 100 oz

Find the missing measure.

4. 24 oz = ____ lb   **5.** ____ oz = 7 lb   **6.** ____ lb = 64 oz   **7.** 5 lb = ____ oz

Metric Measurement

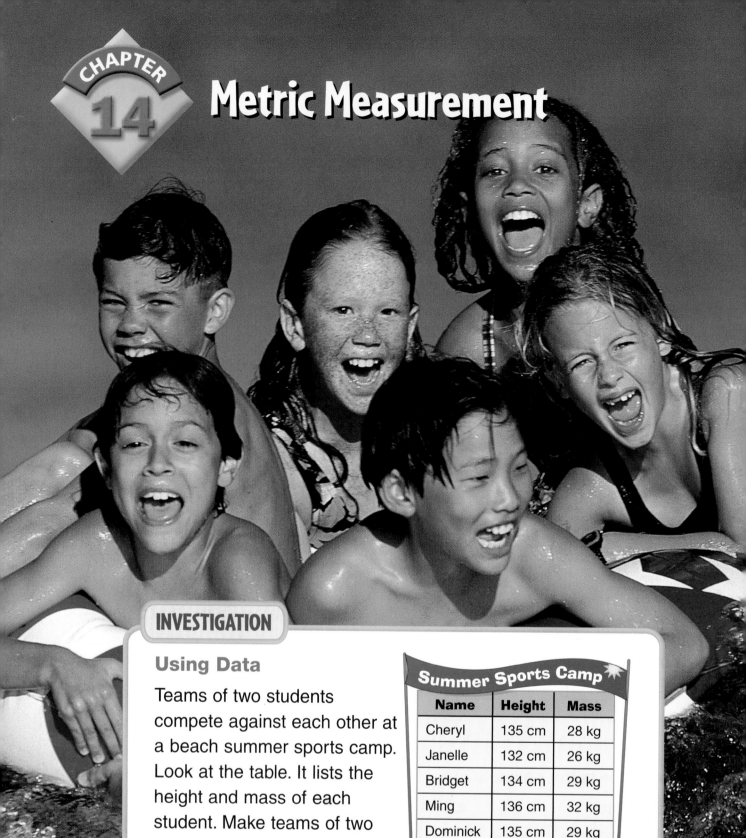

INVESTIGATION

Using Data

Teams of two students compete against each other at a beach summer sports camp. Look at the table. It lists the height and mass of each student. Make teams of two so that the teams are as even as possible. How did you decide which two students to put together on each team?

Summer Sports Camp

Name	Height	Mass
Cheryl	135 cm	28 kg
Janelle	132 cm	26 kg
Bridget	134 cm	29 kg
Ming	136 cm	32 kg
Dominick	135 cm	29 kg
Eduardo	133 cm	31 kg

VOLLEY International

Use What You Know

**Use this page to review and remember
what you need to know for this chapter.**

VOCABULARY

Choose the best term to complete each sentence.

1. A _____ is a metric unit used to measure capacity.

2. The amount of matter in an object is its _____.

3. A _____ is a metric unit used to measure length.

Vocabulary

liter

mass

meter

kilogram

CONCEPTS AND SKILLS

**Which unit does each tool measure?
Write *grams*, *milliliters*, or *centimeters*.**

4.    5.    6.

**Write *true* or *false* for each sentence. If false, rewrite the
sentence so it is true.**

7. You can measure the length of a baseball bat
   in kilograms.

8. You can measure the height of a ceiling in meters.

9. A centimeter is longer than a kilometer.

Write About It

10. Describe 3 different ways to measure a fish
    tank. For each way, list the measurement
    and the tool you would use.

Facts Practice, See page 670.

Centimeter and Millimeter

Objective Measure length in metric units.

Vocabulary
millimeters (mm)
centimeters (cm)
decimeters (dm)

Materials
For each pair:
centimeter ruler

Work Together

Many countries around the world use the metric system of measurement.

Millimeters (mm), **centimeters (cm)**, and **decimeters (dm)** are metric units of length.

Work with a partner to measure the lengths and widths of small objects in millimeters and centimeters.

STEP 1

Estimate the length of the shell.

- How many finger widths long do you think it is?

STEP 2

Use your finger to measure the shell.

- How many finger widths long is the shell?
- How close is that to your estimate?

STEP 3

Measure the length of the shell in centimeters. Line up the shell with the 0 mark on the ruler.

Find the centimeter mark closest to the other end of the shell.

- What is the length of the shell to the nearest centimeter?
- Is this measurement exact? Explain.

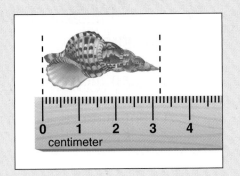

STEP 4

Look at the ruler again. The smaller marks in between the centimeter marks are called millimeters.

- What is the length of the shell to the nearest millimeter? How did you find the measure?

▶ **You can measure longer lengths in decimeters.**

STEP 1

Measure the driftwood to the nearest decimeter.

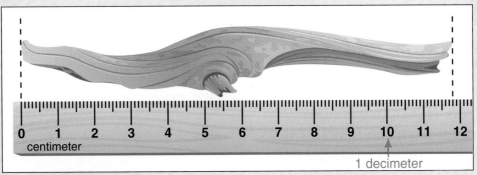

• To the nearest decimeter, how long is the driftwood?

STEP 2

Now measure the driftwood to the nearest centimeter.

• Compare the centimeter and decimeter measurements. Which measurement is more exact? Explain.

Metric Units of Length

1 centimeter	= 10 millimeters
1 decimeter	= 10 centimeters

On Your Own

Estimate. Then measure to the nearest centimeter.

1.

2.

Choose the better estimate.

3. width of your thumb
   1 cm or 1 mm

4. width of your foot
   60 cm or 6 cm

5. length of your leg
   5 cm or 5 dm

Compare. Write >, <, or = for each ⬤.

6. 5 mm ⬤ 5 cm

7. 20 cm ⬤ 4 dm

8. 3 cm ⬤ 30 dm

Talk About It • Write About It

You learned how to measure using millimeters, centimeters, and decimeters.

9. Suppose you measure a pencil in millimeters, centimeters, and then in decimeters. Will there be more millimeters, centimeters, or decimeters? Explain.

10. Is a length more exact if it is measured to the nearest millimeter or centimeter? Explain. When might this be important?

Lesson 2

Meter and Kilometer

Objective Measure longer lengths in metric units.

Vocabulary

meters (m)

kilometers (km)

Learn About It

Fran and her family live near the ocean. Her house is about 1 kilometer from the beach. The door of her house is 1 meter wide.

You can measure longer lengths in **meters (m)** and **kilometers (km)** .

It takes Fran about 10 minutes to walk 1 kilometer to the beach.

Metric Units of Length

1 meter = 10 decimeters
1 meter = 100 centimeters
1 kilometer = 1,000 meters

Guided Practice

Choose the unit you would use to measure each. Write *m* or *km*.

1. length of a room

2. length of a sail

3. depth of an ocean

4. distance to the sun

5. length of a rowboat

6. length of a river

Ask Yourself

- Do I need a small or large unit?

- Which is the smaller unit? the larger unit?

Explain Your Thinking ▶ Would you measure the distance from your home to school in meters or kilometers? Explain your choice.

Extra Help at **eduplace.com/map**

Choose the unit you would use to measure each.
Write _m_ or _km_.

7. width of a classroom

8. distance across U.S.

9. distance airplane flies

10. height of a door

11. distance across town

12. length of a ship

Choose the better estimate.

13. length of a water ski
2 m or 2 km

14. length of a bridge
200 km or 2 km

15. height of a lifeguard
2 m or 20 m

16. height of a lighthouse
25 m or 25 km

17. distance a car travels
90 m or 90 km

18. length of a motorboat
5 m or 50 m

Copy and complete.

19. 5 m = __ cm

20. 8,000 m = __ km

21. 10 km = __ m

22. 1 m = __ dm

23. 3 km = __ m

24. 200 cm = __ m

Compare. Write >, <, or = for each ⬤.

25. 8 km ⬤ 80 m

26. 500 cm ⬤ 5 m

27. 3 km ⬤ 300 m

28. 2 m ⬤ 200 dm

29. 4 km ⬤ 3,500 m

30. 950 cm ⬤ 10 m

31. Estimate It took Rory 33 minutes to walk to the beach nature trail. About how far did he walk? Explain.

32. Multistep Diana sailed a 3-kilometer race one week and a 2,500-meter race the next week. How many meters did Diana sail altogether?

Mixed Review and Test Prep ✓

Open Response
Complete. (Ch. 13, Lesson 3)

33. 6 ft = ■ yd   **34.** 24 in. = ■ ft

35. 4 yd = ■ ft   **36.** 36 in. = ■ ft

Multiple Choice

37. How many meters are in 4 kilometers? (Ch. 14, Lesson 2)

A 4   **B** 40   **c** 400   **D** 4,000

Audio Tutor 2/9 Listen and Understand

Metric Units of Capacity

Objective Measure capacity in metric units.

Learn About It

Many aquariums rescue and raise baby animals.

This baby flamingo is drinking food from a dropper. The dropper holds about 10 milliliters of liquid.

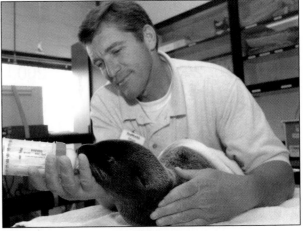

This baby sea lion is drinking food from a baby bottle. A bottle used for baby animals can hold about 1 liter of liquid.

Liter (L) and **milliliter (mL)** are metric units of capacity.

Metric Units of Capacity
1 liter = 1,000 milliliters

This water bottle holds 1 liter of water.

This dropper holds 1 milliliter of liquid.

Try this activity to estimate and measure using liters.

Materials: 1-liter container, other containers

STEP 1 Pick 3 containers. Estimate which of the containers holds less than, more than, or about 1 liter.

STEP 2 Use water and the 1-liter container to check your estimates.

STEP 3 Pick one of your containers. Does it hold more, less, or about 1,000 milliliters? Explain how you know.

Choose the better estimate for the capacity of each.

Ask Yourself
• Do I need a small unit or a large unit?
• Which is the smaller unit? the larger unit?

1.

2.

3.

3 L or 30 mL   1 L or 5 L   14 L or 14 mL

Choose the unit you would use to measure the capacity of each. Write *mL* or *L*.

4. bathtub   5. a spoon   6. a container of milk

Explain Your Thinking ▶ Would you need a larger container to hold 500 mL or to hold 1 L? Explain.

Practice and Problem Solving

Choose the better estimate for the capacity of each.

7.

8.

9.

100 L or 100 mL   20 L or 2 L   200 mL or 200 L

Choose the unit you would use to measure the capacity of each. Write *mL* or *L*.

10. a pail   11. a soup can   12. a drinking glass

13. a pond   14. a small vase   15. a watering can

Solve.

16. Nick poured 2,300 mL of water into a bowl. Then Rea poured 3 L of water into the same bowl. How much water in milliliters is in the bowl now?

17. **Reasoning** Celia's bottle holds more water than Tim's bottle. One bottle has a red label and holds 2 liters. The other has a blue label and holds 1,500 mL. What color is the label on Tim's bottle?

Go On

Copy and complete.

18. 2 L = __ mL

19. 500 mL = __ L

20. 2,000 mL = __ L

21. 3 L = __ mL

22. 10,000 mL = __ L

23. 15 L = __ mL

Compare.
Write >, <, or = for each ●.

24. 25 mL ● 2 L

25. 8 L ● 8,000 mL

26. 1,500 mL ● 2 L

27. 1 L ● 800 mL

28. 12,000 mL ● 12 L

29. 4 L ● 4,000 mL

30. 2,500 mL ● 2 L

31. 7,000 mL ● 70 L

32. 400 mL ● 3 L

Use the picture at the right for Problems 33–36.

33. Is 30,000 mL of milk enough to feed a baby whale calf for one day? Explain how you know.

34. **Analyze** In how many days will a baby whale calf drink 1,200 L of milk?

35. **What's Wrong?** Claire thinks she drinks as much water each day as the whale calf drinks milk. Claire drinks about 1,000 mL of water each day. Why is she wrong? Explain.

36. How many centimeters long can a baby whale calf be at birth? Is a baby whale calf longer than your classroom? Explain your thinking.

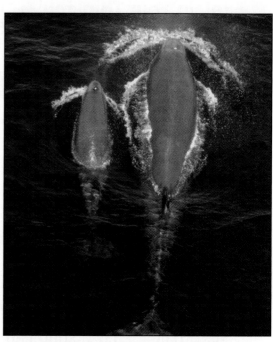

At birth a baby whale calf can be 8 meters long. It can drink 300 liters of milk each day.

Mixed Review and Test Prep

Open Response
Write each time. (Ch. 12, Lesson 3)

37.

38.

39. You need 3 L of water for a science project. Your container holds 500 mL. How can you use it to measure 3L?

(Ch. 14, Lesson 3)

Extra Practice See page 399, Set C.

Real World Connection
Converting Measurements

You can compare customary and metric units of measure.

Use the pictures and the chart for Problems 1–4.

Measurement Conversions
1 inch is a little less than 3 centimeters.
1 yard is a little less than 1 meter.
1 quart is a little less than 1 liter.

1. About how many yards wide is the window?

2 meters

2. One quart of juice serves 4 people. About how many people will one liter of juice serve?

3. Does the flag measure more or less than 60 centimeters?

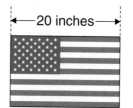

←20 inches→

4. Juan's poster is 3 meters tall. Ned's poster is 3 yards tall. Whose poster is taller?

Check your understanding of Lessons 1–3.

Quick Check

Choose the unit you would use. Write *mm, cm, dm, m,* or *km.* (Lessons 1, 2)

1. length of a crayon

2. width of a hand

3. length of an ant

Choose the unit you would use. Write *cm, m, dm,* or *km.* (Lessons 1, 2)

4. length of a truck

5. length of a field

6. distance to school

7. height of a kitten

8. distance to the sea

9. width of a door

Choose the better estimate. (Lessons 1–3)

10. drinking glass
300 mL or 3 mL

11. in-line skates
2 dm or 2 m

12. a toothbrush
14 mm or 140 mm

13. length of a shoe
20 mm or 20 cm

14. length of a table
2 m or 20 m

15. width of a tack
10 mm or 10 cm

Problem-Solving Strategy
Work Backward

Objective Solve a problem by working backward.

Problem Kareem is helping his father build their sailboat. They cut a board into 2 equal pieces. Then they cut 8 centimeters off one piece. The piece that is left is 32 centimeters long. How long was the original board?

UNDERSTAND

This is what you know.

- They cut the board into 2 equal pieces.
- They cut 8 centimeters off one piece.
- The final piece is 32 centimeters long.

PLAN

You know the final amount, so you can work backward to solve the problem.

SOLVE

- Start with the final length of the piece.
- Work back through each cut that was made.

Final Length				Original Length
32 centimeters	**+ 8**	**40 centimeters**	**+ 40**	**80 centimeters**
8 cm was cut off to get this length.	**Work backward. Add 8.**	The original board was cut into 2 equal pieces to get this length.	**Work backward. Add 40.**	

Solution: The original board was 80 centimeters long.

LOOK BACK

Look back at the problem.

How can you check your answer?

Guided Practice

Use the Ask Yourself questions to help you solve each problem.

1. Kareem's dad cuts a piece of wire into 3 equal pieces. He cuts 2 inches off one piece to make it 7 inches long. How long was the original piece of wire?

2. Kareem cuts a piece of ribbon in half and cuts each of those pieces in half again. Each piece is now 30 inches long. How long was the original piece of ribbon?

   Hint How many pieces of ribbon did he have after all the cuts?

Ask Yourself

UNDERSTAND **What facts do I know?**

PLAN
- **Do I know the final amount?**
- **Can I work backward?**

SOLVE
- **Did I start with the final amount?**
- **What operations should I use?**

LOOK BACK **Did I check my answer by starting with my answer and working forward?**

Independent Practice

Work backward to solve each problem.

3. Kareem bought some bottled water for a boat trip. He drank 3 of the bottles. Then he bought 5 more bottles and drank 2 of those. If he has 4 bottles left, how many bottles did he have at the start?

4. Kareem weighed a bag of boat screws. He added 2 pounds of screws to the bag. After he took out 3 pounds of screws, the bag weighed 4 pounds. How much did the bag weigh at the start?

5. Amy spent $6 for a sailboat kit and $4 for markers at a craft store. Her dad gave her $5. Amy then had $7. How much money did Amy have when she arrived at the craft store?

6. At 7 P.M., there are 11 boats in the harbor, 5 more than there were at 5 P.M. At 3 P.M. there were half as many boats as there were at 5 P.M. How many boats were there at 3 P.M.?

Go On

Mixed Problem Solving

Solve. Show your work. Tell what strategy you used.

7. Philip has a red ribbon and a blue ribbon. The red ribbon is 2 inches longer than the blue ribbon. Together the ribbons are 30 inches long. How long is each ribbon?

8. The Paley family spent $14.35 for gas on Saturday. On Sunday, they spent $1.25 more than they did on Saturday. How much did they spend for gas altogether?

9. Joey added 24 inches of track to his train track. Then he removed 8 inches. This made his track 120 inches long. How long was the track before he began changing it?

You Choose

Strategy
- Guess and Check
- Solve a Simpler Problem
- Use Logical Reasoning
- Work Backward
- Write a Number Sentence

Computation Method
- Mental Math
- Estimation
- Paper and Pencil
- Calculator

Data Use the pictograph to solve Problems 10–14.

The pictograph shows the number of goals each team in a soccer league scored this season.

10. How many goals did the Ospreys score?

11. Which team scored 10 goals?

12. How many more goals did the Dolphins score than the Sharks?

13. Which team scored twice as many goals as the Pelicans?

14. How many goals were scored by the teams altogether?

Number of Soccer Goals

Team	Goals
Dolphins	⚽ ⚽ ⚽ ⚽ ⚽ ⚽
Sharks	⚽ ⚽ ⚽ ⚽ ⚽
Pelicans	⚽ ⚽ ⚽
Ospreys	⚽ ⚽ ⚽ ⚽

Each ⚽ stands for 2 goals.

Problem Solving on Tests

Choose the letter of the correct answer. If the correct answer is not here, choose NH.

1. For a fundraiser, Ella's class will walk a total of 20,000 meters. If 15 students each walk 1 kilometer, how many kilometers are left for the other students to walk?

   A 5 kilometers   **C** 25 kilometers

   B 15 kilometers   **D** 50 kilometers

   (Chapter 14, Lesson 2)

2. John's dog drinks 500 mL of water a day. In 4 days, how many liters of water will it drink?

   F 1 L   **G** 3 L   **H** 5 L   **J** NH

   (Chapter 14, Lesson 3)

Open Response

Solve each problem.

3. For breakfast, Trudy has her choice of eggs or French toast as her meal and orange juice, apple juice, or milk as her drink. How many different combinations of breakfast can she order?

   Represent Use an organized list to help you solve the problem.

   (Chapter 8, Lesson 7)

4. How many △ will balance ▱ ?

   Explain How did you solve the problem?

   (Chapter 11, Lesson 6)

Constructed Response

5. Suppose you are planning a party for your sister. You make a list of things that need to be done to prepare for the party.

   > **Party "To-Do" List**
   > ① Bake the cake
   > ② Make invitations to fit the envelopes.
   > ③ Make fruit punch.
   > ④ Buy 3 pounds of apples.
   > ⑤ Make grab bags for prizes.

Information you need:

a. Which measurement tools would you use for each item on the list? How would you use the tool?

b. On the invitations you plan to write that the party will begin at 2:15 P.M. and end at 3:45 P.M. How long do you plan for the party to last?

c. You plan to make 5 grab bags for prizes. You want to put 4 pieces of gum, 2 tiny toys, and a lollipop in each bag. How many pieces will there be altogether in all the bags? Show how you know.

(Chapter 13, Lesson 6)

 Education Place

See **eduplace.com/map** for more Test-Taking Tips.

◎ **Audio Tutor 2/10** Listen and Understand

Metric Units of Mass

Objective Measure the mass of an object in metric units.

Vocabulary
gram (g)
kilogram (kg)
mass

Materials
balance scale
1-kilogram mass

Learn About It

Manuel and his family are having a picnic at the beach. The picnic basket's mass is 5 kilograms. One of Manuel's grapes is about 1 gram.

Gram (g) and **kilogram (kg)** are metric units used when measuring the **mass**, or the amount of matter, in an object.

Metric Units of Mass

1 kilogram = 1,000 grams

100 grams   *18 kilograms*   *1 kilogram*   *160 grams*

Try this activity to estimate and measure mass.

STEP 1 Find 3 small objects in your classroom. Estimate which of the objects are less than, more than, or about a kilogram.

STEP 2 Use the scale and kilogram mass to check your estimates.

STEP 3 Pick one of your objects. Do you think it is more than, less than, or about 1,000 grams? Explain how you know.

Choose the unit you would use to measure the mass of each. Write *g* or *kg*.

Ask Yourself

• Do I need a small or large unit?

• Which is the smaller unit? the larger unit?

1.

2.

3.

Choose the better estimate.

4. a grapefruit
   500 g or 5 kg

5. a boat
   1,000 g or 1,000 kg

6. a penny
   300 g or 3 g

Explain Your Thinking ▶ Do you think a large item always has a greater mass than a small item?

Practice and Problem Solving

Choose the unit you would use to measure the mass of each. Write *g* or *kg*.

7.

8.

9.

10. a canoe

11. a beach ball

12. a pair of goggles

Choose the better estimate.

13. pair of sunglasses
    150 g or 2 kg

14. a horse
    6 kg or 600 kg

15. a quarter
    5 g or 500 g

16. a piece of chicken
    500 g or 5 kg

17. a paper clip
    1 g or 1 kg

18. a watermelon
    40 g or 4 kg

Did You Know?

1 kilogram is a little more than 2 pounds.

Solve.

19. Manuel and his mother went fishing. Manuel caught a fish with a mass of 2 kilograms. Did the fish weigh more or less than 4 pounds?

20. **Estimate** Manuel's mother once caught a fish that weighed 10 pounds. About what was the mass of the fish in kilograms?

Copy and complete.

21. 4,000 g = __ kg   **22.** $\frac{1}{2}$ kg = __ g   **23.** 3 kg = __ g

24. 500 g = __ kg   **25.** 10,000 g = __ kg   **26.** 12 kg = __ g

Compare. Use >, <, or = for each ●.

27. 65 g ● 6 kg   **28.** 5 kg ● 500 g   **29.** 7 kg ● 7,000 g

30. 900 g ● 1 kg   **31.** 18,000 g ● 18 kg   **32.** 1,700 g ● 2 kg

Data Kites come in all shapes and sizes. Use the information shown about kites for Problems 33–36.

33. Is the mass of the box kite greater or less than 1 kg? How much greater or less? Explain your reasoning.

34. Linh makes 5 box kites. What would be the mass of the 5 kites?

35. How much taller is a Chula kite than a Pakpao kite?

36. **Estimate** A tail for a Pakpao kite can be 60 decimeters long! About how long in meters would the kite and the tail be?

37. **Write About It** Write a rule that gives you the number of grams when you know the number of kilograms.

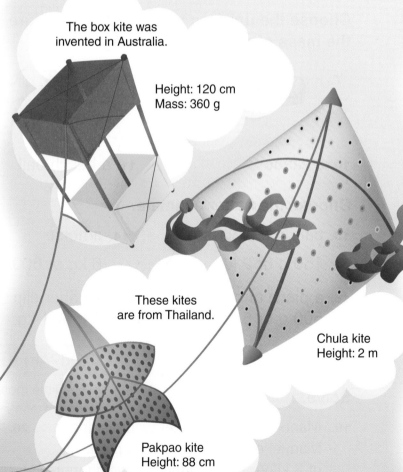

The box kite was invented in Australia.

Height: 120 cm
Mass: 360 g

These kites are from Thailand.

Chula kite
Height: 2 m

Pakpao kite
Height: 88 cm

Extra Practice See page 399, Set D.

Real World Connection
Missing Ingredients!

Chris spilled water on his favorite recipe. Luckily, he remembers some things about the recipe. Use what he remembers to help you complete the recipe. Use the measurements *tablespoon, teaspoon, cup, pint,* or *quart*.

Vegetable Soup

2	chicken broth
2	diced vegetables
1	crushed tomatoes
1	salt
3	lemon juice

Mmm, I remember that:
- each ingredient is measured in a different unit
- there is more chicken broth than any other ingredient
- there is the same amount of vegetables as tomatoes
- 1 tablespoon = 3 teaspoons
- there is less salt than lemon juice

Math Challenge
Missing Units!

Pick two different measurement units to complete each number sentence. You may use each unit more than once.

> in. cm ft
> dm m yd
> km

1. 36 ___ = 1 ___

2. 2,100 ___ > 2 ___

3. 19 ___ < 2 ___

4. 30 ___ = 3 ___

Brain Teaser

Complete each number sentence.

1. 10 mm + ___ = 3 cm

2. 600 m + ___ + ___ = 2 km

3. 2000 g + ___ = 4 kg

4. 300 mL + ___ + ___ = 3 L

5. 20 cm + ___ + ___ = 2 m

Education Place

Check out **eduplace.com/map** for more brain teasers.

Chapter Review/Test

VOCABULARY

Choose the best term to complete each sentence.

Vocabulary
grams
milliliter
kilometer
centimeter
decimeter

1. The width of a finger is about a ___.

2. It takes about 10 minutes to walk 1 ___.

3. An eye dropper can hold about 1 ___.

4. The mass of a sandwich is about 100 ___.

CONCEPTS AND SKILLS

Estimate. Then measure the object to the nearest centimeter. (Lesson 1, pp. 382–383)

5. ———— 6. ———————— 7. ————————

Choose the unit you would use to measure each. Write *cm*, *km*, *mL*, *L*, *g*, or *kg*.
(Lessons 1–3, 5 pp. 382–388, 394–396)

8. length of a paper clip 9. mass of a pencil 10. capacity of a tea cup

Choose the better estimate. (Lessons 1–3, 5 pp. 382–388, 394–396)

11. height of a person
    2 cm or 2 m

12. bottle of bubble soap
    6 mL or 60 mL

13. mass of a hat
    30 kg or 30 g

Copy and complete. (Lessons 1–3, 5, pp. 382–388, 394–396)

14. 1,000 g = ___ kg 15. 90,000 mL = ___ L 16. 5 m = ___ cm

17. 20 dm = ___ m 18. 30 km = ___ m 19. 5 L = ___ mL

PROBLEM SOLVING

Solve. (Lesson 4, pp. 390–392)

20. Dora spent $2 in one store and $4 in another. Her mother gave her $10. Dora then had $12. How much money did Dora have at the start?

Write About It

Show You Understand

Your school is having a relay race.
• The race is 2 km long.
• Each person will run 100 m.
How many people should be on each team? Explain your answer.

Extra Practice

Set A (Lesson 1, pp. 382–383)

Estimate. Then measure to the nearest centimeter, then millimeter.

1.

2.

Choose the better estimate.

3. width of your palm

a. 5 cm   b. 5 dm

4. height of a coffee mug

a. 120 cm   b. 12 cm

5. length of a pencil

a. 15 dm   b. 15 cm

Set B (Lesson 2, pp. 384–385)

Choose the better estimate.

1. width of a refrigerator

a. 1 km   b. 1 m

2. length of a car

a. 5 m   b. 50 m

3. distance to the store

a. 2 m   b. 2 km

Copy and complete.

4. 1,000 m = ___ km

5. 30 mm = ___ cm

6. 700 cm = ___ m

Set C (Lesson 3, pp. 386–388)

Choose the unit you would use to measure the capacity. Write _mL_ or _L_.

1. fish tank

2. raindrop

3. baby bathtub

Compare. Write <, >, or = for each ⬤.

4. 500 mL ⬤ 1 L

5. 3 L ⬤ 2,900 mL

6. 6,000 mL ⬤ 6 L

Set D (Lesson 5, pp. 394–396)

Choose the better estimate.

1. slice of bread

a. 30 kg   b. 30 g

2. tricycle

a. 9 kg   b. 90 kg

3. piece of paper

a. 1 g   b. 100 g

Copy and complete.

4. 8,000 g = ___ kg

5. 6 kg = ___ g

6. 3,000 g = ___ kg

Extra Practice at **eduplace.com/map**

A Really Cool Place

If you're planning a spring visit to Ilulissat, Greenland, you'd better pack warm clothing. The temperature in March is around −22°F. That makes this town a perfect home for the Ilulissat ice shelf. The ice shelf is a large plate of ice that spreads out over the ocean.

Chunks of ice that break off the ice shelf are called icebergs. These icebergs can move fast—up to 12 kilometers a day! Most of them are small, but sometimes they tower more than 100 meters above the surface of the water.

Iceland

Greenland

Arctic Circle

Ilulissat

Canada

Problem Solving

Use the diagram for Problems 1–2.

20 Meters

1 Most of an iceberg is underwater. The tip of the iceberg shown is 3 meters above the water. How much of the iceberg is underwater?

2 A building in Greenland is 198 decimeters tall. Which is greater, the total height of the iceberg shown or the height of the building?

3 During winter in Ilulissat there are very few hours of daylight. On January 15th, the sun rises at 10:49 A.M. and sets at 12:21 P.M. How many hours and minutes of daylight is that?

4 Suppose it took 3 weeks for an iceberg to travel 150 miles in the ocean. How many days is that?

5 On September 3rd the temperature in Ilulissat is 15°C. Should you dress for a possible snowstorm or wear a light jacket?

Education Place

Visit Weekly Reader Connections at **eduplace.com/map** for more on this topic.

Enrichment: Regrouping Measurements

A Slow-Growing Cactus

The Saguaro cactus is found in deserts and grows very slowly. The most it can grow in a year is 8 inches. If it is given enough time, though, it can grow to be 50 feet tall!

Problem In Arizona, a Saguaro cactus that was 21 inches tall grew another 8 inches this year. What is the new height of the cactus in feet?

Find 21 inches + 8 inches.

STEP 1	STEP 2
Find the total number of inches.	Regroup inches into feet.
21 inches	29 inches = 12 inches + 12 inches + 5 inches
+ 8 inches	2 feet
29 inches	So, 29 inches = 2 feet + 5 inches.

Remember:
There are 12 inches in 1 foot.

Solution: The new height of the cactus is 2 feet 5 inches.

Try These!

Find each sum. Write the answer in feet and inches.

1. 10 in.
    8 in.
    + 7 in.

2. 26 in.
    15 in.
    + 13 in.

3. 16 in.
    35 in.
    + 22 in.

4. 14 in.
    15 in.
    + 5 in.

5. 23 in.
    11 in.
    + 12 in.

6. **Challenge** Briana is 4 feet 8 inches tall. Each year she compares her height to a cactus that grows near her house. This year the cactus is 42 inches tall. Is it as tall as Briana? Explain your thinking.

Technology Time

Fascinating Facts

Use your calculator to solve the problems below.

Did you know that some kinds of bamboo can grow an inch every hour?

1. If a 12-inch bamboo plant grows an inch every hour, how many inches tall would it be after a day? a week? a month? How many feet is this?

2. Few bamboo plants grow taller than 100 feet. How many days would it take a bamboo plant to reach this height? Explain how you got your answer.

Did you know that the bee hummingbird is the smallest living bird?

3. Hummingbirds eat about twice their weight each day. About how long would it take each type of hummingbird to eat a kilogram?

4. The world's largest bird, the ostrich, weighs about 130 kilograms. About how many of each type of hummingbird equal one ostrich?

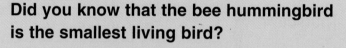

Hummingbird Weights	
Hummingbird	**Weight**
Bee	2 grams
Ruby-throated	4 grams
Giant	20 grams

Did you know that a cow can produce about 8 gallons of milk in a day?

5. If a cow produces 8 gallons of milk a day, how many quarts is that? How many quarts could it produce in a year? How many pints?

6. In Carnation, WA there is a statue of a cow that produced 16,500 quarts of milk. How many gallons is this?

Unit 5 Test

VOCABULARY (Open Response)

Choose the best term to complete each sentence.

1. There are 3 feet in a ____.

2. A kilogram is heavier than a ____.

3. Two cups are equal to 1 ____.

Vocabulary

pint

liter

yard

gram

CONCEPTS AND SKILLS (Open Response)

Look at each pair of times. Write how much time has elapsed. (Chapter 12)

4. Start: 4:30 P.M.

   End: 5:30 P.M.

5. Start: 1:30 A.M.

   End: 2:45 A.M.

Use the calendar to answer Questions 6–7.
(Chapter 12)

6. What is the date of the second Thursday?

7. What is the date two weeks from May 7?

May

Sun.	Mon.	Tue.	Wed.	Thu.	Fri.	Sat.
1	2	3	4	5	6	7
8	9	10	11	12	13	14
15	16	17	18	19	20	21
22	23	24	25	26	27	28
29	30	31				

Write each temperature in degrees Fahrenheit or degrees Celsius. Then write *hot*, *warm*, *cool*, or *cold* to describe each temperature. (Chapter 12)

8. °F 110° 100°

9. °F 60° 50°

10. °C 20°

Choose the better estimate. (Chapters 13–14)

11. the length of a classroom

   a. 10 m   **b.** 10 km

12. the amount of milk in a glass

   a. 1 gal   **b.** 1 c

13. the mass of a nickel

   a. 5 g   **b.** 5 kg

404

Find the missing measure. (Chapters 13–14)

14. 6 yd = ___ ft

15. 2 lb = ___ oz

16. 3,000 mL = ___ L

PROBLEM SOLVING (Open Response)

17. Sonia is 52 inches tall. Rose is 10 inches taller than Sonia. Claire is 4 inches shorter than Rose. Is Claire more than 5 feet tall?

18. Kate bought 3 packs of stickers that cost $2 each. She waited in line at the store for 5 minutes. How much did Kate spend on stickers?

19. Dean cut a piece of fabric into 3 equal pieces. Then he cut 2 yards off one piece. This piece is now 4 yards long. How long was the original piece of fabric?

20. Kathleen uses a 1-gallon pitcher to make punch. She mixes 8 cups of orange juice and 1 quart of cranberry juice. How many quarts of punch does Kathleen make?

Performance Assessment
(Extended Response)

Planetarium Show Schedule		
Show	**Start Times**	**End Times**
The Solar System	9:30 A.M.	10:00 A.M.
	2:00 P.M.	2:30 P.M.
Astronaut Life	11:00 A.M.	12:00 P.M.
	12:45 P.M.	1:45 P.M.
Blast Off!	10:15 A.M.	10:45 A.M.
	2:45 P.M.	3:15 P.M.

Task Mr. Dell's science class is taking a trip to the planetarium. Use the schedule and the information at the right. Decide which 2 shows Mr. Dell's class should see. Tell which time they should see each show. Explain your thinking.

Information You Need
- The class arrives at 9:45 A.M.
- Lunch is between 11:45 A.M. and 12:15 P.M.
- The bus back to school leaves at 3:00 P.M.

Cumulative Test Prep

Solve Problems 1–10.

Test-Taking Tip

Sometimes drawing a picture can help you understand a problem.

Look at the example below.

Tracy puts a fence post on both sides of her yard and 1 post every 3 feet in between. If her yard is 18 feet long, how many posts does she use?

A 6 posts   C 8 posts

B 7 posts   D 9 posts

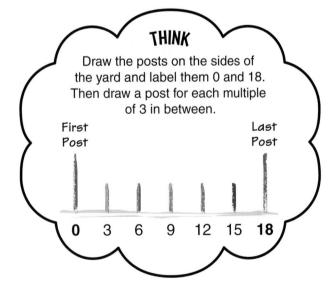

THINK

Draw the posts on the sides of the yard and label them 0 and 18. Then draw a post for each multiple of 3 in between.

First Post   Last Post

0   3   6   9   12   15   18

Multiple Choice

1. There are 2 baskets on a table. There are 6 apples in each basket. Which number sentence tells how many apples there are?

A $3 \times 6 = \blacksquare$ C $2 + 6 = \blacksquare$

B $2 \times 3 = \blacksquare$ D $6 + 6 = \blacksquare$

(Chapter 8, Lesson 1)

2. Dana has a 36-inch piece of ribbon. She cuts it into 6 equal pieces. Then she cuts each of those pieces in half. How long is each piece?

F 6 in.   H 4 in.

G 5 in.   J 3 in.

(Chapter 11, Lesson 6)

3. Which division sentence matches the repeated subtraction shown on the number line below?

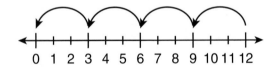

A $12 \div 1 = \blacksquare$ C $12 \div 3 = \blacksquare$

B $12 \div 2 = \blacksquare$ D $12 \div 12 = \blacksquare$

(Chapter 10, Lesson 2)

4. Alex has $4.66. Dora has $2.20. How much do they have together, rounded to the nearest dollar?

F $7   G $6   H $4   J $1

(Chapter 3, Lesson 5)

For Test-Taking Tips, see page 659.

5. What is the greatest possible number that can be made using the digits 5, 6, 9, and 6?

   (Chapter 2, Lesson 1)

6. Alfonso bought 8 packs of juice. Each pack had 6 bottles. How many bottles of juice did Alfonso buy?

   (Chapter 9, Lesson 3)

7. Which of the following times is closer to 6:15 P.M.?

   | 5:25 P.M.   or   7:10 P.M. |

   (Chapter 12, Lesson 4)

8. What ordered pair tells the location of Point *A* on the grid? Explain what each number in the ordered pair represents.

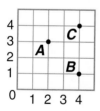

   (Chapter 6, Lesson 7)

9. What is the difference in height between Mt. Mitchell and Mt. Rogers? Explain how to use estimation to check your answer.

Mountain	Height
Mt. Mitchell, NC	6,684 ft
Mt. Rogers, VA	5,729 ft

   (Chapter 5, Lesson 6)

10. Kenny and Sarah are playing a game using the spinners below. The winner of the game is the person whose spinner lands on the number 1 first.

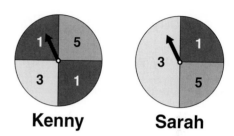

Kenny   **Sarah**

A What number is Kenny's spinner most likely to land on?

B What number is Sarah's spinner most likely to land on?

C Is this a fair game? Why or why not?

D How would you change one spinner to make the game fair?

E Is there a way to make the game fair without changing either spinner? Explain your answer.

   (Chapter 7, Lesson 4)

Education Place

Look for Cumulative Test Prep at **eduplace.com/map** for more practice.

Vocabulary Wrap-Up for **Unit 5**

Look back at the big ideas and vocabulary in this unit.

Big Ideas

25°F means it is freezing, but 25°C means it is warm.

You can buy milk in a 1-gallon bottle.

You can buy water in a 1-liter bottle.

Key Vocabulary
- gallon
- liter

Math Conversations

Use your new vocabulary to discuss these big ideas.

1. Explain how to find the amount of time that has passed from 2:25 P.M. to 8:10 P.M.

2. Explain how to use a ruler to measure the width of a book in inches.

3. **Write About It** Read the newspaper to keep track of the high and low temperatures every day for a week. Make a line graph to show the changes in the high temperatures or the low temperatures for the week.

My backpack is about a foot long.

You could also say it is about 12 inches long.

UNIT 6

Geometry and Measurement

Reading Mathematics

Reviewing Vocabulary

Here are some math vocabulary words that you should know.

area	the number of square units that cover a figure
perimeter	the distance around a closed plane figure
plane figure	a figure that has two dimensions
solid figure	a figure that has three dimensions

Reading Words and Symbols

When you read mathematics, you need to know the words that identify figures. Look at the different names of the figures below.

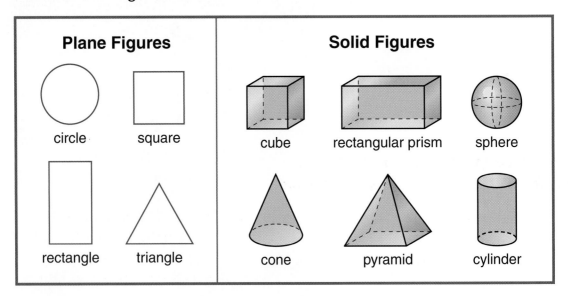

Plane Figures	Solid Figures
circle · square	cube · rectangular prism · sphere
rectangle · triangle	cone · pyramid · cylinder

Write *true* or *false*.

1. A triangle has 4 sides.

2. A sphere is a solid figure.

Reading Test Questions

Choose the correct answer for each.

3. Which pair of figures are triangles?

a.

c.

b.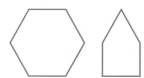

d.

Pair means "two" or "couple."

---

4. Which figure has the same shape as a beach ball?

  a. circle   **c.** rectangle

  b. cylinder   **d.** sphere

Figure means "shape."

5. Which shape has the fewest number of sides?

  a. hexagon   **c.** square

  b. rectangle   **d.** triangle

Fewest means "least."

Learning Vocabulary

Watch for these words in this unit. Write their definitions in your journal.

ray

angle

polygon

quadrilateral

volume

Education Place

At **eduplace.com/map** see eGlossary and eGames—Math Lingo.

Literature Connection

Read "Snowflakes" on Page 653. Then work with a partner to answer the questions about the story.

Plane and Solid Figures

Using Data

The entrance to the Louvre Museum in Paris, France, is a glass pyramid designed by architect I. M. Pei. The four sides are made of 673 panes of glass. It is a square pyramid, which means that its base is a square. Look at the model. What shape is each side? Name some other pyramids or pyramid shapes you have seen or heard about.

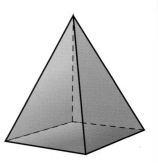

Use What You Know

**Use this page to review and remember
what you need to know for this chapter.**

VOCABULARY

Choose the best word to complete each sentence.

1. A sail on a sailboat has 3 straight sides like
a _____.

2. A penny looks like a _____.

3. A _____ has the same shape as a soup can.

4. A magazine cover is in the shape of a _____.

> **Vocabulary**
> circle
> cylinder
> sphere
> triangle
> rectangle

CONCEPTS AND SKILLS

Use the list below. Write the name of each figure.

circle	cone	cube	cylinder	pyramid
rectangle	rectangular prism	sphere	square	triangle

5.

6.

7.

8.

9.

10.

11.

12.

13.

14.

15.

16.

17.

18.

19.

Write About It ▶

20. Find 3 objects in your classroom that
are in the shape of a rectangle.

Facts Practice, See page 670.

Audio Tutor 2/11 Listen and Understand

Lines, Line Segments, Rays, and Angles

Objective Identify and compare lines, line segments, rays, and angles.

Vocabulary
line
line segment
ray
angle
right angle
parallel lines
intersecting lines
perpendicular lines

Learn About It

The Rock and Roll Hall of Fame is in Cleveland, Ohio. It was designed by the architect I.M. Pei. You can find many familiar geometric figures in the Hall of Fame.

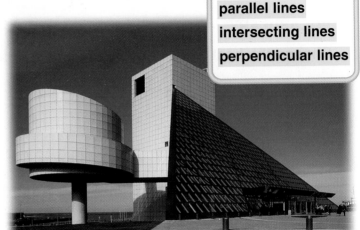

Geometric Figures

Line	A **line** is a straight path that goes on without end in two directions.	*The arrows show that the line does not end.*
Line segment	A **line segment** is part of a line. It has two endpoints.	
Ray	A **ray** is part of a line. It has one endpoint. A ray goes on without end in one direction.	or
Angle	An **angle** is formed by two rays with the same endpoint.	

A **right angle** has a square corner. It measures 90°.

Some angles are less than a right angle.

Some angles are greater than a right angle.

▶ You can also find examples of different lines in the Rock and Roll Hall of Fame.

Parallel lines are the same distance apart and never meet.

Intersecting lines cross at a common point.

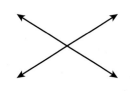

Perpendicular lines cross at right angles.

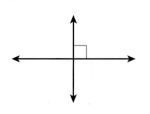

Guided Practice

Tell whether each figure is a *line, line segment,* or *ray*.

Ask Yourself
- Does the figure have any endpoints?
- Does the angle have a square corner?

1.

2.

3.

4.

Tell whether each angle is *a right angle, less than a right angle,* or *greater than a right angle*.

5.   6.   7.   8.

Tell whether each pair of lines is *parallel, intersecting,* or *perpendicular*.

9.   10. 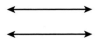   11.   12.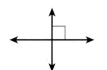

Explain Your Thinking ▶ Do you think you could measure a line? a line segment? a ray? Explain why or why not.

Write whether each figure is a *line*, *line segment*, or *ray*.

13.

14.

15.

16.

Tell whether each angle is a *right angle, less than a right angle,* or *greater than a right angle.*

17.

18.

19.

20.

Tell whether each pair of lines is *parallel, intersecting,* or *perpendicular.*

21.

22.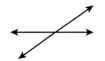

23.

24.

Use the figure on the right for Problems 25–28.

25. How many line segments are shown?

26. How many right angles are shown?

27. How many angles greater than 90° are shown?

28. How many angles less than 90° are shown?

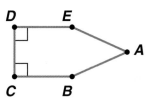

Write *true* or *false* for each.
Draw a picture to explain your answer.

29. A line has one endpoint.

30. A ray is part of a line.

31. A right angle measures 180°.

32. A line segment has two endpoints.

33. Parallel lines cross at right angles.

34. Intersecting lines never meet.

Use the sign for Problems 35–38.

35. How many line segments are in the word "FAME"?

36. How many right angles are in the word "HALL"?

37. How many angles greater than a right angle are in the word "FAME"?

38. How many angles less than a right angle are in the word "HALL"?

Solve.

39. Look at the Rock and Roll Hall of Fame floor plan at the right. Write the location of 2 different kinds of angles you see. Describe the angles.

40. Represent Make a floor plan of your classroom. Label all of the right angles you draw.

41. Analyze At what hourly times do the hands on a clock form right angles?

42. Mila drew two line segments that did not intersect and were not parallel. If the line segments were lines, would they ever intersect? Explain your reasoning.

ROCK AND ROLL HALL OF FAME

Floor Plan for the Rock and Roll Hall of Fame

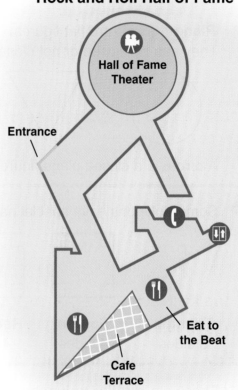

Hall of Fame Theater

Entrance

Eat to the Beat

Cafe Terrace

Mixed Review and Test Prep

Open Response

Compare. Order the numbers from least to greatest. (Ch. 1, Lesson 6; Ch. 2, Lesson 2)

43. 7,684   6,947   7,253

44. 1,293   1,247   1,920

45. 14,678   16,872   14,758

Multiple Choice

46. Which letter is made up of two right angles and two line segments? (Ch. 15, Lesson 1)

A W   **c** D

B T   **D** L

Audio Tutor 2/12 Listen and Understand

Classify Plane Figures

Objective Identify and describe different plane figures.

Vocabulary
plane figure
polygon
side
vertex (vertices)
regular polygon
irregular polygon

Learn About It

Look at this picture of the White House in Washington, D.C. You can find different plane figures in the picture. How many plane figures do you recognize?

▶ **Plane figures** are flat figures. They can be closed or not closed.

A **circle** is a closed plane figure.

▶ **Polygons** are closed plane figures that have three or more line segments.

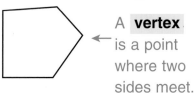

Each line segment is called a **side**.

A **vertex** is a point where two sides meet.

▶ Some polygons have special names.

   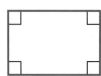

| **Triangle** | **Square** | **Rectangle** | **Pentagon** | **Hexagon** | **Octagon** |
| 3 sides | 4 sides | 4 sides | 5 sides | 6 sides | 8 sides |

▶ These are **regular polygons.**

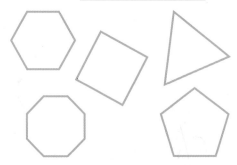

All sides are the same length. All angles are the same size.

▶ These polygons are **irregular polygons**.

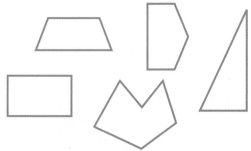

The sides can be different lengths. The angles can be different sizes.

Guided Practice

Tell whether each figure is a polygon. If it is, write its name.

Ask Yourself

- Is the figure closed?
- How many sides does the figure have?

1.

2.

3.

4.

5.

6.

7. Which polygons above are regular polygons?

Explain Your Thinking ▶ Is a circle a polygon? Explain why or why not.

Practice and Problem Solving

Tell whether each figure is a polygon. If it is, write its name.

8.

9.

10.

11.

12.

13.

14.

15.

16. Which polygons above are regular polygons?

17. A ten-sided polygon is called a decagon. Draw a decagon. Is your decagon a regular or irregular polygon?

The Capitol Building in Washington, D.C. also has many plane figures.

Go On

Use the plane figures at the right to answer Questions 18–22.

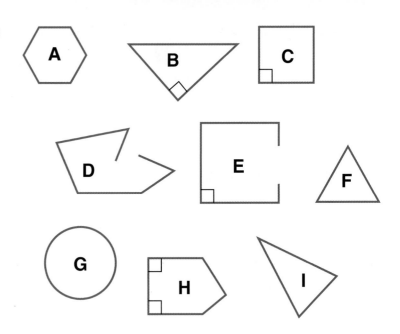

18. Which plane figures have right angles?

19. Which plane figures have fewer than four sides?

20. Which plane figures are closed figures?

21. Which plane figures have more than 4 angles?

22. Which plane figures are regular polygons?

 Data Use the graph to solve Problems 23–27.

Ms. Diaz asked her class to record the kinds of polygons they found in their classroom. The graph at the right shows the results.

23. How many triangles did the class find? Explain how you know.

24. Why do you think there is no X over the hexagon?

25. Which polygon did the class find most often?

26. How many polygons did the class find in all?

27. **Predict** Which shape do you think the students in another classroom would find most often? Explain your reasoning.

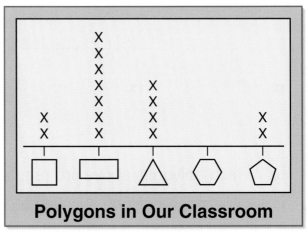

Polygons in Our Classroom

Use the picture at the right to answer Questions 18-22.

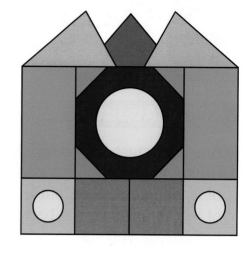

28. What colors are the triangles?

29. What is the special name for the blue polygons?

30. What color is the pentagon?

31. Are the red polygons regular or irregular? What is their special name?

32. What color is the figure that is not a polygon? What is the name of that figure?

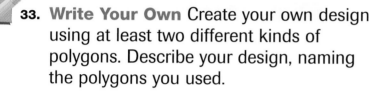

33. **Write Your Own** Create your own design using at least two different kinds of polygons. Describe your design, naming the polygons you used.

Solve.

34. Look at the bird's-eye view of the building at the right. It is the Pentagon in Washington, D.C. Describe the polygons you see.

35. **Analyze** Pia drew 3 polygons. The first had two more sides than the second and twice as many sides as the third. All four sides and angles in the second were equal. Which polygons did Pia draw?

Mixed Review and Test Prep

Open Response

Choose the better estimate.
(Ch. 14, Lessons 2 and 3)

36. height of a house

    12 m or 120 cm

37. capacity of a bathtub

    50 mL or 500 L

38. mass of an apple

    90 g or 9 kg

39. Miss Lao drew the figure below. Is it a polygon? Explain why or why not. (Ch. 15, Lesson 2)

Classify Triangles

Objective Identify, describe, and classify different triangles.

Learn About It

A bridge must hold heavy loads. Bridge engineers often use the shape of a triangle to even out the weight of the vehicles so the bridge will not break. Can you see the different kinds of triangles in this bridge?

▶ Some triangles have special names.

Equilateral Triangle	**Isosceles Triangle**	**Right Triangle**	**Scalene Triangle**
All of the sides have equal lengths.	Two of the sides have equal lengths.	One angle is a right angle.	Each side is a different length.

Guided Practice

Name the kind of triangle shown. Write *equilateral, isosceles, right,* or *scalene.*

Ask Yourself
- Are any of the sides the same length?
- Are any of the angles right angles?

1.

2.

3.

4.

5.

6.

Explain Your Thinking ▶ Are all triangles polygons? Are all polygons triangles? Explain your reasoning.

Practice and Problem Solving

Name the kind of triangle shown. Write *equilateral, isosceles, right,* or *scalene.*

7.

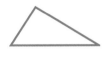

8.

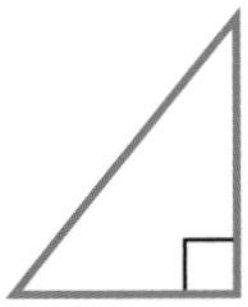

9.

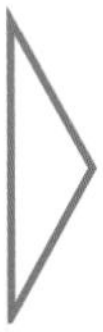

10.

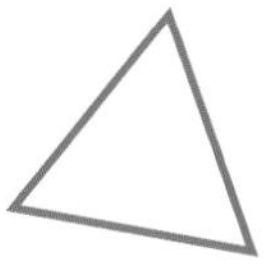

11.

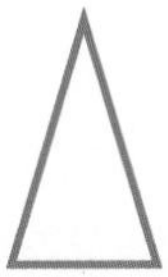

12.

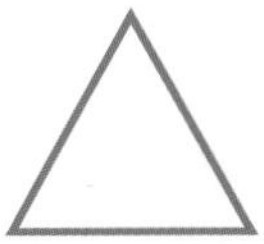

13.

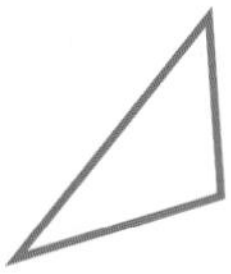

14.

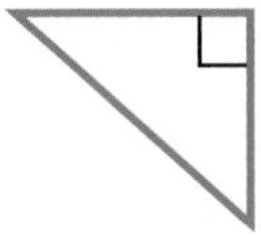

Use the triangles at the right for Problems 15–17.

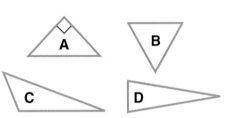

15. Which triangles have at least 2 sides that are equal in length?

16. Which triangles have an angle that is less than a right angle?

17. Which triangle has an angle that is greater than a right angle?

Solve.

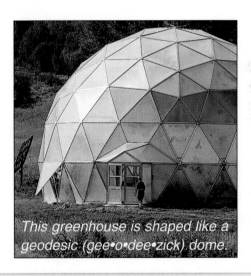

This greenhouse is shaped like a geodesic (gee•o•dee•zick) dome.

18. **Predict** Look at the equilateral triangles in the picture at the right. What do you think is true about their angles?

19. **Represent** Can a triangle have a right angle and be an isosceles triangle? Use a drawing to explain your answer.

20. Can a triangle have two sides that are parallel? Explain your reasoning.

Mixed Review and Test Prep

Open Response

Write the value of the underlined digit in each number. (Ch. 1, Lesson 7)

21. 954

22. 589,851

23. 4,378

24. 11,607

25. 12,311

26. 308,825

Multiple Choice

27. Which word could NOT describe a triangle?
(Ch. 15, Lesson 3)

A plane figure

B four-sided

C polygon

D equilateral

Extra Practice See page 439, Set C.

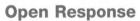

Classify Quadrilaterals

Objective Identify, describe, and classify different four-sided figures.

Vocabulary

quadrilateral
parallelogram
rectangle
square
diagonal

Learn About It

The building in the picture at the right is the Broward County Library. It is located in Fort Lauderdale, Florida.

The architect for this library, or the person who designed it, used different kinds of quadrilaterals.

A **quadrilateral** is a polygon with 4 sides and 4 angles.

▶ Some quadrilaterals have special names.

Quadrilateral	**Parallelogram**	**Rectangle**	**Square**
• 4 sides	• 4 sides	• 4 sides	• 4 equal sides
• 4 angles	• 4 angles	• 4 right angles	• 4 right angles
	• opposite sides are parallel	• opposite sides are parallel	• opposite sides are parallel

▶ A **diagonal** connects two vertices of a polygon that are not next to each other.

You can make triangles by drawing a diagonal in a quadrilateral.

Ask Yourself
- How many sides are there?
- Are the sides parallel?
- Are there four right angles?

**Tell whether the figure is a quadrilateral.
If it has a special name, write it.**

1.  2. 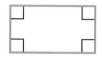 3.

**Write *true* or *false* for each.
Draw a picture to explain your answer.**

4. A triangle is a quadrilateral.

5. A square has 2 pairs of parallel sides.

6. A rectangle is a parallelogram.

7. All quadrilaterals have 4 right angles.

Explain Your Thinking ▶ Explain why a square is both a rectangle and a parallelogram.

Practice and Problem Solving

**Tell whether the figure is a quadrilateral.
If it has a special name, write it.**

8.  9.   10.   11.

12.  13.   14. 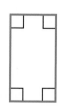 15.

16. Describe two different ways to sort the figures above into two groups.

Copy the figure at the right for Problems 17–19.

17. Draw a diagonal from A to C.
How many triangles are there?

18. Draw another diagonal from B to D.
Now how many triangles are there?

19. Can you draw another diagonal?
Explain why or why not.

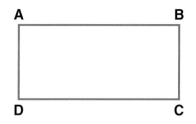

Write *true* or *false* for each. Draw a picture to explain your answer.

20. Some polygons are quadrilaterals.

21. Some rectangles are squares.

22. All quadrilaterals are parallelograms.

23. No triangles have parallel sides.

 Data **Use the grid to solve Problems 24–27.**

24. Which letter is at (2, 1)?

25. Write the ordered pair for *R*.

26. What polygon could you form by using line segments to connect *S, T,* and *U*?

27. Write About It You can make a square by connecting all the points on the grid. Explain how you know it is a square.

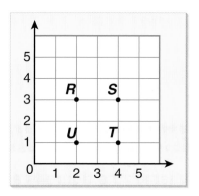

Solve.

28. Write the names of the different quadrilaterals you see in the photo on the right.

29. Represent Design your own building. Draw it using only quadrilaterals and diagonals. Label the different quadrilaterals you draw.

Trees grow inside the Broward County Library in Florida.

Extra Practice See page 439, Set D.

Visual Thinking
Placing Polygons

Look at the Venn diagram.

- Polygons with right angles are in one oval.

- Different kinds of quadrilaterals are in the other oval.

What figures are in both ovals?

Polygons with Right Angles **Different Kinds of Quadrilaterals**

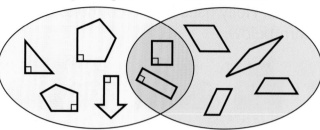

Decide where in the Venn diagram each polygon belongs. Write *yellow*, *blue*, or *green*.

1.

2.

3.

4.

Check your understanding of Lessons 1–4.

Name the figures. Write *line*, *line segment*, *ray*, or *right angle*. (Lesson 1)

1.

2.

3.

Decide whether each figure is a polygon. If it is, write its name. (Lessons 2–4)

4.

5.

6.

7.

Name the triangles. Write *isosceles*, *equilateral*, *scalene*, or *right triangle*. (Lesson 3)

8.

9.

10.

Extra Practice at **eduplace.com/map**

Problem-Solving Strategy
Find a Pattern

Objective Solve problems by finding and completing patterns.

Problem Holly uses blocks to make the pattern below.

Suppose she continues her pattern. What are the next 3 stacks of blocks likely to be?

> **UNDERSTAND**
>
> **This is what you know.**
>
> The blocks are arranged in a pattern.

> **PLAN**
>
> **You can find a pattern to help you solve the problem.**

> **SOLVE**
>
> • Holly's pattern has 1 block, then 3, then 5, then 7.
>
>
>
> > **Think**
> > How does each stack differ from the one before it?
>
> • Each stack has 2 more blocks than the stack before it, with one more on top and one more on the bottom.
>
> • To continue the pattern, the next three stacks should be
>
>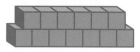
>
> **Solution:** The next three stacks of blocks should be 9 blocks, 11 blocks, and 13 blocks.

> **LOOK BACK**
>
> **Look back at the problem.**
> Does the solution answer the question?

Use the Ask Yourself questions to help you solve each problem.

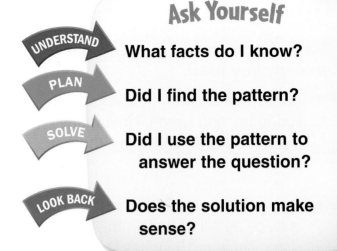

Ask Yourself

UNDERSTAND **What facts do I know?**

PLAN **Did I find the pattern?**

SOLVE **Did I use the pattern to answer the question?**

LOOK BACK **Does the solution make sense?**

1. Leo is making the necklace shown here. If he continues his pattern, what colors are the next two beads likely to be?

2. Pilar created a pattern using letters. If she continues the pattern, what are the next three letters likely to be? Explain how you know.

A   B   B   A   C   C   A   D   D   A

(Hint) How do the letters change each time?

Independent Practice

Use a pattern to solve each problem.

3. **Represent** Look at the pattern of shapes at the right. Draw the next 3 shapes in the pattern.

4. Diego is building a figure with 9 cans at the base. Each row has one less can than the row below. How many cans are in the fifth row he builds?

5. Mike reads the first 10 pages of his book on Monday. He reads 3 pages more each day than the day before. How many pages will he read on Friday?

6. **Create and Solve** Rearrange the number cards at the right to make your own pattern. Then predict the next 2 cards in the pattern.

Go On

Mixed Problem Solving

Solve. Show your work. Tell what strategy you used.

7. Felipe has 3 different color blocks: red, blue, and green. How many different ways can he put them in a row?

8. Dana's brother is 25 inches tall. Dana is twice as tall as her brother. Their sister Angie is 15 inches shorter than Dana. How tall is Angie?

9. **Explain** Three paths form a triangle in a park. If one side of the triangle is perpendicular to the other side, what kind of triangle is it? Tell how you know.

You Choose

Strategy
- Act It Out
- Draw a Picture
- Make a Table
- Use Logical Reasoning
- Write a Number Sentence

Computation Method
- Mental Math
- Estimation
- Paper and Pencil
- Calculator

Data Use the graph for Problems 10–13.

10. Lynn's class voted on the polygon they liked the best. Which polygon received the most votes?

11. How many more students chose squares than chose triangles?

12. If each student voted for one polygon, how many students are in Lynn's class?

13. **What's Wrong?** Sue says octagons got three more votes than pentagons. Why is she wrong?

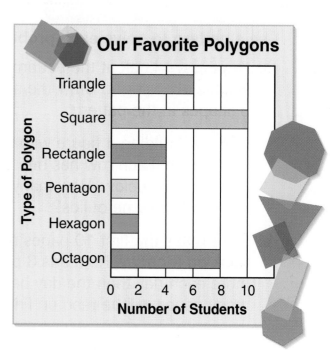

Our Favorite Polygons

Problem Solving on Tests

Choose the letter of the correct answer. If correct answer is not here, choose NH.

1. Which building is located at (3, 1) on the grid?

   A store

   B library

   C school

   D home

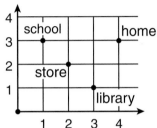

(Chapter 6, Lesson 7)

2. Jo uses a pan balance to measure the mass of a dictionary. If its mass is 3,000 grams, how many kilogram bars will balance it?

   F 1   **G** 3   **H** 6   **J** 9

   (Chapter 14, Lesson 5)

Open Response

Solve each problem.

3. Think of two different kinds of triangles. What do you know about sides and angles that makes your triangles different? Draw your triangles.

   (Chapter 15, Lesson 3)

4. What rule describes how the output is related to the input?

Input	Output
0	2
1	3
4	6
7	9

   (Chapter 10, Lesson 9)

Constructed Response

5. Some friends saw these items at a street fair. They are being sold by the package.

Street Fair Sale	
Item	**Number in Package**
Marbles	27
Soccer Cards	10
Pencils	15
Rings	30

   a. Which of the items in the packages listed can 3 friends share equally with no items left over? How many of each item would each friend receive?

   b. Which of the items can 5 friends share equally with no items left over? How many of each item would each friend receive?

   c. Which items can be shared equally by 3 and by 5 friends? Explain by using multiplication or division number sentences.

   d. Suppose 4 friends want to share soccer cards equally. What is the least number of packs they need to buy so there are no cards left over? Explain.

   (Chapter 9, Lesson 7)

Education Place

See **eduplace.com/map** for more Test-Taking Tips.

Audio Tutor 2/13 Listen and Understand

Solid Figures

Objective Identify, describe, and classify solid figures.

Vocabulary

solid figure

rectangular prism

cube

sphere

cone

cylinder

pyramid

Learn About It

The figures below are **solid figures**. They are 3-dimensional, not flat like plane figures.

Solid Figures

| rectangular prism | cube | sphere | cone | cylinder | pyramid |

▶ Complex solid figures are made up of two or more solid figures.

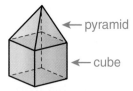
← pyramid
← cube

This figure is made up of a pyramid and a cube.

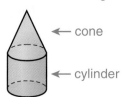
← cone
← cylinder

This figure is made up of a cone and a cylinder.

Guided Practice

Name the solid figure or figures.

1.

2.

3.

Ask Yourself

• Is the figure made up of more than one solid figure?

Explain Your Thinking ▶ Look at the solid figures above. Describe how you can sort the figures in two different ways.

Extra Help at eduplace.com/map

Name the solid figure that each object looks like.

4.

5.

6.

7.

8.

9.

10.

11.

Name the solid figures that make up each object.

12.

13.

14.

15.

Solve.

16. Devika's basketball fit perfectly in a box. What solid figure did the box most likely look like?

17. What's Wrong? Mona said that a sphere is the only solid figure that can roll. Explain why she is wrong.

18. At the grocery store, Josh bought items in the shape of a sphere, a cylinder, and a rectangular prism. What 3 items could he have bought?

19. Write About It A cube is a special kind of rectangular prism. Describe what makes a cube different from other rectangular prisms.

Mixed Review and Test Prep

Open Response

Write the number in standard form.

(Ch. 1, Lesson 4)

20. three thousand ninety-nine

21. 7,000 + 500 + 2

22. 4 hundreds 1 ten 6 ones

Multiple Choice

23. Which solid figure best describes the shape of a shoebox? (Ch. 15, Lesson 6)

A cylinder   **C** cube

B pyramid   **D** rectangular prism

Explore Solid Figures

Objective Use models to relate solid figures to plane figures.

Vocabulary
face
edge
vertex (vertices)

Materials
solid figure models
paper
pencil
Learning Tool 26

Work Together

Look at the rectangular prism below.
It has **faces**, **edges** and **vertices**.

A **vertex** is a point where edges meet. →

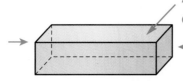

A **face** is a flat surface of a solid figure.

← An **edge** is formed when two faces meet.

You can use models to explore solid figures.

STEP 1
Trace around the faces of a rectangular prism.

- What shape are the faces?
- How many faces are there?

STEP 2
Count the number of edges. Then count the number of vertices.

- How many edges are there?
- How many vertices?

Record your answers in a table like the one below.

STEP 3
Repeat with the cube and the pyramid to complete the table.

Model	Shapes of Faces	Number of Faces	Number of Edges	Number of Vertices
Rectangular Prism				
Cube				
Pyramid				

STEP 4 Use your table to answer these questions.

- Are all the faces of the cube the same shape?
- Are all the faces of the pyramid the same shape?
- Which models have the same number of edges?
- Which models have the same number of vertices?

You can use plane figures and line segments to draw solid figures.

STEP 1 Draw two rectangles of the same size and shape like the ones shown at the right.

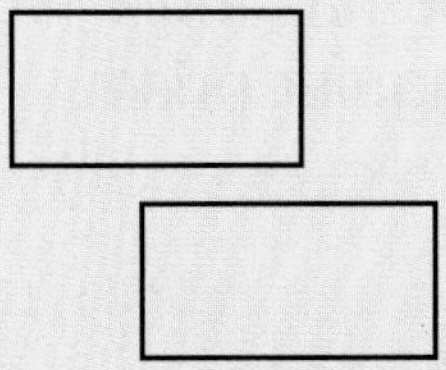

STEP 2 Then connect the vertices of the rectangles with line segments.

- What solid figure did you draw?

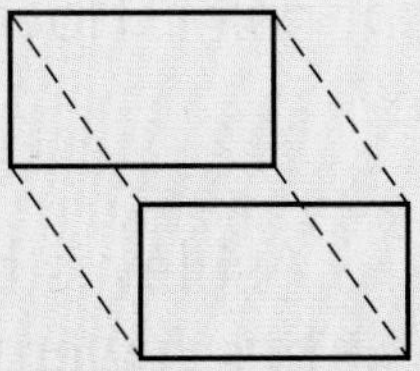

On Your Own

Copy the plane figures. Then connect with line segments to make solid figures. Name the solid figures you drew.

1.

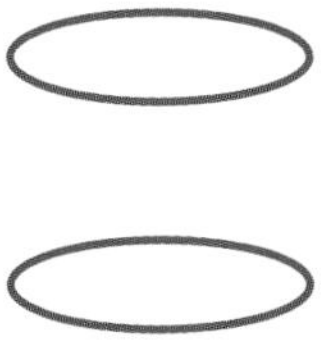

2.

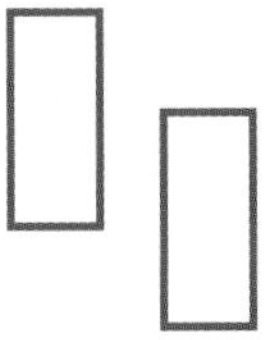

3.

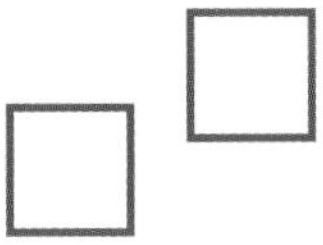

Name the solid figures that have the faces shown.

4.  △△△△

5.

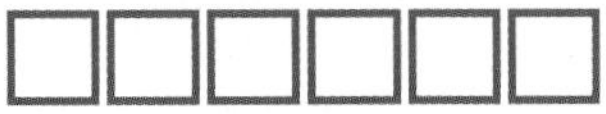

6.

Write *true* or *false* for each.
If false, write a statement that is true.

7. The towers in the picture at the right are shaped like cylinders.

8. The top of each tower in the picture is shaped like a sphere.

9. An edge is formed when 2 faces meet.

10. A tennis ball looks like a cone.

11. A cube has more faces than a rectangular prism.

Solve.

12. Drew made a wooden box shaped like a cube. He painted each face a different color. How many colors did he use?

13. **Analyze** Ashley is holding a solid figure. It has fewer faces than a cube. One of its faces is a square. The other faces are all the same shape. Which solid figure is it?

14. Look around your classroom. What two solid shapes could you use to build a solid shape similar to the one shown here?

The Alcazar is a medieval castle in Segovia, Spain.

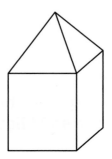

 Talk About It • Write About It

You have learned how solid figures are related to plane figures.

15. Which of the models at the right have a face that is a triangle? a rectangle? a circle?

16. Do any of the models at the right have more vertices than edges? Explain your thinking.

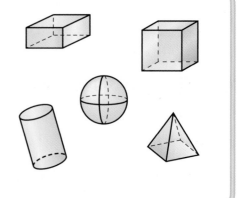

Visual Thinking
Pattern Blocks

Blocks can be used to make patterns based on size and shape.

What is the next block in the pattern?

1.

2.

3.

4. Use or draw blocks to create your own pattern. Have a classmate place or draw the next 3 blocks in the pattern.

Logical Thinking
Analogies

An **analogy** is a comparison of objects that are related to each other.

> A party hat is to a cone as a tennis ball is to a _____.
>
> **A** pyramid   **C** cone
>
> **B** sphere   **D** cube

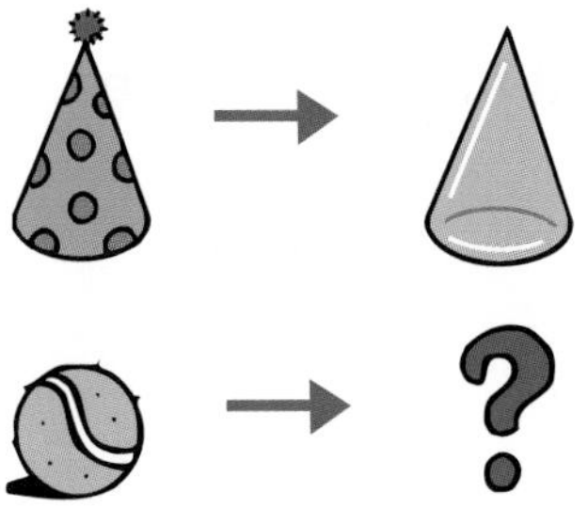

A party hat and a cone are the same shape. The answer is B because a tennis ball and a sphere are the same shape.

1. A wheel is to a circle as a dollar bill is to a _____.

   A square   **C** triangle

   B octagon   **D** rectangle

2. A quadrilateral is to 4 sides as a hexagon is to _____ sides.

   A 3   **C** 5

   B 6   **D** 8

Extra Practice at eduplace.com/map

Chapter Review/Test

VOCABULARY

1. A regular polygon with 3 vertices is an ____.

2. A part of a line that has one endpoint is a ____.

3. A can of tuna is shaped like a ____.

4. A shoebox is shaped like a ____.

Vocabulary

ray

cylinder

rectangular prism

quadrilateral

equilateral triangle

CONCEPTS AND SKILLS

Identify each figure. If it has a special name, write it.

(Lessons 1–2, pp. 414–421)

5.   6.   7.   8.   9.

Write the name of each figure. Tell whether it is a regular polygon.

(Lessons 2–4, pp. 418–426)

10.   11.   12.   13.   14.

Name the solid figure or figures. (Lesson 6–7, pp. 432–436)

15.   16.   17.   18.   19.

PROBLEM SOLVING

Solve. (Lesson 5, pp. 428–430)

20. What are the next three shapes in this pattern?

Write About It

Show You Understand

Think about a quadrilateral, a rectangle, and a square. How are they the same? How are they different?

Extra Practice

Set A (Lesson 1, pp. 414–417)

Tell whether each angle is a *right angle*, *less than a right angle*, or *greater than a right angle*.

1.
2.
3.

Set B (Lesson 2, pp. 418–421)

Tell whether each figure is a polygon. If it is, write its name.

1.
2.
3.
4.

Set C (Lesson 3, pp. 422–423)

Name the kind of triangle shown. Write *equilateral*, *isosceles*, *right*, or *scalene*.

1.
2.
3.
4.

Set D (Lesson 4, pp. 424–426)

Tell whether the figure is a quadrilateral. If it has a special name, write it.

1.
2.
3.
4.

Set E (Lesson 6, pp. 432–433)

Name each solid figure.

1.
2.
3.
4.

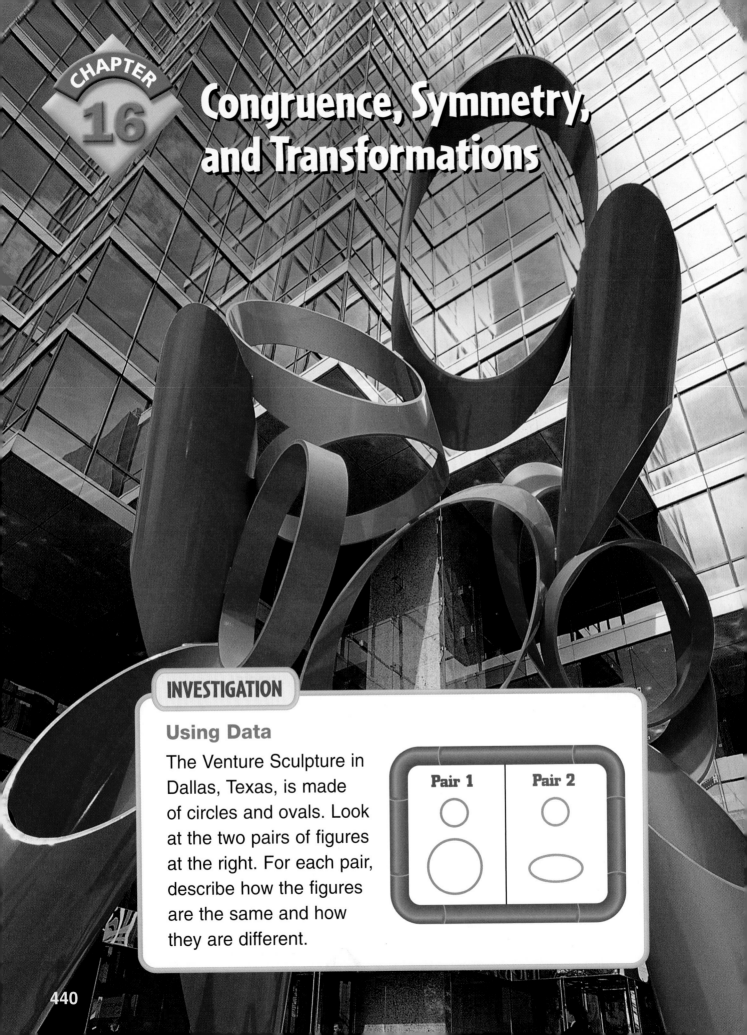

Congruence, Symmetry, and Transformations

INVESTIGATION

Using Data

The Venture Sculpture in Dallas, Texas, is made of circles and ovals. Look at the two pairs of figures at the right. For each pair, describe how the figures are the same and how they are different.

Pair 1   Pair 2

Use What You Know

**Use this page to review and remember
what you need to know for this chapter.**

VOCABULARY

Choose the best term to complete each sentence.

1. Another name for flat geometric figures
   is ____.

2. Any polygon with 3 sides and 3 angles is
   called a ____.

3. A plane figure with no edges or vertices
   is a ____.

> **Vocabulary**
> circle
> triangle
> rectangle
> plane figures
> solid figures

CONCEPTS AND SKILLS

**Classify each as a plane figure or a solid figure.
Then name each figure.**

4.

5.

6.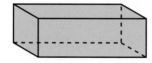

7.

8.

9.

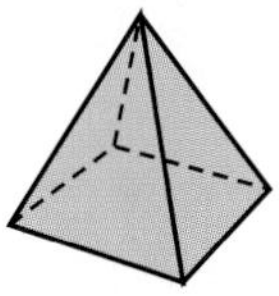

 **Write About It**

10. Look at the pair of figures below.
    Are they exactly the same? Explain
    why or why not.

Facts Practice, See page 669.

Hands On Lesson 1

Congruent Figures

Objective Learn about figures that are the same size and shape.

Vocabulary
congruent

Materials
pattern blocks
construction paper
tracing paper

Work Together

Plane figures with the same size and shape are **congruent.**
Work with a partner to draw figures that are congruent.

STEP 1 Choose a pattern block. Trace around the edges of the block on construction paper. Then trace around the same block on tracing paper.

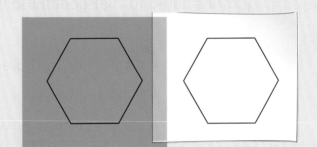

STEP 2 Compare the two figures you traced. Does the outline of the figure on the tracing paper fit exactly over the outline on the construction paper?

- Are the figures the same size?

- Are the figures the same shape?

- Are the figures congruent?

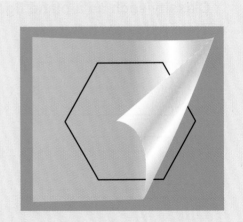

Other Examples

A. Different Sizes

The figures are not congruent. They are not the same size.

B. Different Shapes

The figures are not congruent. They are not the same shape.

Trace one of the two figures. Place the traced figure on top of the other figure. Are the figures congruent?

1.

2.

3.

Trace the first figure. Place the traced figure on top of the other figures. Then choose the figure that is congruent to it. Write a, b, or c.

4.

a. b. c.

5.

a. 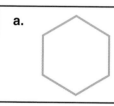 b.  c.

6.

a. b. c.

Talk About It • Write About It

You learned that figures that have the same size and shape are congruent.

7. Not all circles are congruent. Explain why.

8. **Represent** Do you think that all rectangles are conguent? Draw pictures to support your answer.

9. **Analyze** Isabel drew an octagon. Marco drew a hexagon. Can Isabel's figure be congruent to Marco's figure? Explain.

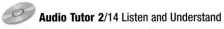 **Audio Tutor 2/14** Listen and Understand

Similar Figures

Objective Learn about figures that are similar.

Vocabulary
similar

Materials
grid paper or Learning
Tool 27

Learn About It

Some art students made a mural. They planned the mural by drawing it on grid paper. The mural is an exact copy of the drawing, but bigger.

Figures that are the same shape, but not necessarily the same size, are **similar**.

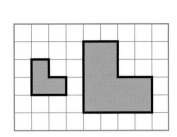

These figures are similar. They are the same shape. They are not the same size.

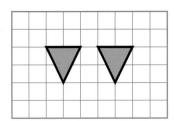

These figures are similar and congruent. They have the same shape and the same size.

Try this activity to draw a figure that is similar to the one shown.

STEP **1** Multiply the length by 2.
$2 \times 6 = 12$

STEP **2** Multiply the height by 2.
$2 \times 4 = 8$

STEP **3** Draw the similar figure. Make the length 12 units and the height 8 units.

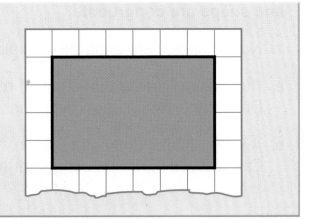

Tell whether the two figures in each exercise are similar.

Ask Yourself
- Are the figures the same shape?
- Are the figures the same size?

1.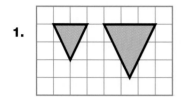

2.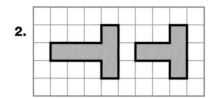

Explain Your Thinking ▶ Are all equilateral triangles similar? Are they congruent? Explain.

Practice and Problem Solving

Tell whether the two figures in each exercise are similar.

3.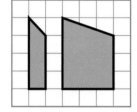

4.

5.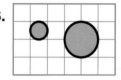

Use the different color figures in the design to answer Questions 6–9.

6. Look at the circles in the design. Are they similar? Are they congruent? Explain.

7. Which quadrilaterals in the design are similar but not congruent?

8. Find two other figures that are similar but not congruent. What shape and color are they?

9. **Analyze** Can you combine two figures in the design to make a figure that is congruent to another figure in the design? Explain how.

Go On

Write *true* or *false* for each sentence. Then write a sentence or draw an example to explain your answer.

10. All circles are similar.

11. All quadrilaterals are similar.

12. All rectangles are similar.

13. All squares are similar.

14. Some triangles are similar.

15. No circles are congruent.

16. Some squares are congruent.

17. Some quadrilaterals are congruent.

Solve.

18. Alex wants to draw a figure similar to the triangles shown. If he makes one side 6 inches long, how long must the other sides be?

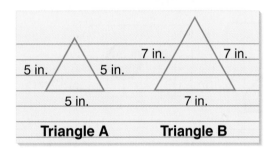

Triangle A   **Triangle B**

19. **What's Wrong?** Leila drew the figures below. She says that she drew congruent figures. What did she do wrong? How do you know?

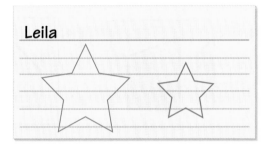

Leila

20. **Explain** Jessie drew a square with sides that were 9 cm long. George drew a square with sides that were 6 cm long. Are the figures that Jessie and George drew similar? Are they congruent?

21. Erin drew a hexagon with sides that were 8 cm long. Mark drew an octagon with sides that were 8 cm long. Are the figures similar? Are they congruent? Explain.

Mixed Review and Test Prep

Open Response

Complete each pattern. (Ch. 1, Lesson 5)

22. 1, 6, 11, 16, _____

23. 26, 23, 20, 17, _____, _____

24. 60, 61, 63, 66, 70, _____, _____

25. 2, 4, 8, 16, _____, _____

26. Are the figures below similar? Are they congruent? Explain how you know. (Ch. 16, Lesson 2)

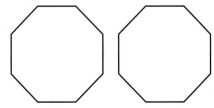

Extra Practice See page 459, Set B.

Visual Thinking
Direction Selection

People often use their sense of direction to keep from getting lost.

Imagine that the directions shown are to a friend's house.

1. Read the directions. Then write directions to explain how to get home.

> Make a left out of your driveway.
> Turn right onto New Freedom Road.
> Then make a left onto Chairville Road.
> Cross Route 70 and make a right onto Stokes Road.
> My house is the second house on the left.

2. Directions can also tell you where to move on a grid. Complete the set of directions to draw this shape.

- Start at (4, 5).
- Move 2 to the right.
- Move 2 down.
- Move 2 to the left.
- Move 2 down
  ?

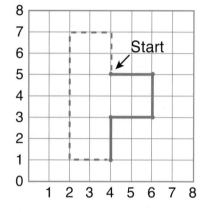

Check your understanding of Lessons 1–2.

Write whether the two figures are congruent or similar. (Lessons 1–2)

1.

2.

3.

4. Sam cuts out an equilateral triangle with sides that are 5 inches long. Sarah cuts out an equilateral triangle with sides that are 8 inches long. Are the two triangles congruent or similar?

5. Jason wants to draw two congruent squares. The first square he draws has sides that measure 8 centimeters. What should the sides of the second square measure?

Line of Symmetry

Objective Learn about figures that have lines of symmetry.

Vocabulary
symmetry
line of symmetry

Materials
pattern blocks
  (hexagon and triangle)
paper
scissors

Work Together

A plane figure that has **symmetry** can be folded along a line so that the two parts match exactly. That line is called a **line of symmetry.**

Work with a partner. Use pattern blocks to draw figures with lines of symmetry.

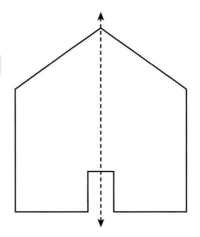

STEP 1 Trace the hexagon pattern block on the piece of paper. Then, trace it again so that the two hexagons make one figure.

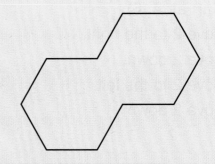

STEP 2 Cut out the figure. Then fold it in half to discover a line of symmetry. Mark the line with a pencil.

STEP 3 Now fold the figure in a different way to find another line of symmetry. Mark it with a pencil.

• How many lines of symmetry are there?

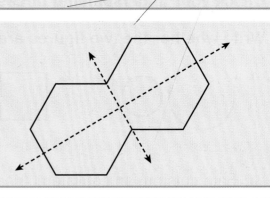

STEP 4 Repeat Steps 1–3 using the triangle pattern block. Be sure to mark the lines of symmetry with a pencil.

• How many lines of symmetry are there?

Trace and cut out each figure. Fold the figure and record the number of lines of symmetry you find.

1.

2.

3.

4.

Tell whether each line appears to be a line of symmetry.

5.

6.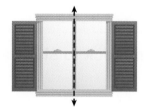

7.

8.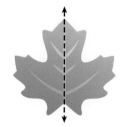

9.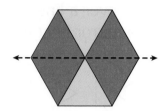

10.

Solve.

11. Draw the number *eight* so that it has two lines of symmetry. Then draw another number that has symmetry.

12. **Analyze** Does a circle have more than one line of symmetry? Draw a circle with lines of symmetry to explain your thinking.

Talk About It • Write About It

You learned that figures that have symmetry can be folded so that the two parts match.

13. Do congruent figures have the same lines of symmetry? Do similar figures have the same lines of symmetry? Explain your thinking.

14. **Represent** Draw a figure that has no lines of symmetry.

Transformations

Objective Learn about flips, slides, and turns.

Vocabulary
slide
flip
turn

Materials
red pattern block
(trapezoid)
dot paper
(Learning Tool 29)

Work Together

You can move figures without changing their size or shape.

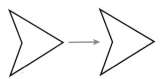 You can **slide** the figure along a straight line.

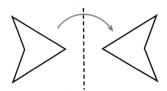 You can **flip** the figure over a line to get a mirror image.

 You can **turn** or move the figure around a point.

Work with a partner. Use a pattern block to show a slide.

 STEP 1

Place the pattern block on dot paper.

Trace around its edges. Then slide the pattern block along the row of dots to the right. Trace around the block again.

- Is the second figure the same size as the first figure? Is it the same shape?

- How does the figure change?

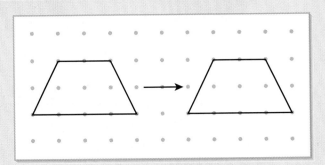

STEP 2

Now slide the figure as shown and trace it again.

- How does the figure change?

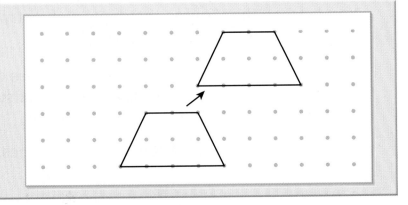

450

Now use the pattern block to show a flip.

 STEP 3

Trace the pattern block again.

Then draw a dotted line above the pattern block. Flip the pattern block over the dotted line. Then trace around the block again. This makes a mirror image.

- Are the two figures congruent?

- Describe how the second figure is different from the first figure.

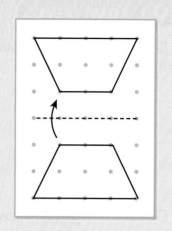

 STEP 4

Trace the pattern block again.

Now flip the pattern block as shown at the right and trace it again.

- How does the figure change each time?

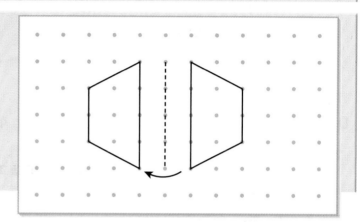

Now use the pattern block to show a turn.

 STEP 5

Trace the pattern block again. Then turn the pattern block a half turn around the point on the dot paper. Then trace around the block again.

- Describe how the figure changed.

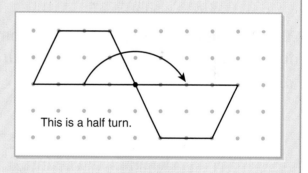

This is a half turn.

 STEP 6

Now turn the block around the point as shown to show turns in other positions. Trace the block each time.

- How does the figure change each time?

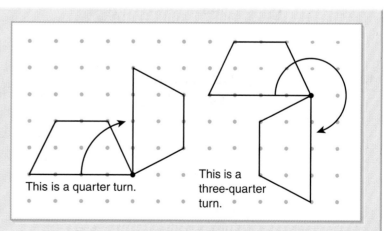

This is a quarter turn.

This is a three-quarter turn.

Go On

Does the figure show a slide? Write *yes* or *no*.

1.

2.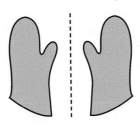

3.

Does the figure show a flip? Write *yes* or *no*.

4.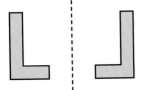

5.

6.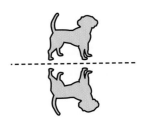

Does the figure show a turn? Write *yes* or *no*.

7.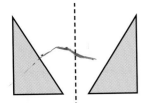

8.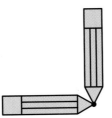

9.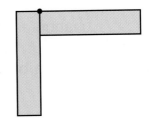

Tell how each figure was moved from Position A to Position B. Write *slide, flip,* or *turn*.

10.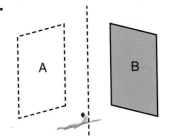

11.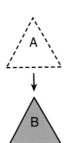

12.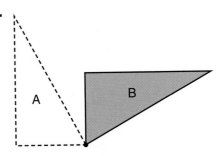

13.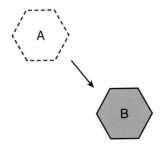

14.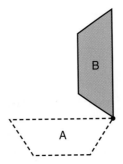

15.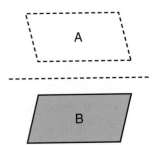

Tell how you would move the last figure to complete the pattern. Write *slide, flip,* or *turn*.

16. 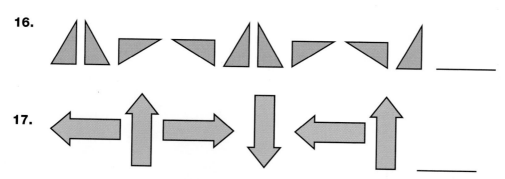 _____

17. _____

18. _____

19. _____

Solve.

20. Look at the pattern at the right. In what position will the twelfth paintbrush be? How do you know?

21. **Create and Solve** Draw a pattern using slides, flips, or turns. Exchange patterns with a partner. Draw the next two figures in the pattern. Then check your partner's drawings.

Talk About It • Write About It

You learned how to slide, flip, and turn plane figures.

22. When you turn a circle, does it look the same as when you flip it? Explain.

23. How would a figure look if you made a full turn?

24. Find examples of slides, flips, and turns in your classroom. Explain how you know what they are.

Problem-Solving Application
Visual Thinking

Objective Solve problems using
visual thinking.

**Sometimes you need to use visual
thinking to solve problems.**

Problem Andy is trying to finish the
modern art jigsaw puzzle shown on the
right. He needs to decide what piece
will complete the puzzle.

▶ **First find the visual clues.**

Look at puzzle pieces that border the missing piece.

You will see that there is a purple circle, a green
triangle and an orange square.

▶ **Then decide which piece completes the puzzle.**

The missing piece must have part of a purple circle
to the left of part of a green triangle. The green
triangle must be above part of an orange square.

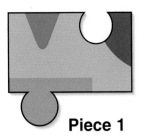
Piece 1

Piece 2

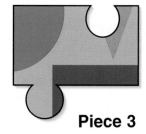
Piece 3

Solution: Piece 2 completes the puzzle.

Look Back Why wouldn't Piece 1 or Piece 3 complete the puzzle?

Extra Help at **eduplace.com/map**

Guided Practice

Use the Ask Yourself questions to help you solve each problem.

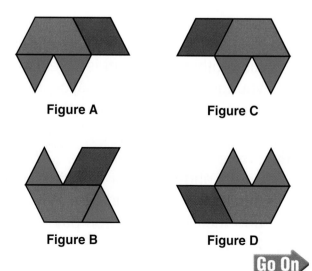

Ask Yourself
- What does the question ask me to find?
- How can I use visual clues to solve the problem?

1. Look at Andy's puzzle pieces again. Decide which piece would complete the puzzle below.

2. Maria is almost finished tiling her kitchen floor. Look at the tile design on the right. Which tiles will complete the floor?

Hint Look for a pattern.

 a.   b.   c.   d.

Independent Practice

Use the pattern blocks below for Problems 3–4.

3. Which two figures show the same design as Figure A, but in different positions? Explain how Figure A was moved each time.

4. **Analyze** Suppose Figure A is directly to your right and does not move. If you move a quarter of a turn to the right, where is Figure A in relationship to you?

Figure A   **Figure C**

Figure B   **Figure D**

Go On

Mixed Strategy Practice

Solve. Show your work. Tell what strategy you used.

5. Lois makes a pyramid using straws for the edges. Her pyramid has one square face. How many straws does she use to make the pyramid?

6. Ms. Finn's class is planting rows of tulips and irises. They want 2 irises for each tulip. Each row of tulips has 4 plants. They plant 3 rows of tulips. How many irises should they plant?

7. Twenty-one parents and teachers help at the school picnic. There are 5 more parents than teachers. How many parents help? How many teachers help?

You Choose

Strategy
- Act It Out
- Draw a Picture
- Guess and Check
- Use Logical Reasoning
- Write a Number Sentence

Computation Method
- Mental Math
- Estimation
- Paper and Pencil
- Calculator

Solve. Tell which method you chose.

8. Ly read 109 pages of a book on Monday, 95 pages on Tuesday, and 185 pages on Wednesday. The book has 598 pages. Has he read more than half of the book?

9. In 1990, the population of Keene, Texas was 3,944 people. In 2000, the population was 5,003 people. How many more people lived there in 2000 than in 1990?

10. **Reasoning** Earl is twice as old as his brother Sam. Sam is 2 years younger than his sister Alice. If Alice is 6 years old, how old is Earl?

11. Paco plants 5 rows of pepper plants and 3 rows of tomato plants in his garden. Each row has 10 plants. How many plants did Paco plant?

12. **Money** A bus ticket costs $7.50 for adults and $4.50 for children. How much would Mr. and Mrs. Allen and their three children pay to ride the bus?

13. On Tuesday, 25,308 people attended a ball game. Wednesday's attendance was 19,463. How many people attended the games?

...

Use Your Memory!

Play this game to practice identifying congruent and similar shapes.

2 Players

What You'll Need • Congruent and similar shape
cards (Learning Tool 28)

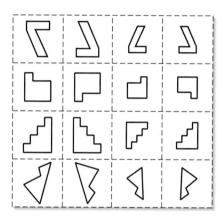

How to Play

1 Cut out the cards on Learning Tool 28.

2 Shuffle the cards. Place them face-down in a 4 × 4 array.

3 The first player turns over any two cards. If the cards are congruent, the player keeps both cards. If not, the player turns the cards back over.

4 Players take turns repeating Step 3 until all the matches have been made.

5 Gather the cards and repeat Step 2. Play the game again, matching similar shapes this time.

6 The player with the most pairs is the winner!

Chapter Review/Test

VOCABULARY

Choose the best term to complete each sentence.

Vocabulary
slide
similar
symmetry
congruent

1. Figures that are the same shape, but not necessarily the same size, are ____.

2. Figures that are the same size and shape are ____.

3. A plane figure that has ____ can be folded along a line so that the two parts match exactly.

CONCEPTS AND SKILLS

Tell whether the two figures in each exercise are similar. If they are similar, tell whether they are congruent. (Lessons 1–2, pp. 442–447)

4.

5.

6.

7.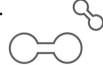

Tell whether the line appears to be a line of symmetry.

(Lesson 3, pp. 448–449)

8.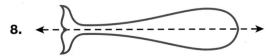

Tell how the figure was moved. Write *slide*, *flip*, or *turn*.

(Lesson 4, pp. 450–453)

9.

PROBLEM SOLVING

Solve. (Lesson 5, pp. 454–456)

10. Which piece completes the puzzle?

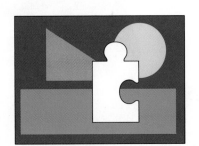

a.

b.

Write About It

Show You Understand

Explain the difference between *congruent* and *similar*. Can two figures be congruent but not similar? Why or why not?

Extra Practice

Set A (Lesson 1, pp. 442–443)

Tell whether the two figures in each exercise are congruent.

1.
2.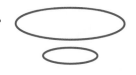
3.
4.

Set B (Lesson 2, pp. 444–447)

Tell whether the two figures in each exercise are similar.

1.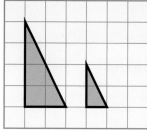
2.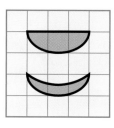
3.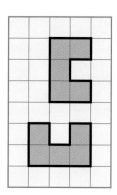
4.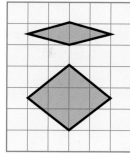

Set C (Lesson 3, pp. 448–449)

Tell whether each line appears to be a line of symmetry.

1.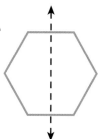
2.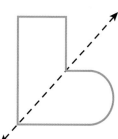
3.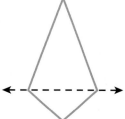
4.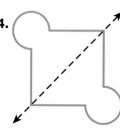

Set D (Lesson 4, pp. 450–453)

Does the figure show a slide, flip, or turn?

1.
2.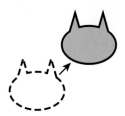
3.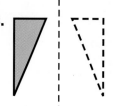
4.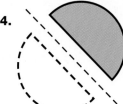

CHAPTER 17

Perimeter, Area, and Volume

INVESTIGATION

Using Data

Nydia and her family are moving into a new apartment. She and her brother Pedro couldn't decide whose room is bigger. The grids below show the size of each room. Whose room is bigger? How can you tell? Make a grid to show a room that is the same size as Nydia's but is a different shape.

Nydia's Room

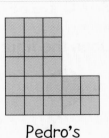

Pedro's Room

Use What You Know

**Use this page to review and remember
what you need to know for this chapter.**

VOCABULARY

Choose the best term to complete each sentence.

Vocabulary
side
plane figure
solid figure
regular polygon
irregular polygon

1. A circle is one kind of ____.

2. A figure that has 3 dimensions is called a ____.

3. Each ____ of an equilateral triangle is the same length.

4. A hexagon with sides that are equal in length is a ____.

CONCEPTS AND SKILLS

Write *plane* or *solid* to identify each figure.

5.

6.

7.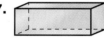

8.

9.

10.

Find each sum.

11. $2 + 3 + 2 + 3$

12. $8 + 7 + 6 + 4$

13. $3 + 8 + 3 + 5 + 6$

14. $2 + 8 + 5 + 2$

15. $4 + 4 + 4 + 4$

16. $5 + 2 + 5 + 2$

17. $8 + 3 + 6 + 5$

18. $5 + 4 + 7 + 3 + 2$

19. $6 + 8 + 6 + 2 + 4$

 Write About It

20. Name a solid figure that you could use to trace a rectangle. Explain why you can use this figure.

Facts Practice, See page 666.

Explore Perimeter

Objective Estimate and measure the distance around a figure.

Vocabulary
perimeter

Materials
For each pair:
small paper clips
toothpicks
string
ruler

Work Together

The distance around a plane figure is called the **perimeter** . You can estimate and measure the perimeter of a book in paper clips and toothpicks.

STEP 1
Trace around one face of a book. Estimate the perimeter using paper clips. Record your estimate in a chart like the one shown.

Perimeter of a Book		
	Estimate	**Measurement**
Number of Paper Clips		
Number of Toothpicks		
Number of Inches		

STEP 2
Place the paper clips end to end around the rectangle you traced. Count and record the number of paper clips you use.

STEP 3
Repeat Steps 1–2 using toothpicks.
• How do the measurements compare?

STEP 4
Now estimate the perimeter of your rectangle in inches. Record your estimate in the chart.

STEP 5
Run a string around the perimeter of the rectangle. Mark the spot where you end on the string.

Then measure the length of the string with the ruler. Record the number in your chart.

• What is the perimeter of the rectangle in inches?

Follow the directions below.

- Copy and complete the chart below. Trace a face of each object.
- Estimate the perimeter of each object. Record your estimates.
- Then measure each using paper clips, toothpicks, and a ruler.

	Object	Objects Used to Measure	Estimate	Measurement
1.	pencil box	paper clips		
		toothpick		
		ruler		
2.	notebook	paper clips		
		toothpicks		
		ruler		
3.	a story book	paper clips		
		toothpicks		
		ruler		
4.	desktop	paper clips		
		toothpicks		
		ruler		

5. How did your estimates compare with your measurements?

6. For each object, compare your measurements with other students in the class. Were your measurements all the same? Explain why or why not.

Talk About It • Write About It

You learned how to estimate and measure the perimeter of a figure.

7. Some people estimate length in feet using their own feet. Estimate the length of your classroom using your feet. How close do you think your estimate will be? Check by measuring with a ruler or yardstick.

8. If you were building a desk or a birdhouse, would you use paper clips, toothpicks, or a ruler to measure? Explain your choice.

Audio Tutor 2/16 Listen and Understand

Find Perimeter

Objective Find the distance around a figure.

Learn About It

The Cruz family is moving into the neighborhood next week! Sam and his friends are making a welcome sign. They plan to put yarn around the edge of the sign as a border. How many inches of yarn do they need?

To solve the problem you need to find the **perimeter**.

The distance around a figure is called the perimeter. To find the perimeter, add the lengths of the sides.

$20 + 32 + 20 + 32 = 104$

The perimeter of the sign is 104 inches.

Solution: The friends need 104 inches of yarn.

20 in.

32 in.

Welcome to the Neighborhood

Other Examples

A. Perimeter of an Irregular Polygon

Add the lengths of each side.

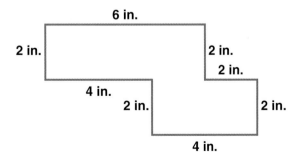

6 in.

2 in.   2 in.

2 in.

4 in.

2 in.   2 in.

4 in.

$6 + 2 + 2 + 2 + 4 + 2 + 4 + 2 = 24$

The perimeter is 24 inches.

B. Measure in Centimeters

Measure each side in centimeters.

$6 + 4 + 6 + 4 = 20$

The perimeter is 20 centimeters.

Ask Yourself
• What will I measure with?
• What numbers do I add?
• How should I label my answer?

Guided Practice

Find the perimeter of each figure. Use a centimeter ruler if side lengths are not given.

1.

2.

3.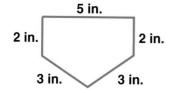
7 ft   2 ft
4 ft
3 ft
7 ft

4.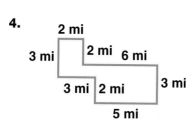
2 mi
3 mi   2 mi   6 mi
3 mi   2 mi   3 mi
5 mi

Explain Your Thinking ▶ Can you find the perimeter of a square if you know the length of one side? Why or why not? Explain.

Practice and Problem Solving

Find the perimeter of each figure.

5.
5 in.
2 in.   2 in.
3 in.   3 in.

6.
6 ft
7 ft   7 ft
10 ft

7.
7 mi
5 mi
9 mi
10 mi

8.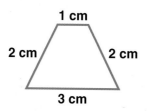
4 in.
6 in.   1 in.
5 in.

9.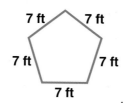
20 mi
20 mi
30 mi
20 mi
20 mi

10.
8 ft
8 ft   8 ft
8 ft   8 ft
8 ft

11.
1 cm
2 cm   2 cm
3 cm

12.
7 ft   7 ft
7 ft   7 ft
7 ft

13.
3 mi
1 mi   1 mi
3 mi

Measure the sides of each figure with a centimeter ruler. Then find the perimeter.

14.   **15.**   **16.**   **17.**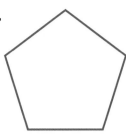

18.

Solve.

19. Multistep The perimeter of an isosceles triangle is 50 inches. Two sides are each 18 inches long. What is the length of the third side?

20. Create and Solve Write a problem that involves finding the perimeter of a shape. Give your problem to a classmate to solve.

21. Represent Use grid paper to draw a rectangle with a perimeter of 16 units. Now draw a different rectangle with the same perimeter.

22. Money At the right is a diagram of Mr. Tate's garden. He wants to put a fence around the boundary of his garden. The fence costs $10 a foot. How much money will Mr. Tate need to pay for the fence?

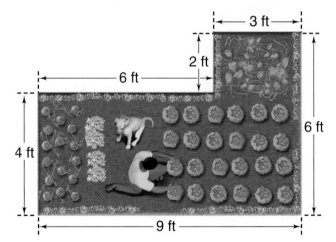

Mixed Review and Test Prep

Open Response

Solve. (Ch. 12, Lesson 5)

23. What is the month just before February?

24. What is the month just after December?

25. What date is one day after August 31?

Multiple Choice

26. Nathan is measuring a square tile. One side is 3 inches. What is the perimeter of the tile?
(Ch. 17, Lesson 2)

A 6 inches   **c** 12 inches

B 9 inches   **D** 15 inches

Extra Practice See page 483, Set A.

Visual Thinking
Coloring Puzzle

Look at the map on the right.

Suppose you want to color the map so that no states that share a border are the same color.

What is the fewest number of colors you could use?

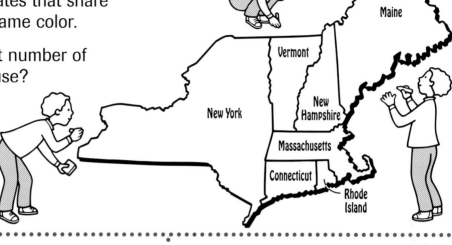

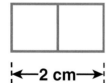

Algebraic Thinking
Perimeter Patterns

Look at the square below.
Its perimeter is 4 cm.

1 cm

Now look at the rectangle below. It was made by connecting 2 squares. What is its perimeter?

←— **2 cm** —→

What would be the perimeter of a rectangle made by connecting

- 3 squares in a row?
- 4 squares in a row?
- 5 squares in a row?

What number pattern do you see?

Brain Teaser

Use these clues to draw and find the perimeter of the mystery figure.

- I am a regular polygon.

- I have more sides than a parallelogram but fewer sides than a hexagon.

- The length of one of my sides in inches is the same as my number of sides.

Education Place

Check out **eduplace.com/map** for more brain teasers.

Explore Area

Objective Estimate the area of a figure.

Vocabulary
area

Materials
For each pair:
1-inch grid paper

Work Together

The **area** of a figure is the number of square units needed to cover the figure without overlapping.

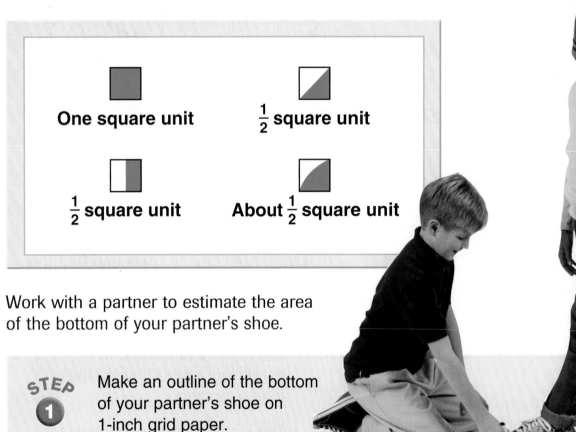

One square unit

$\frac{1}{2}$ square unit

$\frac{1}{2}$ square unit

About $\frac{1}{2}$ square unit

Work with a partner to estimate the area of the bottom of your partner's shoe.

STEP 1 Make an outline of the bottom of your partner's shoe on 1-inch grid paper.

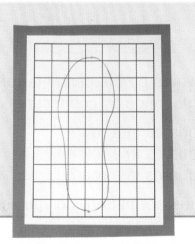

STEP 2 Count the number of whole square units inside the outline of the shoe. Two partly covered squares can be counted as one square unit.

- How many square units did you count?

- Record the number of square units.

Estimate the area of each figure. Each **= 1 square unit.**

1.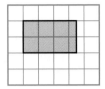

2.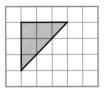

3.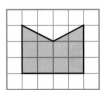

4.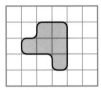

5.

6.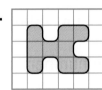

7.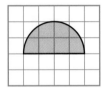

8.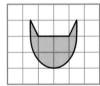

9.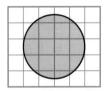

Use one-inch grid paper for Problems 10 and 11.

10. Trace around one of your hands on grid paper. Estimate the area. Then count the square units inside the outline to find the area.

11. Draw a square. Draw a line of symmetry. Estimate the area of each part. What is true about the estimated areas? Explain why.

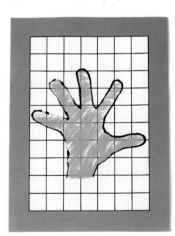

Talk About It • Write About It

You learned how to estimate the area of a figure.

12. Look at Exercises 1 and 5. Is it easier to estimate the area of a rectangle or a heart? Explain.

13. What is the difference between area and perimeter?

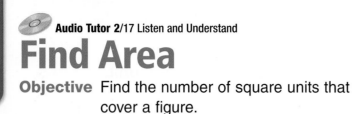

Audio Tutor 2/17 Listen and Understand

Find Area

Objective Find the number of square units that cover a figure.

Vocabulary

area

Learn About It

The Cruz family had a new tile floor put in their kitchen before they moved in. The tiles are square. What is the **area** of the floor?

You can count the number of square tiles to find the area of the floor.

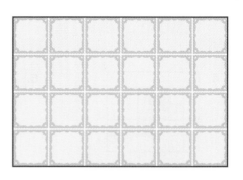

Each tile or ☐ = 1 square unit.

There are 24 square units.

1	2	3	4	5	6
7	8	9	10	11	12
13	14	15	16	17	18
19	20	21	22	23	24

Solution: The area of the floor is 24 square units.

▶ **You can also find area on a geoboard.**

Look at the rectangle at the right.

Each ▦ = 1 square unit.

The area of the rectangle is 4 square units.

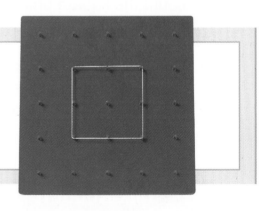

Other Examples

A. Area of an Irregular Figure

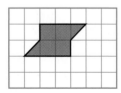

Each ■ =1 square unit
So the area is 5 square units.

B. Area of a Right Triangle

Each ▦ =1 square unit.
So the area is $4\frac{1}{2}$ square units.

Extra Help at **eduplace.com/map**

Guided Practice

Find the area of each figure. Label your answer in square units. Each  or  = 1 square unit.

1. 

2. 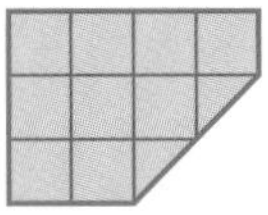

3. 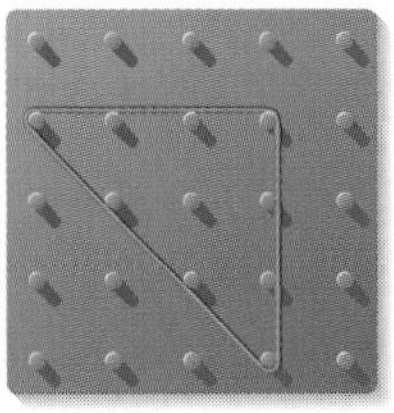

Ask Yourself

- How do I find area?
- What do I do with the half squares?
- Did I label my answer?

Explain Your Thinking ▶ Look at the triangle in Exercise 3 above. If two of these triangles were put together to form a square, what would be the area of the square? Explain.

Practice and Problem Solving

Find the area of each figure. Label your answer in square units. Each  or  = 1 square unit.

4. 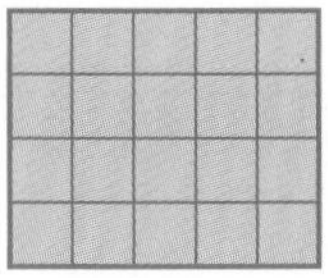

5. 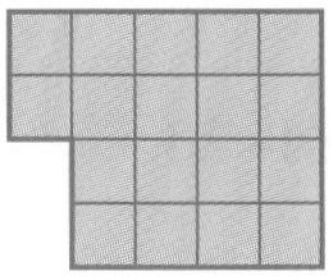

6. 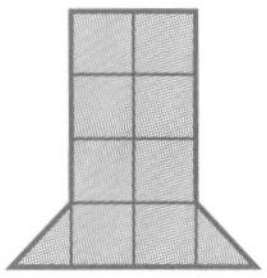

7. 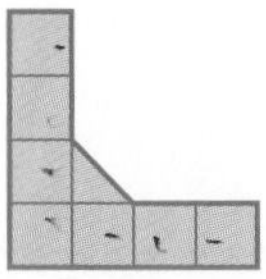

8. 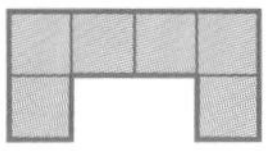

9. 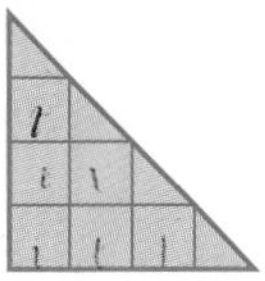

10. 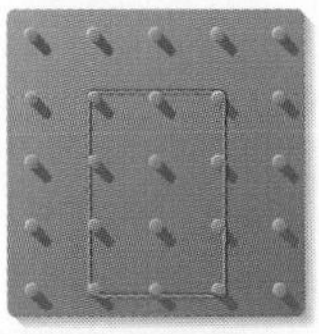

11. 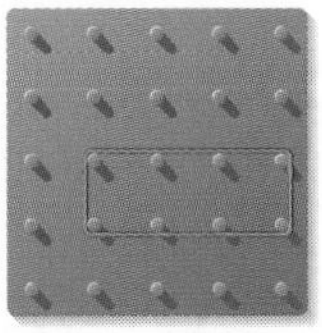

12. 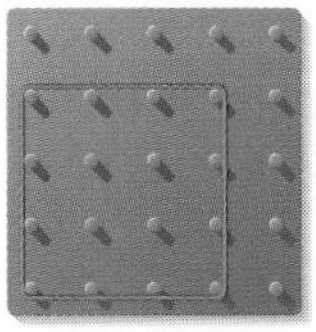

13. 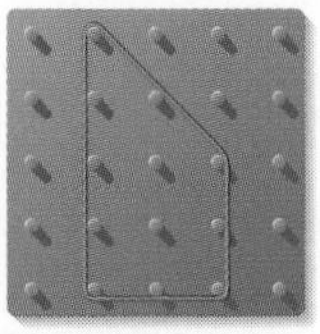

14. 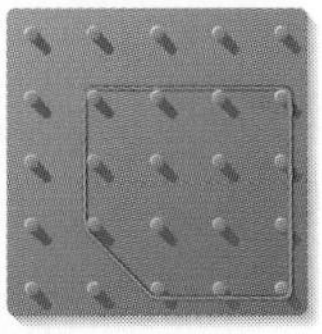

15. 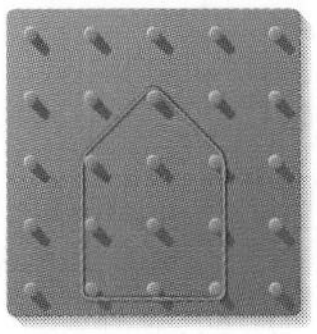

16. How could you find the area of the figure in Exercise 4 without counting each square?

17. **Write About It** Draw two congruent figures on grid paper. Do they have the same area? Explain.

Go On

**Cut out the squares from grid paper.
Place squares on your Workmat to make
shapes with the given area.**

18. A square with an area of 16 square units

19. A rectangle with an area of 24 square units

20. A different rectangle with an area of 24 square units

21. Any figure with an area of 17 square units.

22. Draw a rectangle on your Workmat. Then use your squares to find its area.

23. **What's Wrong?** Jill says that polygons with the same area will have the same perimeter. Show what's wrong with her thinking. Draw two different polygons, each with a different perimeter and each with an area of 15 square units.

Data Use the diagram for Problems 24–28.

24. The diagram shows the design of a tiled pool deck. The deck goes all the way around the pool. What is the area of the deck? Explain your answer.

25. Which has a greater area, the deck or the pool? How much greater?

26. **Money** Ms. Jacobs buys new deck tiles. The tiles cost $3 each. How much does it cost to buy all new tiles?

27. **Predict** Ms. Jacobs wants to alternate between blue and white tiles on the deck. How many of each color tile should she buy?

28. Suppose each side of the squares in the diagram is 1 foot. What is the perimeter of the pool? What is the perimeter of the deck?

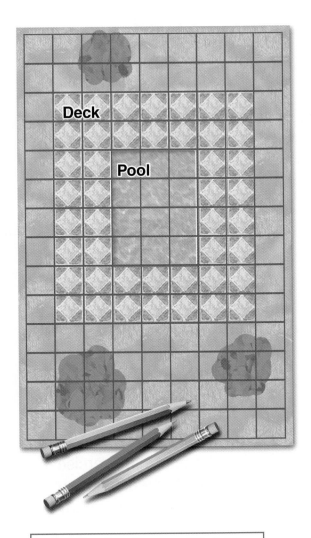

Extra Practice See page 483, Set B.

Math Challenge
Area of a Rectangle

You can count the number of square units to find the area of the rectangle at the right.

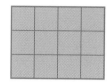

You can also think of the rectangle as an array that is 3 rows of 4 squares each. It is 3 units by 4 units.

You can add or multiply to find the number of square units.

$$4 + 4 + 4 = 12$$

$$3 \times 4 = 12 \text{ square units}$$

The area of the rectangle is 12 square units.

Think
Area = length × width
= 4 units × 3 units
= 12 square units

Multiply to find the area of each rectangle.

1.

2.
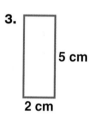
4 in.
3 in. 3 in.
4 in.

3.
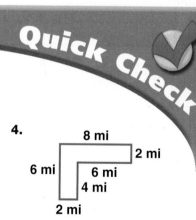
5 cm
2 cm

Check your understanding of Lessons 1–4.

Find the perimeter of each figure. (Lessons 1–2)

1.
10 in.
10 in. ☐ 10 in.
10 in.

2.
12 ft
6 ft ▭ 6 ft
12 ft

3.
3 cm 3 cm
3 cm   3 cm
3 cm

4.
8 mi
2 mi
6 mi   6 mi
4 mi
2 mi

Find the area of each figure. Label your answer in square units. Each ☐ or ▨ = 1 square unit. (Lessons 3–4)

5.

6.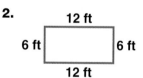

7.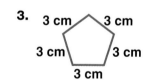

8.

Problem-Solving Application
Use Measurement

Objective Use what you know about perimeter and area to solve problems.

Problem The Cruz family plans to build a treehouse in their backyard. Mr. Cruz wants the floor of the treehouse to be at least 20 square feet. Which plans have enough floor area for the treehouse?

1 foot
1 foot

1 square foot
Each side has a length of 1 foot

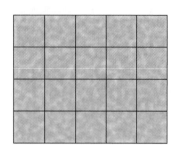
Plan A

Plan B

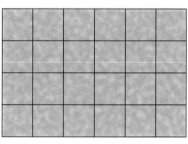
Plan C

UNDERSTAND

This is what you know.

The floor needs to have an area of at least 20 square feet.

PLAN

You can count squares to find the area of each floor plan.

SOLVE

Find the number of squares shown in each plan.
Then compare each area to 20 square feet.

• Plan A has a floor area of 20 square feet.

• Plan B has a floor area of 18 square feet.

• Plan C has a floor area of 24 square feet.

Solution: Plan A and Plan C have enough floor area.

LOOK BACK

Look back at the problem.

Which plan should Mr. Cruz choose? Explain your choice.

Use the Ask Yourself questions to help you solve each problem.

1. **Represent** A treehouse window is 2 feet wide and 2 feet high. Draw it on grid paper. Let 1 square stand for 1 square foot. What is the area of the window?

2. If Mr. Cruz puts a frame around the window, how many feet of framing material will he need?

(**Hint**) The answer is not in square feet.

Ask Yourself

UNDERSTAND → Do I need to find perimeter or area?

PLAN → Did I count units?

SOLVE →
• Did I use the correct units?
• Do I need to label my answer?

LOOK BACK → Did I answer the question?

Independent Practice

Use the diagrams to solve each problem.

3. Bob wants to carpet the floor of his pet's doghouse. Will $32 be enough to buy carpeting? Explain.

Doghouse Floor

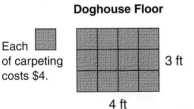

Each ▨ of carpeting costs $4.

3 ft

4 ft

4. Bob is putting a chain-link fence around the pet play area below. How much fencing is needed if the entrance has a wooden gate that is 2 ft wide?

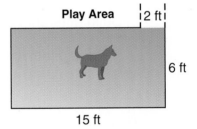

Play Area

2 ft

6 ft

15 ft

5. Mrs. Cruz wants a wallpaper border along the top of the walls in Ann's room. How much border will she need?

Ann's Bedroom

10 ft

12 ft

6. Mr. Cruz wants a rope border around the top of this planter box. How much rope will he need?

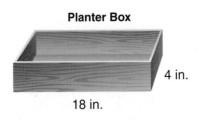

Planter Box

4 in.

18 in.

Explore Volume

Objective Estimate the volume of a figure.

Vocabulary
volume

Materials
For each group:
unit cubes
small box
various containers

 Work Together

The number of unit cubes that make up a solid figure is the **volume** of the figure.

Work with a partner to estimate the number of unit cubes that will fill a small box.

 STEP 1
Estimate how many cubes it will take to fill the box. Record your estimate.

 STEP 2
Fill the box with cubes. Count the cubes as you fill the box to find its volume. Record the number of cubes you used.

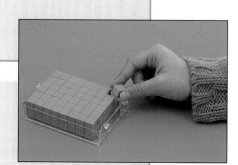

- What is the volume of the box? How does your estimate compare with the volume?

STEP 3
Now use all of the cubes from the box to build a solid figure.

- What is the volume of the figure?

Build different figures with the same number of cubes.

- What is the volume of each figure?

 STEP 4
Estimate the volume of the solid figure below. Record your estimate.

Now use cubes to build the same figure.

- What is the volume of the figure?

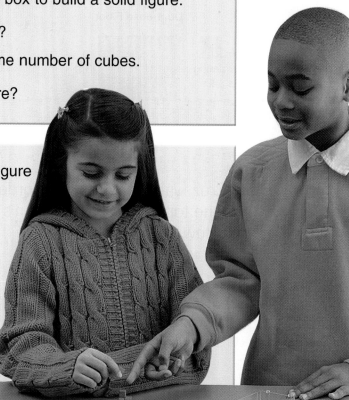

Follow the directions below.

- Copy the chart to the right.

- Find containers like those listed in the chart.

- Estimate how many cubes you will need to fill each container. Record your estimate.

- Now fill each container with cubes. Record the number of cubes you use.

Containers	Estimate	Number of Cubes
1. Gift Box		
2. Spaghetti Box		
3. Small Cereal Box		
4. Cup		
5. Soup Can		

Estimate the volume of each figure. Then build it with cubes. Write the estimate and the number of cubes you used.

6.

7.

8.

9.

10.

11.

Talk About It • Write About It

You learned how to estimate the volume of a figure.

12. Suppose two solid figures have the same volume. Must they have the same shape? Explain.

13. Do you think that the number of cubes used to fill the soup can is greater than or less than the actual volume of the can? Explain your answer.

14. Explain how finding the volume of a container is different from finding the area of a plane figure.

Find Volume

Objective Find the volume of a solid figure.

Learn About It

This is a unit cube. It has a volume of 1 **cubic unit** . **Volume** is the number of cubic units that make up a solid figure.

To find the volume of a solid figure, count the cubic units that make up the solid figure.

1 cubic unit
Each edge has a length of 1 unit.

▶ **Find the volume of the figure at the right.**

- How many layers of cubes are there?
- How many cubes are in each layer?

The volume is 8 cubic units.

▶ **Find the volume of the figure at the right.**

- How many cubes are in the bottom layer?
- How many cubes are in the top layer?

The volume is 8 cubic units.

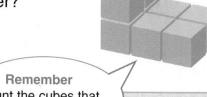

Remember
Count the cubes that are hidden.

Guided Practice

Find the volume of each figure.

Each **= 1 cubic unit.**

1.

2.

Ask Yourself
- How can I find the volume of a solid?
- How many cubes are hidden?

Explain Your Thinking ▶ Why can different solid figures have a volume of 8 cubic units? Explain.

Find the volume of each figure. Each = 1 cubic unit.

3.

4.

5.

6.

7.

8.

Estimate the volume of each container in unit cubes.

9.

10.

11.

12.

13.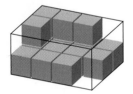

14.

Use the diagram for Problems 15–17.

15. Look at the box on the right. Mrs. Cruz packs one cup into each cube. How many does she pack in the box?

16. What is the volume of the box in cubic units?

17. **Analyze** Suppose Mrs. Cruz only packs half of the box with cups. Would the volume of the box change? Explain.

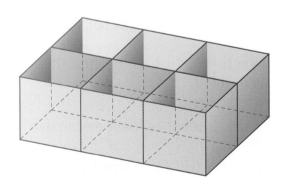

Go On

Use the figures on the right for Problems 18–19.

18. What is the volume of each figure in cubic units?

19. **Predict** How many cubes would likely make up the next figure? Explain your thinking.

Write *true* or *false* for each sentence. Draw or write an example to support your answer.

20. Solid figures with the same volume look the same.

21. If you know the length of one side of a square, you can find the area.

22. If you know the length and width of a rectangle, you can find the perimeter.

23. If you know the perimeter of a shape, you can draw the shape.

Use the figure at the right for Problems 24–25.

24. What is the volume of the figure at the right?

25. **Analyze** Is there a way to find the volume of the figure on the right without counting every unit cube? Explain your answer.

📊 **Data** Use the sign for Problems 26–28.

26. Which freezer has the greatest volume?

27. Which freezer is least expensive?

28. **Analyze** Mr. Cruz wants to get the best deal. Which freezer has the most cubic feet for the least amount of money?

Freezer Sale!

Freeze King
8 cubic feet
$20 per cubic foot

Freeze King Jr.
4 cubic feet
$25 per cubic foot

Extra Practice See page 483, Set C.

Open Response

Look at each pair of times. Write how much time has passed. (Ch. 12, Lesson 4)

29. Start: 7:00 A.M.
End: 7:30 A.M.

30. Start: 11:15 P.M.
End: 11:55 P.M.

31. Start: 9:00 A.M.
End: 11:15 A.M.

32. Start: 12:15 P.M.
End: 3:45 P.M.

33. What is the volume of this figure? (Ch. 17, Lesson 7)

Each = 1 cubic unit.

Problem Solving

Visual Thinking
Tessellations

Some figures can form a tessellation. A tessellation is a pattern made of a figure that repeats with no gaps or holes. A bee's honeycomb is a tessellation of hexagons.

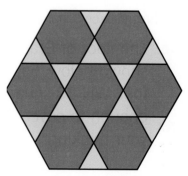

Decide whether each figure will form a tessellation. Write *yes* or *no*.

1.

2.

3.

4. Design your own tessellation. Use a triangle and a hexagon as in the design on the right. Or make a design using other figures that tessellate.

This tessellation is made of 2 figures.

Chapter Review/Test

VOCABULARY

Choose the best term to complete each sentence.

1. The distance around a figure is called the ____.

2. The number of cubic units that make up a solid figure is the ____.

3. The number of square units needed to cover a figure is the ____.

Vocabulary

area

volume

perimeter

cubic unit

CONCEPTS AND SKILLS

Find the perimeter of each figure. (Lesson 2, pp. 464–466)

4. 3 ft 3 ft
   2 ft 2 ft
   5 ft

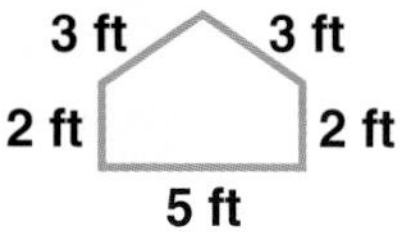

5. 7 cm
   1 cm
   3 cm
   2 cm
   6 cm

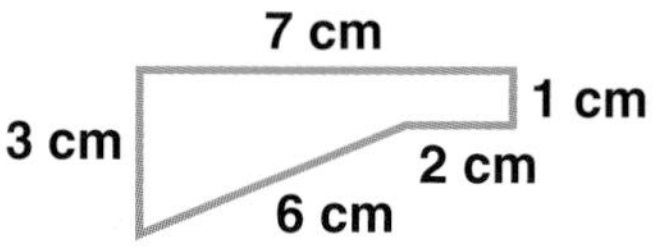

Find the area. Label your answers in square units.
Each = 1 square unit. (Lesson 3–4, pp. 468–472)

6.

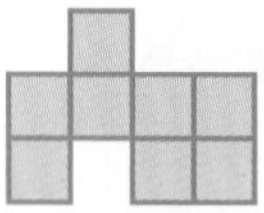

7.

Find the volume. Each ▪ = 1 cubic unit. (Lesson 6–7, pp. 476–480)

8.

9.

PROBLEM SOLVING

Solve. (Lesson 5, pp. 474–475)

10. The floor of Evan's kitchenette is shown below. Each ☐ = 1 square foot. Will 30 square feet of tiles be enough to cover this floor? Explain your thinking.

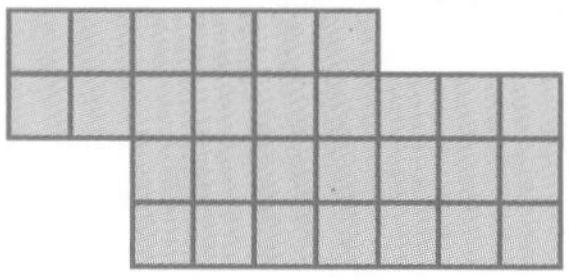

Write About It

Show You Understand

Describe the differences between perimeter, area, and volume. Can you find the volume of a square? Explain.

Extra Practice

Set A (Lesson 2, pp. 464–466)

Find the perimeter of each figure.

1.
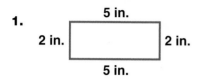
5 in.
2 in.   2 in.
5 in.

2.
12 in.
9 in.   9 in.
8 in.   8 in.

3.
4 ft
5 ft   5 ft
4 ft

4.
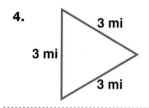
3 mi
3 mi
3 mi

5.
3 km
1 km   4 km
2 km

6.
2 cm   2 cm
1 cm
3 cm   3 cm
2 cm

Set B (Lesson 4, pp. 470–472)

Find the area of each figure. Label your answers in square units.
Each ▢ **or** ▨ **= 1 square unit.**

1.

2.

3.

4.

5.

6.

Set C (Lesson 7, pp. 478–480)

Find the volume of each figure. Each ⬛ **= 1 cubic unit.**

1.

2.

3.

Estimate the volume of each container in unit cubes.

4.

5.

6.
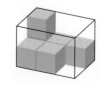

Garden Geometry

What object do you think of when you picture a cube? Perhaps you think of a building block or a number cube. But would you think of a tree? If you visit a topiary garden you might see just that—a tree in the shape of a cube.

Topiary is the art of trimming plants into unusual shapes. Plants can be cut into cube, cone, and spiral shapes. Some are sculpted to look like objects, such as a table and chairs or animals, like rabbits and birds.

Problem Solving

The drawing at the right shows a plan for a topiary garden. Use the drawing for Problems 1–5.

Topiary Garden Plan

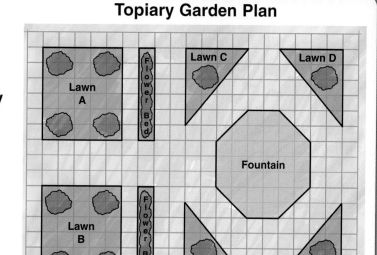

1 What geometric figures do you see in the garden plan? Are any of the figures congruent? Explain.

2 Do the geometric figures in the plan show flips? slides? turns? If so, describe them.

3 What is the shape of the fountain? If each square in the grid represents 1 square foot, what is the area of the fountain?

4 What is the perimeter of the garden? Explain how you found your answer.

5 If you folded the garden plan in half, from the top to the bottom, would the fold be a line of symmetry? Explain why or why not.

Education Place

Visit Weekly Reader Connections at **eduplace.com/map** for more on this topic.

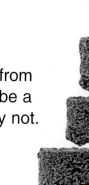

Enrichment: Nets

3-D Puzzles

Vocabulary
net

Materials
Learning
  Tools 31-34
scissors
tape

A **net** is a pattern that can be cut
out and folded to form a solid figure.

The net below is for a cube.

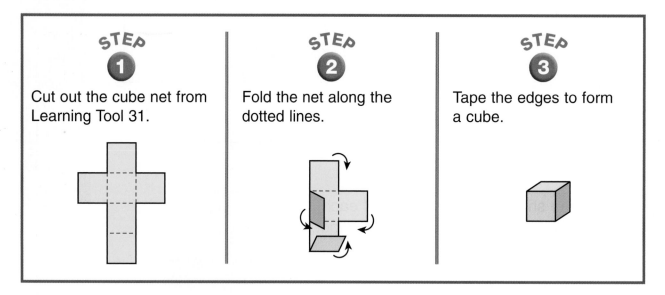

STEP 1
Cut out the cube net from
Learning Tool 31.

STEP 2
Fold the net along the
dotted lines.

STEP 3
Tape the edges to form
a cube.

Try These!

Look at each of the nets below. Write the shape you think each
of the nets will form. Check by using Learning Tools 32–34.

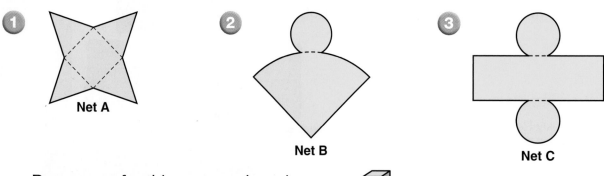

1 Net A

2 Net B

3 Net C

4. Draw a net for this rectangular prism.
   How did you decide on the shapes of
   each face?

Area of Irregular Figures

You can use a calculator when finding the area of irregular figures.

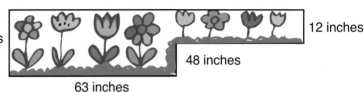

24 inches

12 inches

48 inches

63 inches

Kevin created this chalk drawing. Find the area of his drawing.

Separate the figure into two rectangles.

24 inches

12 inches

48 inches

63 inches

Use a calculator to find the area of each rectangle.

Use this formula: *length × width = area*

Area of the large rectangle

24 × 63 = 1,512

Area = 1,512 square inches

Area of the small rectangle

48 × 12 = 576

Area = 576 square inches

Add both areas to find the area of the whole figure.

1,512 square inches + 576 square inches = 2,088 square inches

The area of the chalk drawing is 2,088 square inches.

Use a calculator to find the area of each irregular figure.

1.
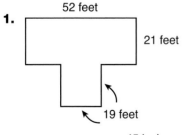
52 feet
21 feet
19 feet

2.
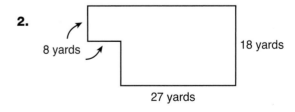
8 yards
18 yards
27 yards

3.
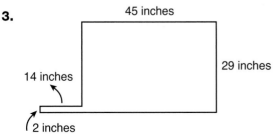
45 inches
14 inches
29 inches
2 inches

4.
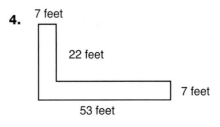
7 feet
22 feet
7 feet
53 feet

Unit 6 Test

VOCABULARY 〔Open Response〕

Choose the best term to complete each sentence.

1. Two rays with the same endpoint form an ____.

2. The number of cubic units in a solid figure is the ____.

3. Figures that are the same shape are ____ figures.

Vocabulary
angle
vertex
volume
similar

CONCEPTS AND SKILLS 〔Open Response〕

Write the special name of each figure. Label any triangle as *equilateral*, *isosceles*, *right*, or *scalene*. (Chapter 15)

4.    5.   6.   7.

Name the solid figure. Use *cube, rectangular prism, cylinder, sphere,* or *pyramid*. (Chapter 15)

8. 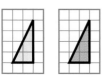   9.    10.

Write whether the figures are *similar* or *congruent*. (Chapter 16)

11.   12.

Tell whether each line shows a line of symmetry. (Chapter 16)

13.    14. 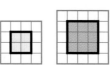   15.

Write whether the second figure shows a slide, flip, or turn. (Chapter 16)

16.   17.   18.

Find the perimeter. (Chapter 17)

19.

Find the area. (Chapter 17)

20.

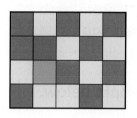

Find the volume. Each = 1 cubic unit. (Chapter 17)

21.

22.

PROBLEM SOLVING (Open Response)

23. At the right is a model of Tia's tile floor. Tia stands on the green tile facing the blue tile. She moves 2 tiles forward and 1 tile to the right. What color tile is she on now?

24. Charlie is sewing fringe along each edge of a square tablecloth. The fringe costs $0.50 a foot. One side of the tablecloth measures 5 feet. How much will the fringe cost?

25. How many sides does each figure in the pattern have? Draw the next figure in the pattern.

Performance Assessment

(Constructed Response)

Task Make a flyer for this month's library theme. The theme is Math and Art.

Use the information at the right to create the flyer. Explain why you drew each shape.

Information You Need

- The flyer should show at least 2 different plane figures and 2 different solid figures.

- The border on the flyer should include at least one slide, flip, or turn of a figure.

- Show at least one figure with two lines of symmetry.

Cumulative Test Prep Practice

Solve Problems 1–10.

Test-Taking Tip

Some problems have more than one step. Work through the problem one step at a time. Use the information from each step to help you.

Look at the example below.

Tina has 4 pieces of string that are each 6 feet long. Zoe has a piece of string that is 8 feet long. How much string do the girls have?

A 24 ft   C 36 ft

B 32 ft   D 60 ft

THINK

First find the length of Tina's string.

4 × 6 ft = 24 ft

Then add the length of Zoe's string.

24 ft + 8 ft = 32 ft

Multiple Choice

1. Change the digit in the hundreds place of the number 2,706 to 4. Then add 2,706 to the new number. What is the sum?

   A 4,112   C 5,112

   B 5,012   D 5,280

   (Chapter 4, Lesson 7)

2. What is the shape of the stop sign?

   F octagon

   G hexagon

   H rectangle

   J pentagon

   (Chapter 15, Lesson 2)

3. Which fact could NOT be used to describe this model?

   A 2 × 6 = 12   C 12 ÷ 2 = 6

   B 6 + 6 = 12   D 24 − 12 = 12

   (Chapter 8, Lesson 2)

4. Which is the best unit to use to measure the mass of a grape?

   F meter   H liter

   G gram   J kilogram

   (Chapter 14, Lesson 5)

For Test-Taking Tips, see page 659.

5. Jun Ming needs 11 meters of rope for a class project. How many centimeters does he need?

(Chapter 14, Lesson 2)

6. Karla's birthday is the second Tuesday after Sunday, July 10. What is the date of Karla's birthday?

(Chapter 12, Lesson 5)

7. What is the mode of the data in this line plot?

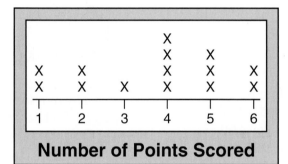

Number of Points Scored

(Chapter 6, Lesson 3)

8. The perimeter of a square is 36 centimeters. What is the length of one side?

(Chapter 17, Lesson 5)

9. Karen has 5 coins in her pocket. Three of the coins are the same. Each of the other 2 coins is different from the rest. What is the least amount of money she could have?

(Chapter 3, Lesson 4)

10. Marlis has 12 shells. She wants to rearrange them to put on display.

A Marlis decides to put the shells into groups of 6. Draw the shells and circle each group of 6.

B What division fact can you use to show how the 12 shells can be placed into groups of 6? How many groups are there?

C Marlis then decides to arrange the shells into groups of 4. How many more groups are there?

D List all of the ways Marlis could arrange the shells so that each group has an equal number of shells.

(Chapter 10, Lesson 1)

Education Place

Look for Cumulative Test Prep at **eduplace.com/map** for more practice.

Vocabulary Wrap-Up for **Unit 6**

Look back at the big ideas and vocabulary in this unit.

Big Ideas

You can identify, describe, and classify plane and solid figures.

You can measure the perimeter, area, and volume of figures.

Key Vocabulary
- plane figures
- solid figures
- perimeter
- area
- volume

Math Conversations

Use your new vocabulary to discuss these big ideas.

1. Use drawings to explain the difference between congruent figures and similar figures.

   The bulletin board is 4 feet high and 5 feet wide.

   We can find its area by multiplying 4 by 5. So the area is 20 square feet.

2. Explain how to use flips, slides, and turns to transform figures. Use drawings to show each type.

3. Explain how to decide if a figure has a line of symmetry. Draw 4 shapes, each with one line of symmetry.

4. Explain how a cube and a square are the same. Explain how they are different. Which one has volume?

5. **Write About It** Make a list of 10 objects in your classroom that look like solid figures. Name the solid figure that each object looks like.

UNIT 7

Fractions and Decimals

Reading Mathematics

Reviewing Vocabulary

Here are some math vocabulary words that you should know.

fraction	a number that names an equal part of a whole or an equal part of a group
one half	one part when a whole or group is divided into two equal parts
one third	one part when a whole or group is divided into three equal parts
one fourth	one part when a whole or group is divided into four equal parts

Reading Words and Symbols

You can show fractions with pictures, symbols, and words.

Model:

Symbol: $\dfrac{1}{2}$ ← part shaded / equal parts

Words: one half is shaded

Model:

Symbol: $\dfrac{3}{4}$ ← red counters / counters in all

Words: three fourths are red

Use words and symbols to answer the questions.

1. How many equal parts does the square have?

2. How many parts of the square are shaded? How many parts are not shaded?

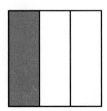

Reading Test Questions

Choose the correct answer for each.

3. Which figure illustrates thirds?

a.   b.    c.   d.

Illustrates means "is an example of" or "shows."

---

4. How many sections of the circle are shaded?

a. 1   c. 3

b. 2   d. 4

Sections means "pieces" or "parts."

5. How can you express three fifths using symbols?

a. $\frac{1}{5}$ c. $\frac{5}{1}$

b. $\frac{3}{5}$ d. $\frac{5}{3}$

Express means "show" or "write."

Learning Vocabulary

Watch for these words in this unit. Write their definitions in your journal.

numerator

denominator

mixed number

decimal

tenths

hundredths

Literature Connection

Read "Uncle Johnathan and The Ice-Skating Contest" on Pages 654–655. Then work with a partner to answer the questions about the story.

Education Place

At **eduplace.com/map**
see eGlossary and
eGames—Math Lingo.

Fraction Concepts

INVESTIGATION

Using Data

Kim is in art class experimenting with different colors and shapes. She painted the picture below. Use words and numbers to compare two of the colors in Kim's picture.

Use What You Know

Use this page to review and remember
what you need to know for this chapter.

VOCABULARY

Choose the best word to complete each sentence.

Vocabulary
thirds
halves
fourths
fractions

1. An apple cut into 2 equal parts has 2 ____.

2. Four ____ make one whole.

3. Equal parts of a whole are called ____ of the whole.

CONCEPTS AND SKILLS

Write the number of parts. Then write whether the parts are *equal* or *not equal*.

4.   5.   6.   7.

What is each figure divided into? Write *halves*, *thirds*, or *fourths*.

8.   9.   10.   11.

Write the fraction.

12. one third   13. three fifths   14. two halves   15. one eighth

16. three fourths   17. one sixth   18. four sevenths   19. two thirds

 **Write About It**

20. Draw a picture to show $\frac{1}{4}$ of a circle. Use the picture to explain what each number in the fraction means.

Facts Practice, See page 668.

Fractions and Regions

Objective Read and write fractions.

Vocabulary
numerator
denominator
fraction

Learn About It

Look at the flag of Lithuania. It has 3 equal parts. One part is red. One part is green. One part is yellow. What **fraction** of the flag is red?

You can use fractions to name equal parts of a region. You can use a fraction to tell what part of the flag is red.

numerator ► 1 ← number of red parts
denominator ► 3 ← total number of equal parts

Read the fraction as "one third."

Solution: One third of the flag is red.

Other Examples

A. Fourths

One fourth or $\frac{1}{4}$ is red.

B. Eighths

Five eighths or $\frac{5}{8}$ is red.

C. Tenths

$\frac{10}{10} =$ 1 whole

Ten tenths or $\frac{10}{10}$ is red.

Guided Practice

Write a fraction for the part of the flag that is yellow. Then write a fraction for the part that is not yellow.

1.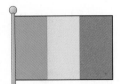

2.

3.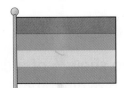

Ask Yourself
• How many parts are there in all?
• How many equal parts are yellow? not yellow?

Explain Your Thinking ► When a whole figure is shaded, what do you know about the fraction's numerator and denominator?

Extra Help at **eduplace.com/map**

Write a fraction for the part that is red.
Then write a fraction for the part that is not red.

4. 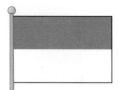   **5.** 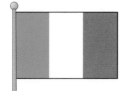   **6.**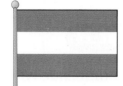

7.   **8.**   **9.**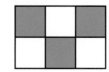

Draw a picture to show each fraction. Then use words to describe the parts that are the numerator and denominator.

10. $\frac{4}{6}$ **11.** $\frac{4}{4}$ **12.** $\frac{7}{8}$ **13.** $\frac{1}{5}$ **14.** $\frac{5}{10}$ **15.** $\frac{2}{6}$

16. three fourths   **17.** two thirds   **18.** four fifths   **19.** five eighths

Solve.

20. What's Wrong? Ava's flag has 1 big piece of blue felt and 1 small red piece. Ava says that half the flag is blue. Why is she wrong?

21. Doug's flag has 9 equal parts. One third of the flag is green. How many parts are green? Explain your thinking.

 22. Write About It Describe how the two figures below are alike and how they are different.

23. The flag of Italy has equal parts of green, white, and red. Write a fraction that describes how much of the Italian flag is not white.

Open Response

Find the missing factors.

(Ch. 9, Lesson 6)

24. $8 \times \blacksquare = 24$ **25.** $\blacksquare \times 2 = 18$

26. $\blacksquare \times 4 = 32$ **27.** $7 \times \blacksquare = 35$

28. $6 \times \blacksquare = 42$ **29.** $\blacksquare \times 9 = 72$

30. Write the fraction for the part that is shaded red.

(Ch. 18, Lesson 1)

Extra Practice See page 517, Set A.

Audio Tutor 2/20 Listen and Understand

Fractions and Groups

Objective Use fractions to name parts of groups.

Learn About It

Ed is making a dinosaur with felt and buttons.
What fraction of the buttons are green?

You can use a fraction to name part of a group or set.

numerator → $\frac{7}{12}$ ← number of green buttons
denominator → ← total number of buttons

Seven out of twelve buttons are green.

Solution: Seven twelfths of the buttons are green.

Try this actvity to model fractions as parts of a group.

Materials: counters

Put 10 counters on your desk so that there are 1 red
counter and 9 yellow counters.

• What fraction of the counters are yellow?

• What fraction of the counters are not yellow?

Guided Practice

Use the picture below to solve.

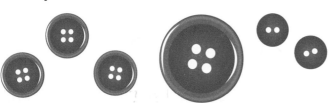

1. What fraction of the buttons have 4 holes?
2. What fraction of the buttons have 2 holes?
3. What fraction of the buttons are red?

Ask Yourself

• How do I decide what number to write as the numerator?

• How do I decide what number to write as the denominator?

Explain Your Thinking ▶ Look at Ed's dinosaur again. What fraction of the buttons are red? Explain how you know.

Write a fraction to name the part of each group that is round.

4.

5.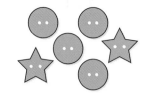

6.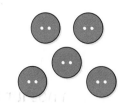

Use the picture on the right for Questions 7–12.

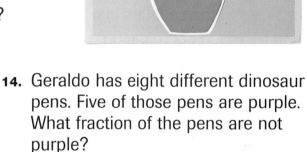

7. What fraction of the flowers are red?

8. Which flower color is $\frac{2}{10}$ of the group?

9. Which flower color is $\frac{3}{10}$ of the group?

10. What fraction of the flowers are not blue?

11. What fraction of the flowers are not pink?

12. What fraction of the flowers are purple?

Solve.

13. Lucy used 5 orange buttons and 5 purple buttons on her dinosaur. What fraction of the buttons are orange?

14. Geraldo has eight different dinosaur pens. Five of those pens are purple. What fraction of the pens are not purple?

15. **Analyze** Ethan used red, white and blue buttons to make a button worm. If he used an equal number of each color, what fraction of the buttons are blue? What fraction are not blue?

16. **What's Wrong?** Doris made a button worm with 3 green buttons, 2 yellow buttons and 5 red buttons. She says that $\frac{3}{7}$ of the buttons are green. Explain why she is wrong.

Mixed Review and Test Prep

Open Response

Complete. (Ch. 14, Lessons 1–3)

17. $1 \text{ m} = \blacksquare \text{ cm}$

18. $2,000 \text{ m} = \blacksquare \text{ km}$

19. $4 \text{ L} = \blacksquare \text{ mL}$

20. $3,000 \text{ mL} = \blacksquare \text{ L}$

21. Claire has 8 beads. Four are red. One half of the remaining beads are white. What fraction of Claire's beads are white?
(Ch. 18, Lesson 2)

Explain how you know.

Fractional Parts of a Group

Objective Find fractional parts of a group.

Learn About It

Sara made a bead bracelet. She used
12 beads. One third are purple.
How many of the beads are purple?

You can use counters to find the answer.

Find $\frac{1}{3}$ of 12.

- Use 12 counters for the total number of beads.
- Put the counters into 3 equal groups.
- Count the number in one of the three groups.

$\frac{1}{3}$ of 12 = 4

Solution: Four of the beads are purple.

Two thirds of Sara's beads are purple or blue.
How many beads are purple or blue?

Find $\frac{2}{3}$ of 12.

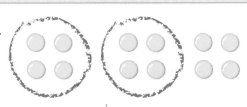

- Use 12 counters for the total number of beads.
- Put the counters into 3 equal groups.
- Count the number in two of the three groups.

$\frac{2}{3}$ of 12 = 8

Solution: Eight of the beads are purple or blue.

Another Example

Parts of a Foot

Use the picture of the ruler to find the number of inches in $\frac{1}{3}$ foot and in $\frac{2}{3}$ foot.

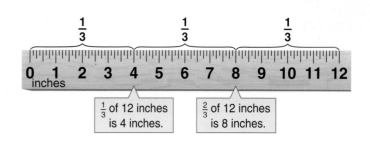

$\frac{1}{3}$ of 12 inches is 4 inches. $\frac{2}{3}$ of 12 inches is 8 inches.

Guided Practice

Use counters to find each answer.

Ask Yourself
- Which number tells how many objects there are in all?
- Which number tells how many equal groups to make?

1. $\frac{1}{2}$ of 10

2. $\frac{3}{5}$ of 5

Draw a picture to find each answer.

3. $\frac{1}{2}$ of 8

4. $\frac{1}{3}$ of 9

5. $\frac{3}{4}$ of 12

Explain Your Thinking ▶ Look back at the ruler. How can you use the ruler to find $\frac{3}{4}$ of 12 inches?

Practice and Problem Solving

Use counters to find each answer.

6. $\frac{1}{4}$ of 8

7. $\frac{2}{3}$ of 15

8. $\frac{1}{5}$ of 10

Draw a picture to find each answer.

9. $\frac{1}{6}$ of 12

10. $\frac{2}{5}$ of 10

11. $\frac{3}{3}$ of 15

12. $\frac{2}{3}$ of 18

13. $\frac{5}{10}$ of 20

14. $\frac{7}{8}$ of 16

Go On

Use the ruler below for Problems 15–19.

15. How many inches equal $\frac{1}{2}$ foot?

16. How many inches equal $\frac{1}{12}$ foot?

17. How many inches equal $\frac{1}{4}$ foot?

18. How many inches equal $\frac{2}{4}$ foot?

19. Your answers to 15 and 18 should be the same. Explain why that is.

Solve.

20. What fraction of the beads on the key chain are green?

21. What fraction of the beads on the key chain are not blue?

22. Calvin has a piece of yarn that is $\frac{1}{2}$ foot long. Rob's yarn measures 7 inches. Whose piece of yarn is shorter?

Data **Use the table for Problems 23–26.**

23. The table shows the beads in a kit. What fraction of the beads are blue?

24. What fraction of the beads are not red?

25. **Reasoning** Gianni has a craft kit with the same number of beads as the one in the table. One third of the beads in Gianni's kit are yellow. Which kit has more yellow beads? How many more?

26. **Create and Solve** Use the table to write a problem using fractions. Give your problem to a classmate to solve.

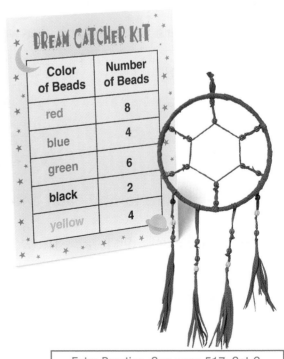

DREAM CATCHER KIT

Color of Beads	Number of Beads
red	8
blue	4
green	6
black	2
yellow	4

Extra Practice See page 517, Set C.

Art Connection
Fraction Quilt

Kendra's mom wants to sew a patchwork quilt. Her kit came with yellow, blue, and green fabric squares and these instructions:

- You must use all 16 of the fabric squares.

- You may not cut the squares.

- $\frac{1}{2}$ of the quilt is yellow.

- The fraction of the quilt that is blue is the same as the fraction that is green.

- No square can share a side with a square that is the same color.

1. How many squares of each color are in Kendra's kit?

2. Represent Draw a picture to show how her quilt will look when it is finished.

WEEKLY WR READER eduplace.com/map

Check your understanding of Lessons 1–3.

Write a fraction to name the part that is shaded blue. (Lessons 1, 2)

1.

2.

3.

4.

5.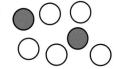

6.

Draw a picture to find each answer. (Lesson 3)

7. $\frac{1}{2}$ of 10

8. $\frac{1}{3}$ of 12

9. $\frac{1}{5}$ of 15

10. $\frac{1}{6}$ of 18

Audio Tutor 2/21 Listen and Understand

Problem-Solving Application
Multistep Problems

Objective Solve problems using more than one step.

Problem Martin's class made kites with tissue paper. Martin had a package with 4 sheets each of red, green, blue, yellow, orange and pink paper. If Martin used $\frac{1}{3}$ of the paper to make his kite, how many sheets did he use?

UNDERSTAND

This is what you know.

- There are 4 sheets of each color.
- There are 6 colors.
- Martin used $\frac{1}{3}$ of the sheets.

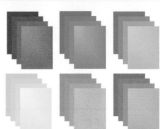

PLAN

You can solve the problem using two steps.

- Find the total number of sheets.
- Then find $\frac{1}{3}$ of that number.

SOLVE

STEP 1

Multiply to find the total number of sheets.

$$\begin{array}{r} 4 \\ \times\ 6 \\ \hline 24 \end{array}$$ ← number of each color
← number of colors
← total number of sheets

There are 24 sheets in all.

STEP 2

Draw a picture to find $\frac{1}{3}$ of 24.

$\frac{1}{3}$ of 24 is 8.

Solution: Martin used 8 sheets of paper.

LOOK BACK

Look back at the problem. How can you use multiplication to check your work?

Use the Ask Yourself questions to help you solve each problem.

1. The class made 10 kites on Monday, 6 kites on Tuesday, and 4 more on Wednesday. On Thursday the class flew $\frac{1}{5}$ of the kites. How many kites did the class fly?

Ask Yourself

UNDERSTAND → **Is this a multistep problem?**

PLAN → **How many steps are in the problem?**

SOLVE → **What should I do first?**

LOOK BACK → **How can I check my work?**

2. Keisha had 4 sheets of stickers. Each sheet had 9 stickers. If Keisha used $\frac{1}{6}$ of the stickers to decorate her kite, how many stickers did she use?

(Hint) Multiply to find the total number of stickers.

Independent Practice

Solve. Show your work.

3. Mrs. Fein arranged some of the kites in 5 rows with 6 kites in each row. Tyrone made $\frac{1}{10}$ of those kites. How many kites did Tyrone make?

4. Anja's kite tail was 7 inches long. Then she made it 5 inches longer. Then she cut $\frac{1}{3}$ off of it. How many inches did she cut off?

5. Look at the tail on Dave's kite at the right. If he continues the pattern and makes 18 triangles, how many will be yellow?

Model Equivalent Fractions

Objective Use different fractions to name the same amount.

Vocabulary

equivalent fractions

Materials

crayons
paper circles
(Learning Tool 37)

Work Together

Fractions that name the same part of a whole are called **equivalent fractions.**

Work with a partner to model equivalent fractions.

 STEP 1 One person should:

- Fold a paper circle in half.
- Draw a line on the fold.
- Color one part of the circle.

How many equal parts are in the circle?

 STEP 2 The other person should:

- Fold a paper circle in half. Fold it in half a second time. Then fold it in half again.
- Draw a line on each fold.
- Color 4 parts of the circle.

How many equal parts are in the circle?

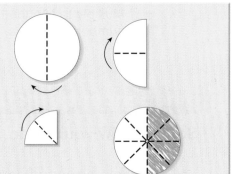

 STEP 3 Compare the 2 circles.

Is the same amount colored in each circle?

What fraction of each circle is colored?

$\frac{1}{2}$ and $\frac{4}{8}$ name the same amount.

$\frac{1}{2}$ and $\frac{4}{8}$ are equivalent fractions.

So $\frac{1}{2} = \frac{4}{8}$.

Write *equivalent* or *not equivalent* to describe the fractions in each pair.

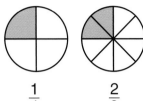 1. $\dfrac{1}{4}$ $\dfrac{2}{8}$

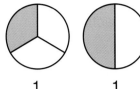 2. $\dfrac{1}{3}$ $\dfrac{1}{2}$

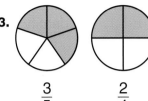 3. $\dfrac{3}{5}$ $\dfrac{2}{4}$

Use the circles to complete the equivalent fractions.

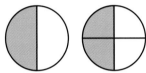 4. $\dfrac{1}{2} = \dfrac{\blacksquare}{4}$

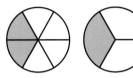 5. $\dfrac{2}{6} = \dfrac{\blacksquare}{3}$

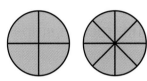 6. $\dfrac{4}{4} = \dfrac{\blacksquare}{8}$

Solve.

7. Jessie made a potholder with 16 fabric squares. All but 4 squares are blue. Write two equivalent fractions for the part of the potholder that is not blue.

8. Dave cut a circle into 6 equal pieces. He colored $\dfrac{1}{2}$ of the pieces purple and $\dfrac{1}{2}$ yellow. How many sixths were yellow?

 Talk About It • Write About It

You have learned how to use different fractions to name the same amount.

9. Write *equivalent* or *not equivalent* to describe the fractions in each pair.

a.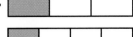

b.

c.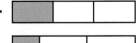

10. Describe how you can tell whether two fractions are equivalent.

Find Equivalent Fractions

Objective Identify equivalent fractions.

Learn About It

You can use fraction strips to help you find equivalent fractions. Remember, equivalent fractions name the same amount.

Look at the fraction strips below.

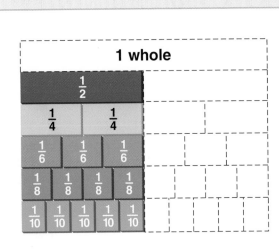

$\frac{1}{2}$ is shaded.

$\frac{2}{4}$ is shaded.

$\frac{3}{6}$ is shaded.

$\frac{4}{8}$ is shaded.

$\frac{5}{10}$ is shaded.

$$\frac{1}{2} = \frac{2}{4} = \frac{3}{6} = \frac{4}{8} = \frac{5}{10}$$

Guided Practice

Name the equivalent fractions shown.

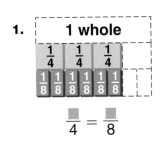

1.
$$\frac{\blacksquare}{4} = \frac{\blacksquare}{8}$$

2.
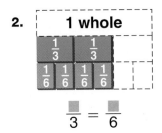
$$\frac{\blacksquare}{3} = \frac{\blacksquare}{6}$$

Ask Yourself

• How many equal parts are in each strip?

• How many parts are shaded?

Explain Your Thinking ▶ Are $\frac{2}{2}$, $\frac{4}{4}$ and $\frac{6}{6}$ equivalent fractions? Why or why not?

Practice and Problem Solving

Name the equivalent fractions shown.

3.

1 whole
$\frac{1}{2}$
$\frac{1}{4}$ $\frac{1}{4}$

$$\frac{1}{2} = \frac{\blacksquare}{4}$$

4.

1 whole
$\frac{1}{5}$ $\frac{1}{5}$ $\frac{1}{5}$
$\frac{1}{10}$ $\frac{1}{10}$ $\frac{1}{10}$ $\frac{1}{10}$ $\frac{1}{10}$ $\frac{1}{10}$

$$\frac{\blacksquare}{5} = \frac{\blacksquare}{10}$$

5.

1 whole
$\frac{1}{6}$ $\frac{1}{6}$ $\frac{1}{6}$ $\frac{1}{6}$ $\frac{1}{6}$
$\frac{1}{12}$ $\frac{1}{12}$ $\frac{1}{12}$ $\frac{1}{12}$ $\frac{1}{12}$ $\frac{1}{12}$ $\frac{1}{12}$ $\frac{1}{12}$ $\frac{1}{12}$ $\frac{1}{12}$

$$\frac{5}{6} = \frac{\blacksquare}{\blacksquare}$$

Draw fraction strips to compare the fractions.
Write *equivalent* or *not equivalent*.

6. $\frac{1}{4}$ and $\frac{3}{8}$ **7.** $\frac{1}{3}$ and $\frac{2}{6}$ **8.** $\frac{1}{2}$ and $\frac{3}{4}$ **9.** $\frac{2}{5}$ and $\frac{1}{4}$

Find each missing number to make equivalent fractions.

10. $\frac{2}{3} = \frac{4}{6} = \frac{8}{12} = \frac{\blacksquare}{24} = \frac{\blacksquare}{48}$

11. $\frac{1}{10} = \frac{2}{20} = \frac{\blacksquare}{30} = \frac{4}{\blacksquare} = \frac{\blacksquare}{\blacksquare}$

 Data Use the table for Problems 12–15.

12. Which two students live the same distance from school?

13. Who lives farther away, Isabel or Jong? Explain how you know.

14. **Analyze** Maya lives closer to school than Karl but farther from school than Jong. What distance could she live from school?

15. **Represent** Draw a map to show where each student lives. Label the school and the homes of each student.

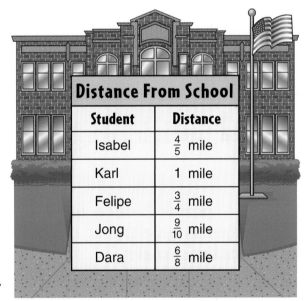

Distance From School

Student	Distance
Isabel	$\frac{4}{5}$ mile
Karl	1 mile
Felipe	$\frac{3}{4}$ mile
Jong	$\frac{9}{10}$ mile
Dara	$\frac{6}{8}$ mile

Mixed Review and Test Prep

Open Response

Multiply or divide. (Ch. 9, Lessons 2, 4; Ch. 11, Lessons 3, 8)

16. 3×9 **17.** 7×4

18. $24 \div 8$ **19.** $18 \div 3$

Multiple Choice

20. Which fraction is equivalent to $\frac{2}{10}$? (Ch. 18, Lesson 6)

A $\frac{10}{2}$ **B** $\frac{1}{2}$ **C** $\frac{1}{5}$ **D** $\frac{2}{5}$

Lesson 7

Mixed Numbers

Objective Identify and write fractions greater than 1.

Vocabulary
improper fraction
mixed number

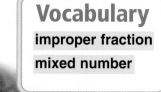

Learn About It

Mr. Fay's art class is making papier-mâché puppets with newspaper. Jim used 5 half-sheets to make his puppet. How many sheets of newspaper did Jim use?

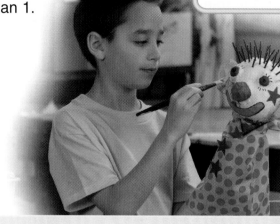

Jim used 5 half-sheets, or $\frac{5}{2}$ sheets of newspaper.

You can also say that Jim used 2 whole sheets and $\frac{1}{2}$ sheet of newspaper, or $2\frac{1}{2}$ sheets.

$\frac{1}{2}$ $\frac{1}{2}$ $\frac{1}{2}$ $\frac{1}{2}$ $\frac{1}{2}$

1 whole   **1 whole** $\frac{1}{2}$

improper fraction → $\frac{5}{2} = 2\frac{1}{2}$ ← mixed number

Solution: Jim used $\frac{5}{2}$ or $2\frac{1}{2}$ sheets of newspaper to make his puppet.

An **improper fraction** has a numerator greater than or equal to its denominator.

numerator → $\frac{5}{2}$
denominator →

A **mixed number** is made up of a whole number and a fraction.

whole number → $2\frac{1}{2}$ ← fraction

Another Example

Mixed Numbers on a Number Line

Jump 5 fifths to land on 1. Jump 3 more fifths to land on $\frac{8}{5}$. You jumped 1, and then another $\frac{3}{5}$. So, $\frac{8}{5} = 1\frac{3}{5}$

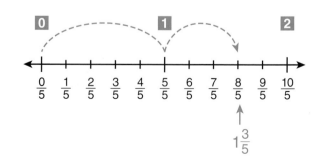

512

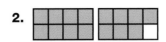

Write an improper fraction, mixed number, or whole number for the shaded parts.

Ask Yourself

• How many whole numbers are shown?

• Are there any fractional parts left?

1.

2.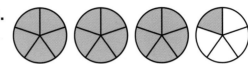

3.

4.

Explain Your Thinking ▶ Is $\frac{4}{3}$ equal to $1\frac{1}{3}$? Draw a picture to explain your answer.

Practice and Problem Solving

Write an improper fraction and a mixed number for the shaded part.

5.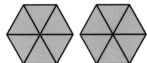

6.

7.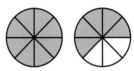

8.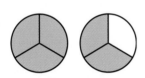

9.

10.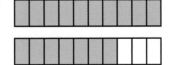

Use the number line to help you write each as a mixed number or a whole number.

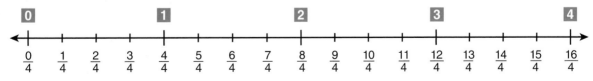

11. $\frac{13}{4}$ 12. $\frac{7}{4}$ 13. $\frac{10}{4}$ 14. $\frac{5}{4}$ 15. $\frac{11}{4}$

16. $\frac{9}{4}$ 17. $\frac{15}{4}$ 18. $\frac{8}{4}$ 19. $\frac{14}{4}$ 20. $\frac{12}{4}$

Go On

Draw a picture to show each improper fraction.
Then write a whole number or a mixed number.

21. $\frac{6}{3}$ **22.** $\frac{7}{6}$ **23.** $\frac{10}{2}$ **24.** $\frac{11}{3}$ **25.** $\frac{9}{4}$

Find each missing number.

26. $\frac{5}{3} = \blacksquare\frac{2}{3}$ **27.** $\frac{11}{4} = 2\frac{\blacksquare}{4}$ **28.** $\frac{6}{\blacksquare} = 2$ **29.** $\frac{\blacksquare}{4} = 3\frac{1}{4}$

30. $\frac{\blacksquare}{2} = 4$ **31.** $2\frac{1}{6} = \frac{\blacksquare}{6}$ **32.** $\frac{\blacksquare}{8} = 1\frac{3}{8}$ **33.** $\frac{12}{5} = \blacksquare\frac{2}{5}$

34. $\frac{17}{6} = \blacksquare\frac{5}{6}$ **35.** $3\frac{1}{7} = \frac{\blacksquare}{7}$ **36.** $4\frac{1}{2} = \frac{\blacksquare}{2}$ **37.** $\frac{31}{6} = \blacksquare\frac{1}{6}$

Solve.

38. Simone used 9 half-sheets of newspaper to make her puppet. What mixed number shows the number of sheets of newspaper she used?

39. **Analyze** Marcus's class used 2 jugs of glue. Suppose each jug was poured into 8 equal cups. How many cups of glue did the class use?

📊 **Data** Use the recipe for Problems 40–43.

40. Is the amount of white glue in the recipe closer to 1 cup or 2 cups?

41. Are $\frac{4}{2}$ cups water enough for the recipe? Explain why or why not.

42. **Analyze** How can you use a $\frac{1}{4}$ cup measuring cup to measure the amount of white glue needed for the recipe?

43. **Represent** Suppose you want to make twice as much papier-mâché. How many cups of water and white glue will you need? Draw a picture to explain your answer.

PAPIER-MÂCHÉ RECIPE

$2\frac{1}{2}$ cups water
$1\frac{1}{4}$ cups white glue

514

Extra Practice See page 517, Set E.

Open Response

Add or subtract. (Ch. 4, Lesson 4; Ch. 5, Lessons 4, 5)

44.   362
         + 539

45.   751
         − 273

46. Write an improper fraction and a mixed number for the shaded part. (Ch. 18, Lesson 7)

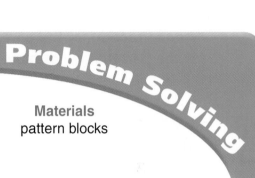

Fractions in Action
Visual Thinking

Materials
pattern blocks

Problem Solving

You can use pattern blocks to model fractions. The yellow hexagon stands for 1 whole.

- You need 2 red quadrilaterals to cover the yellow hexagon. Each red block is $\frac{1}{2}$ of the yellow block.

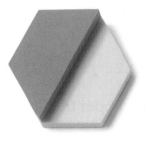

- You need 3 blue parallelograms to cover the yellow hexagon. Each blue block is $\frac{1}{3}$ of the yellow block.

1. How many green triangles do you need to cover the yellow hexagon? What fraction describes each green block?

2. Use one red, one blue, and one green block to cover the yellow hexagon. What fraction of the hexagon does each represent?

Chapter Review/Test

VOCABULARY

1. The number under the fraction bar is the ____.

2. A whole number and a fraction make up a ____.

3. When fractions are equal, they are ____.

Vocabulary

numerator

equivalent fractions

denominator

mixed number

CONCEPTS AND SKILLS

Write a fraction for the part that is blue. Then write a fraction for the part that is not blue. (Lessons 1 and 2, pp. 498–499, 500–501)

4.

5.

6.

7.

Draw a picture to find each answer. (Lesson 3, pp. 502–504)

8. $\frac{4}{9}$ of 9   9. $\frac{2}{6}$ of 18   10. $\frac{4}{5}$ of 10   11. $\frac{3}{3}$ of 12   12. $\frac{1}{4}$ of 16

Write *equivalent* or *not equivalent*. (Lesson 6, pp. 510–511)

13. $\frac{5}{10}$ and $\frac{1}{2}$ 14. $\frac{3}{7}$ and $\frac{1}{6}$ 15. $\frac{3}{4}$ and $\frac{7}{8}$ 16. $\frac{3}{9}$ and $\frac{1}{3}$

Write an improper fraction and mixed number for the shaded parts.

(Lesson 7, pp. 512–514)

17.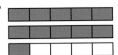

18.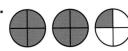

PROBLEM SOLVING

Solve. (Lesson 4, pp. 506–507)

19. The Roy family ate $\frac{2}{3}$ of a pumpkin pie. If the whole pie had 6 pieces, how many pieces were not eaten?

20. Tom had 16 markers. Four of them didn't work. What fraction of them worked?

Write About It

Show You Understand

Kelly made a pizza and cut it into 8 slices. $\frac{4}{8}$ of the pizza had pepperoni, and $\frac{8}{8}$ of the pizza had double cheese. Is this possible?

Draw a picture and explain.

Extra Practice

Set A (Lesson 1, pp. 498–499)

Draw a picture to show each fraction.

1. $\frac{3}{6}$ **2.** $\frac{1}{2}$ **3.** $\frac{5}{5}$ **4.** one seventh   **5.** two ninths

Set B (Lesson 2, pp. 500–501)

Write a fraction to name the part of each group that is blue.

1.   **2.**   **3.**   **4.**

Set C (Lesson 3, pp. 502–504)

Use counters to find each answer.

1. $\frac{2}{3}$ of 9   **2.** $\frac{4}{4}$ of 8   **3.** $\frac{1}{4}$ of 12   **4.** $\frac{3}{5}$ of 10

Draw a picture to find each answer.

5. $\frac{1}{8}$ of 16   **6.** $\frac{1}{2}$ of 18   **7.** $\frac{3}{3}$ of 9   **8.** $\frac{2}{7}$ of 14

Set D (Lesson 6, pp. 510–511)

Write *equivalent* or *not equivalent*. Draw fraction strips to support your answer.

1. $\frac{1}{6}$ and $\frac{9}{9}$ **2.** $\frac{3}{7}$ and $\frac{5}{8}$ **3.** $\frac{1}{5}$ and $\frac{2}{10}$ **4.** $\frac{4}{5}$ and $\frac{8}{10}$

Set E (Lesson 7, pp. 512–514)

Write an improper fraction and mixed number for the parts shown.

1. 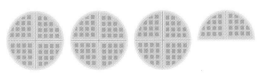   **2.**

Extra Practice at **eduplace.com/map**

Work With Fractions

INVESTIGATION

Using Data

Tameka is measuring ingredients to make blueberry muffins. The recipe she is using is at the right. If Tameka only had a $\frac{1}{4}$ cup measure and a $\frac{1}{2}$ cup measure how might she measure the correct amount of sugar and blueberries?

Blueberry Muffins

$\frac{1}{2}$ cup butter

2 cups flour

$1\frac{1}{4}$ cups sugar

$1\frac{1}{2}$ cups blueberries

$\frac{1}{2}$ cup milk

2 eggs

2 tsp baking powder

$\frac{1}{2}$ tsp salt

Use What You Know

**Use this page to review and remember
what you need to know for this chapter.**

VOCABULARY

Choose the best term to complete each sentence.

Vocabulary

numerator

denominator

mixed number

improper fraction

equivalent
fractions

1. The fraction $\frac{13}{5}$ is an ____.

2. A number made up of a whole number and a
   fraction is called a ____.

3. In the fraction $\frac{1}{3}$, 1 is the ____.

4. Fractions that name the same amount are ____.

CONCEPTS AND SKILLS

Write a fraction for the shaded part.

5.   6.   7.   8.

Write *equivalent* or *not equivalent* to describe the fractions.

9. $\frac{2}{3}$ and $\frac{3}{6}$ 10. $\frac{2}{4}$ and $\frac{1}{2}$ 11. $\frac{1}{3}$ and $\frac{3}{4}$ 12. $\frac{2}{10}$ and $\frac{1}{5}$

Draw a picture to find each answer.

13. $\frac{3}{4}$ of 4   14. $\frac{3}{5}$ of 5   15. $\frac{1}{2}$ of 6   16. $\frac{2}{3}$ of 12

Write an improper fraction and a mixed number for the shaded part.

17.   18.   19.

 **Write About It**

20. Explain how $\frac{4}{4}$ and $\frac{6}{6}$ can both
    represent one whole.

Facts Practice, See page 669.

Audio Tutor 2/23 Listen and Understand

Compare Fractions

Objective Compare fractions with like and unlike denominators.

Learn About It

It's Multicultural Day at school! Hilda and Anna each brought in Greek honey cake to share with their classmates. Each cake was the same size. Is there more of Hilda's or Anna's cake left over?

You can compare fractions that have the same denominator.

Anna's cake
$\frac{3}{8}$ left

Hilda's cake
$\frac{4}{8}$ left

Different Ways to Compare $\frac{3}{8}$ and $\frac{4}{8}$

Way 1 Use fraction strips.

$\frac{3}{8}$ is less than $\frac{4}{8}$. $\frac{3}{8} < \frac{4}{8}$

$\frac{4}{8}$ is greater than $\frac{3}{8}$. $\frac{4}{8} > \frac{3}{8}$

Way 2 Use a number line.

$\frac{4}{8}$ is to the right of $\frac{3}{8}$.

So $\frac{4}{8} > \frac{3}{8}$.

Solution: More of Hilda's cake is left.

You can also compare fractions with different denominators.

Different Ways to Compare $\frac{1}{3}$ and $\frac{1}{2}$

Way 1 Use fraction strips.

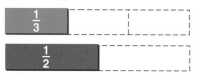

$\frac{1}{3}$ is less than $\frac{1}{2}$. $\frac{1}{3} < \frac{1}{2}$

$\frac{1}{2}$ is greater than $\frac{1}{3}$. $\frac{1}{2} > \frac{1}{3}$

Way 2 Use a number line.

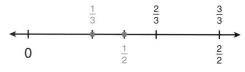

$\frac{1}{2}$ is to the right of $\frac{1}{3}$.

So $\frac{1}{2} > \frac{1}{3}$.

Extra Help at **eduplace.com/map**

Guided Practice

Compare. Write > or < for each ⬤.

- If the denominators are the same, which numerator is greater?

- Which fraction represents the greater part of a whole?

1.

| $\frac{1}{4}$ | $\frac{1}{4}$ | $\frac{1}{4}$ | |

| $\frac{1}{4}$ | | |

$$\frac{3}{4} \;⬤\; \frac{1}{4}$$

2.

| $\frac{1}{4}$ | | | | |

| $\frac{1}{6}$ | | | | | |

$$\frac{1}{4} \;⬤\; \frac{1}{6}$$

Explain Your Thinking ▶ The circles are the same size. Which is greater, $\frac{1}{3}$ or $\frac{1}{4}$? How do you know?

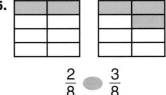

Practice and Problem Solving

Compare the fractions. Write > or < for each ⬤.

3.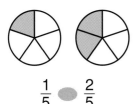

$$\frac{1}{5} \;⬤\; \frac{2}{5}$$

4.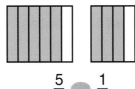

$$\frac{5}{6} \;⬤\; \frac{1}{2}$$

5.

$$\frac{2}{8} \;⬤\; \frac{3}{8}$$

Compare. Write > or < for each ⬤.
Use fraction strips or a number line if needed.

6. $\frac{1}{2} \;⬤\; \frac{2}{2}$ **7.** $\frac{6}{8} \;⬤\; \frac{3}{8}$ **8.** $\frac{5}{5} \;⬤\; \frac{4}{5}$ **9.** $\frac{1}{3} \;⬤\; \frac{1}{8}$

10. $\frac{1}{3} \;⬤\; \frac{1}{4}$ **11.** $\frac{7}{10} \;⬤\; \frac{10}{10}$ **12.** $\frac{1}{3} \;⬤\; \frac{1}{5}$ **13.** $\frac{7}{8} \;⬤\; 1$

14. Analyze Keb ate one fourth of a pizza. Austin ate one sixth of the same pizza. Who ate more pizza?

15. Anita brought $\frac{4}{10}$ of the muffins. Alex brought $\frac{6}{10}$ of the muffins. Who brought more muffins?

Mixed Review and Test Prep ✓

Open Response
Complete the division sentences.
(Ch. 11, Lessons 3–8)

16. $35 \div \blacksquare = 7$ **17.** $\blacksquare \div 7 = 3$

18. $64 \div \blacksquare = 8$ **19.** $\blacksquare \div 4 = 4$

20. $28 \div \blacksquare = 4$ **21.** $\blacksquare \div 6 = 3$

Multiple Choice
22. Which sentence is **not** true?
(Ch. 19, Lesson 1)

A $\frac{4}{5} > \frac{1}{3}$ **C** $\frac{3}{6} > \frac{5}{6}$

B $\frac{4}{10} < \frac{1}{2}$ **D** $\frac{1}{3} > \frac{1}{5}$

Order Fractions

Objective Order like and unlike fractions.

Learn About It

Look at the tacos that Carlos, Mike, and Rose brought for Multicultural Day.

$\frac{1}{6}$ of Carlos's tacos have sour cream.

$\frac{5}{6}$ of Mike's tacos have sour cream.

$\frac{3}{6}$ of Rose's tacos have sour cream.

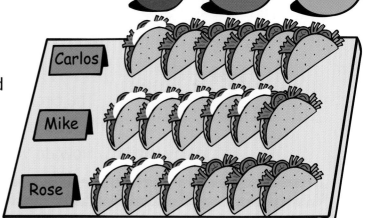

Write the fractions in order from least to greatest.

Different Ways to Order $\frac{1}{6}$, $\frac{5}{6}$, and $\frac{3}{6}$

Way ① Use fraction strips.

| $\frac{1}{6}$ | | | | | |

| $\frac{1}{6}$ | $\frac{1}{6}$ | $\frac{1}{6}$ | $\frac{1}{6}$ | $\frac{1}{6}$ | |

| $\frac{1}{6}$ | $\frac{1}{6}$ | $\frac{1}{6}$ | |

$\frac{1}{6}$ is the least. $\frac{5}{6}$ is the greatest.

So $\frac{1}{6} < \frac{3}{6} < \frac{5}{6}$.

Way ② Use a number line.

$\frac{1}{6} < \frac{3}{6}$

$\frac{3}{6} < \frac{5}{6}$

So $\frac{1}{6} < \frac{3}{6} < \frac{5}{6}$.

Think

$\frac{1}{6}$ is farthest to the left.

$\frac{5}{6}$ is farthest to the right.

$\frac{3}{6}$ is in the middle.

Solution: The order from least to greatest is: $\frac{1}{6}$ $\frac{3}{6}$ $\frac{5}{6}$

Another Example

Order $\frac{1}{8}$, $\frac{2}{3}$, and $\frac{1}{6}$ from greatest to least.

Think

$\frac{2}{3} > \frac{1}{6} > \frac{1}{8}$

The order from greatest to least is: $\frac{2}{3}$ $\frac{1}{6}$ $\frac{1}{8}$.

Order the fractions from least to greatest.

Ask Yourself
- If the denominators are the same, which numerator is the greatest?
- Which fraction represents the least part of a whole?

1.
$\frac{2}{5}$ | $\frac{1}{5}$ | $\frac{1}{5}$
$\frac{4}{5}$ | $\frac{1}{5}$ | $\frac{1}{5}$ | $\frac{1}{5}$ | $\frac{1}{5}$
$\frac{1}{5}$ | $\frac{1}{5}$

2.
$\frac{1}{6}$ | $\frac{1}{6}$
$\frac{1}{8}$ | $\frac{1}{8}$
$\frac{1}{4}$ | $\frac{1}{4}$

Explain Your Thinking ▶ Look at the fractions in Exercise 2. Why does the least fraction have the greatest denominator?

Practice and Problem Solving

Order the fractions from greatest to least.

3.
$\frac{3}{8}$ | $\frac{1}{8}$ | $\frac{1}{8}$ | $\frac{1}{8}$
$\frac{7}{8}$ | $\frac{1}{8}$ | $\frac{1}{8}$ | $\frac{1}{8}$ | $\frac{1}{8}$ | $\frac{1}{8}$ | $\frac{1}{8}$ | $\frac{1}{8}$
$\frac{1}{8}$ | $\frac{1}{8}$

4.
$\frac{1}{2}$ | $\frac{1}{2}$
$\frac{1}{3}$ | $\frac{1}{3}$
$\frac{1}{4}$ | $\frac{1}{4}$

5.
$\frac{1}{5}$ | $\frac{1}{5}$
$\frac{1}{3}$ | $\frac{1}{3}$
$\frac{1}{4}$ | $\frac{1}{4}$

Order the fractions from least to greatest. Use fraction strips or draw a number line.

6. $\frac{1}{4}$ $\frac{1}{8}$ $\frac{1}{2}$

7. $\frac{4}{5}$ $\frac{2}{5}$ $\frac{3}{5}$

8. $\frac{1}{2}$ $\frac{1}{3}$ $\frac{1}{5}$

9. $\frac{6}{8}$ $\frac{5}{8}$ $\frac{2}{8}$

Solve.

10. Kirsten ate $\frac{1}{6}$ of the tacos. Tim ate $\frac{1}{3}$ of the tacos. Tara ate $\frac{3}{6}$ of the tacos. Who ate the least number of tacos?

11. **Explain** Cookbooks that usually cost $8.95 are marked with stickers showing $\frac{1}{2}$ off, $\frac{1}{4}$ off, $\frac{1}{3}$ off. Which sticker gives the best buy?

Mixed Review and Test Prep

Open Response
Write each time as minutes before and after the hour. (Ch. 12, Lesson 3)

12.

13.

14. Order the fractions $\frac{1}{10}$, $\frac{7}{10}$, and $\frac{3}{10}$ from greatest to least. Draw pictures to show your answer.
(Ch. 19, Lesson 2)

Problem-Solving Strategy
Act It Out

Objective Solve a problem by using models.

Problem Sonia and Lamont ate sushi on Multicultural Day. Each California roll is cut into 6 equal pieces. Sonia ate $\frac{1}{2}$ of a California roll. Lamont ate $\frac{2}{3}$ of a roll. Who ate more?

UNDERSTAND

This is what you know.

- Each California roll is cut into 6 equal pieces.
- Sonia ate $\frac{1}{2}$ of a California roll.
- Lamont ate $\frac{2}{3}$ of a California roll.

PLAN

You can use fraction strips to help you compare the fractions.

SOLVE

- Use fraction strips to model how much each person ate.

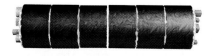

- Line up the fraction strips and compare.

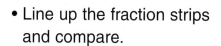

$$\frac{2}{3} > \frac{1}{2}$$

Solution: Since $\frac{2}{3}$ is greater than $\frac{1}{2}$, Lamont ate more.

LOOK BACK

Look back at the problem.

Does the answer make sense? Is $\frac{2}{3}$ to the right of $\frac{1}{2}$ on a number line?

Use the **Ask Yourself questions** to help you solve each problem.

1. Christine drank $\frac{5}{10}$ liter of water. Sheri drank $\frac{1}{2}$ liter. Did they drink the same amount? How do you know?

2. Jorge puts $\frac{1}{3}$ cup of celery, $\frac{3}{4}$ cup of carrots, and $\frac{1}{2}$ cup of onions in the pot. Which vegetable is there the least amount of in the pot?

(Hint) Compare three fraction strips in the same way you compare two.

Ask Yourself

UNDERSTAND
- **What facts do I know?**

PLAN
- **Did I use the correct fraction strips?**

SOLVE
- **Did I line up the fraction strips correctly?**

LOOK BACK
- **Does my answer make sense?**

Independent Practice

Use models to solve each problem.

3. Do $\frac{2}{3}$ and $\frac{1}{2}$ make more or less than 1 whole?

4. **Reasoning** If $\frac{1}{4}$ of 8 is 2, what is $\frac{3}{4}$ of 8?

5. Jodie, Ken, and Greta walk to school. Jodie walks $\frac{2}{3}$ mile, Ken walks $\frac{1}{6}$ mile, and Greta walks $\frac{7}{10}$ mile. Who walks the farthest to school?

6. Dalia's scarf is $\frac{1}{3}$ yellow. Emily's scarf is $\frac{4}{6}$ yellow. Susan's scarf is $\frac{1}{2}$ red and $\frac{1}{2}$ yellow. If each scarf is the same size, whose scarf has the most yellow?

Go On

Mixed Problem Solving

Solve. Show your work.
Tell what strategy you used.

7. A cake has 12 colored stripes. The stripes are in this order: blue, yellow, pink, blue, yellow, pink. If the pattern continues, how many yellow stripes does the cake have?

8. Silvie traveled from Avon to Troy. She arrived in Troy at 4:45 P.M. If the train ride was 2 hours and 5 minutes long, at what time did the train leave Avon?

9. Moe, Al, and Sue are flying kites. Moe's kite is twice as high as Al's kite. Al's kite is 100 feet lower than Sue's kite. If Sue's kite flies at 250 feet, how high is each kite?

10. Joy bought materials for a kite. After she spent $11 on fabric and $4 on string, she had $5 left. What fraction of her money did Joy spend?

You Choose

Strategy
- Make a Table
- Draw a Picture
- Find a Pattern
- Act It Out
- Work Backward

Computation Method
- Mental Math
- Estimation
- Paper and Pencil
- Calculator

Data Use the table for Problems 11–13. Then tell which method you chose.

11. **Analyze** Is the highest recorded temperature of Australia closer to the highest recorded temperature of Europe, or of North America?

12. Compare the highest recorded temperatures of North America and South America. Which is greater? By how many degrees is it greater?

13. About how many degrees difference is there between the highest and lowest temperatures in the table?

World's Highest Recorded Temperatures	
Continent	**Temperature**
Africa	136°F
Antarctica	59°F
Asia	129°F
Australia	123°F
Europe	122°F
North America	134°F
South America	120°F

Problem Solving on Tests

Multiple Choice

Choose the letter of the correct answer. If the correct answer is not here, choose NH.

1. Rita has 306 postcards in her collection. If 137 of her postcards are from the United States, how many are not from the United States?

   A 213   **B** 269   **C** 271   **D** NH

   (Chapter 5, Lesson 7)

2. Matt picks up all his marbles. Bo picks up $\frac{3}{4}$ of hers, Andy picks up $\frac{1}{3}$ of his, and Lisa picks up $\frac{1}{2}$ of hers. If each person started with the same number of marbles, who picked up the fewest marbles?

   F Bo   **G** Lisa   **H** Andy   **J** Matt

   (Chapter 19, Lesson 2)

Open Response

Solve each problem.

3. Marco and Safina buy one whole pizza to share. Marco eats $\frac{1}{2}$ of the pizza. Safina eats $\frac{1}{4}$ of the pizza. How much pizza is left?

   (Chapter 19, Lesson 3)

4. Players toss a cube numbered 3–8. Player 1 gets a point if the number rolled is even. Player 2 gets a point if the number rolled is odd. Is the game fair? How do you know?

   (Chapter 7, Lesson 4)

Extended Response

5. Kim's class is playing a math game. To win, she needs to cross off ten fractions on her card.

   Kim's Card

$\frac{2}{8}$	$\frac{1}{3}$	$\frac{5}{10}$	$\frac{6}{9}$	$\frac{4}{2}$
$\frac{1}{2}$	$\frac{3}{6}$	$\frac{1}{4}$	$\frac{3}{5}$	$\frac{3}{4}$
$\frac{8}{6}$	$\frac{3}{2}$	$\frac{2}{7}$	$\frac{3}{8}$	$\frac{7}{8}$
$\frac{2}{4}$	$\frac{2}{6}$	$\frac{1}{8}$	$\frac{4}{5}$	$\frac{2}{9}$
$\frac{4}{6}$	$\frac{4}{9}$	$\frac{7}{3}$	$\frac{3}{8}$	$\frac{5}{7}$

   A. First, the teacher says to cross off all improper fractions. Which fractions can Kim cross off? How do you know they are improper?

   B. Next, the teacher says to cross off all fractions equivalent to $\frac{1}{2}$. Which fractions can Kim cross off? Draw a number line to show these fractions.

   C. Finally, the teacher says to cross off all fractions that are less than $\frac{5}{8}$. Which fractions can Kim cross off?

   D. Can Kim be a winner? Explain your thinking.

   (Chapter 19, Lesson 2)

Education Place

See **eduplace.com/map** for more Test-Taking Tips.

Audio Tutor 2/24 Listen and Understand

Add Fractions

Objective Add fractions with like denominators.

Learn About It

Some students brought in hero sandwiches on Multicultural Day. The sandwich at the right is cut into 6 equal pieces. Sue ate $\frac{2}{6}$ of the sandwich, and Dave ate $\frac{3}{6}$ of the sandwich. What fraction of the sandwich did Sue and Dave eat?

Add. $\frac{2}{6} + \frac{3}{6} = \blacksquare$

The hero, which originated in Italy, is also known as a grinder, a hoagie, a submarine, and a poor boy.

Different Ways to Add $\frac{2}{6} + \frac{3}{6}$

Way ❶ Use fraction strips.

- Start with the fraction strip for 1 whole.
- Place two $\frac{1}{6}$ fraction pieces below it.
- Add three $\frac{1}{6}$ fraction pieces.

$$\frac{2}{6} + \frac{3}{6} = \frac{5}{6}$$

Way ❷ Write a number sentence.

When the denominators are the same, you can just add the numerators.

$\frac{2}{6} + \frac{3}{6} = \frac{5}{6}$ ← Add numerators.
← Denominators stay the same.

Solution: Sue and Dave ate $\frac{5}{6}$ of the hero sandwich.

Another Example

Find $\frac{5}{8} + \frac{3}{8}$.

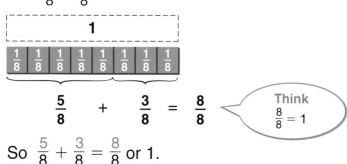

$$\frac{5}{8} + \frac{3}{8} = \frac{8}{8}$$

Think $\frac{8}{8} = 1$

So $\frac{5}{8} + \frac{3}{8} = \frac{8}{8}$ or 1.

Guided Practice

Use the fraction strips to help you add.

1.

1

| $\frac{1}{5}$ | $\frac{1}{5}$ | $\frac{1}{5}$ | | |

$$\frac{2}{5} + \frac{1}{5} = \blacksquare$$

2.

1

| $\frac{1}{3}$ | $\frac{1}{3}$ | $\frac{1}{3}$ |

$$\frac{2}{3} + \frac{1}{3} = \blacksquare$$

Ask Yourself
- How can I use fraction pieces to add?
- Does the sum equal 1?

Add. Use fraction strips or draw a picture to help you.

3. $\frac{1}{4} + \frac{1}{4}$ **4.** $\frac{2}{5} + \frac{3}{5}$ **5.** $\frac{5}{8} + \frac{2}{8}$ **6.** $\frac{7}{9} + \frac{1}{9}$

Explain Your Thinking ▶ How can you use what you know about adding whole numbers to help you add fractions with like denominators?

Practice and Problem Solving

Add.

7.

1

| $\frac{1}{6}$ | $\frac{1}{6}$ | $\frac{1}{6}$ | $\frac{1}{6}$ | | |

$$\frac{3}{6} + \frac{1}{6} = \blacksquare$$

8.

1

| $\frac{1}{4}$ | $\frac{1}{4}$ | $\frac{1}{4}$ | |

$$\frac{2}{4} + \frac{1}{4} = \blacksquare$$

9.

1

| $\frac{1}{5}$ | $\frac{1}{5}$ | $\frac{1}{5}$ | $\frac{1}{5}$ | |

$$\frac{3}{5} + \frac{1}{5} = \blacksquare$$

10.

1

| $\frac{1}{6}$ | $\frac{1}{6}$ | $\frac{1}{6}$ | | | |

$$\frac{2}{6} + \frac{1}{6} = \blacksquare$$

11.

1

| $\frac{1}{8}$ | $\frac{1}{8}$ | $\frac{1}{8}$ | $\frac{1}{8}$ | $\frac{1}{8}$ | $\frac{1}{8}$ | | |

$$\frac{3}{8} + \frac{3}{8} = \blacksquare$$

12.

1

| $\frac{1}{6}$ | $\frac{1}{6}$ | $\frac{1}{6}$ | $\frac{1}{6}$ | $\frac{1}{6}$ | $\frac{1}{6}$ |

$$\frac{4}{6} + \frac{2}{6} = \blacksquare$$

Add. Use fraction strips or draw a picture to help you.

13. $\frac{1}{3} + \frac{1}{3}$ **14.** $\frac{2}{9} + \frac{3}{9}$ **15.** $\frac{1}{8} + \frac{3}{8}$ **16.** $\frac{2}{4} + \frac{1}{4}$

17. $\frac{3}{6} + \frac{2}{6}$ **18.** $\frac{2}{5} + \frac{3}{5}$ **19.** $\frac{5}{8} + \frac{2}{8}$ **20.** $\frac{2}{7} + \frac{5}{7}$

21. Look back at your answers for Exercises 13–20. In which exercises is the sum equal to 1? Explain why.

Go On ▶

Write the letters for the fraction pieces you can use to make exactly one whole.

22. | 1 | a. | $\frac{1}{2}$ | b. | $\frac{1}{4}$ | $\frac{1}{4}$ | $\frac{1}{4}$ | c. | $\frac{1}{4}$ | $\frac{1}{4}$ |

23. | 1 | a. | $\frac{1}{4}$ | $\frac{1}{4}$ | $\frac{1}{4}$ | b. | $\frac{1}{3}$ | $\frac{1}{3}$ | c. | $\frac{1}{8}$ | $\frac{1}{8}$ |

24. | 1 | a. | $\frac{1}{5}$ | $\frac{1}{5}$ | $\frac{1}{5}$ | b. | $\frac{1}{5}$ | $\frac{1}{5}$ | c. | $\frac{1}{6}$ | $\frac{1}{6}$ | $\frac{1}{6}$ |

✖ Algebra • Variables Find the value of *n*.

25. $\frac{1}{4} + \frac{n}{4} = \frac{2}{4}$

26. $\frac{n}{8} + \frac{1}{8} = \frac{6}{8}$

27. $\frac{4}{5} + \frac{n}{5} = \frac{5}{5}$

28. $\frac{5}{9} + \frac{n}{9} = \frac{8}{9}$

29. $\frac{n}{7} + \frac{4}{7} = \frac{6}{7}$

30. $\frac{2}{6} + \frac{n}{6} = \frac{5}{6}$

31. $\frac{2}{7} + \frac{n}{7} = \frac{5}{7}$

32. $\frac{3}{9} + \frac{n}{9} = \frac{8}{9}$

33. $\frac{1}{5} + \frac{n}{5} = \frac{3}{5}$

Solve.

34. **Explain** A cake is cut into six equal pieces. Al eats $\frac{2}{6}$ of the cake, Sal eats $\frac{3}{6}$, and Hal eats $\frac{1}{6}$. Are there any pieces left? If so, how many?

35. Ji and Ruby are painting a fence. Ji paints $\frac{2}{8}$ of the fence, Ruby paints $\frac{3}{8}$. Together, did Ruby and Ji paint more than half the fence?

Use the picture at right for Problems 36–37.

36. Ivan made the stained-glass window at the right. Write a number sentence with fractions to show how much of the window is red or purple.

37. Write a number sentence using fractions to show how much of the window is purple or green.

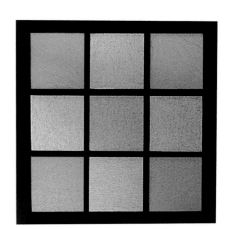

530

Extra Practice See page 537, Set C.

Science Connection
Comparing Lengths of Insects

Have you ever come across a Green Stink Bug or a Buffalo Treehopper? Use fraction strips to answer the questions about these and other insects.

Twice-Stabbed Lady Beetle	Pyralis Firefly	Green Stink Bug	Buffalo Treehopper

$\frac{1}{4}$ inch long	$\frac{1}{2}$ inch long	$\frac{3}{4}$ inch long	$\frac{3}{8}$ inch long

1. Which insect is the longest?

2. Which insect is the shortest?

3. Which insect is twice as long as a Lady Beetle?

4. Write the names of the insects in order from shortest to longest.

WEEKLY ⓌⓇ READER eduplace.com/map

Check your understanding of Lessons 1–4.

Write > or < for each ⬤. (Lesson 1)

1. $\frac{1}{7}$ ⬤ $\frac{3}{7}$

2. $\frac{5}{8}$ ⬤ $\frac{1}{6}$

3. $\frac{1}{8}$ ⬤ $\frac{1}{5}$

Order the fractions from least to greatest. (Lesson 2)

4. $\frac{4}{6}$ $\frac{3}{6}$ $\frac{6}{6}$

5. $\frac{1}{2}$ $\frac{1}{8}$ $\frac{1}{4}$

Find each sum. (Lesson 4)

6. $\frac{3}{5} + \frac{1}{5}$

7. $\frac{1}{8} + \frac{3}{8}$

8. $\frac{2}{4} + \frac{1}{4}$

9. $1 + \frac{1}{7}$

Solve. (Lesson 3)

10. Is $\frac{1}{2}$ ft greater than or less than $\frac{9}{12}$ ft? Use a ruler to explain your answer.

<table>
<tr><td>

**Lesson
5**

</td><td>

Subtract Fractions

Objective Subtract fractions with like denominators.

</td><td>

</td></tr>
</table>

Learn About It

Larry wants to make Southern corn bread for Multicultural Day. The recipe says he needs $\frac{4}{8}$ of a stick of butter for the bread. Larry has $\frac{7}{8}$ of a stick of butter. How much butter will Larry have left after he makes the corn bread?

Subtract. $\frac{7}{8} - \frac{4}{8} = $ ■

Different Ways to Subtract $\frac{7}{8} - \frac{4}{8}$

Way ① Use fraction strips.

- Start with the fraction strip for 1 whole.
- Place seven $\frac{1}{8}$ pieces below it.
- Subtract four $\frac{1}{8}$ pieces.

$$\frac{7}{8} - \frac{4}{8} = \frac{3}{8}$$

Way ② Write a number sentence.

Since the **denominators** are the same, you can just subtract the **numerators**.

$\frac{7}{8} - \frac{4}{8} = \frac{3}{8}$ ← Subtract numerators.

← Denominators stay the same.

Solution: Larry will have $\frac{3}{8}$ of a stick of butter.

Another Example

Find $1 - \frac{4}{6}$.

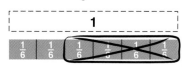

$$\frac{6}{6} - \frac{4}{6} = \frac{2}{6}$$

Think
$\frac{6}{6} = 1$

So $1 - \frac{4}{6} = \frac{2}{6}$.

Ask Yourself

- Which fraction pieces should I use?

- How will the denominator help me write a fraction equivalent to 1?

Use the fraction strips to help you subtract.

1.

$$\frac{2}{3} - \frac{1}{3} = \blacksquare$$

2.

$$\frac{5}{6} - \frac{3}{6} = \blacksquare$$

3.

$$\frac{5}{7} - \frac{1}{7} = \blacksquare$$

4.

$$\frac{5}{8} - \frac{3}{8} = \blacksquare$$

Subtract. Use fraction strips or draw a picture to help you.

5. $\frac{4}{6} - \frac{1}{6}$ **6.** $\frac{7}{8} - \frac{2}{8}$ **7.** $1 - \frac{1}{9}$ **8.** $\frac{1}{4} - \frac{1}{4}$

Explain Your Thinking ▶ Look at Exercise 7. Why should you write 1 as $\frac{9}{9}$ before you subtract?

Practice and Problem Solving

Subtract.

9.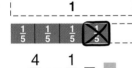

$$\frac{4}{5} - \frac{1}{5} = \blacksquare$$

10.

$$\frac{2}{4} - \frac{1}{4} = \blacksquare$$

11.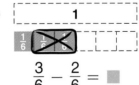

$$\frac{3}{6} - \frac{2}{6} = \blacksquare$$

12.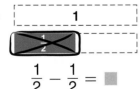

$$\frac{1}{2} - \frac{1}{2} = \blacksquare$$

13.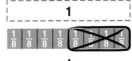

$$1 - \frac{4}{8} = \blacksquare$$

14.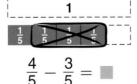

$$\frac{4}{5} - \frac{3}{5} = \blacksquare$$

15. Reasoning Isaac says that $1 - \frac{4}{4}$ is 0. Leisha says that the difference is $\frac{0}{4}$. Are they both correct? Draw pictures or use fraction strips to explain your answer.

Go On

Subtract. Use fraction strips or draw a picture to help you.

16. $\dfrac{3}{4} - \dfrac{1}{4}$ **17.** $\dfrac{3}{5} - \dfrac{2}{5}$ **18.** $\dfrac{6}{7} - \dfrac{5}{7}$ **19.** $1 - \dfrac{4}{8}$

20. $\dfrac{8}{9} - \dfrac{3}{9}$ **21.** $\dfrac{6}{8} - \dfrac{4}{8}$ **22.** $\dfrac{4}{6} - \dfrac{3}{6}$ **23.** $\dfrac{8}{9} - \dfrac{5}{9}$

✗ Algebra • Variables Find the value of *n*.

24. $\dfrac{3}{5} - \dfrac{n}{5} = \dfrac{2}{5}$ **25.** $\dfrac{n}{8} - \dfrac{1}{8} = \dfrac{7}{8}$ **26.** $\dfrac{6}{9} - \dfrac{n}{9} = \dfrac{4}{9}$

27. $\dfrac{3}{6} - \dfrac{n}{6} = \dfrac{2}{6}$ **28.** $\dfrac{n}{3} - \dfrac{1}{3} = \dfrac{2}{3}$ **29.** $\dfrac{6}{7} - \dfrac{n}{7} = \dfrac{2}{7}$

30. Raul cut his sandwich into 4 equal pieces. He gave $\dfrac{1}{4}$ to his brother, $\dfrac{1}{4}$ to his sister, and ate the rest. How much of the sandwich did Raul eat?

📊 Data Use the recipe for Problems 31–34.

31. Explain If you combine the raspberries and the blueberries, will you have more than 1 cup of berries?

32. If Joel doubles the amount of yogurt the recipe calls for, how much yogurt will he use?

33. Suppose Joel puts the fruit in the bowl in the order of the greatest to the least amounts. Which fruit would go in first? Which fruit would go in last?

34. While making the recipe, Joel ate $\dfrac{1}{4}$ cup of the raspberries. What amount of raspberries did he have left for the recipe?

Fabulous Fruit Snack

$\dfrac{1}{2}$ cup bananas

$\dfrac{1}{4}$ cup blueberries

$\dfrac{3}{4}$ cup raspberries

$\dfrac{1}{3}$ cup vanilla yogurt

1 teaspoon shredded coconut

In a bowl cut up the bananas. Add the blueberries and raspberries. Top with yogurt. Sprinkle with coconut.

Serves 2.

534

Extra Practice See page 537, Set D.

Open Response

Name each solid figure. (Ch. 15, Lesson 6)

35.   36.   37.

38. **Subtract.** $\frac{4}{7} - \frac{2}{7}$

(Ch. 19, Lesson 5)

A $\frac{2}{7}$ C $\frac{2}{4}$

B $\frac{6}{14}$ D $\frac{6}{7}$

Game

Activity

Fraction Bingo

2 Players

What You'll Need • 32 counters (16 per player) • game boards (Learning Tool 39) • fraction addition problems (Learning Tool 40) • fraction strips (Learning Tool 35)(optional)

How to Play

1 Use Learning Tools 39 and 40. Place the addition problems face-down in a pile.

2 Players take turns picking problems from the top of the pile. Each player adds, then finds the sum on his or her game board, and places a counter on top of the correct answer. You can use fraction strips to help you.

3 Repeat Step 2 until one player has four counters in a row. The row can be horizontal, vertical, or corner to corner.

Chapter Review/Test

VOCABULARY

Chose the best term to complete each sentence.

Vocabulary
numerators
denominator
improper fraction
equivalent fractions

1. The number below the bar in a fraction is the _____.

2. When fractions name the same amount, they are _____.

3. To add two fractions with the same denominator, you add the _____.

4. $\frac{7}{5}$ is an _____.

CONCEPTS AND SKILLS

Write > or < for each ⬤. (Lesson 1, pp. 520–521)

5. $\frac{2}{3}$ ⬤ $\frac{1}{3}$ 6. $\frac{2}{4}$ ⬤ $\frac{5}{8}$ 7. $\frac{6}{6}$ ⬤ $\frac{1}{6}$

8. $\frac{1}{10}$ ⬤ $\frac{3}{5}$ 9. $\frac{3}{4}$ ⬤ $\frac{1}{4}$ 10. $\frac{2}{3}$ ⬤ $\frac{2}{6}$

Order the fractions from least to greatest. (Lesson 2, pp. 522–523)

11. $\frac{4}{5}$ $\frac{2}{5}$ $\frac{1}{5}$ 12. $\frac{1}{6}$ $\frac{6}{6}$ $\frac{3}{6}$ 13. $\frac{2}{4}$ $\frac{2}{8}$ $\frac{2}{2}$

Add or subtract. Use fraction strips or draw a picture to help you.
(Lessons 4–5, pp. 528–534)

14. $\frac{2}{9} + \frac{3}{9} = $ ■   15. $\frac{1}{7} + \frac{6}{7} = $ ■   16. $\frac{1}{5} + \frac{1}{5} = $ ■

17. $\frac{4}{6} - \frac{3}{6} = $ ■   18. $\frac{2}{4} - \frac{2}{4} = $ ■   19. $1 - \frac{1}{2} = $ ■

PROBLEM SOLVING

Solve. (Lesson 3, pp. 524–526)

20. Yun blows out 10 magic candles on her cake. Suppose $\frac{2}{5}$ light again. How many candles are now lit?

 **Write About It**

Show You Understand

Verna thinks that $\frac{1}{2}$ is less than $\frac{1}{4}$ because 2 is less than 4. Is this correct? Draw pictures to explain your answer.

Extra Practice

Set A (Lesson 1, pp. 520–521)

Write > or < for each ⬤.

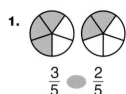

1. $\dfrac{3}{5}$ ⬤ $\dfrac{2}{5}$

2. $\dfrac{2}{3}$ ⬤ $\dfrac{3}{3}$

3. $\dfrac{1}{4}$ ⬤ $\dfrac{1}{8}$

4. $\dfrac{1}{4}$ ⬤ $\dfrac{3}{4}$

5. 1 ⬤ $\dfrac{3}{5}$

6. $\dfrac{3}{6}$ ⬤ $\dfrac{6}{6}$

7. $\dfrac{1}{4}$ ⬤ $\dfrac{1}{3}$

8. $\dfrac{5}{7}$ ⬤ $\dfrac{4}{7}$

Set B (Lesson 2, pp. 522–523)

Order the fractions from least to greatest.

1. $\dfrac{2}{4}$ $\dfrac{1}{4}$ $\dfrac{3}{4}$

2. $\dfrac{2}{5}$ $\dfrac{3}{5}$ $\dfrac{1}{5}$

3. $\dfrac{5}{7}$ $\dfrac{4}{7}$ $\dfrac{6}{7}$

4. $\dfrac{7}{9}$ $\dfrac{2}{9}$ $\dfrac{8}{9}$

5. $\dfrac{1}{2}$ $\dfrac{1}{10}$ $\dfrac{1}{5}$

6. $\dfrac{1}{2}$ $\dfrac{2}{6}$ $\dfrac{2}{3}$

7. $\dfrac{7}{8}$ $\dfrac{2}{4}$ $\dfrac{2}{2}$

8. $\dfrac{1}{4}$ $\dfrac{3}{4}$ $\dfrac{1}{2}$

Set C (Lesson 4, pp. 528–530)

Add.

1.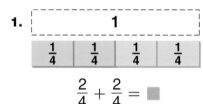

$\dfrac{2}{4} + \dfrac{2}{4} = $ ■

2.

$\dfrac{2}{5} + \dfrac{1}{5} = $ ■

3.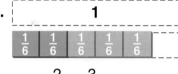

$\dfrac{2}{6} + \dfrac{3}{6} = $ ■

4. $\dfrac{1}{7} + \dfrac{5}{7} = $ ■

5. $\dfrac{7}{9} + \dfrac{1}{9} = $ ■

6. $\dfrac{3}{8} + \dfrac{2}{8} = $ ■

7. $\dfrac{1}{3} + \dfrac{2}{3} = $ ■

Set D (Lesson 5, pp. 532–534)

Subtract.

1.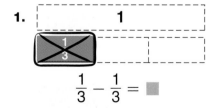

$\dfrac{1}{3} - \dfrac{1}{3} = $ ■

2.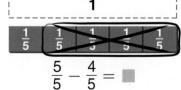

$\dfrac{5}{5} - \dfrac{4}{5} = $ ■

3.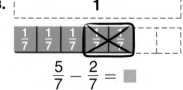

$\dfrac{5}{7} - \dfrac{2}{7} = $ ■

4. $\dfrac{2}{6} - \dfrac{1}{6} = $ ■

5. $1 - \dfrac{2}{5} = $ ■

6. $\dfrac{8}{8} - \dfrac{3}{8} = $ ■

7. $\dfrac{3}{4} - \dfrac{1}{4} = $ ■

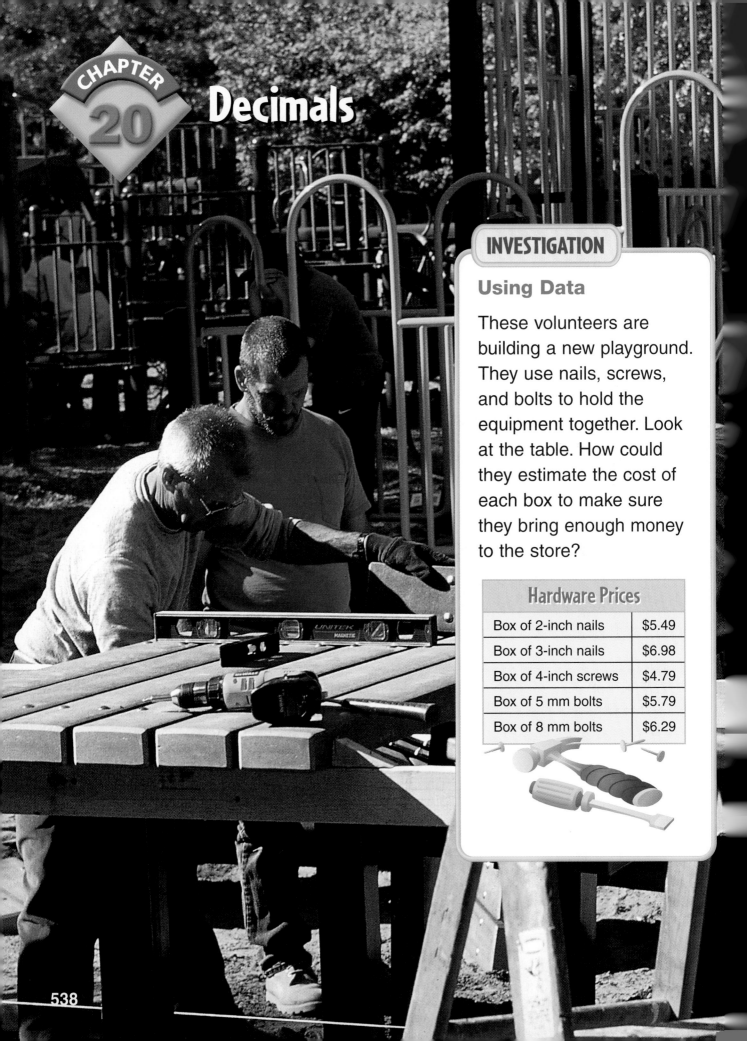

INVESTIGATION

Using Data

These volunteers are building a new playground. They use nails, screws, and bolts to hold the equipment together. Look at the table. How could they estimate the cost of each box to make sure they bring enough money to the store?

Hardware Prices	
Box of 2-inch nails	$5.49
Box of 3-inch nails	$6.98
Box of 4-inch screws	$4.79
Box of 5 mm bolts	$5.79
Box of 8 mm bolts	$6.29

Use What You Know

**Use this page to review and remember
what you need to know for this chapter.**

VOCABULARY

Choose the best term to complete each sentence.

Vocabulary
halves
tenths
fraction
mixed number
decimal point

1. When you write a money amount, you use a ____ to separate the dollars from the cents.

2. A number containing a whole number part and a fraction part is a ____.

3. A whole divided into ten equal parts shows ____.

4. A number that names part of a region or part of a group is a ____.

CONCEPTS AND SKILLS

Write a fraction for the shaded part.

5.   6.    7.   8.   9. ☆ ☆ / ★ ☆

Use a dollar sign and decimal point to write the value of the coins.

10. 1 dime   11. 1 quarter   12. 1 nickel   13. 3 quarters   14. 1 penny

15. 5 quarters   16. 4 nickels   17. 6 dimes   18. 9 pennies   19. 10 dimes

 Write About It

20. Explain how you could show $\frac{35}{100}$ using a model. How many equal parts would there be? How many parts would you shade?

Facts Practice, See page 670.

Tenths

Objective Write fractions with denominators of 10 as decimals.

Vocabulary
decimal
decimal point
tenths

Learn About It

A **decimal** is a number that can have one or more digits to the right of a **decimal point**.

Simon is painting a section of the playground fence. Look at the section of fence shown. It has 10 equal parts. Three of the parts are blue.

What part of the fence is blue?

Different Ways to Show Parts of a Whole

You can use a model.	You can write a fraction.	You can write a decimal.
	$\dfrac{3}{10}$ ← blue parts ← parts in all	

ones	tenths
0 .	3

↑ decimal point

Write 0.3

Read three **tenths**

Solution: $\dfrac{3}{10}$ or 0.3 of the fence is blue.

Guided Practice

Write a fraction and a decimal for each shaded part.

1.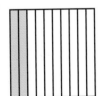

2.

3.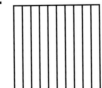

Ask Yourself

• How many equal parts are there?

• How many parts are shaded?

Explain Your Thinking ▶ What does the 0 to the left of the decimal point tell you?

Write a fraction and a decimal for each shaded part.

4. 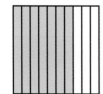   5.    6.   7.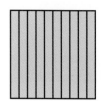

Write each as a decimal.

8. $\frac{9}{10}$ 9. $\frac{1}{10}$ 10. $\frac{6}{10}$ 11. $\frac{3}{10}$ 12. $\frac{8}{10}$ 13. $\frac{4}{10}$

14. one tenth   15. eight tenths   16. five tenths   17. two tenths

Write each as a fraction.

18. 0.3   19. 0.5   20. 0.9   21. 0.6   22. 0.1   23. 0.2

24. nine tenths   25. six tenths   26. four tenths   27. seven tenths

Solve.

28. What is the greatest digit you can have in the tenths place?

29. Explain how to write the fraction $\frac{1}{2}$ as a decimal.

30. **Represent** Show how you would shade a model to show 10 tenths. What is the decimal for 10 tenths? Explain your thinking.

31. **What's Wrong?** Jo painted 7 out of 10 fence sections. She said she had 0.2 left to paint. What mistake did she make?

32. Look at the number 0.3. Why is there a 0 before the decimal point?

Mixed Review and Test Prep

Open Response

Multiply. (Ch. 9, Lessons 2–6)

33. 3×9 34. 7×8 35. 6×5

36. 9×4 37. 5×3 38. 8×2

39. Do 0.5 and 5.0 represent the same amount?

Explain your thinking.
(Ch. 20, Lesson 1)

Extra Practice See page 565, Set A.

Hundredths

Objective Write fractions with denominators of 100 as decimals.

Learn About It

A group of 100 students volunteered to help build a playground. They put their photos on this display.

• On Monday there were 9 photos displayed.

• On Friday there were 81 photos.

What part of the display is filled with photos on each of the two days?

You can use decimal models to show each part.

Monday	Friday
$\frac{9}{100}$	$\frac{81}{100}$

ones	tenths	hundredths
0 .	0	9

ones	tenths	hundredths
0 .	8	1

Write 0.09
Read nine **hundredths**

0.09 of the display is filled.

Write 0.81
Read eighty-one hundredths

0.81 of the display is filled.

Guided Practice

Write a fraction and a decimal for the shaded part.

1.

2.

3.

Explain Your Thinking ▶ Do 0.50 and 0.5 represent the same amount?

542

Write a fraction and a decimal for the shaded part.

4.

5.

6.

7.

Write each as a decimal.

8. $\dfrac{78}{100}$ **9.** $\dfrac{52}{100}$ **10.** $\dfrac{4}{100}$ **11.** $\dfrac{60}{100}$ **12.** $\dfrac{98}{100}$ **13.** $\dfrac{12}{100}$

14. one hundredth   **15.** thirty-seven hundredths   **16.** fifty-three hundredths

Write each as a fraction.

17. 0.49   **18.** 0.23   **19.** 0.07   **20.** 0.40   **21.** 0.78   **22.** 0.10

23. four hundredths   **24.** forty-four hundredths   **25.** fourteen hundredths

Data Use the graph for Problems 26–28.

26. How many students volunteered to work on the playground?

27. What decimal represents the third-grade volunteers?

28. How many more fifth- and sixth-graders volunteered than third- and fourth-graders?

29. Represent Draw models to show 0.9 and 0.09. Is 0.9 greater than 0.09? Explain why or why not.

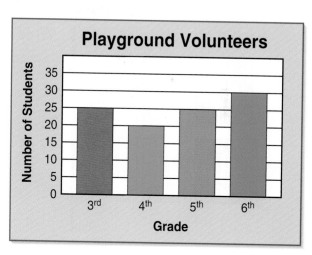

Playground Volunteers

Number of Students / Grade

Mixed Review and Test Prep

Open Response

Add. (Ch. 19, Lesson 4)

30. $\dfrac{1}{8} + \dfrac{3}{8}$ **31.** $\dfrac{1}{6} + \dfrac{4}{6}$

32. $\dfrac{1}{3} + \dfrac{1}{3}$ **33.** $\dfrac{2}{4} + \dfrac{1}{4}$

Multiple Choice

34. Which decimal shows $\dfrac{45}{100}$?
(Ch. 20, Lesson 2)

A 45   **C** 0.45

B 4.5   **D** 0.4

Extra Practice See page 565, Set B.

Decimals Greater Than 1

Objective Write decimals greater than 1.

Learn About It

Some of the parents are building wooden decks for the picnic area in the playground. They already painted $3\frac{5}{10}$ decks.

There are different ways to show the number of decks that are painted.

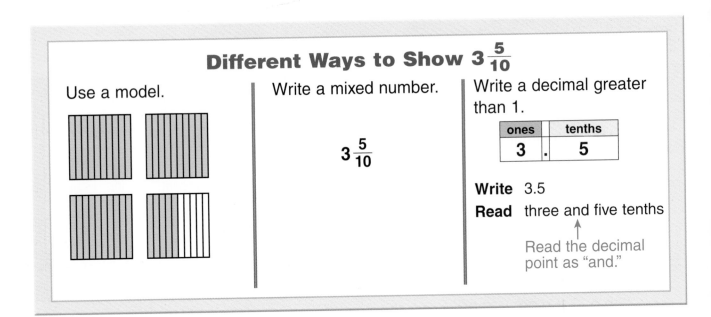

Different Ways to Show $3\frac{5}{10}$

Use a model.	Write a mixed number.	Write a decimal greater than 1.

Write a decimal greater than 1.

ones	tenths
3	5

$3\frac{5}{10}$

Write 3.5

Read three and five tenths

↑ Read the decimal point as "and."

Another Example

Decimal With Hundredths

Use a model.   Write a mixed number.   Write a decimal greater than 1.

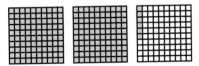

$2\frac{6}{100}$

ones	tenths	hundredths
2	0	6

Write 2.06

Read two and six hundredths

Write a mixed number and a decimal for the shaded part.

1.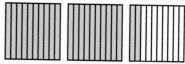

2.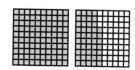

Ask Yourself

- How many wholes are there?

- How many tenths or hundredths are there?

Explain Your Thinking ▶ Why is 2.04 a different value than 2.40?

Practice and Problem Solving

Write a mixed number and a decimal for the shaded part.

3.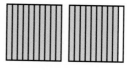

4.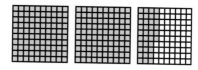

5.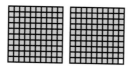

Write each as a decimal.

6. $5\frac{18}{100}$ **7.** $7\frac{8}{10}$ **8.** $9\frac{75}{100}$ **9.** $3\frac{2}{10}$ **10.** $2\frac{6}{100}$ **11.** $1\frac{39}{100}$

12. six and nine tenths **13.** one and six tenths **14.** four and two hundredths

Solve.

15. Mr. Case uses 3 whole cans and $\frac{8}{10}$ of another can of paint to paint all the benches. Write a decimal that shows the total number of cans Mr. Case uses.

16. Reasoning Ernie walks exactly 2 kilometers around the park. If he walks another 0.5 kilometer back to his house, does he walk more or less than 3 kilometers? Explain.

Mixed Review and Test Prep

Open Response

Order the fractions from least to greatest. (Ch. 19, Lesson 2)

17. $\frac{5}{8}$ $\frac{1}{8}$ $\frac{3}{8}$

18. $\frac{1}{2}$ $\frac{1}{3}$ $\frac{1}{8}$

19. $\frac{2}{5}$ $\frac{4}{5}$ $\frac{1}{5}$

20. $\frac{1}{10}$ $\frac{1}{2}$ $\frac{1}{4}$

21. How are $3\frac{60}{100}$ and 3.6 different? How are they alike? (Ch. 20, Lesson 3)

Use pictures, symbols, or words to explain your answer.

Extra Practice See page 565, Set C.

Problem-Solving Decision

Reasonable Answers

Objective Decide whether an answer to a problem makes sense.

You should always look back at a problem to decide whether or not your answer is reasonable.

Problem Carl and his dad are planting shrubs in their backyard. They each planted $\frac{3}{10}$ of the shrubs. Carl said that $\frac{5}{10}$ of the shrubs still need to be planted. Is that reasonable?

Follow these steps to decide.

STEP 1 Find how many of the shrubs were planted.

$$\frac{3}{10} + \frac{3}{10} = \frac{6}{10}$$

$\frac{6}{10}$ were planted.

STEP 2 Use what you know about fractions to decide if it is reasonable that $\frac{5}{10}$ are left.

You know $\frac{6}{10} + \frac{4}{10} = \frac{10}{10}$ or 1.

Since $\frac{5}{10}$ is greater than $\frac{4}{10}$, it is not reasonable that $\frac{5}{10}$ of the shrubs are left.

Solution: Carl's statement is not reasonable.

Try These

Solve. Decide whether the answer is reasonable or not.

1. Luz began filling a sandbox with sand. She made two trips, using $\frac{1}{6}$ of the pile of sand each time. Joe says that $\frac{3}{6}$ of the pile is left. Is this reasonable?

2. Lionel is building birdhouses. He used $\frac{2}{5}$ of a piece of wood for one house and $\frac{1}{5}$ for the other. He thinks that $\frac{2}{5}$ of the piece of wood is left. Is this reasonable?

Calculator Connection
Decimal Decoder

Use your calculator to change the fractions to decimals.

To show $\frac{2}{5}$ as a decimal press: 0.4

Match each answer to a letter below to solve the riddle.

1. $\frac{1}{2}$ **2.** $\frac{3}{4}$ **3.** $\frac{1}{5}$ **4.** $\frac{4}{5}$ **5.** $\frac{1}{4}$ **6.** $\frac{3}{10}$

7. $\frac{1}{10}$ **8.** $\frac{2}{5}$ **9.** $\frac{7}{10}$ **10.** $\frac{3}{5}$ **11.** $\frac{9}{10}$ **12.** $\frac{1}{20}$

Key:	0.05	0.1	0.2	0.25	0.3	0.4	0.5	0.6	0.7	0.75	0.8	0.9
	A	D	E	H	K	O	P	S	T	U	W	Y

Riddle: Why couldn't the calculator fall asleep?

___ ___   ___ ___ ___   ___ ___ ___   ___ ___ ___ ___ ___   ___ ___
 5 3   4 12 10   9 8 8   6 3 11 3 7   2 1

Check your understanding of Lessons 1–4.

Write a fraction and a decimal for each shaded part. (Lessons 1–2)

1.   **2.** **3.** **4.**

Write each mixed number as a decimal. (Lesson 3)

5. $1\frac{38}{100}$ **6.** $2\frac{7}{100}$ **7.** $4\frac{3}{10}$ **8.** six and one hundredth **9.** five and two tenths

Solve. (Lesson 4)

10. Tim put $\frac{6}{10}$ of his stickers on a notebook. He thinks he has $\frac{5}{10}$ of his stickers left to use. Is this reasonable?

Audio Tutor 2/27 Listen and Understand

Compare and Order Decimals

Objective Compare and order decimals.

Learn About It

Students are painting the handball wall on the playground. They paint 0.6 yellow and 0.4 white. Is a greater part of the wall painted yellow or white?

Compare 0.6 and 0.4.

Different Ways to Compare 0.6 and 0.4.

Way ① Use models.

0.6 has more parts shaded than 0.4.

0.6   0.4

So 0.6 > 0.4

Way ② Use a place-value chart.

Start at the left. Compare digits in each place.

ones		tenths
0	.	6
0	.	4
	↑ same	↑ 6 > 4

0.6 > 0.4

Solution: A greater part of the wall is painted yellow.

▶ **You can also use a place-value chart to order decimals.**

Order 0.35, 0.38, and 0.27 from least to greatest.

STEP 1 Line up the decimal points. Start at the left. Compare digits in the same place.

STEP 2 When digits are the same, compare digits to the right.

This is the order of the decimals from least to greatest: 0.27 0.35 0.38

ones		tenths	hundredths
0	.	3	5
0	.	3	8
0	.	2	7

↑ same   ↑ 2 < 3, so 0.27 is the least.   ↑ 5 < 8, so 0.35 < 0.38

0.27 < 0.35 < 0.38

Extra Practice at **eduplace.com/map**

Ask Yourself

• Which decimal is greater?

• Which decimal is less?

Compare. Write >, <, or = for each ⬤.

1.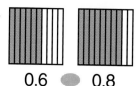

0.6 ⬤ 0.8

2.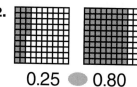

0.25 ⬤ 0.80

Explain Your Thinking ▶ Which is greater, 0.8 or 0.08? Explain.

Practice and Problem Solving

Compare. Write >, <, or = for each ⬤.

3.

0.3 ⬤ 0.2

4.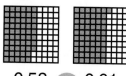

0.58 ⬤ 0.61

5.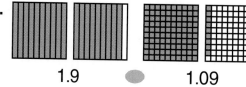

1.9 ⬤ 1.09

6. 1.2 ⬤ 1.5

7. 0.39 ⬤ 0.32

8. 0.40 ⬤ 0.4

9. 0.99 ⬤ 0.90

10. 2.09 ⬤ 2.9

11. 0.8 ⬤ 0.08

Order the decimals from least to greatest.

12. 0.48   0.86   0.64

13. 2.1   1.3   1.9

14. 1.00   1.10   1.01

Solve.

15. The path from the gate to the picnic area is 7.5 meters long. The path from the gate to the swings is 7.08 meters long. Which path is longer?

16. **Analyze** Delia hopped 3.9 meters. Tyrone hopped 1m farther than Delia and 1m less than Orlando. Did anyone hop farther than 6m?

Mixed Review and Test Prep

Open Response

Subtract. (Ch. 19, Lesson 5)

17. $\frac{7}{8} - \frac{3}{8}$

18. $\frac{5}{6} - \frac{2}{6}$

19. $\frac{2}{3} - \frac{1}{3}$

20. $\frac{3}{4} - \frac{1}{4}$

21. $\frac{4}{5} - \frac{2}{5}$

22. $\frac{9}{10} - \frac{3}{10}$

Multiple Choice

23. Which decimal is greater than 1.3? (Ch. 20, Lesson 5)

A 0.5

C 1.1

B 0.9

D 2.0

Compare and Order Fractions and Decimals

Vocabulary
compare
order

Objective Compare and order fractions and decimals.

Learn About It

You can use models or a place-value chart to help you **compare** and **order** fractions and decimals.

Different Ways to Compare 0.7 and $\frac{3}{10}$

Way ❶ Use models.

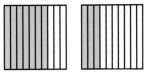

$0.7 > \frac{3}{10}$

Way ❷ Use a place-value chart.

Write $\frac{3}{10}$ as 0.3.
Then compare digits.

ones		tenths
0	.	7
0	.	3

    same   7 > 3

$0.7 > \frac{3}{10}$

▶ You can use what you know about ordering decimals to order fractions and decimals.

Order $\frac{28}{100}$, 0.59, and 0.51 from least to greatest.

STEP 1 First, write the fraction as a decimal. $\frac{28}{100} = 0.28$

STEP 2 Then starting at the left, compare digits in the greatest place. Continue comparing the other digits.

ones		tenths	hundredths
0	.	2	8
0	.	5	9
0	.	5	1

    same   2 < 5   9 > 1

0.28 is least.   0.59 is greatest.

This is the order from least to greatest: $\frac{28}{100}$ 0.51 0.59.

Compare. Write >, <, or = for each ⬤.

1. 0.1 ⬤ $\frac{8}{10}$ **2.** 0.78 ⬤ $\frac{7}{100}$ **3.** 0.60 ⬤ $\frac{9}{10}$

Ask Yourself
- Did I write the fraction as a decimal?
- Can a place-value chart help to compare?

Explain Your Thinking ▶ Which is greater, 8.41 or $8\frac{40}{100}$? Explain your thinking.

Practice and Problem Solving

Compare. Write >, <, or = for each ⬤.

4. $\frac{7}{10}$ ⬤ $\frac{5}{10}$ **5.** 0.01 ⬤ $\frac{3}{100}$ **6.** $\frac{2}{10}$ ⬤ 0.2   **7.** 0.8 ⬤ $\frac{9}{10}$

8. $\frac{59}{100}$ ⬤ 0.60   **9.** $\frac{8}{100}$ ⬤ 0.08   **10.** $\frac{5}{10}$ ⬤ 0.3   **11.** 0.45 ⬤ $\frac{9}{100}$

Order the numbers from least to greatest.

12. $\frac{8}{100}$ 0.02   0.11   **13.** $\frac{7}{100}$ 0.04   0.20   **14.** $\frac{3}{100}$ $\frac{1}{100}$ 0.42

15. $\frac{62}{100}$ 0.57   0.65   **16.** 0.73 $\frac{39}{100}$ 0.30   **17.** $\frac{9}{10}$ 0.6 $\frac{7}{10}$

 Data Use the table for Problems 18–20.

18. On which day does Alicia walk the longest distance? Explain your reasoning.

19. On which day does Alicia walk twice as far as on Monday?

20. On which day does Alicia walk half as far as on Friday?

Alicia's Walking Record

Day	Distance
Monday	$\frac{1}{4}$ mi
Tuesday	0.6 mi
Wednesday	$\frac{1}{2}$ mi
Thursday	1.5 mi
Friday	1.0 mi

Mixed Review and Test Prep ✓

Open Response

Divide. (Ch. 11, Lessons 3–5, 7–9)

21. 30 ÷ 6   **22.** 18 ÷ 3   **23.** 32 ÷ 8

24. 49 ÷ 7   **25.** 36 ÷ 4   **26.** 54 ÷ 9

27. Order these lengths from shortest to longest.

(Ch. 20, Lesson 6)

0.58 m $\frac{82}{100}$ m   0.70 m

Relate Decimals, Fractions, and Money

Materials
play money
tenths and hundredths
models (LT 42, 43)

Objective Relate money to fractions and decimals.

Work Together

You can use what you know about money to help you understand fractions and decimals.

Work with a partner. Use play money to see how different coins can be thought of as parts of a dollar.

 STEP 1

Use pennies to show $1. One hundred pennies are worth 100¢.

- What fraction of a dollar is 1 cent?

- How do you show 1 penny by using a dollar sign and a decimal point?

Record your work in a table like the one started below.

Name of Coin	Number of Cents	Fraction of a Dollar	Value as a Decimal
Penny	1¢	$\frac{1}{100}$	$0.01
Nickel			
Dime			
Quarter			
Half-Dollar			

 STEP 2

Repeat Step 1 using nickels, dimes, quarters, and half-dollars to show $1. Record your work in your table.

Now use decimal models to show parts of a dollar.

 STEP 3 Use a hundredths model.
Shade a model to show $0.25.

- How many parts out of 100 are shaded? What fraction can you write?

 STEP 4 Use a tenths model.
Shade a model to show $0.60.

- How many parts out of 10 are shaded? What fraction can you write?

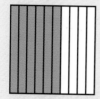

On Your Own

Match each group of coins with the correct value.

1. $\frac{50}{100}$ of a dollar

2. $\frac{3}{10}$ of a dollar

3. $0.75

4. $0.05

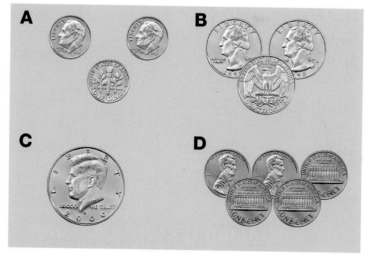

A

B

C

D

Shade hundredths models to show each part of $1.00.
Write fractions to represent each model.

5. $0.17   6. $0.22   7. $0.45   8. $0.53

Shade tenths models to show each part of $1.00.
Write fractions to represent each model.

9. $0.70   10. $0.30   11. $0.40   12. $0.80

Copy and complete the table below. Use play money to help you.

Coins	Number of Cents	Fraction of a Dollar	Value as a Decimal
13. 10 pennies			$0.10
14. 8 dimes		$\frac{80}{100}$ or $\frac{8}{10}$	
15. 2 quarters	50¢		
16. 75 pennies			
17. 4 nickels			
18. 2 half-dollars			

Write each amount as a fraction of a dollar.

19. $0.15 = _____ of a dollar

20. $0.25 = _____ of a dollar

21. $0.75 = _____ of a dollar

22. $0.80 = _____ of a dollar

23. $0.40 = _____ of a dollar

24. $1.00 = _____ of a dollar

25. $0.01 = _____ of a dollar

26. $0.50 = _____ of a dollar

27. $0.36 = _____ of a dollar

28. $0.99 = _____ of a dollar

Talk About It • Write About It

You have learned how to relate money to fractions and decimals.

29. Would you rather have $\frac{7}{10}$ of a dollar or $\frac{75}{100}$ of a dollar? Explain your thinking.

30. To show $0.40 you can use either a hundredths model or a tenths model. To show $0.45 it is better to use a hundredths model. Explain why.

Visual Thinking
Percents

Percent means "out of one hundred." The symbol for percent is **%**.

The design below covers 50 out of 100 squares.

So, $\frac{50}{100}$ or **50%** of the grid is covered.

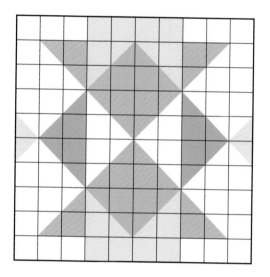

Solve.

1. The design above covers 50% of the grid. How many squares would be covered if a design used 100% of the grid?

2. Suppose a model is divided into ten equal sections. If 50% of the model is green, how many sections are green?

Math Reasoning
Early European Decimals

People in parts of Europe use a comma instead of a decimal point to separate the ones and tenths places. Many years ago, Europeans had other ways of writing decimals.

This is how the mathematician Simon Stevin (1548–1620) would have written the number 259.34.

Explain his method.

Brain Teaser

- Julio bought 0.25 of a dollar's worth of nuts.

- Dara bought three times that amount.

- Val spent twice as much as Julio and Dara spent together for nuts.

What is the total amount of money spent?

Education Place
See **eduplace.com/map**
for more brain teasers.

Add and Subtract Decimals

Objective Add and subtract decimals.

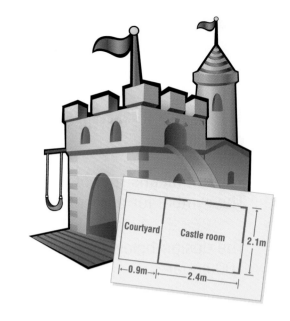

Learn About It

The castle playhouse at the playground has a courtyard and 1 room. The room is 2.4 meters long. The courtyard is 0.9 meters long. What is the total length of the room and the courtyard?

Add. 2.4 + 0.9 = ▦

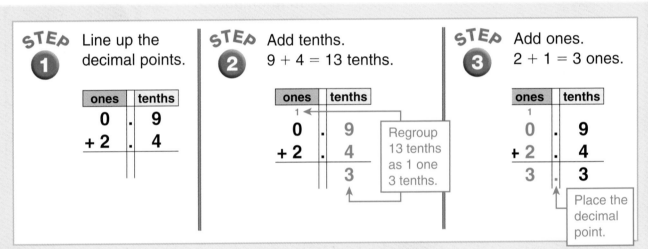

STEP 1 Line up the decimal points.

ones	tenths
0 .	9
+ 2 .	4

STEP 2 Add tenths. 9 + 4 = 13 tenths.

ones	tenths
1 ←	
0 .	9
+ 2 .	4
	3

Regroup 13 tenths as 1 one 3 tenths.

STEP 3 Add ones. 2 + 1 = 3 ones.

ones	tenths
1	
0 .	9
+ 2 .	4
3 .	3

Place the decimal point.

Solution: The room and the courtyard are 3.3 meters long.

▶ How much wider is the courtyard than it is long?

Subtract. 2.1 − 0.9 = ▦

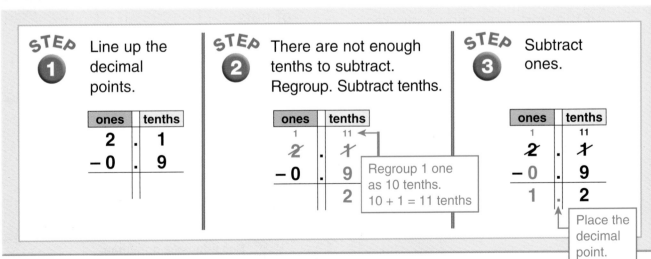

STEP 1 Line up the decimal points.

ones	tenths
2 .	1
− 0 .	9

STEP 2 There are not enough tenths to subtract. Regroup. Subtract tenths.

ones	tenths
1	11 ←
2̶ .	1̶
− 0 .	9
	2

Regroup 1 one as 10 tenths. 10 + 1 = 11 tenths

STEP 3 Subtract ones.

ones	tenths
1	11
2̶ .	1̶
− 0 .	9
1 .	2

Place the decimal point.

Solution: The courtyard is 1.2 meters wider than it is long.

Other Examples

A. Adding Hundredths

$$\begin{array}{r} \overset{1}{5}.62 \\ +\ 2.43 \\ \hline 8.05 \end{array}$$

B. Subtracting Hundredths

$$\begin{array}{r} 6.\overset{8\,12}{\cancel{9}\cancel{2}} \\ -\ 2.35 \\ \hline 4.57 \end{array}$$

Guided Practice

Add or subtract.

1. $\begin{array}{r} 1.3 \\ +\ 2.5 \\ \hline \end{array}$

2. $\begin{array}{r} 8.08 \\ +\ 1.71 \\ \hline \end{array}$

3. $\begin{array}{r} 3.52 \\ +\ 0.67 \\ \hline \end{array}$

4. $\begin{array}{r} 4.8 \\ -\ 3.1 \\ \hline \end{array}$

5. $\begin{array}{r} 3.62 \\ -\ 1.23 \\ \hline \end{array}$

6. $\begin{array}{r} 6.07 \\ -\ 2.63 \\ \hline \end{array}$

7. $1.10 + 1.01$

8. $2.2 + 0.9$

9. $9.0 - 0.9$

> ### Ask Yourself
> • Which digits should I add or subtract first?
> • Do I need to regroup?
> • Did I write the decimal point in the answer?

Explain Your Thinking ▶ How do you decide where to place the decimal point in the answer?

Practice and Problem Solving

Add or subtract.

10. $\begin{array}{r} 5.4 \\ +\ 2.3 \\ \hline \end{array}$

11. $\begin{array}{r} 1.5 \\ +\ 4.9 \\ \hline \end{array}$

12. $\begin{array}{r} 3.8 \\ +\ 2.8 \\ \hline \end{array}$

13. $\begin{array}{r} 5.49 \\ -\ 4.16 \\ \hline \end{array}$

14. $\begin{array}{r} 7.38 \\ -\ 5.23 \\ \hline \end{array}$

15. $\begin{array}{r} 6.35 \\ -\ 0.27 \\ \hline \end{array}$

16. $4.99 + 2.00$

17. $9.6 + 2.4$

18. $11.2 - 1.1$

19. $4.56 + 2.34$

20. $6.19 - 4.28$

21. $9.09 + 0.91$

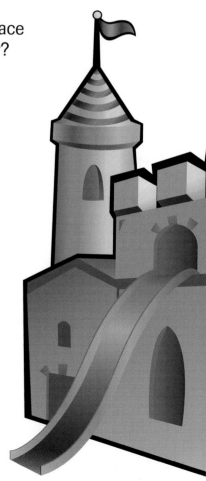

Go On

Algebra • **Functions** Complete each table by following the rule.
If the rule is not given, write the rule.

	Rule: Add 1.5	
	Input	Output
22.	1.0	▨
23.	1.5	▨
24.	▨	3.5
25.	3.0	▨

	Rule: Subtract 0.5	
	Input	Output
26.	5.5	▨
27.	▨	4.0
28.	3.5	▨
29.	2.5	▨

30.

Rule: _____	
Input	Output
2.3	4.6
3.3	5.6
4.3	6.6
6.3	8.6

Data Use the picture at the right for Problems 31–33.

31. How tall is the first floor of the castle?

32. The children decide to put flags along the top of the castle. If the flags are 0.3 meters tall, how far from the ground are the tops of the flags?

33. The castle has a rectangular window on the second floor. What is the perimeter of the window?

34. **Estimate** It cost $83.75 for lumber and $12.95 for nails to build a fence around the castle. Was $100.00 enough to pay for the lumber and the nails?

Mixed Review and Test Prep

Open Response

Compare. Write > or < for each ●.

(Ch. 19, Lesson 1)

35. $\frac{7}{8}$ ● $\frac{1}{8}$

36. $\frac{2}{4}$ ● $\frac{3}{4}$

37. $\frac{1}{3}$ ● $\frac{3}{3}$

38. $\frac{1}{5}$ ● $\frac{1}{10}$

39. Alex rides his bicycle 1.5 miles in the morning and 1.7 miles in the afternoon. How many miles does he ride?

(Ch. 20, Lesson 8)

Extra Practice See page 565, Set F.

Visual Thinking
Estimating Fractions and Decimals

You can use a number line to decide if a fraction or decimal is closer to 0 or 1.

If a fraction is less than $\frac{1}{2}$, it is closer to 0 than to 1.

$\frac{2}{5}$ is to the left of $\frac{1}{2}$.

$\frac{2}{5}$ is less than $\frac{1}{2}$.

So $\frac{2}{5}$ is closer to 0 than to 1.

If a fraction is greater than $\frac{1}{2}$, it is closer to 1 than to 0.

$\frac{4}{5}$ is to the right of $\frac{1}{2}$.

$\frac{4}{5}$ is greater than $\frac{1}{2}$.

So $\frac{4}{5}$ is closer to 1 than to 0.

If a decimal is less than 0.5, it is closer to 0 than to 1.

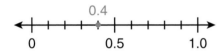

0.4 is to the left of 0.5.

0.4 is less than 0.5.

So 0.4 is closer to 0 than to 1.

If a decimal is greater than 0.5, it is closer to 1 than to 0.

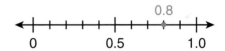

0.8 is to the right of 0.5.

0.8 is greater than 0.5.

So 0.8 is closer to 1 than to 0.

Tell if the fraction marked by the point is closer to 0 or to 1.

1.

2.

Name the decimal for each marked point.
Then tell if the decimal is closer to 0 or to 1.

3.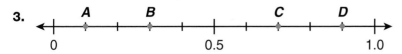

Problem-Solving Application

Use Money

Objective Solve problems by adding, subtracting, multiplying, and dividing money.

Problem Clara Canary flies over to the new playground for a snack. She orders carrot soup and a birdseed muffin at the *Animal Snack Bar*. If she pays with a 10-dollar bill, how much change should she get?

Animal Snack Bar

Birdseed muffin	$ 1.75
Carrot soup	$ 3.60
Duck treats	$ 2.95
Squirrel snacks	$ 2.00
Acorn pie	$ 3.25

UNDERSTAND

What do you know?

- Carrot soup costs $3.60.
- A birdseed muffin costs $1.75.
- Clara pays with a 10-dollar bill.

PLAN

- First, add the cost of the carrot soup to the cost of the birdseed muffin to find the total cost.
- Then subtract the total cost from the amount Clara pays.

SOLVE

STEP 1

$$
\begin{array}{r}
\overset{1}{\$3.60} \leftarrow \text{cost of soup} \\
+ \ \$1.75 \leftarrow \text{cost of muffin} \\
\hline
\$5.35 \leftarrow \text{total cost}
\end{array}
$$

STEP 2

$$
\begin{array}{r}
\$10.00 \\
- \$5.35 \\
\hline
\$4.65
\end{array}
$$

Solution: Clara Canary should get $4.65 in change.

LOOK BACK

Look back at the problem.

Is your answer reasonable? Check by estimating.

Guided Practice

Use the *Animal Snack Bar* menu on Page 560 to solve each problem.

1. Dwayne Duck buys duck treats and an acorn pie. He pays with a 5-dollar bill and 5 quarters. How much change should he get?

2. Sam Squirrel orders 6 packs of squirrel snacks. He gives the clerk a 10-dollar bill, a 1-dollar bill, 2 quarters, and 3 dimes. How much more money does Sam Squirrel owe?

 Hint Use basic multiplication facts to find the total cost of the snacks.

Ask Yourself

UNDERSTAND Is more than one operation needed to solve the problem?

PLAN Did I use the correct information from the sign?

SOLVE
- How much does the food cost?
- How much is paid?

LOOK BACK Is the answer reasonable?

Independent Practice

Data **Use the craft store prices for Problems 3–6.**

3. Darren buys scissors and glue at the craft store. He pays with a 20-dollar bill. How much change should he get?

4. Rosa buys string and paper. She gives the cashier two 1-dollar bills and 6 quarters. Her brother pays the remaining amount. How much does her brother pay?

5. Neng buys 4 rolls of tape. He gives the cashier two 10-dollar bills. How much change should he get?

6. Whitney has a 10-dollar bill and four 1-dollar bills. She wants to buy as much glitter as she can. How many cans of glitter can she buy?

Arts & Crafts

Price List

Glue	$2.80
Roll of Tape	$3.00
String	$2.75
Scissors	$3.25
Paper	$3.95
Glitter	$2.00

Go On

Mixed Strategy Practice

Solve. Show your work. Tell what strategy you used.

7. Jon, Pam, Leon, and Gina are lining up to go out for recess. Jon is first. Pam is in front of Leon but behind Gina. List the students in order from first to last in line.

8. **Money** Franco ordered a tuna sandwich that cost $2.40. He paid the clerk with three 1-dollar bills. He received 5 dimes and 4 nickels in change. Did he get the correct change? Explain.

9. Troy rode his bicycle 22 miles last weekend. He rode 6 more miles on Saturday than on Sunday. How many miles did he ride each day?

You Choose

Strategy
- Act It Out
- Draw a Picture
- Guess and Check
- Use Logical Reasoning
- Write a Number Sentence

Computation Method
- Mental Math
- Estimation
- Paper and Pencil
- Calculator

📊 **Data** Use the pictograph for Problems 10–12. Then tell which method you chose.

10. How many children chose the trumpet as their favorite instrument?

11. If 82 children chose the guitar as their favorite instrument, how many more children chose the guitar than chose the piano?

12. How many more children chose the trumpet and the drums than chose the piano?

Favorite Kinds of Musical Instruments

Trumpet	🧍🧍🧍
Piano	🧍🧍🧍🧍🧍
Drums	🧍🧍🧍🧍🧍

Each 🧍 stands for 12 children.

Real World Connection
Dewey Decimal System

Libraries that use the Dewey Decimal Classification System label their books with decimals.

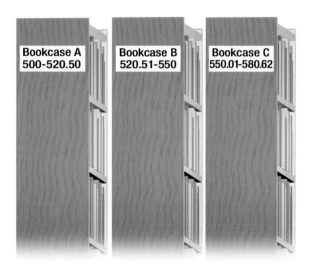

Bookcase A
500–520.50

Bookcase B
520.51–550

Bookcase C
550.01–580.62

Tell where each book below should be placed.
Write *Bookcase A, Bookcase B,* or *Bookcase C.*

1. 550.79

2. 519.99

3. 501.09

4. 520.60

5. 572.15

6. 506.48

7. Make a visit to a library. Find examples of the Dewey Decimal System. Write a word problem that has something to do with the Dewey Decimal System. Give your problem to a classmate to solve.

Chapter Review/Test

VOCABULARY

Vocabulary

tenths

decimal

hundredths

numerator

Choose the best term to complete each sentence.

1. A fraction can also be written as a ____.

2. An object that is divided into ten equal parts is divided into ____.

3. An object that is divided into a hundred equal parts is divided into ____.

CONCEPTS AND SKILLS

Write as a fraction or mixed number, and as a decimal. (Lessons 1–3, pp. 540–545)

4. two tenths

5. eight hundredths

6. six and five tenths

7. twenty and two hundredths

8. seven and eleven hundredths

Compare. Write >, <, or = for each ⬤. (Lessons 5–6, pp. 548–551)

9. 1.9 ⬤ 1.7

10. 0.05 ⬤ 0.5

11. 0.04 ⬤ $\frac{4}{100}$

Order the numbers from least to greatest. (Lessons 5–6, pp. 548–551)

12. 0.17   0.71   0.70

13. 3.03   3.3   3.13

14. $\frac{8}{10}$ 0.7 $\frac{11}{100}$

Add or subtract. (Lesson 8, pp. 556–558)

15. $\begin{array}{r} 3.4 \\ + \ 7.2 \\ \hline \end{array}$

16. $\begin{array}{r} 6.71 \\ + \ 2.56 \\ \hline \end{array}$

17. $\begin{array}{r} 8.51 \\ - \ 2.30 \\ \hline \end{array}$

18. $\begin{array}{r} 5.24 \\ - \ 1.15 \\ \hline \end{array}$

19. $\begin{array}{r} 4.00 \\ - \ 2.67 \\ \hline \end{array}$

PROBLEM SOLVING

Solve. (Lessons 4, 9, pp. 546, 560–562)

20. Dad buys 2 shirts for $11.50 each. He gives the cashier two 20-dollar bills. Is it reasonable to get two 10-dollar bills as change?

Write About It

Show You Understand

If a quarter is $\frac{1}{4}$ of a dollar, what fraction of a dollar is 3 quarters?

Explain your reasoning.

Extra Practice

Set A (Lesson 1, pp. 540–541)

Write as a decimal.

1. $\frac{5}{10}$
2. $\frac{8}{10}$
3. $\frac{2}{10}$
4. three tenths
5. six tenths

Set B (Lesson 2, pp. 542–543)

Write as a fraction.

1. 0.09
2. 0.13
3. thirty hundredths
4. six hundredths

Set C (Lesson 3, pp. 544–545)

Write each as a decimal.

1. $5\frac{8}{10}$
2. $2\frac{34}{100}$
3. six and six tenths
4. three and eighty hundredths

Set D (Lesson 5, pp. 548–549)

Compare. Write >, <, or = for each ⬤.

1. 1.8 ⬤ 1.9
2. 0.03 ⬤ 0.3
3. 6.06 ⬤ 0.66
4. 0.53 ⬤ 0.35

Set E (Lesson 6, pp. 550–551)

Order the numbers from least to greatest.

1. 0.6   0.16 $\frac{6}{100}$
2. 0.53 $\frac{35}{100}$ 5.30
3. 0.84 $\frac{8}{100}$ $\frac{8}{10}$

Set F (Lesson 8, pp. 556–558)

Add or subtract.

1. 6.5 + 1.3
2. 9.45 + .45
3. 8.7 − 2.5
4. 5.80 − 4.33
5. 3.74 − .88

6. 3.0 − 0.7
7. 6.05 − 0.95
8. 7.7 + 6.3
9. 2.18 + 0.55
10. 5.92 + 3.89

Extra Practice at **eduplace.com/map**

Creatures of the Sea

Fish are not the only animals that live in water. Sea otters and polar bears spend much of their lives in the ocean. Whales and dolphins, which are not fish, live in water all the time. All these creatures are sea mammals.

Unlike fish, sea mammals have to hold their breath underwater. Like humans, they breathe air through their lungs. Have you ever tried holding your breath? You can't do it for very long. Sea mammals can do it for much longer. Some can stay underwater for as long as 2 hours!

Sea Otter

├─4 feet─┤

Dolphin

├─6 feet─────┤

Walrus

├─12 feet──────────┤

Elephant Seal

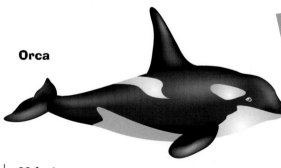

├─16 feet──────────────┤

Orca

├─20 feet──────────────────┤

Education Place

Visit Weekly Reader Connections at **eduplace.com/map** for more on this topic.

Problem Solving

The diagrams show the estimated length of five sea mammals. Use them for Problems 1–3.

1. Which sea mammal is $\frac{1}{4}$ the length of the elephant seal?

2. What fraction of all of the animals shown are longer than 15 ft?

3. The combined length of which two sea mammals is $\frac{1}{2}$ the length of the orca?

4. An elephant seal held its breath for $1\frac{4}{10}$ hours. Write this as a decimal.

5. A beluga whale held its breath for $\frac{3}{10}$ of an hour. A gray whale held its breath for 0.25 hours. Which whale held its breath longer?

It's All Equal!

Look at the figure on the right.
What fraction of the figure is shaded?

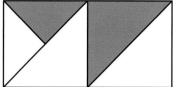

You can follow these steps to find out.

- First divide the figure into equal parts.

- Then count the total number of equal parts.

- Finally count the number of equal parts that are shaded.

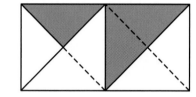

$\frac{3}{8}$ of the figure is shaded.

THINK
3 of the equal parts are shaded.
There are 8 equal parts.

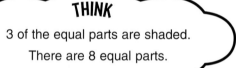

Try These!

**Draw each figure and divide it into equal parts.
Then tell what fraction of the figure is shaded.**

1.

2.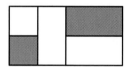

3.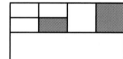

4.

5.

6.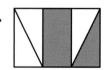

Explain Your Thinking Peter says that
$\frac{2}{4}$ of the figure at the right is green. Is
he right? Why or why not?

Prepare to Compare!

Suppose Damian walks $\frac{3}{5}$ of a mile to school and Patricia walks $\frac{2}{6}$ of a mile. Who walks farther?

You can use the fractions models found on Education Place at **eduplace.com/map** to help you find out.

Make a fraction strip to represent Damian's walk.

- Put your pointer over the picture of the workmats. Click on the fraction strip.

- Put your pointer over the **scissors** and select $\frac{1}{5}$.

- Click the top strip to cut it into fifths.

- Click **Fill.** Then click the first 3 sections of the fraction strip.

  The fraction strip now shows $\frac{3}{5}$.

Make a fraction strip to represent Patricia's walk.

- Use the **scissors** to select $\frac{1}{6}$.

- Click the second strip to cut it into sixths.

- Click **Fill.** Then click the first 2 sections of the fraction strip.

  The fraction strip now shows $\frac{2}{6}$.

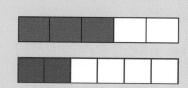

Solution: Since $\frac{3}{5}$ is longer than $\frac{2}{6}$, Damian walks farther.

Use the fraction models. Write $>$, $<$, or $=$ for each ⬤.

1. $\frac{3}{5}$ ⬤ $\frac{2}{3}$ 2. $\frac{5}{8}$ ⬤ $\frac{8}{12}$ 3. $\frac{1}{3}$ ⬤ $\frac{1}{2}$ 4. $\frac{2}{4}$ ⬤ $\frac{1}{5}$

5. $\frac{6}{12}$ ⬤ $\frac{5}{10}$ 6. $\frac{1}{8}$ ⬤ $\frac{1}{6}$ 7. $\frac{1}{4}$ ⬤ $\frac{2}{5}$ 8. $\frac{3}{10}$ ⬤ $\frac{4}{12}$

 Unit 7 Test

VOCABULARY (Open Response)

Choose the best term to complete each sentence.

Vocabulary

tenths

equivalent fractions

hundredths

mixed number

1. Fractions that name the same part of a whole are called ____.

2. A number that is made up of a whole number and a fraction is called a ____.

3. You can read 0.55 as fifty-five ____.

CONCEPTS AND SKILLS (Open Response)

**Write a fraction for the part of the drawing that is yellow.
Then write a fraction for the part that is not yellow.** (Chapter 18)

4.

5.

6.

Write *equivalent* or *not equivalent* to describe the fractions. (Chapter 18)

7. $\frac{1}{2}$ and $\frac{2}{4}$

8. $\frac{4}{5}$ and $\frac{2}{10}$

9. $\frac{1}{3}$ and $\frac{3}{9}$

10. $\frac{2}{8}$ and $\frac{1}{4}$

Write an improper fraction and a mixed number for the shaded part. (Chapter 18)

11.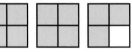

12.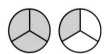

13.

Order the fractions or decimals from greatest to least. (Chapters 19–20)

14. $\frac{4}{6}$ $\frac{5}{6}$ $\frac{1}{6}$

15. $\frac{1}{3}$ $\frac{1}{2}$ $\frac{1}{4}$

16. $\frac{3}{8}$ $\frac{1}{8}$ $\frac{4}{7}$

17. 1.3 2.4 2.3

18. 1.20 2.3 0.3

19. 0.45 0.13 0.21

5. Fred ran 0.7 of a mile. Amanda ran $\frac{4}{10}$ of a mile. Who ran farther?

(Chapter 20, Lesson 6)

6. Lupe drew all the lines of symmetry in a square. How many lines did she draw? Explain your reasoning.

(Chapter 16, Lesson 3)

7. Lou placed the points on this grid.

Where should he place the last point to form a square?

(Chapter 6, Lesson 7; Chapter 15, Lesson 2)

8. Fong is playing a game using the spinner below. He receives a point every time he spins a 2. What is the probability of Fong receiving a point?

(Chapter 7, Lesson 3)

9. Olanda and Maria each have a 1-gallon can of paint. Olanda uses $\frac{5}{8}$ of her can. Maria uses $\frac{3}{8}$ of her can. How much more paint does Olanda use than Maria?

(Chapter 19, Lesson 5)

10. Andy's father is building a fence around his backyard. He made a drawing to help him find the amount of fence he will need.

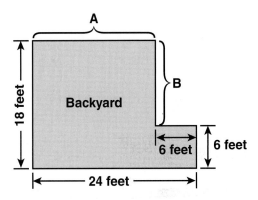

A How many feet of fence will Andy's father need for the side labeled A? for the side labeled B? Explain how you decided.

B What is the perimeter of the backyard? Write your answer in feet.

C Andy's father plans to buy the fence in 6-foot sections. How many sections will he have to buy to fence in the backyard? Explain your thinking.

(Chapter 17, Lesson 2)

Education Place

Look for Cumulative Test Prep at **eduplace.com/map** for more practice.

Vocabulary Wrap-Up for Unit 7

Look back at the big ideas and vocabulary in this unit.

Big Ideas

You can represent an equal part of a whole or an equal part of a group using a fraction.

You can name the same amount using an improper fraction or a mixed number.

You can name the same amount using a fraction or a decimal.

Key Vocabulary

fraction

improper fraction

mixed number

decimal

Math Conversations

Use your new vocabulary to discuss these big ideas.

1. Explain how $\frac{3}{6}$ and $\frac{1}{2}$ are related. Use pictures or fraction strips.

2. Explain how to order $\frac{8}{10}$, 0.2, and 0.6 from least to greatest.

3. Explain the steps you follow to find $\frac{1}{5} + \frac{3}{5}$.

4. Explain the steps you follow to find $6.9 - 3.2$.

5. **Write About It** If you wanted to find out how $\frac{5}{4}$ looks like as a mixed number, how could pictures or fraction strips help you?

$\frac{1}{10}$ of the kids in our class have been to the dentist this month.

You could also write that as the decimal 0.1

Multiply by 1-Digit Numbers

page 578

Divide by 1-Digit Divisors

page 608

Multiplication and Division by 1-Digit Numbers

Reading Mathematics

Reviewing Vocabulary

Here are some math vocabulary words that you should know.

dividend   the number that is divided

divisor   the number that divides the dividend

factors   the numbers that are multiplied

product   the answer to a multiplication problem

quotient   the answer to a division problem

Reading Words and Symbols

You can describe an array using both words and symbols. There are 4 rows of hearts with 6 hearts in each row.

$$4 \times 6 = 24$$

number of groups   number in each group   total number

$$24 \div 4 = 6$$

total number   number of groups   number in each group

Use words and symbols to answer the questions.

1. How many groups of stars are there? How many stars are in each group?

2. What multiplication sentence can you write to describe the group of stars? What division sentence can you write?

Reading Test Questions

Choose the correct answer for each.

3. Determine which picture represents 12 ÷ 2.

a. [☐ ☐ ☐ ☐ ☐ ☐]
[☐ ☐ ☐ ☐ ☐ ☐]

b. [☐ ☐ ☐]
[☐ ☐ ☐]

c. [☐ ☐]
[☐ ☐]
[☐ ☐]
[☐ ☐]

d. [☐ ☐]
[☐ ☐]

Determine means "decide" or "figure out."

---

4. Ed has 18 cherries. He separates them into 3 equal portions. How many cherries are in each portion?

a. 3   **b.** 6   **c.** 8   **d.** 9

Portion means "part" or "section."

5. Which symbol makes the number sentence true?

$$5 \bullet 7 = 35$$

a. +   **c.** ×

b. −   **d.** ÷

True means "correct" or "right."

Learning Vocabulary

Watch for these words in this unit. Write their definitions in your journal.

regroup

remainder

Literature Connection

Read "Elephants on the Move" on Page 656. Then work with a partner to answer the questions about the story.

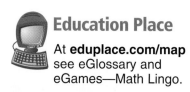

Education Place

At **eduplace.com/map**
see eGlossary and
eGames—Math Lingo.

Multiply by 1-Digit Numbers

INVESTIGATION

Using Data

This student is at a museum making huge bubbles with a bubble maker. The recipe below is for bubble solution that you can make at home. What could you use to measure the "parts" in the recipe?

Bubble Recipe
40 parts water
4 parts dish soap
1 part glycerine
1 part white corn syrup
Makes 1 batch.

Use What You Know

Use this page to review and remember what you need to know for this chapter.

VOCABULARY

Vocabulary
array
factor
multiple
product

1. A number that is multiplied is called a ____.

2. The answer to a multiplication problem is called the ____.

3. When you multiply a number by any whole number you get a ____ of that number.

CONCEPTS AND SKILLS

Find the product.

4. $\begin{array}{r} 2 \\ \times\ 0 \\ \hline \end{array}$

5. $\begin{array}{r} 10 \\ \times\ 1 \\ \hline \end{array}$

6. $\begin{array}{r} 3 \\ \times\ 8 \\ \hline \end{array}$

7. $\begin{array}{r} 7 \\ \times\ 2 \\ \hline \end{array}$

8. $\begin{array}{r} 10 \\ \times\ 5 \\ \hline \end{array}$

9. $\begin{array}{r} 6 \\ \times\ 0 \\ \hline \end{array}$

10. $\begin{array}{r} 7 \\ \times\ 7 \\ \hline \end{array}$

11. $\begin{array}{r} 9 \\ \times\ 3 \\ \hline \end{array}$

12. 5×5

13. 7×4

14. 4×8

15. 9×6

Round to the place of the underlined digit.

16. <u>8</u>4

17. <u>2</u>5

18. <u>3</u>24

19. $<u>9</u>.27

 Write About It

20. Write at least 3 number sentences that describe the array below.

Facts Practice, See page 668.

Multiply Multiples of 10, 100, and 1,000

Objective Use patterns and basic facts to multiply.

Learn About It

On March 6, 1876 Alexander Graham Bell spoke to his assistant using his invention, the telephone. Today, some sales people make over 200 telephone calls a day!

If Mrs. Cohen makes 200 telephone calls a day, how many calls will she make in 4 days?

You can use basic facts and patterns of zeros to help you multiply **multiples** of 10, 100, and 1,000.

Use the basic fact.

Then use a pattern of zeros.

$4 \times 2 = 8$
$4 \times 20 = 80$
$4 \times 200 = 800$

Think
To find the product first write the product of the basic fact. Then add on the same number of zeros as in the **factors**.

Solution: Mrs. Cohen will make 800 telephone calls in 4 days.

Guided Practice

Use a basic fact and patterns to find each product.

1. $3 \times 2 = \blacksquare$
   $3 \times 20 = \blacksquare$
   $3 \times 200 = \blacksquare$
   $3 \times 2,000 = \blacksquare$

2. $4 \times 3 = \blacksquare$
   $4 \times 30 = \blacksquare$
   $4 \times 300 = \blacksquare$
   $4 \times 3,000 = \blacksquare$

3. $5 \times 6 = \blacksquare$
   $5 \times 60 = \blacksquare$
   $5 \times 600 = \blacksquare$
   $5 \times 6,000 = \blacksquare$

Ask Yourself

• What basic fact can help me find the product?

• What pattern of zeros can help me?

Explain Your Thinking ▶ Use $4 \times 5 = 20$ to find $4 \times 5,000$. What can you predict about the product when there is a zero in the basic fact?

Use a basic fact and patterns to help you find each product.

4. $1 \times 9 = \blacksquare$
$1 \times 90 = \blacksquare$
$1 \times 900 = \blacksquare$
$1 \times 9{,}000 = \blacksquare$

5. $2 \times 6 = \blacksquare$
$2 \times 60 = \blacksquare$
$2 \times 600 = \blacksquare$
$2 \times 6{,}000 = \blacksquare$

6. $3 \times 7 = \blacksquare$
$3 \times 70 = \blacksquare$
$3 \times 700 = \blacksquare$
$3 \times 7{,}000 = \blacksquare$

7. $4 \times 4 = \blacksquare$
$4 \times 40 = \blacksquare$
$4 \times 400 = \blacksquare$
$4 \times 4{,}000 = \blacksquare$

8. $7 \times 5 = \blacksquare$
$7 \times 50 = \blacksquare$
$7 \times 500 = \blacksquare$
$7 \times 5{,}000 = \blacksquare$

9. $8 \times 5 = \blacksquare$
$8 \times 50 = \blacksquare$
$8 \times 500 = \blacksquare$
$8 \times 5{,}000 = \blacksquare$

Find each product.

10. 2×50

11. 3×60

12. 6×60

13. 6×600

14. 5×300

15. 5×800

16. 9×900

17. $3 \times 3{,}000$

18. $4 \times 6{,}000$

19. $7 \times 8{,}000$

20. $5 \times 6{,}000$

21. $9 \times 4{,}000$

Solve.

22. A new 8-story office building has 40 telephones installed on each floor. How many telephones are there in the building?

23. **Mental Math** Mr. Cox drives a bus from Lenox to Carson and back again using the route on the right. If he made the round trip 5 times in May, how many miles did he drive in that month?

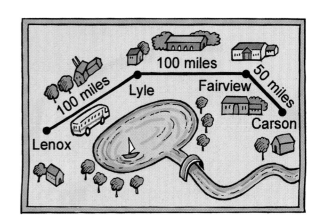

Mixed Review and Test Prep

Open Response

Multiply or divide. (Ch. 8, Lessons 4, Ch. 9, Lessons 3, 5, Ch. 10, Lessons 6, Ch. 11, Lessons 5, 9)

24. $18 \div 6$

25. 5×4

26. 6×6

27. $81 \div 9$

28. $35 \div 5$

29. 4×8

30. When a number is multiplied by 3, the product is 27,000. What is the number?
(Ch. 21, Lesson 1)

What basic fact did you use to find the number?

Extra Practice See page 607, Set A.

Audio Tutor 2/30 Listen and Understand

Model Multiplication

Objective Use base-ten blocks to multiply numbers.

Vocabulary
product
regroup

Materials
base-ten blocks

Work Together

You can use base-ten blocks to help you multiply
a two-digit number by a one-digit number.

▶ **Use base-ten blocks to find 3 × 23.**

STEP 1 Show 3 groups of 23.

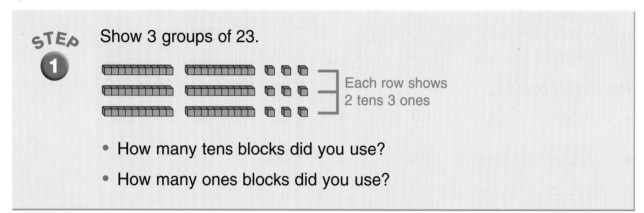

Each row shows
2 tens 3 ones

- How many tens blocks did you use?

- How many ones blocks did you use?

STEP 2 Record your answer
in a chart like the
one on the right.

Tens	Ones
6	9

23 ← number in each group
× 3 ← number of groups
69

- What is the **product** of 3 and 23?

▶ **Now use base-ten blocks to find 3 × 24.**

STEP 3 Show 3 groups of 24.

- How many tens blocks did
you use?

- How many ones blocks did
you use?

STEP 4 When the number of ones blocks is 10 or greater than 10, you need to **regroup** 10 ones as 1 ten.

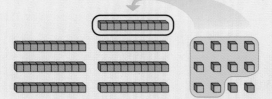

Tens	Ones
7	2

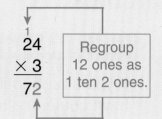

$$\begin{array}{r} \overset{1}{24} \\ \times\, 3 \\ \hline 72 \end{array}$$

Regroup 12 ones as 1 ten 2 ones.

- How many tens blocks and ones blocks do you have now?

- What is the product of 3 and 24?

On Your Own

Tell what multiplication sentence is shown by the blocks.

1.

2.

Use base-ten blocks to help you find each product.

3. 4×22 4. 2×24 5. 2×46 6. 3×15

7. 2×35 8. 4×13 9. 5×12 10. 2×38

11. Look back at Exercises 3–10. When did you have to regroup? How do you know when to regroup just by looking at the factors?

12. **Create and Solve** Write a problem that requires regrouping ones, and another that does not. Give your problems to a classmate to solve.

Talk About It • Write About It

You have learned how to model multiplication using base-ten blocks.

13. How many tens are in the product of 3 and 25?

14. How much greater is the product of 4 and 22 than the product of 3 and 22?

Lesson 3

Estimate Products

Objective Round numbers to estimate products.

Learn About It

If you bought milk in the 1800s, it would have come in glass bottles. Now we have paper cartons that don't shatter.

The head of the cafeteria of Baker School orders 285 cartons of milk each day. About how many cartons does she order in 5 days?

"About" means an estimate, or an answer that is close to the exact answer. One way to estimate is to round and multiply.

The picture shows one of the first milk cartons ever to be used. It was invented in 1915.

Estimate. $5 \times 285 = \blacksquare$.

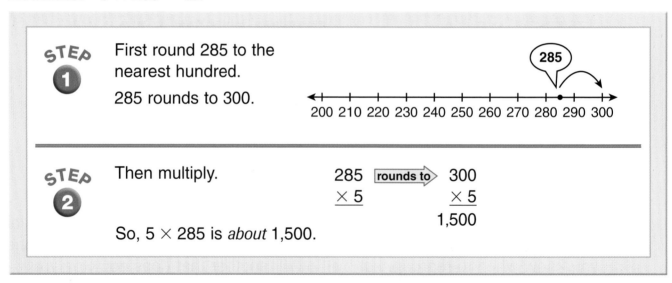

STEP 1 First round 285 to the nearest hundred.

285 rounds to 300.

200 210 220 230 240 250 260 270 280 290 300

STEP 2 Then multiply.

$$\begin{array}{r} 285 \\ \times 5 \end{array} \quad \text{rounds to} \quad \begin{array}{r} 300 \\ \times 5 \\ \hline 1,500 \end{array}$$

So, 5×285 is *about* 1,500.

Solution: The head of the cafeteria of Baker School orders about 1,500 cartons of milk in 5 days.

Other Examples

A. Estimate $7 \times 53 = \blacksquare$.

$$\begin{array}{r} 53 \\ \times 7 \end{array} \quad \text{rounds to} \quad \begin{array}{r} 50 \\ \times 7 \\ \hline 350 \end{array}$$

7×53 is *about* 350.

B. Estimate $6 \times 35 = \blacksquare$.

$$\begin{array}{r} 35 \\ \times 6 \end{array} \quad \text{rounds to} \quad \begin{array}{r} 40 \\ \times 6 \\ \hline 240 \end{array}$$

6×35 is *about* 240.

Remember
If the ones digit is 5 or more, round up to the next ten.

Try this activity to learn how to use a part to estimate a whole.

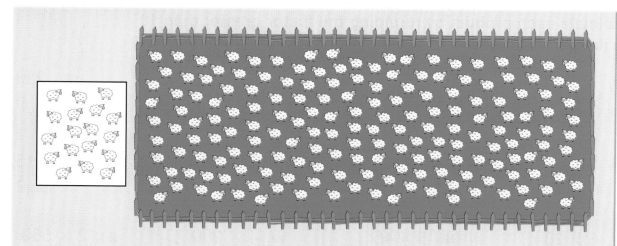

STEP 1 Count the sheep in the smaller picture. Then use the smaller picture to estimate the number of sheep in the larger picture.

- How many sheep are in the smaller picture?
- About how many groups like that are in the larger picture?
- About how many sheep are in the larger picture?

STEP 2 Now count the exact number of sheep in the larger picture.

- How many sheep are in the larger picture?
- How close was your estimate to the exact number?

Guided Practice

Estimate each product by rounding the factor greater than 10 to its greatest place.

1. 65
   × 2

2. 24
   × 7

3. 432
   × 3

4. 6 × 28

5. 9 × 93

6. 4 × 550

Ask Yourself
- Did I round to the nearest 10 or 100?
- Did I use basic multiplication facts to help me find the product?

Explain Your Thinking ▶ Look back at Exercise 1. How can you tell if the estimated product is greater than or less than the exact answer?

Go On

Practice and Problem Solving

Estimate each product by rounding the factor greater than 10 to its greatest place.

7. 42
    × 5

8. 85
    × 6

9. 28
    × 8

10. 385
    × 3

11. 223
    × 6

12. 37
    × 2

13. 75
    × 2

14. 584
    × 6

15. 458
    × 3

16. 615
    × 5

17. 6 × 28

18. 5 × 45

19. 4 × 280

20. 2 × 550

21. 5 × 24

22. 3 × 498

23. 8 × 127

24. 5 × 358

X Algebra • Symbols Compare. Write >, <, or = for each ●.

25. 6 × 30 ● 3 × 60

26. 3 × 481 ● 3 × 500

27. 10 × 88 ● 100 × 88

28. 37 × 3 ● 30 × 3

29. 7 × 31 ● (6 × 31) + 31

30. 18 × 52 ● 20 × 52

Solve.

31. A dairy farm operates seven days a week. It makes 465 gallons of milk each day. About how many gallons does the farm make in one week?

32. Mr. Lin's class drank 21 cartons of milk each day for 4 days. Ms. Colton's class drank 29 cartons of milk each day for 3 days. Estimate to find the class that drank more milk.

Data Use the sign for Problems 33–35.

33. Maureen bought a pint of milk, 8 ounces of cheese, and 1 pound of butter. About how much money did she spend?

34. Bill, Leroy, and Tony each want to buy a pint of milk and an ice cream cone. About how much money will they need in all?

35. Ethan bought 3 gallons of milk. He gave the clerk $10. About how much change did he get?

Dairy Prices	
Gallon of Milk	$ 2.19
Pint of Milk	$ 0.79
8 Ounces of Cheese	$ 1.99
Pound of Butter	$ 3.99
Ice Cream Cone	$ 1.75
Pint of Ice Cream	$ 3.69

Extra Practice See page 607, Set B.

Math Challenge

Case of the Missing Digits

Detective Dibble is hot on the trail of the missing digits. His only clues are the numbers left behind. Help him find the missing digits.

1. $\begin{array}{r} \blacksquare\blacksquare \\ \times\ 2 \\ \hline 82 \end{array}$

2. $\begin{array}{r} \blacksquare 3\blacksquare \\ \times\ 4 \\ \hline 5\blacksquare 8 \end{array}$

3. $\begin{array}{r} \blacksquare 4 \\ \times\ \blacksquare \\ \hline 42 \end{array}$

4. $\begin{array}{r} \blacksquare\blacksquare \\ \times\ 5 \\ \hline 60 \end{array}$

5. $\begin{array}{r} \blacksquare\blacksquare\blacksquare \\ \times\ 3 \\ \hline 756 \end{array}$

6. $\begin{array}{r} \blacksquare\blacksquare\blacksquare \\ \times\ 2 \\ \hline 694 \end{array}$

Check your understanding of Lessons 1–3.

Use a basic fact and patterns to help you find the product. (Lesson 1)

1. $3 \times 3 = \blacksquare$
   $3 \times 30 = \blacksquare$
   $3 \times 300 = \blacksquare$
   $3 \times 3,000 = \blacksquare$

2. $8 \times 2 = \blacksquare$
   $8 \times 20 = \blacksquare$
   $8 \times 200 = \blacksquare$
   $8 \times 2,000 = \blacksquare$

3. $2 \times 4 = \blacksquare$
   $2 \times 40 = \blacksquare$
   $2 \times 400 = \blacksquare$
   $2 \times 4,000 = \blacksquare$

Round to estimate each product by rounding the factor greater than 10 to its greatest place. (Lesson 3)

4. $\begin{array}{r} 71 \\ \times 7 \\ \hline \end{array}$

5. $\begin{array}{r} 35 \\ \times 5 \\ \hline \end{array}$

6. $\begin{array}{r} 234 \\ \times 6 \\ \hline \end{array}$

7. $\begin{array}{r} 771 \\ \times 3 \\ \hline \end{array}$

8. $\begin{array}{r} 578 \\ \times 6 \\ \hline \end{array}$

9. $\begin{array}{r} 884 \\ \times 4 \\ \hline \end{array}$

Solve. (Lesson 2)

10. When you multiply 36×3, how do you regroup the ones?

Multiply 2-Digit Numbers by 1-Digit Numbers

Objective Multiply 2-digit numbers by 1-digit numbers with and without regrouping.

Learn About It

Johannes Gutenberg invented the printing press in 1436. Before that, books had to be written by hand. Imagine how long that took!

Suppose Gutenberg wanted to print 3 copies of 14 different books. How many books would he print?

Multiply. $3 \times 14 = $ ■

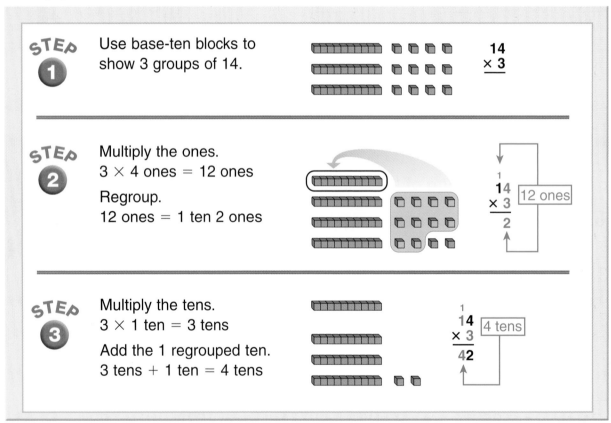

STEP 1	Use base-ten blocks to show 3 groups of 14.	$\begin{array}{r} 14 \\ \times\ 3 \\ \hline \end{array}$
STEP 2	Multiply the ones. 3×4 ones = 12 ones Regroup. 12 ones = 1 ten 2 ones	$\begin{array}{r} \overset{1}{1}4 \\ \times\ 3 \\ \hline 2 \end{array}$ 12 ones
STEP 3	Multiply the tens. 3×1 ten = 3 tens Add the 1 regrouped ten. 3 tens + 1 ten = 4 tens	$\begin{array}{r} \overset{1}{1}4 \\ \times\ 3 \\ \hline 42 \end{array}$ 4 tens

Solution: Gutenberg would print 42 books.

Other Examples

A. No Regrouping

$$\begin{array}{r} 32 \\ \times\ 3 \\ \hline 96 \end{array}$$

B. Regrouping Tens as Hundreds

$$\begin{array}{r} 82 \\ \times\ 4 \\ \hline 328 \end{array}$$

4×8 tens = 32 tens
32 tens = 3 hundreds 2 tens

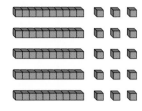

Ask Yourself

- What do I multiply first?
- Do I need to regroup ones? tens?
- Do I need to add any regrouped tens?

Use base-ten blocks to help you find each product.

1. 4×15

2. 5×13

Multiply.

3.	4.	5.	6.	7.
21	45	17	51	32
$\times 4$	$\times 2$	$\times 5$	$\times 4$	$\times 3$

Explain Your Thinking ▶ What is the greatest number of ones you can have before you need to regroup ones?

Practice and Problem Solving

Find each product.

8. 4×13

9. 3×15

10. 4×16

11.	12.	13.	14.
23	34	21	33
$\times 2$	$\times 2$	$\times 5$	$\times 2$

15.	16.	17.	18.
42	14	38	21
$\times 4$	$\times 5$	$\times 2$	$\times 7$

19. 2×41 **20.** 3×25 **21.** 4×32 **22.** 5×41

23. 3×53 **24.** 5×18 **25.** 7×31 **26.** 2×93

Go On

Algebra • **Functions** Complete each table.

Rule: Multiply by 6	
Input	Output
21	126
27. 15	▪
28. 12	▪
29. ▪	60

Rule: Multiply by 3	
Input	Output
30. ▪	30
72	216
31. 85	▪
32. 90	▪

33. | Rule: Multiply by ▪ | |
| --- | --- |
| Input | Output |
| 55 | 110 |
| 42 | 84 |
| **34.** 25 | ▪ |
| **35.** 18 | ▪ |

 Data Use the graph for Problems 36–40.

36. Carla's school voted on their favorite type of reading material. Each student voted only once. How many students voted?

37. How many students chose books as their favorite reading material? How many chose magazines?

38. **Represent** Write a number sentence to show the total number of students who did not choose magazines.

39. **Explain** How many more students chose books than chose magazines? How did you figure out the answer?

40. **Write About It** Suppose 9 more students chose books. What would the new row for books look like? Explain your reasoning.

Favorite Things to Read	
Type of Reading Material	Number of Students
Book	🧍🧍🧍🧍🧍🧍
Magazine	🧍🧍🧍🧍🧍
Newspaper	🧍🧍🧍
Each 🧍 stands for 6 students.	

Mixed Review and Test Prep

Open Response

Look at the figure below.

(Ch. 17, Lessons 2, 4)

41. What is the perimeter of the square?

42. What is the area of the square?

1 ft
1 ft

Multiple Choice

43. There are 8 rows of students in a school picture. Each row has 22 students. How many students are in the picture?

(Ch. 21, Lesson 4)

A 30   C 176

B 66   D 1,616

Extra Practice See page 607, Set C.

Math Reasoning

Multiply in a Different Way

You don't always have to use the standard method to multiply.

The models show how to multiply in a different way.

Standard Method:	**Multiply 4 × 12 in a different way.**

Multiply 4 × 12.

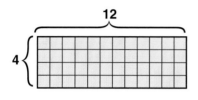

$4 \times 12 = \blacksquare$

$4 \times 12 = 48$

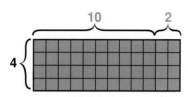

$4 \times 12 = \blacksquare$

$4 \times (10 + 2) = \blacksquare$

$(4 \times 10) + (4 \times 2) = \blacksquare$

$40 + 8 = 48$

How does writing 12 as 10 + 2 help to multiply the numbers?

You can also use an array to show the multiplication.

Standard Method:

$4 \times 12 = 48$

$4 \times 12 = \blacksquare$

$(4 \times 10) + (4 \times 2) = \blacksquare$

$40 + 8 = 48$

Find each product. Use one of the methods shown above and the standard method.

1. 38
   × 2

2. 61
   × 4

3. 43
   × 3

4. 29
   × 2

5. 72
   × 4

6. **Analyze** How are the methods alike? How are they different?

Multiply 3-Digit Numbers by 1-Digit Numbers

Vocabulary

regroup

Objective Multiply when one factor is a 3-digit number.

Learn About It

A school supply store sold 3 boxes of ballpoint pens last week. Each box had 126 pens. How many ballpoint pens did the store sell last week?

Multiply. $3 \times 126 = $ ▨

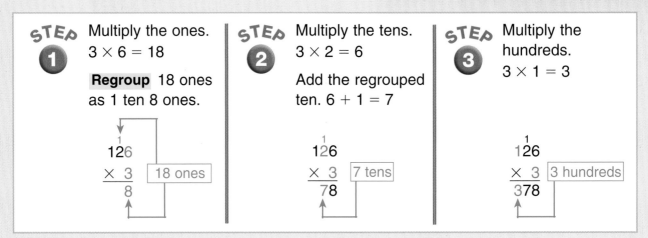

STEP 1 Multiply the ones.
$3 \times 6 = 18$

Regroup 18 ones as 1 ten 8 ones.

$$\begin{array}{r} \overset{1}{12}6 \\ \times\ 3 \\ \hline 8 \end{array}$$ 18 ones

STEP 2 Multiply the tens.
$3 \times 2 = 6$

Add the regrouped ten. $6 + 1 = 7$

$$\begin{array}{r} \overset{1}{12}6 \\ \times\ 3 \\ \hline 78 \end{array}$$ 7 tens

STEP 3 Multiply the hundreds.
$3 \times 1 = 3$

$$\begin{array}{r} \overset{1}{12}6 \\ \times\ 3 \\ \hline 378 \end{array}$$ 3 hundreds

Solution: $3 \times 126 = 378$

Other Examples

A. No Regrouping

$$\begin{array}{r} 103 \\ \times\ 2 \\ \hline 206 \end{array}$$

B. Regrouping Tens

$$\begin{array}{r} \overset{2}{2}70 \\ \times\ 3 \\ \hline 810 \end{array}$$
3×7 tens = 21 tens
21 tens = 2 hundreds 1 ten

Guided Practice

Find each product.

1. $\begin{array}{r} 234 \\ \times\ 2 \\ \hline \end{array}$
2. $\begin{array}{r} 218 \\ \times\ 4 \\ \hline \end{array}$
3. $\begin{array}{r} 140 \\ \times\ 7 \\ \hline \end{array}$
4. $\begin{array}{r} 121 \\ \times\ 5 \\ \hline \end{array}$

Ask Yourself
• Do I need to regroup ones? tens?
• Do I need to add any regrouped numbers?

Explain Your Thinking ▶ Compare multiplying with 3-digit numbers to multiplying with 2-digit numbers.

Find each product.

5. 202
   × 4

6. 394
   × 2

7. 109
   × 4

8. 413
   × 2

9. 116
   × 2

10. 184
    × 2

11. 124
    × 4

12. 262
    × 3

13. 130
    × 5

14. 241
    × 3

15. 2 × 317

16. 3 × 143

17. 5 × 115

18. 6 × 112

19. 7 × 114

20. 4 × 150

21. 2 × 493

22. 3 × 329

Algebra • **Symbols** Compare. Write >, <, or = for each ●.

23. 512 × 4 ● 4 × 512

24. 82 × 2 ● 100 + 50 + 4

25. 0 × 8,379 ● 8 × 379

26. 8 × 301 ● (8 × 300) + (8 × 1)

27. 4 × 223 ● 4 × 232

28. 39 × 4 × 8 ● 39 × 3 × 8

29. Last week Mr. Masumoto sold 215 ballpoint pens. He sold 4 times as many pencils as pens. How many pencils did he sell?

30. **Analyze** Is the product of a 2-digit number and a 1-digit number always a 3-digit number? Explain your thinking.

31. Last year Ned collected 204 ballpoint pens. This year he collected 3 times as many as last year. How many pens does Ned now have in his collection?

32. **Reasoning** A Ferris wheel has 16 seats. Each seat holds 2 people. If every seat is filled for each ride and no one rides twice, how many people can ride in 4 rides?

Mixed Review and Test Prep

Open Response

Write each fraction as a decimal.

(Ch. 20, Lessons 1, 2, 3)

33. $\frac{3}{10}$

34. $\frac{13}{100}$

35. $\frac{1}{2}$

36. $1\frac{6}{10}$

37. $2\frac{68}{100}$

38. $3\frac{4}{10}$

39. A town's new park is in the shape of a regular pentagon. Each side is 119 feet. What is the perimeter of the park?

(Ch. 21, Lesson 5)

Explain your reasoning.

Audio Tutor 2/33 Listen and Understand

Problem-Solving Strategy
Solve a Simpler Problem

Objective Use a simpler problem to help you solve complex problems.

Problem Mike invents a machine that does homework. He uses the machine 339 times. His best friend Joe uses it 265 times. The machine uses 7 pieces of paper each time. How many pieces of paper are used in all?

UNDERSTAND

This is what you know.

- Mike uses the machine 339 times.

- Joe uses it 265 times.

- The machine uses 7 pieces of paper each time.

PLAN

You can use easier numbers to help you decide how to solve the problem.

SOLVE

STEP 1
Choose easier numbers to decide how to solve the problem.

What if Mike used it 3 times and Joe used it 2 times?

Add.	Then multiply.
3	5
+ 2	× 7
5	35

STEP 2
Reread the problem. Solve using the original numbers.

Add.	Then multiply.
	2
339	604
+ 265	× 7
604	4,228

So, 4,228 pieces of paper are used.

LOOK BACK

Look back at the problem.

Does the solution answer the question?

Use the Ask Yourself questions to help you solve each problem.

1. The regular price of a box of paper is $9.99. The sale price is $7.59. If Mike buys 4 boxes on sale, how much money will he save?

2. Suppose Mike's machine used 5 pieces of paper each time. If Mike used it 155 times, Joe used it 284 times, and Ana used it 262 times, how many sheets were used?

   (Hint) Decide which operation to use first.

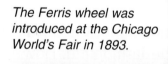

Ask Yourself

UNDERSTAND **What do I know?**

PLAN **Can I work with easier numbers?**

SOLVE **Which operations should I use?**

LOOK BACK **Does my answer make sense?**

Independent Practice

Use easier numbers to help you solve each problem.

3. The original Ferris wheel measured 790 feet around. Suppose you rode it 4 times, and each ride took you around twice. How many feet did you travel?

4. The original Ferris wheel held 2,160 people. On one ride, there were 1,165 empty seats. On another ride, there were 1,250 empty seats. How many seats were full during the two rides?

5. If the London Eye Ferris wheel can carry 800 passengers in a half hour, how many people can it carry in 4 hours?

The Ferris wheel was introduced at the Chicago World's Fair in 1893.

The London Eye opened in the year 2000.

Mixed Problem Solving

Solve. Show your work. Tell what strategy you used.

6. **Money** Jan has twice as much money as Sam. Sam has $2 less than Pam. If Pam has $10, how much money does Jan have?

7. Vinnie folded a piece of paper in half and then in half again. Next he punched 2 holes in the folded paper. How many holes were in the paper when Vinnie unfolded it?

8. Sue is stacking boxes. There are 8 boxes in the bottom row and 1 box in the top row. If each row has one less box than the row below it, how many boxes are there?

You Choose

Strategy
- Act It Out
- Draw a Picture
- Find a Pattern
- Solve a Simpler Problem
- Work Backward

Computation Method
- Mental Math
- Estimation
- Paper and Pencil
- Calculator

 Data Use the price list for Problems 9–12. Then tell which method you chose.

9. Mrs. Rodriguez bought two fruit baskets at the farm stand. How much did she spend?

10. Martin bought 3 loaves of bread, 2 apple pies, and a jar of jam. Andrew bought a fruit basket. Which boy spent more money?

11. Carmen bought 3 jars of jam and a loaf of bread. She gave the clerk $10. How much change should she get?

12. **You Decide** Joan wants to buy 3 different items. She has $16. What items can she buy?

Farm Stand Price List	
Jar of Jam	$1.59
Apple Pie	$3.95
Loaf of Bread	$1.65
Fruit Basket	$12.89

Problem Solving on Tests

Multiple Choice

Choose the letter of the correct answer.

1. Use the pictograph. How many students in the survey chose grilled cheese as their favorite lunch?

Favorite Lunches	
hot dogs	♀♀
grilled cheese	♀♀♀♀♀
pizza	♀♀♀

Each ♀ = 4 students.

A 5   **B** 20   **C** 40   **D** 200

(Chapter 6, Lesson 5)

2. Marta is 3 feet 2 inches tall. Petros is 3 inches shorter than Daniel. Daniel is 8 inches taller than Marta. How tall is Petros?

F 2 ft 9 in.   **H** 3 ft 7 in.

G 2 ft 11 in.   **J** 3 ft 11 in.

(Chapter 13, Lesson 4)

Open Response

Solve each problem.

3. Smoothies cost $2.19. Mrs. Yee has $8.00 to buy a smoothie for herself and 3 for her children. Does she have enough money? Explain.

(Chapter 3, Lesson 4)

4. Carly lives $\frac{1}{2}$ mile east of school. Nan lives $\frac{2}{3}$ mile east of school. Molly lives between Carly and Nan. Who lives closest to the school?

(Chapter 19, Lesson 3)

Constructed Response

5. John earns $3.00 each Monday and each Wednesday by raking. On Sundays, he earns $5.00 for pulling weeds. He is saving his money to buy skateboards.

Skateboards	
Great Board	$39.99
Super Board	$59.99
Super-Deluxe Board	$99.99

a. How much money can he earn in one week? Show how you know.

b. Estimate how many weeks it will take him to earn enough money to buy each of the skateboards.

c. John wants to buy the Super Board for himself and the Great Board for his sister. How many weeks does he need to work?

(Chapter 3, Lesson 4)

Education Place

See **eduplace.com/map** for more Test-Taking Tips.

Regrouping Twice

Objective Multiply and regroup more than once.

In 1760, Ben Franklin made the first bifocals so he could see near and far.

Learn About It

Suppose an eyeglass factory shipped 185 pairs of glasses to an optometrist each month. How many eyeglasses did they ship to her in 5 months?

Multiply. $5 \times 185 = $ ■

Different Ways to Find 5×185

Way ① You can use paper and pencil.

STEP 1 Multiply the ones.
$$5 \times 5 = 25$$

Regroup 25 ones as 2 tens 5 ones.

$$\begin{array}{r} {}^{2} \\ 185 \\ \times\ 5 \\ \hline 5 \end{array}$$ 25 ones

STEP 2 Multiply the tens.
$$5 \times 8 = 40$$

Add the 2 regrouped tens.
$$40 + 2 = 42$$

Regroup 42 tens as 4 hundreds 2 tens.

$$\begin{array}{r} {}^{4\,2} \\ 185 \\ \times\ 5 \\ \hline 25 \end{array}$$ 42 tens

STEP 3 Multiply the hundreds.
$$5 \times 1 = 5$$

Add the 4 regrouped hundreds.
$$5 + 4 = 9$$

$$\begin{array}{r} {}^{4\,2} \\ 185 \\ \times\ 5 \\ \hline 925 \end{array}$$ 9 hundreds

---

Way ② You can use a calculator.

Press:

Display:  925

Solution: The factory shipped 925 eyeglasses.

Another Example

Multiply With 4-Digit Numbers

$$\begin{array}{r} {}^{1} \\ 8{,}734 \\ \times\quad 2 \\ \hline 17{,}468 \end{array}$$

Multiply the thousands. $2 \times 8 = 16$
Add the regrouped thousand. $16 + 1 = 17$
Regroup 17 thousands as 1 ten thousand, 7 thousands.

Guided Practice

Find each product. Regroup if needed.

Ask Yourself

- Do I need to regroup ones, tens, or hundreds?
- Do I need to add any regrouped numbers?

1. 125
    × 4

2. 243
    × 2

3. 714
    × 6

4. 2,416
    ×   3

5. 1,721
    ×   5

6. 2,621
    ×   4

Explain Your Thinking ▶ When regrouping is needed, what must you do with the numbers you regroup?

Practice and Problem Solving

Multiply. Regroup if needed.

7. 137
    × 6

8. 526
    × 3

9. 351
    × 4

10. 323
    ×   3

11. 1,123
    ×   3

12. 1,562
    ×   3

13. 3,215
    ×   4

14. 7,151
    ×   6

15. 8 × 116

16. 5 × 521

17. 5 × 221

18. 3 × 312

19. 7 × 1,413

20. 9 × 2,811

21. 6 × 6,251

22. 3 × 7,128

✗ **Algebra • Symbols** Compare the products. Write >, <, or = in the ●.

23. 4 × 316 ● 3 × 330

24. 3 × 691 ● 2 × 372

25. 4,391 × 5 ● 6 × 3,391

26. 2,925 × 3 ● 4 × 1,092

Go On ▶

Find the missing digit. Show your work.

27.
$$137 \times 8$$
$$1{,}09\blacksquare$$

28.
$$313 \times 6$$
$$1{,}8\blacksquare8$$

29.
$$5{,}621 \times 4$$
$$22{,}\blacksquare84$$

30.
$$4{,}016 \times 5$$
$$2\blacksquare{,}080$$

Solve.

31. All 2,392 students at Orange Elementary School had both of their eyes checked by the nurse. Seven teachers also had their eyes checked. How many eyes did the nurse check?

32. Earl is picking new frames for his glasses. He can choose from 3 silver frames, 2 gold frames, and 5 brown frames. If he picks a frame without looking, which color will he most likely get?

33. Mr. Wu needs 500 key chains for his shop. He ordered 6 boxes. Each box has 72 key chains. Did he order enough? How do you know?

34. Danielle spent $3.75 on snacks. Andrew spent twice as much as Danielle. How much did they both spend together?

35. **What's Wrong?** Look at Miriam's work at the right. It shows how Miriam multiplied 6 × 315. What did she do wrong?

> Miriam
>
> $$315 \times 6$$
> $$1{,}860$$

Mixed Review and Test Prep ✓

Open Response

Add or subtract. (Ch. 20, Lesson 8)

36.
$$1.4 + 0.5$$

37.
$$6.02 + 1.01$$

38.
$$7.0 - 0.7$$

39.
$$7.44 - 0.89$$

Multiple Choice

40. Bill's calculator shows the product 4,314. Which of these examples did he do?
(Ch. 21, Lesson 7)

A 7 × 618   C 8 × 728

B 6 × 719   D 5 × 832

Extra Practice See page 607, Set E.

Real–World Connection

Miles to Go

Three students walk a different number of miles in a walk-a-thon. How many feet did each travel?

Complete the table.

If Sergio walks 6 miles, how many yards does he walk? How did you find the answer?

| 1 mile = 5,280 feet |
| 1 mile = 1,760 yards |

Name	Number of miles walked		Number of feet walked
Abe	3	3 × 5,280	
Shondra	7	7 × 5,280	
Rosario	5		

Logical Thinking

Ten Times the Weight

- Atlas lifts weights. He lifts 4 pounds. Then he lifts ten times as much. How much does he lift?

- Atlas lifts ten times as much weight again. How much does he lift?

- Finally, Atlas tries to lift ten times as much weight again. How much does he try to lift?

What do you notice about the pattern of zeros each time Atlas lifted ten times as much weight?

Brain Teaser

Look at these four digits.

7 4 1 8

- Use the digits to make a three-digit number and a one-digit number so that their product is the *greatest* possible.

- Now use the digits to make a three-digit number and a one-digit number so that their product is the *least* possible.

Education Place

Check out **eduplace.com/map** for more brain teasers.

Multiply Money

Objective Multiply with money.

Learn About It

Long ago, people saved their coins in pots made of clay called pygg. They called these pots piggy banks. Today piggy banks are shaped like pigs and can be made of many different materials.

Scott has an empty piggy bank. He puts $2.25 per week into the bank for 3 weeks. How much money is in his piggy bank?

Use what you know about multiplying whole numbers to multiply money.

Different Ways to Find 3 × $2.25

Way ➊ You can use paper and pencil.

STEP 1 Multiply as if you were multiplying whole numbers.

$$\begin{array}{r} \overset{1}{2}25 \\ \times\ \ 3 \\ \hline 675 \end{array}$$

STEP 2 Write the dollar sign and decimal point in the product.

$$\begin{array}{r} \overset{1}{2}.25 \\ \times\ \ 3 \\ \hline \$6.75 \end{array}$$

> Write the decimal point in the product in the same place as the decimal point is in the money amount.

Way ➋ You can use mental math.

STEP 1 Multiply the dollars and the cents separately.

$$3 \times \$2.25 = (3 \times \$2) + (3 \times \$0.25)$$
$$= \quad \$6 \quad + \quad \$0.75$$

STEP 2 Then add.

$$\$6 + \$0.75 = \$6.75$$

Solution: Scott has $6.75 in his piggy bank.

Ask Yourself

• Do I need to regroup?

• Where will I place the dollar sign and the decimal point in the product?

Guided Practice

Find each product. Regroup if needed.

1. $3.24
    × 2

2. $1.15
    × 3

3. $1.13
    × 5

4. $3.18
    × 4

5. $4.53
    × 3

6. $2.25
    × 4

Explain Your Thinking ▶ Which is a reasonable answer for 2 × $1.50, $300 or $3.00? Explain how you know.

Practice and Problem Solving

Estimate, then multiply.

7. $7.24
    × 2

8. $8.11
    × 3

9. $9.23
    × 2

10. $1.16
    × 2

11. $1.92
    × 3

12. $2.41
    × 4

13. $2.81
    × 4

14. $1.19
    × 6

15. 6 × $2.51

16. 3 × $1.35

17. 2 × $3.87

18. 3 × $2.78

19. 9 × $2.17

20. 8 × $7.29

21. 6 × $9.55

22. 4 × $8.88

23. Stella has $4.45 in her piggy bank. Dan has $0.50 less than Stella. Al has twice as much money as Dan. How much money does Al have?

24. Samuel wants to buy 3 slices of pizza. If each slice costs $1.75, about how much money will he need? Explain your reasoning.

Solve.

25. Luisa wants to go on 6 rides at a fair. Each ride ticket costs $1.75. If Luisa pays for the tickets with a $20 bill, how much change should she get?

26. It costs $2.25 to see the Variety Show at the fair. Seven friends want to see it. If they received $4.25 in change, what was the total amount they first paid?

27. The first act of a play went from 8:15 P.M. to 9:00 P.M. Then there was a half-hour intermission. The second act lasted for an hour. At what time did the play end?

28. Each piggy bank below is 24 cm long. If a store displayed 9 of the banks on a shelf, tail-to-nose, how long would the line of banks be?

𝒳 Algebra • Functions Complete each table.

Rule: Multiply by 2	
Input	**Output**
$6.25	$12.50
29. $4.49	▦
30. $5.35	▦
31. ▦	$5.00

Rule: Multiply by 5	
Input	**Output**
$2.29	$11.45
32. $3.31	▦
33. ▦	$8.00
34. $5.05	▦

35.

Rule: Multiply by ▦	
Input	**Output**
$1.25	$5.00
$3.00	$12.00
36. $4.00	▦
37. $4.54	▦

Choose a Computation Method

Mental Math • Estimation • Paper and Pencil • Calculator

Solve.

38. Gerry's mom makes piggy banks to sell at a craft fair. She uses 4 corks on each bank for the legs. If she made 24 piggy banks, how many corks did she use?

39. Sari is having a birthday party. She buys 4 small piggy banks as party favors. Each bank costs $3.50. How much does Sari spend on the banks?

40. The Save-A-Buck Bank gives piggy banks to children who open accounts there. If 210 banks are given out each month, about how many are given out in 3 months?

41. A toy company orders shipments of piggy banks from a factory. There are 3,579 banks in each shipment. How many banks are there in 7 shipments?

Extra Practice See page 607, Set F.

Open Response

Find the sum. (Ch. 4, Lesson 1)

42. $4 + 5 + 1 + 6 + 5$

43. $3 + 2 + 7 + 8 + 7$

44. $1 + 7 + 9 + 3 + 8$

Multiple Choice

45. Which is the product?

(Ch. 21, Lesson 8)

$$\$1.43 \times 6$$

A $8.48   **C** $9.58

B $8.58   **D** $ 858

Calculator Connection

Problem Solving

NO Problem!

Suppose your calculator's multiplication key is broken. You can think of multiplication as repeated addition. Here is another way to find products with a calculator.

Find 5 × 7.

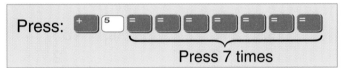

Press 7 times

Find 27 × 4.

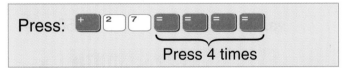

Press 4 times

Use this method to find each product. Check your answers by using the multiplication key.

1. 5×6 **2.** 7×19 **3.** 8×45

4. 7×225 **5.** 4×542 **6.** 6×343

Chapter Review/Test

VOCABULARY

Choose the best word to complete each sentence.

Vocabulary

factors

product

regroup

multiples

1. The numbers 30 and 80 are ____ of 10.

2. The numbers 5 and 2 are ____ of 10.

3. When you multiply two numbers, you get a ____.

CONCEPTS AND SKILLS

Estimate each product by rounding the greater factor to its greatest place.
(Lesson 3, pp. 584–586)

| 4. 79 × 3 | 5. 62 × 5 | 6. 127 × 8 | 7. 380 × 2 | 8. 551 × 6 |

Find each product. (Lessons 1, 4, 5, 7, 8, pp. 580–581, 588–593, 598–604)

| 9. 60 × 4 | 10. 800 × 7 | 11. 27 × 3 | 12. 42 × 4 |

| 13. 61 × 5 | 14. 112 × 8 | 15. 217 × 3 | 16. 463 × 2 |

17. 552 × 3   **18.** 328 × 6   **19.** 1,771 × 2   **20.** 2,163 × 4

21. $1.14 × 8   **22.** $0.79 × 5   **23.** $3.09 × 7   **24.** $2.56 × 4

PROBLEM SOLVING

Solve. (Lesson 6, pp. 594–596)

25. The Southborough School bus route is 9 miles. One year, Ms. Sato drove the bus 332 times, and Mr. Harding drove it 218 times. How many miles did the school bus travel that year?

Write About It

Show You Understand

When you multiply a three-digit number by a one-digit number, will you always get a three-digit product? Give examples to support your answer.

Extra Practice

Set A (Lesson 1, pp. 580–581)

Find each product.

1. 4×20 2. 3×500 3. 9×300 4. $8 \times 5{,}000$

Set B (Lesson 3, pp. 584–586)

Estimate each product.

1.	27 $\times\ 2$	2.	83 $\times\ 4$	3.	512 $\times\ 6$	4.	755 $\times\ 3$	5.	398 $\times\ 5$

Set C (Lesson 4, pp. 588–590)

Find each product.

1.	13 $\times\ 3$	2.	62 $\times\ 4$	3.	28 $\times\ 2$	4.	22 $\times\ 5$	5.	93 $\times\ 7$

Set D (Lesson 5, pp. 592–593)

Find each product.

1.	102 $\times\ 4$	2.	171 $\times\ 5$	3.	329 $\times\ 3$	4.	183 $\times\ 2$	5.	114 $\times\ 6$

Set E (Lesson 7, pp. 598–600)

Multiply. Regroup if needed.

1.	217 $\times\ 6$	2.	405 $\times\ 3$	3.	1,302 $\times\ 7$	4.	2,108 $\times\ 4$	5.	6,215 $\times\ 2$

Set F (Lesson 8, pp. 602–604)

Estimate, then multiply.

1.	$ 4.23 $\times\ 2$	2.	$3.19 $\times\ 5$	3.	$1.08 $\times\ 7$	4.	$5.86 $\times\ 2$	5.	$1.67 $\times\ 3$

Divide by 1-Digit Divisors

INVESTIGATION

Using Data

Volunteers are planting shrubs and flowers in front of a museum. The graph shows the types of flowers they planted. Each type of flower is planted in more than one row and each row has the same number of flowers. How might they plant the Zinnias?

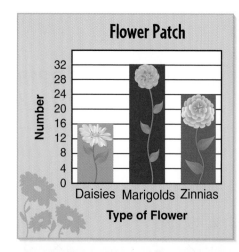

Flower Patch

Number

32
28
24
20
16
12
8
4
0

Daisies Marigolds Zinnias

Type of Flower

Use What You Know

**Use this page to review and remember
what you need to know for this chapter.**

VOCABULARY

Choose the best term to complete each sentence.

1. The number that is to be divided in a division problem is the ____.

2. The answer in a division problem is the ____.

3. The number dividing another number is the ____.

4. You can sometimes use a ____ fact to help you divide.

> **Vocabulary**
> divisor
> multiple
> dividend
> quotient
> multiplication

CONCEPTS AND SKILLS

Find each product.

5. 3×90

6. 4×55

7. 6×10

8. 2×35

9. 4×22

10. 3×32

11. 5×42

12. 7×15

Divide.

13. $7\overline{)49}$

14. $6\overline{)24}$

15. $8\overline{)56}$

16. $9\overline{)45}$

17. $16 \div 2$

18. $9 \div 3$

19. $36 \div 4$

20. $20 \div 5$

21. $72 \div 9$

22. $64 \div 8$

23. $63 \div 7$

24. $30 \div 6$

 Write About It

25. Explain how to divide the money shown into 3 equal groups. How much money is in each group?

Facts Practice, See page 670.

Use Mental Math to Divide

Objective Use patterns and basic facts to help you divide.

Vocabulary
dividend
divisor
quotient

Learn About It

A crowd of 1,600 people was divided into 8 large sections along a parade route. How many people are in each section?

Divide.   1,600   ÷   8 = ■ ← quotient

↑   ↑
dividend   divisor

You can use basic facts and patterns of zeros to help you divide multiples of 10, 100, and 1,000.

Use the basic fact.	$16 \div 8 = 2$
Then use a pattern of zeros.	$160 \div 8 = 20$
	$1,600 \div 8 = 200$

Think
The quotient has the same number of zeros as the dividend unless there is a zero in the basic fact.

Solution: There are 200 people in each section.

Another example: $40 \div 5 = 8$

$400 \div 5 = 80$

$4,000 \div 5 = 800$

Guided Practice

Use a basic fact and patterns to find each quotient.

1. $30 \div 6 = $ ■
$300 \div 6 = $ ■
$3,000 \div 6 = $ ■

2. $42 \div 7 = $ ■
$420 \div 7 = $ ■
$4,200 \div 7 = $ ■

Ask Yourself

- What basic fact can help me?

- How many zeros should be in the quotient?

Explain Your Thinking ▶ Use $20 \div 4 = 5$ to find $200 \div 4$.
What can you predict about the quotient when there is a zero in the basic fact?

Use a basic fact and patterns to find each quotient.

3. $36 \div 6 = \blacksquare$
   $360 \div 6 = \blacksquare$
   $3,600 \div 6 = \blacksquare$

4. $24 \div 3 = \blacksquare$
   $240 \div 3 = \blacksquare$
   $2,400 \div 3 = \blacksquare$

5. $20 \div 4 = \blacksquare$
   $200 \div 4 = \blacksquare$
   $2,000 \div 4 = \blacksquare$

Divide.

6. $270 \div 9$
7. $350 \div 7$
8. $490 \div 7$
9. $320 \div 8$

10. $240 \div 6$
11. $720 \div 8$
12. $200 \div 5$
13. $300 \div 6$

14. $1,800 \div 2$
15. $5,600 \div 7$
16. $3,000 \div 5$
17. $1,000 \div 2$

18. There are 150 cheerleaders marching in the parade in 5 equal groups. If each group has the same number of cheerleaders, how many are in each group?

19. The Fourth of July celebrations will feature a "Battle of the Bands." The 8 winning bands will share equally the total prize money of $2,400. How much will each band receive?

20. There were 350 balloons, but 30 burst. Eight clowns share the remaining balloons equally. How many balloons will each clown carry to give away at the parade?

21. **Analyze** There are 7 more children than adults running in the relay race. If 25 people are running in the race, how many of them are children? Explain how you know.

Open Response
Name each polygon. (Ch. 15, Lesson 2)

22.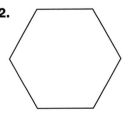

23.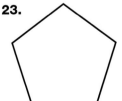

Multiple Choice
24. Third graders received a donation of 160 books. If each student received 2 books, how many third graders are there?
(Ch. 22, Lesson 1)

A 8

c 800

B 80

D 8,000

Audio Tutor 2/35 Listen and Understand

Model Division With Remainders

Objective Find remainders in division problems.

Vocabulary
remainder

Materials
counters

Work Together

At a library used-book sale, Alicia and her 3 friends buy a box of 25 books. Each friend wants to take home the same number of books. What is the greatest number of books each friend can take?

Work with a partner. Use counters to help you solve the problem.

 STEP 1

Divide 25 counters into 4 equal groups. Put any leftover counters aside.

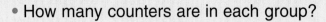

- How many counters are in each group?

- How many counters are left over?

Sometimes when you divide, you have a number left over. This is the **remainder**. The remainder must be less than the divisor.

How many books will each friend take home?

How many books are left over?

 STEP 2

Divide to show what you did.

number in
each group

Remember
R stands for
remainder.

number of
equal groups →

$$4\overline{)25}^{\,6\ R1}$$

number
left over

number
being divided

Extra Help at **eduplace.com/map**

STEP 3

Use 25 counters. Try making 5, 7, and 9 equal groups. Use the greatest number possible in each equal group. Record your work in a table like the one shown.

Total Number of Counters (Dividend)	Number of Groups (Divisor)	Number in Each Group (Quotient)	Number Left Over (Remainder)	Show the Division
25	4	6	1	6 R1 4)25
25	5			
25	7			
25	9			

- Look back at your table. Are the remainders less than, equal to, or greater than the divisors?

- Which division has a remainder of 0?

▶ You divided by making equal groups. Now try using repeated subtraction to find quotients and remainders.

Find 19 ÷ 3.

STEP 1

Use 19 counters. Remove 3 counters at a time until you cannot remove a full group of 3. Count how many groups of 3 you removed.

- How many groups of 3 counters did you remove?
- How many counters are left over?

STEP 2

Record the subtraction. Then show the division. Record the remainder if there is one.

```
                groups
  19
 - 3  ———→  1
  16
 - 3  ———→  2
  13
 - 3  ———→  3
  10
 - 3  ———→  4
   7
 - 3  ———→  5
   4
 - 3  ———→  6
   1  ———→  remainder
```

            6R1
         3)19

Go On

Use the picture to divide.

1.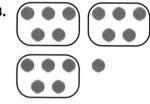

2.

3.

4.

Divide. Use counters and repeated subtraction to help you.

5. 18 ÷ 3

6. 15 ÷ 2

7. 16 ÷ 4

8. 29 ÷ 5

9. 21 ÷ 3

10. 19 ÷ 4

11. 24 ÷ 5

12. 29 ÷ 3

13. 22 ÷ 4

14. 28 ÷ 5

15. 30 ÷ 8

16. 18 ÷ 7

Divide. Use counters or draw a picture to help you.

17. Divide 18 into 3 equal groups.

18. Divide 18 into 4 equal groups.

19. Divide 16 into 4 equal groups.

20. Divide 16 into 3 equal groups.

21. Divide 20 into 5 equal groups.

22. Divide 20 into 6 equal groups.

23. Divide 15 into 3 equal groups.

24. Divide 15 into 4 equal groups.

Talk About It • Write About It

You learned how to find remainders in division problems.

25. Diane said that $5\overline{)16}$ $^{3\ R1}$. Jack said that $5\overline{)16}$ $^{2\ R6}$.
Who is right? Explain your answer.

26. What is the greatest remainder you can have when
the divisor is 5? How do you know?

Activity

Remainder Race

2 Players

What You'll Need

- a number cube labeled 1 to 6
- a game board like the one shown (Learning Tool 44)

How to Play

1 The first player rolls the number cube. He or she then writes the number rolled in an empty □ on the game board.

2 The first player then names the quotient and remainder for that problem. The other player checks that the quotient and remainder are correct.

3 The remainder is the number of points scored. If there is no remainder, the player scores 10 points.

4 Players take turns, repeating Steps 1–3. The first player to reach a total of 30 points wins.

5)3□	2)1□	3)2□	4)3□
3)1□	4)2□	5)2□	6)4□
5)1□	4)1□	6)4□	7)5□
8)6□	9)5□	7)4□	8)5□

Estimate Quotients

Objective Estimate quotients.

Vocabulary

compatible numbers

Learn About It

Volunteers at the Senior Center deliver meals to house-bound people. In the last 3 weeks, Mr. Sell delivered 54 meals. He delivered the same number each week. About how many meals did he deliver each week?

Since the problem asks for "about how many meals," you do not need an exact answer.

You can use compatible numbers to estimate the quotient.

MEALS ON WHEELS

Estimate. $54 \div 3 = \blacksquare$

Compatible numbers are numbers that are easy to divide.

Think of a number that is close to 54 that is easy to divide by 3.

Think

$$3\overline{)54} \rightarrow 3\overline{)60}^{\,20}$$

So $54 \div 3$ is about 20.

Solution: Mr. Sell delivered about 20 meals each week.

Other Examples

A. Estimate $118 \div 6$.

Think

$$6\overline{)118} \rightarrow 6\overline{)120}^{\,20}$$

So $118 \div 6$ is about 20.

B. Estimate $205 \div 4$.

Think

$$4\overline{)205} \rightarrow 4\overline{)200}^{\,50}$$

So $205 \div 4$ is about 50.

C. Estimate $383 \div 2$.

Think

$$2\overline{)383} \rightarrow 2\overline{)400}^{\,200}$$

So $383 \div 2$ is about 200.

Guided Practice

Estimate. Write the compatible numbers you used.

Ask Yourself
• What compatible numbers should I use?

1. $4\overline{)75}$ 2. $3\overline{)82}$ 3. $3\overline{)123}$ 4. $8\overline{)163}$

5. $9\overline{)190}$ 6. $7\overline{)623}$ 7. $146 \div 5$ 8. $251 \div 6$

9. $591 \div 3$ 10. $199 \div 7$ 11. $315 \div 8$ 12. $114 \div 4$

Explain Your Thinking ▶ If you estimate the quotient for $164 \div 4$ using the compatible numbers $160 \div 4$, will the estimate be greater than or less than the exact quotient? How do you know?

Practice and Problem Solving

Estimate. Write the compatible numbers you used.

13. $3\overline{)64}$ 14. $4\overline{)89}$ 15. $3\overline{)95}$

16. $4\overline{)79}$ 17. $2\overline{)177}$ 18. $3\overline{)208}$

19. $552 \div 8$ 20. $795 \div 4$ 21. $925 \div 3$

22. $396 \div 5$ 23. $214 \div 4$ 24. $150 \div 7$

Solve.

25. Last week Senior Center volunteers delivered 432 meals. If they delivered the same number of meals each day, about how many meals did they deliver each day?

26. Special boxes keep meals warm until they are delivered. One box has 48 meals in it, one box has 53 meals in it, and another box has 56 meals in it. About how many meals are there in all?

Go On

Estimate to decide if each quotient is greater than 50 or less than 50. Use this division example to help you: 250 ÷ 5 = 50.

27. 285 ÷ 5   **28.** 248 ÷ 5   **29.** 315 ÷ 5

30. 245 ÷ 4   **31.** 265 ÷ 3   **32.** 260 ÷ 6

𝒳 Algebra • Expressions Estimate to compare. Use > or < for each ⬤.

33. 73 ÷ 2 ⬤ 73 ÷ 5   **34.** 112 ÷ 5 ⬤ 212 ÷ 5

35. 550 ÷ 6 ⬤ 101 ÷ 2   **36.** 89 ÷ 3 ⬤ 45 ÷ 4

37. 231 ÷ 7 ⬤ 138 ÷ 3   **38.** 372 ÷ 4 ⬤ 434 ÷ 3

Solve.

39. The Senior Center stores 238 meal trays in 6 boxes. About how many meal trays are stored in each box?

40. Write a division problem with a quotient between 40 and 50. Explain how you chose the divisor and dividend.

📊 Data Use the bar graph for Problems 41–45.

41. About how many senior citizens went swimming this week?

42. Which activity was the most popular?

43. Which activity was twice as popular as bowling?

44. **Mental Math** Last week there were 11 fewer painters than this week. How many senior citizens painted last week?

45. **Create and Solve** Use the bar graph to write a word problem. Exchange problems with a classmate and solve.

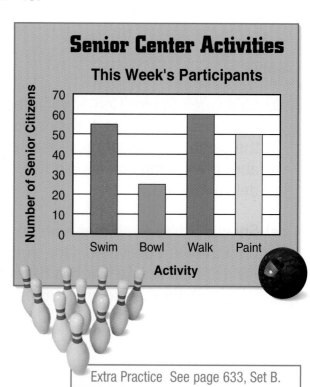

Senior Center Activities

This Week's Participants

Number of Senior Citizens

Activity: Swim, Bowl, Walk, Paint

Extra Practice See page 633, Set B.

Math Challenge

Divisor Puzzle

Find three different paths to get to number 60.

- Each path starts at a corner of the big triangle.

- Use the corner number as a divisor.

- Cross only sides of small triangles.

- Move to the next triangle only if its number can be divided by your divisor and give a remainder of zero.

What do you notice about all the divisors and the number 60?

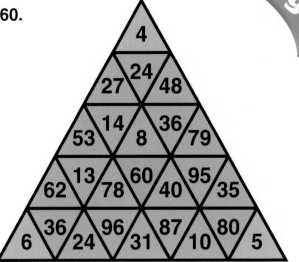

Check your understanding of Lessons 1–3.

Divide. (Lessons 1–2)

1. $240 \div 3$
2. $300 \div 5$
3. $800 \div 2$

4. $23 \div 3$
5. $25 \div 6$
6. $18 \div 4$

Estimate. Write the compatible numbers you used. (Lesson 3)

7. $78 \div 4$
8. $61 \div 2$
9. $185 \div 3$

Solve. (Lesson 3)

10. A local store has donated $75 to your sports team. Your team will use the money to buy new uniform shirts. The shirts cost $9 each. About how many new shirts can your team buy?

Extra Practice at **eduplace.com/map**

Lesson 4

Two-Digit Quotients

Objective Use base-ten blocks to show division with two-digit quotients.

Vocabulary

quotient

dividend

divisor

remainder

Learn About It

Forty-six police officers have new duties. Teams of 4 officers each run self-defense classes or train new recruits. The remaining officers are on bicycle patrol. How many teams are there? How many officers are on bicycles?

Divide. $46 \div 4 = $ ■ or $4\overline{)46}$

STEP 1 Use base-ten blocks to show 46.

  ← **quotient** (number of teams)

$4\overline{)46}$ ← **dividend** (officers in all)

↑

divisor (number of officers)

STEP 2 Divide 4 tens into 4 equal groups. Put 1 ten into each group.

$$\begin{array}{r} 1 \\ 4\overline{)46} \\ -4 \\ \hline 0 \end{array}$$

← Write 1 in the tens place.

← Multiply. 1×4 tens = 4 tens

← Subtract. $4 - 4$

Compare. $0 < 4$

STEP 3 Divide the 6 ones. Put 1 one into each group. There are 2 ones left over. The remainder is 2.

$$\begin{array}{r} 11 \\ 4\overline{)46} \\ -4\downarrow \\ \hline 06 \\ -4 \\ \hline 2 \end{array}$$

← Write 1 in the ones place.

← Bring down 6 ones.

← Multiply. 4×1 ones = 4 ones

← Subtract. $6 - 4$

Compare. $2 < 4$

← **remainder**

Check Your Work

Multiply the quotient by the divisor. Then add the remainder.

$$\begin{array}{r} 11 \\ \times 4 \\ \hline 44 \\ +2 \\ \hline 46 \end{array}$$

Solution: There are 11 teams.
There are 2 officers on bicycles.

Ask Yourself
- Can I divide the tens?
- Can I divide the ones?
- Are any ones left over?

Divide. Use base-ten blocks to help you divide.

1. $3\overline{)66}$ 2. $2\overline{)63}$ 3. $4\overline{)85}$ 4. $2\overline{)83}$

5. $58 \div 5$ 6. $73 \div 7$ 7. $62 \div 3$ 8. $68 \div 6$

Explain Your Thinking ▶ Look at Exercise 4 above. How can you use estimation to check your answer?

Practice and Problem Solving

Use base-ten blocks to help you divide.

9. $3\overline{)99}$ 10. $4\overline{)88}$ 11. $3\overline{)63}$ 12. $2\overline{)68}$ 13. $2\overline{)86}$

14. $2\overline{)87}$ 15. $3\overline{)65}$ 16. $5\overline{)59}$ 17. $4\overline{)49}$ 18. $3\overline{)95}$

19. $57 \div 5$ 20. $49 \div 2$ 21. $89 \div 4$ 22. $87 \div 4$ 23. $67 \div 3$

✖ **Algebra • Symbols** Use >, <, or = for each ⬤.

24. $80 \div 4$ ⬤ 30 25. 30 ⬤ $55 \div 5$ 26. 40 ⬤ $160 \div 4$

27. $48 \div 2$ ⬤ 20 28. $240 \div 6$ ⬤ 40 29. $200 \div 5$ ⬤ 50

Solve.

30. There are 83 officers at a special dinner. They sit in groups of 8. The remaining officers are speakers. How many filled tables will there be? How many speakers?

31. **Estimate** Four officers share a dinner bill of $43 equally. About how much will each officer pay? Is the exact amount greater than or less than your estimate?

Mixed Review and Test Prep

Open Response
Multiply. (Ch. 21, Lesson 4)

32. 8×16 33. 7×24

34. 2×63 35. 5×21

36. 4×34 37. 3×46

38. Wayne has 84 cards. He wants to put the same number into 4 boxes. How many cards should he put into each box? Explain how you got your answer.
(Ch. 22, Lesson 4)

Problem-Solving Application
Interpret Remainders

Objective Decide what a remainder means.

**When a problem has a remainder, you need
to decide what the remainder means.**

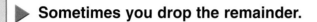

▶ **Sometimes you drop the remainder.**

Firefighters are having a pancake breakfast. There
are 38 pancakes ready to be served. Firefighter John puts
4 pancakes on each plate. How many plates can he fill?

$$\begin{array}{r} 9 \text{ R2} \\ 4\overline{)38} \\ -36 \\ \hline 2 \end{array}$$

There are 4 pancakes on each plate.
There are 9 full plates with 2 pancakes
left. Drop the remainder.

John can fill 9 plates.

▶ **Sometimes the remainder is the answer.**

There are 32 firefighters who will work at the breakfast.
Teams of 5 firefighters are needed to prepare food. The
rest will sell tickets. How many firefighters will sell tickets?

$$\begin{array}{r} 6 \text{ R2} \\ 5\overline{)32} \\ -30 \\ \hline 2 \end{array}$$

Six teams of firefighters will prepare
food. The 2 firefighters not on teams will
sell tickets. The remainder is the answer.

Two firefighters will sell tickets.

▶ **Sometimes you increase the quotient.**

A volunteer is driving 44 senior citizens to the breakfast. If the
van can take 8 passengers, how many trips does the volunteer
need to make?

$$\begin{array}{r} 5 \text{ R4} \\ 8\overline{)44} \\ -40 \\ \hline 4 \end{array}$$

The volunteer can take
40 people in 5 trips.
So increase the quotient.

Six trips are needed for 44 senior citizens.

Ask Yourself
• Should I increase the quotient?
• Should I drop the remainder?
• Is the remainder the answer?

Guided Practice

Use the Ask Yourself questions to help you solve each problem.

1. There are 20 firefighters who will give safety lessons to students. There are 3 schools. An equal number of firefighters will go to each school. How many firefighters will not go to schools?

2. There are 18 community buildings that need to be inspected for fire safety. If the fire inspector checks 4 buildings a day, how many days will it take for the inspector to check all 18 buildings?

Independent Practice

Solve.

3. There are 35 firefighters attending a meeting. Most of them are seated at tables. There are 8 firefighters at each table. The others are standing. How many are standing?

4. The firefighters bought Sparky the Dalmatian several bags of doggy treats. A bag holds 25 treats. If Sparky gets 3 treats a day, on what day will a new bag have to be opened?

5. A landlord has 11 smoke alarms. She needs to put 2 smoke alarms on each floor of a 5-floor building. How many alarms will be unused?

6. There are 41 new helmets at the fire station. Each cubbyhole holds 6 helmets. How many cubbyholes are needed so that all of the helmets can be put away?

Three-Digit Quotients

Objective Divide a three-digit number by a one-digit number.

Learn About It

There were 351 people who volunteered to clean up 3 parks on Earth Day. If an equal number of people worked at each park, how many people cleaned each park?

Divide. $351 \div 3 = \blacksquare$ or $3\overline{)351}$

STEP 1 Divide the hundreds.

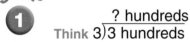

Think $3\overline{)3 \text{ hundreds}}$

$$\begin{array}{r} 1 \\ 3\overline{)351} \\ -3 \\ \hline 0 \end{array}$$

← Write 1 in the hundreds place.
← Multiply. 3 × 1 hundred
← Subtract. 3 − 3
Compare. 0 < 3

STEP 2 Bring down the tens.
Divide the tens.

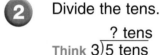

Think $3\overline{)5 \text{ tens}}$

$$\begin{array}{r} 11 \\ 3\overline{)351} \\ -3\downarrow \\ \hline 05 \\ -3 \\ \hline 2 \end{array}$$

← Write 1 in the tens place.

← Bring down 5 tens.
← Multiply. 3 × 1 ten
← Subtract. 5 − 3
Compare. 2 < 3

STEP 3 Regroup leftover tens as ones.

Think 2 tens 1 one = 21 ones

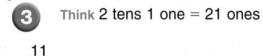

$$\begin{array}{r} 11 \\ 3\overline{)351} \\ -3\downarrow \\ \hline 05 \\ -3 \\ \hline 21 \end{array}$$

← Bring down 1 one.
Regroup 2 tens 1 one as 21 ones.

STEP 4 Divide the ones.

Think $3\overline{)21 \text{ ones}}$

$$\begin{array}{r} 117 \\ 3\overline{)351} \\ -3 \\ \hline 05 \\ -3 \\ \hline 21 \\ -21 \\ \hline 0 \end{array}$$

← Write 7 in the ones place.

← Multiply. 3 × 7 ones
← Subtract. 21 − 21
Compare. 0 < 3

Solution: 117 people cleaned each park.

Check your work.

Multiply the quotient by the divisor.

$$\begin{array}{r} 117 \\ \times\ 3 \\ \hline 351 \end{array}$$

Divide and check.

1. 4)464̄

2. 3)951̄

3. 5)567̄

4. 856 ÷ 4

5. 894 ÷ 2

6. 974 ÷ 3

Ask Yourself
• Do I need to regroup?
• Is there a remainder?

Explain Your Thinking ▶ Look back at Exercise 6. How many digits will the quotient have? How do you know?

Practice and Problem Solving

Divide and check.

7. 5)595̄

8. 3)372̄

9. 3)642̄

10. 2)652̄

11. 2)831̄

12. 5)575̄

13. 5)580̄

14. 4)868̄

15. 3)957̄

16. 4)469̄

17. 476 ÷ 4

18. 696 ÷ 6

19. 452 ÷ 2

20. 644 ÷ 3

21. 936 ÷ 3

22. 872 ÷ 4

23. 876 ÷ 2

24. 585 ÷ 5

25. There are 438 new benches to be placed in 4 sections of Devon. Each section of town gets the same number of benches. About how many benches will be placed in each section?

26. **Analyze** At the end of Earth Day, 15 plastic bags were left over. One group of volunteers used 49 bags, one group used 54 bags, and the third group used 62 bags. How many bags were there to start?

Mixed Review and Test Prep ✓

Open Response

Multiply. (Ch. 21, Lesson 5)

27. 4 × 237

28. 5 × 163

29. 3 × 267

30. 4 × 325

31. 6 × 219

32. 7 × 123

33. 2 × 473

34. 8 × 134

Multiple Choice

35. A farmer has 434 pounds of apples to load equally onto 2 trucks. How many pounds will be on each truck?

(Ch. 22, Lesson 6)

A 436 **B** 212 **C** 217 **D** 21

Audio Tutor 2/38 Listen and Understand

Place the First Digit

Objective Decide where to place the first digit in the quotient.

Learn About It

Six children planted 138 flowers in a community garden. Each child planted the same number of flowers. How many flowers did each child plant?

Divide. $138 \div 6 = \blacksquare$ or $6\overline{)138}$

STEP 1 Decide where to place the first digit in the **quotient**.

Think $6\overline{)1}$? hundreds
$6\overline{)1}$ hundreds

$6\overline{)138}$ $1 < 6$ There are not enough hundreds to divide.

$13 > 6$ Place the first digit of the quotient in the tens place.

STEP 2 Divide the tens.

Think $6\overline{)13}$? tens
$6\overline{)13}$ tens

$\begin{array}{r} 2 \\ 6\overline{)138} \\ -12 \\ \hline 1 \end{array}$ ← Multiply. 6×2 tens
← Subtract. $13 - 12$. Compare. $1 < 6$

STEP 3 Bring down the ones. Divide the ones.

Think $6\overline{)18}$? ones
$6\overline{)18}$ ones

$\begin{array}{r} 23 \\ 6\overline{)138} \\ -12\downarrow \\ \hline 18 \\ -18 \\ \hline 0 \end{array}$ ← Multiply. 6×3 ones
← Subtract. $18 - 18$ Compare. $0 < 6$

Solution: Each child planted 23 flowers.

Guided Practice

Divide. Check your answers.

1. $4\overline{)328}$
2. $2\overline{)138}$
3. $5\overline{)175}$
4. $6\overline{)324}$

Explain Your Thinking ▶ When you divide a 3-digit number by a 1-digit number, can you ever have a 1-digit quotient?

Ask Yourself

• Where should I write the first digit in the quotient?

Divide. Check your answers.

5. $2\overline{)122}$ 6. $3\overline{)273}$ 7. $4\overline{)168}$ 8. $4\overline{)456}$ 9. $3\overline{)102}$

10. $3\overline{)141}$ 11. $5\overline{)120}$ 12. $6\overline{)198}$ 13. $2\overline{)284}$ 14. $4\overline{)476}$

15. $5\overline{)320}$ 16. $6\overline{)552}$ 17. $3\overline{)282}$ 18. $3\overline{)369}$ 19. $4\overline{)892}$

20. $480 \div 5$ 21. $282 \div 6$ 22. $291 \div 3$ 23. $388 \div 4$ 24. $236 \div 2$

✖ Algebra • Equations Solve for *n*.

25. $192 \div 2 = n$ 26. $64 \div 2 = n$ 27. $224 \div 2 = n$ 28. $256 \div 2 = n$
    $192 \div 4 = n$ $64 \div 4 = n$ $224 \div 4 = n$ $256 \div 4 = n$
    $192 \div 8 = n$ $64 \div 8 = n$ $224 \div 8 = n$ $256 \div 8 = n$

Solve.

29. Look back at Exercises 25–28. What do you notice about the quotients as the divisors increase?

30. There are 24 rose bushes to plant in 3 equal rows. How many bushes will be in each row?

31. A square garden has a perimeter of 92 feet. How long is one side of the garden?

32. Patrick worked 3 hours to plant 88 tulip bulbs. About how many tulip bulbs did he plant each hour?

Mixed Review and Test Prep

Open Response

Write whether the event is impossible, unlikely, likely, or certain. (Ch. 7, Lesson 1)

33. Landing on red

34. Landing on green

35. Landing on blue

36. A theater has 128 seats. There are 8 seats in each row. How many rows of seats are there? (Ch. 22, Lesson 7)

Explain how you got your answer.

Divide Money

Objective Divide amounts of money.

Learn About It

Elena, Bobby, Lori, and Joe have $5.88 to buy snacks at the Community Fair. They want to share the money equally. How much will each friend receive?

Divide. $5.88 ÷ 4 = ■   or   4)$5.88

STEP 1 Divide the dollars.

```
    1
4)$5.88
  − 4
    1
```

Think
1 × 4 dollars

STEP 2 Divide the dimes.

```
    1 4
4)$5.88
  − 4
    18
  − 16
     2
```

Think
4 × 4 dimes

STEP 3 Divide the pennies.

```
    1 47
4)$5.88
  − 4
    18
  − 16
     28
   − 28
      0
```

Think
4 × 7 pennies

STEP 4 Write the dollar sign and the decimal point in the quotient.

```
  $1.47
4)$5.88
```

The decimal point separates the dollars and cents.

Check your answer.

```
 $1.47
 × 4
 $5.88
```

Solution: Each friend will have $1.47 to spend.

Another Example

A. Quotient less than $1.00

```
  $0.65
4)$2.60
 − 2 4
    20
  − 20
     0
```

B. Zero in the quotient

```
  $2.08
3)$6.24
 − 6
   2
 − 0
   24
 − 24
    0
```

Divide. Model with coins and bills if you wish.

Ask Yourself

- Where should I place the first digit?
- Did I place the dollar sign and the decimal point in the quotient?

1. $2\overline{)\$8.46}$

2. $4\overline{)\$4.84}$

3. $\$5.65 \div 5$

4. $\$9.50 \div 5$

5. $\$6.81 \div 3$

6. $\$2.28 \div 3$

Explain Your Thinking ▶ If you took away the decimal point in $3.45, how much money would there be?

Practice and Problem Solving

Divide. Model with coins and bills if you wish.

7. $3\overline{)\$6.93}$

8. $2\overline{)\$4.14}$

9. $2\overline{)\$2.56}$

10. $6\overline{)\$6.72}$

11. $4\overline{)\$3.92}$

12. $3\overline{)\$6.45}$

13. $\$6.50 \div 2$

14. $\$8.64 \div 4$

15. $\$8.74 \div 2$

16. $\$6.81 \div 3$

17. $\$5.55 \div 5$

18. $\$2.24 \div 4$

✖ **Algebra** • **Functions** Copy and complete each table. If the rule is not given, write the rule.

	Rule: Divide by 5	
	Input	**Output**
19.	$3.50	▣
20.	$5.75	▣
21.	▣	$0.80
22.	$5.15	▣
23.	▣	$0.45

	Rule: ____	
	Input	**Output**
	$6.33	$2.11
	$9.69	$3.23
	$2.46	$0.82
25.	$6.45	▣
26.	$2.76	▣

24.

Go On

✗ Algebra • Equations Solve for *n*.

27. $n \div 3 = \$3.00$

28. $\$4.26 \div 2 = n$

29. $n \div 2 = \$3.24$

30. $n \div 3 = \$2.21$

31. $\$6.24 \div 4 = n$

32. $n \div 3 = \$1.21$

33. Write About It What is a reasonable answer for $\$5.16 \div 4$, $\$129$ or $\$1.29$? Explain your thinking.

34. What's Wrong? This is how Daria divided $\$9.25$ by 5. What did she do wrong? Show the correct way to do the division.

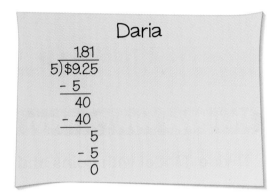

Daria

$$\begin{array}{r} 1.81 \\ 5\overline{)\$9.25} \\ -5 \\ \hline 40 \\ -40 \\ \hline 5 \\ -5 \\ \hline 0 \end{array}$$

Choose a Computation Method

Mental Math • Estimation • Paper and Pencil • Calculator

Use the sign for Problems 35–38. Then tell which method you chose.

35. At the Community Fair, tickets for games and rides were sold in blocks of 8. How much did each ticket cost?

36. Mr. Sell has twenty dollars. Does he have enough money to buy 100 tickets? If not, how many tickets can he buy?

37. On Saturday, $\$352$ was collected from ticket sales at the fair. How many blocks of tickets were sold?

38. You Decide What games and rides would you want to try? How many tickets will you have to buy? How much will it cost?

Community Fair
8 Tickets For $2.00

GAMES

Ring Toss	3 Tickets
Pop the Balloon	3 Tickets
Dunk The Clown	5 Tickets

RIDES

Ferris Wheel	3 Tickets
Swings	3 Tickets
Spinning Cups	5 Tickets

Extra Practice See page 633, Set F.

Open Response

Copy and complete. (Ch. 14, Lesson 2)

39. 8 m = _____ cm

40. 7,000 m = _____ km

41. 5 cm = _____ mm

42. 400 cm = _____ m

43. Martin buys 4 pens for a total of $6.76. Each pen costs the same. How much does one pen cost?

(Ch. 22, Lesson 8)

Calculator Connection

Problem Solving

Mental Math vs. Machine

Sometimes it's quicker to solve a problem with a calculator. Sometimes it's quicker to solve it mentally.

Work with a partner.

1. Copy the problems shown onto index cards. Shuffle the cards. Place them face down in a pile.

| 49 ÷ 7 | 48 ÷ 9 | 240 ÷ 4 | 320 ÷ 8 | 694 ÷ 3 |
| 974 ÷ 3 | 350 ÷ 5 | 600 ÷ 3 | 674 ÷ 6 | 897 ÷ 2 |

2. Decide who will use the calculator and who will use mental math.

3. Turn over a card. The first person to correctly solve the problem keeps the card. The player with the most cards wins.

4. **Write About It** What type of problem is easier to solve mentally? What type is easier to solve with a calculator?

VOCABULARY

Choose the best term to complete each sentence.

Vocabulary

divisor

quotient

multiple

dividend

remainder

1. In the division sentence 6 ÷ 3 = 2, 2 is the ____.

2. In the division sentence 8 ÷ 2 = 4, 2 is the ____.

3. In the division sentence 10 ÷ 5 = 2,
10 is the ____.

4. In the division problem 7 ÷ 3, there is a ____ of 1.

CONCEPTS AND SKILLS

Estimate each quotient. Write the compatible numbers you used.

(Lesson 3, pp. 616–618)

5. $4\overline{)35}$

6. $5\overline{)41}$

7. $7\overline{)523}$

8. $9\overline{)800}$

Divide and check. (Lessons 1, 4, 6–8, pp. 610–611, 620–621, 624–630)

9. 600 ÷ 6

10. 640 ÷ 8

11. 84 ÷ 4

12. 37 ÷ 3

13. $2\overline{)28}$

14. $5\overline{)585}$

15. $3\overline{)927}$

16. $4\overline{)804}$

17. $4\overline{)249}$

18. $6\overline{)426}$

19. $7\overline{)214}$

20. $3\overline{)297}$

21. $2\overline{)\$5.16}$

22. $3\overline{)\$6.54}$

23. $3\overline{)\$8.76}$

24. $4\overline{)\$6.56}$

PROBLEM SOLVING

Solve. (Lesson 5, pp. 622–623)

25. A club is going on a field trip. There are 27 club members that will ride in vans. Each van holds 6 people. How many vans does the club need?

 Write About It

Show You Understand

Often when you divide you need to decide what to do with a remainder.

- Describe a situation when you would drop the remainder.

- Describe a situation when you would increase the quotient.

Extra Practice

Set A (Lesson 1, pp. 610–611)

Divide.

1. $50 \div 5$ 2. $420 \div 6$ 3. $810 \div 9$ 4. $360 \div 6$

5. $270 \div 3$ 6. $5,600 \div 8$ 7. $1,400 \div 7$ 8. $3,200 \div 4$

Set B (Lesson 3, pp. 616–618)

Estimate. Write the compatible numbers you used.

1. $3\overline{)29}$ 2. $4\overline{)22}$ 3. $9\overline{)351}$ 4. $2\overline{)127}$ 5. $6\overline{)418}$

Set C (Lesson 4, pp. 620–621)

Divide. Use base-ten blocks to help if you wish.

1. $2\overline{)48}$ 2. $5\overline{)55}$ 3. $2\overline{)86}$ 4. $4\overline{)49}$ 5. $3\overline{)95}$

Set D (Lesson 6, pp. 624–625)

Divide and check.

1. $2\overline{)498}$ 2. $3\overline{)657}$ 3. $4\overline{)852}$ 4. $5\overline{)565}$ 5. $3\overline{)923}$

6. $4\overline{)432}$ 7. $3\overline{)621}$ 8. $2\overline{)854}$ 9. $2\overline{)693}$ 10. $5\overline{)580}$

Set E (Lesson 7, pp. 626–627)

Divide. Check your answers.

1. $2\overline{)164}$ 2. $4\overline{)128}$ 3. $5\overline{)155}$ 4. $3\overline{)218}$ 5. $6\overline{)429}$

6. $3\overline{)276}$ 7. $7\overline{)504}$ 8. $4\overline{)228}$ 9. $2\overline{)187}$ 10. $3\overline{)423}$

Set F (Lesson 8, pp. 628–630)

Find the quotient.

1. $2\overline{)\$6.48}$ 2. $3\overline{)\$6.51}$ 3. $4\overline{)\$2.88}$ 4. $\$9.27 \div 3$ 5. $\$8.65 \div 5$

Jump for Joy!

If you think that jumping rope began in America, you're wrong. It was brought to America in the 1600s by Dutch settlers. Jumping rope was different in those times. Mostly boys jumped rope then.

By the 1800s more girls began jumping rope. Over the years singing games and tricks were invented, and jumping rope became more popular. Today there are serious jump rope competitions. One day you might see jumping rope become an Olympic sport!

Double Dutch involves two people turning two jump ropes for one or more jumpers. The table shows some Double Dutch tricks and the number of points each trick is worth. Use the table for Problems 1–3.

Double Dutch Tricks	
Trick	**Points**
Scissor Jump	8
Push-Ups	9
Cartwheel	10
Aerial	12

1 Jenna is practicing some jump rope tricks. She is able to do 3 scissor jumps, 2 cartwheels, and 2 aerials. How many points does she earn?

2 Mike earned 27 points doing only one kind of trick. Which trick is it? How did you find the answer?

3 Suppose the Blue Team earned 110 points for doing the cartwheel trick. How many times did they do the trick?

4 If a single rope turns 187 times in 1 minute, about how many times, to the nearest hundred, will the rope turn in 4 minutes?

5 Kizzie spent $8.76 on two jump ropes for the competition. Both jump ropes cost the same amount. How much did each jump rope cost?

6 There are 251 students going to see the South City Jumping Rope Competition. There are 5 buses. Each bus holds 45 students. Are there enough buses for all the students? Explain your thinking.

Education Place

Visit Weekly Reader Connections at **eduplace.com/map** for more on this topic.

Enrichment: Logical Thinking

ALL, Some, and None Statements

Sentences with the words *all*, *some*, and *none* are used in logical thinking.

- *All* means "every one" in a group.
- *Some* means "at least one" in a group.
- *None* means "not any" in a group.

You can use these ideas to tell if a statement is true or false.

Look at the picture of the students above.

These statements are true.	**These statements are false.**
• All of the students are dressed up in costumes. • Some of the students are dressed up as animals. • None of the students are wearing face paint.	• All of the students are dressed up like people. • Some of the students are not wearing costumes. • None of the students are dressed like animals.

Use the picture below. Tell whether each statement is true or false. If the statement is false, rewrite it to make it true.

1. All of the students are dressed up like animals.

2. None of the students are dressed up like farm animals.

3. All of the students are wearing face paint.

4. Some of the students are dressed up like 4-legged animals.

Curious Calculations

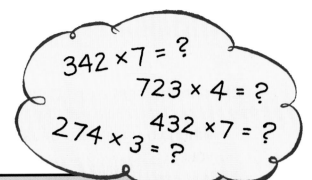

$342 \times 7 = ?$
$723 \times 4 = ?$
$432 \times 7 = ?$
$274 \times 3 = ?$

Arrange the digits below to make the greatest possible product. Use your calculator to help you.

1. **Digits:** 2, 5, 6, 7
   ☐ ☐ ☐ × ☐

2. **Digits:** 1, 3, 7, 9
   ☐ ☐ ☐ × ☐

3. **Digits:** 0, 4, 6, 8
   ☐ ☐ ☐ × ☐

4. **Digits:** 1, 2, 4, 6
   ☐ ☐ ☐ × ☐

5. **Digits:** 3, 4, 5, 7
   ☐ ☐ ☐ × ☐

6. **Digits:** 0, 1, 6, 9
   ☐ ☐ ☐ × ☐

7. **Write About It** How can you order the digits to always get the greatest product?

Use your calculator to solve the riddle:

- Divide each number in Exercises 8–13 by the numbers 2 through 9 to find the *greatest* quotient with no remainder.

- Match that quotient with a letter in the key.

- Then write that letter above the matching exercise number in the riddle to solve the riddle.

I'm outta here!

Me too!

8. 96   9. 87   10. 95   11. 102   12. 150   13. 161

KEY:

15	19	21	23	29	30	32	34	48	50	51	75
D	E	H	I	L	M	N	O	P	R	S	T

RIDDLE: What did the number say when it was divided in half?

___ ___ ___ ___ , ___   ___ ___ ___ ___ ___ ___ !
9   10   12   11   11   8   9   13   12

✓ Unit 8 Test

VOCABULARY (Open Response)

Choose the best word to complete each sentence.

Vocabulary
product
regroup
quotient
multiples
remainder

1. When you name 16 ones as 1 ten and 6 ones, you ____.

2. When you divide, the answer is the ____.

3. The numbers 200, 400, and 600 are all ____ of 100.

4. When you divide 8 by 3, there is a ____ of 2.

CONCEPTS AND SKILLS (Open Response)

Estimate each product or quotient. (Chapters 21–22)

5.
$$\begin{array}{r} 46 \\ \times\ 3 \\ \hline \end{array}$$

6.
$$\begin{array}{r} 72 \\ \times\ 4 \\ \hline \end{array}$$

7.
$$\begin{array}{r} 315 \\ \times\ 2 \\ \hline \end{array}$$

8.
$$\begin{array}{r} 238 \\ \times\ 4 \\ \hline \end{array}$$

9. $4\overline{)86}$

10. $5\overline{)118}$

11. $6\overline{)375}$

12. $3\overline{)239}$

13. 18×6

14. 32×9

15. 712×6

16. $42 \div 5$

17. $85 \div 9$

18. $127 \div 6$

Find each product or quotient. (Chapters 21–22)

19. 4×70

20. 6×80

21. 2×500

22. 8×300

23. $4 \times 9,000$

24. $90 \div 3$

25. $900 \div 3$

26. $480 \div 6$

27. $320 \div 8$

28. $3,200 \div 8$

29.
$$\begin{array}{r} 28 \\ \times\ 5 \\ \hline \end{array}$$

30.
$$\begin{array}{r} 35 \\ \times\ 6 \\ \hline \end{array}$$

31.
$$\begin{array}{r} 236 \\ \times\ 3 \\ \hline \end{array}$$

32.
$$\begin{array}{r} \$1.92 \\ \times\ 5 \\ \hline \end{array}$$

33.
$$\begin{array}{r} \$3.14 \\ \times\ 2 \\ \hline \end{array}$$

34. $2\overline{)58}$

35. $3\overline{)76}$

36. $4\overline{)896}$

37. $7\overline{)\$1.54}$

38. $3\overline{)\$7.35}$

39. Cups are set up by the punch bowl. The right side has 103 stacks of cups, and the left side has 97 stacks of cups. Each stack has 8 cups. How many cups are there in all?

40. To serve the pasta, 23 large spoons are needed. These spoons come in boxes of 5. How many boxes need to be purchased? How many extra spoons will there be?

Performance Assessment

Constructed Response

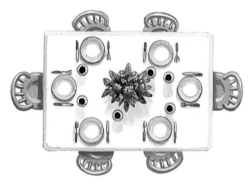

welcome to the SPAGHETTI FUNDRAISER!

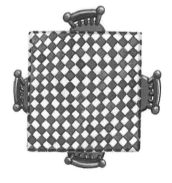

Square Table
Seats 4

Rectangular Table
Seats 6

Circular Table
Seats 8

Task Ms. Owens needs to decide how many of each shape table to use for the spaghetti dinner fundraiser.

Use the information above and at the right. How many tables of each shape should she use? Explain your thinking.

Information You Need

- There must be exactly 184 seats.
- There are 10 square tables available.
- There are 12 rectangular tables available.
- There are 15 circular tables available.

Cumulative Test Prep

Solve Problems 1–10.

Test-Taking Tip

Sometimes you can test the answer choices to select the correct one.

Look at the example below.

$$3 \times \blacksquare + 4 = 10$$

A 1   C 3

B 2   D 4

THINK

Multiply each answer choice by 3, and then add 4, to find which will give an answer of 10.

$3 \times 2 + 4 = 10$
So choice **B** is the correct answer.

1. Which shape is a right triangle?

   A   C

   B   D

   (Chapter 15, Lesson 3)

2. Mateo wants to use three numbers to write related multiplication and division sentences. Which set of numbers can he use?

   F 3, 8, 11   H 5, 10, 15

   G 4, 4, 16   J 6, 12, 24

   (Chapter 10, Lesson 3)

3. Tevy bought the same number of stickers each day. After 6 days, she had 24 stickers in all. How many stickers did she buy each day?

   A 1   B 2   C 3   D 4

   (Chapter 10, Lesson 5)

4. Which fraction is equivalent to 0.06?

   F $\dfrac{10}{6}$ H $\dfrac{60}{100}$

   G $\dfrac{6}{10}$ J $\dfrac{6}{100}$

   (Chapter 20, Lesson 2)

For Test-Taking Tips, See page 659.

5. Aaron bought 240 crayons. There are 8 crayons in each box. How many boxes did he buy?

(Chapter 22, Lesson 1)

6. Rob has 5 dimes and 2 pennies. Luisa has 1 quarter and 3 dimes. Debbie has 2 quarters and 1 penny. Order the amounts from greatest to least. Who has the most money?

(Chapter 3, Lesson 4)

7. How many vertices does the pyramid shown below have? How many faces does it have?

(Chapter 15, Lesson 7)

8. A football player runs 19 yards. A baseball player runs 90 feet from home plate to first base. Who runs farther? How much farther?

(Chapter 13, Lesson 3)

9. Which of the figures below has a greater area?

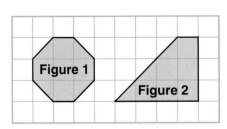

Figure 1

Figure 2

(Chapter 17, Lesson 4)

10. Tuan, Lisa, and Marc each baked a pie for the school bake sale. The shaded sections show how many pieces each student sold.

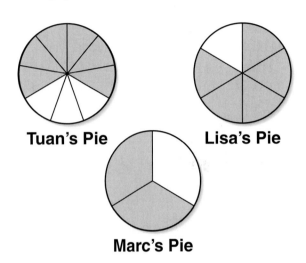

Tuan's Pie   Lisa's Pie

Marc's Pie

A Write a fraction to show what portion of pie each student sold.

B Which student sold the greatest amount of pie?

C Which two students sold equal portions of pie? Explain how you know.

D Did the student who sold the most pieces of pie also sell the most pie? Explain your answer.

(Chapter 19, Lesson 1)

Education Place

Look for Cumulative Test Prep at **eduplace.com/map** for more practice.

Vocabulary Wrap-Up for **Unit 8**

Look back at the big ideas and vocabulary in this unit.

Big Ideas

Sometimes when you multiply, you need to regroup.

Sometimes when you divide, there is a remainder.

You can use mental math to multiply or divide.

Key Vocabulary

regroup

remainder

mental math

Math Conversations

Use your new vocabulary to discuss these big ideas.

1. Explain how to estimate the product of 4 × 327.

2. Explain how you know that 25 ÷ 6 has a remainder.

3. Explain how you can use base-ten blocks to help you find the product of 3 × 26.

4. Explain where to place the first digit of the quotient when finding the answer to 145 ÷ 5.

5. **Write About It** You use multiplication and division frequently in your daily life. Brainstorm a list of some activities that require you to multiply or divide.

I need to multiply 7 by 300 to solve this problem.

Try using mental math to solve it.

Student Resources

Table of Measures

Customary Units of Measure

Metric Units of Measure

Length

1 foot (ft)	=	12 inches (in.)
1 yard (yd)	=	36 inches
1 yard	=	3 feet
1 mile (mi)	=	5,280 feet
1 mile	=	1,760 yards

1 centimeter (cm)	=	10 millimeters (mm)
1 decimeter (dm)	=	10 centimeters (cm)
1 meter (m)	=	100 centimeters
1 meter	=	10 decimeters
1 kilometer (km)	=	1,000 meters

Capacity

1 pint (pt)	=	2 cups (c)
1 quart (qt)	=	2 pints
1 gallon (gal)	=	4 quarts

1 liter (L)	=	1,000 milliliters (mL)

Weight/Mass

1 pound (lb)	=	16 ounces (oz)
1 ton (T)	=	2,000 pounds

1 kilogram (kg)	=	1,000 grams (g)

Units of Time

1 minute (min)	=	60 seconds (s)
1 quarter-hour	=	15 minutes
1 half-hour	=	30 minutes
1 hour	=	60 minutes
1 day (d)	=	24 hours
1 week (wk)	=	7 days

1 year (yr)	=	12 months (mo)
1 year	=	52 weeks
1 year	=	365 days
1 leap year	=	366 days
1 decade	=	10 years
1 century	=	100 years

Money

1 penny	=	1 cent (¢)
1 nickel	=	5 cents
1 dime	=	10 cents

1 quarter	=	25 cents
1 half-dollar	=	50 cents
1 dollar ($)	=	100 cents

A Is for Abacus

BY DAVID M. SCHWARTZ *from G Is for Googol*

Hundreds of years before calculators were invented, people in China discovered they could add and subtract quickly by sliding beads back and forth on strings. They put seven beads on a string and put a few of these strings in a wooden frame. We call the device an abacus.

Today many people in China and Japan still use abacuses. The strings represent place values (1s, 10s, 100s, etc.). The positions of the beads along the string represent the number of 1s, 10s, or 100s being used.

If you think pushing beads back and forth is slow work, think again. In contests between people using calculators and people using abacuses to add and subtract, the abacus users usually win! Some Chinese and Japanese shopkeepers don't even need a real abacus. They just move their hands in the air, sliding imaginary beads back and forth on imaginary strings. But they still get a real answer!

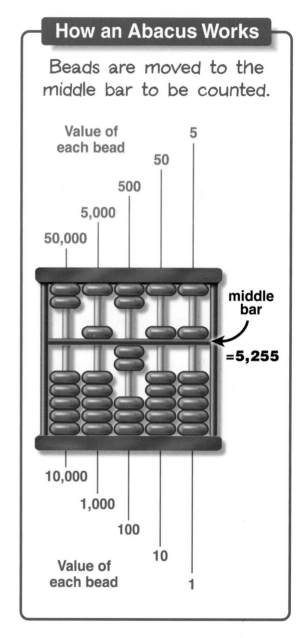

How an Abacus Works

Beads are moved to the middle bar to be counted.

Value of each bead

5
50
500
5,000
50,000

middle bar

=5,255

10,000
1,000
100
10
1

Value of each bead

---

 1 How many abacus beads would you use to represent the number 4,000? How about 4,002?

2 Do you think you would ever use an abacus to do everyday math? Why, or why not?

The School Is One Big Bird Feeder!

Birds can be interesting and fun to watch. You can attract birds by enticing them with tasty treats. Many people do this by making bird feeders. There are several common ways to make a bird feeder. You might want to try one of these with your class, and hang them in trees around your school.

When choosing a place to hang your bird feeder, think about where the birds will feel safe from cats or squirrels. Try to hang it in a tree with protective bushes nearby. Birds can perch and gather courage before daring to try your treat.

Here are instructions on how you can make your own bird feeder. Choose the type you like best, or try them both!

Here are a few birds that you might see if you build a bird feeder!

Pinecone Bird Feeders

Materials:

- 1 pinecone
- 4 tablespoons peanut butter
- 1 piece of string
- 1 cup of birdseed

Mix the birdseed with the peanut butter in a bowl. Then spread the mixture onto the pinecone. Put the pinecone into the refrigerator so that the peanut butter mixture can harden. This way it will be less messy! Then tie a string to the tip of the pinecone, and hang the feeder outside on a tree.

Milk Carton Bird Feeders

Materials:

- 1 half-gallon milk carton
- 1 piece of string
- 1 dowel rod
- Scissors
- Birdseed

Clean the carton well, then cut large windows into opposite sides of the carton. Leave 2 inches at the top and bottom of the windows. Ask your teacher to use the scissors to poke a hole below each window so you can push the dowel rod through. This gives the birds something to perch on as they eat the seeds you pour inside. Poke a small hole in the top of the carton and string it up! Enjoy!

Shayla hangs one of the peanutty pinecones.

1. If you wanted to make 2 pinecone bird feeders, how many tablespoons of peanut butter would you need? Write a number sentence to solve.

2. If your class made 12 pinecone bird feeders and 15 milk carton bird feeders, how many bird feeders were made?

3. Why do you need to carefully choose where to hang a bird feeder?

Frog or Toad: How to Tell

BY ELIZABETH A. LACEY
from The Complete Frog

Frogs and toads have the same overall shape and often seem much alike in color and habits. Both of these amphibians, for instance, usually lay their eggs in or near water.

Generally speaking, if you find it in a pond, it's the common frog, and if you find it in the woods, it's the common toad. But there are other clues as well.

The Common Frog	The Common Toad
Smooth, soft skin	Thick, bumpy skin
Long ridges down each side of back	Short ridges on top of head, large bumps behind eyes
Large, round "ears" under eyes on each side	Very small, round "ears" below eyes
Slender body, long legs, speedy swimmer	Plump body, shorter legs, slower moving
Lives in or very near water	Lives inland in woods

1 According to the information in the chart, where are the toad's ears located?

2 If a toad and a frog were to run a 50-yard race, which animal would win? How do you know this?

Leaders of the Pack

from National Geographic Explorer

"A wolf pack is basically a family that stays together while the 'children' learn to live on their own," says Dr. I. David Mech. He is a wolf biologist who has been studying wolf behavior for many years. The wolf pups have a lot to learn before they can make it without their parents.

"Wolves learn the ropes by watching other members of the pack," says Mech. First the new pups learn the basics. They learn how to ask for food. They learn how to howl and how to beat a brother at wrestling! Meanwhile 'teenagers' take more advanced classes. They learn how to hunt for small prey such as rabbits and mice. By early fall, the pack's youngest pups are ready to travel. The pack spends the fall and winter roaming its territory in search of moose and elk. The lessons get harder as the young face large animals with dangerous antlers and hooves.

When they're ready to hunt alone, the older "children" leave. Some travel hundreds of miles to find mates and raise families. It's their turn to be leaders of the pack!

continued on next page

By the Numbers

- 1 litter of pups is born each year in a typical pack.

- 3 times bigger than a coyote, the gray wolf is the largest wild member of the dog family.

- 22 pounds of meat may be eaten at one wolf's meal.

- 40 miles an hour is a wolf's top running speed.

1 About how many pounds of meat might a pack of 8 wolves eat at one meal? Write a number sentence to solve.

2 If there are 6 pups in every litter, how many pups would be born in 3 years?

3 Why do you think wild animals live together in packs?

READING MATH

The Big Chill

Winters in Alaska can be amazingly cold. In February 1999, the temperature in the town of Fairbanks was as low as ⁻47 degrees Fahrenheit.

People who live in such climates have learned how to stay warm. They can do a number of things, from making a fire to bundling up in fleece and down. Animals also live in cold Alaskan climates. How do they survive such cold weather?

continued on next page

Arctic Animals

The fur on a caribou grows in two layers. The caribou has fur all over its body, except for a small area around its eyes and lips. This double-coat keeps the caribou from freezing.

The musk ox has fur that grows as long as 3 feet. This long shaggy coat is also waterproof, which helps to protect it from the rain and snow. Its body has a thick layer of fat, another natural device to keep it warm.

The polar bear's fur coat is also thick. It has two layers, just like the caribou. One is an outer layer of long, dense hairs, and one is an undercoat of short, wooly hairs. Even though its fur is white, a polar bear's skin is black, a color that absorbs more heat. Under its skin is a layer of blubber, or fatty tissue, which keeps it warm in icy waters as well as on land. (Polar bears are excellent swimmers!)

An arctic bird called the ptarmigan has brown feathers in the summer. These feathers change to white in the winter. This white color helps the ptarmigan blend into the snowy background so that its enemies cannot see it as easily.

The Arctic fox also changes color with the seasons. In the summer it is brown to match the grasses, and in the winter it is white to match the snow. This is called camouflage. Changing color helps the Arctic fox to hide from predators, while making it easier for the fox to sneak up on its prey.

1. If the temperature went from ⁻40 degrees Fahrenheit to ⁻47 degrees Fahrenheit, would it be getting warmer or colder?

2. What are three things animals have that help them live in a cold climate?

3. Compare the climate where you live with the climate of Alaska. How is it alike or different?

Snowflakes

BY DAVID McCORD
from Sing a Song of Popcorn

Sometime this winter if you go
To walk in soft new-falling snow
When flakes are big and come down slow

To settle on your sleeve as bright
As stars that couldn't wait for night,
You won't know what you have in sight —

Another world — unless you bring
A magnifying glass. This thing
We call a snowflake is the king

Of crystals. Do you like surprise?
Examine him three times his size:
At first you won't believe your eyes.

Stars look alike, but flakes do not.
No two the same in all the lot
That you will get in any spot

You chance to be, for every one
Come spinning through the sky has none
But his own window-wings of sun:

Joints, points, and crosses. What could make
Such lacework with no crack or break?
In billion billions, no mistake?

1 What types of shapes can you identify in the snowflakes on this page?

2 Are all the snowflakes on the page symmetrical? How do you know?

3 What are some other examples of patterns that are found in nature?

Uncle Johnathan

and the

Ice-Skating Contest

BY GRETCHEN WOELFLE *from Never Go Home Without a Fish*

Christopher and his Uncle Johnathan go fishing. While they wait and wait and wait for a bite, Uncle Johnathan tells about an event that took place on that very lake.

"Tell me about the ice-skating contest," Christopher said. It was his favorite story and it happened right here on the lake.

"All the other skaters were young and lean. I was middle-aged and not lean." His uncle chuckled. "They dragged logs onto the ice and took turns jumping. One log, then two, four, eight, twelve logs. They laughed every time I took my turn, but I laughed back."

Christopher could picture Uncle Johnathan heaving his big body from side to side, swinging his arms back and forth.

"At sixteen logs only five skaters were left, and one was me. At nineteen logs only three skaters were left, and one was me. At nineteen logs another man fell.

Then there was just young Peter Bixby and me. We both jumped twenty logs. Then at twenty-one, Peter caught his skate and skidded for fifty feet."

Christopher loved what came next.

"Then it was my turn," Uncle Johnathan continued, "and I cleared it. For good measure, I went and jumped over another one. Twenty-two logs. No one has beaten my record yet."

Uncle Johnathan chuckled. "Life gives you things you never expect," he mused, "and sometimes it doesn't give you what you have every right to expect — like fish for dinner!"

1 If there were ten skaters in the ice-skating contest, what fraction of the skaters were left at sixteen logs?

2 Write the fraction of skaters left at nineteen logs as a decimal.

3 Do you think Uncle Johnathan's story was true? Why or why not?

READING MATH

Elephants on the Move

from Weekly Reader

What weighs 12,000 pounds and carries its own trunk when it moves? An African elephant!

About 1,000 African elephants are moving. They are going from a national park in South Africa to nearby countries. There, the elephants will help fill a new park.

The new park is in three countries: South Africa, Mozambique, and Zimbabwe. It covers an area a little larger than Maryland.

The move reduces the number of elephants in Kruger National Park in South Africa. It has about 9,000 elephants. Animal experts say that is too many big animals for the size of the park.

Crispian Olver, an official in South Africa, says the move will be done by 2004. The move will not only help the elephants, he says. It will also make money from tourists who visit the new park.

1 If 20 elephants are moved every day for 7 days, how many will be moved? Write a multiplication sentence to solve.

2 If each of the three countries received the same amount of animals, about how many would each receive?

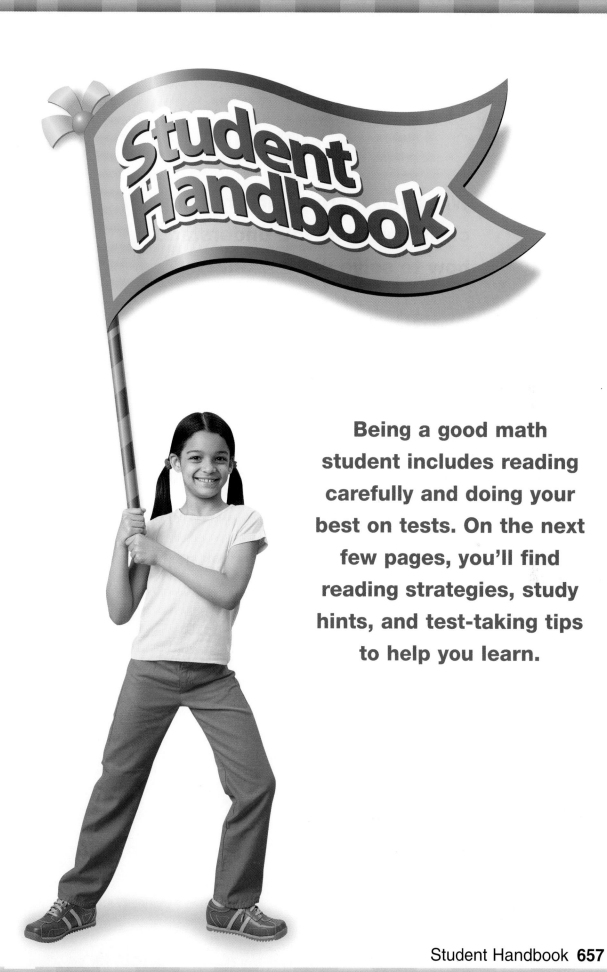

Student Handbook

Being a good math student includes reading carefully and doing your best on tests. On the next few pages, you'll find reading strategies, study hints, and test-taking tips to help you learn.

Use Reading Strategies to Think About Math

What you learn during reading class can help you understand how to solve word problems.

Understand What the Question Is

Read the problem once to be sure it makes sense to you. Ask yourself the question in your own words. Picture the situation and make a drawing if it helps.

Think About the Words

As you read the problem, pay attention to the mathematical words. If you don't understand a word, try to decide what it means by looking at the words around it.

Be Sure You Have Enough Information

Identify the information. You may need to look at a table or a graph as well as the words. Think about information you already know that may help.

Plan What You Will Do

Think about the problem-solving plan and strategies. Decide what computation method is needed. Then make a plan and follow it.

Evaluate Your Work

Look back at what the question asked, and check that your answer really answers that question. Be sure you have labeled your answer.

Strategies for Taking Tests

You need to think differently about how to answer various kinds of questions

All Questions

If you can't answer a question, go on to the next question. You can return to it if there is time.

Always check your computation.

Multiple-Choice Questions

Estimate the answer. This can help eliminate any unreasonable choices.

On bubble sheets, be sure you mark the bubble for the right question and for the right letter.

Short-Answer Questions

Follow the directions carefully. You may need to show your work, write an explanation, or make a drawing.

If you can't give a complete answer, show what you do know. You may get credit for part of an answer.

Long-Answer Questions

Take time to think about these questions because you often need to explain your answer.

When you finish, reread the question and answer to be sure you have answered the question correctly.

Student Scoring Rubric

Your teacher may use a scoring rubric to evaluate your work. An example is on the next page. Not all scoring rubrics are the same, so your teacher may use a different one.

Scoring Rubric

Rating	My work on this problem
Exemplary **(full credit)**	• has no errors, has the correct answer, and shows that I checked my answer. • is explained carefully and completely. • shows all needed diagrams, tables, or graphs.
Proficient **(some credit)**	• has small errors, has a close answer, and shows that I checked only the math. • is explained but may have missing parts. • shows most needed diagrams, tables, or graphs.
Acceptable **(little credit)**	• has some errors, has an answer, and shows that I did not check my answer. • is not explained carefully and completely. • shows few needed diagrams, tables, or graphs.
Limited **(very little credit)**	• has many errors and may not have an answer. • is not explained at all. • shows no needed diagrams, tables, or graphs.

TWO Important Things You Can Do Before a Test

• Get plenty of sleep the night before.
• Eat a good breakfast in the morning.

Your Plan For Problem Solving!

Follow this four-part plan and you'll become a problem-solving superstar!

Remember!

Always START at the "Understand" step and move on. But if you can't get an answer don't give up. Just go back and start again!

Understand
Plan
Solve
Look Back

UNDERSTAND

Always be sure you know what the question means! Here are some hints to help you:

- Read the problem and imagine the situation. Draw a picture if it helps.

- Replace any hard names you can't read with easier ones.

- Identify what the question is asking.

- Look for words that help you decide whether to add, subtract, multiply, or divide.

**Start by making a plan!
Ask yourself:**

- What strategy should I use?

- Do I have too much or too little information?

- Should I do more than one step?

- Which operation should I use?

- Should I use paper and pencil, mental math, or a calculator?

You Choose

Strategy
- Act It Out
- Draw a Picture
- Find a Pattern
- Guess and Check
- Make an Organized List
- Make a Table
- Solve a Simpler Problem
- Use Logical Reasoning
- Work Backward

Finally! Now you're ready to solve the problem!

- Carry out your plan.

- Test your method and strategy.

- Adjust your plan if needed.

- Check your calculations.

Congratulations! You've solved the problem. But is it correct? Once you have an answer, ask:

- Is my answer reasonable?

- Is my answer labeled correctly?

- Did I answer the question that was asked?

- Do I need to explain how I found the answer?

Study Skills

Knowing how to study math will help you do well in math class.

> ## To be a good math student, you need to learn
>
> ★ **how to listen when your teacher is teaching.**
>
> ★ **how to work alone and with others.**
>
> ★ **how to plan your time.**

Listening Skills

Listen carefully when your teacher is showing the class how to do something new. Try to understand what is being taught as well as how to do each step.

If you don't understand what your teacher is showing the class, ask a question. Try to let your teacher know what you don't understand.

Listening carefully will also help you be ready to answer any questions your teacher may ask. You may be able to help another student by explaining how you understand.

Working Alone and with Others

When you work alone, try to connect the math you are learning to math you already know. Knowing how parts of mathematics fit together helps you remember and understand.

When you work with others help as much as you can. Cooperating is another word for working together. When people cooperate, they often learn more because they share ideas.

Planning Your Time

Doing your homework on time is part of being a good math student. Make sure that you take the assignment home with you.

Have a place at home to do your homework—it could be in your room or at the kitchen table or anywhere that works for your family.

Get extra help if you are having trouble. Write questions about what you don't understand. This will help your teacher give you the extra help you need.

Addition and Subtraction

- To practice counting on or counting back, do Columns A and B.
- To practice adding doubles or doubles plus one and the related subtraction facts, do Columns C and D.
- To practice making a ten, do Column E and F.
- For mixed practice, choose rows to do.

	Column A	Column B	Column C	Column D	Column E	Column F
Row 1	4 + 2	6 − 2	0 + 0	9 − 4	7 + 5	11 − 4
Row 2	7 + 1	5 − 1	3 + 4	4 − 2	3 + 8	15 − 6
Row 3	3 + 6	9 − 2	5 + 5	11 − 6	4 + 6	14 − 8
Row 4	2 + 5	8 − 3	9 + 9	16 − 8	5 + 8	13 − 9
Row 5	1 + 8	10 − 3	7 + 6	15 − 7	9 + 6	18 − 9
Row 6	9 + 3	7 − 1	8 + 9	17 − 8	8 + 4	16 − 9
Row 7	8 + 2	11 − 2	6 + 6	14 − 7	7 + 9	14 − 5

More Practice

Work with a partner. Make flash cards for the facts that give you trouble. Practice your facts by quizzing each other with the flash cards.

More Addition and Subtraction

- **For addition practice, do Columns A, C, and E.**
- **For subtraction practice, do Columns B, D, and F.**
- **For mixed practice, choose rows to do.**

You Choose

Strategy
- Count On
- Count back.
- Use doubles.
- Use doubles plus one.
- Make a ten.
- Use related addition and subtraction facts.

	Column A	Column B	Column C	Column D	Column E	Column F
Row 1	4 + 4	11 − 7	9 + 1	12 − 6	0 + 5	13 − 8
Row 2	6 + 1	10 − 6	5 + 4	14 − 9	2 + 6	11 − 3
Row 3	3 + 2	12 − 5	7 + 3	13 − 5	8 + 0	12 − 8
Row 4	8 + 7	14 − 6	4 + 9	15 − 9	3 + 3	8 − 2
Row 5	9 + 0	13 − 6	5 + 6	10 − 8	6 + 8	16 − 8
Row 6	7 + 7	10 − 5	8 + 8	16 − 7	7 + 4	12 − 9
Row 7	5 + 3	17 − 9	2 + 7	13 − 7	5 + 9	15 − 8

More Practice

See how many fact families you can write in 3 minutes.

Mixed Addition and Subtraction

- To practice adding, do Columns A, C, and E of Rows 1–5.
- To practice subtracting, do Columns B, D, and F of Rows 1–5.
- For mixed practice, choose rows to do.

	Column A	Column B	Column C	Column D	Column E	Column F
Row 1	6 + 3	10 − 4	3 + 9	8 − 6	5 + 1	14 − 9
Row 2	2 + 4	13 − 4	9 + 5	16 − 7	4 + 3	10 − 3
Row 3	9 + 4	14 − 5	4 + 0	11 − 5	5 + 5	15 − 8
Row 4	7 + 7	16 − 9	8 + 5	10 − 9	6 + 9	9 − 0
Row 5	8 + 3	12 − 3	6 + 7	14 − 6	8 + 8	17 − 9
Row 6	7 + 0	15 − 7	12 − 6	7 + 8	14 − 8	13 − 7
Row 7	11 − 9	13 − 9	5 + 7	10 − 7	9 + 8	12 − 7
Row 8	16 − 8	5 + 6	13 − 4	4 + 7	18 − 9	2 + 9
Row 9	6 + 6	4 + 8	9 + 7	14 − 7	15 − 9	11 − 8
Row 10	12 − 4	17 − 8	9 + 9	15 − 6	8 + 6	13 − 8

Multiplication

- To practice skip counting by 2 and 3, do Column A.
- To practice multiplying by 0 and 1, do Column B.
- To practice skip counting by 5 and 10, do Column C.
- To practice using doubles, do Columns D and E.
- To practice multiplying by 7 and 9, do Column F.
- For mixed practice, choose rows to do.

	Column A	Column B	Column C	Column D	Column E	Column F
Row 1	3 ×2	6 ×1	5 ×3	1 ×1	2 ×2	7 ×3
Row 2	2 ×5	3 ×0	10 ×2	3 ×3	3 ×4	9 ×3
Row 3	3 ×6	2 ×1	10 ×5	4 ×4	4 ×5	7 ×5
Row 4	2 ×7	8 ×1	5 ×1	5 ×5	6 ×5	9 ×6
Row 5	8 ×2	9 ×0	10 ×7	6 ×6	6 ×7	9 ×4
Row 6	3 ×8	1 ×7	9 ×5	7 ×7	8 ×7	7 ×9
Row 7	2 ×9	0 ×5	5 ×8	8 ×8	9 ×9	9 ×8

More Practice

Work with a partner. Make flash cards for the facts that give you trouble. Practice your facts by quizzing each other with the flash cards.

More Multiplication

- To practice with 0, 1, and 2, do Column A.
- To practice with 3, 4, and 5, do Column B.
- To practice with 6 and 7, do Column C.
- To practice with 8 and 9, do Column D.
- For mixed practice, choose Columns E and F or choose rows to do.

You Choose

Strategy
- Use skip counting.
- Use doubles.
- Draw an array.

	Column A	Column B	Column C	Column D	Column E	Column F
Row 1	1 ×3	3 ×5	5 ×6	6 ×8	4 ×7	3 ×9
Row 2	2 ×4	4 ×9	3 ×7	9 ×2	4 ×3	5 ×5
Row 3	0 ×0	7 ×4	6 ×9	8 ×8	2 ×8	6 ×4
Row 4	1 ×4	8 ×5	8 ×6	5 ×9	7 ×9	7 ×2
Row 5	7 ×0	4 ×6	7 ×8	8 ×3	6 ×6	5 ×4
Row 6	9 ×1	5 ×7	7 ×6	9 ×9	8 ×4	9 ×6
Row 7	6 ×2	4 ×8	9 ×7	8 ×9	8 ×7	7 ×7

More Practice

Make a multiplication table. See how fast you can complete all of the multiplication facts.

Division Facts

- To practice dividing by 1, 2 and 3, do Column A.
- To practice dividing by 4 and 5, do Column B.
- To practice dividing by 6 and 7, do Columns C and D.
- To practice dividing by 8 and 9, do Columns E and F.
- For mixed practice, choose rows to do.

You Choose

Strategy
- Use related multiplication facts.
- Use doubles.
- Draw a picture.

	Column A	Column B	Column C	Column D	Column E	Column F
Row 1	$2\overline{)14}$	$4\overline{)16}$	$6\overline{)18}$	$7\overline{)0}$	$9\overline{)18}$	$8\overline{)8}$
Row 2	$3\overline{)12}$	$4\overline{)28}$	$7\overline{)21}$	$6\overline{)36}$	$8\overline{)40}$	$8\overline{)56}$
Row 3	$2\overline{)10}$	$5\overline{)30}$	$6\overline{)42}$	$7\overline{)63}$	$9\overline{)36}$	$9\overline{)0}$
Row 4	$3\overline{)24}$	$4\overline{)32}$	$7\overline{)35}$	$6\overline{)6}$	$8\overline{)72}$	$9\overline{)54}$
Row 5	$3\overline{)27}$	$4\overline{)36}$	$7\overline{)14}$	$6\overline{)48}$	$9\overline{)81}$	$8\overline{)32}$
Row 6	$1\overline{)6}$	$5\overline{)20}$	$6\overline{)54}$	$7\overline{)49}$	$8\overline{)24}$	$9\overline{)72}$
Row 7	$2\overline{)16}$	$5\overline{)45}$	$6\overline{)30}$	$7\overline{)56}$	$9\overline{)63}$	$8\overline{)64}$

More Practice

Work with a partner. Make flash cards for the facts that give you trouble. Practice your facts by quizzing each other with the flash cards.

More Division

- To practice dividing by 1, 2 and 3, do Column A.
- To practice dividing by 4 and 5, do Column B.
- To practice dividing by 6 and 7, do Column C.
- To practice dividing by 8 and 9, do Column D.
- For mixed practice, choose Columns E and F, or choose rows to do.

You Choose

Strategy
- Use related multiplication facts.
- Use doubles.
- Draw a picture.

	Column A	Column B	Column C	Column D	Column E	Column F
Row 1	2)0̄	5)40̄	7)28̄	9)27̄	3)9̄	1)8̄
Row 2	1)9̄	5)15̄	6)54̄	9)9̄	2)14̄	3)15̄
Row 3	3)6̄	4)12̄	6)0̄	8)48̄	8)32̄	5)10̄
Row 4	1)1̄	5)25̄	7)42̄	8)72̄	9)45̄	7)63̄
Row 5	3)18̄	4)24̄	7)7̄	9)36̄	4)28̄	7)49̄
Row 6	3)21̄	4)20̄	6)12̄	8)16̄	8)56̄	6)54̄
Row 7	2)18̄	5)35̄	7)56̄	9)63̄	6)30̄	9)81̄

More Practice

Make triangular flash cards for multiplication and division fact families. Place all cards face down. Without looking at the numbers, pick a card up by a corner so one of the numbers is covered up. Use the numbers you can see to decide what the unknown number is.

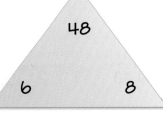

Multiplication and Division

- To practice multiplication, do Columns A, B, and C of Rows 1–5.
- To practice division, do Columns D, E, and F of Rows 1–5.
- For mixed practice, choose rows to do.

	Column A	Column B	Column C	Column D	Column E	Column F
Row 1	4×6	3×7	5×3	$32 \div 8$	$16 \div 2$	$27 \div 9$
Row 2	7×6	8×5	2×6	$8 \div 1$	$0 \div 9$	$24 \div 8$
Row 3	4×9	7×4	6×9	$5 \div 5$	$36 \div 6$	$63 \div 9$
Row 4	6×5	5×7	7×8	$45 \div 9$	$9 \div 9$	$49 \div 7$
Row 5	8×9	9×9	6×8	$24 \div 6$	$81 \div 9$	$64 \div 8$
Row 6	$28 \div 4$	$54 \div 9$	7×2	$6 \div 6$	8×4	6×3
Row 7	5×4	6×6	$0 \div 7$	0×8	$54 \div 6$	$36 \div 9$
Row 8	9×7	$56 \div 8$	$35 \div 7$	3×4	$40 \div 8$	3×9
Row 9	$48 \div 8$	$16 \div 4$	9×5	$56 \div 7$	1×9	7×7
Row 10	9×2	8×3	$42 \div 7$	8×8	$72 \div 9$	$30 \div 6$

Glossary

addend A number to be added in an addition expression or equation.

Example: 5 + 6 = 11

addends

addition An operation on two or more numbers that gives the sum.

angle A figure formed by two rays with the same endpoint.

area The number of square units in a region.

Area = 8 square units

array An arrangement of objects, pictures, or numbers in columns and rows.

Associative Property of Addition The property which states that the way in which addends are grouped does not change the sum. It is also called the *Grouping Property of Addition*.

Example: (2 + 3) + 4 = 2 + (3 + 4)

Associative Property of Multiplication The property which states that the way in which factors are grouped does not change the product. It is also called the *Grouping Property of Multiplication*.

Example: (5 × 4) × 3 = 5 × (4 × 3)

bar graph A graph that uses bars to show data.

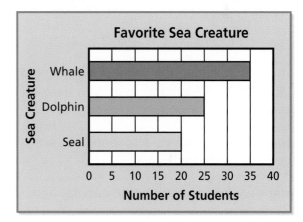

capacity The amount a container can hold.

centimeter (cm) A metric unit of length equal to 10 millimeters.

1cm = 10mm

Glossary 673

circle A plane figure that forms a closed path so that all points on the path are the same distance from a point called the center.

Commutative Property of Addition The property which states that the order of addends does not change the sum. It is also called the *Order Property of Addition*.

Example: 6 + 7 = 7 + 6

Commutative Property of Multiplication The property which states that the order of factors does not change the product. It is also called the *Order Property of Multiplication*.

Example: 4 × 3 = 3 × 4

compare Examine the value of numbers to find if they are greater than, less than, or equal to one another.

compatible numbers Numbers that are easy to compute mentally.

cone A solid figure with one circular flat surface and one curved surface.

congruent figures Figures that have the same size and shape.

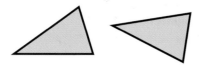

cube A solid figure that has six square faces of equal size.

cubic unit A cube used to measure volume. Each edge is equal to a unit of measure.

cylinder A solid figure with two congruent, circular faces and one curved surface.

data A set of information.

decimal A number with one or more digits to the right of a decimal point.
Examples: 0.5, 0.06, and 12.679 are decimals.

decimal point (.) The point separating the parts from the wholes in a number.

decimeter (dm) A metric unit of length equal to 10 centimeters.

degree Celsius (°C) The metric unit of temperature.

degree Fahrenheit (°F) The customary unit of temperature.

denominator The number below the bar in a fraction.

Example: $\frac{1}{5}$ ← denominator

diagonal A line segment connecting two vertices of a polygon that are not next to each other.

difference The answer to a subtraction problem.

> *Example:* $10 - 7 = 3$
>   ↑
>   difference

digit Any of the symbols 0, 1, 2, 3, 4, 5, 6, 7, 8, 9 in the base-ten numeration system.

Distributive Property of Multiplication The property which states that multiplying a sum by a number is the same as multiplying each addend by the number and adding the products.
Example: $2 \times (3 + 4) = (2 \times 3) + (2 \times 4)$

divide To separate an amount into smaller, equal groups to find the number of groups or the number in each group.

dividend The number that is divided in division.

division An operation that results in a quotient.

divisor The number that divides the dividend.

edge The line segment where the faces of a solid figure meet.

← edge

elapsed time The amount of time that passes between the start and the end of an activity.

equally likely Having the same probability of happening.

equilateral triangle A triangle that has three congruent sides.

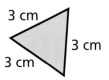
3 cm
3 cm
3 cm

equivalent amounts Amounts that are equal or worth the same are equivalent.

equivalent fractions Fractions that name the same part of a whole.
Example: $\frac{2}{3}$ and $\frac{10}{15}$ are equivalent fractions.

estimate To find an answer that is close to the exact amount.

expanded form A way to write a number that shows the value of each digit.
> *Example:* $3{,}000 + 400 + 9$ is the expanded form of 3,409.

face A flat surface of a solid figure.

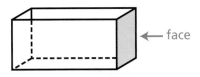
← face

fact family Related facts using the same numbers.

A fact family for 2, 4, and 6:
$2 + 4 = 6 \qquad 4 + 2 = 6$
$6 - 4 = 2 \qquad 6 - 2 = 4$

A fact family for 3, 5, and 15:
$3 \times 5 = 15 \qquad 5 \times 3 = 15$
$15 \div 5 = 3 \qquad 15 \div 3 = 5$

factors Numbers that when multiplied together give the product.

flip To turn something over, front to back.

fourths One or more of four equal parts of a whole.

fraction A number that names a part of a set or a part of a region.
Examples: $\frac{1}{2}$, $\frac{3}{4}$, and $\frac{2}{3}$ are fractions.

front-end estimation A method of estimating sums, differences, products, and quotients using front digits.

gram (g) The basic metric unit of mass.

greater than (>) The symbol used to compare two numbers.
Example: 5 > 4 means 5 is greater than 4.

halves One or more of two equal parts of a whole.

hexagon A six-sided plane figure.

hundreds

513,249

2 hundreds

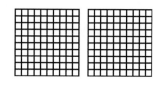

hundred thousands

513,249

5 hundred thousands

hundredths One or more of one hundred equal parts of a whole.

one hundredth →

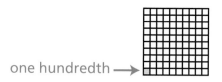

improper fraction A fraction that is greater than or equal to 1. The numerator in an improper fraction is greater than or equal to the denominator.
Examples: $\frac{5}{5}$ and $\frac{8}{7}$ are improper fractions.

intersecting lines Lines that cross each other at a common point.

irregular polygon A polygon whose sides are not all the same length, or whose angles are not all the same measure.

is equal to (=) Is the same in value as.

is not equal to (≠) Is not the same in value as.

isosceles triangle A triangle that has two sides equal in length.

4 in.   4 in.

key The code that tells what each symbol represents.

kilometer (km) A metric unit of length equal to 1,000 meters.

leap year A year with 366 days which occurs every 4 years.

less likely Has less of a chance to happen.

less than (<) The symbol used to compare two numbers.
Example: 4 < 5 means 4 is less than 5.

line A straight path that goes on without end in opposite directions.

line of symmetry The line on which a figure can be folded so that the two halves match exactly.

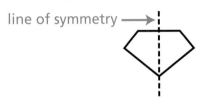

line plot A diagram that organizes data using a number line.

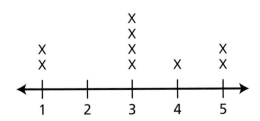

line segment Part of a line. A line segment has two endpoints.

liter (L) The basic metric unit of capacity.

mass A measurement of the amount of matter in an object. It is often measured using grams or kilograms.

mean The average of numbers in a set of data.

measuring cup A tool used to measure capacity.

median The middle number in a set of ordered numerical data.
Example: In the set 2, 3, 6, 7, 7, the median is 6.

meter (m) The basic metric unit of length.

mile (mi) A customary unit of length.

millimeter (mm) A metric unit of length that is $\frac{1}{1,000}$ of a meter.

mixed number A number containing a whole number part and a fraction part.
Examples: $2\frac{1}{2}$ and $5\frac{3}{7}$ are mixed numbers.

mode The number that occurs most often in a set of data.

more likely Has more of a chance to happen.

multiple The product of a number and any other number.

multiplication An operation that finds the total number of items that are in equal groups.

multiply To combine equal groups.

negative A word used to describe numbers that are less than zero.

net A pattern that can be cut out and folded to form a solid figure.

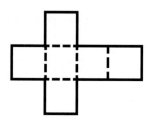

numerator The number above the bar in a fraction.

Example: $\frac{1}{5}$ ← numerator

octagon An eight-sided plane figure.

ones

513,249

9 ones

order Arranging numbers from greatest to least or least to greatest.

ordered pair A pair of numbers used to locate a point.

ordinal number A number used to show order or position, such as *first, second, third, fourth, fifth.*

ounce A small customary unit of capacity.

outcome A result in a probability experiment.
Example: In tossing a coin, heads and tails are the two possible outcomes.

parallel lines Lines that are the same distance apart and never meet.

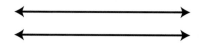

parallelogram A quadrilateral whose opposite sides are parallel.

pentagon A five-sided plane figure.

perimeter The distance around a plane figure.
Example: The perimeter of this rectangle is 20 inches.

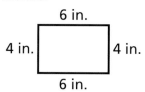

6 in.

4 in.   4 in.

6 in.

perpendicular lines Lines that intersect at right angles.

pictograph A graph that uses pictures to show data.

Fish in Eric's Tank	
Guppies	
Mollies	
Neons	

Each stands for 5 fish.

place value The value assigned to the place that a digit occupies in a number.

Example: In 346, the digit 3 is in the hundreds place and has a value of 300.

plane figure A geometric figure that is flat and has two dimensions.

polygon A simple, closed plane figure made up of three or more line segments.

Examples:

probability The chance of an event occurring.

product The answer to a multiplication problem.

Example: 4 × 5 = 20

product

Property of One The property that states that the product of any number and 1 is that number.

Example: 4 × 1 = 4

pyramid A solid figure whose base is a polygon and whose other faces are triangles with a common vertex.

quadrilateral A polygon with four sides.

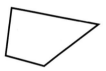

quotient The answer in a division problem.

Example: 32 ÷ 4 = 8

quotient

range The difference between the greatest number and the least number in a set of data.

ray A part of a line that has one endpoint and goes on without end in one direction.

rectangle A quadrilateral with 4 right angles.

rectangular prism A solid figure whose faces are all rectangular.

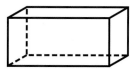

regroup To use place value to exchange equal amounts when renaming a number.

regular polygon A polygon whose sides are all the same length, and whose angles are the same measure.

remainder The number left over when a number cannot be divided evenly.

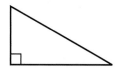

right angle An angle that measures 90°.

right triangle A triangle with one right angle.

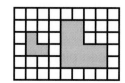

round To find about how many or how much by expressing a number to the nearest ten, hundred, thousand, and so on.

scale A system of marks at equal intervals and in a given order. Used on graphs to help show numerical data.

scalene triangle A triangle with sides of all different lengths.

side (of a polygon) A line segment that is part of a polygon.

side of a polygon ⟶

similar Having the same shape, but not necessarily the same size.

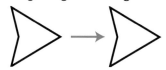

slide Moving a figure along a line.

solid figure A figure that has three dimensions.

sphere A solid figure that is shaped like a round ball.

square A rectangle with four equal sides and four right angles.

square number The product of a whole number multiplied by itself.

Example: $3 \times 3 = 9$; 9 is a square number.

standard form A way to write a number using only digits.

subtraction An operation on two numbers that involves separating a part from a whole and that gives the difference.

sum The answer to an addition problem.

Example: $5 + 6 = 11$

$\uparrow$

sum

survey One method of collecting information.

symmetry A figure has symmetry if it can be folded along a line so that the two parts match exactly.

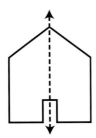

tally mark A mark on a tally chart that stands for **1** of something.

tens

513,249

4 tens

ten thousands

513,249

1 ten thousand

tenths One or more of ten equal parts of a whole.

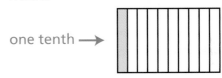

one tenth

thousands

513,249

3 thousands

triangle A three-sided plane figure.

turn To rotate a figure around a point.

unit cost The cost of one item.

vertex (vertices) of a polygon A point common to two sides of a polygon.

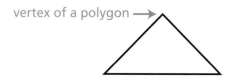

vertex of a polygon →

vertex (vertices) of a solid figure A point common to the edges of a solid figure.

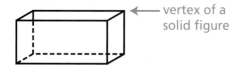

← vertex of a
solid figure

volume The number of cubic units that fit inside a solid figure.

weight The measure of how heavy something is.

word form The form of a number that is written using words.

Zero Property of Addition The property which states that the sum of any number and 0 is that number.

  Example: $8 + 0 = 8$

Zero Property of Multiplication The property which states that the product of any number and 0 is 0.

  Example: $7 \times 0 = 0$

Index

meaning of, 410, 468
modeling (including tiling),
    468–473
use gridded region to determine,
    471–472, 473, 474–475

Arrays
division, 264–265, 270–271,
    288–289, 295
multiplication, 208–209, 216,
    234–235, 240, 251, 264–265,
    288–289, 295, 473, 591

Assessment, *See also* Test Prep
Chapter Test, 24, 42, 60, 104, 132,
    172, 190, 228, 256, 282, 314,
    350, 378, 398, 438, 458, 482,
    516, 536, 564, 606, 632
Performance Assessment, 67, 139,
    197, 321, 405, 489, 571, 639
Quick Check, 13, 35, 55, 89, 127,
    157, 187, 215, 245, 269, 295,
    339, 363, 389, 427, 447, 473,
    505, 531, 547, 587, 619
Unit Test, 66–67, 138–139,
    196–197, 320–321, 404–405,
    488–489, 570–571, 638–639
Use What You Know, 3, 27, 45, 75,
    107, 147, 175, 205, 231, 259,
    285, 329, 353, 381, 413, 441,
    461, 497, 519, 539, 579, 609

Associative Property
of addition, 76–77
of multiplication, 252–253

Audio Tutor, 4, 6, 10, 28, 30, 32,
    48, 50, 76, 78, 86, 90, 110, 112,
    116, 128, 154, 158, 168, 176, 182,
    206, 210, 216, 224, 232, 234, 240,
    250, 260, 262, 266, 272, 286, 288,
    290, 300, 304, 336, 346, 358, 360,
    364, 370, 372, 384, 386, 394, 414,
    418, 432, 444, 464, 470, 478, 498,
    500, 506, 512, 520, 528, 532, 542,
    548, 556, 580, 582, 584, 588, 594,
    610, 612, 616, 620, 626

Bar graph
definition of, 144
making, 164–166, 179
scale, 164–166

using, 38–39, 42, 67, 69, 92, 179,
    185, 190, 191, 193, 197, 222,
    294, 430, 543, 608, 618

Base-ten blocks
to model addition, 82, 137

to model division, 620–621
to model multiplication, 582–583,
    588–589
to model subtraction, 116

Basic Facts
addition, 72–73, 76–77, 110–111,
    665–667
division, 260–261, 262–263,
    264–265, 266–267, 270–271,
    272–273, 278–280, 286–287,
    288–289, 290–291, 292–294,
    295, 296–298, 304–305,
    306–307, 308, 670–672
multiplication, 206–207, 208–209,
    210–211, 212–214, 216–217,
    218–219, 224–226, 232–233,
    234–235, 236–238, 239,
    240–241, 242–244, 246–247,
    248, 264–265, 668–669, 672
subtraction, 72–73, 110–111,
    665–667

Benchmarks
capacity
    customary units, 370
    metric units, 386
length
    customary units, 360
    metric units, 384
mass, 394
temperature, 346
weight, 372

Brahmi numerals, 269

Brain Teasers, 41, 131, 153, 299,
    397, 467, 555, 601

Calculator, *See also* Calculator
Connections; Technology Time
choose a computation method, 16,
    40, 92, 100–101, 126, 160, 222,
    276, 302, 366, 392, 430, 456,
    526, 562, 596, 604, 630
division with, 294, 637
find area of irregular figure with,
    487

multiple operations with, 403
multiplication with, 362, 598, 637
order of operations on, 319
subtraction with, 124

Calculator Connections
addition patterns, 89
calculator or mental math, 631
change fractions to decimals, 547
multiply using repeated addition,
    605
mystery numbers, 127
number sentences, 313
place-value addition, 13

Calendar, 326, 340–343

Capacity
benchmarks, 370, 386
customary units, 368–369,
    370–371
metric units, 386–388

Celsius temperature, 346–348
benchmarks, 346

Centimeter, 382–383, 384–385

Cent sign, 1b

Certain event, 176–177

Challenge
area of a rectangle, 473
divisors, 619
equal amounts of money, 55
estimate differences, 131
exercises, 53, 65, 194, 299, 402
measurement units, 397
missing numbers, 587
place value, 41

Chance, meaning of, 145

Change, making, 50–51

Checking
addition, 82, 86, 94, 98
division, 620, 624, 628
subtraction, 117, 120

Choose a computation method,
16, 40, 92, 100–101, 126, 160,
222, 276, 302, 366, 392, 430, 456,
526, 562, 596, 604, 630

Choose the operation, 268

Choose a strategy, 16, 40, 92, 160,
222, 276, 302, 366, 392, 430, 456,
526, 562, 596, 662, 666, 669–671

Circle, 418–421

reading, 154–156
using, 184, 276, 420

Lines, 414–417
intersecting, 415–417
parallel, 415–417
perpendicular, 415–417

Line segment, 414–417

Line of symmetry, 448–449

List-making, strategy, 220–222

Liter, 386–388

Literature Connection, 1c, 73, 145,
203, 327, 411, 495, 577, 645–656

Logical Thinking,
See also Measurement Sense;
   Reasoning; Visual Thinking
all, some, none statements, 636
analogies, 437
multiples of 10, 601
non-standard units, 377
using to solve problems, 364–366,
   376–377
Venn Diagram, 299

Make an Organized List, strategy,
220–222

Make a Table, strategy, 158–160

Manipulatives, *See also* Place-value
blocks
balance scale and weights, 372, 394
base-ten blocks, 582–583
coins, 178
containers, 368–369, 386,
   476–477
counters, 206–207, 260–261, 500,
   535, 612–614
decimal models, 552–553
fraction strips, 510–511, 520–521,
   522–523, 524–525, 528–530,
   531, 532–534, 535
geoboards, 470–471
index cards, 375
number cards, 309
number cubes, 59, 97, 615
paper circles, 508–509
pattern blocks, 442, 448, 450–451,
   515
play money, 59, 552–554

real-world objects, 181, 354–357,
   462–463
rulers, 355–357, 358–359,
   382–383, 462–463, 465–466
snap cubes, 150–152
solid figure models, 434–435
spinners, 178–180
symbol cards, 309
thermometers, 347
tracing paper, 442–443
unit cubes, 476–477

Maps,
coloring with fewest colors, 467
using a map, 88, 112, 130, 139

Mass, 394–396
benchmarks, 394

Math Challenge *See* Challenge

Math Conversations, 70, 142, 200,
324, 408, 492, 574, 642

Math Reasoning *See* Reasoning

Mean, modeling, 150–152, 153

Measure, unit of, 327

Measurement
area, 470–473, 474–475
   estimating, 468–469
capacity
   benchmarks, 370, 386
   customary units, 368–369,
      370–371
   metric units, 386–388
converting metric and customary
   units, 398
formula (for area), 473, 487
game, 375
length
   benchmarks, 360, 384
   customary units, 354–357,
      358–359, 360–363
   fractions of a foot, 503
   metric units, 382–383,
      384–385
   to the nearest centimeter,
      382–383
   to the nearest half-inch,
      358–359
   to the nearest inch, 354–357
   to the nearest millimeter,
      382–383
   to the nearest quarter-inch, 363

mass, 394–396
   benchmarks, 394
   with non-standard units, 354, 377,
      462–463
perimeter, 462–463, 464–467,
   474–475
   estimating, 462–463
temperature, 346–348
   benchmarks, 346
time, 330–331, 332–333, 344–335,
   336–339, 340–343
   using, 474–475
volume, 476–477, 478–480
   estimating, 476–477
weight, 372–374
   benchmarks, 372

Measurements, adding, 402,
464–466

Measures, table of, 644

Measures of central tendency *See*
Mean; Median; Mode; Range

Median
from a line plot, 154–156
modeling, 150–152, 153

Mental math
addition, 76, 85, 88, 122
choose a computation method, 16,
   40, 92, 100–101, 126, 160, 222,
   276, 302, 366, 392, 430, 456,
   526, 562, 596, 604, 630
division, 610–611
exercises, 88, 92, 126, 581, 618
multiplication, 224–226, 580–581,
   602
subtraction, 122, 123, 126
versus using a calculator, 631

Meter, 384–385

Metric units
capacity, 386–388
   benchmarks, 386
converting to customary units, 389
extra practice, 399
length, 382–383, 384–385
   benchmarks, 384
mass, 394–396
   benchmarks, 394
temperature, 346–348
   benchmarks, 346

Mile, 360–362

Milliliter, 386–388

Pictograph
choosing a display, 167
definition of, 144
key, 162
making, 162–163
using, 16, 40, 160, 219, 244, 302, 392, 562, 590

Picture
using data from, 321, 396, 421, 496, 501, 558
drawing to solve problems, 300–302

Pint, 368–369, 370–371

Place value
to add and subtract decimals, 556–558
to compare decimals, 548–549
to compare fractions and decimals, 550–551
to compare whole numbers, 28–29
decimal, 540–541, 542–543, 544–545
extra practice, 25
hundredths, 542–543
money and, 46–47
to order decimals, 548–549
to order fractions and decimals, 550–551
to order whole numbers, 30–31
puzzle, 41
tenths, 540–541
through hundreds, 6–7
through hundred thousands, 20–22
through ten thousands, 18–19
through thousands, 10–12

Place-value blocks
modeling addition, 82
modeling division, 620–621
modeling multiplication, 582–583, 588–589
modeling numbers, 7
modeling subtraction, 116
modeling whole numbers, 1b

Place-value chart
to add and subtract decimals, 556
to compare decimals, 548
to compare fractions and decimals, 550
to compare whole numbers, 28
decimals greater than one on, 544
money amounts on, 46
to order decimals, 548

to order fractions and decimals, 550
to order whole numbers, 30
to tenths, 540
through hundreds, 6
through hundred thousands, 20
through hundredths, 542
through ten thousands, 18
through thousands, 10

Plane figures
classifying, 418–421, 427
meaning of, 410
relationship to solid figures, 434–436

Plots
choosing a display, 167
line plot, 154–156

P.M., 330–331

Polygons, 418–421

Pound, 372–374

Practice Games *See* Games

Prediction
exercises, 89, 160, 244, 420, 423, 472, 480
from an experiment, 184–186
from a pattern, 14–15, 23
game, 181
using probability, 181

Prism, 432–433, 434–436
net for, 486

Probability, 174–200
combinations, 220–222
equally likely outcomes, 178–180
event, 176
experimental, 178–180
extra practice, 191
fairness and, 188–189
game, 181
identifying outcomes, 178–180
likelihood of an event, 176–177
meaning of, 176
of an outcome, 182–183
prediction and, 181, 184–186
using, 188–189

Problem-solving *See* Choose a computation method; Choose a strategy; Different ways; Problem-solving applications; Problem-solving

decisions; Problem-solving strategies; Test-taking tips

Problem-solving applications
interpret remainders, 622–623
make change, 50–51
multistep problems, 506–507
use a bar graph, 38–39
use money, 560–562
use probability, 188–189
use a schedule, 344–345
visual thinking, 454–455

Problem-solving decisions
choose the operation, 268
estimate or exact answer, 102
explaining answers, 130
multistep problems, 254–255
reasonable answers, 546
too much or too little information, 376–377

Problem-solving features
algebraic thinking, 23, 103, 153, 157, 215, 245, 281, 298, 299, 467
art connection, 484–485, 505
brain teaser, 41, 131, 153, 299, 397, 467, 555, 601
calculator connection, 13, 89, 313, 547, 605, 631
logical thinking, 299, 377, 437, 601
math challenge, 41, 55, 131, 397, 473, 587, 619
math reasoning, 81, 85, 115, 123, 131, 167, 187, 555, 591
number sense, 239
reading connection, 255
real world connection, 171, 339, 389, 397, 563, 601
science connection, 192–193, 316–317, 343, 363, 400–401, 531, 566–567
social studies connection, 35, 41, 62–63, 119, 134–135, 227, 269, 295, 634–635
visual thinking, 153, 349, 427, 437, 447, 467, 481, 515, 555, 559

Problem-solving strategies
act it out, 524–526
draw a picture, 300–302
find a pattern, 14–16, 428–430
guess and check, 90–91
make an organized list, 220–222

Rules
  division, 278–280
  rounding, 36
  subtraction, 108–109

Scale, graph, 164–166

Scalene triangle, 422–423

Schedule
  using, 344–345

Sides
  finding perimeter by measuring,
    464–466
  of polygons, 418
  of quadrilaterals, 424–426
  of triangles, 422–423

Similar, meaning of, 444

Similar figures, 444–446
  game, 457

Skip counting
  to divide, 262
  to multiply, 210, 212, 216, 218,
    234

Slides, 450–453

Solid figures, 432–433, 434–436
  classifying, 432–433
  complex, 432–433
  drawing, 434–436
  meaning of, 410
  nets for, 486
  relationship to plane figures,
    434–436

Solve a Simpler Problem, strategy,
  594–596

Sphere, 432–433

Square, 418, 424–426

Square number, 251

Square unit, 468–469, 474

Standard form numbers, 6–7,
  10–12, 18–19, 20–22

Statistics *See* Data; Graphs; Mean;
  Median; Mode; Probability; Range

Strategies *See* Problem-solving
  strategies

Student Handbook, 657–664

Subtraction
  across zeros, 128–129
  using a calculator, 124
  checking, 117, 120
  decimal, 556–558
  definition of, 72
  estimating differences, 112–115
  extra practice, 133
  fact families, 110–111
  facts practice, 665–667
  with fractions, 532–534
  greater numbers, 124–126
  mental math, 122, 123, 126
  modeling, 110, 116, 532–534
  with money, 112–113, 115,
    117–118, 120–122, 125
  patterns, 126
  regrouping, 116–118, 120–122,
    123, 124–126, 128–129,
    556–558
  relation to addition, 110–111
  repeated to divide, 262–263, 266,
    270, 272, 290, 296
  rules for, 108–109
  whole number, 106–133
  with zero, 108–109

Sums, 72
  estimating, 78–81

Survey
  conducting, 148–149
  using data from, 154, 162, 195

Symbol, meaning of, 1c

Symbols
  cent sign, 1b
  decimal point, 1b, 540
  dollar sign, 1b
  inequality, 28

Symmetry, line, 448–449

Table, *See also* Function table;
  Multiplication table; Tally chart
  using data from, 7, 12, 19, 22, 26,
    31, 44, 74, 106, 114, 118, 135,
    139, 204, 226, 284, 312, 335,
    374, 380, 504, 511, 526, 538,
    551

making
  to record work, 8, 207, 232,
    462, 463, 477, 552, 554, 613
  to solve problems, 158–160

Table of Measures, 644

Talk About It, 9, 149, 152, 163, 166,
  180, 207, 233, 251, 261, 287, 357,
  369, 383, 436, 443, 449, 453, 463,
  469, 477, 509, 554, 583, 614

Tally chart
  choosing a display, 167
  definition of, 144
  making, 148–149, 178, 180, 186
  organizing data in, 148–149
  using, 146, 149, 153, 174,
    184–186

Tally mark, 144

Technology, *See also* calculator;
  Calculator Connections; Technology
  Time
  Audio Tutor, 4, 6, 10, 28, 30, 32,
    48, 50, 76, 78, 86, 90, 110, 112,
    116, 128, 154, 158, 168, 176,
    182, 206, 210, 216, 224, 232,
    234, 240, 250, 260, 262, 266,
    272, 286, 288, 290, 300, 304,
    336, 346, 358, 360, 364, 370,
    372, 384, 386, 394, 414, 418,
    432, 444, 464, 470, 478, 498,
    500, 506, 512, 520, 528, 532,
    542, 548, 556, 580, 582, 584,
    588, 594, 610, 612, 616, 620,
    626
  Internet connections, 1c, 6, 13, 17,
    25, 27, 32, 35, 41, 43, 45, 50, 55,
    61, 63, 65, 69, 73, 76, 89, 93,
    105, 110, 119, 127, 131, 133,
    135, 137, 141, 145, 153, 157,
    161, 168, 173, 182, 187, 191,
    193, 195, 199, 203, 206, 215,
    223, 227, 229, 234, 245, 255,
    257, 262, 269, 277, 281, 283,
    286, 295, 299, 303, 313, 315,
    317, 323, 327, 339, 343, 346,
    349, 351, 358, 363, 367, 377,
    379, 384, 393, 397, 399, 401,
    407, 411, 427, 431, 432, 437,
    439, 447, 454, 459, 467, 470,
    473, 481, 483, 485, 491, 495,
    498, 505, 515, 517, 520, 527,
    531, 537, 547, 548, 555, 563,
    565, 567, 569, 573, 577, 580,

587, 597, 601, 605, 607, 612, 619, 633, 635, 641

Technology Time
calculator
    area of irregular figures, 487
    multiple operations, 403
    multiplication and division, 637
    order of operations, 319
    comparing fractions, 569
    comparing money amounts, 65
    make a bar graph, 195
    use base-ten blocks to add, 137

Temperature, 346–348
benchmarks, 346

Tens, rounding to, 32–34, 36–37

Tenth, 540–541

Tessellation, 481

Test prep, *See also* Test-Taking Tips
constructed-response questions, 139, 161, 197, 199, 277, 303, 323, 393, 431, 489, 491, 573, 597, 639
extended-response questions, 17, 67, 69, 93, 141, 223, 321, 367, 405, 407, 527, 571, 641
multiple-choice questions, 7, 17, 19, 22, 29, 47, 58, 68, 77, 84, 93, 122, 140, 161, 198, 211, 219, 223, 227, 238, 247, 263, 267, 273, 277, 281, 289, 298, 303, 307, 322, 333, 343, 367, 371, 385, 393, 406, 417, 423, 431, 433, 466, 490, 511, 521, 527, 543, 549, 572, 590, 597, 600, 605, 611, 625, 640
open-response questions, 5, 7, 17, 19, 22, 29, 31, 37, 47, 49, 58, 66, 67, 69, 77, 80, 84, 93, 96, 99, 101, 109, 111, 114, 119, 122, 129, 138, 139, 141, 161, 170, 177, 183, 196, 197, 199, 209, 211, 217, 219, 223, 227, 235, 238, 241, 247, 253, 263, 265, 267, 271, 273, 277, 281, 289, 291, 298, 303, 305, 307, 313, 320, 321, 323, 331, 333, 335, 343, 349, 359, 367, 371, 374, 385, 388, 393, 404, 405, 407, 417, 421, 423, 431, 433, 446, 466, 481, 488, 489, 491, 499, 501, 511, 515, 521, 523, 527,

535, 541, 543, 545, 549, 551, 558, 563, 570, 571, 573, 581, 590, 593, 597, 600, 605, 611, 621, 625, 627, 631, 638, 639, 641
Problem Solving on Tests, 17, 93, 161, 223, 277, 303, 367, 393, 431, 527, 597
Student Handbook, 657–664

Test-Taking Tips, 68, 140, 198, 322, 406, 490, 572, 640

Thermometer, 326

Thousands
modeling, 8–9
place value through, 10–12
rounding to, 36–37

Three-dimensional figures *See* Solid figures

Time
after the hour, 332–333, 334–335
A.M. and P.M., 330–331
before the hour, 332–333, 334–335
calendar, 340–342, 343
elapsed, 336–338
estimating, 338–339
extra practice, 351
leap year, 343
reading and writing, 330–331, 332–333, 334–335
schedule, 344–345
telling
    to five minutes, 332–333
    to the hour, half-hour, quarter-hour, 330–331
    to the minute, 334–335
units of, 330, 340

Time line, 349

Trading *See* Regrouping

Transformations, 450–453

Translation *See* Slides

Triangles, 418
classifying, 422–423

Turns, 450–453

Two-dimensional figures *See* Plane figures

Unfair and fair games, 188–189

Unit cost, 318

Unit Test, 66–67, 138–139, 196–197, 320–321, 404–405, 488–489, 570–571, 638–639

Unlikely, 176–177

Value, meaning of, 1c

Variables, 103, 225, 227, 245, 274, 279, 281, 298, 304, 306–307, 310, 530, 534

Venn diagram, 299, 427

Vertex (Vertices)
of a polygon, 418
of a solid figure, 434–436

Visual Thinking, 454–455
estimating fractions and decimals, 559
following directions, 447
fractional parts, 568
maps, 467
modeling fractions, 515
pattern blocks, 437
percent, 555
rounding decimals, 559
rounding fractions, 559
tally chart, 153
tessellation, 481
using a time line, 349
Venn diagrams, 427

Vocabulary
Reading Math, 1b–1c, 72–73, 144–145, 202–203, 326–327, 410–411, 494–495, 576–577
Wrap-Up, 70, 142, 200, 324, 408, 492, 574, 642

Volume, 476–477, 478–480
estimating, 476–477
extra practice, 483
meaning of, 476, 478

Credits

PERMISSIONS ACKNOWLEDGMENTS
Houghton Mifflin Mathematics © 2005, Grade 3 PE/TE

"A is for Abacus" from *G Is For Googol: A Math Alphabet Book*, by David M. Schwartz. Text copyright © 1998 by David M. Schwartz. Reprinted by permission of Tricycle Press.

"The Big Chill" is excerpted from *TIME For Kids*, News Scoop Edition, February 12, 1999 Issue. Copyright © 1999 by Time, Inc. Used with permission from TIME For Kids magazine.

"Elephants on the Move" from *Weekly Reader*, November 16, 2001 Issue. Copyright © 2001 by Weekly Reader Corporation. Reprinted by permission of Weekly Reader Corporation. Weekly Reader is a federally registered trademark of Weekly Reader Corp.

"Frog or Toad: How to Tell" is excerpted from *The Complete Frog*, by Elizabeth A. Lacey. Text copyright © 1989 by Elizabeth A. Lacey. Reprinted by permission of HarperCollins Publishers.

"Leaders of the Pack," by Terry Krautwurst from *National Geographic World*, November 2001 Issue. Copyright © 2001 by National Geographic Society. Used with permission.

"The School is One Big Bird Feeder!" excerpted from *TIME For Kids*, February 12, 1999 Issue. Copyright © 1999 by Time, Inc. Used with permission from TIME For Kids magazine.

"Snowflakes" from *One At A Time*, by David McCord. Copyright © 1966 by David McCord. Reprinted by permission of Little, Brown and Company (Inc.). Electronic rights granted by The Estate of David T.W. McCord.

"Uncle Johnathan and the Ice-Skating Contest," by Gretchen Woelfle, originally published as "Never Go Home Without A Fish" from *Stories From Where We Live: The North Atlantic Coast*. Copyright © 2000 by Gretchen Woelfle. Reprinted by permission of the author.

Untitled Haiku "old and quiet pond..." from *Grass Sandals: The Travels of Basho*, by Dawnine Spivak. Text copyright © 1997 Dawnine Spivak. Reprinted with the permission of Atheneum Books for Young Readers, an imprint of Simon & Schuster Children's Publishing Division.

Cover © Gail Shumay/Getty Images.

PHOTOGRAPHY
vi AP/Wide World Photos. **viii** (bl) © Naturfoto Honal/CORBIS. (bm) Michaelturco.com. (br) Frans Lanting/Minden. **xv** (bm) Richard Cummins. **xvi** (t) © Mark E. Gibson. (b) © Lincoln Russell/Stock, Boston Inc./PictureQuest. **xvii** © DigitalVision/PictureQuest. **xxi** (t) Ron Sherman/Getty Images. (b) © Philip Rostron/Masterfile. **2** © Richard Nowitz/CORBIS. **4** (t) NASA (JPL42582 MRPS78052). (tm) NASA (S62-08774). (bm) © CORBIS. (b) NASA (JPL p45424). **6** NASA. **7** NASA (ISS004-E-5269). **10** NASA (STS-111, EC02-0131-3). **11** NASA (STS-1, GPN-2000-000650). **18** NASA (STS-96 Starshine1). **20** PlaceStockPhoto.com. **26** AP/Wide World Photos. **28** © James Marshall/CORBIS. **32** National Theater of the Deaf. **33** National Theater of the Deaf. **35** Wendy Chan/Getty Images. **36** AP/Wide World Photos. **37** Angelo Cavalli/agefotostock. **40** Bob Winsett/Index Stock. **44** PhotoDisc/Getty Images. **51** PhotoDisc/Getty Images. **56** © Arthur Tilley/i2i Images/PictureQuest. **62-3** © Angelo Hornak/CORBIS. **62(b)** Luis Castaneda/Getty Images. **63(b)** © Araldo de Luca/CORBIS. **74** Thomas Dressler/agefotostock. **77** EyeWire/Getty Images. **78** © John Foster/Masterfile. **79** Ted Wood/Getty Images. **82** Chip Henderson/Index Stock. **84** PhotoDisc/Getty Images. **86** Frans Lanting/Minden. **90** (l) © Naturfoto Honal/CORBIS. **90** (r) Bristol City Museum/naturepl.com. **91** (t) Mike Moffet/Minden. (m) © A. H. Rider/Photo Researchers, Inc. (b) Michaelturco.com. **94** Michael Newman/PhotoEdit. **95** PhotoDisc/Getty Images. **96** DK Images. **98** Royalty-Free/CORBIS. **99** Royalty-Free/CORBIS. **100** Erik Aeder/Pacific Stock. **101** © Jonathan Blair/CORBIS. **106** © Miles Ertman/Masterfile. **116** State of North Carolina Department of Transportation, Ferry Division. **117** State of North Carolina Department of Transportation, Ferry Division. **122** © 2003, John K. Nakata, sightandsound.com. **124** Mark Wagner/Getty Images. **125** MaXx Images/Index Stock. **128** © Peter Christopher/Masterfile. **130** F. Jack Jackson/Alamy. **134-5** ©AFP/CORBIS. **146** David Young-Wolff/PhotoEdit. **156** Royalty Free/CORBIS. **163** Jim Cummins/Getty Images. **164** AP/Wide World Photos. **165** © Orban Thierry/CORBIS SYGMA. **192-3** Georgette Douwma/Getty Images. **192** (t) KARL & JILL WALLIN/Getty Images. **193** (t) BRIAN SKERRY/Getty Images. **195** Royalty Free/CORBIS. **197** (cr) PhotoDisc/Getty Images. **203** (tr) PhotoDisc/Getty Images. **204** © Peter Beck/CORBIS. **227** Antonio M. Rosario/Getty Images. **230** Frans Lanting/Minden. **235** Michael Patricia Fogden/Minden. **236** G. Brad Lewis/Getty Images. **237** Phil Coleman. **240** (b) Chris Matheson/agefotostock. **242** © Tom Schumm. **254** Frans Lanting/Minden. **258** © Douglas Scott Chapin/Workbook Stock. **263** (t) DK Images. **263** (b) J & P Wegner/Animals Animals. **264** PhotoDisc/Getty Images. **268** © Kevin Fleming/CORBIS. **270** AP/Wide World Photos. **284** Tony Freeman/PhotoEdit. **293** Stockbyte. **307** Brand X Pictures. **313** (tl) © Seattle Art Museum/CORBIS. (tr) (bl) (br) © The Seattle Art Museum, Duncan MacTavish Fuller Memorial Collection. Photo: Paul Macapia. **317** (t) © Ralph A. Clevenger/CORBIS. **316-7** George Lepp/Getty Images. **317** (b) Courtesy of Wendy Thomson. **330** (r) Raymond Forbes/agefotostock. **343** National Baseball Hall of Fame. **363** Digital Vision/Getty Images. **380** John C. Russell/Teamworks. **384** (l) Kindra Clineff/Index Stock. (r) Jeff Greenberg/Index Stock. **386** © SeaWorld San Diego. **388** Flip Nicklin/Minden. **390** (t) Richard Cummins. **391** Gary D'Ercole/Index Stock. **392** ComstockKLIPS. **400-1** Getty Images. **401** (b) Gerben Oppermans/Getty Images. **402** (tr) PhotoDisc/Getty Images. **403** (br) Kunst & Schiedulin/Firstlight.ca. **412** Will & Deni McIntyre/Getty Images. **414** © Bill Ross/CORBIS. **418** © James Lemass. **419** © Richard Sisk/Panoramic Images. **421** PhotoDisc/Getty Images. **422** Lincoln Russell/Stock, Boston Inc./PictureQuest. **423** © Mark E. Gibson. **424** Broward County Libraries Division-Fort Lauderdale, Florida. **426** Broward County Libraries Division-Fort Lauderdale, Florida. **436** © Peter Bowater/Photo Reearchers, Inc. **440** Chuck Pefley/Stock Boston. **481** Jeff Foott/Discovery Images/PictureQuest. **484-5** © Michael Boys/CORBIS. **485** (b) Courtesy of Larry Albee/Longwood Gardens. **496** FLASHLIGHT!/Stock Boston. **498** Stockbyte. **518**

Credits continued

Bob Daemmrich/Stock Boston. **524** Conrad & Company Photography/Stock Food. **526** PhotoDisc/Getty Images. **534** (b) PhotoDisc/Getty Images. **535** (l) DigitalVision/PictureQuest. (ml) James Lloyd/Animals Animals. (mr) Ken Cole/Animals Animals. (r) © Ed Reschke/Peter Arnold, Inc. **538** Glenn Kulbako/Index Stock. **541** Comstock. **546** © Richard Hutchings/CORBIS. **551** ImageState RF. **555** The Granger Collection. **558** sweetland-outdoor.com. **562** PhotoDisc/Getty Images. **566-7** Kim Westerskov/Getty Images. **566** (b) Lightwave Photography, Inc./Animals Animals/Earth Scenes. **567** (b) Michio Hoshino/Minden Pictures. **578** Photo courtesy of Science World British Columbia. **580** The Granger Collection. **584** Elopak, Inc. **588** North Wind Picture Archives. **595** (t) North Wind Picture Archives. (b) © Paul Hardy/CORBIS. **596** © Sandy King/Getty Images. **598** © Bettmann/CORBIS. **602** Burke/Tiolo/Brand X Pictures/Alamy. **608** Jeff Greenberg/Index Stock. **610** Ron Sherman/Getty Images. **612** D. Young-Wolff/PhotoEdit/PictureQuest. **616** David R. Frazier. **617** Bob Daemmrich/Stock Boston/PictureQuest. **618** ComstockKLIPS. **621** © Philip Rostron/Masterfile. **622** Syracuse Newspapers/Albert Fanning/The Image Works. **624** David Young-Wolff/PhotoEdit. **625** Michael J. Doolittle/The Image Works. **626** Bob Daemmrich/The Image Works. **627** ChromaZone Images/Index Stock. **628** (t) © Tom & Dee Ann McCarthy/CORBIS. **634-5** Richard Hutchings/PhotoEdit. **646** (t) Frank Siteman/Index Stock Imagery. (b) © Ann States/CORBIS. **647** © Ann States/CORBIS. **648** (l) © Randy M. Ury/CORBIS. (r) © Paul Wenham-Clarke/ImageState/Alamy Images. **649** (t) © Art Wolfe/Getty Images. (b) © Tom Brakefield/CORBIS. **650** © Art Wolfe/Getty Images. **651** © Chris Arend/Alaska Stock. **653** © Scott Camazine/Photo Researchers, Inc. **656** © Stan Osolinski/Getty Images.

ASSIGNMENT PHOTOGRAPHY

643 © HMCo./Jade Albert.

220, 224 (tr), **464** (t), **531, 552** (b) © HMCo./Greg Anthony.

xxvi, xxix, 661, 664 © HMCo./Joel Benjamin.

197 (br), **321** (tr)(br), **487** (bl), **639** (tr)(br) © HMCo./Ray Boudreau.

xxx (cr), **72, 144** (tr), **202, 326, 410, 494, 576** © HMCo./Dave Bradley.

vii (bl), **50** (tr), **52** (t), **174, 218, 304, 332, 334, 336, 340, 344, 345, 347, 420, 460, 502, 506, 512, 520** © HMCo./Angela Coppola.

ix (br), **xi** (br), **xvii** (br), **8, 9, 71** (br), **97, 123, 131, 142, 148, 150-153, 168, 170, 176, 181, 184, 188, 187, 200, 206** (b), **212, 213, 216, 232, 234, 238, 240** (t), **249** (b), **250, 252, 260, 262, 267, 287, 291, 296, 309** (b), **325, 330** (l) (ml) (mr), **354** (tr) (br), **355** (b), **358, 364, 368, 372** (tr) (br), **375, 376, 387, 408, 425, 428** (tr), **434, 457, 462, 476, 492, 508, 540, 575, 582, 615, 631, 642** © HMCo./Carol Kaplan.

xxii, xxv, xxvii, xxviii, 658, 660, 662 © HMCo./Allan Landau.

xv (br), **xviii** (b), **55, 57, 178** (b), **182, 183, 186, 297, 300, 328, 352, 390** (b), **468** (t), **514, 525, 528, 532, 592** © HMCo./Michael Indresano.

67 (tr)(c)(b), **70** (tr), **196** (tr), **320** (tr), **404** (tr)(bl), **489** (tr) © HMCo./Dave Starrett.

66 (bl), **142** (tr), **492** (tr) © HMCo./Ron Tanaka.

ILLUSTRATION

viii, 13, 16, 26, 31, 39, 74, 76, 92, 114, 118, 129 (bl), **153** (br), **154, 157, 214, 219, 222, 226, 253, 258, 269, 276, 294-5, 298-9, 328, 335, 371, 380, 386-7, 389** (tl), **389, 430, 477, 511, 586, 590, 608, 630** Argosy. **136, 139, 320** (bl), **405** (c), **638** (bl) Steve Attoe. **397** (tr) Robin Boyer. **13, 339, 343, 369-70, 417** (c), **470, 475** Ken Batelman. **153** (bl), **265, 366** Estelle Carol. **570** (br) Michael Cho. **49, 54, 120, 298** (t), **312, 466, 472, 480, 648** Joel Dubin. **337** Rob Dunlavey. **xxi, 21, 46, 125, 158, 273, 275, 365, 620** Julie Durell. **110, 290** John Edwards Inc. **xv, 5, 108, 338, 359, 384, 394-5, 542, 544, 548, 581, 611** Ruth Flanigan. **274, 363** Patrick Gnan. **80** Jim Gordon. **xiii, 288, 313, 587** Mike Gordon. **408** (tr)(cr) Jeff Grunewald. **xiii, 84, 278-9, 280, 560** Tim Haggerty. **xiv, 305, 310, 333, 348** Jenny B. Harris. **vi (cl), xii, xx, 23, 89, 131, 221, 242, 298** (c), **299, 547, 555, 601, 605** Ken Hensen. **600** Nathan Jarvis. **324** (tr), **574, 642** Kelly Kennedy. **ix, x, 38, 113, 129** (c), **159** Dave Klug. **200** (tr), **404** (cr), **569, 637** Bernadette Lau. **17, 93, 302, 367, 393, 467** Ruth Linstromberg. **vi (tr), 14, 15** Ethan Long. **66** (tr) Tadeusz Majewski. **88, 112, 652** Ortelius. Design. **65** (br), **199** (bl), **319, 326** (cr)(br), **570** (tr), **577** (cl), **638** (tr) Jun Park. **488** (tr) Clarence Porter. **306** Precision Graphics. **433, 522,** Chris Reed. **41, 119, 512, 524, 563, 599, 604** Brucie Rosch. **654-55** Goro Sasaki. **102, 215, 360, 362, 377, 594** Alfred Schrier. **12, 19, 22, 160, 189, 302, 373-4, 417** (t), **645** Rob Schuster. **121, 168, 170** Steve Snider. **255** Winson Trang. **35, 266, 272, 474** George Ulrich. **247** Joe Veno. **292, 505** Bari Weissman.

All tech art by Pronk & Associates